CRAFTS MOVEMENT IN THE NORTH WEST OF ENGLAND

A Handbook

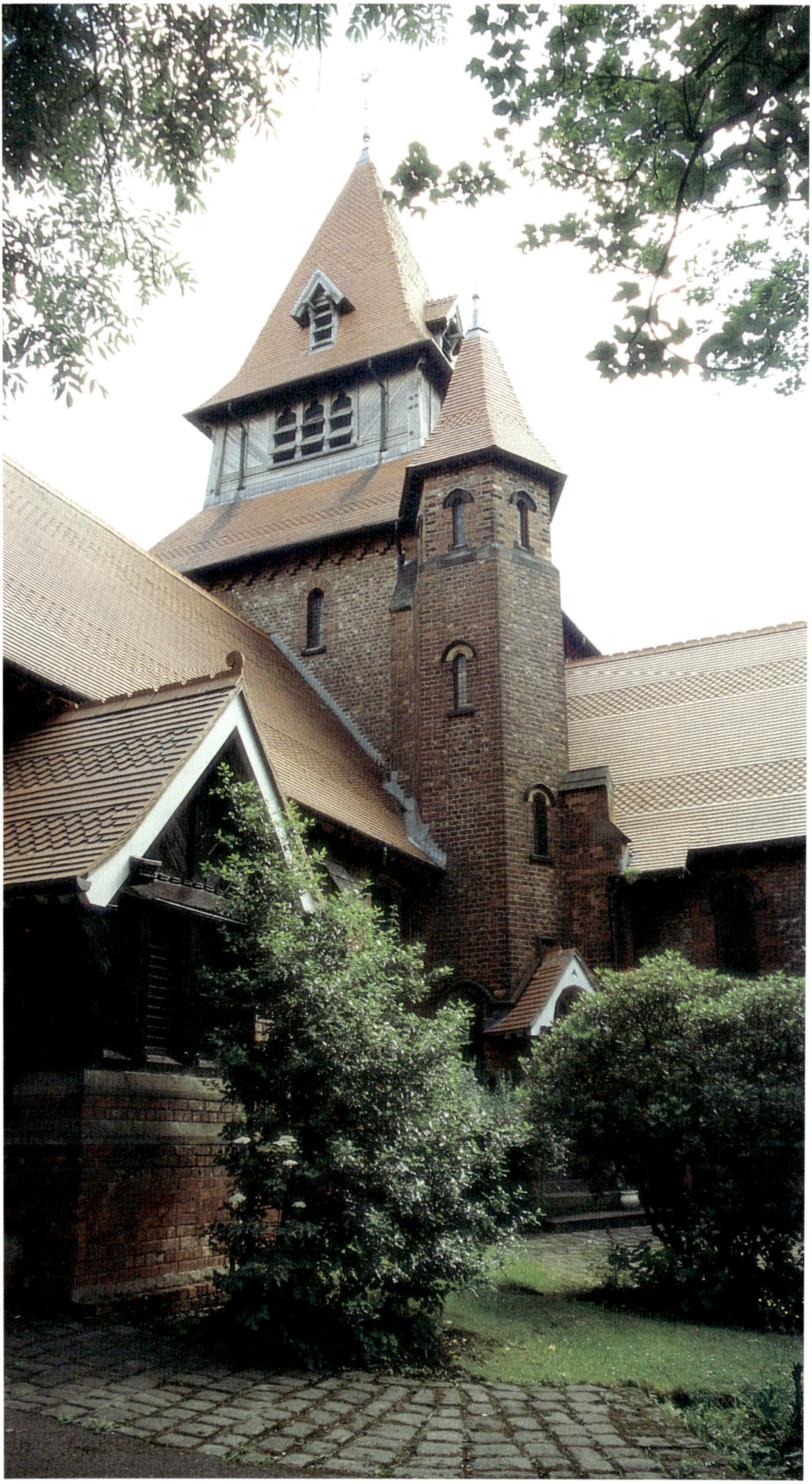

THE ARTS AND CRAFTS MOVEMENT IN THE NORTH WEST OF ENGLAND

A Handbook

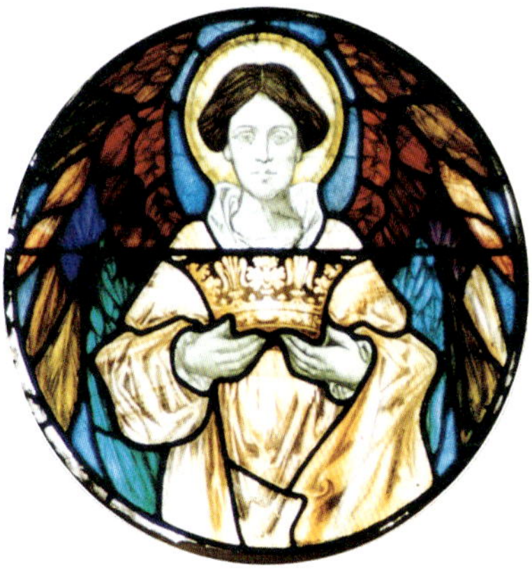

BARRIE AND WENDY ARMSTRONG

OBLONG

Cover Illustration: ***Peacock Frieze designed by W. Dennington for Shand Kydd, c. 1900.*** *© Whitworth Art Gallery, Unuiversity of Manchester.*

Frontispiece: ***St Anne, Haughton, by J. M. Taylor, 1882.***

Title Page: ***Christ Church, Chadderton. Detail of the Ainley memorial window, c. 1902.***

First published for the authors in 2005 by Oblong Creative Ltd, 416B Thorp Arch Estate, Wetherby LS23 7BJ, UK

ISBN 0 9536574 6 9

Published with the generous assistance of the Mark Fitch Fund

Designed and produced in the UK by Oblong Creative Ltd

CONTENTS

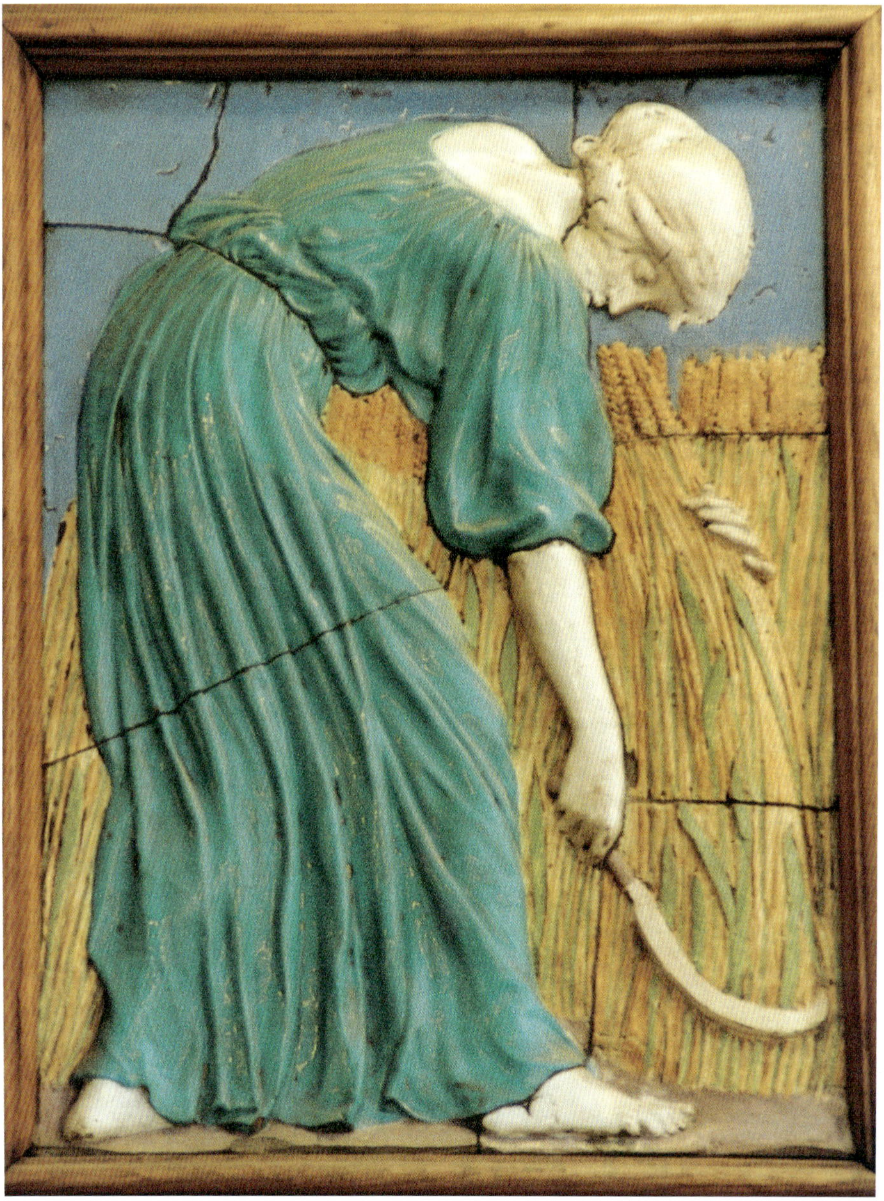

Central Library, Birkenhead. 'The Reaper'. Della Robbia plaque designed by Conrad Dressler.
Courtesy of Birkenhead Library and Wirral Library Services

PREFACE

We have set out to make this book a good companion and a useful guide for those going in search of the legacy of the Arts and Crafts Movement in the North West of England. The Gazetteer has been compiled over the last seven years during which we visited more than eight hundred sites travelling countless miles between the Solway Firth and the Potteries, the Pennines and the Irish Sea. These visits were not the result of random ramblings but were planned after extensive preparatory and on-going research.

We began by looking first of all for references to work carried out in the North West by men and women who were well-known in the Arts and Crafts Movement and whose output is well-documented. This relatively easy task was soon expanded to include the work of members of The Art-Workers' Guild and the Arts and Crafts Exhibition Society, many of whom were less well-known and consequently less well catalogued. From there we spread our net even wider to include members of the short-lived Northern Art Workers' Guild many of whom, despite producing excellent work were unrecognised and virtually unrecorded. We also looked for the work of artists and designers, including many women, who were not admitted to or did not join organisations but were trained in the Arts and Crafts manner.

Our bibliography gives some indication of the extent of our efforts to locate the work of our architects, artists, designers and craftsmen from contemporary and modern published sources. We also spent a considerable time in various Public Record Offices and national and county archives. We visited art galleries and museums, university and public libraries and the Diocesan Record Offices of the region. Last but not least, we were grateful to receive many suggestions and recommendations from scholars, curators, vicars, vergers, church wardens, friends and helpful passers-by.

Serendipity was our constant companion. We were surprised and delighted by the number of occasions on which a visit to confirm the continued existence of one piece of work revealed another totally unexpected 'find'. This suggests that there is more work still to be discovered in the region. Among these 'finds' were works deserving of the highest praise whose provenance, despite our initial research, we have had to attribute for the time being to 'Anon'.

Art and architectural historians generally date the Arts and Crafts Movement to the years between 1880 and the Great War. We have taken a broader view in order to include some of the influential work done between 1860 and 1880 while the Movement was developing. This includes the work of William Morris and his Pre-Raphaelite circle and a number of architects who set the trend towards a freer use of the principles of Gothic architecture. While fashions changed and the demand for Arts and Craft work diminished after the Great War many architects, artists, designers and craftsmen lived on and continued to work well into the 1940s and we have followed the work of some of our people up to, and in some cases, beyond the Second World War. We have not included the work of people who started their careers after 1920.

Art Nouveau in the 'Continental' style was not generally appreciated in contemporary England but we did find and include the occasional 'whiplash curve' in decorative motifs. (More than 'occasional' if we include the flowing robes in the stained glass designed by Burne Jones for Morris & Co). The Art Deco style came into vogue as most things Arts and Crafts were going out of fashion and so for the most part we have omitted it.

The Arts and Crafts Movement has been compared to a tapestry in which some of its threads are long and brightly coloured, others short and muted. Some are very long but make short or intermittent appearances on the front of the tapestry. So it is with the workers in the Movement, especially in the North West where there were perhaps insufficient clients to sustain a wholly 'Arts and Crafts' practice and where artists, architects, designers and craftsmen were obliged to take a more pragmatic approach to earning their living.

There is very little published research into the region's decorative art and architecture during this period and even less about the Arts and Crafts connections. We have therefore been pragmatic, some may say 'creative', in our approach to including some of the work of such architects as James Medland Taylor, Paley & Austin, R. B. Preston, R. K. Freeman, John Douglas of Chester and C. J. Ferguson of Carlisle, to name but a few. The output of most of these architects was vast, each deserving of a separate book. We have therefore included what we considered their best Arts and Crafts work on its own merits but some of their other buildings were often included because of the presence of other people's decorative art.

Inevitably, a project of this kind is shaped to a large extent by the availability of the source material and the extent of public access to the work identified. There is little point for instance in listing furniture or other artefacts in private houses or including buildings with exciting interiors if they are not accessible to the public. Nor was it practicable to seek out the many intriguing houses hidden behind high and well-clipped hedges in villages or on the outskirts of towns throughout the region. Such factors as these have combined to produce an ecclesiastical bias in the Gazetteer. However, what unexpected treasure-houses of the decorative arts and crafts so many churches and chapels have proved to be! Among these treasures there is a preponderance of marvellous stained glass. Our visits to churches provided opportunities to see many beautiful works of art in the tranquility of their intended surroundings. Such occasions were always enjoyable and often inspiring experiences frequently enhanced by welcoming and helpful members of the church. Sadly many churches are kept locked for security reasons except for services or during particular opening times. For this reason we have provided the telephone number of the church minister or parish office at the end of each entry in the Gazetteer. We hope it will not be too much of an imposition for them to point callers in the direction of an appropriate key holder. These numbers were correct at the time of going to press but, should there be changes, Church Directories can be found at most public libraries and the Diocesan or Head Office phone numbers at the end of this preface should be helpful.

When we began our research in 1998 we were well aware of the inadequacies of access for people with mobility problems in many of the buildings we visited. From 2004 however almost all public buildings including churches are expected to provide access and most have done so. We are sure that people who deal with this inconvenience on a daily basis will not need to be told it is always safer to telephone beforehand to check on access — and also to check that your planned visit does not coincide with a wedding, christening or funeral.

The latest changes in local government boundaries have created some minor problems in arranging the Gazetteer geographically since Warrington, Halton and Wirral were released from the control of their administrative counties. For the sake of tidiness we have, with apologies, returned Wirral to Merseyside and Warrington and Halton to Cheshire.

Living in East Cheshire we are very aware of the Arts and Crafts treasures just a short distance away in North Staffordshire and so we have chosen to add them to the Gazetteer with a nodding apology to Staffordshire people if they are not happy to be linked to the North-West in this way. We think the rarity value and the quality of the work listed in the Gazetteer will be sufficient justification for our straying over the border.

When we were arranging the routes for our hundreds of visits we used a combination of the Philip's – Ordnance Survey Street Atlases and the Landranger Series of maps. We have included O.S. Grid References for every entry in the Gazetteer and recommend the use of the appropriate O.S. Street Atlases.

As we progressed through the region we found ourselves confronted by a 'new name' almost every day and we decided to develop a 'Who's Who'. Neither of us will now own up to having suggested the idea because it has grown immense and has consumed a huge amount of time. We have given less space to those people who are already well known and much written about in order to include the less well known and to give at least a mention to those about whom we know next-to-nothing. We hope that the sometimes minimal information we have been able to gather about individuals may help to make linkages in the 'people-network' of the period and inspire others to dig deeper. Who knows anything for instance about the Grasmere Hermit other than that he is said to have carved the over-mantle in the dining room of the Langdale Chase Hotel in 1892?

All the names included in the 'Who's Who' are printed in bold type in the Gazetteer and the places where the work of individuals can be found are listed at the end of each 'Who's Who' entry. We hope this cross-reference will be useful and simple to use.

Nowhere in the book have we tried to define the Arts and Crafts Movement or seek to explain how it came about. We did not have the space and it has already been done by more experienced hands than ours. So for those readers who are not familiar with the Movement we have asterisked those books in the bibliography which will be particularly useful in giving an overview of the subject. Of course there is nothing quite like actually getting out and seeing things to help gain an understanding and the purpose of this book is to show you where to look in the North-West.

We know that this book is not a complete guide to absolutely everything that is Arts and Crafts in the North West of England — time and space would not permit it — but we would be pleased to hear of things we have missed or to receive information on people or organisations about whom we know very little. In the meantime we hope the Gazetteer is fit for the purpose, vernacular in style and of exacting quality. It has certainly been satisfying to compile.

Barrie & Wendy Armstrong
Bollington
March 2005

C. of E. Diocesan Telephone numbers

Carlisle (for Cumbria)	01228 522 573
Blackburn (for most of Lancashire)	01254 54421
Bradford	01535 650555
Manchester	0161 828 1400
Chester (includes Cheshire, parts of Merseyside & Greater M/c)	01244 620 444
Lichfield Diocesan Secretary	01543 306030
Liverpool (includes Warrington, Widnes & Wigan)	0151 709 9722

R. C. Diocesan Telephone Numbers

Diocese of Lancaster Administration office (inc Cumbria)	01524 384820
Diocese of Salford Curia	0161 8340005
Archdiocese of Liverpool Central information office	0151 522 1000
Archdiocese of Birmingham Administration office (inc. Staffs)	0121 230 6237

Non-Conformist Church Telephone Numbers

North Western Baptist Association	01942 221595
Methodist Church	020 7486 5502
United Reform Church	020 7916 2020
Unitarian Church	020 7240 2384

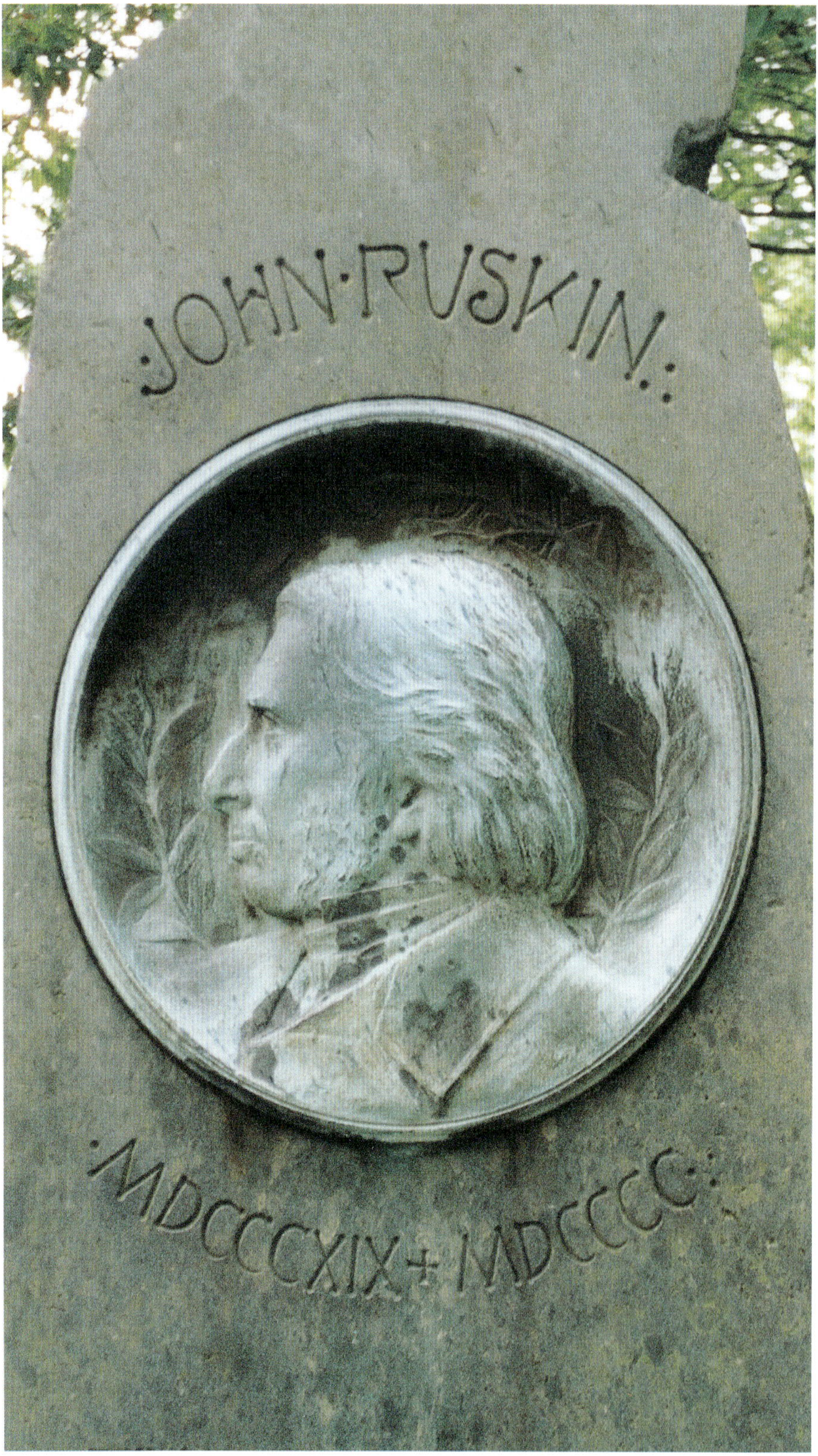

John Ruskin's memorial at Friars Crag, Derwentwater. Sculpture by A. C. Lucchesi, c. 1901.

INTRODUCTION

MUCH OF WHAT HAS BEEN WRITTEN about the Arts and Crafts Movement has focused on events, organisations and personalities in London, the Home Counties and the Cotswolds which were from the 1880s, the main centres of attention and activity for the architects, artists, designers and craftsmen involved with its development. Although recent publications[1] have highlighted the work of some of Lakeland's Arts and Crafts organisations, we found, while doing the research for this book, that most of the North West was unexplored and unreported. We had set out to do no more than identify the buildings and decorative arts associated with the Arts and Crafts in the region but we soon found ourselves asking questions about the people involved and how the Movement had developed in the North West. The 'people' questions have been answered in more detail in our 'Who's Who' and we have set out below what is a brief account of some of the events, people and organisations that contributed to the progress of the Movement in the Region.

In Cumbria, the Lake District had been imbued with its own particular culture of poetry and art long before the opening of the last quarter of the nineteenth-century. By that time, however, industrialisation elsewhere in the country had led to the demise of many of the area's traditional crafts and cottage industries. In 1872 John Ruskin bought 'Brantwood', a house overlooking Coniston Water and for the last twenty-seven years of his life spent more and more time there. Around him assembled a circle of philanthropic friends and acquaintances who admired his teachings and were able to implement them in practical ways. In so doing they developed Lakeland's own appropriate brand of Arts and Crafts.

In 1884, the redoubtable vicar of Crosthwaite H. D. Rawnsley (who had been a student of Ruskin's at Oxford) and his talented, artistic wife Edith established evening classes in their parish hall teaching handicrafts which provided creative and useful occupations for the unemployed and those in seasonal employment. The classes,

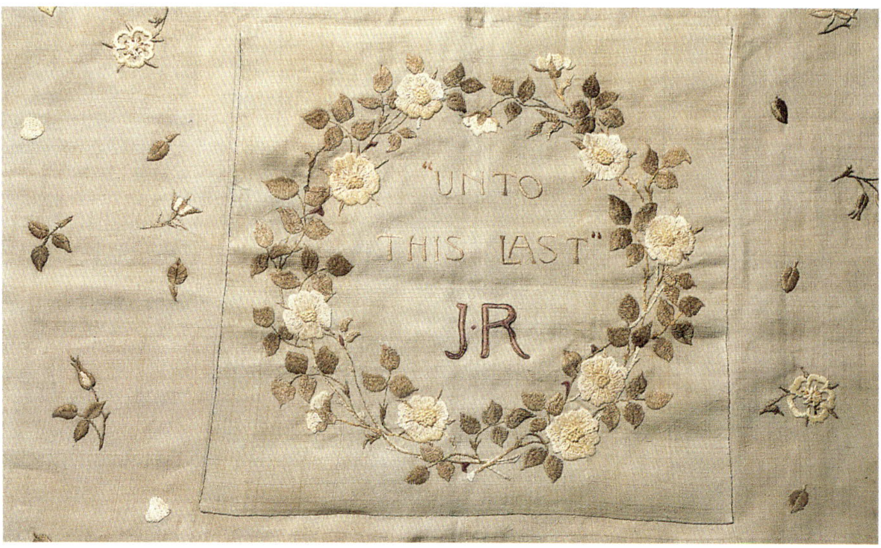

Ruskin's pall, designed by Edith Rawnsley and Harold Stabler and made by Marian Twelves and workers at the Ruskin Linen Industry, 1900. *© Ruskin Museum, Coniston.*

which came to be known as the Keswick School of Industrial Arts, grew so large and commercially successful that in 1894 the School moved into its own purpose-built premises. Best known for making repoussé copper, brass and silver wares, the School continued in business until 1984. Among the many excellent teachers who worked there was Harold Stabler who had trained at the Kendal School of Art while apprenticed to Arthur Simpson. He became the Keswick School of Industrial Arts' first head teacher.

Also in 1884, while the Art-Workers' Guild was being established in London, the Langdale Linen Industry was established in Elterwater by Albert Fleming a London solicitor and his housekeeper Marian Twelves, who had moved from the south to live in Skelwith Bridge. Both were devoted Ruskinians whose objectives were to retrieve the lost skills of hand-spinning and weaving once common in Westmorland and Cumberland and to offer the women of Langdale the opportunity to enhance the quality of their lives through the practice of these crafts and the art of embroidery. Elizabeth Pepper took over the creative management of the industry in 1889 when Marian Twelves left Langdale to do similar work in connection with the Keswick School of Industrial Arts. In 1894 Miss Twelves set up her own Ruskin Linen Industry at High Hill, Keswick under the auspices of the St George's Guild.

Inspired by the work at Langdale, Annie Garnett started a similar spinning, weaving and embroidery class in her home town of Windermere. By 1891 the class had become commercially viable and under the trade name of 'The Spinnery' produced some exquisite woven linens and silks as well as embroidery. Many years later in 1920 Ann Macbeth, the celebrated embroiderer and teacher at the Glasgow School of Art chose to spend her retirement in the Lake District. The only example of her work we found outside the museum collections hangs in her local church, St Patrick's, Patterdale. The Coniston Museum has a particularly fine collection of work by the Langdale and Ruskin Linen Industries while the Abbot Hall Gallery and Museum in Kendal owns a unique collection of Annie Garnett's work.

The spinning and weaving of linen was by no means confined to Langdale, Windermere and Keswick. Across the county at Cockermouth Jonathan Harris and Sons were producing machine-woven linens at the Derwent Mill by the 1870s and had shops in London, Manchester, Birmingham and abroad.[2] They produced over fifty shades of coloured cloth and yarn and during the 1880s and '90s sold a range of artistically designed domestic furnishings which they showed at national exhibitions in 1889 and 1890.

Working on a similar scale in the north of the county was the firm of Thomas Clarkson which had earlier been based at Bannister Hall, near Preston where they had block-printed the first fabrics sold by Morris, Marshall Faulkner & Co. in 1868. The firm moved from Preston to Carlisle in the 1880s where they were fabric printers mostly of Arts and Crafts designs. They did not resume printing for Morris & Co. until 1904.[3] To-day the successor firm, Stead MacAlpin & Co., in Cummersdale, Carlisle still prints Morris's patterns under licence for Liberty's and Sanderson but the original Morris blocks are now kept in the William Morris Gallery, Walthamstow. Alexander Morton & Co., makers of woven textiles, moved their business from Scotland to Carlisle in 1900. They had contracts with Butterfield and Voysey but also bought designs from other leading designers of the day. From 1906, under the name of Morton Sundour Fabrics, they also produced printed textiles in Carlisle in a factory designed for them by Robert Lorimer.

Carlisle can claim association with the early Arts and Crafts Movement through George Howard, Ninth Earl of Carlisle, friend and patron of William Morris and Edward Burne-Jones. They carried out important commissions for him at his London house and at Naworth Castle where they were frequent visitors. The Tullie House Museum in Carlisle continues this association with a wonderful collection of Pre-Raphaelite paintings and even some work by George Howard himself.

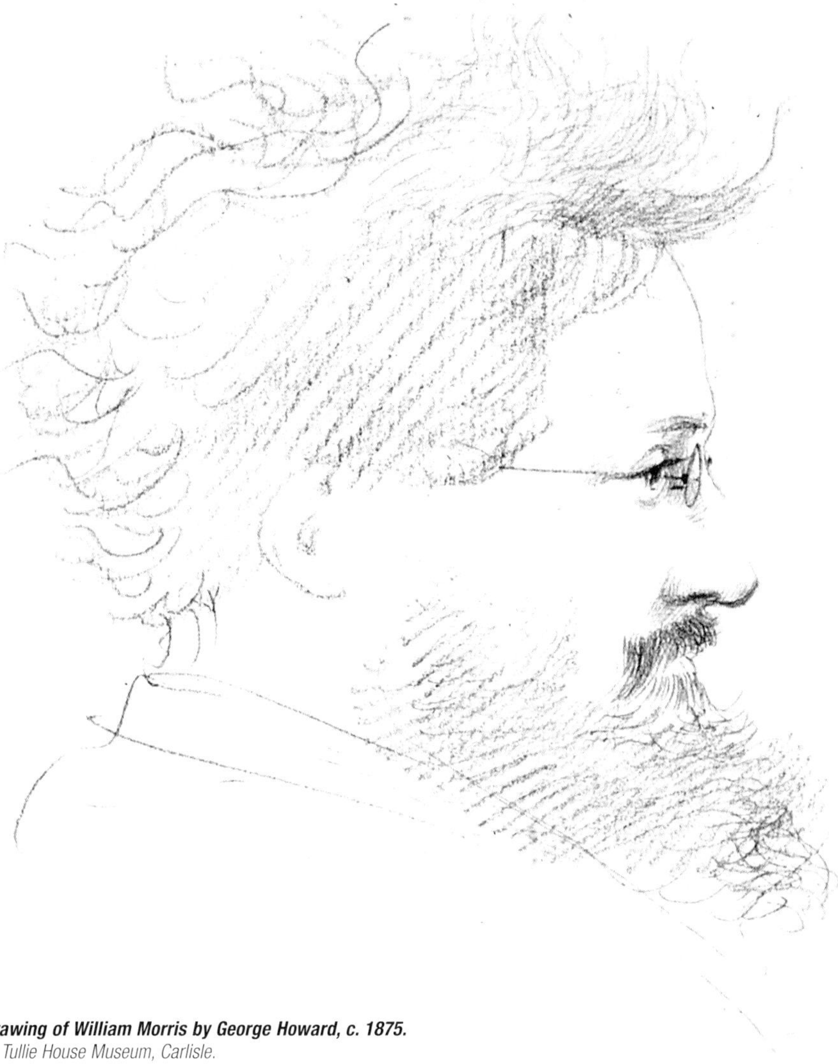

Drawing of William Morris by George Howard, c. 1875.
© Tullie House Museum, Carlisle.

A.W. Simpson ran his furniture making and wood-carving business in Kendal from 1885 to 1922 and is probably now the best known of the Cumbrian craftsmen. Despite working in and managing a very successful business he made time to pass on his craft skills by giving classes in many of the surrounding villages and running a summer school at Ghyll Head 1893–1901. In 1901 he set up 'The Handicrafts', a shop near the railway station in Windermere to sell his own wares and the pottery, metalwork and fabrics of other craftsmen. He also held annual exhibitions in Kendal to show his own work and that of his students alongside the paintings and drawings of local artists, including Arthur Severn and Edith and William Collingwood. William Collingwood was Ruskin's secretary and one of his former students at Oxford.

There is much to be discovered about many other skilled wood-workers and carvers in Cumbria who perhaps worked in a similar way to Simpson but whose lives and work have not been recorded. The work of Joseph Kilbride who had a workshop in Windermere but retired to Barbon has been identified in a number of churches thanks to his obituary in the village church, but less is known of the work of John Carlisle also of Barbon and of George Black of Carlisle, who appears for a time at least to

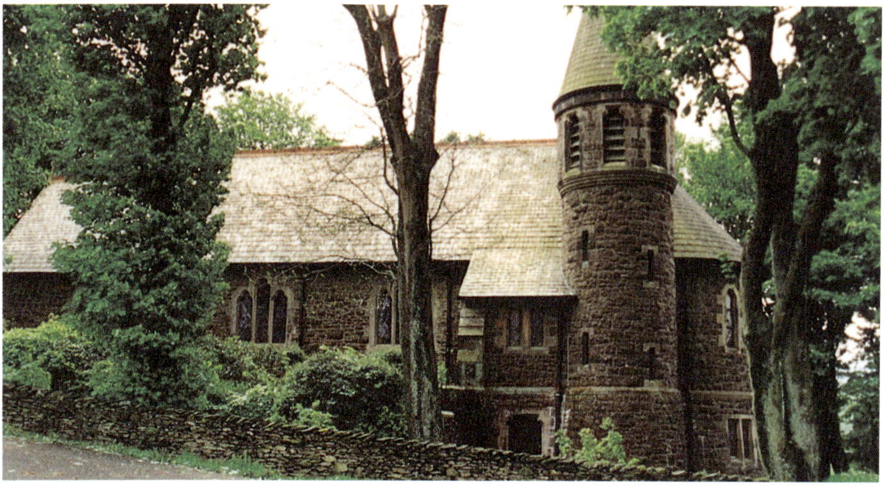

St James, Tebay by C. J. Ferguson, c.1885.

have been Charles Ferguson's favoured woodworker. George Fendley, whose work can be seen in Calthwaite church, is known to have had a woodworking school in Carlisle and to have taught both at the Carlisle School of Art and the Keswick School of Industrial Arts.

Whilst C. F. A. Voysey and M. H. Baillie Scott famously designed houses on the shores of Windermere, Cumbria could boast its own Arts and Crafts architects. C. J. Ferguson of Carlisle was a sponsor of the Arts and Crafts Exhibition Society in London in 1888 and was elected to the Art-Workers' Guild in 1893. Little has been published about his career and we have confined ourselves in the Gazetteer to his ecclesiastical work. On the west coast, Arthur Huddart set up his practice in Whitehaven *c.* 1892 where he had trained under T. L. Banks and C. Harrison Townsend. He designed a number of restrained free-style buildings in the area including two District Banks but his major work was in Eskdale Green where he built a number of houses in the village and the large country house 'Gatehouse' for the Liverpool merchant J. H. Rea. John Flavel Curwen, whose main interests were restoring old country houses and archaeology, was based in Kendal 1886–1912 where he designed some

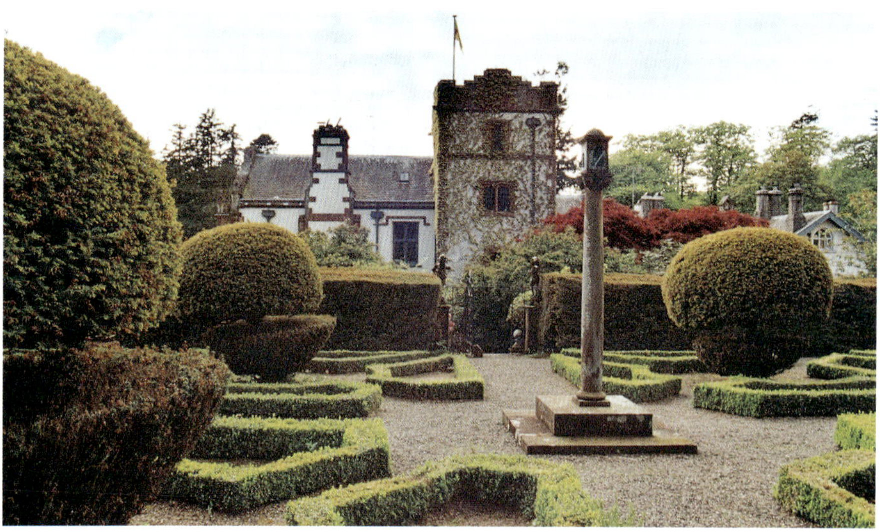

Garden at Graythwaite Hall by T. H. Mawson, 1889.

smaller Arts and Crafts houses on the outskirts of the town. Dan Gibson was a Lincolnshire man who was based in Windermere from *c.* 1900 where he built a number of country houses around the lakes and for a brief time worked in partnership with the landscape architect Thomas Mawson. His impact on Lakeland architecture was cut short when he died at the age of forty-one.

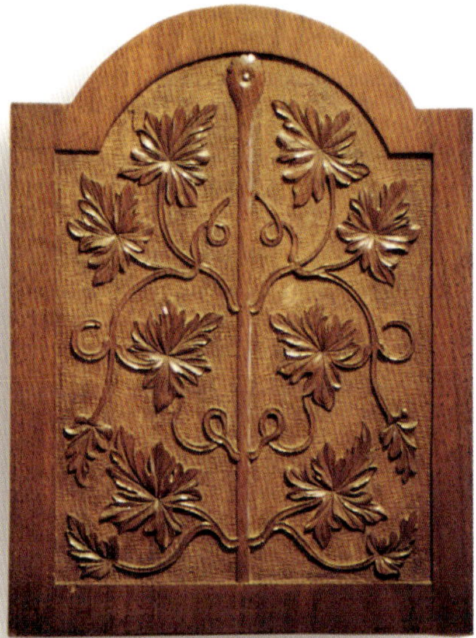

Panel from Coniston Woodworking Class, c. 1890.
Courtesy of Brantwood, Coniston

T. H. Mawson became a member of the Art-Workers' Guild in 1905 although he had been running his landscape and garden design business in Windermere since 1888. He designed his first private garden at Graythwaite, Sawrey in 1889 and it remains one of the most intact of the nineteen Lakeland gardens he is known to have planned and executed. Gardens change enormously in a hundred years and very few if any can claim to be as they were originally intended. Nevertheless many still retain their original structure and architectural features even if the planting schemes have changed.

From the later 1880s up to the time of the First World War there was a continual succession of Arts and Crafts exhibitions both nationally and locally. Like the many local evening classes[4] these were often staged by the Home Arts and Industries Association,[5] by various art-workers' groups or by the Art or Technical Schools. The most prestigious of these were the Arts & Crafts Exhibition Society's shows in London and the Home Arts and Industries Association Annual Exhibition at the Albert Hall. The Langdale and Ruskin Linen Industries, the Spinnery and the Keswick School of Industrial Arts were frequent exhibitors as were, for a short time, The Lyswick Hall School of Art led by its shadowy Principal J. W. Oddie and the Kirkby Lonsdale classes organized by local squire Alfred Harris and his wife. Kirkby Lonsdale's prize exhibitor in pottery was the intriguing John Firth[6] while leather work and bindings were exhibited by his daughter Susannah and Miss Annie M. Harris. A considerable amount of original research is needed not only into some of these elusive figures but also into the true extent and importance of this exhibition network.

From the mid-1870s the ecclesiastical stained glass in Cumbria was all 'imported' until the late 1920's when Bernard and Beatrice Walmsley moved their studio from St Anne's on Sea to Little Langdale and even then their output appears to have been relatively small. We have highlighted ten sets of Morris & Co.'s windows in churches, including some of the firm's most memorable work at Troutbeck and Staveley and almost three times as many windows designed by Henry Holiday. This is an unsurprising ratio given that Holiday spent many of his holidays in the Lake District, developed a wide circle of connections and eventually built a holiday home there. The Christopher Whall School has eleven windows in Cumbria only two of which were by the maestro himself: his 'Nativity' in Carlisle Cathedral and the glorious east window at Killington church.

In the days of the flowering of the Arts and Crafts Movement the Red Rose County of Lancashire included what are now the Greater Manchester and Merseyside conurbations as well as the Furness area of Cumbria. Much of what is to be found in present-day Lancashire can be said to have come out of Lancaster in the architectural work of Paley & Austin, the stained glass of Shrigley & Hunt, the

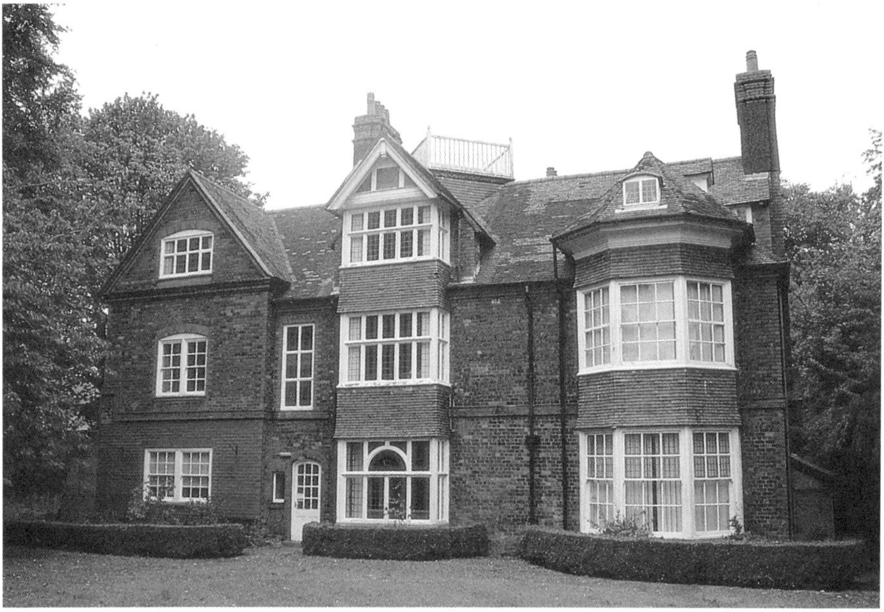

The Knoll, Westbourne Road, Lancaster, by Hubert Austin, 1879. *Courtesy of Lancashire County Council.*

woodwork of James Hatch & Co. and the furniture and furnishings of Waring & Gillow.

Whilst no-one doubts the quality of Hubert Austin's architecture few have sought to place him within the Arts and Crafts Movement. It is not an obvious conclusion to be drawn from his ecclesiastical work. Nevertheless, over a period of forty years he produced a bevy of beautiful churches, many in a progressive Neo-Gothic style, which have a degree of lightness, elegance, eccentricity, respect for the quality of their materials, and excellence in the detail of their decoration and furnishings, which should set the firm, at least retrospectively, in the Arts and Crafts fold. A visit to his house, 'The Knoll' in Westbourne Rd, Lancaster would add weight to this opinion.

Paley & Austin's preferred source of stained-glass work was Shrigley & Hunt, who were established in Lancaster by 1874. A. W. Hunt had trained with Heaton Butler & Bayne[7] in the late 1860s where he may have been influenced by the work of Henry Holiday and through him, perhaps, forged his life-long links with Carl Almquist. From the beginning Hunt's firm produced work of high quality in its design, materials and craftsmanship. The firm's commercial longevity is witness to Hunt's pragmatism. He was prepared to fulfil orders for rows of saints standing on pedestals in canopied niches as well as the free-flowing pictorial designs more indicative of an Arts and Crafts practice. In some minds this 'mixed' approach to style and technique may rule out the possibility of Arts and Crafts credentials: others, particularly if they had seen the firm's work at Pownall Hall in Wilmslow, would disagree.

Lancaster supported six other stained-glass manufacturers in the early years of the twentieth century and, of these, the one with the closest links with the Arts and Crafts Movement was Barrowclough & Sanders. Barrowclough trained with Shrigley and Hunt, and Sanders attended the Birmingham Municipal School of Art under Henry Payne before going to work for the Bromsgrove Guild. The firm was established in Lancaster in 1920. Its work remains uncatalogued.

The family business of James Hatch & Co. was founded in Lancaster in 1841. It was another firm favoured by Paley & Austin for the high quality of its craftsmanship but this time in woodwork and carving. No records of the firm's work have yet been uncovered to help identify the extent of its work but it was sufficiently well-known and respected for it to be commissioned by architect Percy Worthington of Manchester to provide the best woodwork that could be found for the Unitarian Church in Ullet Road, Liverpool and by architects William & Segar Owen for William Lever's church in Port Sunlight.

The firm of Gillows, decorators, cabinet-makers and upholsterers, had a long history dating from 1769 — becoming Waring and Gillow in 1900. It was not a firm particularly noted for its Arts and Crafts production but one which moved with the times, had a good apprentice school, and received prestigious commissions from the leading architects of the day including work for A. W. N. Pugin at the New Palace of Westminster, from G. G. Scott for the Grand Midland Hotel and St Pancras Station and from W. Burges for the Marquis of Bute's properties. It also commissioned designers and architects like E.W. Godwin, Bruce Talbert, T. E. Collcutt and J. Henry to design furniture. The firm featured prominently in the 1903 Exhibition catalogue of the Northern Art Workers' Guild as executing work designed by one of its members, Sidney Houghton.

Thomas Mawson built his experimental Westfield Village, in Lancaster thanks to the generous patronage of Herbert Lushington Storey, a member of one of the city's most wealthy families, who manufactured oilcloth and baize. This model village, with its associated workshops provided homes and workplaces for ex-soldiers disabled in the Great War and displayed some of the social conscience often associated with the Arts and Movement. Mawson began work on Westfield Village after completing plans for a very different project, Blackpool's huge and successful Stanley Park in 1922. Not only did he design its vast acres of parkland, gardens and recreational amenities but he also controlled the quality of the housing development surrounding the park by providing suggestions for house designs and by vetting the designs submitted by other architects.

Blackpool like the rest of the Fylde coast from Lytham to Fleetwood has churches, hotels and hidden Arts and Crafts houses, which were a fruitful source of commissions for the North West's architects and stained-glass artists. New to us was the Cleveleys Cottages Exhibition of 1906 in which architects and builders were invited to submit designs for houses based on the Letchworth Garden City experience. The houses were then built on a prepared site in Cleveleys and opened to visitors as a huge sales promotion. Today the houses are an integral part of Cleveleys village.

In 1891 Lancashire was home to the largest Art Pottery in the North West. This was Pilkington's tile factory opened in Clifton by manager William Burton and expanded in 1903 to make their beautiful Lancastrian Ware pots. Although Burton commissioned nationally known designers including Walter Crane, Lewis F. Day, and C. F. A. Voysey, he also established a talented team of artists who had been working in the Potteries. Foremost among them were: John Chambers, Gordon Forsyth, Richard Joyce and W. S. Mycock. There are marvellous collections of Pilkington's Lancastrian Ware, especially at the Peter Scott Gallery in Lancaster University (which also has the John Chambers archive), at the Bury Art Gallery and at the Salford Museum which displays only a small part of its collection but also holds the Walter Mycock archive.

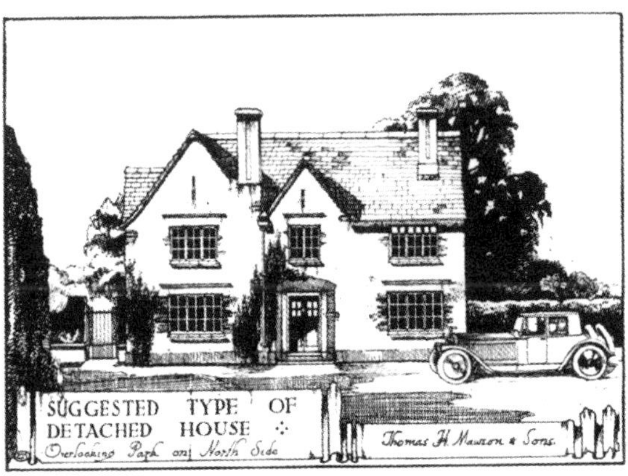

Stanley Park, Blackpool. Suggested house design by T. H. Mawson. *Courtesy of Blackpool Civic Tust.*

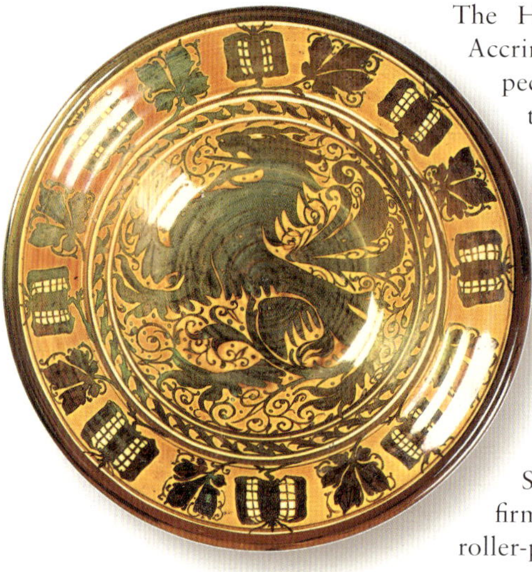

The Haworth Museum and Art Gallery in Accrington is home to a fabulous and unexpected attraction. It has the largest collection of Tiffany glass outside the USA beautifully displayed in an Arts and Crafts house designed by Walter Brierley.

In the 1880s Lancashire meant textiles, especially cotton. While most of this was mass-produced using steam power there were some smaller firms which experimented using new techniques in weaving, dyeing and printing. For example, Turnbull and Stockdale in Stubbins near Ramsbottom was a small firm of textile-printers who used block and roller-printing methods. From 1881 Lewis F. Day was engaged as its Art Director and it became one of the most successful art-fabric printers of the day with large contracts from Liberty, Maples and Goodyers. In 1888 Arthur H. Lee, the son of a Bolton mill owner, set up his own weaving firm in Warrington (then in Lancashire) encouraged by his brother-in-law George Faulkner Armitage who designed the firm's first fabrics. A. H. Lee & Son produced quality jacquard woven wool, silk and cotton furnishing fabrics designed by Day, Crane, Haité, Mackmurdo and Voysey. Their fabrics, like Turner and Stockdale's, were shown at the Arts and Crafts Exhibitions. In 1904 the firm moved to Birkenhead.

Rachel Kay Shuttleworth of Gawthorpe Hall, Padiham is an unsung heroine in the cause of craftwork. She studied art in Paris and became an expert needlewoman. Living close to the cotton mills of Lancashire she could see the ill-effects of industrialisation and the value of creative hand-work in helping to alleviate some of them. She lectured on craftwork and established craft classes in London where she worked and at Barbon near Kirby Lonsdale *c.* 1903 where her family had a country house. During the Great War she set up craft classes to help with the war effort in her home town of Padiham, Lancashire. In 1921 she was instrumental in setting up the North-West branch of the Embroiderer's Guild writing articles for their monthly magazine. During the 1920s she set up many craft clubs all over Lancashire to enable unemployed people to learn arts and crafts. It was not until the 1950s that she achieved her life's ambition of setting up a Craft College at Gawthorpe Hall. The vast range of textiles and embroideries she collected as visual aids for her lectures along with some of her

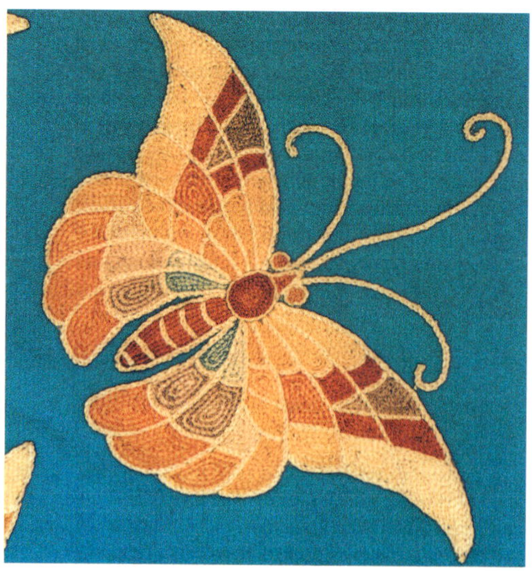

above: ***Royal Lancastrian Ware, a charger designed by Gordon Forsyth, 1909.*** *© Peter Scott Gallery, Lancaster Univbersity.*

right: ***Embroidered butterfly. Detail from a curtain attributed to Ruth Day (daughter of Lewis F. Day).*** *Courtesy of R. Kay-Shuttleworth Trust.*

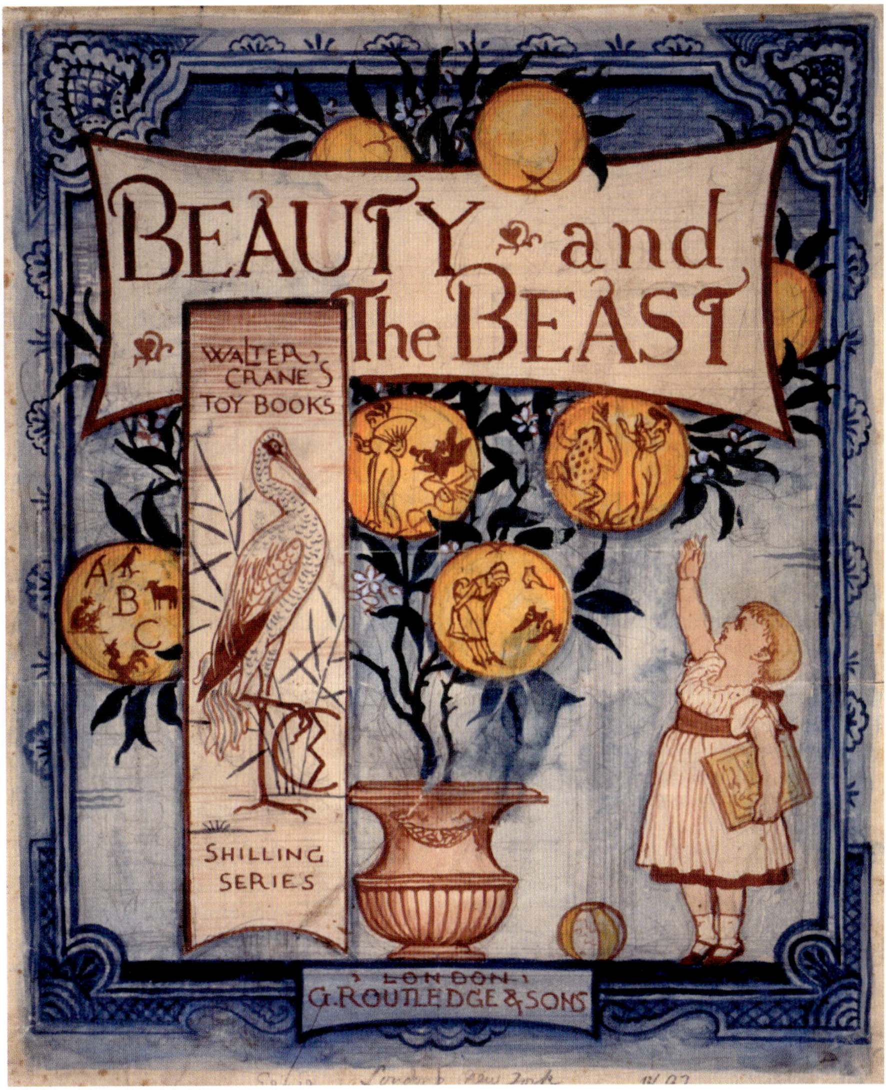

***Title page illustration by Walter Crane from* Beauty and the Beast.** *© Whitworth Art Gallery, Manchester University.*

own work now form the Rachel B. Kay-Shuttleworth collection and can be visited by appointment at Gawthorpe Hall.

In Manchester it may be said that the Arts and Crafts made a first showing in 1883[8] when Morris & Co. opened a branch of its business there. Then in 1887 the city staged its Great Jubilee Exhibition, supported with enthusiasm by the Corporation, to celebrate the city's progress in industry and the arts. Conveniently, Ford Madox Brown was still painting the murals in the Manchester Town Hall, so he was asked to decorate the spandrels in the domed exhibition hall which had been designed by George Faulkner Armitage, the well-known architect and designer. Armitage featured prominently in the exhibition for he designed the Council Chamber and a suite of sumptuous rooms with much mahogany, carving and panelling and 'rich silk curtains' Another of his displays, sponsored by Neville Clegg of Altrincham featured furnished rooms for the artisan under the seriously Arts and Crafts' title 'Beauty is not incompatible with economy'.[9] The furniture was made by A. W. Simpson.[10] The exhibition attracted firms from across the country but few individual craftsmen. The Century

Guild brought the avant garde to the city with their much-applauded[11] furnished drawing room and Morris & Co. displayed decorative furnishings nearby. It is interesting that even in Manchester in 1887, Morris was described as 'a poet and decorative artist, the great high priest and dictator in such points of taste'.[12] The next display belonged to Kendal Milne who became the Manchester agents for Morris & Co. when they shut their Manchester shop in 1887. The Manchester Municipal School of Art had a stand to exhibit students' work and it is reported that one enterprising student John Cassidy offered to model *in situ* anyone who had the courage to sit for him.[13] He went on to become one of Manchester's leading sculptors.

A new Municipal School of Art was built in 1888 and eventually extended in 1897 by the addition of an Art Gallery and Museum. The extension was made possible by a grant of £10,000 from the profits of the Jubilee Exhibition. In 1893, under the chairmanship of Charles Rowley, a printer and socialist friend of William Morris and Ford Madox Brown, the School Committee appointed Walter Crane as the Director of Design at the School after which it became a focus for much of the Arts and Crafts activity in the city. Crane's task was to advise the committee on ways of reforming design education and to teach some classes in design. He also assisted Rowley in spending some of the Jubilee money on the purchase of many magnificent items for the School's Gallery and Museum. These items now form part of the Manchester Metropolitan University's collection held in the Sir Kenneth Green Library. A splendid Walter Crane collection and archive is held by the Whitworth Art Gallery.

During the 1890s the School of Art ran a series of lectures given by prominent national Arts and Crafts artists in the week preceding the Autumn session. They were aimed at teachers and professionals but were also open to the public. The school was highly successful in winning national gold and silver medals and trained many students who made their contribution to the Arts and Crafts in the North West, including architects F. H. Crossley (1897–98) and John Cocker (1901–02), designers Sidney Mawson (1884–87) and Thomas Wardle junior (1889–92), Joseph Lawton (1900–03) artist and designer who taught briefly at Liverpool City School of Art (1920–21) and the sculptors John Cassidy (1884–87), Jenny Delahunt (1898–1901) and Walter Marsden (1907–11). The Wigan-born sculptor John Millard taught at the school for many years.[14]

Crane's short time in Manchester, only one week per month over the period 1893–96, was put to good use for, in addition to his work at the School, he played a major part in the founding of the Northern Art Worker's Guild in 1896. It aimed to 'bring together those who are engaged in all the practical Arts and Crafts' and its first Master was the architect Edgar Wood. It was supported by highly regarded honorary members including Robert Anning Bell, Henry Wilson, Lewis F. Day and Frederic Shields as well as Walter Crane himself. It drew its membership from among the commercial craft workers of the area, the staff and ex-students of the Manchester School of Art, architects and the managers of sizeable craft industries. The Guild did not achieve the stature of its London brother but it organised a programme of regular meetings each year and held exhibitions of work in 1898, 1903 and 1911 but then appears to have dwindled away by 1912. Leading members of the Guild, including William and Joseph Burton from Pilkington's, Edgar Wood, W. J. Pearce and representatives of George Wragge Ltd and Armitage & Wolff, sat on the School of Art's sectional and advisory committee's at various times from *c.* 1907 to 1930.

George Wragge not only ran a successful stained-glass studio at 'The Crafts' in Salford but also had a much larger metalwork business, started sometime in the 1890s, which included both art metalwork and metalwork supplied to the architectural trade. He worked closely with his architect friend Edgar Wood who designed many beautiful pieces of metalwork produced by the firm. Wragge employed two talented Scottish designers: J. E. C. Carr, who opened the stained glass studio *c.* 1898 and the

Glasgow-School designer E. A. Taylor 1906–11. Apart from the sole survivor of a suite of windows at the Midland Hotel in Manchester and a small window in Blackpool Town Hall, all we have been able to identify as the work of these artists is two brass commemorative plaques devoid, in the one case, of the six stained-glass windows that accompanied it and the other deprived of the wonderful Art-Nouveau figures that once supported it. All of their work can not have been destroyed in the Second World War or the great slum clearance boom of the 1960s and the '70s, or can it?

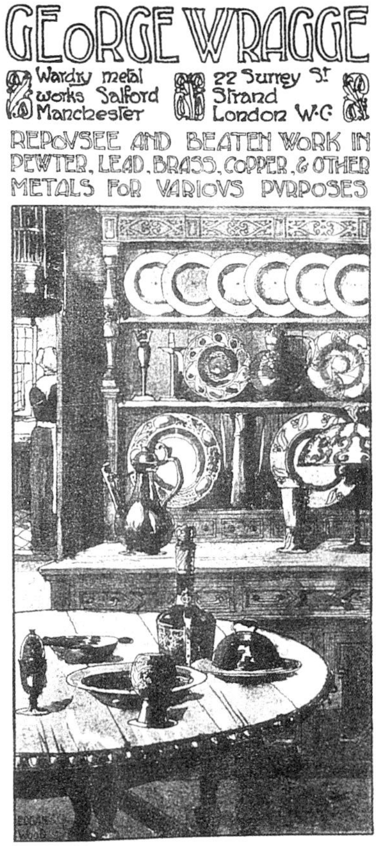

Page from George Wragge catalogue, illustrated by Edgar Wood. *Courtesy of the National Art Library, V&A Museum/V&A Images.*

Walter J. Pearce was the Master of the Northern Art Workers' Guild in its 1903 exhibition year when the joint secretary was H. Gustave Hiller. Both men were stained-glass artists. Hiller appears to have learnt his trade in the Manchester firm of Reuben Bennett from about 1895 before setting up on his own in Liverpool *c.* 1904. Pearce came to Manchester *c.* 1890 after working with an unknown London firm of decorators and stained-glass window makers[15] but his firm does not appear in the Trade Directories until 1898. Both Pearce and Hiller produced distinctive windows until *c.* 1940. Reuben Bennett showed plasterwork 'modelled by the artist's own hand' at the 1887 Jubilee Exhibition, exhibited wrought iron work with the Northern Art Workers' Guild in 1911 and was still making stained-glass windows after the Great War.

It is generally supposed that the driving force of the Guild was its first Master, Edgar Wood who is considered by many to have been the leading Arts and Crafts architect in the North of England and influential on an international scale. Most of his early buildings were based on vernacular tradition but he always managed to express his individuality and inventiveness either in design or ornamentation in ways which help to make his work recognisable. In addition to his many houses in Middleton and south Manchester he built what is the iconic Arts and Crafts building in Greater Manchester, The First Church of Christ Scientist, in Daisy Bank Road. Wood entered into an informal partnership with James Henry Sellers *c.* 1903. Both architects were interested in building with reinforced concrete and were at the cutting edge of architectural design in the first decade of the twentieth-century. Sellers, like Wood, was a talented furniture designer.

The 1860s saw the arrival in Manchester of the architect James Medland Taylor. His output, over a fifty-year period, was huge and variable in style. His architectural philosophy is undocumented and we have not seen enough of his work to vouch for his Arts and Crafts credentials, however given the quality and individuality of his churches at Haughton and Haughton Green, and his simple little St James's at Gatley, we think his work is worthy both of inclusion here and of further investigation. There are other architects like R. K. Freeman and R. B. Preston who, like Taylor, seem to approach the Arts and Crafts and then move off again. More research is needed to determine their place in the order of things. There is much more to be learnt also

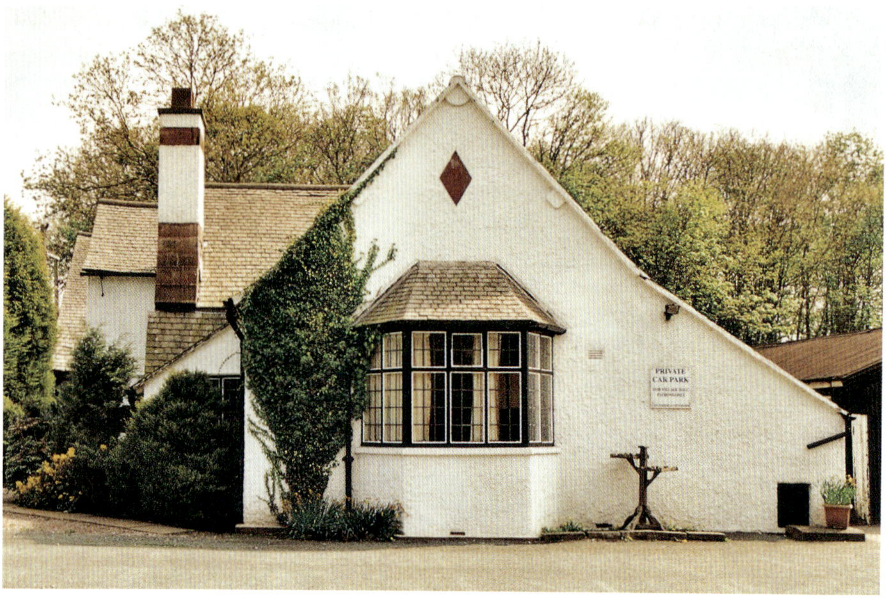

Cranage Village Hall, Cheshire, by Percy Worthington, 1907.

about the interesting work of Frank B. Dunkerley who lived in Cheshire and had his office in Manchester.

Percy Worthington however has a clearer place in the Arts and Crafts story. During the early part of his career he was responsible for a number of Arts and Crafts buildings in the North West including the Unitarian Church at Sefton Park, Liverpool, country houses in Cumbria, the village hall in Cranage, Cheshire, and George Wragge's house in Knutsford.

George Faulkner Armitage of Altrincham, architect and designer, provided a wide range of services. His business, set up in 1873, offered a comprehensive decoration and furnishing service, much on the lines of Morris, Marshall, Faulkner & Co. His designs were executed in wood, metal, plasterwork and embroidered textiles and sold and exhibited widely in England and on the Continent. He conducted most of his business from his home where he had built drawing offices and workshops. Given the nature, style and contemporary prestige of Armitage's work it is interesting that he did not join the Northern Art Workers' Guild or exhibit with them.

Unlike Manchester, Liverpool did not set up an Art-Workers' Guild and the reason for that may well be that in 1894 the University College, Liverpool established the first combined School of Architecture and Applied Arts in England and it was around this institution that the Arts and Crafts flourished for about a decade. The new Professor of Architecture was F. M. Simpson and it was not by accident that the inaugural address at the School's opening was given by his friend, the architect Thomas Graham Jackson. It was Jackson and Richard Norman Shaw who had written so passionately, in 1892, about the qualifications and training of architects. They opposed the existing system and argued in favour of a common foundation course for architecture and the building arts and crafts.[16] The new School provided the opportunity to do just that. Simpson who had been a member of the Art-Workers' Guild since 1887 appointed some of the most committed and talented artists and craftsmen as instructors including three who were also members of the Art-Workers Guild. They were Robert Anning Bell who became instructor in painting and drawing, Charles Allen who taught sculpture and Richard Llewellyn Rathbone who gave evening classes in metalwork and had a workshop in Liverpool. The Glasgow architect and designer Herbert

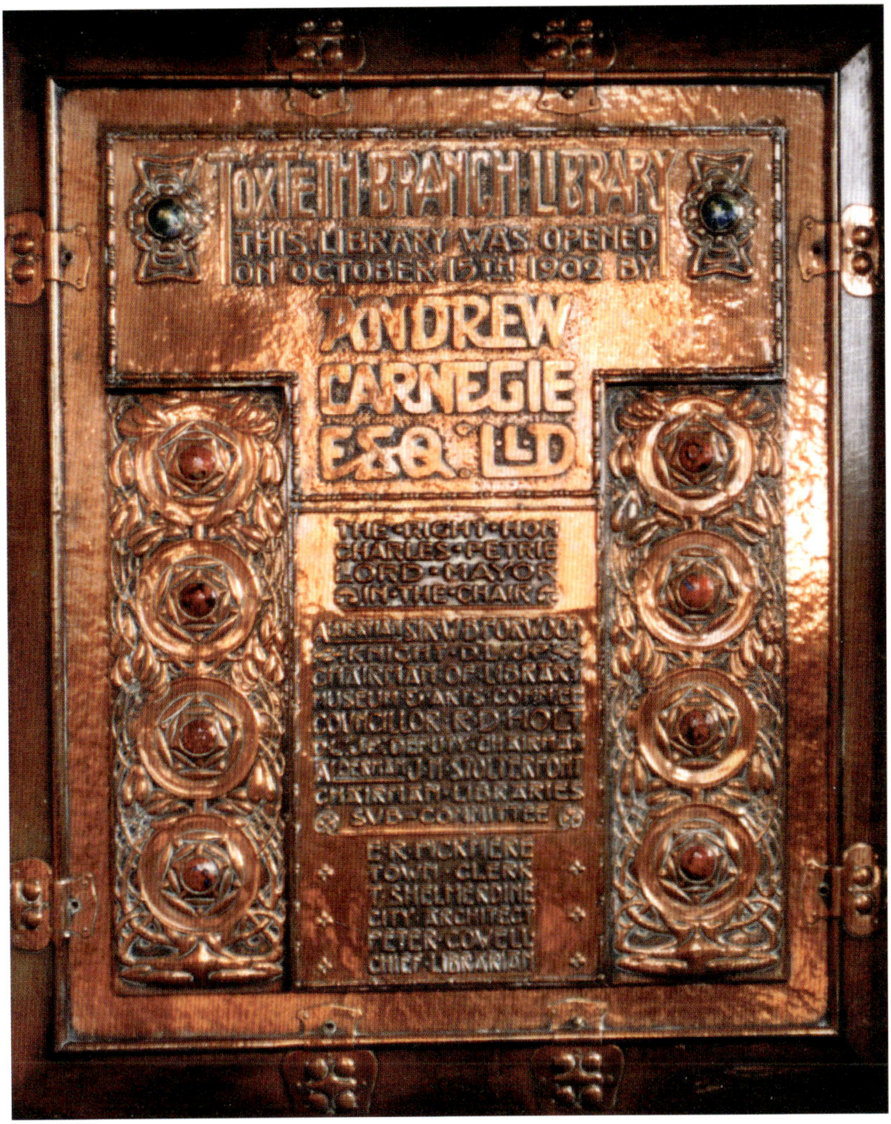

Toxteth Library, Liverpool. Commemorative plaque by C. E. Thompson, 1902.
Courtesy of Liverpool Libraries and Information Services.

MacNair arrived in 1898 as an instructor in design including stained glass. His wife Frances Macdonald MacNair gave private classes in embroidery and in 1901–02 was herself a student of enamelling for two nights a week. Also in 1901–02 Augustus John briefly added his charismatic presence to the teaching staff.

The school was a Mecca not just for young ambitious apprentices, artists and craft workers but also for older experienced craftsmen like Henry Bloomfield Bare and Charles Edward Thompson, who produced some of Merseyside's most beautiful repoussé metal work. Bloomfield Bare was also an architect and occasional correspondent for the *Studio* but in the case of Thompson we have found no evidence of his work in the North West before 1901 or after 1911.

Among those students who went on to make their names was Phoebe McLeish the sculptress and modeller who met her future husband Harold Stabler here. They became one of the most successful partnerships in the Arts and Crafts business. Ruth Bare the daughter of Henry Bloomfield Bare became a pottery designer and modeller,

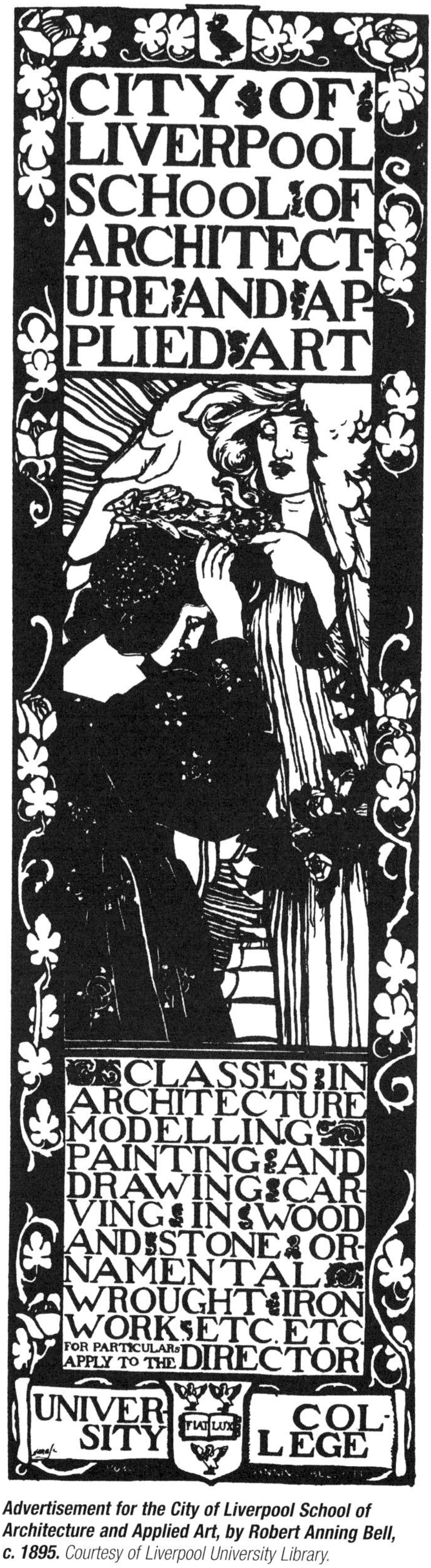

Advertisement for the City of Liverpool School of Architecture and Applied Art, by Robert Anning Bell, c. 1895. *Courtesy of Liverpool University Library.*

W. Alison Martin made a career as a painter and mural artist and Clinton Balmer went to the U.S.A. where he worked as a book illustrator. Two student sculptors went on to have very successful careers in Liverpool: Edward Carter Preston who did some of his finest work in the Anglican Cathedral and George Herbert Tyson Smith, noted for the Liverpool Cenotaph on St George's Plateau and for the sculpture on many other beautiful Great War memorials. Members of the Lee family who had moved their successful textile factory from Warrington to Birkenhead in 1904 also attended classes.[17]

The staff and students were a strong and cohesive group who worked in what became known as 'The Art Sheds' from 1894 to 1905. In the early days the students held annual exhibitions at the Walker Art Gallery. They also exhibited at the Walker's Spring and Autumn exhibitions. For fun they staged plays and tableaux in which first Anning Bell and then the MacNairs were especially involved. Anning Bell and his students also illustrated the University student magazine *The Sphinx*. The Department's lasting memento is the flamboyant Philharmonic Hotel in Hope St decorated for the brewery owner Robert Cain *c.* 1900 with decorative plasterwork and copper repoussé panels.

When F. M. Simpson left the Department in 1903 he was succeeded by C. H. Reilly and in 1905 it was decided that the School of Architecture would be separated from the Applied Arts' Department and that the latter would be joined with Liverpool School of Art in Mount Street to form the City School of Art. Some of the staff and students, who were not happy about this new arrangement opted out and formed their own school at the Sandon Studios in the old Blue Coats School. Among the teaching staff who went to the Sandon Studios were Herbert MacNair and the painter Gerard Chowne. This arrangement lasted only a short time before a shortage of new students meant the MacNairs needed to find other work and so returned to Glasgow. The Sandon Studios Society, which was formed by one of the students Fanny Lister Dove, later Calder, continued to be the most progressive of societies, supporting the Arts in the city throughout the twentieth-century.

The City School of Art, despite its uncomfortable start, prospered under its Principal Fred Burridge and Vice-Principal C. J. Allen. Over the years well-known local and national artists and craftsmen taught there including Léon Solon, May Cooksey, a former student at the Liverpool School of Art, Joseph Hodel of the Bromsgrove Guild, the architect Gordon Hemms, former pupil William Medcalf and Frank Norbury who had a woodworking business in Liverpool.[18]

In addition to the Schools of Art, the other great influence on the development of the Arts and Crafts Movement in Liverpool was its wealthy, philanthropic merchants who were patrons of the Arts and of Education. Liverpool had a long history of patronage of the Arts. Local business men John Miller and George Rae had bought paintings by the Pre-Raphaelites in the 1850s and 60s and had supported the city's own small circle of Pre-Raphaelite painters. A past mayor of the city, the brewer Andrew Barclay Walker, donated the Walker Art Gallery which opened in 1877. In the 1880s such men as William and Philip Rathbone, George Holt, John Brunner, C. S. Jones and Henry Tate would have been actively involved in promoting trade through fairs like the International Exhibition of Navigation and Manufacture 1886 and the first Congress of the National Association for the Advancement of Art and its Application to Industry in 1888. They also funded many of the University buildings and the sculpture with which they and many other buildings elsewhere in the city were decorated. The sculpture came to symbolise the wealth and success of Liverpool.

It was the 'New Sculptors' like C. J. Allen, George Frampton, F. W. Pomeroy, Alfred Gilbert, and W. Goscombe John, all members of the Art-Workers' Guild, who were commissioned for much of this work although it was the Bromsgrove Guild who designed and made the famous Liver Birds on the Liver Insurance Building. The patrons, who were generous supporters of Art in their lifetimes were themselves commemorated in death by statues set up in the city and by plaques and medals in the university buildings. All the Liverpool Museums have excellent displays of sculpture and of paintings by the Pre-Raphaelites and their circle.

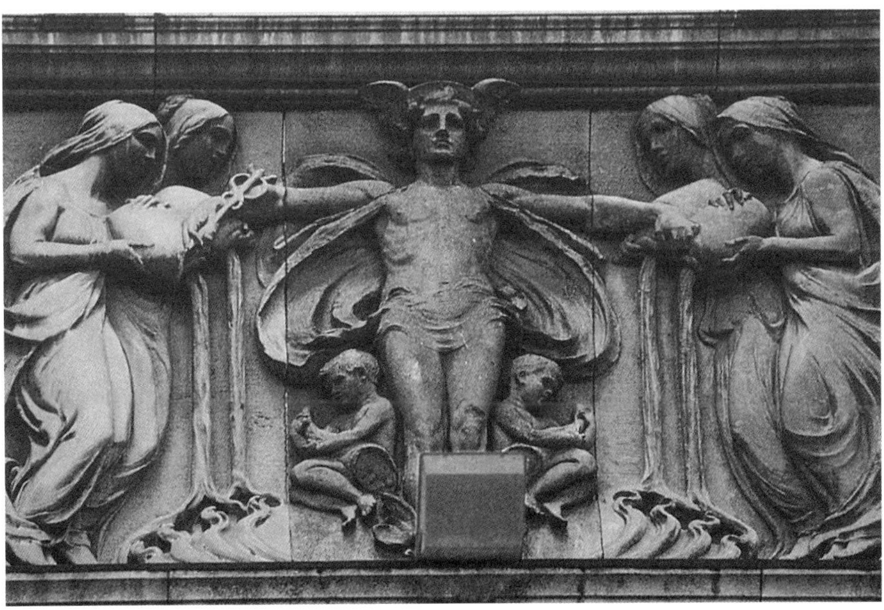

Relief on the Royal Insurance Building, Dale St, Liverpool by C. J. Allen, 1903.

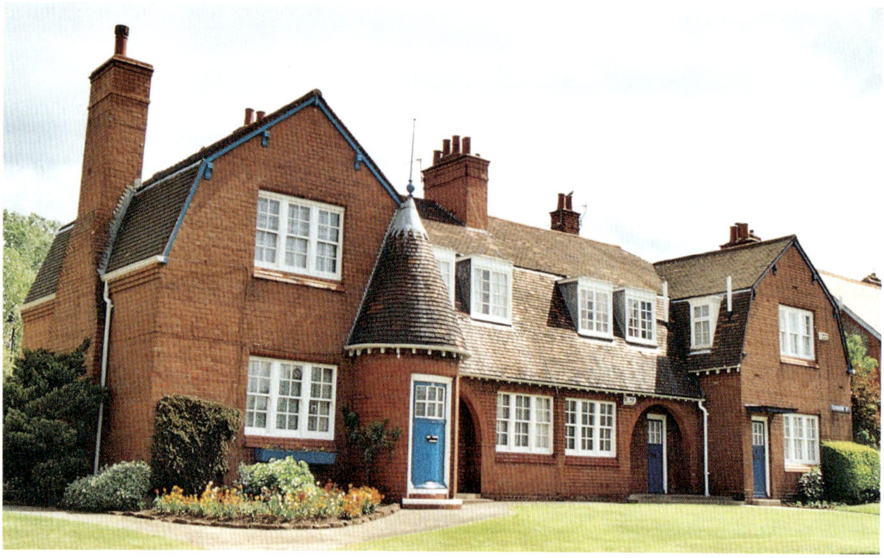

61–67 Corniche Road, Port Sunlight, by Huon Matear, 1898.

Of artists and craftsmen not directly connected with the Art Schools we found only one stained-glass artist working consistently in Liverpool. This was Henry Gustave Hiller, who had moved from Manchester to set up a studio and workshop in Seel St in the centre of the city *c.* 1903. His distinctive work in stained glass, murals and gesso-work can be seen all round the North West in churches, public buildings and even public houses. It was not until 1916 that Trena M. Cox opened her stained glass studio in Birkenhead before moving to Chester in 1923.

In 1894 the highly individual Della Robbia pottery studio was set up by Harold Rathbone and Conrad Dressler in Birkenhead to supply architectural faience but it was their highly decorative domestic ware which was most successful. As well as locally-trained women decorators the firm employed many designers including Ellen Rope, Ruth Bare and Cassandia Walker. Examples of Della Robbia Pottery can be seen in Birkenhead at the Wirral Museum in Hamilton Square and the Williamson Art Gallery in Slatey St which has the largest Della Robbia collection in the U.K.

Merseyside had a wealth of architects who for at least a part of their careers designed in an Arts and Crafts manner but their work is for the most part not well-documented. The best known is probably that of Grayson & Ould during the 1890s and early 1900s. J. F. Doyle collaborated with his former master Richard Norman Shaw on some of the major buildings in the city and on his own account is worth following if only because of his choice of decorative artists. Edmund Kirby a former pupil of John Douglas ran one of the biggest practices in the city and on rare occasions, such as at High Legh in Cheshire, sought to emulate his mentor. Charles Deacon deserves more attention than we have been able to given him. Edmund Rathbone was the northern representative of the Century Guild in the 1880s and this, together with his family connections placed him at the centre of Liverpool's Arts and Crafts scene but little of his architecture, including that produced during his partnership with Edmund Ware, has been identified. T. H. Shelmerdine was the City Council's Surveyor for forty-one years and as such headed the architecture department. It is his name which appears among the 'credits' on the beautiful repoussé panels commemorating the opening of the Andrew Carnegie Libraries built in the city in a variety of Arts and Crafts styles.

In 1889–90 the first houses were built in the ambitious Port Sunlight village which was devised by William Lever, the Sunlight Soap king who later became Lord Leverhulme. This was not simply a project to house the workers near Lever's soap works. It was both a high-quality architectural 'collection' and an object lesson in 'enlightened self-interest'. The amenities of the village were unsurpassed and the 850 houses were designed by more than thirty hand-picked architects — some local, some national — in what was certainly the North West's answer to Letchworth, if not the Hampstead Garden Suburb. The local architects involved in the project included Jonathan Simpson of Bolton, a close friend of Lever and his son James Lomax-Simpson who trained at Liverpool and had a practice there. Huon Matear was another Liverpool man who trained with Francis Doyle and was in practise with him before joining up with F. W. Simon. William and Segar Owen practised in Warrington and William designed the first of the houses on the Port Sunlight site. John Joseph Talbot who practised in Bolton and Liverpool with William Gilmour Wilson was perhaps the most consistently 'Arts and Crafts' of the local architects but his career was cut short by his early death in 1902.

One of the finest amenities in the village is the Lady Lever Art Gallery which houses Lever's magnificent art collection. There are marvellous Pre-Raphaelite paintings and many fine examples of 'New Sculpture.'

The Wirral, apart from having another of Lever's housing projects at Thornton Hough, is sprinkled with small towns and villages, Heswall, Caldy, Hoylake, West Kirby, Bidston, Prenton and Oxton to name but a few where as well as having interesting churches there are many interesting apparently Arts and Crafts houses, no doubt designed by any one of the region's architects, but discreetly hidden out of reach behind walls or hedges. The same applies to other parts of Merseyside particularly on the coast around Southport and Formby.

What Lord Leverhulme was to Port Sunlight so the First Duke of Westminster was to the Grosvenor Estates in and around Chester. Unlike Leverhulme he employed only one architect for most of the work and that was John Douglas and again unlike Leverhulme he worked on a large number of villages. The work was another expression of 'enlightened self-interest' providing sound and well-designed farm houses, estate-workers' houses, schools, churches, halls and pubs. The Duke's home, Eaton Hall was

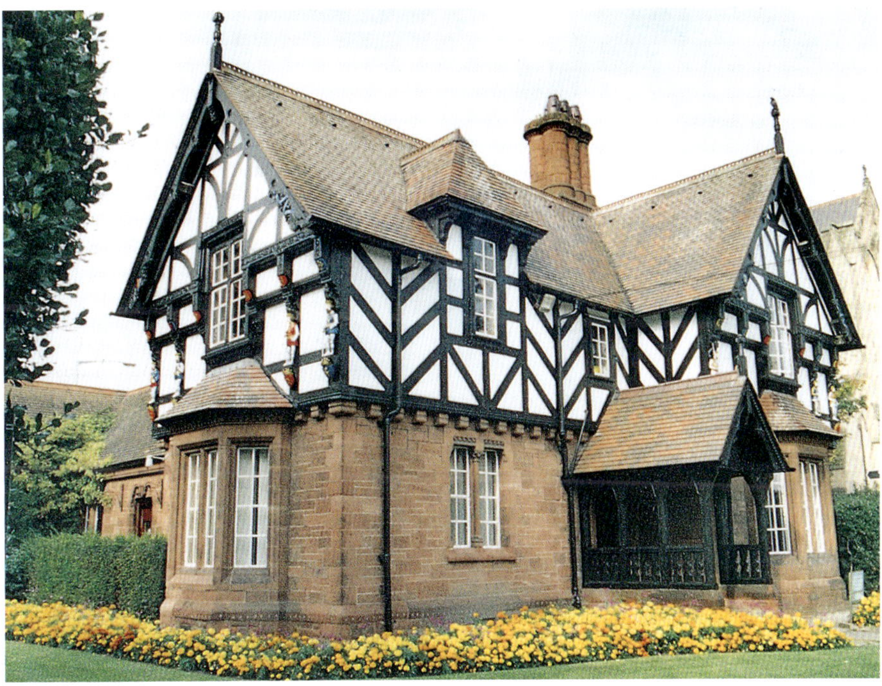

Grosvenor Park Lodge, Chester, by John Douglas, 1865.

built by Alfred Waterhouse as was the stable and the huge chapel which is full of the most glorious Arts and Crafts work. It is especially remarkable for the superb stained-glass and mosaics designed by Frederic Shields. The gardens of the house were designed by numerous Arts and Crafts designers, including Edwin Lutyens, Detmar Blow and C. E. Mallows.

John Douglas designed buildings in Chester and around the county for over fifty years and is especially renowned for his half-timbered black and white buildings. He was not a publicist and said nothing about his architectural philosophy but his work speaks volumes for him in terms of the use of traditional methods and materials, the fitness for purpose of his buildings, his vernacular style and the quality of the workmanship he exacted from his builders and craftsmen. His influence is shown in the many half-timbered houses built in the years up to the Great War — and beyond.

Chester had a Guild of Handicraft which is undocumented apart from a *Studio* report of its 1902 exhibition at the Grosvenor Museum. There was also an active and talented Embroidery Society. From the late 1890s Robert Hilton, a member of the Northern Art Workers' Guild worked in Chester and made some of the most beautiful enamel and silver work in the country. His silver work was registered at the Chester Assay Office and his commissions frequently came from churches. He had two talented daughters, Agnes and Dorothy, who both trained as artists and both showed their work at local exhibitions. Hilton and his family moved to Keswick in 1905 when he became director of the Keswick School of Industrial Arts.

By 1903 locally born Gilbert Gamon, who trained with Shrigley & Hunt in Lancaster, had established his own stained-glass business in Chester. He worked in partnerships first with G. W. Humphry *c.* 1903 and later as Gamon and Williams. Trena Cox who had previously worked for Gamon moved her studio from Birkenhead to Chester in 1923.

At the other side of the county James Smithies, a member of the Northern Art Workers' Guild ran a successful art metalwork shop with showrooms in Wilmslow and Manchester. He made his name for his distinctive repoussé copper and brass work. Six miles away in Macclesfield, there was a flourishing silk industry and a successful School of Art. In 1882 one of the town's most progressive silk industrialists, Joshua Nicholson, added to the facilities of the town by establishing a School of Embroidery in his Hope St Mill. It was run by a Miss Tweedale on the same lines as the Royal School of Needlework which had been established in 1872 in London. The School trained embroiderers who could then find good jobs at Nicholson's or in other local mills. The designs executed by the School were frequently provided by the prize winners from the Art School while others came from George Faulkner Armitage. The Hope St Mill had been producing many of Morris & Co.'s damask silks since *c.* 1875.[19]

Just over the border from Cheshire in North Staffordshire stands the moorland town of Leek which made contact with the Arts and Crafts Movement in 1875 when William Morris arrived to learn the art of using vegetable dyes from mill owner Thomas Wardle. Wardle printed fourteen of Morris's fabric designs in the 1870s and also bought designs for his own use from many leading designers of the day including Crane, Butterfield, Voysey and Sidney Mawson. Morris's lengthy visits to the area 1875–78 seem to have had a substantial impact on the town because from the 1880s several of the more avant garde business men of Leek were responsible for commissioning Arts and Crafts architects for building houses and altering their churches. Not least among the architects were Richard Norman Shaw and J. D. Sedding. Morris is said to have been responsible for encouraging Elizabeth Wardle, Thomas's wife, to establish the Leek Embroidery Society *c.* 1880 which became world-renowned for its ecclesiastical embroidery. Inspired by Morris, the Leek-based architect William Larner Sugden became a member of the SPAB and his architectural partnership with his father left an interesting Arts and Crafts legacy to their home town. John Edgar Platt, once Head of Applied Art at Edinburgh School of Art, war artist and President of the Society of Gravure Printers in Colour 1939–53, was born in Leek. He was Head of the Leek School of Art between 1910 and 1917 and made his contribution to the decoration of Norman Shaw's wonderful All Saints church in the town.

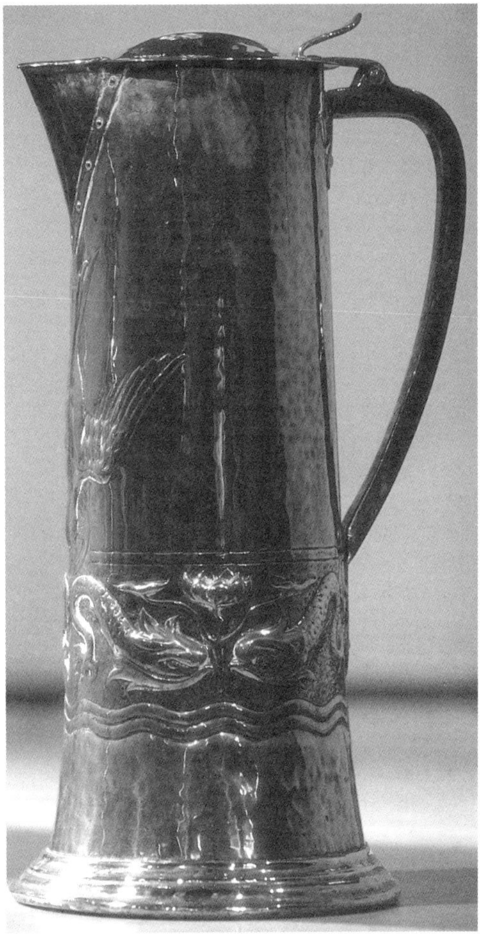

Copper baptismal jug in Christ Church, Chester, by James Smithies, c. 1905.

Stoke on Trent is the home of large pottery manufacturers like Minton, Doulton and Wedgwood. These firms set up art pottery studios to respond to the growing demand for art pottery in the second half of the nineteenth century. Doulton's was based in Lambeth in London as was Minton's until it burnt down in 1875 and was then transferred to the Minton works in Stoke-on-Trent. Here Leon Solon and John Wadsworth (a former student at Macclesfield School of Art) developed 'Secessionist' ware which was successfully produced from 1900 to 1914. Charlotte and Alfred Powell from the Cotswolds were commissioned to do designs for Wedgwood's art-pottery from 1906 into the 1930s. Smaller art potteries flourished at the turn of the century. Among them were the under-researched Foley potteries who commissioned artists as different in style as Frederick Rhead and George Logan to design for them. Bernard Moore developed his own brand of flambé glazes 1905–15. William Moorcroft, who worked as a potter and designer for James MacIntyre & Son from 1897 until 1913, set up his own business in Cobridge having already made a name for himself with the fabulous tube-lined pots which sold at Liberty's and all over the world under his name. The work of William Moorcroft can be seen in the Moorcroft factory's own museum in Cobridge and at The Potteries Museum at Hanley which also has a splendid collection of art pottery.

One of the crafts we did not find based anywhere in the region was that of the private press, printing limited high-quality editions of books. Given how few presses all over England were doing this at the end of the nineteenth-century we should not have been surprised. We did find marvellous examples of the work of the five main private Arts and Crafts presses of the period: Kelmscott, The Vale, The Doves, Ashendene and Essex House all of which are well-represented at most of the large libraries in the region. So too are examples of the related art of book illustration at which some artists like Arthur Rackham could make a full-time living but for most others, like the stained glass designers Harry Clarke and Paul Woodroffe and all-round designers like Walter Crane it was just another craft at which they were very accomplished. North-West-born illustrators included Clinton Balmer, John Edgar

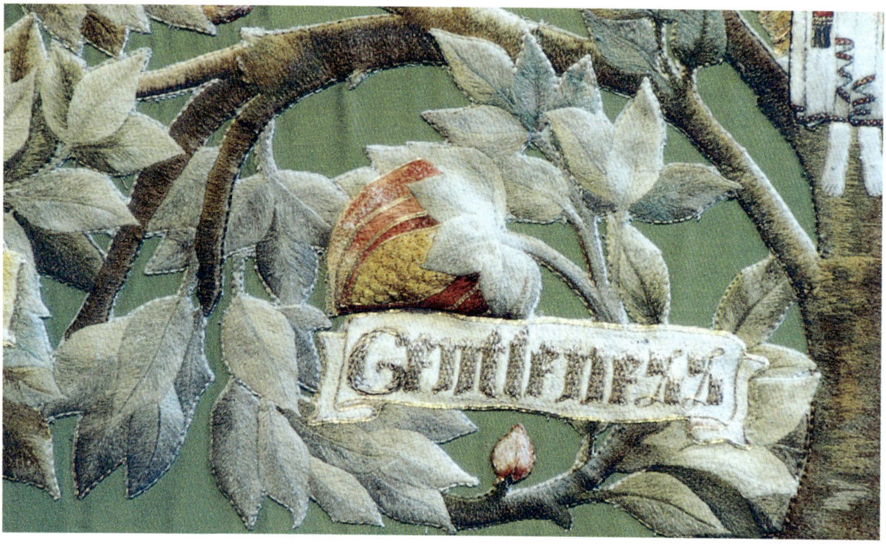

Leek embroidery altar frontal designed by Gerald Horsley for Longdon Church, Nr Leek, c. 1905.

Platt and Frederic Shields, but we have found little about Will Mellor who appears frequently in The Northern Art Workers' Guild Exhibition of 1911 as a book binder and illuminator or about H. C. D. Chorlton, who printed catalogues, posters and other work for the Northern Art Workers' Guild of which he was a member.

These then are some of the people and organisations that gave shape to the Arts and Crafts Movement in the North-West of England. Many were local but we also identified work executed by artists, architects, designers and craftsmen with national reputations who were based outside our region. Their work was often reported in the contemporary technical journals and featured in such periodicals as the *Studio* and *Country Life*. Their influence on practitioners in the North-West and on those commissioning new work is difficult to gauge but must have made a major contribution to the development of the Arts and Crafts in the North-West.

In this introduction we have drawn on information we gathered more or less as a by-product of our principal research and it has served well enough to produce this simple sketch of events, organisations and people. However, we realise we have raised more questions than we have been able to answer, and that in itself leads to the conclusion that much more research is needed to trace developments in the North West. Dozens of potential projects spring to mind as intimidating as 'how did changes in the art education system in the 1890s actually influence the Arts and Crafts Movement in the North West?' and as intriguing as 'what was A. H. Mackmurdo doing in Liverpool in the 1880s?' We hope this book will help its readers to enjoy the legacy of the Arts and Crafts Movement in the region and encourage them to seek answers to the many questions we have had to leave hanging in the air.

NOTES

1 See Bibliography for work by Bruce, Brunton, Chapman and Haslam, S.
2 Parry, Linda, *Textiles of the Arts and Crafts Movement*, p. 126, 1987.
3 Archives Stead & MacAlpin, Cummersdale.
4 Classes have been identified from various sources, including contemporary newspapers, at Barbon, Burneside, Coniston, Gatebeck, Hawkshead, Heversham, Milnethorpe, Penrith, Sedbergh, Torver, Windermere
5 Set up by Mrs Eglantyne Jebb of Ellesmere, Shropshire in 1884 to establish classes all over the country, run by amateur volunteer teachers. By 1889 the Association was running some 450 classes with 5000 students and in the 1890s the number of students doubled. The centre piece of the Association's programme was its huge annual exhibition at the Albert Hall.
6 John & Susannah Firth and Annie M Harris showed at the Arts and Crafts Exhibition in 1889 under their own names.

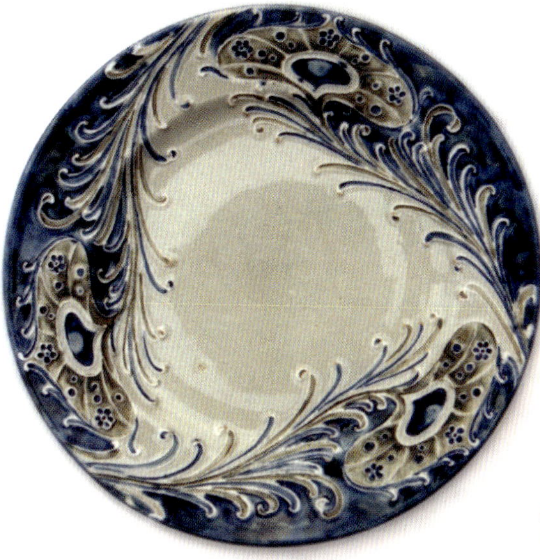

Moorcroft Florian Ware plate, c. 1900.

[7] Waters, William, Stained Glass from Shrigley & Hunt.
[8] Morris & Co. first appear in the *Manchester Trade Directories* in 1883 at 21 John Dalton St as 'cabinet makers and general house furnishers'. In 1884 the firm appears as 'art decorators, art furniture manufacturers and designers, 16 Albert Square and at 449 Oxford St London' and as 'cabinet makers' at 25 Brazenose St. In 1886 and '87 they appear simply as 'cabinet makers 25 Brazenose St' and there are no further entries.
[9] Archive material on George Faulkner Armitage at Sale Library, GMC.
[10] *Manchester Jubilee Exhibition Catalogue*, 1887.
[11] Described as 'Probably the most unique and original of the Furniture exhibits' by the *Journal of Decorative Art*, Nov 1887, p. 172.
[12] *Jubilee Exhibition Catalogue*, 1887.
[13] David Jeremiah, *A Hundred Years and More*,1980, Manchester Polytechnic Dept of Printing Technology
[14] Staff and student information from the School of Art archives at the Sir Kenneth Green Library, Manchester Metropolitan University.
[15] Information supplied by David Pearce, grandson of Walter J. Pearce.
[16] R. N. Shaw and T. G. Jackson, *Architecture a Profession or an Art*, London, 1892.
[17] Liverpool University. Attendance Registers for the Art Sheds, 1900–1904.
[18] Morris C., 'History of Liverpool Regional College of Art 1825–1970', M.Phil.
[19] *Macclesfield Courier Herald*, 3 Feb 1883.

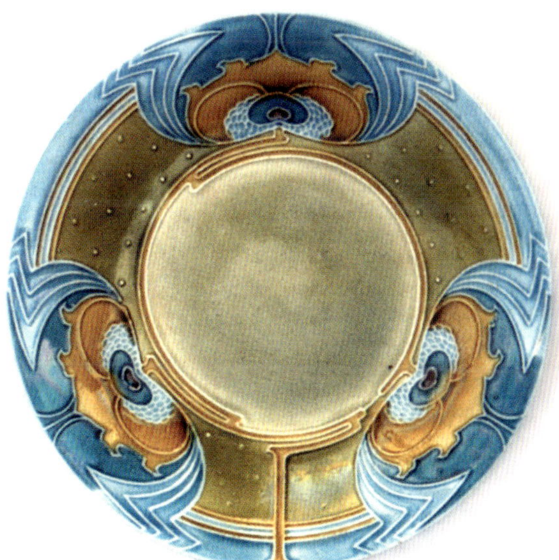

Minton Secessionist plate, c. 1902.

CUMBRIA

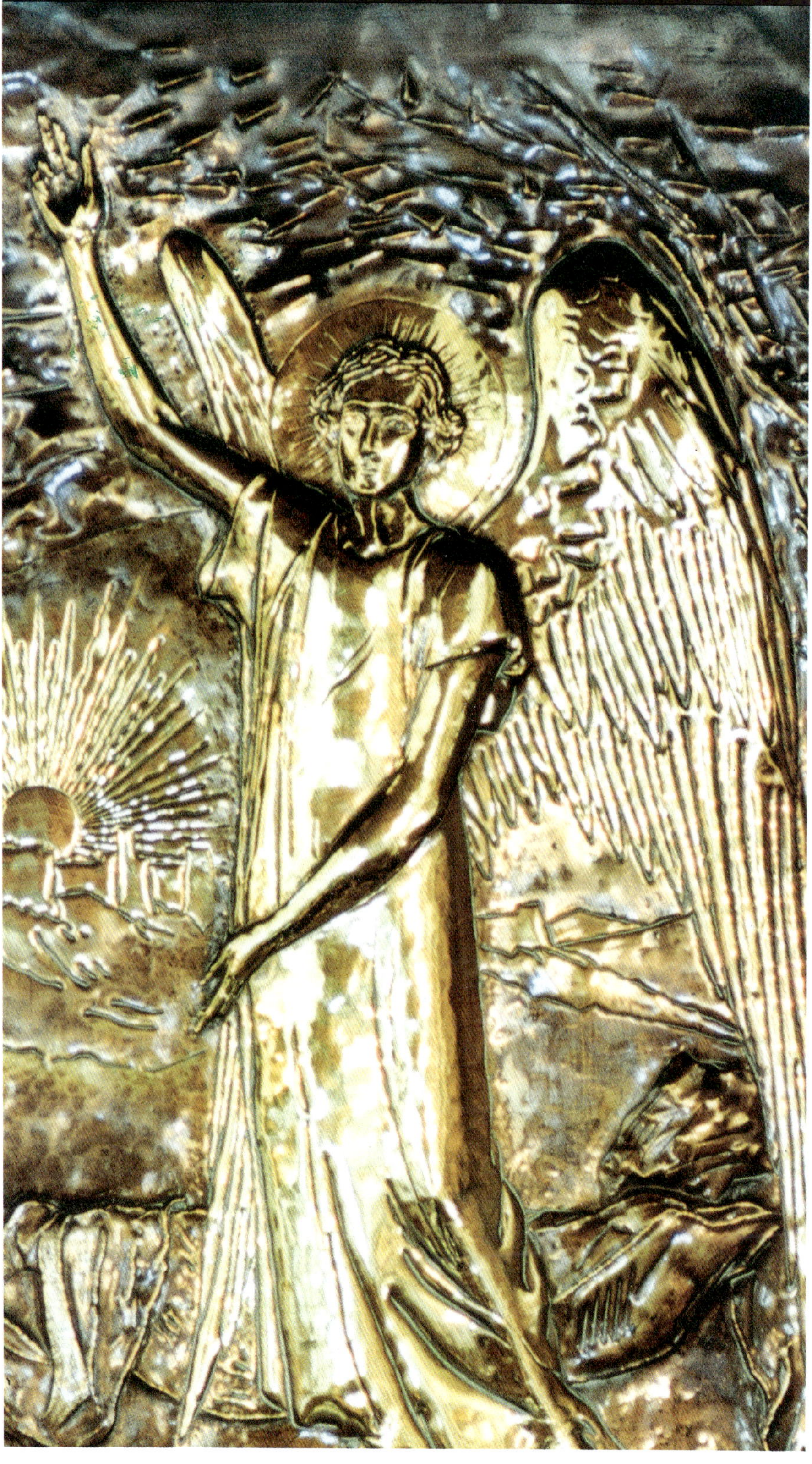

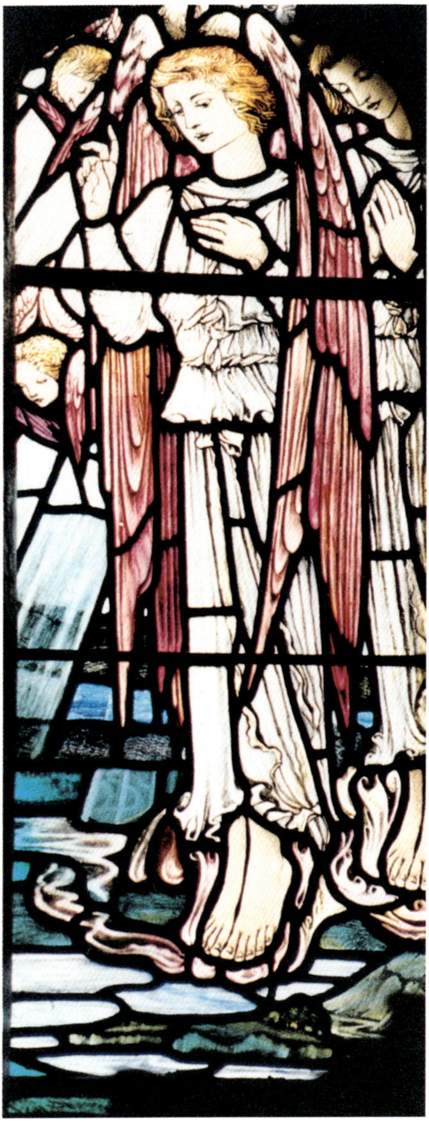

St Cuthbert's, Aldingham. Detail of the angel of the Lord. Veronica Whall, 1934.

ALDINGHAM is off the A5087 between Bardsea and Newbiggin overlooking Morecambe Bay.

St Cuthbert's (SD285710) is aptly described in its own leaflet as 'an exquisite little church'. The earliest parts of the building date from the late C12 and there are C14 and C15 additions. The pulpit was carved in an Arts and Crafts manner in about 1905 but it is unattributed. The east-facing window in the south aisle was beautifully designed and executed in 1934 by **Veronica Whall**. It shows a shining throng of angels announcing the Nativity to the amazed shepherds, a border collie and two attentive lambs.

Access: Usually open. Vicarage Tel. 01229–581383.

AMBLESIDE lies at the head of Lake Windermere on the A591.

The Armitt Library and Museum (NY376047) lies to the east of the A591 between Ambleside and Rydal. The library was founded by Mary Armitt of Ambleside and opened in 1912. It has a large collection of books about Cumbria and its notable residents and organisations. These include not only the Armitt sisters but also Harriet Martineau, Charlotte Mason, Beatrix Potter, **William G. Collingwood** and John Ruskin.

The Museum has a number of exhibits of Arts and Crafts interest including a watercolour 'The Knoll', painted in 1855 by 16 year-old **Henry Holiday**. There is a selection of **Ruskin Lace** worked by the **Langdale Linen Industry** and paintings by **W. G. Collingwood**. There are some of **Ruskin's** paintings, a lock of his hair and a plaster bust modelled by Collingwood's daughter Barbara.

Access: Library: Open Mon–Fri. 10.00–16.00, closed for lunch 12.30–13.30.

Museum: Open daily 10.00–17.00. Last admission 16.30.

Tel. for both 015394–31212.

St Mary's, Vicarage Rd (NY374044), built 1850–54 by G. G. Scott, can be located from all over the town by its huge tower and spire. The west-most window in the south aisle 'Angels with Children', 1889 and the west-most window in the north aisle 'Christ Blessing the Children', 1891 were both designed by **Henry Holiday** and made by **James Powell of**

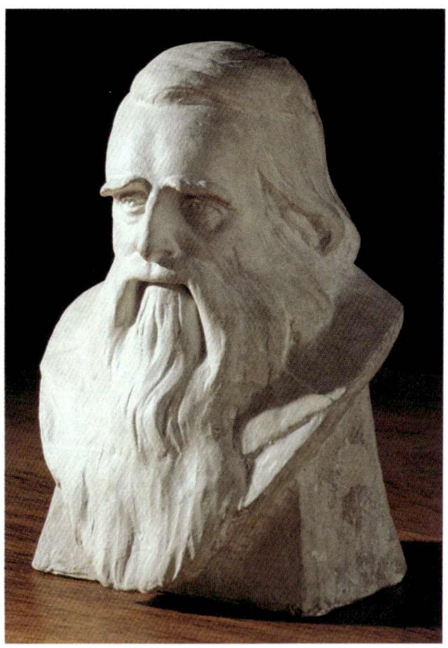

Armitt Library and Museum. Plaster bust of John Ruskin by Barbara Collingwood. *Copyright The Armitt Trust*

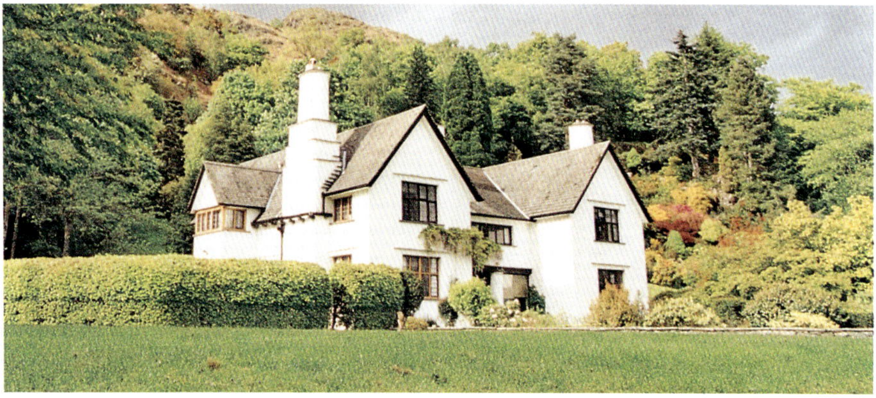

'White Craggs', Ambleside. Designed by Dan Gibson, c. 1900.

Whitefriars. The second window from the east in the south aisle, 'St Anne and St Mary', was made in 1952 by **B. & B. D. Walmsley** in nearby Langdale. The excellent wood-carving of the northern English saints on the choir stalls and other woodwork on the reredos was executed by **Bridgeman of Lichfield** 1895–99 while **Shrigley & Hunt** made the mosaic panels for the reredos.

Access: Usually open. Vicarage Tel. 015394–33205.

The Methodist Church built 1898 in Millam Park (NY376046) and its nearby free style church hall by William Mason 1903 are soon to be flats. The church's impressive Art Nouveau – style stained glass west window will however remain a feature and will be back-lit at night.

Access: Minister Tel. 015394–33232.

Ashley Green (NY357038), designed in 1906 by **Percy Worthington**, stands high above the A593 about a mile west of Ambleside. It has a Lakeland-slate roof, rendered walls and stone-mullioned windows. The house has magnificent views of Lake Windermere.

Access: Private dwellings.

White Craggs (NY364036), hidden from view high up on the northern side of the A593 at Clappersgate, was designed *c.* 1900 by **Dan Gibson**. It has many Gibsonian features including vernacular cylindrical chimney-stacks, overhanging eaves, rendered walls and straight mouldings above the stone-mullioned windows.

Access: Private dwellings.

Betty Fold, Hawkshead Hill, Ambleside (SD342994) was built 1907–08 for **Henry Holiday**, his wife Kate and daughter Winifrid. Henry, supremely self-confident though not an architect designed the house himself and employed an architect to produce the working drawings and supervise the work.

Access: This is a private house, although it does have a holiday apartment to let. Tel. 015394–3661.

ARMATHWAITE is in the maze of narrow lanes and tiny villages east of the M6, about half way between Penrith and Carlisle.

The Chapel of Christ and Mary (NY505463) is a small C17 church. At the west end there is a single-light window by **A. K. Nicholson** dating from the 1930s showing Christ and the little children.

Access: Usually open in the summer. Vicarage Tel. 016974–73320.

ARNSIDE lies at the north end of Morecambe Bay and is reached by the B5282 off the A6.

St James's (SD459787) has two windows by **Edward Payne**. His 'Good Shepherd' spreads across a three-light window in the south wall while a single lancet in the north wall contains 'The Nativity'. Both windows were made in 1948.

Access: Usually open in the summer. Vicarage Tel. 01524–761319.

BARBON lies to the east of the A683 Sedbergh to Kirkby Lonsdale road 3 or 4 miles north of Kirkby Lonsdale.

St Bartholomew's (SD627825) is an excellent example of the 1893 vintage work of **Paley & Austin** of Lancaster, who used local craftsmen to execute the furnishings. The architects' glaziers of choice were their fellow-townsmen **Shrigley & Hunt** who supplied all the stained glass here except for the west window which was designed for **Powell of Whitefriars** by F. Mann. It shows 'Christ the Good Shepherd' surrounded by beautifully drawn, adoring angels with bindweed in their hair. The 'Mary and Martha' window at the west end of the north aisle was designed by **Carl Almquist** for **Shrigley & Hunt**. 'Fortitude' and 'Pax' in the two-light window in the north aisle were also made by **Shrigley & Hunt** using designs purchased from **Henry Wilson**. The grisaille pictures in the cusp of each light were designed by Henry's brother Patten Wilson. The eagle

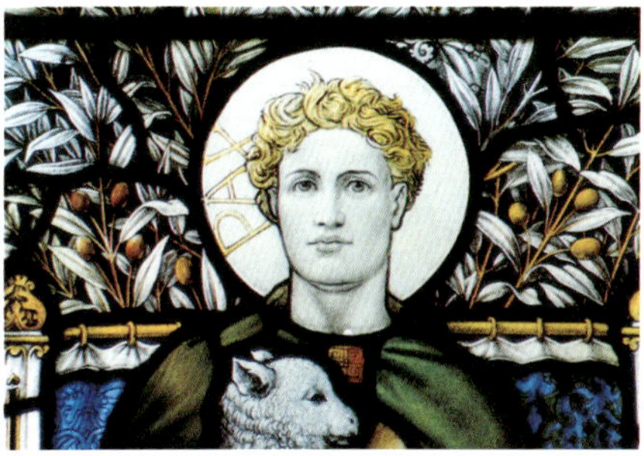

St Bartholomew's, Barbon. 'PAX'. Detail of stained glass designed by Henry Wilson for Shrigley & Hunt, c. 1920.

lectern was carved by **J. M. Kilbride** whose obituary is framed on the south wall at the back of the church. A second obituary attributes the woodwork in the chancel to Mr J. Mattison of Burton. The Chancel screen and the font cover are also attributed to local craftsmen including, no doubt, **John Carlisle**.

Access: Usually open in the summer. Parish office Tel. 01524–271320.

BARDSEA overlooks Morecambe Bay and is approached by the A5087 from Ulverston.

Holy Trinity (SD301746) has a polygonal apse containing three very unusual lancet windows. They were designed by **Wilhelmina Geddes** and made-up by her colleague **Michael Healy** in Dublin. The windows were installed in 1924 and represent the Baptism, Crucifixion and Resurrection of Jesus. The colours are very dark so the window is best seen on a bright morning. The west-most window dated 1903 in the north nave shows Jesus with Martha and Mary and was designed by **Carl Almquist** for **Shrigley & Hunt**.

Access: Vicarage Tel. 01229–583174.

BARROW in FURNESS stands on the edge of the Irish Sea at the end of the A590.

Abbey House in Abbey Rd (SD216720) about 2 miles from the town centre, was designed by **E. L. Lutyens** in 1913. It was built of local red sandstone in a simplified Elizabethan style as a guest-house for the shipbuilding firm of Vickers. It is now a hotel lying within a bow shot of the ruins of Furness Abbey. There have been changes in the furnishing and interior decoration but it remains essentially a Lutyens house.

Access: Open to non-residents. Tel. 01229–838282.

St James's, Blake St (SD195700) is said by Pevsner to be the best church in Barrow. It was built 1867–69 by E. G. Paley and is a splendid brick church. There are three windows which date from the 1950s by G. E. R. Smith in the apse and in the baptistery. On the west wall, there is a wonderful **Keswick School of Industrial Arts** brass repoussé plaque dated 1901 which commemorates John Sawyer a former verger. A small gilded and enamelled cast metal plaque hangs on the south chancel wall. It is dated 1930 but the maker's mark is not clear. The woodwork in the chancel is very fine but unattributed. The reredos, installed in 1919, has especially well-carved figures of St

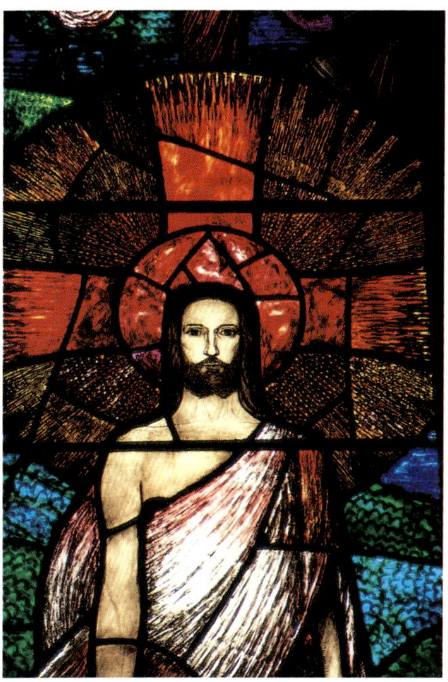

Holy Trinity, Bardsea. Detail of east window by Wilhelmina Geddes, 1924.

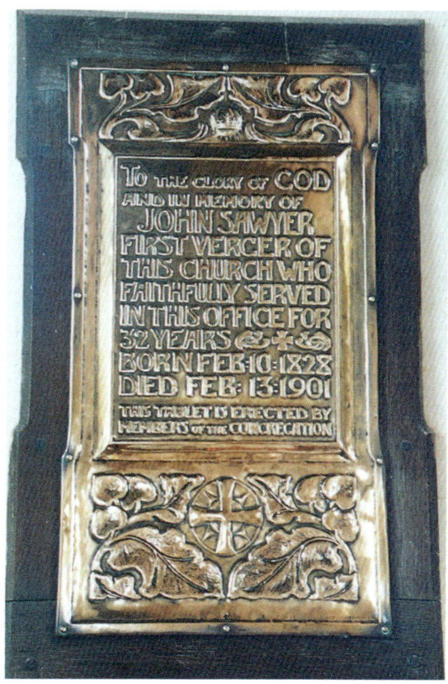

St James's, Barrow in Furness. Memorial plaque by the KSIA, 1901.

Peter and St James. The west window holds six stained-glass panels, brought here in 2002 from the redundant church of St John in Windermere, which are now set in clear quarries. The outer lights illustrate the parable of 'The Pearl of Great Price', on the left and of 'The Lost Penny Found', on the right. Both were designed by the painter **James Clark**. The remaining panels were made by **Henry Holiday** and include a single-light version of 'The Light of the World' and a three-light representation of the parable of 'The Rich Man's Feast'. They are splendid in their new setting and are a worthy acknowledgement of the vision and tireless persistence of the people who succeeded in bringing them here.

Access: Vicarage Tel. 01229–821475.

St George the Martyr in St George's Square (SD 203687) is another **E. G. Paley** church from the 1860s. Volume 39 of The Studio, p. 171, has an illustration and description of a banner designed by **Edith Rawnsley** for the Church Congress in Barrow in 1906. The banner was given into the safe keeping of St George's at that time, but is not currently on display.

Access: Vicarage Tel. 01229–821641.

There are two blocks of red sandstone tenement buildings at the northern end of **Michaelson Rd** (SD200691) which look as if they have been lifted out of Glasgow and dropped here. They were built for Vickers in 1884. Was the architect a Glaswegian? No surprisingly perhaps, it was **Paley & Austin**.

Vickerstown lies across the bridge from Barrow in Furness on Whalney Island and was begun in 1901 as the Vicker's version of Port Sunlight. It must be said however, that while Vickers did not have Leverhulme's flair for architectural variety, he did have a greater sense of urgency so that by 1904 Vickerstown was a community of some 930 houses. However, unlike Port Sunlight, the settlement did not have a huge range of social facilities.

BASSENTHWAITE is about 6 miles north-west of Keswick.

Armathwaite Hall, (NY208325) off the B5291 is a stone-built house which was adapted and extended by **C. J. Ferguson** on a grand scale in a free Tudor style in 1881. It sits in its imposing setting at the head of Bassenthwaite and is now used as a hotel.

Access: Open to non-residents Tel. 017687–76551.

St John's (NY229317) is south of the village at the side of the A591. There is a very elegant worked-metal memorial plaque on the north wall of the nave which is beautifully fashioned but unsigned. **W. H. Ward** designed the Great War Memorial in the churchyard. It is made of smooth, green Lakeland stone decorated with a

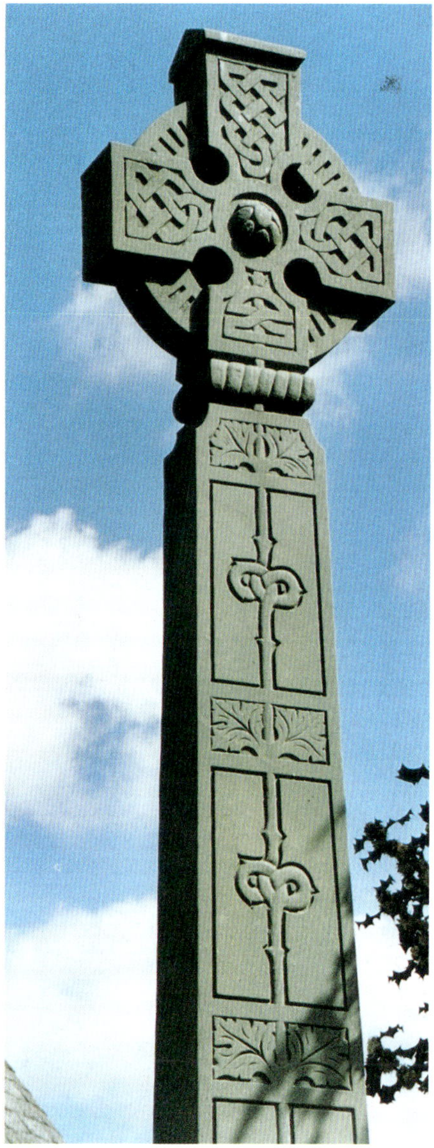

St John's, Bassenthwaite. Detail of the Great War Memorial. W. H. Ward, c. 1920.

stylized vine which climbs unerringly up the shaft towards the entrelac cross at its head.

Access: Usually open. Vicarage Tel. 016973–71541.

BEETHAM is just west of the A6 about a mile south of Milnthorpe.

St Michael and All Angels is a small stone church dating back to C12 but with C15 and C16 additions. It was restored in the 1870s by **Paley & Austin**. This was the church attended by **Robert Hilton** who came to live at nearby Hale when he retired from the Keswick School of Industrial Arts. He wrote a history of the church assisted by his daughter **Agnes Hilton**

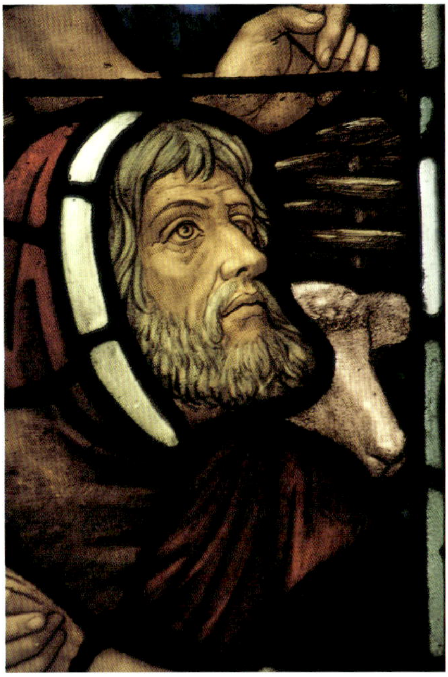

St Michael's, Bootle. Detail of 'Adoration of the Shepherds' window. Henry Holiday, 1900.

which was published in 1933. It was Agnes who created the beautifully decorated Roll of Honour listing the men who served in the Great War. The church also has some beautifully embroidered altar frontals and some fine and elaborate carving on the chancel screen.

Access: Parsonage Tel. 015395–62216.

BOOTLE is on the A595 about 7 miles north of Millom.

St Michael's church (SD108884) is 'ancient' but has a C19 tower and transepts. The striking 'Adoration of the Shepherds' window in the north chancel was designed and executed by **Henry Holiday** in 1900.

Access: Usually open. Vicarage Tel. 01229–718223.

BOWNESS on WINDERMERE is on the east side of the lake south of Windermere town.

St Martin's Bowness (SD402969), has recently re-opened after an extensive refurbishment. It is a C15 church extended in 1870 containing much High-Victorian painted decoration. The west end of the north aisle boasts a three-light window by **A. K. Nicholson** dated 1915 depicting Ss John, Mark and George. The east end of the south aisle has been converted to a chapel using portions of the rood-screen brought here from the redundant St John the Evangelist up the road. The carving was designed by the local architect **Dan Gibson** and executed by the vicar of St John's, the Rev. E. S. Robertson and his parishioners from 1896 onwards. There is also a bookcase designed by **A. W. Simpson** and given as a memorial to **Dan Gibson**. At the east end of the north aisle are curtains made by war-disabled craftsmen employed by Painted Fabrics Ltd and given in 1936. The reading desk in the Lady Chapel was made by **J. M. Kilbride**.

Access: Open 10.00–16.00 (30 March–30 Sept.) otherwise Rectory Tel. 015394–43063.

Blackwell (SD400945) stands on the western side of the B5360 just south of the junction with the A5074. It was designed in 1899 by **M. H. Baillie Scott** as a holiday home for the Manchester brewer Sir Edward Holt who was later to become Lord Mayor of Manchester. To-day, it is owned by the Lakeland Arts Trust and is open to the public. The principal ground floor rooms have been restored to their former glory and provide a feast of decorative art and design in woodwork, stained glass, ceramics, metalwork, furniture and architecture – all that

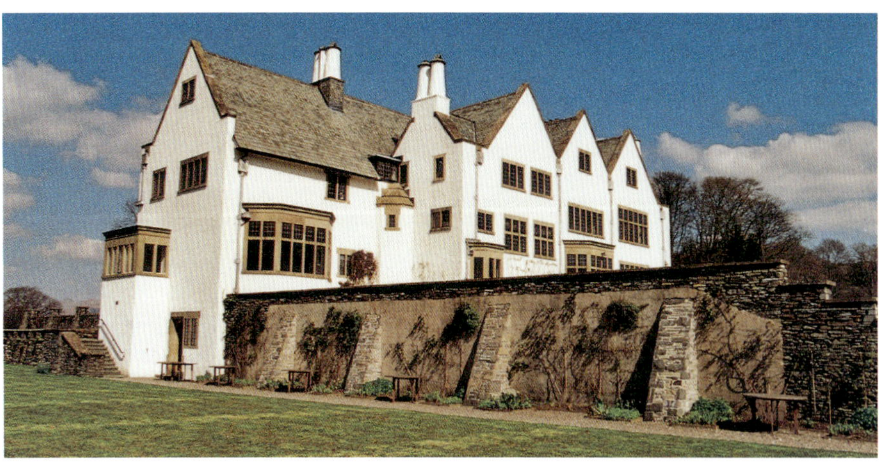

'Blackwell', Bowness on Windermere. North Front. M. H. Baillie Scott, 1899. *Courtesy of the Lakeland Arts Trust*

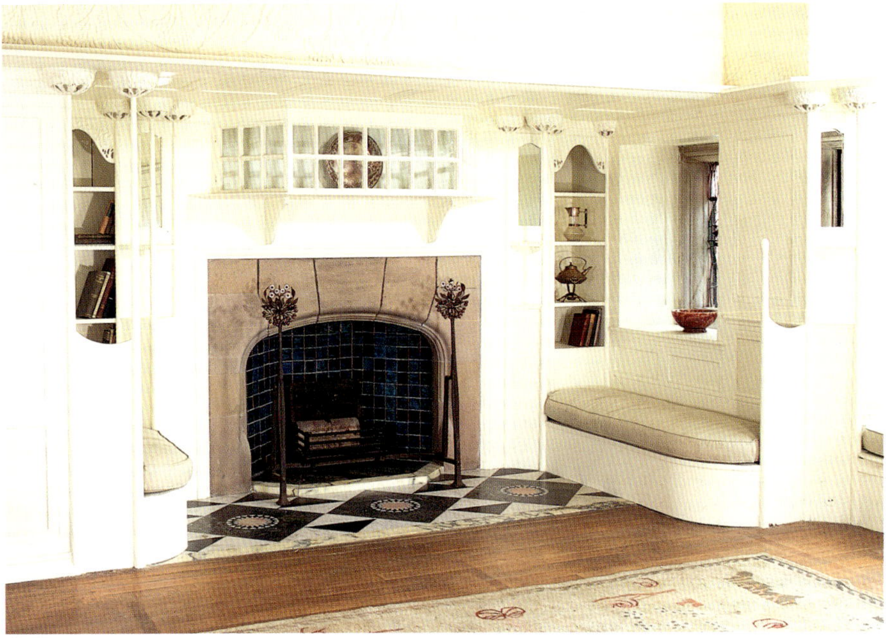

'Blackwell', Bowness on Windermere. The white drawing-room. *Copyright Lakeland Arts Trust*

is best about the Baillie Scott ethos. The Living Hall at the centre of all Baillie Scott's houses is a show piece. At one end there is a large inglenook with built-in seating, a delft-tiled fireplace and a chimney piece of Westmorland slate and limestone. Above the inglenook is a small room reached from the main stairs, with unglazed openings, profusely carved with foliage and small birds, which provide a look-out over the proceedings in the hall below. **Baillie Scott** designed the birds-and-tulips stained glass in the panels of the sliding doors in the passage screen. He also designed the Manxman piano. At the other end of the room the double-height ceiling has been lowered and the focus moves to the striking, peacock wallpaper-frieze printed by Shand Kydd in 1900. Old photographs show that here stood a billiard table, lit by six lights with copper domed shades, before a well-carved alcove which provided raised seating for spectators.

The dining-room which leads off the hall still retains its hessian wall-covering with mountain ash, small birds, bluebells and daisies designed by **Baillie Scott**. There is an inglenook with a similar fireplace to that in the hall and small Art Nouveau stained-glass windows on either side of the inglenook.

The white drawing room is at the west end of the house overlooking both lake and hills. It is a masterpiece which has to be seen to be appreciated. Beneath its moulded-plaster ceiling and frieze a narrow plate-shelf runs around the room supported by the slenderest of pillars with pierced basket-like capitals profusely carved with flowers, foliage and birds. The inglenook here is the most decorative in the house. The fireplace is of stone and ceramic tiles. Above the mantelshelf is a display cupboard with small glazed windows and at either side are elegant shelves and benches. On the marble-mosaic hearth stand the most striking pair of wrought-iron fire dogs decorated with enamelled foliage and berries.

The upper floors of the house are used for temporary decorative art exhibitions but these rooms also contain **Baillie Scott's** stained glass and have fireplaces with **William De Morgan** tiles. Throughout the house there are interesting window catches and door handles. The house is a shining example of Baillie Scott's work and it has been cleverly complemented by Arts and Crafts furnishings acquired by or on loan to the Lakelands Arts Trust.

It is unfortunate that most of Baillie Scott's practice documentation was lost when his studio caught fire, for it is difficult now to name the craftsmen responsible for carrying out the work in the house. It is known, however, that **A. W. Simpson** was responsible for the carved mountain ash frieze in the great hall, a motif which is repeated all over the house.

The garden was designed by **Thomas Mawson** and it must have been one of his simpler plans bearing in mind it was for a holiday home. Only the basic structure now remains. Outside apart from taking a good look at the interesting elevations of the house and the vernacular chimneys, look out for the specially designed lead work of the rain-water heads and down-pipes. This is the only Baillie Scott house in the country permanently open to visitors and is not to be missed.

Access: Open 10.30–17.00 daily (16.00 in Feb and Mar, Nov and Dec). Closed for a short period at Christmas. Admission charges. Tel. 015394–46139.

Broadleys (SD393934) stands between the A592 and the eastern shore of Lake Windermere about 2 miles south of Bowness. It was built in 1898 by **C. F. A. Voysey** as a holiday home for A. Currer-Briggs of Leeds. It is a masterful 'small' country house with many of the engaging external features which make Voysey's houses so readily identifiable including white rough-cast walls, overhanging eaves, extravagant gutter brackets, buttresses, stone-mullions and horizontal bands of windows. The house is built on an L-shaped plan creating a sheltered courtyard for the main entrance. An open entrance porch leads through a wide and sturdy oak-studded door with distinctive iron hinges into a small low-ceilinged lobby and from there into the imposing double-height hall fitted out with fine, oak panelling and flooring. The room is dominated by a high, stone-mullioned bow window offset to the right of the room. At one end there is a large stone inglenook with built-in seats, a stone hearth and a copper canopy over the iron fire-grate. The principal rooms on both floors of the house have marvellous bow windows looking out over the lake. The dining-room is oak-panelled and retains its Voysey-designed tiled fireplace. The sitting-room, much altered over time, was originally wall- papered and had a French window opening onto the terrace overlooking the sunken garden. It has a restored Voysey fireplace above which is one of his decorative ventilation grills. Throughout the house Voysey's metal work designs can be seen on the windows, doors and fireplaces with his notable use of the heart motif. Even the staircase has lead hearts set into the balusters. On the lake side of the house the garden is partially terraced and down at the lake is the boathouse which was also designed by Voysey.

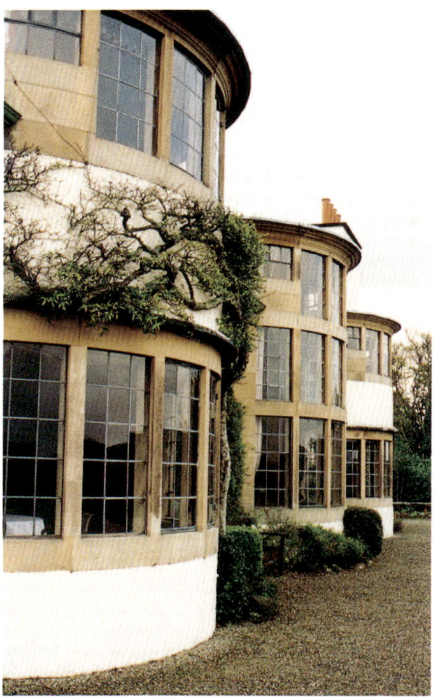

'Broadleys', Bowness on Windermere. Detail, west front. C. F. A. Voysey, 1898. *Courtesy of the Windermere Power Boat Club.*

Access: The house is currently the home of the Windermere Power Boat Club and is open to visitors from April–Sept on Thursdays 10.00–12.00 by appointment. The Club offers mid-week Bed and Breakfast accommodation to non-members. Tel. 015394–43284.

Moor Crag (SD392925) is another house designed by **C. F. A. Voysey** less than half a mile from Broadleys. It was built in 1898 as a holiday home for J. W. Buckley, a Manchester textile manufacturer. It has since been converted into two private dwellings.

Access: Private houses.

Fairfield House in Brantfell Rd, (SD404968) was the home of **Annie Garnett** and is now a hotel. The sitting room has a **Voysey** fireplace which is set, oddly enough, beneath a window. The gardens, which were designed by Annie, are now much reduced. **The Spinnery**, once a hive of industry, has been converted into self-contained holiday apartments while the erstwhile Spinnery Shop, at the foot of Brantfell Road, is now a restaurant.

Access: Tel. 015394–46565.

Gilpin Lodge Hotel, Crook Road, (SD429959) lies to the north of the B5284 just to the east of Windermere Golf Club. The original house was successfully enlarged and improved in 1901 and again more recently. The sitting-room still has the beautiful polished wood and leaded-glass fireplace surround and overmantel made by **A. W. Simpson**.

Access: Open to non-residents. Tel. 015394–88819.

Dawstones off Lickbarrow Road, (SD420974), Windermere was built in 1904 by **Dan Gibson** for the Liverpool merchant Alexander Millington Singh. It has a Lakeland slate roof with overhanging eaves, massive vernacular chimney-stacks and long ranges of horizontal windows set against sparkling white harling. It sits beautifully in its gardens which merge at the margins into the natural landscape. The house has been divided into three sections, the middle one of which, now known as **Gillthwaite Rigg**, retains many original fireplaces and decorative plasterwork. It offers excellent Bed

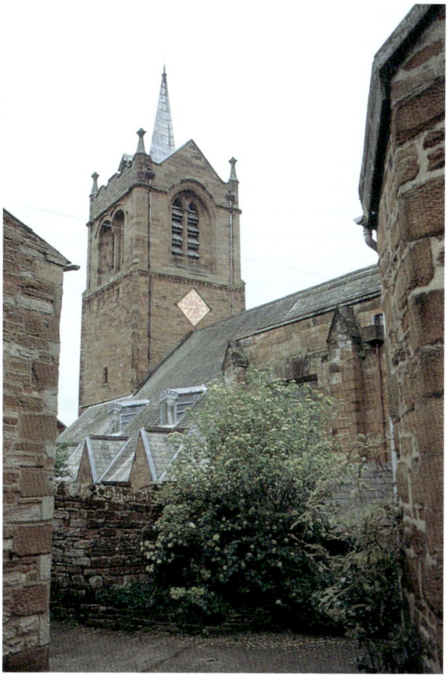

St Martin's, Brampton. Philip Webb 1874. Tower by George Jack, 1906.

and Breakfast and a rare opportunity to spend time in a Dan Gibson house.

Access: Gillthwaite Rigg, Tel: 015394–46212 for B&B.

BRAMPTON lies on the A69 about 7 miles east of Carlisle. The village has a by-pass but is well signposted from the main road.

St Martin's, Front St (NY527610) was built 1874–78 by **Phillip Webb** who was proposed for the commission by George Howarth of nearby Naworth Castle. This is the only church that Philip Webb built and his collaboration with **Burne-Jones** and **Morris** in this church over a twenty year period has produced an outstanding example of unity in the arts which was one of the major objectives of the Arts and Crafts Movement. The church is full of interest in its architecture and decoration.

The church is built of the local red sandstone and has a Westmorland slate roof. The north side, which faces Front St, is remarkable for its three gables with their sloping merlons. To the east of them is the rather square, undecorated two storey vestry and to the west stands the tower with its still 'temporary' spire. On the south side the land rises steeply from the base of the low south wall and the roof falls in a single grand sweep from the ridge to the eaves broken only by a range of dormer windows.

The north-west porch door opens directly into a surprisingly low-ceilinged baptistery under the tower. It has all the welcoming ambience and scale of a domestic entrance hall and immediately creates the impression that something very special is afoot. The great volume of the body of the church comes as a great surprise. In contrast to the baptistery the nave is very high. The roof trusses are hidden by a panelled ceiling which is enlivened by planted wooden fan-vaulting. Interesting though it is, it is not the ceiling which first catches the eye when leaving the baptistery, it is the sumptuous east window installed by **Morris & Co.** in 1881.

The centre light is filled with 'Christ the Good Shepherd' who is supported on either side by an angelic orchestra and the Saints Martin, Mary, Dorothea and George. Beneath the Good Shepherd, is the unique panel of a pelican on its nest feeding four chicks with its own blood. The figures, the pelican, the chicks and the stubby Art Nouveau tree were all designed by **Burne-Jones** but it was **Morris** who produced the background and the brilliant colour scheme. On a sunny morning this window is glorious.

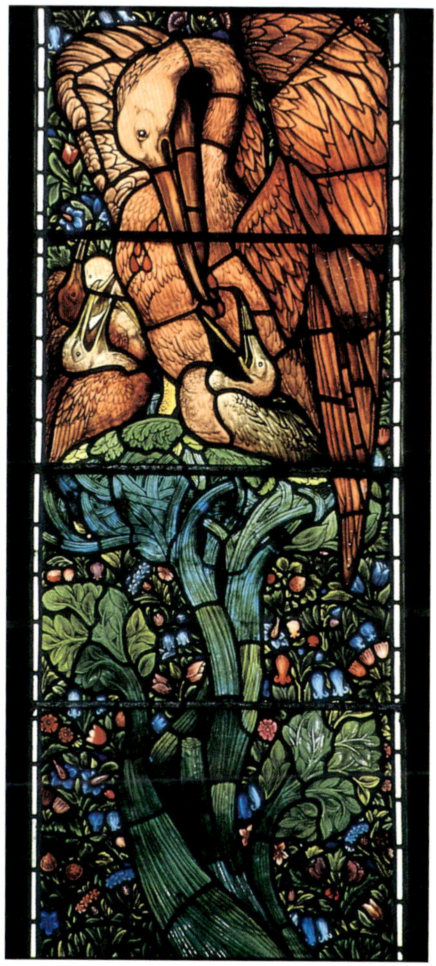

St Martin's, Brampton. Detail of east window by Morris & Co., 1880–81.

The gilded gesso reredos beneath the window is also by **Morris & Co.** and may have been executed by **Kate Faulkner**.

In the north aisle Webb chose to use cross-gables to raise the height of the north wall and so install three sets of tall windows to increase the natural lighting. **Morris & Co.** installed stained glass in them but as single figures set in clear-glass quarries. The two west-most windows made in 1878 feature Old Testament prophets while the third window 1880–81 shows Ss John, Peter, Luke and Paul. All were designed by **Burne-Jones**. A shortage of floor space prompted **Webb** to build a two storey vestry at the east end of the north aisle supported on the south side by the chancel pillars. He used the under croft of the vestry to create what is now the War Memorial Chapel.

The south face of the roof is brought down in a single slope over the nave and aisle. In consequence the south wall is quite low and the windows are relatively small. Webb has introduced a range of domestic-scale dormer windows over the south aisle which, not only solve the lighting difficulty but add to the visual interest. He has coved and panelled the ceiling but exposed the tie beams, which are supported by the aisle arcade, creating another decorative feature. The stained glass windows in this aisle are all by **Morris & Co.** and all designed by **Burne-Jones**. With the exception of the swirling Art Nouveau 'Hope, Charity and Faith' in the east-most window of 1887, the rest have small picture-panels set in clear quarries and were made 1888–97. The remaining **Morris & Co.** windows at the west end of the church are of later date. The font is older than the church and was brought from another place and provided with a cover by the **Keswick School of Industrial Arts** *c.* 1909.

The tower proposed by Webb was not topped out until 1906 under the supervision of **George Jack**. In the same year, **Ellen Mary Rope** was commissioned to make the terracotta St Martin which is fixed in a niche to the left of the door in the north-west porch.

Access: Usually open. Vicarage Tel. 016977–42182.

St Martin's Church Hall, which stands next to the church, was built 1895 by **C. J. Ferguson** who used the red sandstone chosen by Webb for the church and although not in the least a stylistic copy, it looks very much at home beside Webb's work. Internally, the floor space was kept free of pillars by supporting the roof on segmental, laminated, wooden arches.

Access: The hall is now an antiques centre and open for business during normal working hours. Tel. 016977–42515.

Green Lanes, in Greenhill, (NY526607) was designed by **Philip Webb** at the same time as St Martin's church. It was to have been the vicarage but was never used as such and is now a nursing home.

Access: Private dwelling.

Four Gables (NY562620) was designed by **Philip Webb** for the Howard Estate and is hidden behind high hedges on the northern side of the A69 about a mile from the centre of Brampton.

Access: Private house.

BRATHAY lies about 1 mile south west of Ambleside west of the B5285.

Holy Trinity in Bog Lane, (NY362033) was built in the 1830s and enlarged in 1905 by **Paley & Austin**. Its tower is covered with Virginia creeper and is a startling scarlet landmark in the autumn. Inside on the north wall of the choir there is a **Keswick School of Industrial Arts** repoussé panel featuring doves and wild roses. It commemorates the Reverend Rawnson, one time incumbent who died in 1899. The church has its original bronze and copper electric light fittings. Four of the two-light windows in the nave were designed by the **Rev E. M. Geldart** and made by Taylor and Clifton, of Berners St, London *c.* 1915. The east window is by Powell of Whitefriars. The woodwork in the screen, chancel, and sanctuary is all beautifully made and was designed by the architect George Redmayne, whose father was a founder of the church.

Access: Usually open. Vicarage: 015394–33205.

BRIDEKIRK is sign-posted off the A595 north of Cockermouth.

St Bridget's (NY118337) was built by **Cory & Ferguson** 1868–70 in a Neo-Norman style. It shares the churchyard with the picturesque ruins of the chancel of the original Norman church and incorporates parts of the old building, including its beautifully carved C12 font. Although it is not unusual in **C. J. Ferguson's** churches, there is a surprising contrast here between the stone exterior and the brick-lined interior. The apse has a blind arcade of intersecting round-headed arches behind the altar, filled with highly glazed tiles bearing Celtic motifs. The chancel has three windows by **Powell of Whitefriars**. 'Fide' was designed by **Henry Holiday** while 'Spes' and 'Caritas' were designed by **G. P. Hutchinson**. 'St Bride' in the south transept is also attributed to Powell.

Access: Vicarage Tel.01900–826557.

BROUGHTON in FURNESS is about 10 miles north of Barrow in Furness at the junction of the A595 and A593.

St Mary Magdalene (SD209874) is an ancient church with many later additions and amendments. There are two good windows in the south aisle. The most easterly of which is a

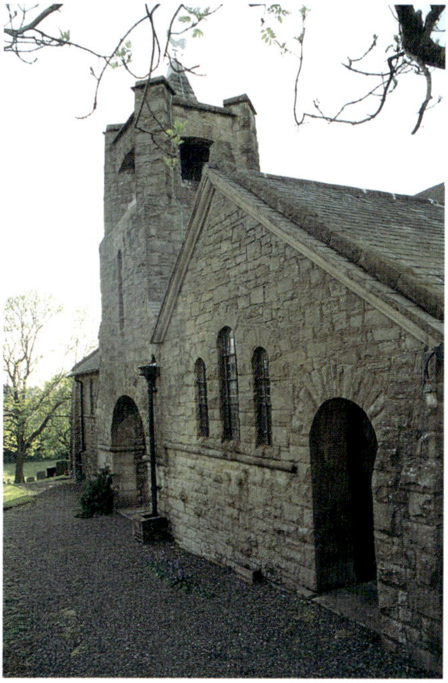

St Columba's, Broughton Moor. Porch and tower. W. D. Caröe, 1905.

three-light window designed by **James Milner Allen** for **Shrigley & Hunt**, which is decorated with floral designs and cheeky sparrows. The third window from the east end is a version of 'Hope' by **Burne-Jones**. According to A. C. Sewter's catalogue of Morris & Co's stained glass, this window was brought here from Redcar after its original home had been demolished.

Access: Usually open. Vicarage Tel. 01229–716305.

BROUGHTON MOOR is south of the A594 between Cockermouth and Maryport.

St Columba's (NY054332) stands at the cross-roads in the village. Its was designed by **W. D. Caröe** 1905 in such a way as to enable the church to be built by unskilled local workers under the supervision of a local mining engineer, who happened to be Caröe's wife's sister's husband. The church has a simple interior, and its rustic exterior, particularly the tower, will raise a smile on the greyest day.

Access: Vicarage Tel. 01900–825317.

BURNESIDE lies to the north of Kendal and is signposted via an unclassified road off the A591, the Kendal to Windermere road.

St Oswald's (SD505957) stands on the main road at the northern end of the village. It was built 1880–81 by **C. J. Ferguson**. The modern utilitarian screening of the north aisle lessens the impact of Ferguson's design. Nevertheless the church retains an extraordinarily tranquil ambience. The fine five-light east window with the figures of St Oswald, the Virgin Mary, Christ, St John and St Kentigern was made by **Caroline Townshend** and **Joan Howson** in 1936. The reredos is a piece of local Arts and Crafts history created in 1890. It comprises twenty-seven panels carved by sixteen students at the village evening class and put together to form a unified design of intertwining foliage. Each panel bears the initials of its carver and their names are listed on a small brass plate hidden to the right of the reredos. Down among the S's is the name of **A. W. Simpson** who tutored the class and, in the previous year, had shown a carved panel at the Arts and Crafts Exhibition Society in London. The catalogue records the piece as 'a carved panel of dog roses'. Is it now part of the reredos? There is other fine woodwork in the church including the later tower screen and at the west end **Ferguson's** stone font has a band of finely carved water lily leaves and flowers below the rim.

Access: Usually open in the summer. Vicarage Tel. 01539–722015.

BUTTERMERE is on the B5289 west of Buttermere Lake.

St James's (NY176170) is a very small church which stands in a superb position at the roadside between Crummockwater and Buttermere. It was built in 1841 but the two-light east window showing Mary, Martha and a delightful cherub's head were designed by **Henry Holiday** in 1893. The church also has much un-attributed but very fine wood carving including an array of angels decorating the wall-plates.

Access: Usually open. Vicarage Tel. 01900–85237.

CALDER BRIDGE is on the A595 about 5 miles south of Egremont.

St Bridget's (NY042062) has a three-lancet east window designed by **Henry Holiday** after 1877

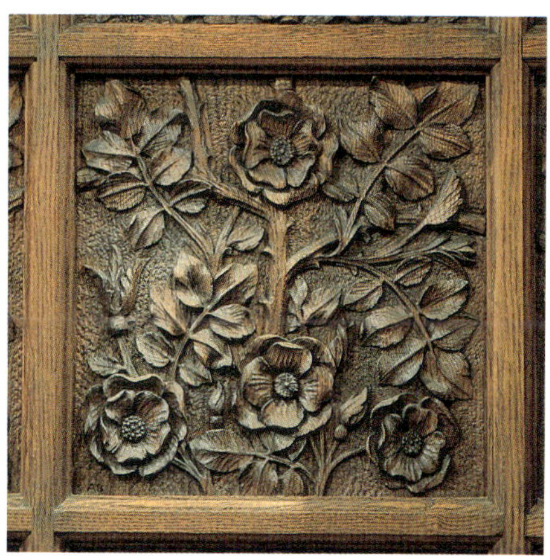

St Oswald's, Burneside. Panel from reredos. Burneside carving class, 1890.

for **Powell of Whitefriars**. It contains seven patterned panels each containing a cartouche illustrating an incident in the life of Christ.

Access: Usually open 9.00–17.00. Vicarage Tel. 01946–841327.

CALTHWAITE lies west of the north bound carriageway of the M6. Access is from the A6 north of Penrith or from the B5305.

All Saints (NY470400) was built in 1913 to designs by **J. H. Martindale**. An unusual feature of the church is its pulpit which is built into the thickness of the wall and has its own window. The church was built by T. Lowthian & Sons who also built Robert Lorimer's church at near-by Plumpton. The excellent carving on the lectern, the choir stalls and the angels looking down over the sanctuary are all the work of **George Fendley** of Carlisle.

Access: Vicarage Tel. 016974–73320.

CARLISLE, straddles the A6 some 10 miles south of the Scottish border.

The Tullie House Museum and Library in Castle St (NY400558) occupies a C17 house with an extension on the Castle St frontage by **C. J. Ferguson** 1892–93. The museum has a collection of work by **Burne-Jones** including cartoons for some of the stained-glass windows in Brampton Church. Other members of the Pre-Raphaelite circle represented in its fine collection include **D. G. Rossetti**, Simeon Solomon and Arthur Hughes. There are pictures by George Howard (9th Earl of Carlisle), embroidery designs by **William Morris** and ceramics by **William De Morgan**, the **Martin Brothers** and others. **The Keswick School of Industrial Arts** is represented here as is **A. W. Simpson**. There are collections, though not on permanent display, of the works of Paul Nash, **Clinton Balmer**, and the Scottish artists John Duncan, Phoebe Anna Traquair and Jessie M. King. Book illustrators are represented with etchings by **F. L. Griggs** paintings and wood cuts by Charles Ricketts and lithographs by C. H. Shannon. The new Millenium Gallery has some of **Harry Redfern's** water colours of pub interiors and a collection of biscuit tins, made by Hudson Scott of Carlisle, some of which reproduce Arts and Crafts designs.

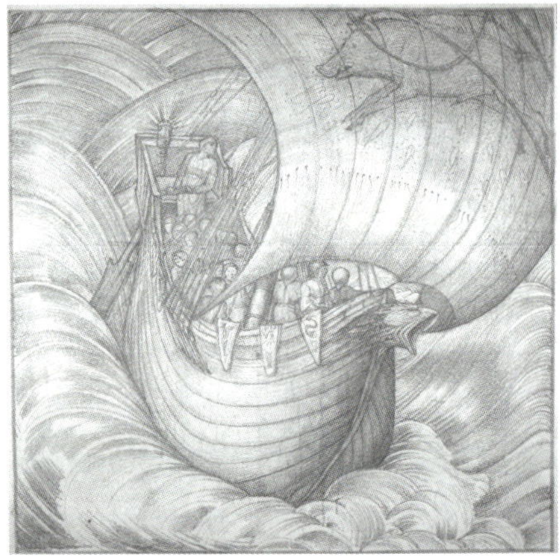

Tullie House, Carlisle. 'Voyage to Vinland the Good' by Edward Burne-Jones, 1884. *Copyright Tullie House Museum of Art Gallery.*

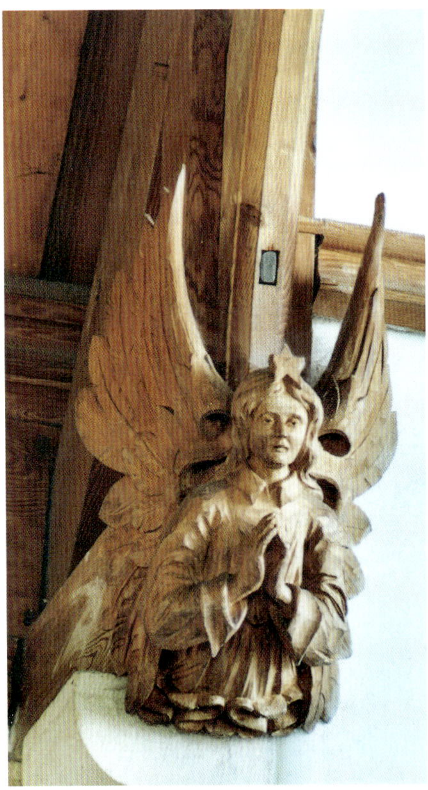

All Saints, Calthwaite. Chancel angel. Carved by George Fendley, c. 1913.

Access: Open daily all year round. For opening times Tel. 01228–534781.

Carlisle Cathedral (NY399558) has been in a state of flux since the C12. Its last restoration was in the 1850s and its internal orientation is a bit confusing, mostly because the length of the nave has been reduced and is now so much smaller than the chancel that the layout feels back-to-front. 'The Nativity' window by **Christopher Whall** high on the south wall of the book shop was dedicated in 1915. The painted C14 wagon roof in the choir was damaged in the C18 and not restored until 1856 when the work was undertaken by Owen Jones – author of the highly influential book *A Grammar of Ornament*. The bishop's throne was designed *c.* 1880 by **G. E. Street** and the elaborate high altar and baldacchino are by **Charles Nicholson**. The nearby two-light window at the eastern end of the south choir

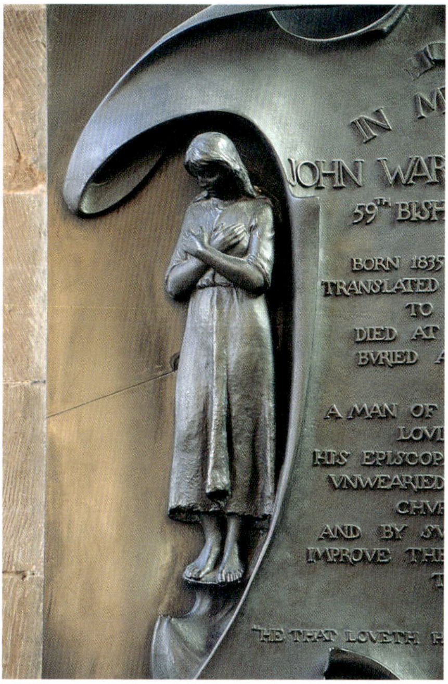

Carlisle Cathedral. Detail of the Bardsley Memorial by A. C. Lucchesi, 1906. *By kind permission of the Dean and Chapter of Carlisle Cathedral*

wall, depicting St George and St Nicholas, is by Charles's brother, **Archibald K. Nicholson**. The second and third south choir windows are by **Powell of Whitefriars** and date from the 1920s and 1930s. They are in a similar style to the Nicholson window. There is a memorial plaque on the wall of the south choir commemorating Canon Rawnsley, who was so involved with the preservation of the Lake District and founding of the Keswick School of Industrial Arts. The designer and maker of the plaque remain anonymous. The monument to Dean Close in the south chancel aisle was executed in 1885 by **H. H. Armstead** while nearby lies the bronze effigy of Bishop Goodwin sculpted in 1891 by **Hamo Thorneycroft**. The bronze tablet commemorating Bishop John Wareing Bardsley was made by **A. C. Lucchesi** in 1906. There is a beautiful bronze war memorial at the southern end of the west wall which is very Arts & Crafts-cum-Art Nouveau but there is no reference to its maker. Arthur Blomfield designed the font which was executed by **F. W. Pomeroy** in 1891.

Access: Open during daylight hours but access may be limited during services. Tel. cathedral office 01228–548151.

St Aidan's in Warwick Rd, (NY410559) was built 1899–1902 by **C. J. Ferguson** and was completed only 2 years before his death. It is an excellent example of his work comprising the church, its hall and the vicarage all designed as-a-piece in red sandstone. The church is also blessed with a wonderful set of windows by **A. K. Nicholson**.

Access: Vicarage Tel. 01228–522942.

St Cuthbert's in St Cuthbert's Lane (NY401557) is just off the market place. It is a red and grey stone C18, galleried church and an unexpected place to find a set of six windows made by **G. E. R. Smith** at the **A. K. Nicholson** Studio. The windows are all in the south aisle and each one illustrates an incident in the life of St Cuthbert. The date of the last dedication is 1956.

Access: Usually open. Vicarage Tel. 01228–521982.

St James's in St James Rd, (NY394549) was built 1865–67 by Andrew and Pepper of Bradford. It has three beautiful windows, two of which are by **A. K. Nicholson** and the other is by **G. E. R. Smith**. The south aisle east-most window, made by **Nicholson** in 1906, shows the

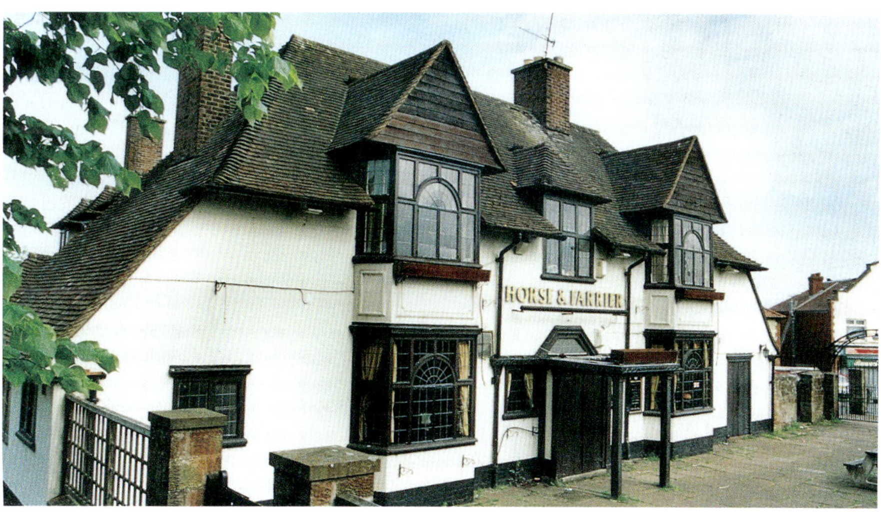

'Horse and Farrier' Carlisle. Harry Redfern, 1928.

Virgin Mary and Dorcas. The north aisle east-most window of St James and St John the Divine dedicated in 1932 is also by **Nicholson**. The south aisle west-most window is by **Smith** and depicts a young David and St George. This is a World War II memorial with the kneeling figures of an airman, a sailor, a nurse and a soldier below the main figures.

Access: Parish Office Tel. 01228–810616.

The Horse & Farrier on the corner of Wigton Rd and Orton Rd (NY383552) was designed by **Harry Redfern** in 1928 with a bowling green attached. While the exterior elevations are still full of interest the interiors have been much altered.

Access: Normal pub hours.

The Magpie, on the corner of Victoria Rd and Duranhill Rd (NY424551) was designed by **Harry Redfern**, whose interplay of gables and dormers give it very interesting roof lines. It has seen considerable change inside.

Access: Normal pub hours.

The Redfern, (NY392572) on Etterby Rd was built in 1938 towards the end of **Redfern's** time as chief architect of the State Management Scheme.

Access: Normal pub hours.

In James Rd at the corner of Empire Rd (NY395550) is the oddly-named house **TUE THUR** designed for James Morton, fabric manufacturer, by **Robert Lorimer** in 1923.

The Crown and Mitre Hotel at 4 English St (NY403557) is by **Oliver & Dodgshun** 1902. The hotel has a fine unattributed Art Nouveau low-relief sculpture above the front door and a number of other well carved external stone decorations. Internally there are wall paintings in the bar and a good ballroom.

Access: Open to patrons of the hotel, its bars and restaurants.

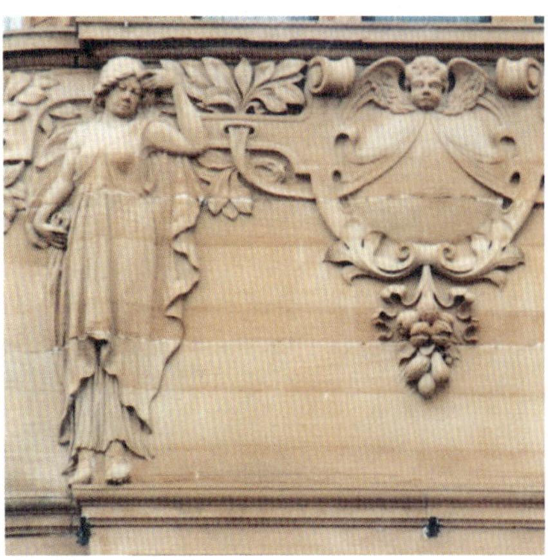

'Crown and Mitre' Carlisle, Relief sculpture, c. 1902.

Rickerby Park, (NY425571) to the east of the city is the site of a simple but very large, stone cenotaph attributed in the National Inventory of War Memorials to **Robert Lorimer**.

CASTERTON is on the A683 about 1 mile north of its junction with the A65.

Holy Trinity (SD625796) was built for Casterton School for the Daughters of Clergymen in 1831

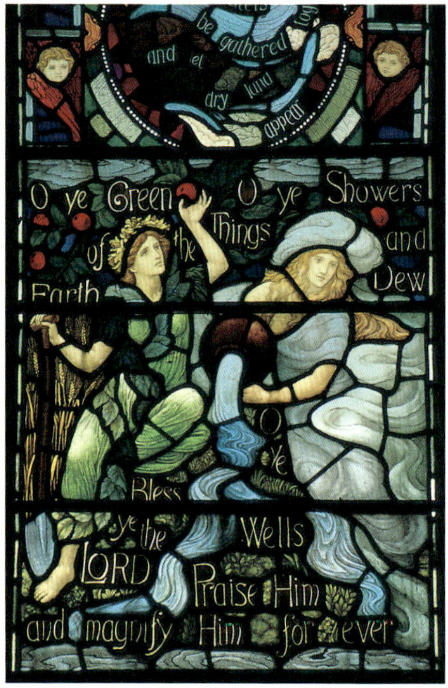

Holy Trinity, Casterton. Detail of the Benedicite window. Henry Holiday, c. 1897

but has a wealth of later decoration. There are wall paintings on both sides of the nave and above the baptistery arch executed by **James Clark** 1901–10. Other paintings above the east window and on the south wall of the chancel are by **Henry Holiday** who also designed and executed the stained glass in the chancel and in the lancets at the west end. All Holiday's work was executed 1894–1897. Some of Clark's paintings representing biblical scenes are a bit difficult to see because of the awkward lighting but they repay the time spent in finding the right place from which to view them. Holiday's two lancets at the west end, which depict the seven days of the Creation accompanied by illustrations of the verses of the Benedicite, are spectacular and must rank among his best work in the North West.

Access: Usually open. Parish office Tel. 01524–71320.

CHAPEL STILE is in Langdale, about 4 miles north-west of Ambleside on the B5343.

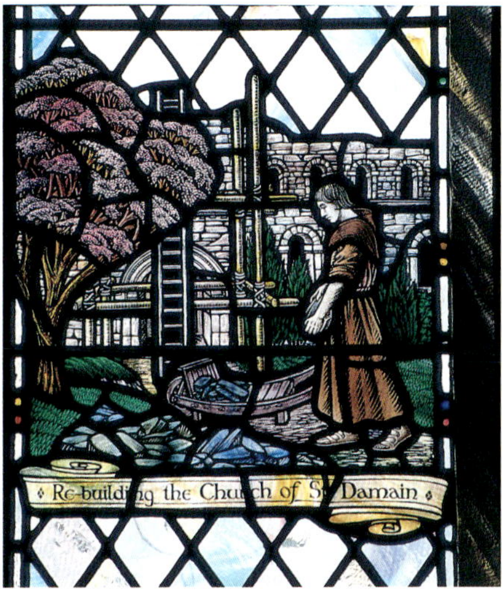

Holy Trinity, Chapel Stile, Langdale. Detail of the St Francis window. B. & B. D. Walmsley, c. 1938.

Holy Trinity (NY321057) is unmistakable in the centre of the village. Unmistakable also is **B. & B. D. Walmsley's** window in the south wall of the nave. It shows Saint Francis surrounded by birds and scenes from his life. The window was made *c.* 1938 at the Walmsleys' St Anne's Studio in the village. The window is unsigned but relatives still living in the village vouch for its authenticity.

Access: Vicarage Tel. 015394–33205.

CLEATOR straddles the A5086 between Egremont and Cleator Moor.

The Church of St Mary and the Grotto (NY014135) was built in 1856 by E. W. Pugin and has an almost complete set of stained-glass windows by the **Earley Studio**. The windows have various commemorative dates ranging 1950–65 and they form a beautiful and sparkling display. The jewel-like colours, mosaic backgrounds and long Byzantine figures are all reminiscent of the style of **Harry Clarke**.

Access: Usually open. Presbytery Tel. 01946–810324.

COCKERMOUTH sits in the angle made by the A595 and the A66.

The Great War memorial stands in South St (NY119306) and is a powerful 'Winged Victory' sculpted by **F. W. Doyle Jones**.

Wood Hall Gardens (NY125324) lie to the east of the A595 north of Cockermouth. They cover 5.5 acres and were designed 1910–20 by **T. H. Mawson** for solicitor Edward Tyson. The original Wood Hall was demolished some 40 years ago but the gardens, once an overgrown ruin, have been much restored over the last 30 years, retaining many of the balustrades, terraces and walls, the original tree species in the pinetum and two aged stone summerhouses.

Access: The gardens can be visited by arrangement. Tel. 01900–823585.

COLTON is a little hamlet on the Furness Fells between the southern tails of lakes Coniston and Windermere.

Holy Trinity (SD317861) huddles in splendid isolation on the hillside above Spark Bridge. It was consecrated in 1578, enlarged in the C18 and eventually Victorianised. It has an unexpected array of C20 stained glass. In the south wall the sanctuary window and the three double-lights in the nave are attributed by the National Association of Decorative and Fine Art Societies survey to **G. P. Gamon & Humphreys** while Jacob's Dream, also in the south wall, is attributed to **H. Warren Wilson**.

Access: Vicarage Tel. 01229–861285.

CONISTON village is at the head of the lake about 8 miles south west of Ambleside on the A593.

St Andrew's churchyard (SD302975) is the last resting place of **John Ruskin** who chose to be

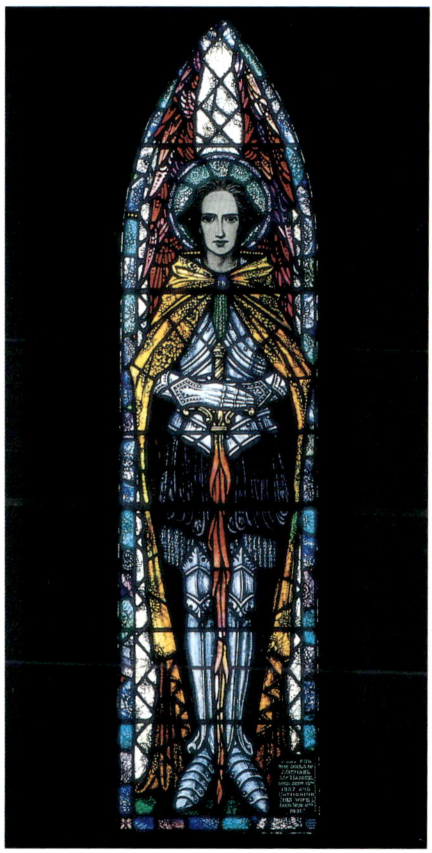

St Mary and the Grotto, Cleator. St Michael by the Earley Studio. No date.

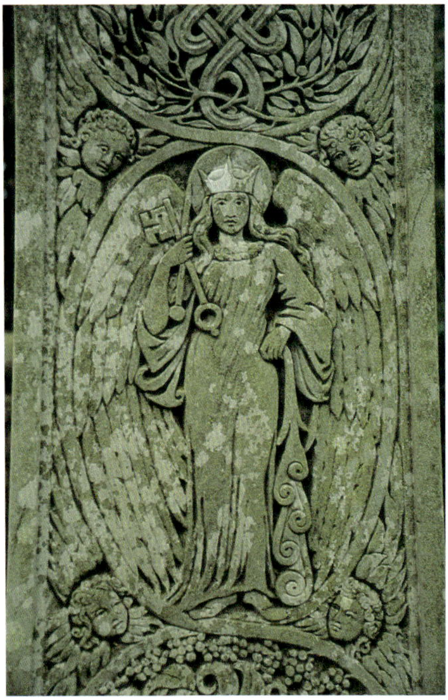

Coniston churchyard. Detail of the John Ruskin Memorial Cross. W. G. Collingwood, 1901.

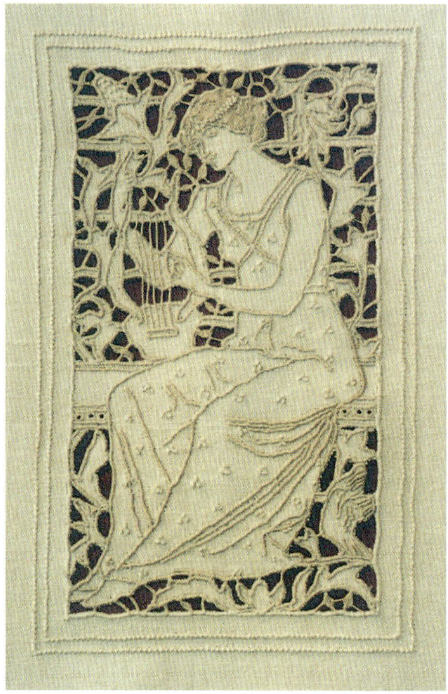

Langdale Linen. St Cecilia panel, a free-hand variation of the Ruskin lace technique, c. 1900. *Photo: authors. Courtesy of the Ruskin Museum, Coniston*

buried here rather than in St Paul's Cathedral. His grave is marked by the Neo-Celtic cross in the north-east corner of the church yard which was designed by **W. G. Collingwood** and carved by **H. T. Miles**. Collingwood's own grave is nearby. The Great War Memorial, also in the churchyard, was designed by **Collingwood**.

Access: There is easy access to the church yard.

Ruskin Museum (SD302978) is in the centre of the village attached to the Village Institute which was set up in 1901 by **W. G. Collingwood** as a memorial to Ruskin. It was the venue of many Arts and Crafts exhibitions in its heyday. The museum has recently been extended and among other things it has a well set out display of Ruskiniana, including some of his paintings and the beautiful pall designed for the great man's funeral by **Edith Rawnsley** and **Harold Stabler**. It was executed by **Marian Twelves** and the women of the **Ruskin Linen Industry**. The **Langdale Linen Industry** is well-represented by a beautifully-displayed collection of its work. Even the spinning-chair made for **Mrs Pepper** by **A. W. Simpson** is on display together with examples of the work of the lesser known Coniston woodworking class. The circular relief bust of Ruskin is a copy of the memorial made by **A. C. Luchesi** for the Friars Cragg memorial on Derwent Water.

Access: Open daily, Easter to Mid-November 10.00–17.30. Winter Wed–Sun 10.30–16.30. Admission charge. Tel. 015394–41164.

Brantwood is 1½ miles south-east of Coniston overlooking the Lake (SD314958). The house was the home of **John Ruskin** from 1872 until his death in 1900. Only a relatively small part of the house is open to the public but it is sufficient, on a quiet day, to allow the shade of the old man to make contact, especially in the corner window looking out over the lake to the Old Man of Coniston. The house has a collection of Ruskin's own drawings and paintings and examples of **Ruskin Lace**. Three carved wooden plaques were made by the woodworking class at the Coniston Institute and there is also a small display of **Ruskin Pottery**.

Access: Open daily mid–Mar to mid–Nov 11.00–17.30 and Wed–Sun mid–Nov to mid–Mar 11.00–16.30. Admission charge. Tel. 015394–41396.

COTEHILL is about 5 miles south-east of Carlisle on an unclassified road east of the A6.

St John the Evangelist (NY470502) was built by Habershon & Brock in 1868. Externally the church has lost its eccentricity by the removal of the beehive-like pigeon loft from the top of the tower but it remains a very attractive building. It has a two-light window at the eastern end of the north nave which Pevsner thinks is 'influenced by Morris but looking like the work of **Powell**' and 'uncommonly good'. The window appears in Powell's order book and was designed in 1871 by **Henry Holiday**. The two lights show St John and St James.

Access: Usually open. Vicarage Tel. 01228–513205.

CROGLIN lies 10 miles south of Brampton on the B6295.

St John the Baptist (NY575472) was built in 1878 and is a low building with Neo-Norman window heads. This very small and simple church contains something rather special. It has four framed and glazed colour prints by the **Fitzroy Picture Society**. There is a triptych of 'The Nativity' by **Heywood Sumner** and a set of three pictures by **Selwyn Image** 'The Annunciation', 'The Sermon on the Mount' and 'The Agony in the Garden'. They were all printed in 1897 by James Ackerman, and published by George Bell & Sons. They are lovely to look at and amazing to find 100 years later in near perfect condition.

Access: Vicarage Tel. 01228–560332.

CROSBY-on-EDEN lies about 3 miles east of Carlisle on the A689.

St John the Evangelist (NY449596) was built in 1852 by T. H. Billings in what Pevsner calls 'a very inventive, rather naughty' style. It is certainly eye catching, especially its bizarre tower roof with its outsized lucarnes and huge disproportionate crockets. These, together with the 'gun-barrel' rainwater spouts, give its silhouette an outlandish, dragon-like quality. The pulpit, priest's stall and prayer desk are the work of **A. W. Simpson's** firm in Kendal. The

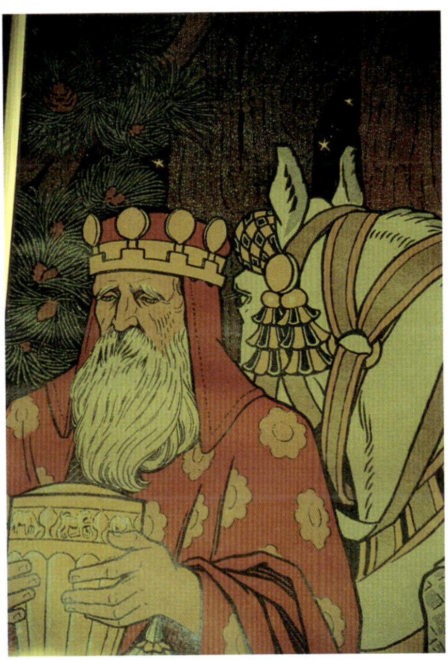

St John's, Croglin. Detail of the 'Adoration of the Magi'. Heywood Summer for The Fitzroy Picture Society, 1897.

pulpit dates from 1925, three years after Simpson's death, but the abundant vines, roses, pomegranates, ears of wheat and acorns are typical of the firm's work. The carving of the good shepherd on the pulpit is attributed to **William Aumonier (Jr)** and the figure on the lectern is of no lesser quality. The nave has unusual moulded glass stars in the window heads dating from the 1950s but the ornate filigree painted 'pelmets' over the nave window openings must be from the 1850s. The little wall-hung Great War memorial is by Hughes and Blocklow of Battleship Wharf, Blyth and Dover St London. The copper work is by the **Keswick School of Industrial Arts**.

Access: Vicarage Tel. 016977–42182.

CROSBY RAVENSWORTH lies off the B6260 between Appleby and Tebay.

St Lawrence's (NY622149) is a C13 church with the chancel by J. S. Crowther dating from 1875. The reredos is a copy, carved in wood, of da Vinci's 'The Last Supper'. It was executed by members of Mrs Webster's carving class in 1897. Mrs Webster was the vicar's wife. This panel is also listed, among the works of **J. M. Kilbride** in his obituary in Barbon church. Was he the tutor to the class?.

Access: Usually open. Vicarage Tel. 01931–715226.

CUMDIVOCK lies about 2 miles south-west of Dalston.

St John's (NY341489) was built in 1871 by **C. J. Ferguson** and is typical of his small nave and chancel churches with a very simple interior. Ferguson placed a window in the north wall by the pulpit which, by design or accident, gives a fine view of his own house, Cardew Lodge. He adopted a freestyle approach to the design of the windows and tracery here and provided another of his unique bellcôtes. The font cover, unsigned and undated, takes the form of a flat wooden platter finely carved with the traditional three fishes of the Trinity. The lych-gate was built in 1906 to plans drawn up by Benwell of Lowther St in Carlisle.

Access: Parish Office Tel. 01228–701215.

DALSTON lies 4 miles south of Carlisle on the B5299.

St Michael's (NY371500) is substantially an 1890s building although there has been a church here since the C12. Externally, its red-sandstone elevations fit very naturally into its surroundings. The double bellcôte, freestyle tracery and the odd positioning of the window opening in the angle of the north transept and chancel, all suggest **C. J. Ferguson's**, involvement. Internally, the church has an exposed, timber roof supported on tall, slender, oak pillars. There is a delightful carved, light-oak font-cover designed by **Robert**

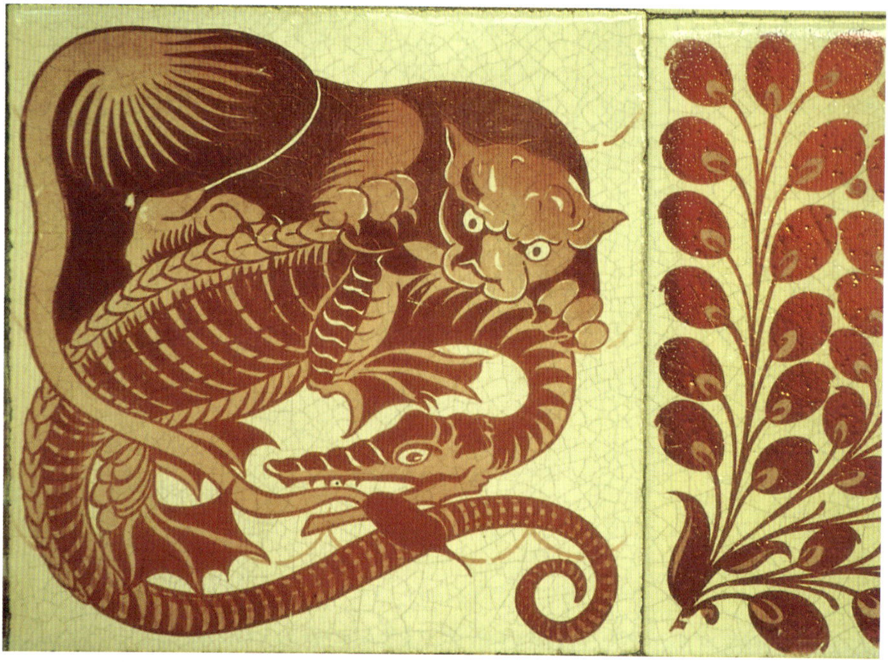

Dalston Hall Hotel. Fireplace tiles by William De Morgan.

Lorimer which was given to the church in 1925. The altar and reredos which seem to date from the 1920s have carved, painted and gilded figures but the work remains unattributed.

Access: Usually open after 10.00. Parish Office Tel. 01228–710215.

Dalston Hall (NY378515) stands to the east of the B5299 about a mile north of Dalston. It is well signposted as the Dalston Hall Country House Hotel and shares a drive with the Golf Club which surrounds the house and an adjoining caravan park. The C17 Hall grew up around a pele tower dating from *c.* 1500 and was given a new and sympathetic entrance front in 1899 by **C. J. Ferguson** who also seems to have refurbished the house. Note the double-height, galleried 'baronial hall' with its inglenook and rather Art Nouveau electroliers, and check the fireplaces for **William De Morgan** tiles.

Access: Open to non-residents. Tel. 01228–710271.

DALTON in FURNESS lies off the A590 between Ulverston and Barrow in Furness.

St Mary's (SD226739) was built in a free Decorated style by **Paley & Austin** in 1884 and looks magnificent. The church has two small but beautiful bronze plaques on the north wall of the south chapel. The first commemorating Anthony Edward Baldwin killed during the Battle of Jutland aged 16; the second is for his brother Hugh killed in action in France in 1918 aged 20. The excellent workmanship is unattributed.

Access: Usually open. Vicarage Tel. 01229–462526.

EAGLESFIELD is reached by a good but unclassified road about 2 miles south of Cockermouth west of the A5086.

St Philip and St James, (NY106282) which is also known as The John Dalton Memorial Church, Mosser, is close to the A5086. The church was designed by **C. J. Ferguson** and built by local builders and craftsmen 1890–91. There is much Arts and Crafts-style carving. The pulpit, credence table and cupboard date from about 1891 and the reredos, which stretches across the width of the church, was given in 1907 by Mrs Sewell of Brandling Hall in memory of her husband. It features fine carving including roses and lilies at either side. It is suggested in the church guide that the work was executed by Mrs Sewell herself. The window in the south wall of the chancel was made in 1931 by **A. K. Nicholson** and shows John the Baptist and St John the Divine.

Access: Vicarage Tel. 01900–603886.

EAMONT BRIDGE is just 1 mile south of Penrith.

The little Boer War memorial on the corner of the B5320 and the A6 (NY523282) has relief sculptures of the two villagers killed in the Boer War and gives the names of the two men who came home safely. The sculptor was **William Grant Stevenson** and the memorial was made in 1900.

EGREMONT is on the A595, 3 or 4 miles south of Whitehaven.

The church of **St Mary and St Michael** (NY011106) was built by **T. Lewis Banks** 1880–83. Fine carving is a major feature of the church and can be seen on the alabaster pulpit, the stonework of the capitals and most particularly in the woodwork of the sanctuary. The figures on the reredos are exceptional but intriguingly, un-attributed. The in-house guide gives them a date of 1928 and they may well have been designed by **W. D. Caröe** who produced designs for the new vestry and chancel in 1926. The unusual white angel font, donated in 1883 appears to be a copy of the Caen stone font made for Edinburgh Cathedral by John B. Rhind.

Access: Usually open 9.00–11.45 daily. Vicarage Tel. 01946–820268/822051.

ESKDALE GREEN straddles the unclassified road which runs down from the Wrynose and Hardknott Passes to Ravenglass.

St Bega's (NY143001) stands beside the road in the centre of the village. It was built 1890 by **T. L. Banks** to a design by **Charles Harrison Townsend**. Internally it is a very plain church which because of the lie of the land stands on top of the church hall and vestry. It has a very decorative and unusual terracotta font which is dated 1904 and signed by **Hope Rea**. Early photographs of the church show it once had a slender spirelet-cum-bellecôte similar to that on Townsend's mission church at Kirkland. Records show that **Arthur Huddart**, who was working in **T. L. Banks's** Whitehaven office in 1890, was responsible for supervising the work.

Access: Usually open. Vicarage Tel. 019467–23242.

Gatehouse, Eskdale Green, (NY149004) was built in 1896 by **Arthur Huddart** of Whitehaven for the shipping-line owner, James Henry Rea of Liverpool. It was built in red granite and red sandstone in Tudor-style with mullioned windows. The square tower at the eastern-end of the building was added later 'by another hand', says Pevsner, in about 1901. The ground-floor room in the tower has a large, inglenook fireplace with two copper repoussé panels showing graceful galleons in full sail. One of the pair is signed **James Smithies** of Wilmslow. Above, on the first floor, is a bedroom with a delightful inglenook, a copper fire-hood and a carved C17 overmantel. The plaster ceiling is decorated with very delicate, low-relief plant-forms. The long gallery on the ground floor has two eye-catching fireplaces, more copper-work and interesting tiles by **Pilkington**. Here, as in the reception rooms in the older part of the house, the ceilings have elaborate, moulded plasterwork. The library, with its oak-panelled walls, has another inglenook-fireplace and a jolly, copper fender decorated with repoussé crabs and lobsters. Off this room is a modern conservatory with a stained-glass window brought here in 1976 from Platt Chapel in Manchester. It commemorates Sigfreid W. Herford, a young mountaineer who was killed in the Great War. The window was made by **Caroline Townshend** and **Joan Howson** in 1921. The landscaped gardens, including the lake in front of the house and the more-distant Japanese Garden (now much overgrown), were created by **T. H. Mawson**.

Access: The house has been an Outward Bound centre since 1949. Subject to availability, it also provides tourist hotel accommodation. Tel. 019467–23281.

FINSTHWAITE lies to the west of Lake Windermere about 2 miles north of Newby Bridge near the Stott Park Bobbin Mill.

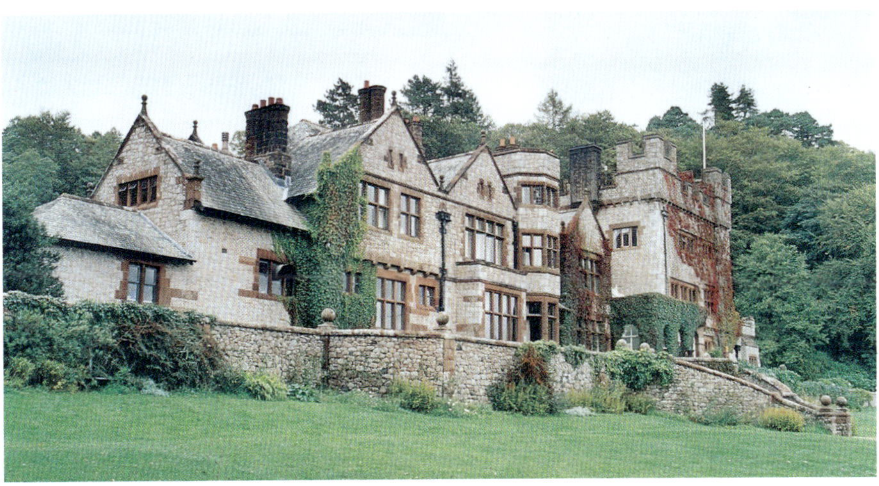

'Gatehouse' Eskdale Green. Garden front. A. Huddart, 1896.

St Peter's church (SD369877) was re-built by **Paley & Austin** 1873–74. It has a massive central tower with a pyramid-like slate covered spire and unusually for **Paley & Austin**, it is very 'Normande' in style. Even so, it seems rooted in its surroundings in this corner of south Lakeland. The Norman features are continued inside the church, with zigzag decoration on the arches and scalloped capitals. The vaults beneath the tower are painted with angels and texts as is the east wall of the sanctuary. The exposed rafters in the chancel are painted with chevrons of red and white, green and black. All the painted work was executed by **Shrigley & Hunt**. The east window is said to have been designed by **Henry Holiday** for **Powell of Whitefriars**. There are other Powell windows in the chancel which when taken with the painted decoration and the ornate metal light-fittings produce an extraordinarily good overall effect.

Access: Usually open. Vicarage Tel. 015395–31476.

FLOOKBURGH is about 1 mile south of Holker Hall on the B5278.

St John's (SD362760) was built 1897–1900 and is one of **Austin & Paley's** best. It is very big with a saddle-back tower at the west end and an apse at the east end. The stained-glass windows in the apse have very unusual colouring for **Shrigley & Hunt** who made all the windows here. There is a small painted and gilded Great War memorial which is very decorative but unsigned.

Access: Usually open. Vicarage Tel. 015395–58245 .

GAMBLESBY lies off the A686 midway between Penrith and Alston.

St John's (NY609394) is a charming sandstone church by **C. J. Ferguson** dating from 1868, one of the first he built after his return from his sojourn in London with G. G. Scott.

Access: Now redundant.

GOSFORTH lies 7 miles south of Egremont on the A595 .

St Mary's (NY072037) has Norman and C14 elements but it is essentially an excellent **C. J. Ferguson** church built 1896–99. In the church yard there is a slender, 15 feet tall, genuine C10 Anglo-Saxon decorated cross.

Access: Usually open. Vicarage Tel. 019467–25251.

GRANGE over SANDS is on the northern shore of Morecambe Bay.

The Clock Tower at the centre of the town (SD408778) was erected in 1912. It may owe some of its inspiration to the work of Edgar Wood but its architect is, to date, undiscovered.

GRASMERE village lies at the head of the lake off the A591 about 4 miles north of Ambleside.

St Oswald's (NY337076) is a mediaeval church in the centre of the village and is more of a place of pilgrimage for Wordsworth afficionados than for the Arts and Crafts. However, aside from the Wordsworth memorial monument, the church has two windows designed and executed by **Henry Holiday**. The east-most window of the south nave wall has two lights with angels bearing scrolls, made in 1893. The second window from the east end in the south wall also has two lights and shows Jesus with Mary and Martha calling Lazarus from the tomb.

Access: Usually open daily 8.00–18.00. Rectory Tel. 015394–35326.

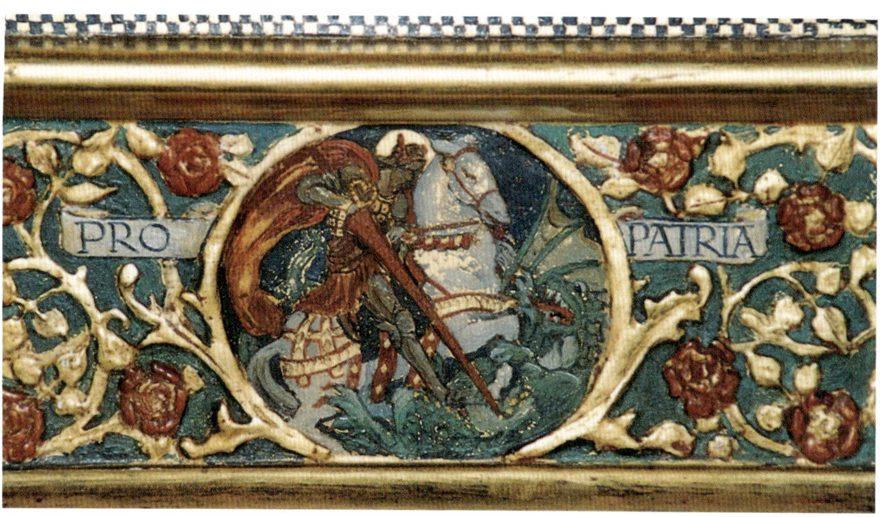

St John's, Flookburgh. Detail of Great War memorial. Unsigned, c. 1920.

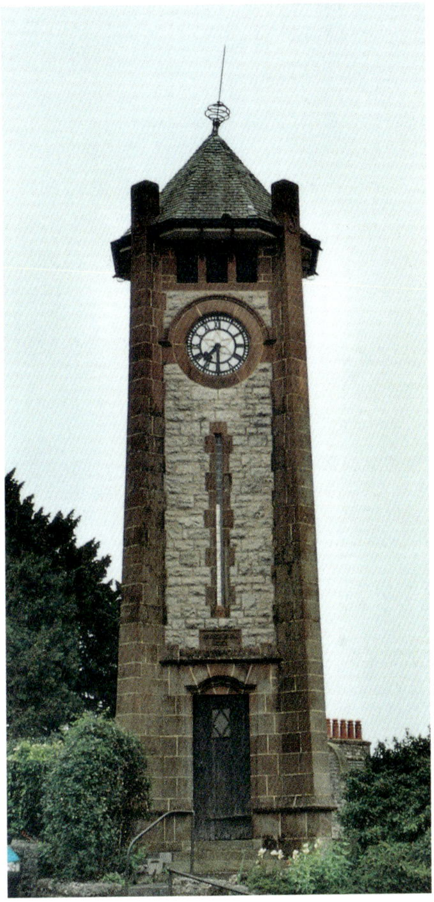

Grange over Sands. Clock tower. Unattributed, 1912.

Grasmere's **Great War memorial** stands on a little grassy knoll in Broadgate Meadow (NY338078). It is a simple and elegant Celtic cross designed by **W. G. Collingwood** and carved from Lakeland stone. It has entrelac patterns on the back while the front has a stylised deer standing on an entrelac serpent.

GRAYTHWAITE is half way between Sawrey and Newby Bridge on the western side of Lake Windermere.

Graythwaite Hall (SD370910) was originally a small Elizabethan house and has been remodelled and extended by many hands including those of **R. K. Freeman** 1887–90 and again after The Great War. It is difficult now to distinguish where one alteration finishes and another starts. The house is set in a well-tended garden designed by **Thomas Mawson** in 1889 for Colonel Myles Sandys. It remains pretty well intact with interesting sun-dials and other garden ornaments designed by **Knill Freeman** and **Dan Gibson**.

Access: The garden is open to the public 10.00–18.00 daily.

GREAT ASBY sits high up on the fells south of Appleby off the B6260 road to Tebay.

St Peter's (NY682132) is an 1860s grey stone church with a two-light window with the figures of St Peter and St Bartholomew dated 1929 and made by **Leonard Walker**. He uses just about every stained-glass technique and although small, the window is worth stopping off to see.

Access: Usually open. Vicarage Tel. 01931–715226.

GREYSTOKE lies beside the B5288 west of Penrith.

St Andrew's (NY445308) stands in the centre of the village. It is a very large and very beautiful church with a long history reaching back to the C13. The great east window has mediaeval glass which was removed for safekeeping during the Civil War and reassembled in a most haphazard but strangely effective way. Look out for the red devil. The Arts and Crafts period interest lies in the three-light window on the north side of the west wall which was designed by **A. K. Nicholson** in 1922. It represents Christ with the Children and St Margaret of Scotland.

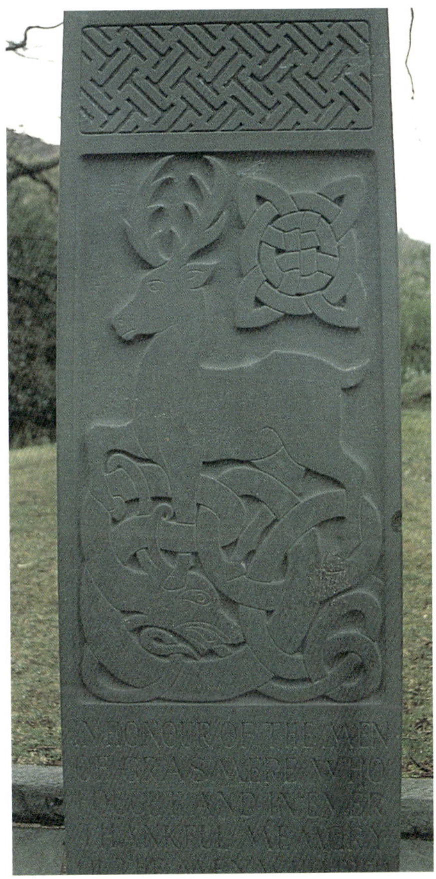

Grasmere Great War memorial. Detail.
W. G. Collingwood, c. 1920.

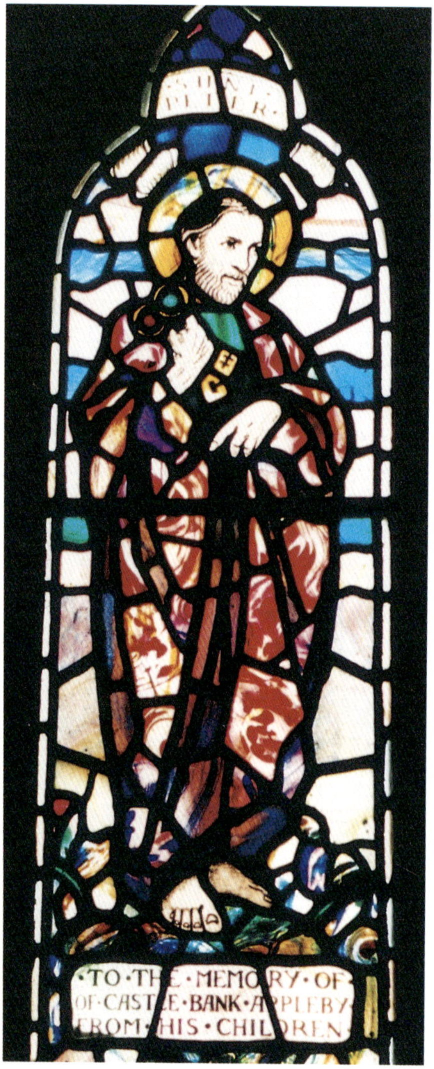

St Peter's, Gt Asby. 'St Peter' by Leonard Walker, 1929.

There is a fine, carved, stone memorial tablet on the west wall commemorating Henry Charles Howard, who died in 1919.

Access: Usually open. Vicarage Tel. 017684–83293.

HAWKSHEAD lies at the junction of the B5284 and the B5285 about 5 miles south of Ambleside.

St Michael and All Angels (SD352980) is a C16 and C17 church and has many interesting older features. Of Arts and Crafts interest are the four windows by **W. H. Lonsdale** (third, fourth, fifth and sixth from the east in the south wall). It is interesting to see the stylistic change between 'The Adoration of the Magi and Shepherds' made in 1884 and 'The Adoration of the Shepherds' made in 1901. He seems to have been ahead of the style in the earlier window and behind the times in 1901. The war memorial cross in the churchyard was designed by **W. G. Collingwood** in 1919.

Access: Usually open. Vicarage Tel. 015394–36301.

Pullwoods (NY365015) stands on the north western shore of Lake Windermere about 2 miles north of Hawkshead on the B5286. It is a magnificent half-timbered house designed by **George Faulkner Armitage** 1890–91 for Sir William Crossley, the owner of an engineering firm in Manchester and a director of the Manchester Ship Canal Co. It has black and white gables and terracotta-coloured plasterwork amidst the half-timbering on the first floor. The ground floor walls are of stone. The house has many of the characteristics of Cheshire's black and white vernacular and Faulkner Armitage has added some of his own idiosyncrasies in the details, including for example, the wonderful ribbon-like wrought iron gutter brackets.

Access: Private house.

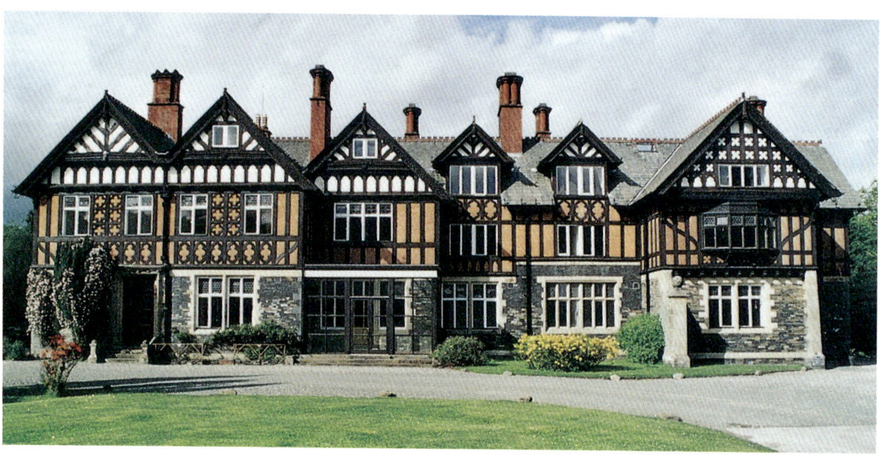

'Pullwood', Hawkshead. Entrance front by G. F. Armitage, 1891.

HEVERSHAM village is signposted off the A6 south of Levens Hall.

St Peter's (SD496834) is well on through the village, but easily seen. It has a huge Early English style west tower but this dates from the **Paley & Austin** restoration 1869–70. The remainder is essentially a Perpendicular building. The west window was designed by **A. K. Nicholson** after 1923 and shows Thomas à Becket and Henry II with St Ursula and St Cecilia. There is good carving on the pew ends.

Access: Open until dusk. Vicarage Tel. 015395–63125.

HOLME lies close to the north-bound lane of the M6 between junctions 35a and 36.

Holy Trinity (SD524788) is a small and plain 1830s church where the delightful three-light east window was designed by **Mary Alice Gordon** and made for her by **A. J. Dix** in the 1920s. It shows a landscape with pictorial representations of Sacrifice, Love Triumphant and Labour.

Access: Vicarage Tel. 01524–781391.

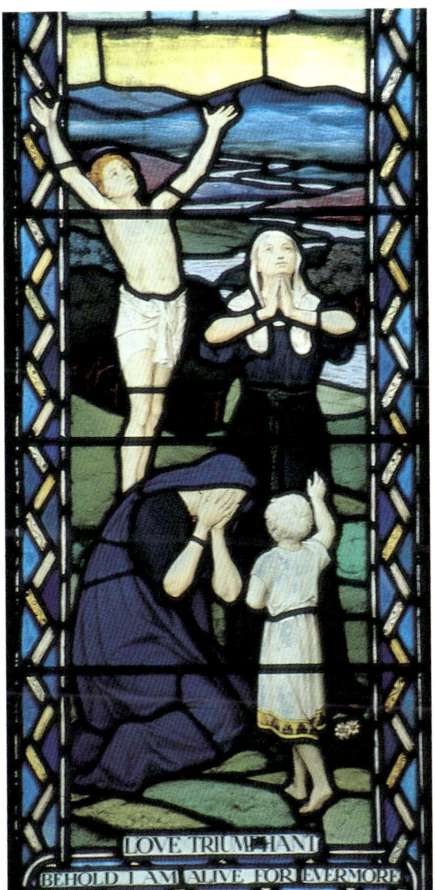

Holy Trinity, Holme. Detail of the east window. Designed by M. Alice Gordon, c. 1920.

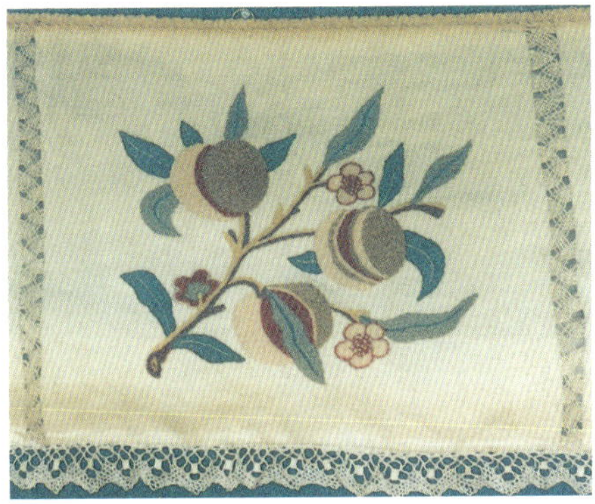

Hutton in the Forest. Detail of the bed hanging. Lady Margaret Vane, undated. *Courtesy of Lord and Lady Inglewood*

HUTTON in the FOREST (NY460355) is a country house about 2½ miles north-west of the M6 Junction 41 on the B5305.

The house began life as a C14 pele tower and was added to in the C17 and C18. Much of the Victorian work was done under the auspices of Anthony Salvin 1832–86. However it was Lady Margaret Vane, the châtelaine of Hutton, who redecorated and refurbished much of the interior in the late C19. She was a talented amateur artist and embroiderer and her work can best be seen in the Lady Darlington bedroom. Here, the **William Morris** 'pomegranate' wallpaper is the inspiration for the bedspread and hangings which were designed and worked by Lady Margaret and are the central feature of the room. Examples of her paintings and decorated pottery are also on display together with a **William De Morgan** charger, a collection of copper ware by the **Keswick School of Industrial Arts** and silver by **W. H. Mawson** and **Harold Stabler**. Some of these pieces stand on elegant little arts and crafts tables. The copper finger-plates on the doors were designed by **J. W. Oddie**. Lady Margaret Vane is also said to have had a hand in the design of the delightful gardens which surround the house.

Access: The house is open 12.30–16.00 in Easter week and on Thurs, Fri, Sun and Bank holidays from 1 May–end of Sept. Gardens open 11.00–17.00 daily, except Sat from Easter–end of Oct. Admission charges. Tel. 017684–84449.

INGS lies about 2 miles east of Windermere on the A591.

St Anne's (SD448987) was built in 1743. It has a very powerful east window designed by **Edward Frampton** and although it is not dated it would appear to have been made in Frampton's own studio. (i.e. after 1881). The splendid, intricate carving on the reredos, lectern and pulpit was executed, over many years, by **Robert Fell** of Applethwaite.

Access: Usually open. Vicarage Tel. 01539–821267.

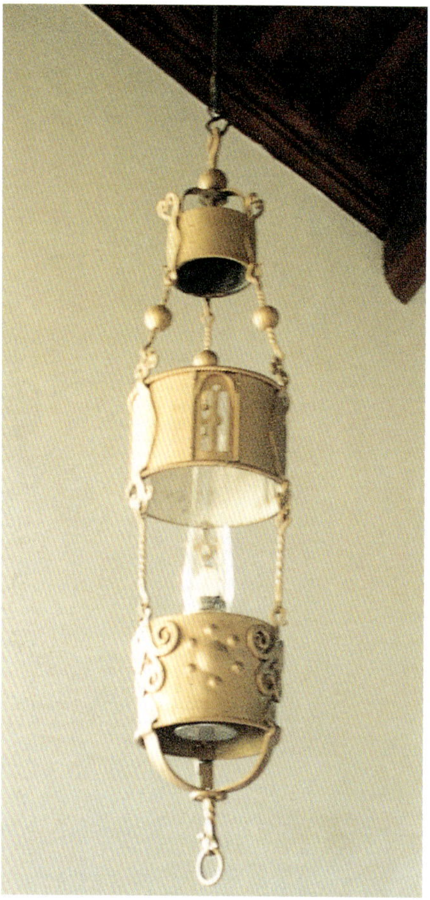

St Michael's, Isel. Hanging lamp by W. Bainbridge Reynolds.

IRTON is at the end of an unclassified road. As you come down from the Hardknott Pass through Eskdale Green the road to Irton is signposted on the left and the church is at the end of a lane on the right just before the village.

St Paul's (NY091005) is an 1850s building with a C9 stone cross in its church yard. It also has two exceptional two-light windows made by **Morris & Co.** in 1887 and 1888. Both windows are in the north wall. One shows St Paul preaching at the altar of the 'Unknown God' and a powerful Tiburtine Sibyl and the other shows St Agnes and St Catherine of Alexandria. They are beautiful windows. St Catherine was designed by **William Morris** and the other three figures are all by **Edward Burne-Jones**. The church has a collection of six embroidered banners dating from the 1870s. The lych-gate is said to be a copy of the ancient lych-gate at St George's in Beckenham, Kent and was made in 1908 by the craftsmen working on the estate.

Access: Usually open. Vicarage Tel. 019467–23242.

ISEL is off the beaten track, so head north-east from Cockermouth on the A595 take the first right off to Blindcrake, turn right in the village, pass Isel Hall, ignoring the signpost to Sunderland on your left. Keep going and you will see the church on your right just a little way off the road.

St Michael's (NY0162334) is a tiny Norman church dating back to 1130. The metal hanging lamps were designed and made by **William Bainbridge Reynolds** whose work is more often seen in such grand places as St Paul's Cathedral and Westminster Abbey. The lamps are not fearfully exciting in themselves but they are very fitting for this very small, very old church. St Michael's also boasts an altar frontal embroidered by the Royal School of Needlework in 1902 which is kept for special occasions.

Access: Usually open. Vicarage Tel. 016973–71541.

KENDAL is about 5 miles west of the M6 on the A684.

The Abbot Hall Museum and Art Gallery (SD516922) is off Kirkland, near the Parish Church. Among the 'Victorian Life in Kendal' exhibits, are collections of furniture made by **A. W. Simpson**, Stanley Davis, Eric Sharpe and Romney Green. There is metal work and jewellery made at the **Keswick School of Industrial Arts** and needle craft by the **Langdale Linen Industries**. There is a particularly fine collection of the work of **Annie Garnett** of The Spinnery at Windermere. Because of the fragile nature of the fabrics they are kept in the museum's store. The museum also holds archive material relating to **Simpson**, Davis, Sharpe and Garnett. The Lakeland Arts Trust which runs Abbot Hall is also responsible for Blackwell in Bowness on Windermere and items from these collections may be displayed from time to time at either venue.

Access: Open daily Apr–Oct 10.30–17.00. Otherwise 10.30–16.00. Check Christmas opening. Admission charges. Tel. 01539–722464.

'Fritillary' fabric woven at the Spinnery. c. 1900–10.
Courtesy of Lakeland Arts Trust

Abbot Hall Park (SD516923) to the east of Abbot Hall has a stone drinking-fountain in the form of an obelisk decorated with a very attractive Celtic entrelac design. In the north-east corner of the park there is another obelisk. This one is of green Westmorland stone and was erected in honour of James Cropper first Chairman of the Westmorland County Council. The obelisk bears a relief bust of Mr Cropper made by **A. C. Lucchesi**. There is confusion over who designed the drinking fountain although the name of **W. G. Collingwood** is offered for both obelisks.

Holy Trinity (SD516922) is across the courtyard from Abbot Hall. It is a huge parish church much restored in the 1850s. The three-light window, third from the west in the south-aisle wall was designed by **Mary Alice Gordon** and made for her by **Shrigley & Hunt**. It is a clever, pictorial representation of the soul's journey to eternal life. The window is dedicated to Mrs Gordon's mother, Mary Wakefield who died in 1922.

Access: Open 9.20–16.30 daily from Easter to the end of Oct. Otherwise open in the mornings. Church Office Tel. 01539–721248.

Carnegie Library, (SD516929) in Highgate is built in a free-style manner in red sandstone with an enormous amount of glass in the north wall. The building was designed by T. F. **Pennington** 1909.

The ex–Westmorland County Council building in Stricklandgate, (SD515931) which houses the Public Record Office has a superb, copper relief bust commemorating James Cropper chairman of the County Council 1890–1900. It was made by **A. C. Lucchesi** in 1901 and is hung to the right of the entrance to the Council Chamber.

Access: Normal office hours. Tel. 01539–773540/773539.

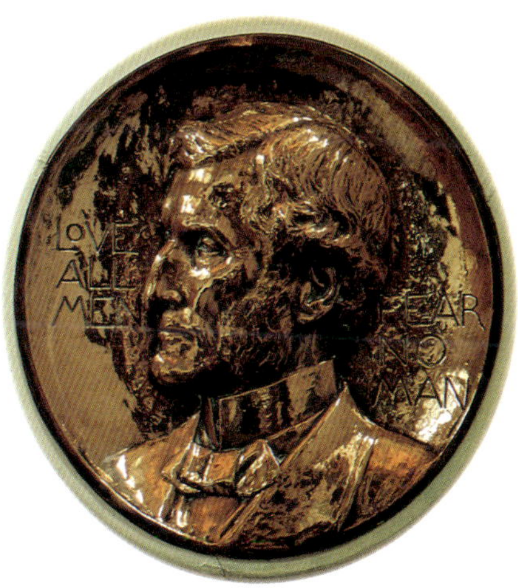

County Hall, Kendal. Relief bust of James Cropper by A. C. Lucchesi, 1901.

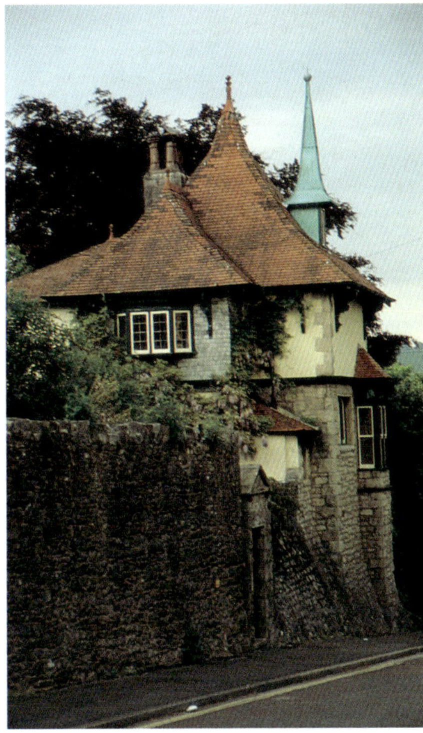

Hill Cot, 80 Gillingate, Kendal.

Littleholme, 3 Sedbergh Rd, Kendal. (SD534929) was built in 1909 by **C. F. A. Voysey** for his friend, local wood-carver and furniture-maker **A. W. Simpson**.

Access: Private residence.

Lynnside, on Gillingate (SD512923), is an extraordinary house designed by **J. F. Curwen** in 1890 for the aerated-water manufacturer F. Crewdson. Across the road at 80 Gillingate is the different, but equally unusual, **Hill Cot**.

Access: Private residences.

K Shoes Great War Memorial (SD517918) stands behind a wall under the trees at the south side of Nether Bridge near the old K Shoe Factory. It is a Westmorland stone cross with an entrelac shaft designed by **W. G. Collingwood** *c.* 1920.

KENTMERE stands at the end of an unclassified road about 5 miles north of Stavely in the Kent Valley.

St Cuthbert's church (NY455042) contains a rather dark bronze tablet set on the wall beside the pulpit. It was made at the **Keswick School of Industrial Arts** in 1901 and commemorates Bernard Gilpin who was born in Kentmere in 1517. He was a Protestant priest who escaped martyrdom only because he suffered a broken leg and was unable to travel to London. By the time he was fit to travel, Queen Mary was dead and Good Queen Bess pardoned him.

Access: Usually open. Vicarage Tel. 01539–821267.

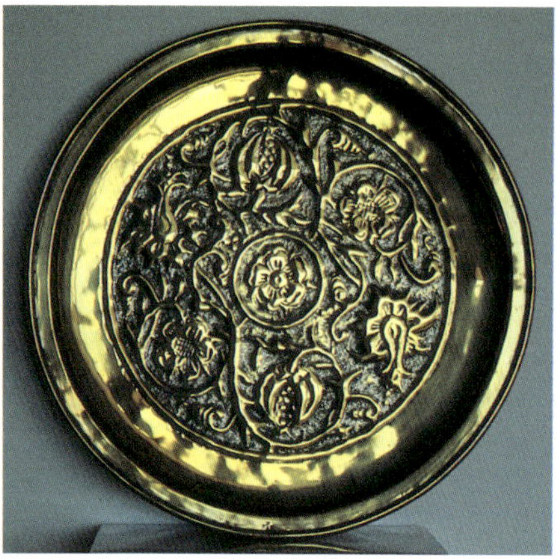

KSIA brass charger deigned by Edith Rawnsley.
Courtesy of the Keswick Museum

KESWICK stands at the head of Derwent Water at the junction of the A591 and the A66.

Keswick Museum in Station Rd, Fitz Park (NY268236) was built in 1897 by **Thomas Hodgson** in an Arts and Crafts manner. It contains a local history collection including a repoussé copper Great War memorial made by **W. H. Mawson** to commemorate Brigham Old Boys killed in the Great War. There is a small collection of **Ruskinian** memorabilia and letters. The exhibition room has six hanging lights made by the **Keswick School of Industrial Art** and there are a number of copper and brass repoussé platters and plaques designed by **Edith Rawnsley** and also made at the **KSIA**.

Access: Open Tues–Sat from 10.00–16.00. Closed 31 Oct.–Good Friday. Tel. 017687–73263.

County Square (NY267235) is the site of the town's stone war memorial on the pedestal of which is an extra copper panel made at the **Keswick School of Industrial Arts**. The panel was originally displayed at the railway station and commemorates the men of the Cockermouth, Keswick and Penrith Railway who were killed in the Great War.

St John the Evangelist (NY269232) is about 400 yards from the town centre on the Keswick to Ambleside Road. The church was built in 1838 by Anthony Salvin who returned to extend it in 1862 and again in 1882. There are many examples of the stained-glass designs of **Henry Holiday**. His earliest work is the six-light, three-tier east window which was made by Powell of Whitefriars in 1879. It depicts Old Testament figures in the bottom tier, New Testament figures in the middle row and above them a host of angels. Ten years later Holiday designed the three-light window opposite the organ in the chancel which illustrates the parables of 'The Lost Penny Found', 'The Good Shepherd' and 'The Seeds Falling on Stony Ground'. In 1890 he added the side windows in the Sanctuary (two evangelists on each side) and St John and St Paul in the third window from the east in the south wall. His last window here is also in the south aisle and depicts 'Christ With the Little Children'. Between Holiday's windows in the south wall is an example of the work of **Veronica Whall**. Her 'Christ and the Little Children' is rich in colours and symbolism and manages to engage the emotions without being over sentimental. At the west end of the south aisle is a window designed by **G. P. Hutchinson**. The window is dated 1918 and shows the two Mary's at the empty tomb receiving the message 'He is not here' from one of the most beautiful angels in the county. The font cover and several memorials in the church are said in the guidebook to have been made at the **Keswick School of Industrial Arts** although the mark is not always apparent. Nevertheless the Great War Memorial looks every square-inch like the work of the KSIA. The guidebook attributes the eagle lectern to George Brooker, one of a family of woodcarvers who, among other things, carved ships' figureheads. It was presented in 1887.

Access: Usually open. Vicarage Tel. 017687–72130.

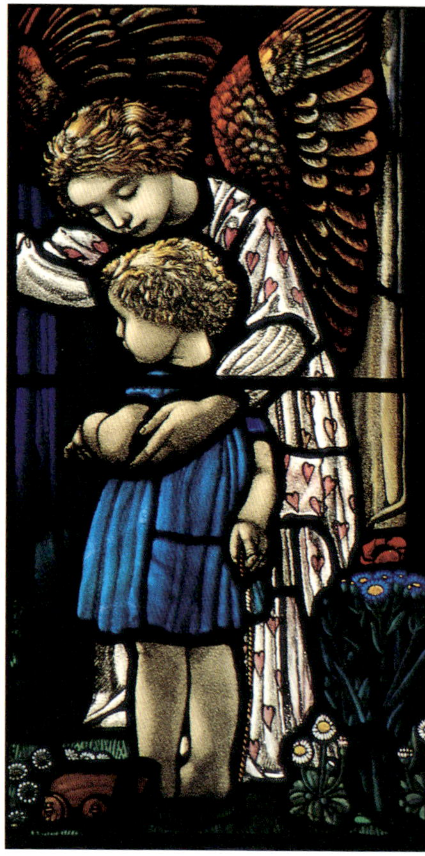

St John's, Keswick. Stained-glass detail by Veronica Whall, 1918.

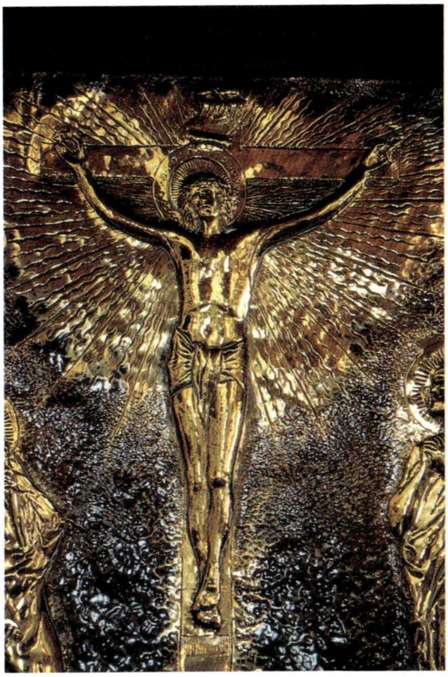

St Kentigern's, Crosthwaite, Keswick. Detail of the reredos by KSIA, 1889.

St Kentigern's, Crosthwaite (NY256244) stands on the western fringe of Keswick on a site which was first used for church building in 553 A.D. The present church dates from 1553 and underwent its restoration in 1844 at the hands of G. G. Scott. The interior of the church contains some wonderful work by the **Keswick School of Industrial Arts**. In H. D. Rawnsley's biography Eleanor, his second wife, claims that all the decoration was designed by **Edith Rawnsley**: the sanctuary mosaics, the altar hangings, the silver backed service books, the pulpit and the carved panels in the porch as well as some crosses and memorial stones. The pièce de résistance is the gleaming reredos. Ian Bruce in *The Loving Eye and Skilful Hand* attributes the execution to **Edith Rawnsley** and **John Birkett** together with A. Litt, R. Temple and G. Dickson. It is made up of three highly polished repoussé panels, which show the Nativity, the Crucifixion and the Resurrection with the text which reads 'My meat is to do the work of him that sent me'. The rest of the reredos has beautifully carved figures in keeping with the quality of the other woodwork in the chancel and choir. **Edith Rawnsley** also designed a festive white altar frontal from a design adapted from a tomb in Ravenna and made from inexpensive woollen material. She strongly believed and demonstrated in her work that beautiful things are not necessarily costly. In 1909 as a memorial to H. D. Rawnsley's 25 years work at Crosthwaite, the font was re-sited in the old vestry and paved and panelled in green slate. There are copper memorial plaques on the north wall and gleaming copper light fittings in the nave and aisles. The design of the light fittings is attributed to **Edith Rawnsley** by Sara E. Haslam in *John Ruskin and the Lakeland Arts Revival, 1880–1920*.

Access: Usually open. Vicarage Tel. 017687–72509.

Crosthwaite Parish Hall, on High Hill (NY264237) was built by **C. J. Ferguson** and was the first home of the **Keswick School of Industrial Arts**. Across the road and on the other side of the bridge stands the building built for the School by **Austin & Paley** in 1894.

The Ruskin Memorial, Friars Cragg, (NY264223) on the shore of Derwentwater, is less than a mile from Keswick town centre and is reached by a footpath at the end of Lake Road. The memorial was designed by **W. G. Collingwood** and the relief bust of Ruskin was sculpted by **A. C. Lucchesi** in 1900.

KILLINGTON is a tiny hamlet tucked away off the B6256 west of Sedbergh. You will need a sharp eye and a bit of intuition because the lanes are narrow and the hedges are high. Such signs as exist are likely to be buried in the hedgerows.

All Saints (SD612891) stands next to Killington Hall part of which is in ruins. The church is C14 or C15 with C18 enlargement. Its glory is the **Christopher Whall** east window which floods the little church with light and colour.

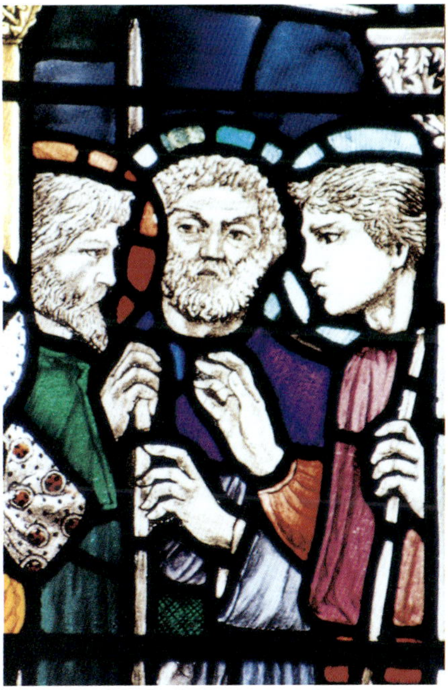

All Saints, Killington. Detail of the east window. Christopher Whall, 1907.

The window dated 1907 is dedicated to Florence Anne Upton-Cottrell-Dormer of Ingmire Hall, Sedbergh. It depicts the sudden appearance of Christ to his disciples in the upper room after his resurrection. On the right the disciples who met the risen Christ at Emmaus have just arrived bursting to tell their news and unaware of His presence are no doubt very put out to be 'shushed' by the disciple half-turned towards them. It is a wonderfully-designed window with a bounty of angels and Old Testament prophets in the tracery.

Access: Open daily 9.30–17.00.

KIRKANDREWS on ESK is in a field east of the A7 about 7 miles north of Carlisle.

St Andrew's (NY391720) is signposted off the A7 between Longtown and Canonbie. The lane becomes a field track but by then the church is reassuringly in sight! It was built in 1776 and was given a new screen, reredos and stained glass by **Temple Lushington Moore** in 1893. The screen is green and gold in an Italianate style and together with the stained-glass windows is evidence of the architect's ability to design in sympathy with the original building. The church has undergone substantial repair and restoration.

Access: Vicarage Tel. 01228–791338.

KIRKBAMPTON lies on the B5307 some 5 miles west of Carlisle.

St Peter's (NY305566) is 800 years old and has a Norman arch. It also has an east window, made in 1871, by **Morris, Marshall, Faulkner & Co.** in which eight of **William Morris's** musical angels surround a Christ by **Burne-Jones**. Unfortunately the colours have weathered and the window has lost much of its appeal.

Access: Usually open. Rectory Tel. 01228–576324.

KIRKBRIDE is on the B5307 about 7 miles east of Carlisle.

St Bride's (NY228564) celebrated its 800th anniversary in 1989. It is essentially a Norman church despite its restoration in the 1890s. The combination pulpit and prayer desk was carved by little-known **George Black** of Carlisle while the window in the south wall of the chancel showing the empty tomb was made in 1896 and designed by the better-known **John Francis Bentley**. The south porch was designed by **Oliver & Dodgshun**.

Access: Usually open. Rectory Tel. 016973–51256.

KIRKBY in FURNESS lies about 3½ miles south-east of Broughton in Furness on the A595.

St Cuthbert's, Beckside, (SD234822) has a two-light window in the north wall of the sanctuary by **Hugh Arnold**. It was erected in 1907 and shows St Aidan and St Cuthbert although the artist has given Cuthbert a book to carry instead of the traditional severed head of St Oswald. The figures are well drawn and the leading of the clear quarries hints at Arnold's skill as a designer of plain decorative glazing.

Access: Vicarage Tel. 01229–889256.

KIRKBY LONSDALE is 5 or 6 miles east of the M6, junction 36, on the A65.

St Mary's (SD613787) has massive, decorated Norman pillars and many other early characteristics which have survived several enlargements and restorations. 'Faith, Hope and Charity' in the east-most three-light window in the south aisle was designed by **Henry Holiday** and executed by Heaton, Butler & Bayne according to Leslie Smith in *Stained Glass in the Anglican Churches of the Diocese of Carlisle*. However, Pevsner asserts they are 'no doubt by Powell'. They have beautiful figures and faces. The north-west corner of the church has been enclosed to form a vestry which makes it difficult to see the windows in that corner which were designed by **Carl Almquist** for **Shrigley & Hunt**.

Access: Usually open. Parish Office Tel. 015242–71320 or 72044.

KIRKBY STEPHEN is a market town on the A685 some 4 miles south of its junction with the A66.

The Parish church (NY778088) has a four-light window in the south side of the west wall

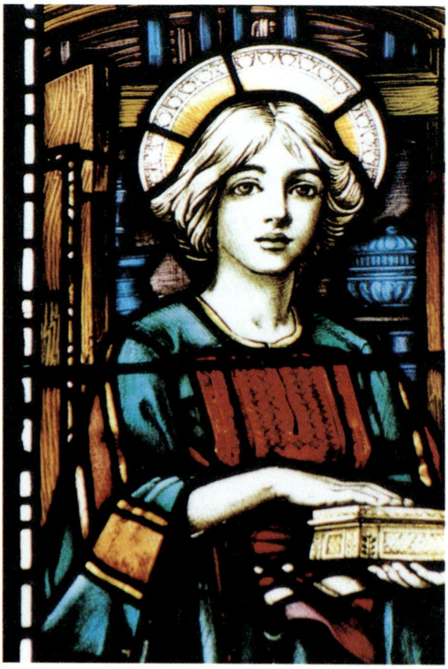

Parish Church, Kirkby Stephen. Detail, Mary of Bethany by James Clarke, 1904.

which was designed by **James Clark** and executed by **A. J. Dix**. The nearby cartoons are signed JC and dated 1903. The figures are Samuel, Mary of Bethany, Eunice & Timothy, and Peter. For a window made in 1903 Mary's face and haircut are surprisingly modern. The spectacular rood-screen was made by **A. W. Simpson** of Kendal *c.* 1920. The organ-screen was carved by **J. M. Kilbride** of Windermere.

Access: Usually open. Church Office Tel. 017683–72910.

KIRKLAND lies 4 or 5 miles north of Cleater Moor on the A5086.

This little **Mission Church** (NY075182) was designed by **C. H. Townsend** during his time with **T. L. Banks** and was built in 1886. Its Arts and Crafts style is reflected in the elegant simplicity of its design. Internally, it has an unusual 'roll-up' screen to separate the chancel with its beamed ceiling from the body of the church, thus making the nave available for more secular use as a church hall. The building bears a striking resemblance to St Bega's at Eskdale Green.

Access: Vicarage Tel. 01946–861310.

KIRKLINTON is about 2 miles east of the A607 south of the river Lyne.

Kirklinton Park Lodge (NY453667) is recorded in the Register of Listed Buildings, as having probably been designed by **J. H. Sellers** *c.* 1900 when he was working in the Carlisle office of G. Dale Oliver.

Access: Private dwelling.

LAMPLUGH lies to the east of the A5086 mid-way between Cockermouth and Egremont.

St Michael's (NY088209) was almost rebuilt in 1870 by **William Butterfield**. It stands outside the village and is a neat example of his simple country-church style. The big bellcôte at the west end, the chimney on the north side and the traceried opening above the chancel arch are characteristic features.

Access: Vicarage Tel. 01946–861310.

LANERCOST is about 2 miles north-east of Brampton.

The Priory Church of St Mary Magdelene at Lanercost (NY557638) has three wonderful windows by **Morris & Co.** all designed by **Burne-Jones**. Two are in the north wall. In the west-most window, made in 1887, the principal figure is St Luke and in a panel below, St Peter and St John are shown healing a cripple at the Beautiful Gate of the Temple. Next to it, but not installed until 1912, is the unusual subject of Moses being carried off by the angels for burial. The third window, 'The First Noël' of 1890 is on the west wall at the end of the north aisle. **Burne-Jones** also designed the scenes in the memorial tablet to Charles Howard and his wife which hangs in the chancel.

Access: Usually open. Vicarage Tel. 016977–2478.

LEVENS lies just north of the A590 at its junction with the A6 about 5 miles south of Kendal.

St John the Evangelist (SD487860) has a beautiful east window made in 1922 by **A. K. Nicholson**. It shows Christ in Glory

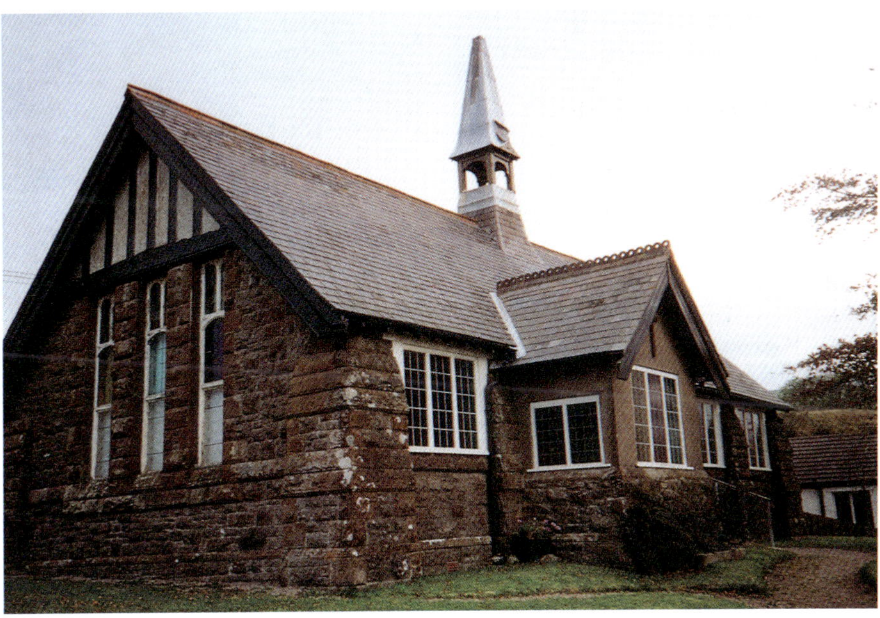

Mission church, Kirkland, C. H. Townsend, 1886.

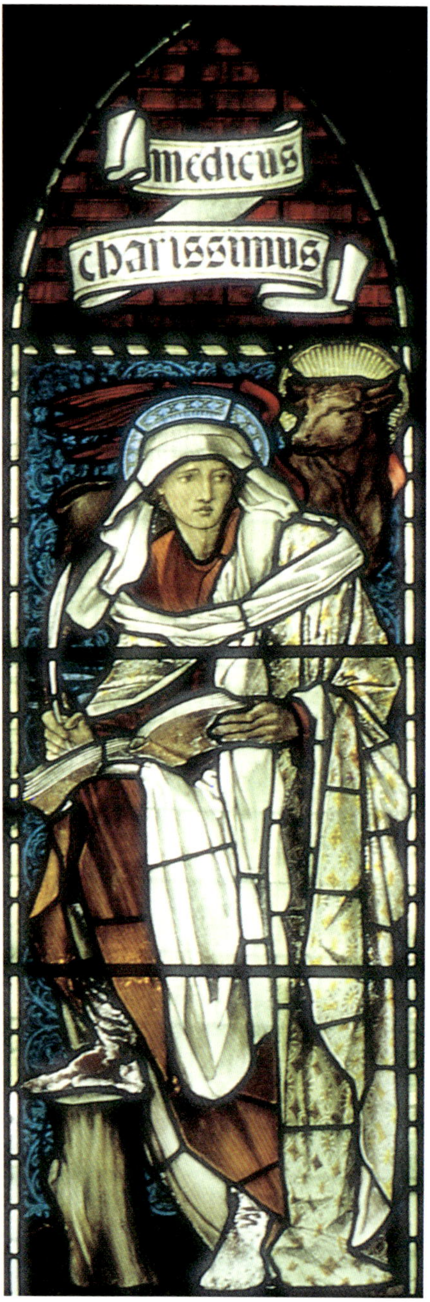

Priory church, Lanercost. St Luke by Morris & Co., 1887.

above a representation of the Crucifixion with Mary and John on either side of the cross. The cross is a living tree bearing 12 different kinds of fruit. Although the colours are more muted than those usually associated with Nicholson's windows, it is no less spectacular. The small lights at the foot of the major panels depict scenes from the life of Jesus. The detail is worth close observation. In the churchyard are three simple headstones designed by **Harold Stabler** for three ladies of the Stabler family; Bertha the organist, Hannah the school teacher and Sarah the wife of George Stabler.

Access: Usually open. Vicarage Tel. 015395–60223.

LOW WRAY lies about 2 miles north of Hawkshead in the lanes off the B5286 near the front gate of Wray Castle.

St Margaret's (NY372006) is part of the view from Wray Castle. It has a simple reredos made by **Arthur Simpson**.

Access: Usually open in the mornings. Vicarage Tel. 015394–36301.

MEALSGATE is on the A595 about 15 miles south-west of Carlisle.

New All Hallows church (NY197424) is about a mile from the A595 on the B5299. It is one of **C. J. Ferguson's** little Neo-Gothic gems. **The Powell of Whitefriars** order book in the Archive of Art and Design attributes St John and the Virgin Mary to **William Aikman**. Who then designed and executed the little St Martin window and the rather good 'Moses in the Bulrushes'?

Access: Vicarage Tel. 016973–71541.

MILBURN is a small village on the fells north of Appleby, probably best approached from the A66 at Temple Sowerby passing through Newbiggin on an unclassified road.

St Cuthbert's (NY652292) lies outside the village where there has been a church in one form or another since Norman times. The east-facing window in the south aisle is attributed by Leslie Smith to **Marjorie Kemp** and **Margaret Chilton** in 1934. They are similarly credited with the' Good Shepherd' and 'David the Shepherd Boy' (1930) while 'St Michael' and 'St Luke' are by **Marjorie Kemp** alone and dated 1946. These are good examples of their work which is rarely seen in the North West.

Access: Open in the summer.
Rectory Tel. 017683–61269.

MILLOM stands in splendid isolation on a loop of the A5093.

Holy Trinity (SD171812) is just north of the town off the A5093. The three-light window in the middle of the south aisle is by **Hugh Arnold**. It dates from 1908 and shows the archangels Gabriel, Michael and Raphael. Michael looks as if his shoulder is a bit stiff. Perhaps his joust with the devil was too robust! There is an interesting memorial bronze plaque with acorns, entrelac, shields and bosses, dated 1907 but with no maker's mark.

Access: Vicarage Tel. 01229–772889.

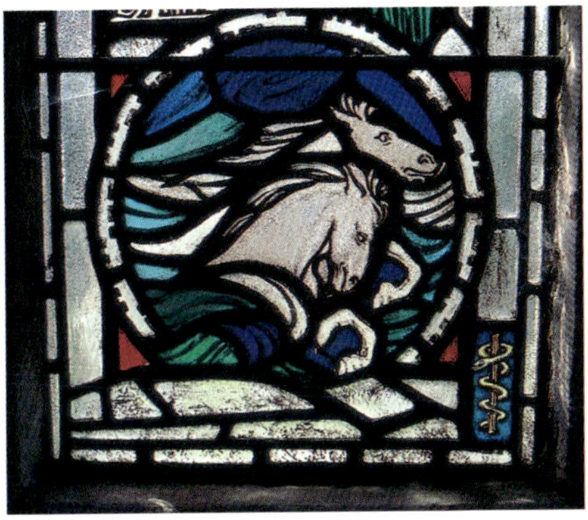

St Cuthbert's, Milburn. Roundel beneath the David panel by Kemp and Chilton, 1930.

MOSSER MAINS lies at the end of a maze of tiny country lanes. Set out from Cockermouth on the A5086 towards Egremont, take the second unclassified road on your left (it will be the second minor crossroad) enter the maze and head for Mosser Mains Farm.

St Michael's (NY116248) is an C18 church and was to have become redundant when the new church was built at Eaglesfield, however, it survives. This very small chapel has a proportionately small single-light east window featuring a dove and foliage by **Joan Howson.**

Access: Ask for the key at Gill Brow Cottage next to Mosser Mains Farm, drive on past the little group of houses and you will see the church on top of a hill. You will have to walk the last 100 yards. Vicarage Tel. 01900–603886.

MUNCASTER is 1 mile west of Ravenglass on the A595.

St Michael's (SD104965) is near the castle. It has five wonderful two-light windows by **Henry Holiday** for **Powell of Whitefriars.** The 'Shepherds' window in the sanctuary and the three pairs of angels in the chancel were erected in 1882 as a memorial to four friends of Lord Muncaster who were killed by brigands in Greece in 1870. The fifth window, made in 1887, is in the middle of the south wall and shows the 'Angel of Judgement' and the 'Angel who Troubled the Waters' (John 5:4).

Access: Usually open. Vicarage Tel. 019467–23242.

The Great War Memorial (SD090967), on the south side of the A595 takes the form of a simple cross on a plinth, designed to be elegant by E. L. Lutyens in 1920.

NATLAND lies on the southern edge of Kendal just off the A65.

St Mark's (SD521892) was built 1909–10 by **Paley & Austin.** The style is Perpendicular with touches of Arts and Crafts decoration. The five-light war-memorial east window made in 1947 by **G. E. R. Smith** is breathtaking. A

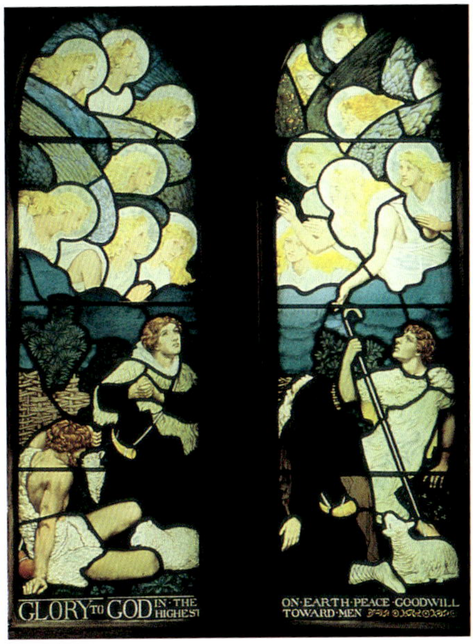

St Michael's, Muncaster. 'The Anunciation to the Shepherds' by Henry Holiday, 1882.

brilliant, if alternative colour-way rainbow arches across all 5 lights and separates the earthly from the heavenly existence. Below the rainbow, St George sits on his charger in front of a rising sun while to his left and right are figures representing the armed forces and civil services who are commemorated by the window. Above the rainbow Christ stands in Glory against a tree of life among His saints and prophets. The figures and the cherubs in the tracery are set against clear quarries with lead lines that represent radiating light. The overall effect of shining brightness is magnificent. So too is the small scale detail such as the robin on the Land-girl's wooden rake. The two-light window in the east end of the south chapel was also made by **G. E. R. Smith** at the A. K. Nicholson studio in 1939. It shows a heavenly host of golden, trumpet-playing, angels standing on a rainbow to welcome home the black- robed monk commemorated by the window. In the south aisle the second window from the west is by H. Martin (of the Celtic Glass Studio Swansea) 1947. It is a memorial to George Keesey who was killed in 1916 in the Great War and to his only son who died in 1944 of wounds received during the Second World War.

Access: Usually open. Vicarage Tel. 015395–60355.

NETHER DENTON lies between the A69 and Hadrian's Wall on a very exposed hill top. Follow the signpost to Low Row about 4 miles east of Brampton, cross the railway and turn right. You will see the signpost to the church (on the left) about 2 miles on.

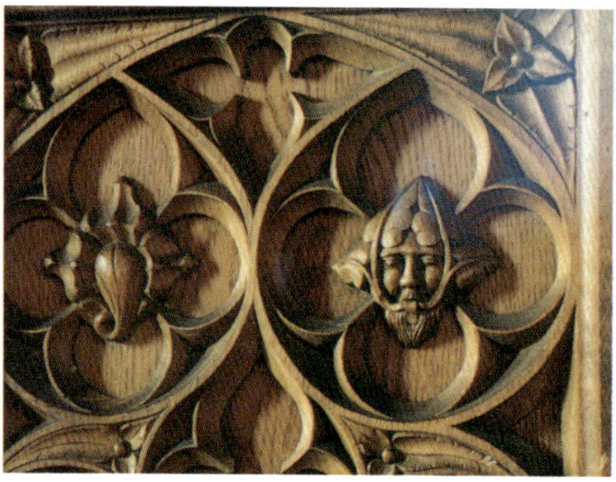

St Cuthbert's, Nether Denton. Detail of pulpit, the green man. Unattributed.

St Cuthbert's (NY616655) was built in 1870 by **C. J. Ferguson** in very simple Early English style with excellent but unattributed carving on the pulpit.

Access: Usually open. Vicarage Tel. 016977–2478.

NEW HUTTON is signposted off the A684 Kendal to Sedbergh Rd. Take the turning nearest to Kendal, it is less complicated.

St Stephen's (SD562911) was built in 1829. The east window was designed and made by **H. G. Hiller** as a memorial to 'Queen Victoria the Good'. It is one of his earliest commissions and is a little bit stiff. Nevertheless, it is a well-balanced design in which the Good Shepherd and St Stephen are set off against a background of grapes and vines with grey-green foliage. The church also has some simple, Arts and Crafts, oak fittings.

Access: Usually open. Vicarage Tel. 01539–824272.

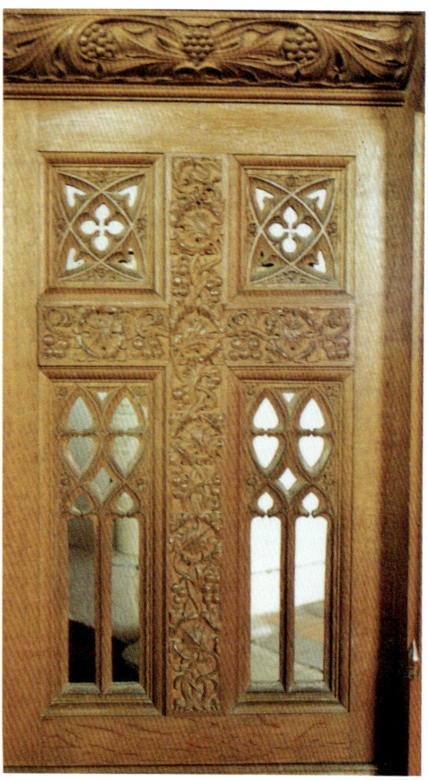

St John's, Old Hutton. Detail of lectern by A. W. Simpson.

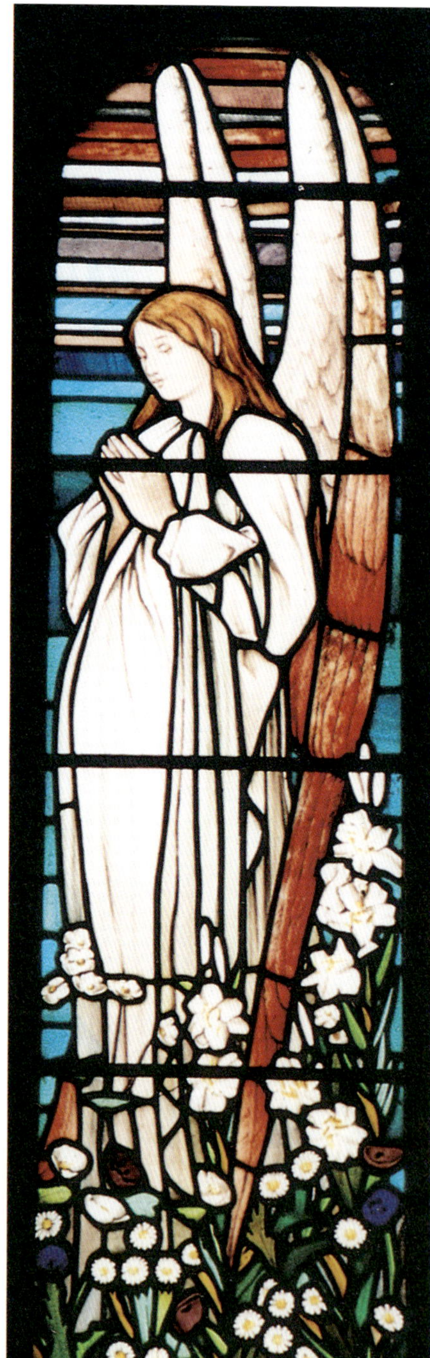

All Saints', Orton. Detail of the Wilson Home window. Beatrice Whistler. 1891.

OLD HUTTON is on the B6254 about 3 miles south-east of Kendal.

St John the Baptist (SD561887) has a lectern carved in 1920 by **A. W. Simpson.**

Access: Vicarage: Tel. 01539–824272.

ORTON village is north of Tebay on the B6260.

All Saints (NY624083) is a C13 church with Perpendicular alterations and an unusual C19 window. It is fitted at the west end of the baptistery and is a memorial to 8 year-old Jane Mary Wilson Holme who died in 1880. It was erected by **Campbell, Smith and Co.** of London in 1891 and is the only window ever designed by **Beatrice Whistler**. There are particularly interesting effects created by the horizontal lead lines and the colours in the sky. It is also interesting that the artist appears to have forsaken the androgeny of at least one of her angels who appears to be developing 'an interesting condition'.

Access: Usually open. Vicarage Tel. 015396–24532.

OXENHOLME is about 2 miles south-east of Kendal on the B6254.

Barrows Green (SD529898) is an impressive building designed in 1906 by **Percy Worthington** and recently converted into luxury apartments. The house now goes under the name of **Highfield Hall**, an appropriate name as it sits high up on the barrow overlooking the Cumbrian countryside. It was built in local stone and slate with interesting porch entrances and stone-mullioned windows.

Access: Private dwellings.

PATTERDALE lies at the southern end of Ullswater on the A592.

St Patrick's (NY393159) lies in the middle of the village on the A592. This is another of Salvin's Lakeland churches built in 1853. It is blessed with three of **Ann Macbeth's** needlework panels. The 'Good Shepherd' is embroidered with the score of Jerusalem, a reminder that Ann Macbeth helped establish the local branch of the Womens Institute in 1921. There are also banners showing a bowl of colourful flowers and a text 'Peace when thou comest and when thou goest may thy footsteps echo peace.' A fourth panel 'The Nativity' is owned by Glasgow Corporation and is displayed at St Patrick's during the summer season. 'The Lakeland Prayer' is by a later pair of hands.

Access: Usually open during the season. Rectory Tel. 017684–82209.

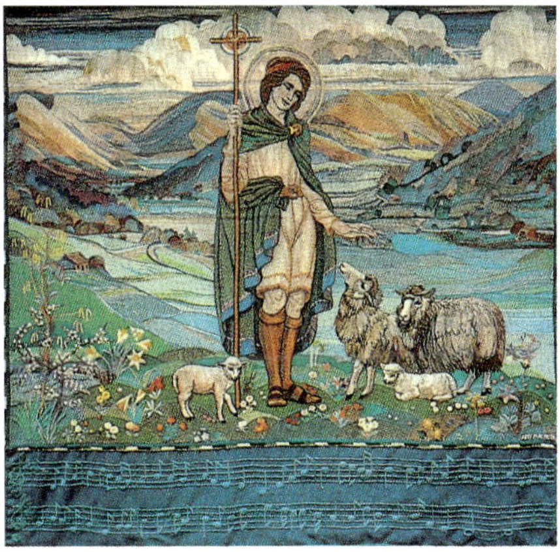

St Patrick's, Patterdale. Embroidered hanging, 'The Good Shepherd' by Ann Macbeth. *Courtesy of the Theo Trust*

PENNINGTON is signposted to the north of the A590 Dalton to Ulverston Rd.

St Michael and the Holy Angels (SD262774) has a set of windows in the north-nave wall by **Powell of Whitefriars** dating from the 1920s and designed by **G. P. Hutchinson**. There is an interesting, almost daily, correspondence in the Public Record Office at Barrow between Hutchinson and the incumbent, Canon Kenworthy, covering the design period. There are heartfelt pleas such as 'Can you make Bede more venerable?' and questions and replies about the symbolism and colours used in the windows. Hutchinson held his own very well in the face of a meticulous client who was obviously clear about what he wanted.

Access: Vicarage Tel. 01229–583174.

PENRITH stands at the major north-south and east-west crossroads of the A6 and M6 with the A66.

The Great War Memorial stands in Castle Park (NY511298). 'The Black Angel' as it is known locally is a winged Victory sculpted by **F. W. Doyle Jones** *c.* 1920 and set upon a stone pedestal.

PLUMBLAND lies east of Maryport between the A596 and the A595 on the B5301 .

St Cuthbert's (NY141392) is a **Cory & Ferguson** church built 1870–71 and is reputedly one of Ferguson's best. Among a huge amount of stained glass are two windows by **A. K. Nicholson** at the west end. The figures are of St George and St Martin with panels showing George slaying his dragon and Martin dividing his cloak.

Access: Usually open. Vicarage: 016973–71541.

PLUMPTON sits at the A6/ B6413 cross roads 5 miles north of Penrith.

St John the Evangelist (NY494373) was built in 1907 by **Robert Lorimer**. It has the easy simplicity that is evidence of the great expertise of its architect who was able to rely on the slight batter of the walls of the stumpy tower and the south porch to lift an otherwise plain

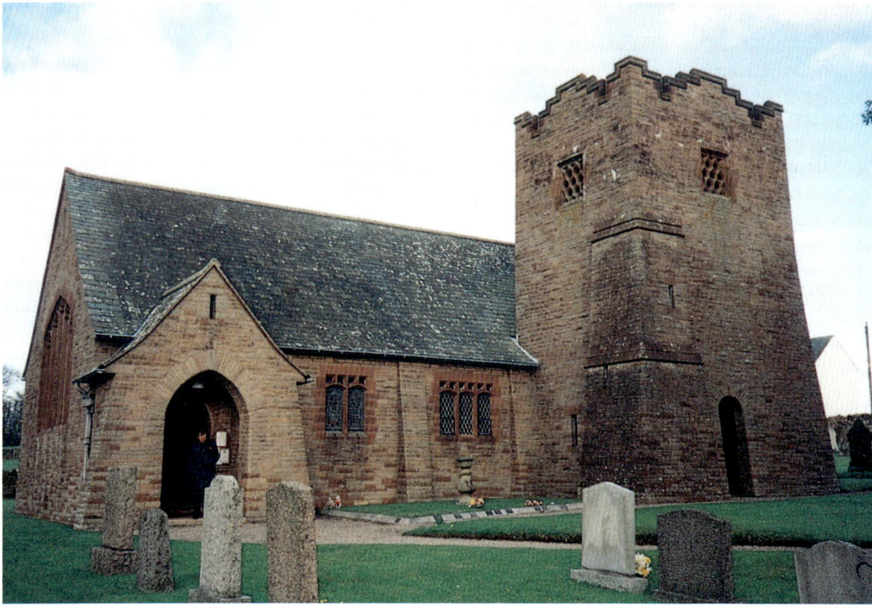

St John's, Plumpton. Robert Lorimer, 1907.

building out of the commonplace. There are two of **Burne-Jones's** musical angels (1908) in the windows next to the door on the south wall. The simplicity of the interior, set off by the grey stone walls, forms a perfect setting for the large reredos, which was designed by **Lorimer** but only installed here in 1999. It arrived in Plumpton by a circuitous route after being rescued 23 years earlier from the redundant St Mary's Mission Church, Bell's Brae, Edinburgh. The paintings have been attributed to William Hole (1846–1917) who did the murals at the Scottish Portrait Gallery and in the Edinburgh City Chambers. The altar with its carving of the pelican and the pulpit were also designed by Lorimer.

Access: Parish Office Tel. 01768–862867.

Lorimer was also responsible for refurbishing the nearby **Brackenburgh Tower** (NY477384) in 1903.

Access: Private house.

PONSONBY lies to the east of the A595 and about a quarter mile south of Calder Bridge.

The Parish church (NY043056) is not in the village at all, but stands on a knoll in a field to the west of the A595. The east window is by **Morris & Co.** from 1877. It comprises three lancets: Peter and John; the Crucifixion and the Nativity; Paul and Barnabas. Barnabas was designed by **Morris** and the others are all by **Burne-Jones**. At the other end of the church there are two lancets in the west tower showing Faith and Charity. They were designed and executed by **Henry Holiday** and dedicated in 1893.

Access: Usually open. Vicarage Tel. 01946–841327.

RAVENSTONEDALE is signposted to the south of the A685 Sedbergh to Tebay Rd.

St Oswald's (NY721041) is an C18 church. The design of the east-most window in the south nave wall is attributed by Leslie Smith (see bibliography) to **J. E. Nuttgens** although it was made by **Powell of Whitefriars** after 1925. It represents St Margaret of Scotland. On the other side of the church is a striking window signed by **Daniel Cottier** showing St Cecilia in very 1890s dress and with a face so contemporary that it could be a portrait of Mary Blanche Hewetson to whom the window is dedicated.

Access: Usually open. Vicarage Tel. 015396–24532.

RUSLAND is a fairly dispersed parish on Furness Fells and the church takes a bit of finding. Head south from Hawkshead to Rusland and the church appears on your right in the middle distance.

St Paul's (SD339896) is an C18 church which was substantially rebuilt in 1868. The simple reredos is by **A. W. Simpson** and there are three windows attributed by Leslie Smith (see bibliography) to **H. W. Lonsdale**. His two-light window in the south wall of the sanctuary shows 'Jesus with the Woman at the Well' while in the south wall of the chancel he depicts Christ and the Apostles. His third window is the east-most in the south wall of the nave and shows St Paul and the Elders.

Access: Usually open. Vicarage Tel. 015394–36301.

RYDAL is about 1 mile north of Ambleside on the A591.

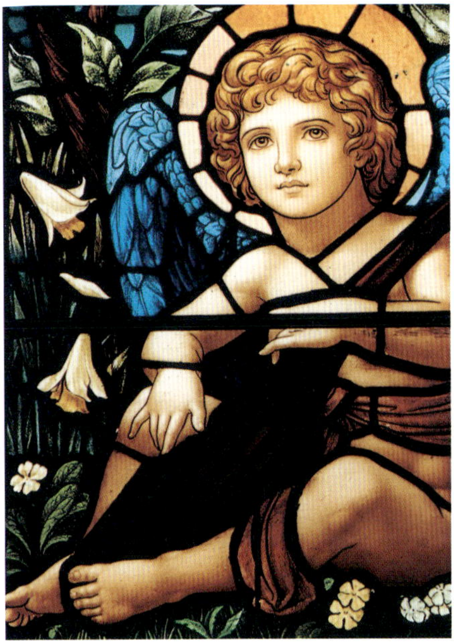

St Mary's, Rydal. Detail of the Quillinan window by Henry Holiday, 1891.

St Mary's (NY364062) dates from 1824 but has a two-light window by **Henry Holiday** made in 1891. It is fixed in the south wall and is a beautifully made memorial to Jemima Catherine and Rotha Quillinan and features naked cherubs, carrying scrolls. The cartoon for this window was used by Holiday as an illustration in his *Stained Glass as an Art*, which was published in 1896. It was a very appropriate choice as it is a very beautiful window.

Access: Usually open. Vicarage Tel. 015394–32050.

Rydal Hall Garden (NY365063) is just up the hill from St Mary's church. The Hall is now the Carlisle Diocesan Conference Centre. The formal garden, which was designed in 1909 by **T. H. Mawson**, is of special interest because many of the structural elements such as the balustrades, pillars, fountain pond, sculptures, steps and pavements are not stone but concrete. Plans are in hand for the renovation of the garden.

Access: Always open. Free.

ST BEES is on the coast 3 miles north-west of Egremont.

St Bee's School Chapel (NX971123) was built by **Paley & Austin** in 1895 in the firm's undemonstrative and very restful version of Perpendicular. The lancet window in the south wall of the chancel is a rare example in the North West of the work of **J. H. Bonnor**. Tidings of great joy are brought to the bemused shepherds by a beautiful, if whimsical, pink winged angel of the Lord. The whole scene is set against the background of a brilliant night sky studded with sparkling, diamond-bright stars. Visit by appontment.

Access: Tel. 01946–828000.

SEASCALE is about 6 miles south of Egremont and is reached by the B5343 which is a loop off the A595.

St Cuthbert's (NY038012) was built in 1890 by **C. J. Ferguson**. It is a big Decorated style, red-sandstone church. The stone came from St Bees 6 miles up the coast. The four-light east window is by **Caroline Townshend** and was installed in 1911. The tracery lights and the top portions of the two outer lights are used to depict the 'Seven Days of the Creation'. The four main lights show: Christ as the Head and

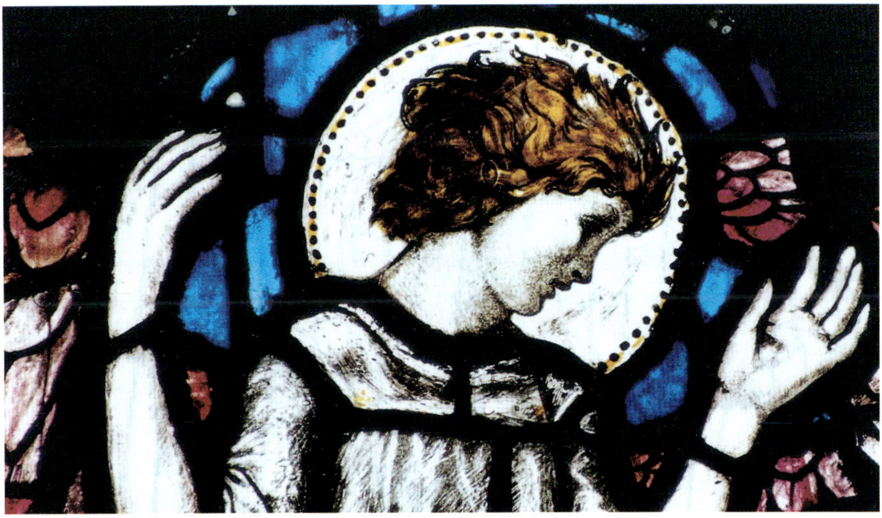

St Bee's School Chapel. Detail of Chancel window. J. H. Bonnor. *Courtesy of St Bee's School*

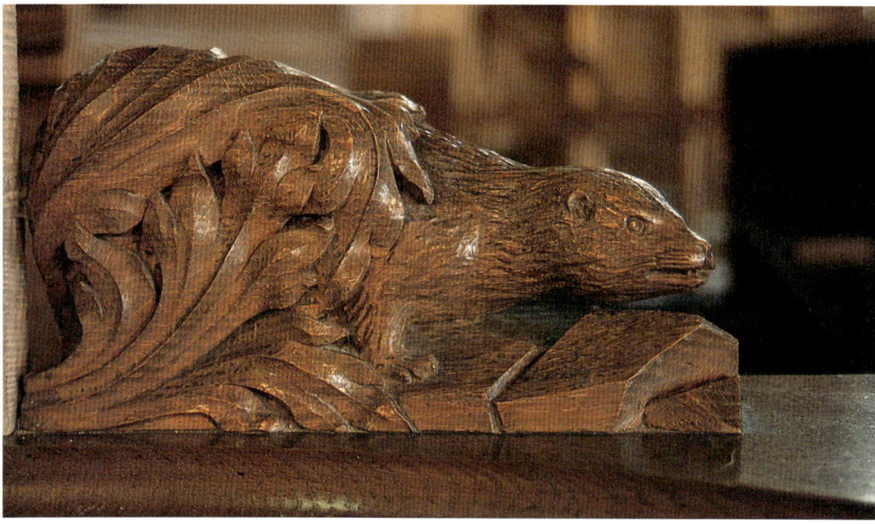

St Cuthbert's, Seascale. Otter by J. Sharp of Whitehaven, c. 1912.

Body of the church; the four Evangelists; Mary and the Christ Child; shepherds, saints and children. The two-light window second from the east in the north nave is also by **Caroline Townshend** and was made in 1912. The replica of Durham Cathedral's St Cuthbert's cross on the altar and the wooden candlesticks are by **Keswick Industrial Arts** (formerly the Keswick School of Industrial Arts). The low chancel screen, designed in 1912 by **J. H. Martindale**, incorporates two clergy stalls decorated with very attractive finials (an otter and a seagull) which were carved, along with the figure work, by **Mr J. Sharp** of Hensingham, Whitehaven. The font cover at the other end of the church was designed by **C. J. Ferguson** in 1899.

Access: Vicarage Tel. 019467–28217.

SHAP village is on the A6 about 15 miles north of Kendal and 10 or 11 miles south of Penrith.

St Michael's (NY564153) has been here in one form or another since about 1200 A.D. although it is now substantially a Victorian building. It has excellent woodwork in the sanctuary, choir and pulpit which is among the works of **J. M. Kilbride** listed in his obituary. Most of the stained glass is by **Shrigley & Hunt** but the Westmorland Gazette (4.3.1899) attributes the design of the archangel Michael in the east-most window in the north aisle to **J. F. Bentley**. The window was designed in 1899 and installed in 1904 after the architect's death.

Access: Vicarage Tel. 01931–716232.

SILLOTH is on the coast about 10 miles west of Wigton at the end of the B5302.

Christ Church (NY111537) was built 1870–71 by Cory & Ferguson but won in competition by **C. J. Ferguson** in 1865 when he was still a pupil of G. G. Scott. It is a big church with a detached porch tower and a tall broached spire that can be seen from many miles away on the Solway plain. The grey stone exterior contrasts with the pale brick inside where Ferguson uses narrow contrasting red brick horizontals to relieve the monotony. The great square stone font with its minimalist fern decoration is very effective.

Access: Usually open. Vicarage Tel. 016973–31413.

SKELSMERGH lies about 2 miles north of Kendal to the east of the A6.

St John the Baptist (SD529954). The centre window in the south wall depicting 'Resurrection Morning' was made by **Joan Howson** in 1937.

Access: Vicarage Tel. 01539–724498.

SKIRWITH is signposted to the east of the A686 and the turn-off is about half a mile east of Langwathby.

St John Evangelist (NY619327) is a mid-Victorian church of little distinction but it has an interesting east window in the Lady Chapel designed by the architect **George Fellowes Prynne** (better known for his work on the south coast of England) and made by Percy Bacon in 1919.

Access: Vicarage Tel. 01768–881212.

SOULBY is signposted from the A685 in Kirkby Stephen.

St Luke's (NY750111) was started in the C17 and restored in about 1870. It has two windows by **Henry Holiday** designed for **Powell's** in 1890. In the north wall at the eastern end is 'The Light of the World' and 'The Good Shepherd' while opposite, on the south wall are

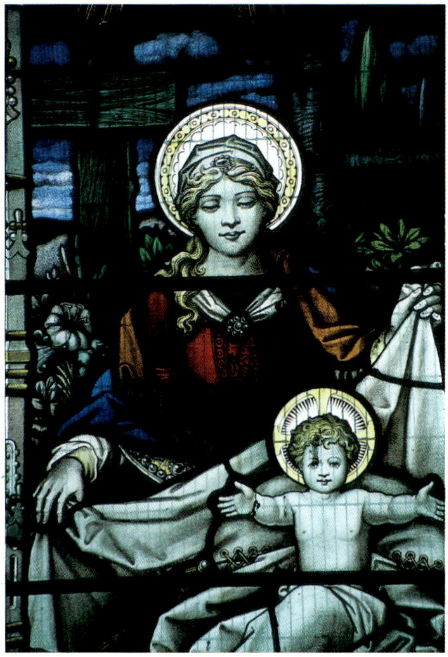

St John's, Skirwith. Detail of the Lady Chapel window. G. Fellows Prynne, 1919.

'Jesus and Mary Magdalene' and 'The Woman at the Well'.

Access: Redundant. Contact Carlisle Diocesan Office.

STAVELEY lies on the north side of the A591 between Kendal and Windermere.

St James's church (SD468986) was built by J. S. Crowther in 1862–65. The stained glass in the three narrow lancets of the east window was made by **Morris & Co.** in 1881. This is one of the most memorable and beautiful of **Morris & Co.** windows in the North West. The left and right lancets each show three of **Morris's** musical angels, floating one above the other. The figures in the central lancet were designed by **Burne-Jones**. The ascended Christ is shown in the upper third of the lancet while the remainder depicts the Crucifixion. Christ on the cross and the angels are set against a midnight blue, star-spangled sky. In the south aisle near the door there are two smaller lancets with figures by **Burne-Jones** representing St Margaret and St James which were made by **Morris & Co.** in 1907. The pulpit and choir stalls are all by **A. W. Simpson** of Kendal.

Access: Usually open. Vicarage Tel. 01539–821267.

TEBAY lies on the A685 near M6 junction 36.

St James's (NY617044) is a picturesque church by **C. J. Ferguson** built in 1880. The apse and round tower with its conical slate roof give it a rather French feel. The grey stone exterior belies the red and white brickwork of the interior. The memorial window in the

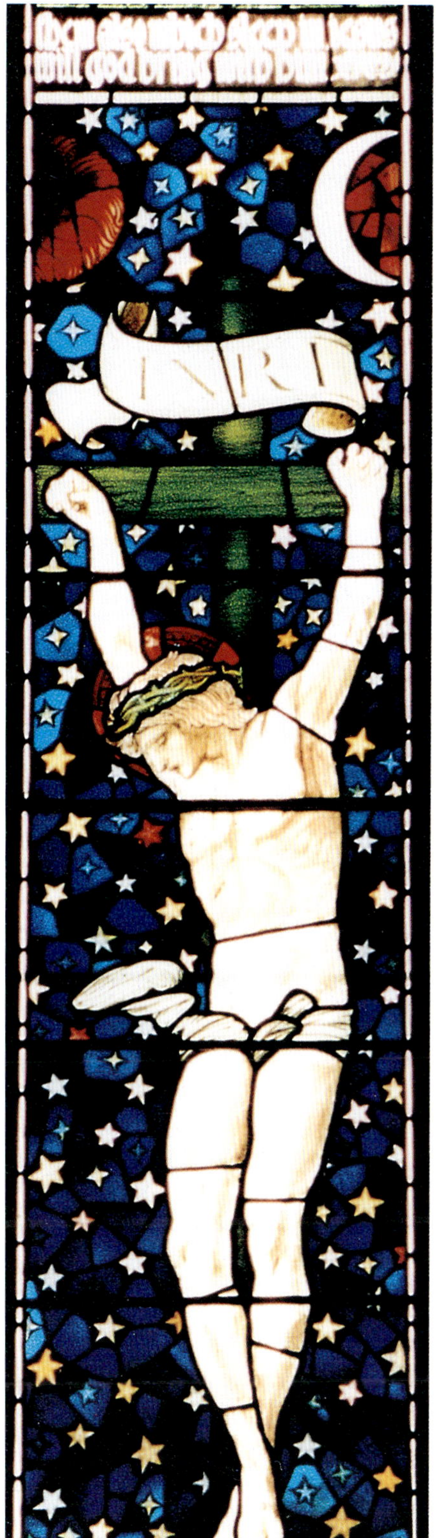

St James's, Staveley. Detail of central lancet east window. Morris & Co., 1881.

baptistery is by **Abbott & Co.**, and dates from 1919. The war memorial window is by Curtis, Ward & Hughes.

Access: Vicarage Tel. 015396–24532.

TEMPLE SOWERBY is about 6 miles east of Penrith on the A66 Appleby road.

St James's (NY613271) is an C18 church restored in the 1870s. The east window was designed by **G. P. Hutchinson** for **Powell of Whitefriars.**

Access: Vicarage Tel. 017683–71204.

TROUTBECK is 3 or 4 miles north of Windermere on the A592.

The **Church of Jesus** (NY412027) stands at the side of the A592 at the edge of the village. It is a small and ancient building with a mid-C18 tower and a most unexpected setting for one of the stained-glass wonders of the Lake District. Its east window was made in 1873 by **Morris, Marshall, Faulkner & Co.** The five-light window contains designs by four of the partners in the firm. **Burne-Jones** designed the main panels including the poignant Christ crucified in the centre light. He also provided the cartoons for two of the smaller figures in the tracery (John the Baptist and Christ as the gardener). **William Morris** designed the four angels in the top row of the tracery lights as well as the Annunciation scene in the row below. This row also contains the figure of Noah provided by **Ford Madox Brown**. A rare treat here is **Phillip Webb's** drawing of fish – trout in the beck – which separate the figures in the tracery. There are four predella like panels at the bottom of the window. Two of these, 'The Baptism of Christ' and 'Christ Blessing the Children', were designed by **Burne-Jones**, while 'Christ's Charge to Peter' and the 'Supper at Emmaus' are **Ford Madox Brown's** work. The detail of the figures and the panels together with the overall arrangement and the colours of the window make it one of the best in the region.

Access: Usually open. Vicarage Tel. 015394–43032.

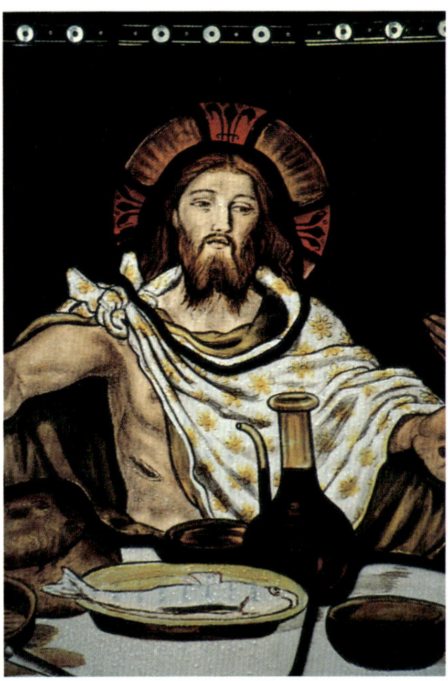

Church of Jesus, Troutbeck. Detail of east window. Ford Maddox Brown for Morris & Co., 1873.

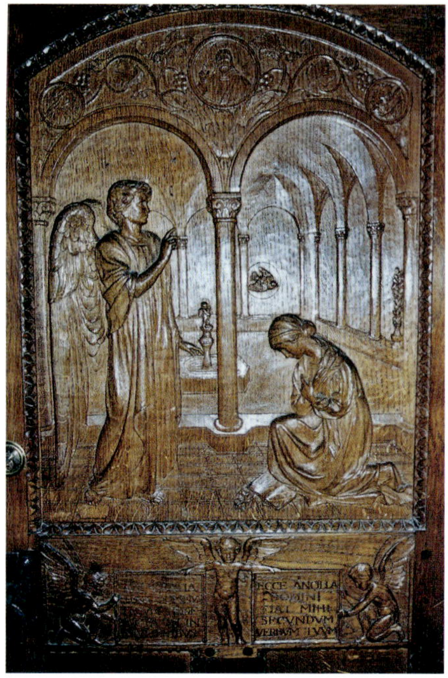

St Mary's, Urswick. Detail, Vestry door. Alex Miller, c. 1910.

URSWICK lies east of Dalton in Furness in the lanes between the A590 and the A5087.

St Mary's (SD269741) is a C13 church extended in the C14 and restored in 1908. **The Guild of Handicraft** did the superb woodwork 1909–12. The work includes the carving on the chancel screen (St James & St John the Baptist) and the choir stall bench-ends decorated with cherubs, garlands and musical instruments. The vestry door is decorated with a carving of 'The Annunciation' and the reredos has 'The Last Supper' supported by carved figures of the Virgin Mary and St George. The figure carving on the screen is by **Alec Miller** of the Guild. **Paul Woodroffe** has a window here, second from the east in the south wall of the nave, showing St Michael as a knight in golden armour and two maidens, Joan of Arc with a mattock and Jepthah's daughter with a lamp. The window was erected in 1913.

Access: Open daily 10.00–15.00.
Rectory Tel. 01229–581383.

VALE of LUNE lies at the junction of the A683 and A684 west of Sedburgh.

St Gregory's Church (SD633922) was built in the early 1860s at the expense of Miss Frances Upton of nearby Ingmire Hall as a permanent base for a preacher previously employed by the LNW Railway Company to minister to the navvies laying the track. It was then, as now, a simple building but it was refurnished *c.* 1900 with Arts and Crafts touches in the woodwork and a spectacular set of stained-glass windows, thought by the Redundant Churches Fund to have been made by **Campbell Smith & Co.** of London. The windows are full of beautifully portrayed plants, animals and birds of the area. In the chancel 'Justice' and 'Fortitude' are by William Morris of Westminster who is not to be confused with **Morris & Co.** The dainty little window of 'Peace' in the porch was made by **Powell of Whitefriars.**

Access: The church is in the care of the Redundant Churches Fund and is open daily from 9.00–17.00.

WALTON is about 2 miles north of Brampton and is signposted off the A6071 Brampton to Longtown road.

St Mary's (NY524647) is one of **Paley & Austin's** big village churches full of architectural interest. There are two stained-glass windows in the north-nave wall by **Heaton, Butler & Bayne.** They have the feel of **Henry Holiday**; in fact the gamekeeper in the second window from the west end even looks like Henry Holiday.

Access: Vicarage Tel. 016977–2478.

WARWICK BRIDGE lies on the A69, the Carlisle to Brampton road, 3 miles east of Junction 43 on the M6.

Our Lady and St Wilfred at Warwick Bridge (NY476567) was designed by **A. W. N. Pugin** and built in 1841. The stained glass is by Hardman who executed Pugin's designs, although these windows post-date Pugin himself. Pevsner marks this church out as the point of departure for the school of archeological accuracy in English Neo-Gothic Architecture. It is very simple Early English in style with delightful stencilled and gilded decoration in the chancel and sanctuary and recent 'cartwheel' light fittings in the nave.

Access: Usually open. Presbytery Tel. 01228–560273.

WARWICK on EDEN is 2 miles east of Carlisle on the A69.

St Leonard's (NY466568) is described by Pevsner as the 'most memorable Norman village church in Cumberland'. It also has a very memorable window in the baptistery at the west end designed by **Henry Holiday** and made by **Powell of Whitefriars.** It shows St Paul preaching to a small group of Romans. It is a little window but cleverly designed and executed.

Access: Parish Office Tel. 01228–603608.

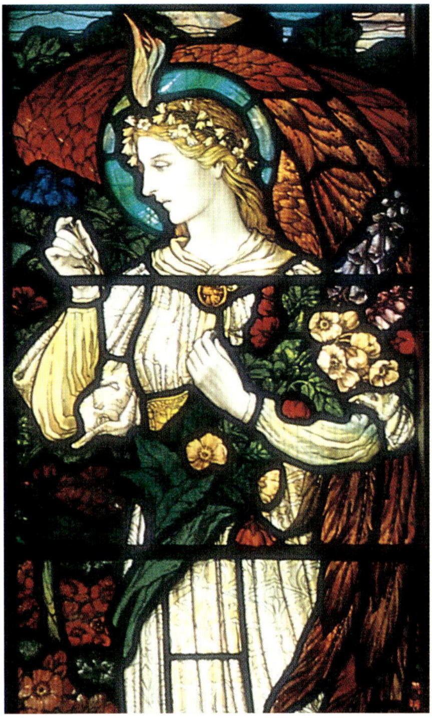

All Saints, Watermillock. Detail of window. William Aikman, 1899.

WATERMILLOCK is about 7 miles south-west of Penrith on the A592.

All Saints (NY432230) was built in 1884 by **C. J. Ferguson** and stands at the end of a leafy lane. It has interesting windows by Burlison & Grylls and Heaton, Butler & Bayne but the star is a two-light window made by **Powell of Whitefriars** in 1899 to a design by **William Aikman.** It shows two angels hovering over a wonderful flower-garden filled with foxgloves, wild roses, yellow poppies and hare bells. Aikman's fees for the window were £3 0s 0d for the sketch in October 1898 and £6 0s 0d for the cartoons in April 1899.

Access: Usually open in the summer. Rectory Tel. 017684–83293.

WINDERMERE lies to the east of the lake at the junction of the A591 and the A592.

St Mary Applethwaite (SD409988) re-opened in the year 2000 after a fire which consumed the roof of the nave and much of its stained glass. It remains essentially a **Paley & Austin** building with a huge tower over the crossing dating from 1881. The second window from the east end in the north wall was made by **A. J. Dix** in 1898 but who designed this beautiful congregation of

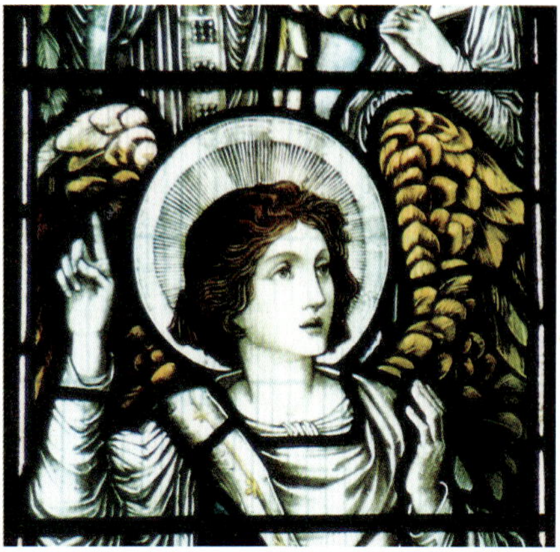

St Mary's, Windermere. Detail of angels executed by A. J. Dix, 1898.

angels? The east window was erected in 1956 and made by **G. E. R. Smith**.

Access: Usually open. Vicarage Tel. 015394–43032.

Brockhole (NY390011) is now the Lake District National Park Visitor Centre on the road from Windermere to Ambleside. The house was built by **Dan Gibson** in 1900 for W. H. A. Gaddum, a wealthy silk merchant from Alderley Edge. The five acres of formal gardens were laid out by **T. H. Mawson** who also landscaped the remaining 25 acres of parkland which run down to the lakeside. Inside the house are visitor centre, exhibition rooms and a café with views over the garden.

Access: The visitor centre is open daily from April to October between 10.00–17.00. The grounds and gardens are open all year. Tel. 015394–46601.

Cragwood, (NY392009) is a country-house hotel near Brockhole on the A59. It was built in 1910 by **Frank Dunkerley** for the industrialist Albert Warburton and nestles into the surrounding woodland. It is a beautifully understated Arts and Crafts house. Internally, the main reception rooms have excellent woodwork and modelled plaster ceilings. There is, however, a certain eccentricity in the decoration of the drawing room ceiling where bats and owls abound. According to the hotel brochure, the magnificent gardens were set out by **T. H. Mawson**.

Access: Open to non residents. Tel. 015394–88177.

Keldwith, (SD407998) is hidden away from view at the end of a private road, high above the A591. It was built *c.* 1900 by **H. L. North** whose work is more often found in Wales. The house, which is many gabled and built with local stone and slate, is now converted into apartments.

Access: Private residences.

Holehird Gardens (NY411008) are in the care of the Lakeland Horticultural Trust and are open to the public every day. The **lodge** was designed by **Dan Gibson**.

Access: Open daily from sunrise to sunset.

Holbeck Ghyll, Holbeck Lane (NY393022) is one mile south of Ambleside off the A591 and a half-mile up Holbeck Lane. This early 19C stone-built house, which looks over Lake Windermere, was 'modernised' *c.* 1900 when it was given some delightful Arts and Crafts features. They start in the entrance porch where the door leading into the entrance hall has a decorative stained glass panel, huge wrought iron hinges on the porch side and a polished copper repoussé lock-plate on the hall side. The large entrance hall is panelled in oak and has an inglenook fireplace. On either side of the fireplace opening there are plaster relief trees in a rather restrained art nouveau-style and the inglenook cornice is decorated with small

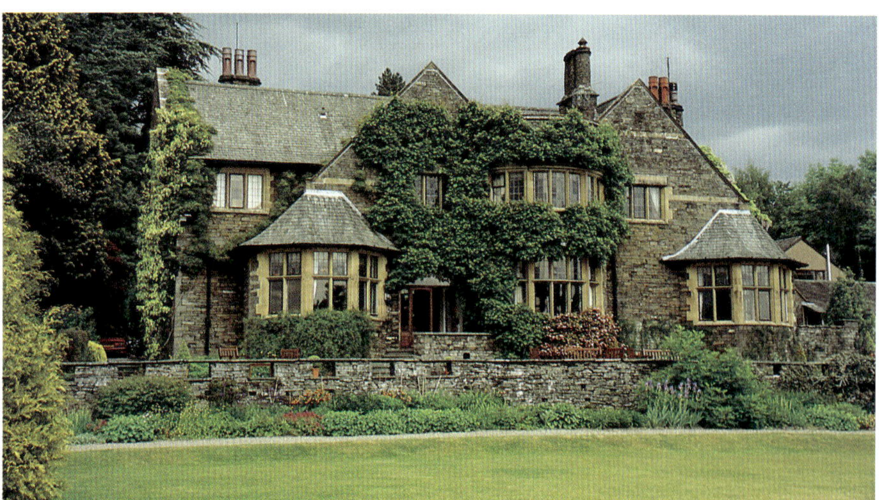

'Cragwood', Windermere by F. B. Dunkerley, 1910.

bosses carved with a tulip motif. This motif is repeated in the cleverly-pierced decoration in the balusters of the oak staircase and the same pattern is to be found on the wooden railings of the veranda outside. The staircase window contains heraldic glass and on the first floor landing is an attractive stained-glass screen. There is a mix of other interesting stained glass downstairs with simple heart and oval-shaped decoration in some windows and more flamboyant brightly-coloured decorative flowers and foliage in others. Amazingly the stylish Edwardian repoussé copper electrics-light switches, bell pushes and socket holders are all in working order. The architect responsible for the alterations is, to date, unknown.

Access: Open to non-residents. Tel. 015394–32375.

Langdale Chase Hotel (NY387018) is 2 miles south-east of Ambleside on the A591and was built in 1891 for a Manchester businessman to designs by **J. L. Ball**, J. T. Lee & Pattison of Manchester in a Neo-Elizabethan style. It has been used as a country-house hotel since 1930. The carved oak fire surround and overmantel in the hall is a C17 piece imported in *c*. 1910 by a previous owner as were the tiles which are attributed to **William De Morgan**. The oak staircase and carving around the hall were the work of **Arthur Jackson Smith** of Sale in Cheshire who settled in Coniston. There is a carved overmantel in the original dining room which was worked in 1892 by the **Grasmere Hermit**. The gardens, as might be expected in Windermere, were planned and laid out by **T. H. Mawson** although there have been many subsequent changes in the planting schemes.

Access: The hotel is open to non–residents. Tel. 015394–32201.

WINSTER lies on the A5074 about 5 miles south of Windermere.

Holy Trinity (SD418930) is a superbly-located little church built in 1875. The east window was designed by **Henry Holiday**. There is a small bronze and enamel memorial plaque by **Harold Stabler** on the south wall which commemorates the life of Joseph Holt of Blackwell, who was killed in the Great War.

Access: usually open. Vicarage Tel. 015395–68276.

Birkett Houses, (SD414930) despite the plural is just one house designed in 1907 by **Dan Gibson** for the Birkett family who were local gentleman farmers.

Access: Private dwelling.

WORKINGTON is on the coast north of Whitehaven and south of Maryport.

The **Great War Memorial** in Vulcan Park (NX999284) was designed in 1928 by **Robert Lorimer** and decorated with relief sculptures by **Alex Carrick**.

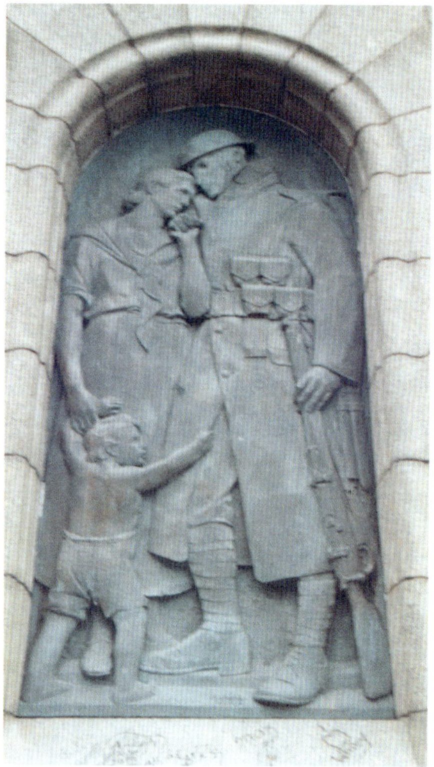

Great War Memorial, Workington. Relief panel by Alex Carrick, c. 1920.

WREAY lies 5 miles south of Carlisle between the M6 and the A6.

St Mary's at Wreay (NY434491) is one of the most original and interesting churches you could wish to see. It is the creation of an independent, well-travelled Victorian lady called Miss Sara Losh (1785–1853). Miss Losh had an interest in architecture and a lively, if eccentric imagination. She gave her talents free-rein in designing and arranging the building of this church as a monument to her dead sister, Katherine and to her parents. Although the work was completed in 1842 it could so easily fit into the Arts and Crafts period 50 years later. It is a basilica church and can best be described as a free-style building which draws on French and Italian Romanesque characteristics. The interior is a feast for the eyes and a challenge to the powers of observation and intellect to find and interpret the surfeit of symbolism hidden within the many objects and ornaments. There are dragons, bats and angels, arrows and pine cones, and the illustrated life cycle of the butterfly. There is an abundance of carving in stone, wood and alabaster of animals, trees and flowers, monsters and insects and a chorus of angels with palm trees above the archway into the apse. The wood used is unusual, for as well

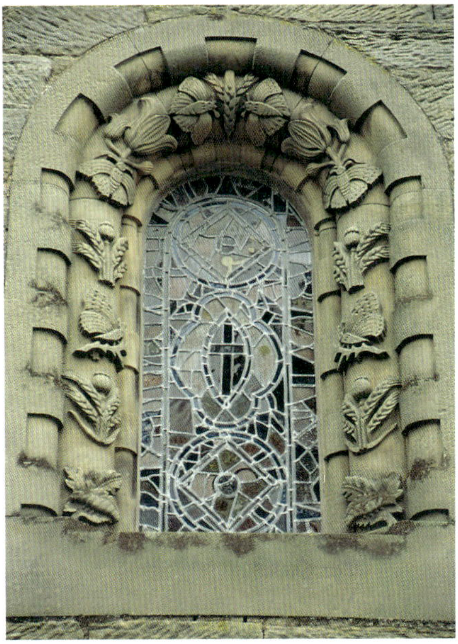

St Mary's, Wreay. Window surround. Sarah Losh, c. 1850.

as oak and Spanish chestnut there is black, earthily-primitive bog oak which is used to create the two striking lecterns, the pulpit and a couple of chairs. Part of the alabaster panelled font was carved by Miss Losh herself while the font cover was done by her cousin, William Losh. It has charming motifs which include a butterfly, a pomegranate and lotus flowers. Adding to what may be called theatrical charm, are the stained-glass windows – there are 84 of them! There are the restrained though striking 'fossil' windows high up in the apse and below them are the 'Seven Lamps of the Spirit' made of orange and yellow glass. In the nave and clerestory are eye-catching non-figural mosaic-mixtures of coloured glass, some of which is said to have been 'rescued' by cousin William from the ruins of an archbishop's palace in Paris after the 1830 revolution. There is much more to delight and bemuse inside this church including a portrait on the west wall of Miss Losh herself. Outside the church a single glance upwards will reveal the unusual gargoyles and inveigle you into walking around the entire church for fear of missing the snake, alligator and tortoise. At ground level is a sun dial, a well and an old font – a reminder of an earlier church on this site. In one corner of the churchyard is a mausoleum containing an alabaster figure of Katherine carved by the Carlisle architect and sculptor David Dunbar. There is also a runic cross set up in memory of the parents of Sara and Katherine and finally the graves of the sisters themselves. This extraordinary building is a monument to Sara's devotion to her sister and to her own intriguing personality.

Access: Usually open. Vicarage Tel. 01228–710215.

WYTHBURN lies 7 miles south of Keswick on the A591 in the shadow of Helvellyn.

This tiny wayside Chapel (NY326135) was restored in 1872. Unexpectedly, it contains small stained-glass windows by three renowned artists. In the apse is 'Christ the Good Shepherd', by **Henry Holiday** (1892) flanked by 'St Peter' and 'David the Shepherd Boy', both by **Hugh Arnold** in 1906. At the other end of the church is a three-light window showing Christ in Glory with St Cuthbert and St Herbert designed by **Temple Lushington Moore** in 1889. **H. Victor Milner** executed much of Moore's stained glass at this time but the link has not been documented here.

Access: Usually open in the summer. Vicarage Tel. 017687–79714.

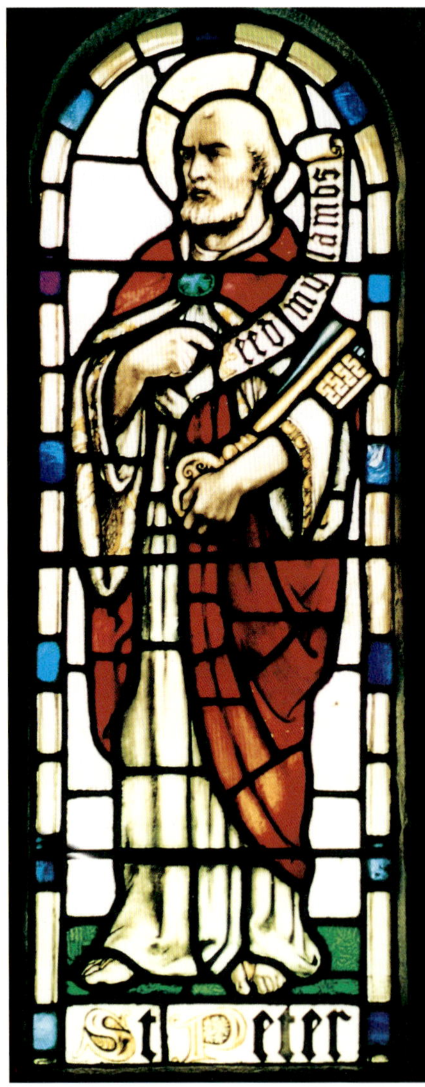

Wythburn Chapel. St Peter by Hugh Arnold, 1906.

LANCASHIRE

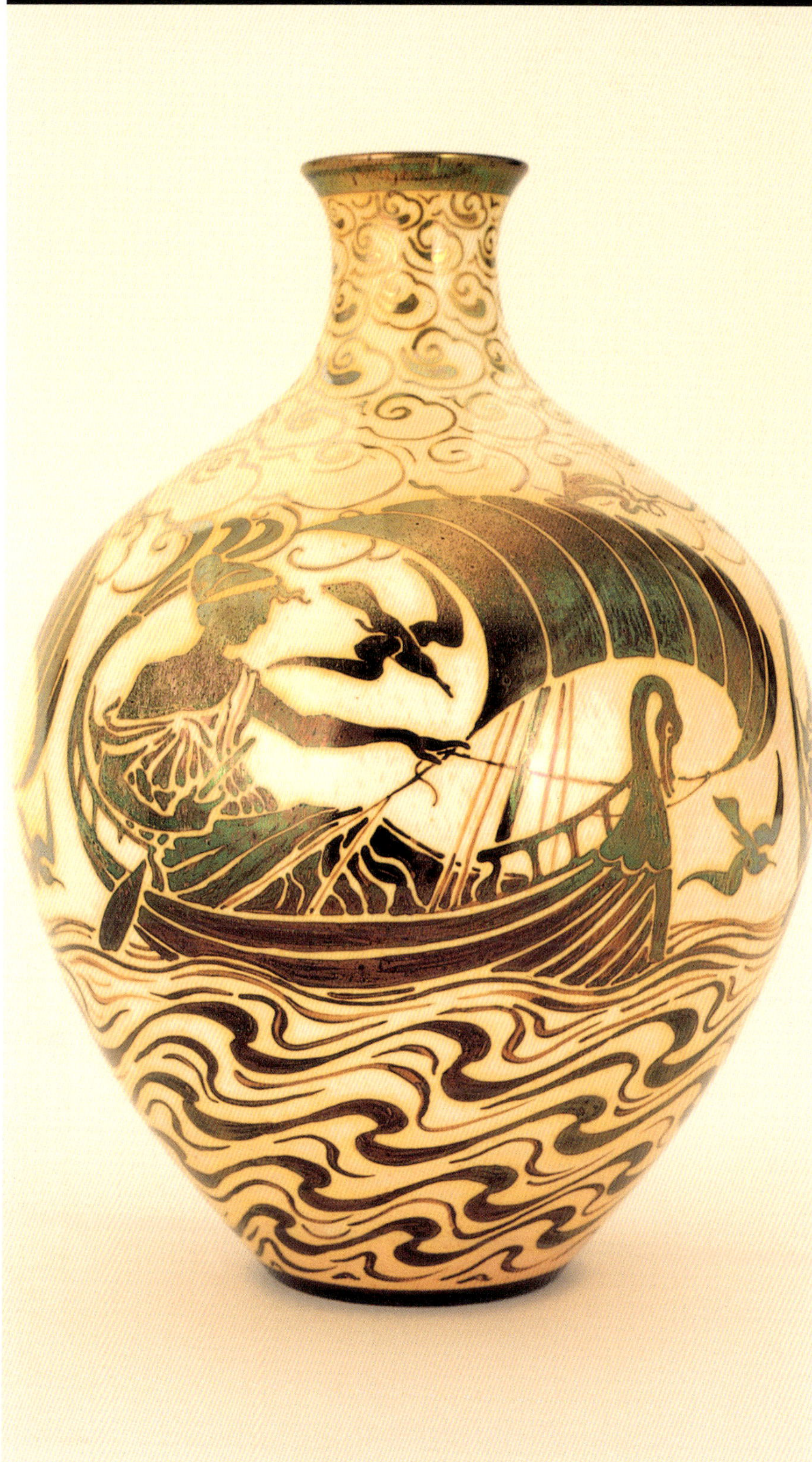

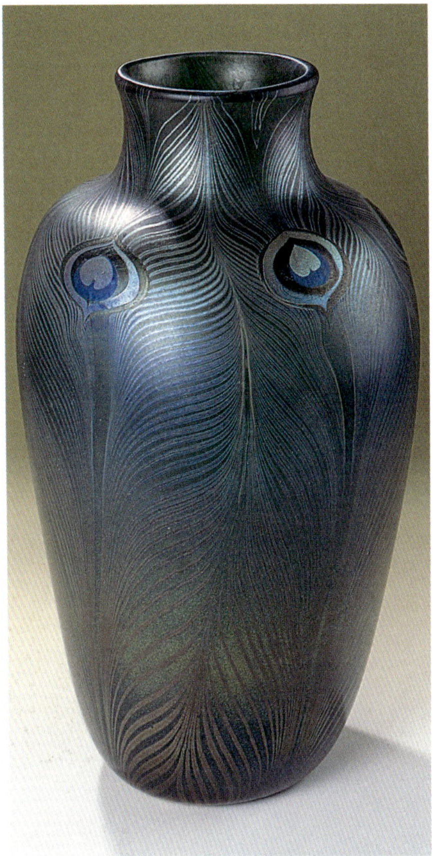

Haworth Museum, Accrington. Tiffany peacock vase.
© Haworth Art Gallery, Hindeburn Borough Council, Accrington

ACCRINGTON is midway between Blackburn and Burnley south of the M65.

Haworth Art Gallery, in Haworth Park, Manchester Rd (SD767272), was originally a house called **Hollins Hill** designed in a Neo-Jacobean style by **W. H. Brierley** in 1909 for William Haworth, an Accrington cotton magnate. It has excellent moulded-plaster ceilings in the reception rooms and fine wood carving throughout, particularly in the billiard room. In addition to fine paintings, the museum houses the largest collection of **Tiffany Glass** outside the USA. It was brought here by Joseph Briggs, an Accrington engraver, who emigrated to New York at the age of seventeen, joined Tiffany and became first a foreman, then the firm's art director and eventually personal assistant to **Louis Comfort Tiffany**. When the firm closed down in 1933 Briggs returned to England with a large selection of the firm's output half of which he donated to the Corporation. It is wonderful to see it here.

Access: Open Wed–Fri 2.00–17.00. Sat and Sun 12.00–16.30. Tel. 01254–233782.

Oakhill Park, (SD765276) is the site of Accrington's War Memorial, designed by **C. H. Reilly** and sculpted by **G. H. Tyson Smith** in 1922. It is essentially a monolith which serves as background to a beautifully sculpted figure of Peace.

Dyke Nook, about a mile north of the town centre on Whalley Rd (SD758294), was designed by **W. H. Brierley** 1910–11. In 1969 Pevsner described it as 'an uncommonly good

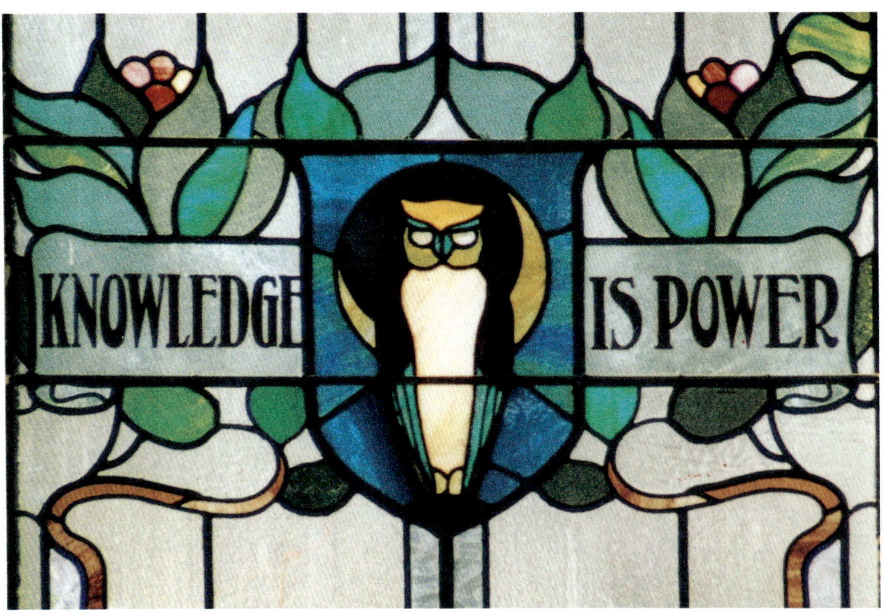

Accrington Library. Detail of staircase window by H. G. Hiller, c. 1908.

Neo-Jacobean house'. It stood empty for some years with its windows boarded up and its Gertrude Jekyll garden reverting to nature, but it has recently been acquired for renovation.
Access: Private house.

St John, Baxendon, (SD772265) has a set of four small two-light windows in the south aisle designed in 1888 by **Henry Holiday**.
Access: Vicarage Tel. 01254–232471.

Accrington Library in St James's St (SD759285) was built 1906–08. The main staircase window was made by **H. G. Hiller**. It has a fine central figure holding up the light of knowledge flanked by two wise owls on leafy branches. The green tiles on the staircase are quietly decorative and were made by J. & M. Wade of Burslem.
Access: Tel. 01254–872385.

ADLINGTON lies on the A6 just south of Chorley and west of the Rivington Reservoir.

St Paul's, Railway Rd (SD604135) was built in 1883 and has two stained-glass windows by **Morris & Co.** The two-light window in the south transept, 'Paul and Stephen' was made in 1895. Opposite stand 'Justice and Humility' made in 1897.
Access: Vicarage: 01257–480253.

AUGHTON is east of the A59, on the Ormskirk to Liverpool Rd.

St Michael's (SD392054) began life with the Normans but there is little remaining of their work. It is essentially a Perpendicular church with C18 and C19 additions and alterations. The remarkable ten-light east window and a three-light window in the north aisle were designed by **W. J. Medcalf** in 1899 while still a student at the Liverpool School of Architecture and Applied Art. One light is illustrated in the short-lived but beautifully produced contemporary student magazine *The Cloud*. The east window shows Christ ascending in the company of an angelic orchestra while the north window shows Christ with two apostles on the road to Emmaus. In the north-tower wall there is a two-light window showing 'The Adoration of the Shepherds' made in 1926 by **A. K. Nicholson**. There is an interesting reredos from about 1899 and good carving on the pew ends in the choir.
Access: Vicarage Tel. 01695–423204.

BAMBER BRIDGE is near the junction of the M6 and M61.

St Saviour's in Church Rd (SD565250), Cuerden was built in 1836 by **Edmund Sharpe** and is said to be his first church. It is Romanesque in style with a west gallery supported on slender iron pillars wrapped in 'Lincrusta' (a heavy-duty embossed wall paper). The chancel and apse were added in 1887 by **T. H. Myres**. The baptistery at the west end has a delightful stone font with a bronze cover given in 1907. Neither the font, carved with beautiful angels, nor the cover with its bronze figure of John the Baptist, is signed, but they are remarkable pieces of work.
Access: Vicarage Tel. 01772–335374.

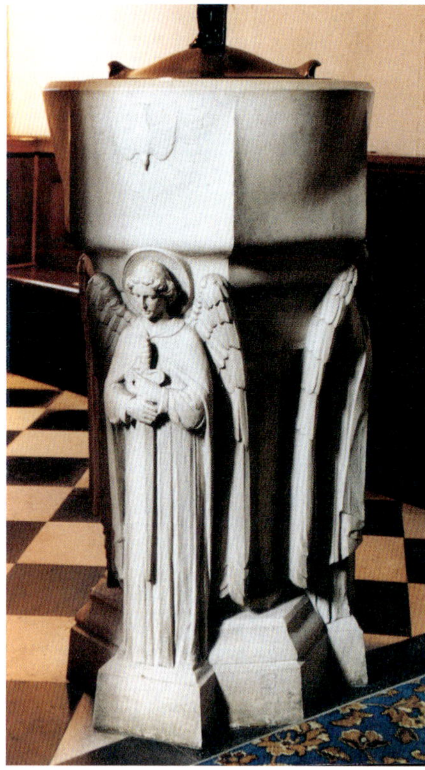

St Saviour's, Bamber Bridge. Font (anon) c. 1907.

BLACKBURN is about 7 miles east of the M6 junction 31.

Blackburn Museum, in Museum St, (SD681283) was built in 1872 by Woodzell and Collcutt. It is decorated externally with relief panels, designed by **G. W. Seale**, representing Art, Science, Agriculture and Industry and there are later decorative opus-sectile panels in the porch designed by **J. W. Brown** for **James Powell & Sons**. In its collection of books and manuscripts the museum has examples of the work of **Morris's Kelmscott Press**, C. R. Ashbee's **Essex House Press** and T. J. Cobden Sanderson's **Doves Press**.
Access: Open Tue–Sat 10.00–16.45. Tel. 01254–667130.

St Silas, Preston New Rd (SD666285) was built by **Austin & Paley** in 1894 and has acquired a feast of stained glass. In the south wall are two late **Morris** windows and a really late treat from **Henry Holiday**. The earliest **Morris** window was made in 1908 and has four lights,

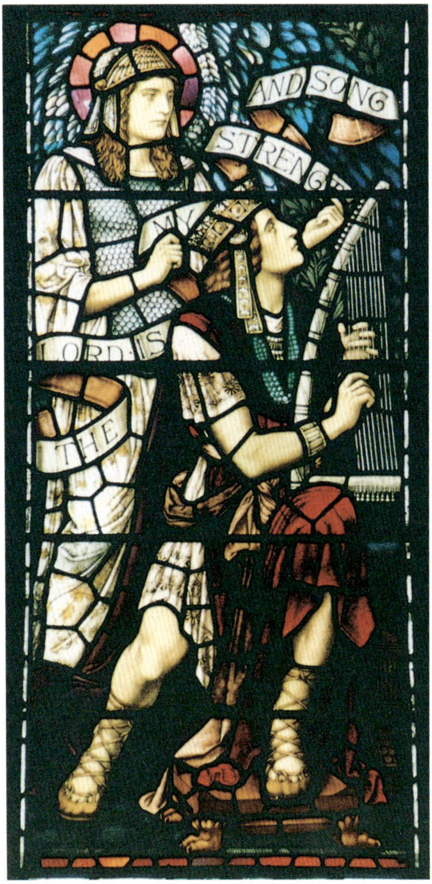

St Silas's, Blackburn. King David by Henry Holiday, 1921.

showing 'St Anne', 'The Adoration of the Magi', 'The Nativity' and 'Simeon'. **William Morris's** cartoon was used for Simeon and the remaining figures are after **Burne-Jones**. To the west of this is a window designed for the firm in 1911 by **J. H. Dearle**. The **Henry Holiday** window stands to the east of the Morris windows. It was made in 1921 and features David, Gideon, Jesse and Jacob accompanied by gorgeous angels. This beautiful window was designed when Holiday was 82 years old and was probably made in the studio of Edward Liddall Armitage who began to execute Holiday's glass from about 1920. The east window is a brash, theatrical but unsigned production.

Access: Vicarage Tel. 01254–671293.

Holy Trinity, Larkhill (SD687284) was built by **Edmund Sharpe** *c.* 1840 with the aid of funds raised in part by selling ceiling space to those willing to pay to display their heraldic devices. It was a good ploy as the whole of the nave and chancel ceiling is covered with painted coats of arms, including Queen Victoria's. The three-light 'St Christopher' in the Baptistery was made by **Veronica Whall** in 1948. The church is redundant but thanks to local efforts it is now in the care of the Churches Conservation Trust.

Access: By appointment. Tel. 01254–53866.

Queen Elizabeth Grammar School, in West Park Rd, (SD674287) is an ancient foundation but a very modern school. The science-block staircase has an unexpected stained-glass window which was made by **Morris & Co.** in 1903 for a nearby country house and given to the school in 1958. It has three lights divided horizontally to form six panels. **Burne-Jones's** figures representing Moon, Earth and Sun sit in the upper panels above Thor, Odin and Frey. Individually, the panels are beautiful and the window as a whole is enchanting. In the school's Great Hall is a series of twelve stained-glass windows made by the Lakeland stained-glass artist **B. D. Walmsley** in the 1920s. The five-light window at the end of the hall represents Queen Elizabeth I granting the school its charter in 1567 watched by courtiers and ladies-in-waiting. The artist has given amazing attention to detail in dressing his figures, especially the Queen's robes and those of her Ladies. Along the side of the room is a range of six two-light windows featuring the great Elizabethan explorers and men of letters. Walmsley's cartoons for Byrd and Greville are displayed at the entrance to the Hall.

Access: Tel. 01254–686300.

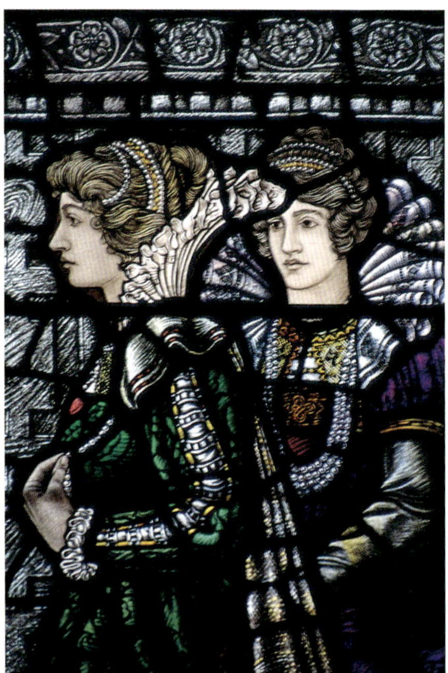

Queen Elizabeth Grammar School, Blackburn. Detail of Charter window. B. D. Walmsley. *Courtesy of the Queen Elizabeth G.S.*

BLACKPOOL The breezy Vegas of the North waits for its visitors at the end of the M55. The resort's iconic image, the **Tower**, does not immediately bring the Arts and Crafts Movement to mind but it was designed by **Maxwell & Tuke** 1891–94. The Empress Building once had twenty-eight **Doulton** ceramic panels designed by **W. J. Neatby** and fixed in niches around the Church St foyer. Eight of the panels survive but are in a part of the building sold off first as a car sales garage and latterly as a bar. The panels are safe in their niches but covered over and not on display – one of these days perhaps.

St Stephen on the Cliffs, in St Stephen's Rd, (SD309388) was built 1925–27 by **Paley & Austin**. The red brick exterior provides a strong contrast to the softness of the pink stone used inside the building where the arcades of the nave and side chapels create interesting and often picturesque internal 'views'. The wood carving in the chancel is very fine and dates from about 1939. There is an Actors Chapel on the north side with a striking stained-glass window designed by **Baron Arild Rosencrantz** in 1935. It has figures representing Persifal, Galahad and Everyman and was placed here in memory of two friends, John Huddlestone the impresario, and John Tiller creator of The Tiller Girls dance troupe. This seems to be the only Rosencrantz window in the North West.

Access: Usually open daily 8.00 to 17.00. Vicarage Tel. 01253–351484.

Warley Road Congregational Church (SD307377), now the United Reformed Church is known as **King's Christian Centre**. It has recently undergone a substantial refurbishment but has retained the six-light east window which was made in about 1914 by **W. J. Pearce**. It features King David the harpist, left of centre, with Old Testament prophets standing by while women and children dance and clash cymbals. To the right stands the Virgin Mary accompanied by St Cecilia at the organ and a bevy of angels. It is a very attractive window but on close inspection is slightly marred by odd facial expressions, some of which are due to deterioration in the colours.

Access: Tel. 01253–290716.

North Shore Methodist Church, Dickson Rd (SD307368) has a wealth of Art Nouveau stained glass. No one has researched the history of this church and its furniture and fittings but it looks very interesting indeed.

Access: Church Office Tel. 01253–294640 (best Mon–Wed).

Blackpool Town Hall in Talbot Square (SD306364) was built 1895–1900. The Council chamber is decorated on three sides with huge murals painted by R. Brown of London in 1901. There is much stained glass by **Abbott &**

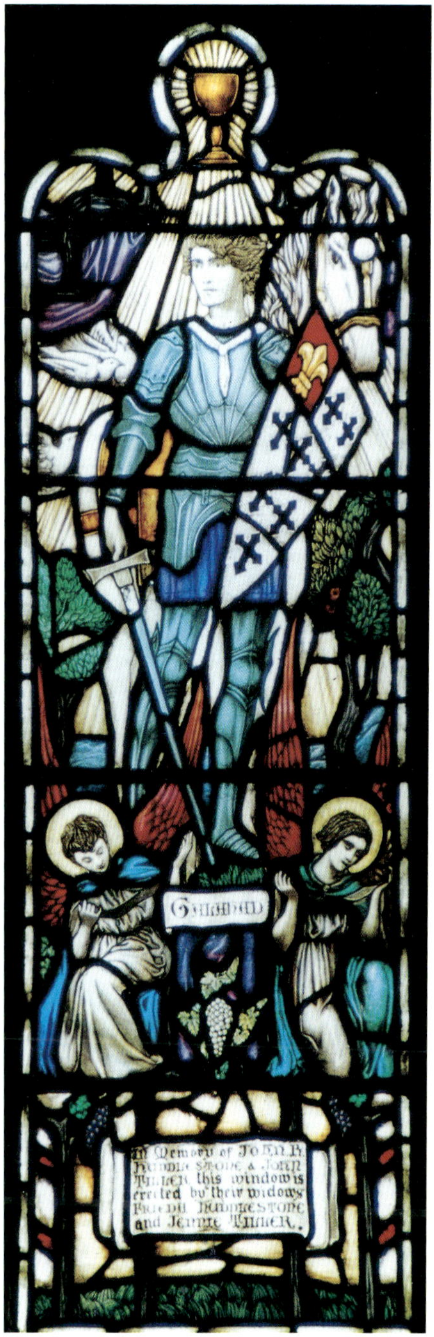

St Stephen's, Blackpool. Galahad by Arild Rosencrantz, 1935.

Co. but, almost hidden on the spiral staircase leading to the public gallery, there is a small monochrome window depicting ancient sailing ships returning to port. It was executed by **George Wragge Ltd** in 1900 some two years after **J. E. C. Carr** came down from Glasgow to help set up Wragge's stained-glass department.

Access: Town Hall Tel. 01253–477477.

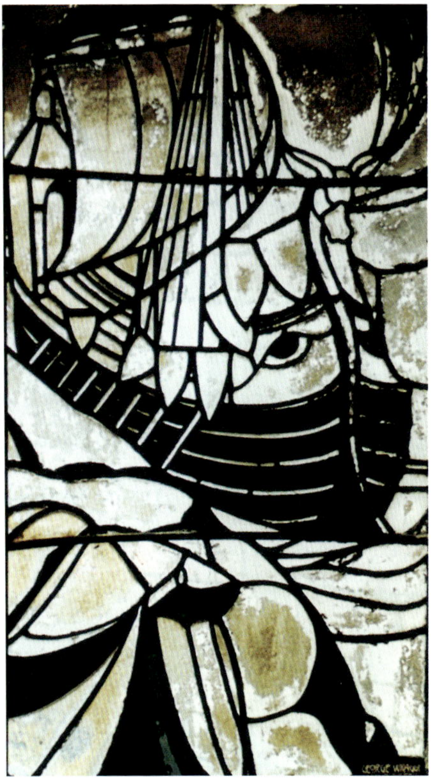

Town Hall Blackpool. Detail stair window by G. Wragge Ltd, 1900.

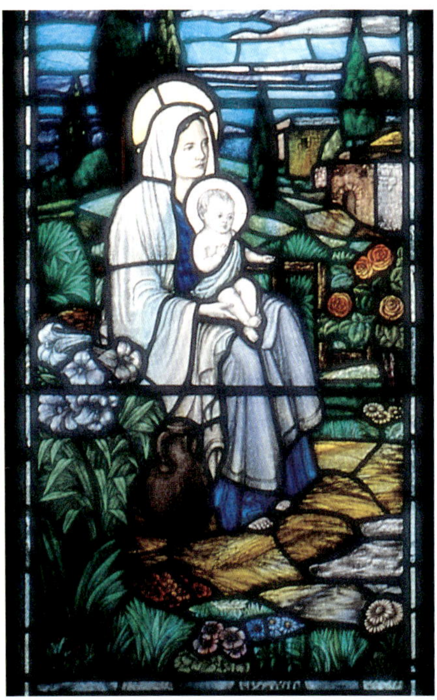

Christ Church, Blackpool. Visit of the Magi. A. Todd, 1935.

Christ Church and All Saints in Palatine Rd (SD311356) was built in 1907 and is a bulky, red-brick building. Among the stained glass is a two-light window in the south wall, made *c.* 1935 and signed by **Arthur Todd** of Heywood. It is a sun-filled, alfresco, 'Adoration of the Magi'.

Access: Vicarage Tel. 01253–391235.

Holy Trinity, in Dean St, South Shore (SD307338) was built in 1895 and according to Pevsner it is **R. K. Freeman's** chef d'oeuvre. Internally it gives an impression of lightness that belies its great size. It is very high with a broad nave and narrow passage aisles on both sides. The chancel has a painted wooden rib-vaulted ceiling and the transepts reach up to the height of the nave. Each transept gable has two great four-light windows divided twice horizontally to give 12 panels. There is clear glass on the north side but the south transept windows were filled by **Shrigley & Hunt** in 1909. Small scale copies of the original sketches are displayed nearby and describe the topics as 'Temple and Church Music' on the right and 'Building the Temple of God' on the left. They show **Shrigley & Hunt** at their picture-book best, working with designs by **Carl Almquist.** The Saints George, Michael and Alban in the South African War Memorial Chapel window were also designed by **Almquist** in 1903.

Access: Vicarage Tel. 01253–347140.

Blackpool War Memorial, on the Prom near Talbot Square, (SD306364), is an imposing obelisk with metal relief panels executed by **Gilbert Ledward** *c.* 1922.

Stanley Park (SD325360) is on the eastern side of the town bordered by North Park Drive, West Park Drive and East Park Drive. The Park was designed by **T. H. Mawson & Sons** for Blackpool County Borough Council in 1922 and opened to great and well-deserved acclaim, in 1926. It was designed to be a park and

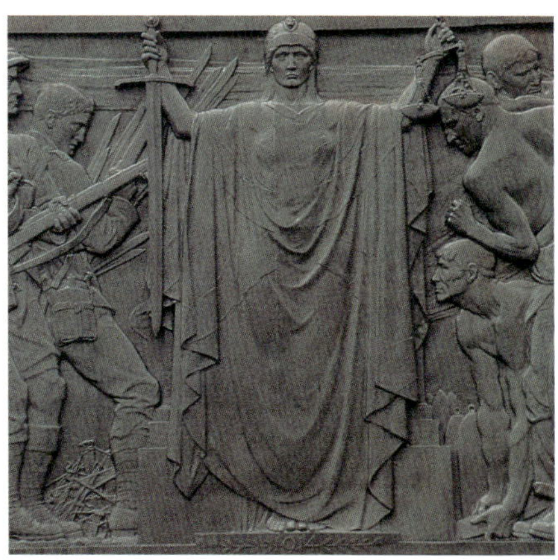

Great War Memorial, Blackpool. Detail of 'Justice' by G. Ledward, 1922.

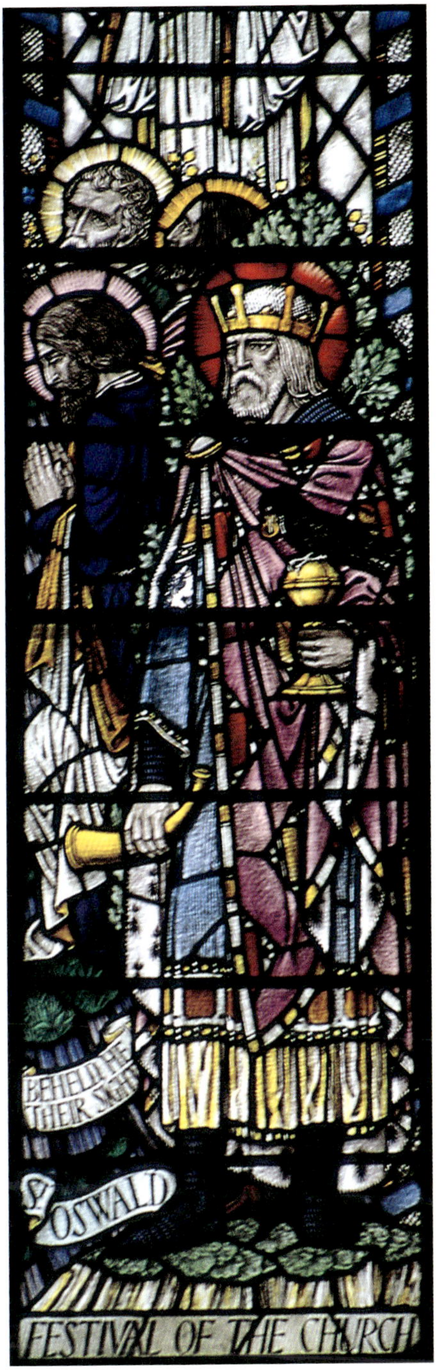

St Cuthbert's, Burnley. St Oswald by J. E. Nuttgens, c. 1929.

recreation area with an 18-hole golf course, a cricket ground, rugby and football pitches, tennis courts and bowling greens. **Mawson** also created a 22 acre boating lake and the usual walks through formal gardens and informal woodlands. The whole site covers 274 acres and remains substantially intact. **Mawson's** plan provided for the land surrounding the park to be sold by the Council as individual building plots to help fund the work. **Mawson** managed to retain control over the quality of the houses built on these plots by producing exemplars for the guidance of local architects and by vetting all applications for building permission before they were considered by the Council. This accounts for the many Voysey 'look-alikes' and other Arts and Crafts derivatives surrounding the Park. The clock tower in the park was designed by **Lionel Budden.**

Access: Dawn until dusk.

BURNLEY is the largest of the string of East Lancs mill towns that follow the Leeds and Liverpool Canal into the Pennines. Junction 10 on the M65 will lead to the town centre.

St Catherine's, Todmorden Rd (SD848324) was built in 1897 by **James Medland Taylor**. It is a big, wide and relatively low church (in a non-liturgical sense). Outside it is faced in stone and has a short tower at the north-west corner topped by an attractive green slate, pyramid roof. The walls are supported by buttresses which are pierced on the southern side to form a passageway to the porch. Internally the church is dramatic. There are no aisles and no chancel-arch. The wide nave gives an uninterrupted view from all parts straight into the apse with its wrought-iron baldacchino backed by the east window. The internal walls are of dark-red brick relieved at the east end by yellow pattern-work either side of the apse arch. Dormer windows, high up in the roof, lighten and add interest to the nave. At the west end there is a small apse for the baptistery. There is an unusual, unsigned and undated three-light 'Resurrection' window in the north wall, which has been executed in a rather curious drawing style.

Access: Vicarage Tel. 01282–424587.

St Cuthbert's in Towneley St (SD849345) has an excellent east window, showing St Cuthbert, Christ Ascending, and St Oswald. All were designed by **Joseph Nuttgens** in about 1929. He also designed two small lancets in the baptistery *c.* 1945 and a larger two-light window in the Lady Chapel, after 1947. 'Mary the Mother of Jesus' is on the left and 'Tabitha' on the right. The commemorative plaque recording the dedication of the church in 1908 bears the **Keswick School of Industrial Arts** mark as does the brass Cuthbert's Cross and the pair of entrelac candlesticks on the altar.

Access: Vicarage Tel. 01282–424978.

Towneley Hall, (SD855308) is east of Todmorden Rd on the south east approach to Burnley. It began life in the Middle Ages but is now essentially a Georgian house which does

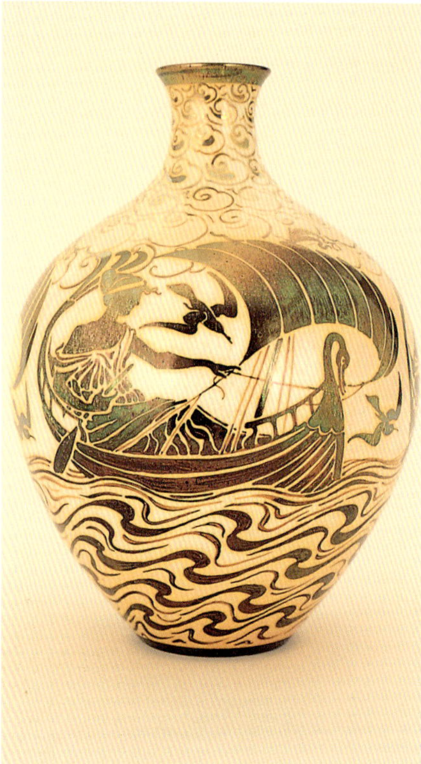

Pilkingtons Royal Lancastrian Lustre Vase, 1906. Designed by Walter Crane and painted by William S. Mycock. *© Towneley Hall Museum and Art Gallery, Burnley Borough Council*

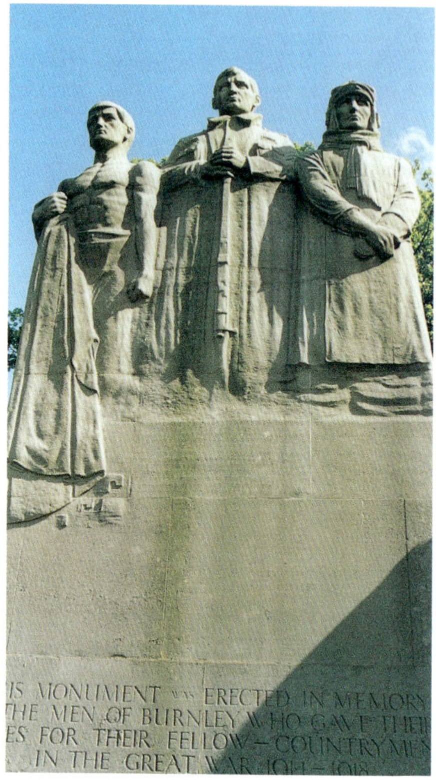

Towneley Park, Burnley. Detail of the Great War Memorial by W. Gilbert, 1926.

duty as The Towneley Hall Art Gallery and Museum. In addition to the gallery's huge collection of oils and watercolours it is the home of a significant collection of **Pilkington** Pottery.

Access: Open Mon–Thur 10.00–17.00, Sat and Sun 12.00–17.00. Tel. 01282–424213.

The Great War Memorial (SD853307) was sculpted by **Walter Gilbert** and stands in the Garden of Remembrance which is reached via the Townely Hall car park. Three figures representing the Navy, the Army and the Air Force emerge from the top of the Portland stone cenotaph, while at either side stands the bronze figure of a woman. On one side is a grief stricken mother and on the other a sister, wife or sweetheart. It was unveiled in 1926.

CALDER VALE village is about 10 miles east of Garstang (as the crow flies) in an idyllic spot on the fringe of the fells.

St John the Evangelist (SD538463) is best approached from Oakenclough unless you fancy a half-mile walk up from the village. The church was built in 1863 with local stone outside and a brick interior. There are three stained-glass windows by **Morris & Co.** The west-most in the north aisle was made in 1907 and has St Martin cutting his cloak and St Michael with a broken lance both by **Burne-Jones.** The three-light west window in the tower was made in 1908 and shows the Crucifixion with Mary and John. The two-light west-most window in the south wall is the Great War Memorial and was made in 1920 from **J. H. Dearle's** cartoons. On the north wall is a framed certificate of merit from the Morecambe Music Festival in 1925 the art work of which bears **Walter Crane's** logo!

Access: Vicarage Tel. 01524–791229.

CHORLEY lies south and west of junction 8 on the M6.

St Peter's, Harper's Lane (SD589184) has a three-light Resurrection window in the east wall made by **J. Nuttgens** in 1951.

Access: Vicarage Tel. 01257–263423.

CHURCH sits in a meander of the Leeds and Liverpool Canal, north of Oswaldtwistle, west of Accrington and just south of Junction 7 on the M65.

St James's in Church St (SD742291) comprises a Perpendicular tower, a Georgian gallericd nave and a late Victorian chancel. Two two-light windows were installed in the south wall by **Morris & Co.**, in 1891, each light showing one of the four Evangelists. Unfortunately, they were all destroyed in 1916 as the result of an explosion at a nearby ammunition factory. Undaunted the congregation had the windows rebuilt by **Morris & Co.** in 1918. The explosion also destroyed the three two-light windows in the south wall of the chancel and these were replaced in 1927 not by Powell of Whitefriars, who made the originals but by **B. D. Walmsley**. James and Andrew; Mary and Martha; Christopher and Nicholas are the brilliantly drawn and coloured saints. There is another, smaller two-light window at the east end of the north wall, in similar style, showing Mary with Jesus after the Resurrection. It was made after 1923 and could also be by **Walmsley**. The reredos takes the form of a huge and stunning opus sectile which stretches from wall-to-wall across the east end. It was most likely made by **Powell of Whitefriars** in 1909.

Access: Vicarage Tel. 01254–236946.

The Great War Memorial stands in front of Elmfield Hall in Getty Park (SD750290) off the A679, Hyndburn Rd. The figure of Peace was sculpted in stone by **Walter Marsden.**

COCKERHAM lies in the flat-lands south of the Lune estuary and west of the M6 Junction 33.

St Michael's (SD462518) stands in splendid isolation in the middle of a field. It was rebuilt in 1900 by **Austin & Paley** who incorporated the C14 tower. The east window was made by **Morris, Marshall, Faulkner & Co.** in 1867 and was dismantled and re-fixed in slightly larger window openings during the **Austin & Paley** rebuilding. The cartoons for Matthew and John were by **Ford Madox Brown.** Mark, in crimson and green, is by **Burne-Jones** while Luke was

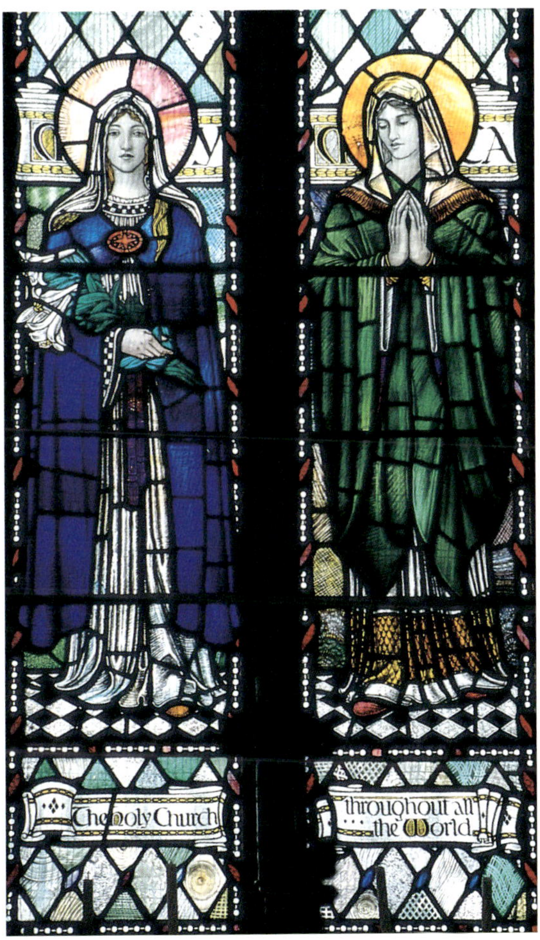

St James's, Church. Mary and Martha by B. D. Walmsley, 1927.

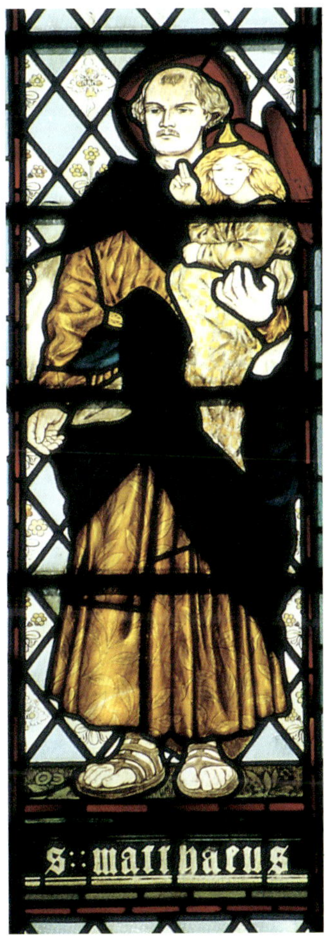

St Michael's, Cockerham. St Matthew by Ford Maddox Brown for Morris, Marshall, Faulkner & Co., 1867.

drawn by **William Morris** who also designed the seraphs and pattern work in the tracery.

Access: Vicarage Tel. 01524–791390.

COLNE is as far as the M65 goes into the East Lancashire Pennines.

Holy Trinity church, Burnley Rd, (SD877393) was built by **R. B. Preston** 1912 in a Romanesque style. The font in the baptistery at the west end has a cover made in 1962 by **Thompson** of Kilburn. The trademark mouse can be seen on the font cover as well as on the chancel screen and the lectern.

Access: Vicarage Tel. 01282–859956. Office Tel. 01282–859476.

DARWEN is south of Blackburn on the A666 to Bolton.

St Peter's is in Church St, (SD694222) off Bolton Rd. In 1978 when the nearby St George's, Darwen became redundant, its clergy stalls and choir stalls were moved to the chancel of St Peter's. At the same time St George's Great War Memorial and its reredos panelling were moved into the Lady Chapel at St Peter's. All of this woodwork was made in **A. W. Simpson's** workshop in 1922.

Access: Rectory Tel. 01254–702411.

DOWNHAM is a lovely village about 3 miles north-east of Clitheroe off the A59.

St Leonard's (SD784443) stands at the start of the village opposite the pub. It is an old site and there have been a succession of alterations and enlargements to the church. What is seen today is essentially a C15 tower and a reconstruction of the remainder by **Mervyn Macartney** 1909–10. The church is very restrained internally. There are no capitals and the mouldings of the arches disappear into the piers. There are similar arrangements for the chancel arch, doorways and other arches. The pew ends in the choir are simple but interesting and there is excellent carving in the decoration of the pulpit and the lectern. The altar and reredos were made later by **Robert Thompson**. The Latin inscription on the five-light east window is interpreted to mean that the window was designed, cut, painted, fired and leaded in 1869 by the brothers Assheton who were local landowners and benefactors. If this is so, it is quite remarkable for its time both in design and colour. It was fitted into the new window opening by Shrigley & Hunt when **Macartney** extended the chancel. Shrigley & Hunt also made the St Leonard window in the west wall in 1911. There is interesting ironwork to the south door. The church has a pair of simple brass vases made by the **Artificers' Guild**.

Access: Vicarage Tel. 01200–458019.

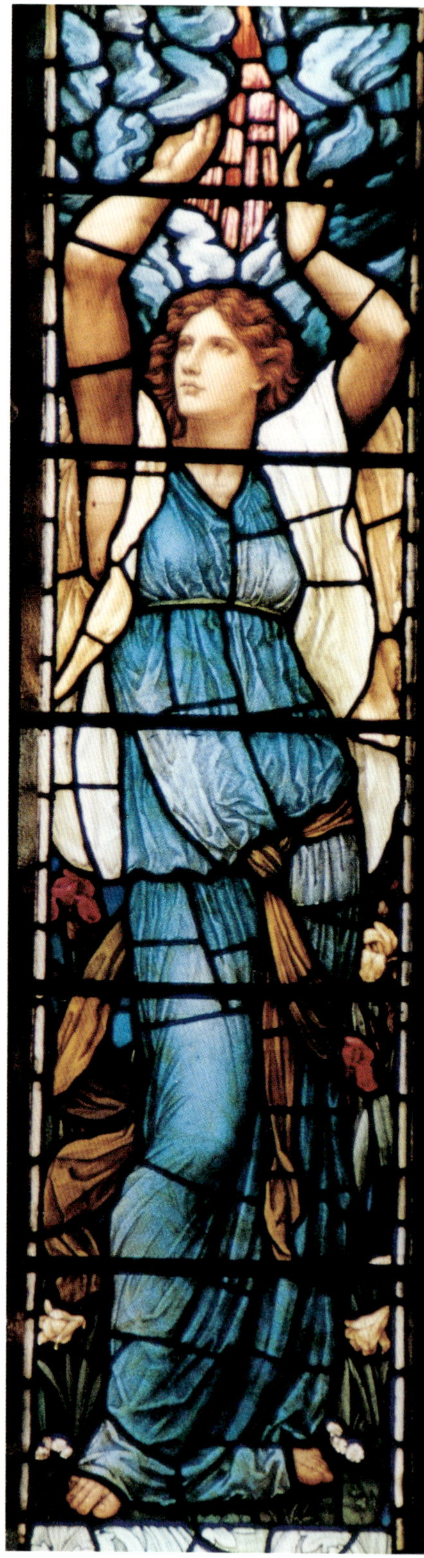

C of E and Methodist Church, Edgeworth. 'Faith' by Henry Holiday. No date.

EDGEWORTH is about 4 miles north of Bolton town centre on the A666.

The Joint C of E and Methodist Church in Bolton Rd (SD739163) has two excellent windows by **Henry Holiday**. In the south wall is a three-light window made in his own studio *c.* 1896 illustrating the parables of 'The Sower' 'The Good Shepherd' and 'The Lost Piece of Silver'. His other window, 'Faith, Love and Hope' is in the apse. Edgeworth does not appear in Winifrid Holiday's list and the date is approximate.

Access: Manse Tel. 01204–852270.

FLEETWOOD is on the north-west corner of the Fylde coast about 6 miles from Blackpool.

Rossall School (SD314448) has buildings in pretty well all of the partnership combinations of the **Paleys & Austins** 1861–1897 and a dining room built by Hubert Worthington in 1931. The library, once the chapel, has heraldic glass by **Trena Cox**. **Robert Lorimer** created the school's Great War Memorial Chapel when he added the south transept to **E. G. Paley's** church 1923–25. The reredos was carved by **Eric Gill** and there is a notable statue of St George, carved in wood by **Alice Meredith Williams**. The carved pew-ends in the chapel and in the nave were executed by **Lorimer's** preferred woodworkers, the brothers **W. & A. Clow** of Edinburgh. The reredos in the chancel was carved by Josephine de Vasconcellos in the 1950s. The second window from the west on the south side of the nave is by **Christopher Whall and Louis Davis**. There are also windows by **A. K. Nicholson** and **J. N. Bewsey** in the north chancel. **Bewsey** also made the main east window and the south and east windows in Lorimer's Memorial Chapel, all in the 1920s.

Access: By appointment with the School Chaplain. Tel. 01253–774201.

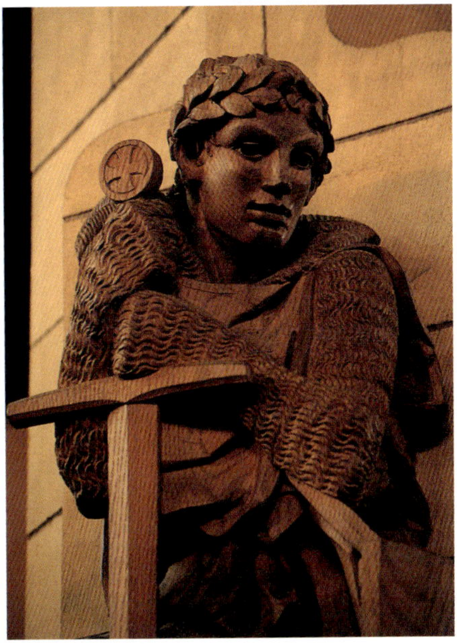

Rossall School Chapel, Fleetwood. Detail of St George by Alice Meredith Williams, c. 1924.

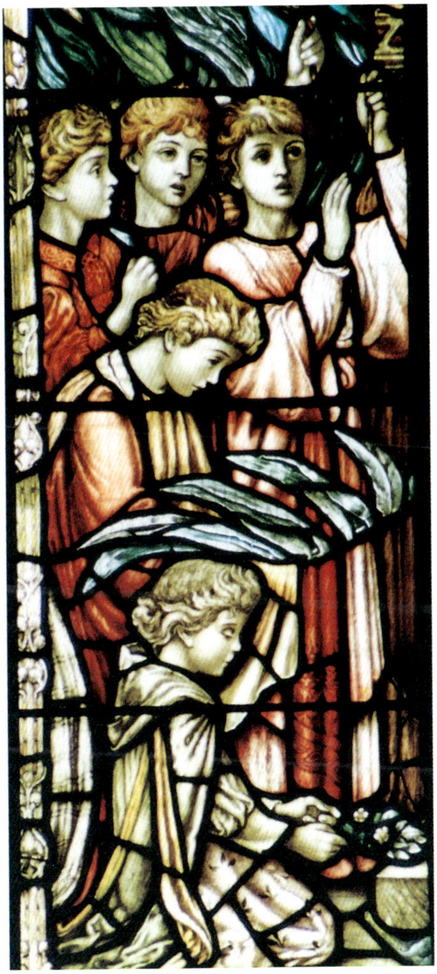

Rossall School Chapel, Fleetwood. Stained glass panel by Louis Davis, c. 1892.

Fleetwood's **Great War Memorial** is in the Memorial Gardens, (SC328473). Made in stone, the classical figure of Victory, crowned with a laurel wreath, holds upright the torch of freedom. The statue stands on a cylindrical base with carved relief panels inset above the list of those who lost their lives. It was sculpted by **G. H. Tyson Smith** in 1921.

FOULRIDGE is about a mile north of Colne on the A56 and has some attractive Arts and Crafts-style houses standing well back above the main road.

St Michael and All Angels, Skipton Rd, (SD890419) is an admirable stone church built

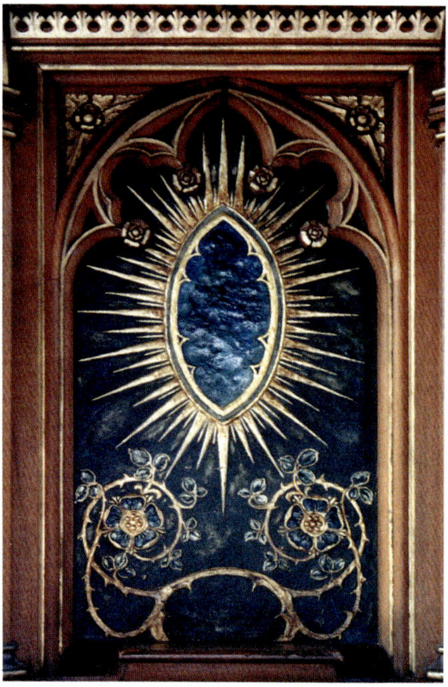

St Michael Foulbridge. Detail of gesso work on the reredos by H. Gustave Hiller, 1904.

by **R. B. Preston** 1903–05. Externally it has a very impressive east end with the vestry in an undercroft beneath the chancel and a tall bell tower at the north-east corner. The north side is given added interest by the two gables of the transept and another on the north-west porch. Internally it has simple stone walls with clear glass at the east and west ends. The architect has made the most of the decorative possibilities of his window shapes and sizes and the exposed woodwork of the roof. The pine pews show the faded remains of what was once a green stain and the simple carving on the choir stalls picks up the motif from the cusps in the window heads. The altar in the Lady Chapel is beautifully carved with lilies. There is only one stained-glass window in the body of the church. It is in the south wall and is by **William Glasby**, made in 1928. There are five painted-gesso panels in the reredos made by **H. G. Hiller** dated 1904. This is a fine church in a beautiful setting.

Access: Vicarage Tel. 01282–864046.

GARSTANG straddles the A6 half way between Preston and Lancaster.

St Thomas's (SD491450) is an C18 church with a chancel added in 1876. The east window featuring a very doubtful Thomas was designed by **Carl Almquist** and made by **Shrigley & Hunt** in 1878. The narthex screen contains some delightful floral stained-glass.

Access: Vicarage Tel. 01995–602162.

GREAT ALTCAR is on the B5195 between Formby and Ormskirk.

St Michael's church (SD320065) was built for Lord Sefton by **John Douglas** in 1879 in his black and white, timber-frame style. It stands on a red brick plinth and is roofed with red tiles. It has a small bell-tower at the west end. The flat-topped window openings have differing details one from another. Internally with the exception of the reredos, much of the decorative appeal of the building comes from the exposed structural woodwork. The reredos is made up of three monochrome, sepia, painted tile-panels which have the 'Supper at Emmaus' in the centre and an archangel in each of the side panels. They were designed in 1879 by **Heaton, Butler & Bayne** and made by Craven Dunnill. There are text panels on either

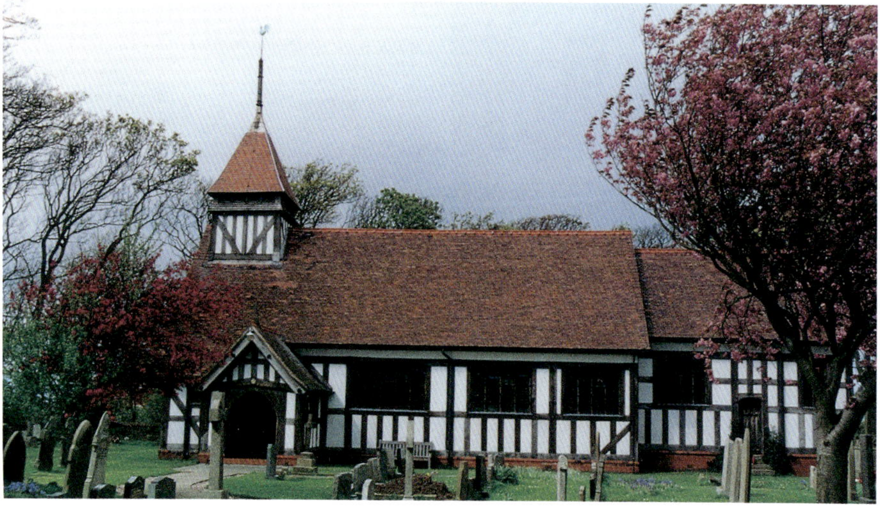

St Michael's, Great Altcar by John Douglas, 1879.

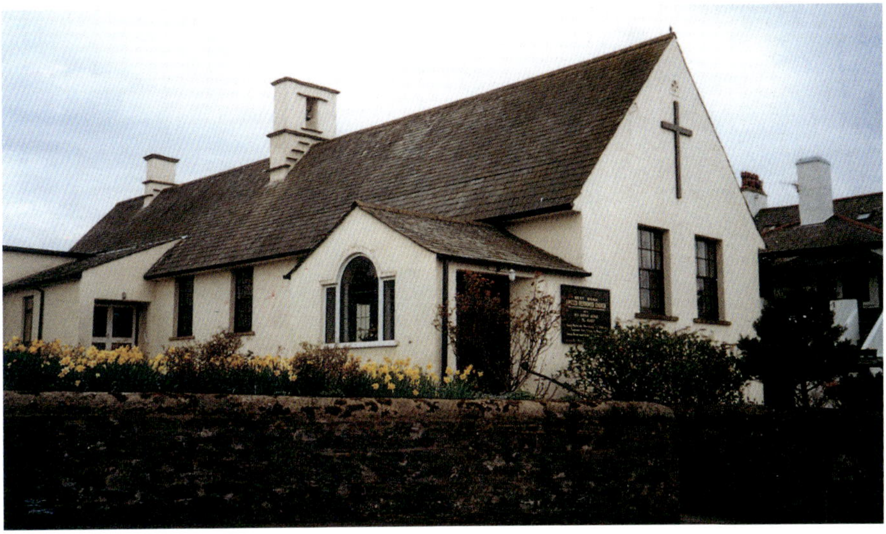

Congregational Church, Hest Bank by Mawson and Gibson, c. 1903.

side of the reredos surmounted by illustrative prints. The exposed beams carry various gilded biblical texts including 'Depart in Peace' over the south-porch door. All of the windows have clear diamond-leaded glass save one panel in the west window signed 'EF 1885' for **Edward Frampton**.

Access: Vicarage Tel. 01704–873304.

GREAT HARWOOD is north of Junction 7 on the M65.

St Bartholomew's (SD734327) is a genuine Perpendicular church but the chancel was extended in 1886. It is fitted with a fine four-light east window: 'The Nativity', 'The Presentation', John and Mary and 'Noli me Tangere'. It was designed by **Henry Holiday** for **Powell of Whitefriars** in 1889.

Access: Vicarage Tel. 01254–884039.

GREAT MITTON is about 3 miles south-west of Clitheroe.

All Hallows' (SD715389) is a mediaeval church which has C19 and C20 stained glass. The two-light window in the south wall of the nave is by **Edward Woore** but from 1938 and lacking his early sparkle. Who, on the other hand, made the exciting, unsigned east window with its red-winged dragon about to receive the coup de grace?.

Access: Waddington Vicarage Tel. 01200–423589.

HASLINGDEN is about 3 miles south of Accrington on the A56.

St Peter's, Laneside, (SD787230) was built in 1890 by **Basil Champneys**. The nave was never completed and a fire in 1988 necessitated much rebuilding. Nevertheless, the altar, pews, pulpit and font remain from **Champneys's** church. He also designed the school behind the church.

Access: Vicarage Tel. 01706–213838.

St John the Evangelist (SD783254) at Stonefold was built in 1885–86 by **Basil Champneys**. It is closed and under threat of demolition.

HEST BANK is a village, once separate from its neighbours Slyne and Bolton le Sands but now part of the ribbon of development that follows the A6 north out of Lancaster on its way to Carnforth. **T. H. Mawson** chose to live here at the height of his career and during his retirement.

Mallards, (SD465661) on the beach at Teal Bay was designed by **Mawson** for his own use as a holiday home with the white walls and round chimney stacks found more often around his home town of Windermere.

The Congregational church, now the URC (SD468663), was built in 1903 by **Mawson** and **Dan Gibson**. Lord Leverhulme was persuaded by Mawson to contribute to the cost of providing a screen. However, the development of the chapel outgrew its original building and when a larger hall was built for worship in the 1920s the original chapel, stripped of such decorative work as there was, became a community hall. Externally it is a visually pleasing building owing something to Voysey.

Applegarth, at the top of the hill on Hest Bank Lane, (SD471662) was designed by **Mawson** as his permanent home in a rather square and substantial Ernest Newton style. Also in Hest Bank Rd is **Bracondale** the house he built for his son Prentice Mawson.

A number of smaller houses near the former Congregational Church, recognisable by their

Voysey or Baillie Scott characteristics, were designed by **Mawson** for what was to have become a model village.

LANCASTER lies to the west of the M6 between junctions 33 and 34.

St Paul's Scotforth Rd (SD480600) was built in 1874–76 by **Edmund Sharpe**. Surprisingly, given Sharpe's fame and expertise in Gothic, it is built in stone in a Neo-Norman style with terracotta dressings to the doors and windows. It has a striking, stone tower with a copper saddleback-roof, circular clerestory-windows, low aisles on both sides and a large apse at the east end. Internally, the church is very light and attractive. The painted ceiling of the apse, the stylised figure of Christ in the central east window, the high vault in the chancel supporting the tower and the yellow, semi-circular, terracotta arches and pillars evoke a sense of Provence, Italy or Byzantium rather than Normandy. While the **Shrigley & Hunt** Catalogue lays claim to the two two-light windows at the east end of the north wall it does not mention the wheel window in the west wall which looks very like their work. The intriguing slightly Byzantine east window is also unsigned but could be by the Lancaster firm Lambert & Butler.

Access: Vicarage Tel. 01524–32106.

Methodist Church, Scotforth Rd, Greaves (SD480603) was built in 1908–09 by **A. G. Chant**. Pevsner suggests the style is most probably inspired by Edgar Wood. Whether or not that is the case the church is a quiet triumph. It is built of stone with a significant tower topped by a slender copper-covered spire and there is an Art Nouveau flourish to the tracery in the windows. The interior is surprisingly light and airy, an impression strengthened by the dormer-style clerestory windows and the use of tall and slender wood-clad steel pillars to support the roof timbers. Only the windows in the apse at the east end have stained glass which was executed as a Great War Memorial by **Barrowclough & Sanders** in 1921.

Access: Manse Tel. 01524–32717.

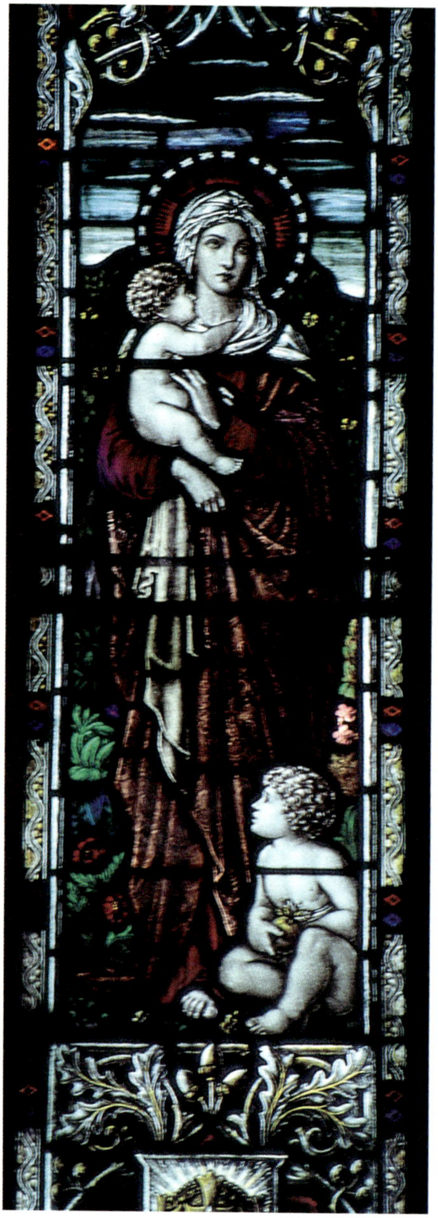

Scotforth Rd Methodist church, Lancaster. Detail of the east window by Barrowclough & Sanders, 1921.

Christ Church in Wyresdale Rd (SD485614) was built 1855–57 and was extended by **Austin & Paley** 1895. It is a good place to see a range of **Shrigley & Hunt** stained-glass windows. **Carl Almquist** was responsible for the five-light west window 1895; 'The Adoration of the Magi' 1905; 'Jairus's Daughter' and 'The Raising of the Widow's Son' in the south aisle and also 1905; 'The Good Shepherd' in the baptistery and the single light 'Good Shepherd' in the west aisle, both 1895. **Edward Holmes Jewitt** designed 'The Rivers of Paradise' 1896 and 'I am Alpha and Omega' 1896 both in the south aisle. He also designed the unusual and powerful 'I am the Light of the World' in the north wall in 1895.

Access: Vicarage Tel. 01524–34430.

Lancaster Town Hall in Dalton Square (SD479615) was built in classical style by E. W. Mountford in 1906–09. It has sculpture by **F. W. Pomeroy** on its front pediment and internally there are ceilings moulded by the **Bromsgrove Guild**.

The Ashton Memorial, in Williamson Park, (SD489614) is the outstanding landmark of

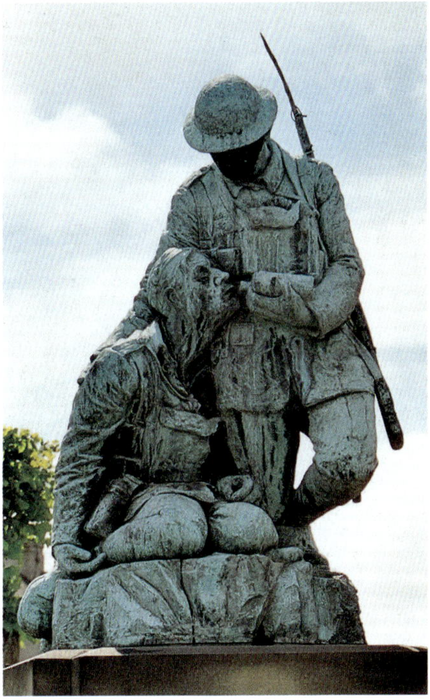

Westfield village, Lancaster. Detail of War Memorial by Jennie Delahunt, 1925.

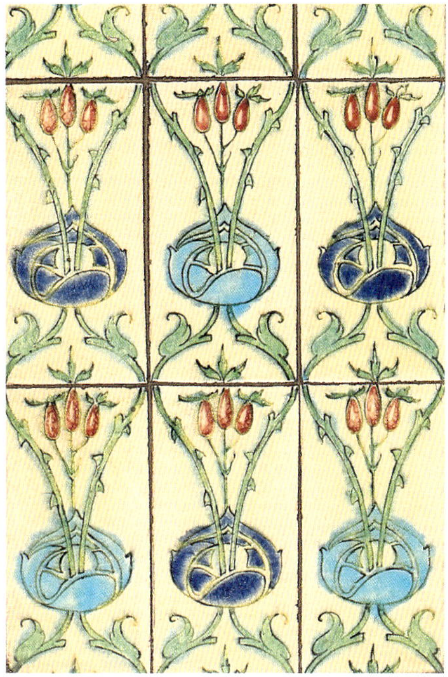

Peter Scott Gallery, Lancaster University. Pilkington Royal Lancastrian Pottery, 'Rosehip' design tiles by John Chambers c. 1906. *© Peter Scott Gallery, Lancaster University*

Lancaster. It was built in 1906 to designs by John Belcher who took the chair at the discussions which led to the establishment of the Art-Workers' Guild. It was his building for the Institute of Chartered Accountants off Moorgate in the City of London which was upheld by many of the Guild's members as a shining example of the 'unity of art', incorporating as it did expressive sculpture into its façade. This exceptional monument in Lancaster however owes less to the Arts and Crafts movement and more to Belle Époque classicism.

Westfield Memorial Village is off West Rd (SD470617) and opposite the Giant Axe Field. The War Memorial at the centre of the village has a sculpture made in 1925 by **Jennie Delahunt**, a teacher at the Lancaster School of Art and the Girls' Grammar School. There is also a commemorative plaque recalling that 'The cottages were built by public and individual subscription. The village was designed by **Thomas Hayton Mawson.**' This is the only example of what Mawson had hoped would be a nationwide approach to the housing of seriously injured ex-soldiers and their families in a village community in which they could also earn a living in associated workshops.

Lancaster University, (SD485575) at Bailrigg to the south of the city is home to **The Peter Scott Gallery**, situated in the Great Hall complex of the University. The Gallery houses the University's international art collection. It also has one of the most splendid displays of **Pilkington** Royal Lancastrian Pottery in the country including the less-often seen tiles designed by John Chambers and a pot by the elusive **John Firth** of Kirby Lonsdale who supplied unglazed pottery to Pilkington when they were establishing their pottery department. The Gallery has recently acquired the archive of John Chambers who was the company's chief designer and head of the architectural pottery department from 1891 until his retirement in 1938.

Access: During univerity term time. Mon–Fri 11.00–16.00 and Thur 18.00–20.30. Admission charge. Tel. 01524–593057.

The Ruskin Library at the University holds the vast amount of material which was collected by John Howard Whitehouse (1813–1955) an educationalist, Liberal MP and one-time Secretary of the Birmingham Ruskin Society. He also bought 'Brantwood' in Coniston and today both the library and the house are managed by the Ruskin Foundation which is based at Lancaster University. The Library collection includes 29 volumes of Ruskin's diaries from 1835–88, over 7000 letters and a complete collection of his published books as well as those written about him. In the public galleries there are changing exhibitions of some of Ruskin's 950 drawings and prints from the collection.

Access: Reading Room by appointment Mon–Fri 10.00–16.30. Tel. 01524–593587. Gallery: open Mon–Sat 11.00–16.00 & Sun 13.00–16.00.

The garden to **Bailrigg House**, which forms part of the university complex, was designed by **T. H. Mawson** although little now remains of his design.

LECK is about 3 miles south-east of Kirby Lonsdale.

St Peter's (SD643766) was built by **Paley & Austin** 1878–79 and fitted out with windows by **Powell of Whitefriars** using cartoons made by **Henry Holiday**. The church was burnt in a catastrophic fire in 1912 and rebuilt according to the original plans. Powell then remade the windows in accordance with Holiday's original cartoons. The east window, two three-light windows in the north aisle and the two-light window at the west end of the north aisle are by **Holiday**.

Access: Vicarage Tel. 015242–21030.

LONGTON is about 5 miles south-west of Preston off the A59 Southport Road.

St Andrew's, on Liverpool Road, (SD485258) was built in 1887 by **J. E. K. Cutts**. It is an excellent building even without its planned tower and spire. On the north side 'the Good Shepherd' and 'Charity' are by **Barrowclough & Sanders** of Lancaster as is the richly coloured and beautifully drawn 'Consider the Lilies of the Field' in the east-most window.

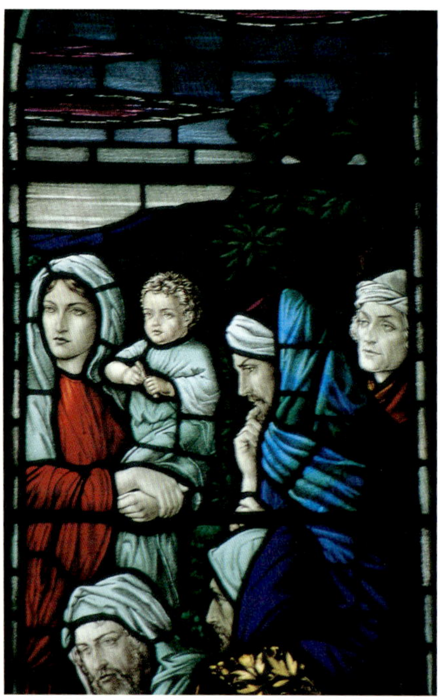

St Andrew's, Longton. Detail north aisle window by Barrowclough & Sanders c. 1927.

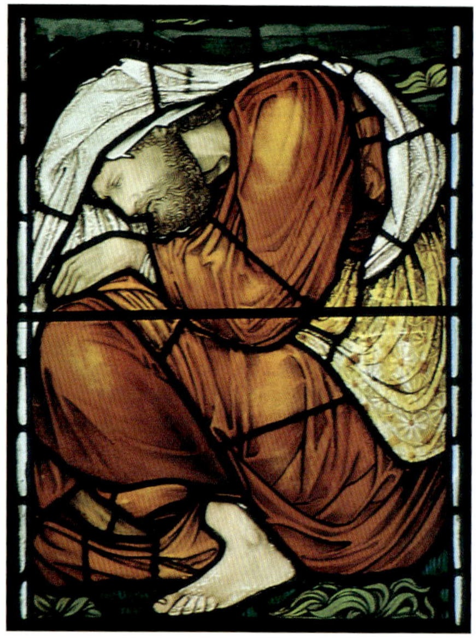

St Cuthbert's, Lytham St Annes. St Peter by Morris & Co. 1875.

Access: Vicarage Tel. 01772–612179 .

LYTHAM St ANNE'S is, about 4 miles south of Blackpool.

St Cuthbert's is in Church Rd, (SD357272) Lytham. The three-light window, second from the east in the south aisle, was made in 1875 by **Morris, Marshal, Faulkner & Co.** from **Burne-Jones's** cartoons. The window shows the 'Transfiguration of Christ' in the centre light with Moses and Elias on either side. Beneath these figures are three crouched, sleeping apostles, James, John and Peter, each one carefully folded into the limited space available in the cleverest and most decorative way. The wall paintings in the sanctuary and the baptistery were executed by Wallace Ward in 1932. Serried ranks of standing, kneeling and trumpet-playing angels line the north, south and east walls of the sanctuary in a truly glorious display. They are more Art Deco than Arts and Crafts but will not be ignored. The repoussé and enamel plaque on the south side of the chancel arch is skilfully designed and executed but unsigned.

Access: Vicarage Tel. 01253–736168.

St Thomas's in St Thomas Rd (SD326284) was built 1899–1905 by **Austin & Paley**. Pevsner damns it with faint praise saying 'Brick faced interior, not of as much interest as many other Austin & Paley churches.' Do not be deceived. The church contains some wonderful surprises. Apart from its architecture it has some magnificent stained glass especially in the

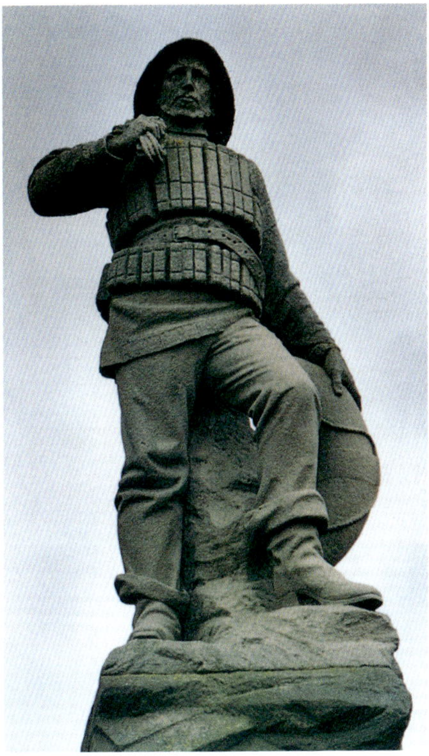

Life boatmen's memorial, Lytham by W. B. Rhind. 1883.

'Benedicite' window at the east end which was designed by **G. P. Hutchinson** for **Powell of Whitefriars** *c.* 1920. It spreads across five lights and is stunning in the composition of its colours, forms and lines. It gives as much pleasure in its totality as it does in the detail of its figures and incidents. The west window is also exceptional, also by **Powell** but designed in 1931 by Carl Edwards. The window has six lights and each light is divided into two panels. The lower panels are filled with the most colourful and beautiful angels each standing beneath a roundel representing one of the days of creation while more angels fill the upper tier of lights and tracery. It is spectacular. There are other notable smaller windows by Carl Edwards at the west end of the aisles. Down the north aisle is a series of four two-light windows also by Powell made in the 1930s which depict incidents in the life of Christ. They are more akin to book illustrations than is usual in Powell's windows.

Access: Vicarage Tel. 01253–723750.

The fine **Great War Memorial** in Ashton Gardens (SD319290) is an angel of Victory standing on a very tall and elegant obelisk which has relief sculptures around its base. It was executed by sculptor **Walter Marsden** in 1923.

The Lifeboat Disaster Memorial (SD318286) on the south Prom, near St Anne's Pier commemorates the loss of the lifeboat *Laura Janet* and twenty-seven souls in December 1886. It was sculpted by **W. B. Rhind** in 1888 and depicts William Johnson the Cox in his sou'wester and cork life-jacket, carved in stone and looking out over the sands of the Ribble estuary.

Fairhaven Church, in South Clifton Drive (SD348274) is known for obvious reasons as the White Church. It was built in 1912 by Briggs, Wolstenholme & Thornley in a Byzantine style with a ground-plan based on a Greek Cross. The whole of the exterior is clad in white faience and presents an exciting and exotic composition of towers and domes. Inside it is the stained-glass windows which make the impact. They were made 1905–12 by **Abbott & Co.** of Lancaster using designs attributed to Charles Elliott of London. Apparently he was given the subjects to work with and suggestions as to the symbolism to employ by Luke S. Walmsley, who was a founder-member of the church. He was also the father of **B. D. Walmsley** who, it is said, was inspired by these windows to take up stained-glass work.

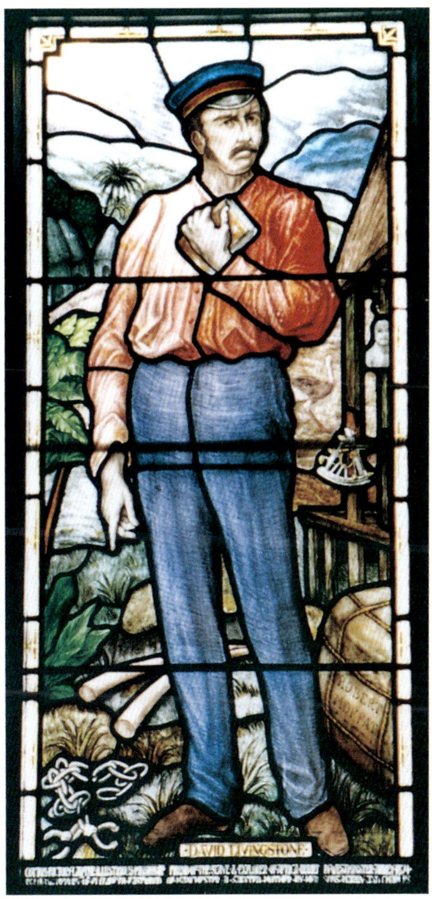

Fairhaven Church, Lytham. 'David Livingstone' panel by Abbott & Co. c. 1912.

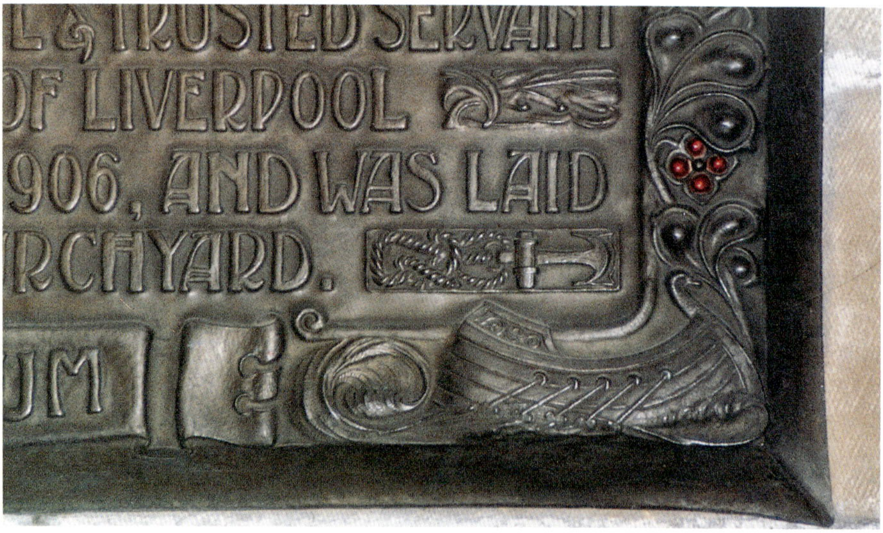

St Peter and St Paul, Ormskirk. Detail of a memorial panel. Unsigned, c. 1906.

There are four window openings and thirty four panels some bearing single figures on a time line ranging from Moses to David Livingstone. Others show more usual scenes such as the Crucifixion and Ascension and some recall less obvious events, such as 'Martin Luther Confronting the Diet of Worms', and 'The Ejectment of a Non-Conformist Minister and his Family From their Home at the Restoration'. The pulpit is decorated with beautiful repoussé copper panels which were made in 1921 by **Walter Marsden** as a memorial to members of the church who were killed in the Great War.

Access: Church office Tel. 01253–739947.

MELLING is 8 miles north-east of Lancaster on the A687.

St Wilfrid (SD599711) has an east window designed by **Henry Holiday** and made by Heaton Butler and Bayne.

Access: Vicarage Tel. 015242–21030.

MELLOR is 2 miles north-west of Blackburn and is reached by unclassified roads linking the A6119 with the A59.

The Methodist church (SD655310) in Mellor Lane was, until recently, a Neo-Gothic building with a ten-light window made in 1900 by **Morris & Co.** All the figures were based on cartoons by **Burne-Jones**. The original church has been demolished and seven of the figures have been splendidly installed in the new building.

Access: Circuit Property Steward Tel. 01254–263267.

MORECAMBE is west of junction 34 of the M6 between Lancaster and the Irish Sea.

The **Midland Hotel**, Marine Road (SD428644) was designed by Oliver Hill and opened in 1933 to excellent architectural reviews. It was the ultimate in Art Deco design with decorative features provided by **Eric Gill** and his son-in-law Denis Tegetmeier. The hotel has been unused for some years and has fallen into disrepair. However, **Eric Gill's** monumental seahorses on the front of the building and his relief sculpture representing 'Odysseus's Welcome by Nausicaa', in the lobby remain undamaged as does the circular 'Triton' panel above the spiral staircase also designed by **Gill** and painted by Tegetmeier. The pair also collaborated on the relief-map of the North West fixed to the wall in what was the children's room.

Access: The hotel is currently undergoing extensive restoration. For progress reports contact www.urbansplash.co.uk.

NELSON is just north-east of Junction 12 on the M65.

St Phillip's, (SD865381) Leeds Rd, was built by **R. B. Preston** 1900–02 in an Early English style. It is a big, stone church which has been re-ordered to provide community facilities. The wooden reredos was designed by Preston in 1921 and according to the NADFAS (The National Association of the Decorative and Fine Arts Societies) survey the carving was undertaken by Mr F. Jackson. It is not known who was responsible for the choir stalls which have a touch of the Arts and Crafts about them. The five-light east window is by **Allen Barrowclough** of Lancaster and was made in 1912 as a memorial to a 14 year old girl who drowned while bathing at St Anne's on Sea.

Access: Vicarage Tel. 01282–698161. Office Tel. 01282–619057.

ORMSKIRK is about 6 miles west of Skelmersdale on the A577.

St Peter & St Paul stands in the centre of the town, (SD414086) unmistakable because of the strange juxtaposition of its west tower and the taller spire sprouting from the south west corner. Under the tower, in the north and west walls are two windows by **Henry Holiday**. To the west is a three-light window 'Christ Stilling the Storm on the Sea of Galilee' which was made in 1892 and is an excellent example of the work Holiday produced in his own studio. In the north wall is a window he designed for **Powell of Whitefriars** in 1880 showing Christ with the little children. It is a touch sentimental, with the attendant adults staring into the middle distance. In the nave the window east of the south door was made by **Joseph Nuttgens** in 1953. It shows Mary and the apostles receiving the gift of the Holy Spirit. In the shadows on the north wall is a plaque in memory of Charles Warlow who died in 1906. The central panel of text is surrounded by a repoussé plant-form border incorporating clusters of red berries with stylised Viking ships at the bottom corners and at the centre top. It is beautiful work and like many memorials, unsigned.

Access: Vicarage Tel. 01695–572143.

OSWALDTWISTLE lies between Blackburn and Accrington.

Immanuel church, in New Lane, (SD734267) is a large, stone church with a solid, square west tower. The church has three windows by **Morris & Co.** Two of them are in the north transept, St Michael, with red wings and wearing armour chased with gold was installed in 1895 while Gabriel in pale green and pink, with blue wings followed in 1897. St Cuthbert was installed in the north side of the nave in 1914. All three figures are based on **Burne-Jones's** cartoons. In the apse of the south chapel are five beautiful but unattributed single lights. In the south wall there is a particularly war-like St Oswald and an equally belligerent St George made by **Shrigley & Hunt**. The Great War Memorial on the south wall, brought here from St Michael's, was made by **W. J. Pearce** 1920.

Access: Parish Office open 9.00–12.00 weekdays. Tel. 01254–382147.

Great War Memorial, at the junction of Union Rd and Rhyddings St (SD741276) was designed by **L. F. Roslyn** in 1921. A bronze winged Victory stands on top of a granite pedestal which also supports a plinth on which a soldier stands protectively astride a fallen comrade. The prow and stern of a ship project from the pedestal and carry bronze figures representing the Royal Navy and the Royal Air Force. It is a very original and emotive composition.

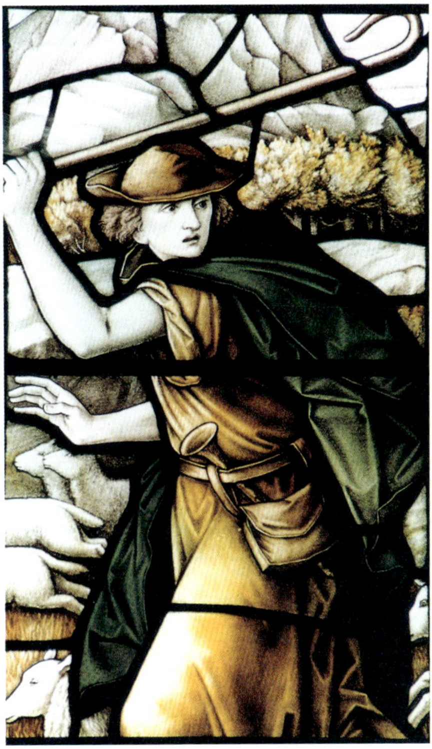

Christ Church, Over Wyresdale. Detail, shepherd window, designed by Carl Almquist for Shrigley & Hunt, c. 1900.

OVER WYRESDALE is a thinly-populated parish centred on the hamlet of Abbeystead some 2 miles east of junction 33 on the M6.

Christ Church is on Abbeystead Rd, (SD551545) and is known locally as 'The Shepherd's Church'. It is a Georgian building, restored in 1894 by **John Douglas**, who added a spire and chancel to the building using carved timber pillars for the chancel arch. All of the stained-glass windows refer to sheep or shepherds and were designed by **Carl Almquist** for **Shrigley & Hunt** 1891–1903. Those in the aisles rely solely on grisaille and silver stain. The church has a 'Breeches Bible' usually kept in a case placed on a table which was carved by the Rev John W. Wood. He also made the Charity box at the rear of the church and executed the text over the lych-gate.

Access: Dolphinholme Vicarage Tel. 01524–792327.

Abbeystead, about a mile east of Christ Church, is a house built in 1886 by **Douglas & Fordham** in Elizabethan style for the Earl of Sefton. It is still a private house owned now by the Grosvenor Estate.

PADIHAM has almost been caught up in the expansion of Burnley and sits just off its north western extremity.

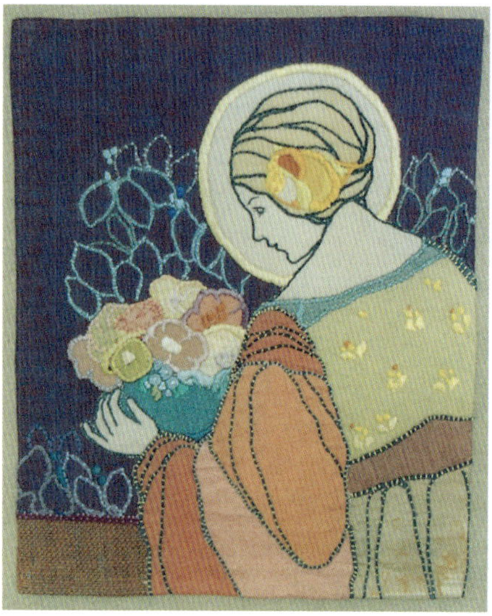

Gawthorpe Hall, Padiham. 'Lady with Posy' by Rachel George. No date. *Courtesy of the Trustees of the Rachel B. Kay-Shuttleworth Collection*

Gawthorpe Hall, off Padiham Rd, (SD806341) is described by the National Trust as 'an Elizabethan gem in the heart of Lancashire.' It was built around 1600 and restored in the middle of the C19 by Charles Barry. It has many notable paintings on loan from the National Portrait Gallery and some incidental Arts and Crafts gems such as the **William De Morgan** tiled fireplace in the long gallery, some **Pilkington** pots and a rather splendid ironwork electric lamp on a newel post which looks like one in the **George Wragge Ltd** catalogue. However, what Gawthorpe is most noted for is the Kay-Shuttleworth collection of needlework which was brought together by **Rachel Beatrice Kay-Shuttleworth** and is privately owned. It is the finest embroidery collection in England outside the V&A Museum. Most of it is in store but the public display has examples of the work of many ages and many countries. The handicraft of the late C19 and early C20 is well represented by the superb work of **Rachel Kay-Shuttleworth** herself and by other leading craftswomen including **Ann Macbeth** of Glasgow School of Art fame and some less well-known but very talented needlewomen.

Access: National Trust property open 1 April–31 Oct 13.00–17.00 daily except Mon and Fri. Tel. 01282–771004.

PRESTON stands, proudly, north of the River Ribble and west of junction 31 of the M6.

St Cuthbert's, Lytham Rd, (SD527313) Fullwood was designed by **Temple Lushington Moore** in 1913 and if the Great War had not intervened it would have been an exceptional cathedral-like building with a huge chancel with central nave and double aisles either side. As it happened work stopped in 1916 with the construction of temporary walls on the south side and at the west end. The tower was never built, the nave was not extended and the temporary walls are still in place. The lack of cash which prevented the completion of the church is reflected internally in minimal decoration. However the absence of stained glass in the range of tall three-light windows in the north wall and the gabled east end, fill the church with light and even now, in its unfinished state, it is a forest of pillars and a maze of arcades always throwing up interesting perspectives.

Access: Vicarage Tel. 01772–717346 .

Harris Museum and Art Gallery, (SD541294) Market Place is housed in an imposing Neo-Classical Grade 1 listed building. Its collection includes a selection of **Doulton & Co.** and **Pilkington Royal Lancastrian Pottery** dating from 1880–1910 and a striking silver plaque of the 'Annunciation' by **Alexander Fisher** dated 1904. 'Alleluia' by **Morris & Co.** to a design by **Burne-Jones** is currently displayed in the Fine Art Gallery and is one of two Burne-Jones tapestries in the collection. The Fine Art Gallery also holds several interesting fin-de-siècle statues including *Guinevere's Redeeming* by **W. Reynolds Stephens** and work by **G. F. Watts, Hamo Thorneycroft, Gilbert Bayes, Goscombe John, Alfred Drury, Alfred Gilbert and Albert Toft**. A stained-glass window by **Henry Holiday** 1904 featuring philosophers, poets and dramatists from Ancient Greece complements the Museum's architecture.

Access: Open Mon–Sat, 10.00–17.00, Sun 11.00–16.00. Admission Free. Tel. 01772–258248.

The Harris Library on the first floor of the Museum and Art Gallery has a Private Press Collection of some six hundred volumes including books by the **Kelmscott, Doves** and **Nonesuch Presses**.

Access: Tel. 01772–532676.

RAWTENSTALL is north of Bury and Rochdale between Haslingden and Bacup on the A681.

St Mary's (SD811228) was built in 1829 and is an unusual place to find a wooden reredos and sanctuary panelling designed by **Henry Wilson** in 1907. The wood and wrought-iron altar-rail donated shortly afterwards may also have been designed by Wilson. The reredos has a special quirk in that the central panels can slide apart to reveal the coat of arms of the donor of the earlier east window. Otherwise the work, though pleasing, is not remarkable.

Access: Chrch office Tel. 01706–231266.

Rawtenstall Carnegie Library, (SD811227) was built in 1906 by **Crouch, Butler & Savage** in

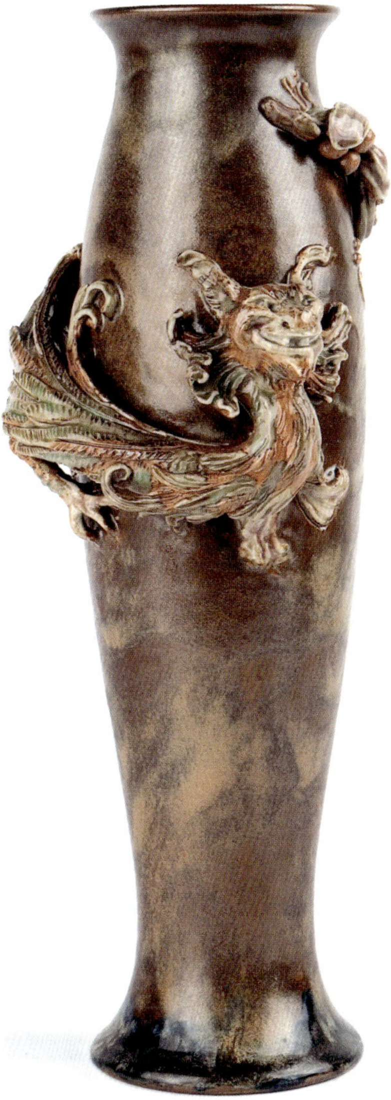

Harris Museum, Preston. Dragon vase designed by Mark Marshall for Doulton & Co., Lambeth c.1900.
© Harris Museum and Art Gallery, Preston

Edwardian style. The ornamental ironwork above the entrance has an Art Nouveau flourish reminiscent of the **Bromsgrove Guild** who executed work for the architects at this time. The same Art Nouveau flourish is repeated in the wrought-iron gates.

Access: Tel. 01706–227911.

The Great War Memorial (SD811227) stands in a small park between the library and St Mary's and takes the form of a simple obelisk bearing four small high-relief bronze panels showing figures in the fighting services as well as those who laboured in their support, including nurses, fishermen and farmers, for example. It is excellent work by **L. F. Roslin**.

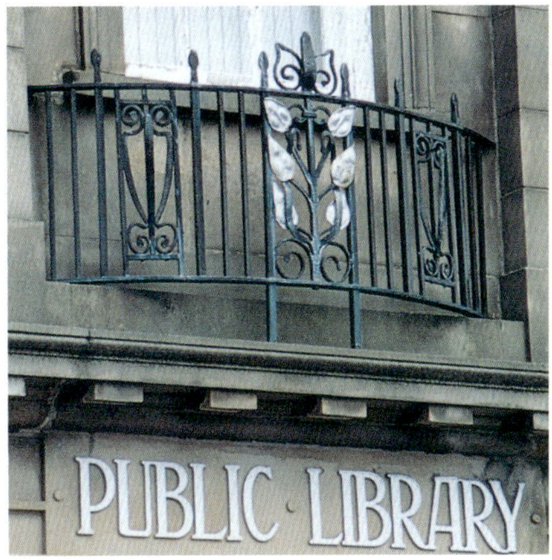

Rawtenstall Library. Detail of ironwork.

SILVERDALE overlooks Morecambe Bay and can be approached from Junction 35 on the M6 through Carnforth and Warton.

St John's (SD463754) was designed in 1886 by **Ball & Elce** of Manchester. It is a large, delightful church built of locally quarried stone which sits very well in its setting. Chief among those subscribing to the cost was Henry Boddington the Salford brewer. The reredos was designed by William Ball and executed by **John Jarvis Millson** who also carved the corbels and capitals. The carved choir stalls, prayer desk, pulpit and oak seating were all by **James Hatch** of Lancaster. Most of the stained glass is by Shrigley & Hunt of Lancaster although the east-most window in the south aisle is by **H. G. Hiller** and was dedicated in 1926.

Access: Usually open. Vicarage Tel. 01524–701268.

STONYHURST lies in a beautiful rural corner of east Lancashire north of Accrington and east of Blackburn about 5 miles west of Clitheroe on the B6243.

Stonyhurst, (SD691391) according to Pevsner 'is the most monumental Elizabethan mansion in the county'. In 1794 it became **Stonyhurst College** and in 1887 **Paul Woodroffe** was numbered among its pupils. He not only designed the college's Boer War Memorial but he also designed and made more than sixty stained-glass panels installed on the main staircase, in the upper refectory, the Sodality Chapel and the upper gallery. All but the Sodality Chapel windows are heraldic devices but worthy of special note in any collection. They are beautifully drawn and coloured and full of interest. There are four **Woodroffe** windows in the Sodality Chapel each of which has two lights with a single transom. The earliest work, from 1911, is on the north side of the chapel and depicts the figures of Saints Helena, Thomas Moore, Francis Borgia and the Blessed Edmund Campion. Next to that is a

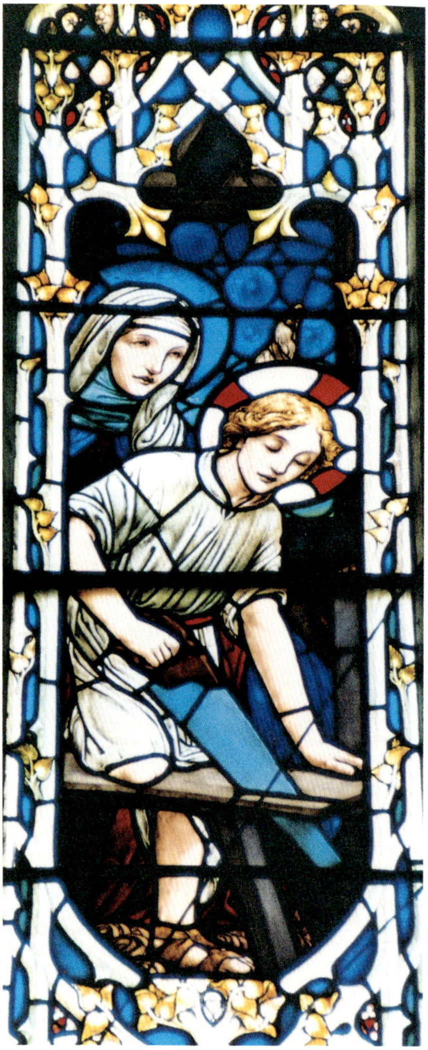

Sodality Chapel, Stoneyhurst College. Detail of the Young Jesus window by P. Woodroffe, 1915. *Courtesy of Stonyhurst College*

window, made in 1920, showing the 'Annunciation' enlivened by the Dove of the Spirit, streaking into the scene like a thunderbolt. On the south side is the 'Adoration of the Shepherds' and the 'Young Jesus Working in his Father's Carpenter's Shop' made in 1915 and set next to the 'Crucifixion and Resurrection' window (1914). Here the dark muted tones of the descent from the cross contrast startlingly with the lightness and brightness of the 'Resurrection'. The College's Great War Memorial was a new Physics Laboratory and a shrine and altar at the end of the upper gallery in the old building. The architectural design-work for this was undertaken by another 'old boy', Major Kirby, of the Liverpool firm of Edmund Kirby & Sons. The relief sculpture in white marble above the altar shrine is by **Gilbert Ledward** and dates from 1923.

Access: The school is open to visitors from mid-July to end August and to organised groups booked in advance. Admission charge. Tel. 01254–826345.

TARLETON is just north of the A565 about 5 miles north of Southport.

Holy Trinity (SD451204) stands in the centre of the village in C14 style but was built in 1886. There is a cheering contrast between its grey and cold exterior and the light, warm, honey colour of the stonework inside. It is a perfect setting for a brilliant east window designed by **A. J. Davies** and made by the **Bromsgrove Guild** in 1921. It is a Crucifixion scene in which the figure of Christ and the angels above him are bathed in light while the apostles and Mary Magdalene, at the foot of the cross, are in gloomy darkness. The middle distance is filled with the heads of the watching crowd. In the early morning of a fine day in summer this window sings like an anthem of praise. In the sanctuary the carved mouse on the back of the bishop's chair marks a piece of **Robert Thompson** furniture made in the 1950s.

Access: Vicarage Tel. 01772–812614.

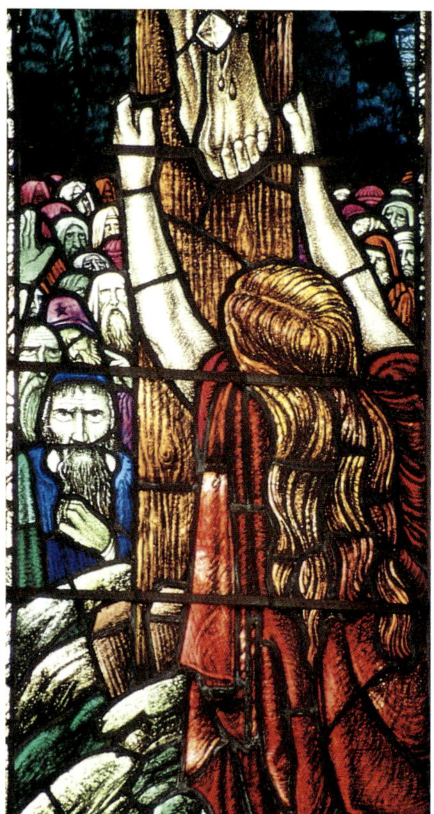

Holy Trinity, Tarleton. Detail of east window by A. J. Davies, 1921.

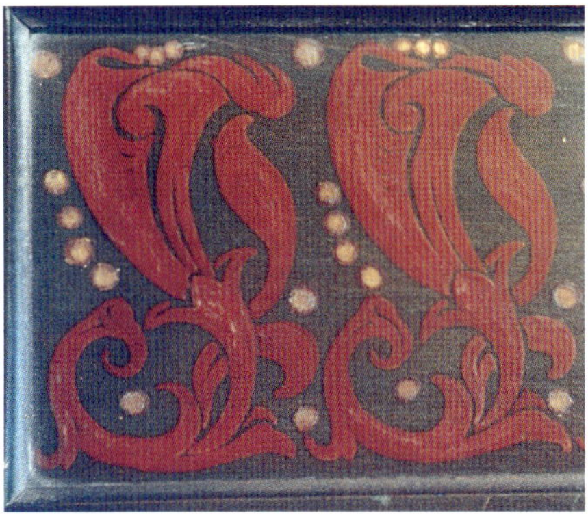

Turton Tower. Detail of decorated wardrobe by C. R. Ashbee. *Reproduced with permission of V&A Museum / V&A Images*

TURTON village is on the B6391 about 5 miles north of Bolton.

St Anne's, High St, (SD734157) Chapeltown, is a mid-C19 church with a reredos added in 1888 by **R. K. Freeman**. The three-light window at the west end of the south wall shows St John in the left light, St Anne in medieval dress in the centre teaching Mary to read and St James the Greater standing on the right. It dates from about 1920 and was designed and executed by **Paul Woodroffe**.

Access: Vicarage Tel. 01204–852222.

Turton Tower (SD731152) is essentially a C15 pele tower extended in succession by the Elizabethans, Georgians and Victorians. Since 1930 it has been the subject of a Trust and used first as the local council offices and more recently as a museum. There is a mix of furnishing styles in the various rooms. The Bradshaw Suite has a comfortable Neo-Tudor four-poster bed and a **C. R. Ashbee** wardrobe.

Access: Tel. 01204–852203.

UPHOLLAND is south of Skelmersdale and west of Orrell on the A577.

St Thomas the Martyr in Church St (SD523051) was once a Benedictine priory and the huge scale of the C14 building can be gauged from the fact that the nave of the present church was the original chancel. The tower was added around 1500 and the chancel in 1882. Along with the chancel came a series of stained-glass windows by **Henry Holiday**. The five-light east window is an excellent version of the 'Ascension' made in 1884 by **Powell of Whitefriars**. In the same year **Holiday** produced the designs for the windows in the north and south walls of the sanctuary. On the north side is a two-light window. The top panels show 'The Baptism of Christ' and 'Paul Baptising the Phillipean Jailer'. The lower panels show 'The Cleansing of Naaman' and 'Noah Greeting the Dove'. On the opposite side is a three-light window in which the top panels show a silver and gold version of 'The Adoration of the Lamb'. The lower panels have a rather cramped 'Last Supper' where, on the right, a halo-less Judas is about to slope off and fulfil his destiny. The north chancel window made *c*. 1904 provides an interesting example of the development of Holiday's style. It is a two-light window with Jonathan and David in the lower panels and above them the lame and the sick are being brought to Jesus to be cured. In the midst of this stained glass and the mediaeval stonework, the low wooden chancel-screen made in 1931 speaks for the quality of the work of later craftsmen.

Access: Rectory Tel. 01695–622936.

WHALLEY is about 5 miles north of Accrington by the A680.

St Mary and All Saints (SD733362) has Norman ancestors but is essentially an Early English Gothic church with a Perpendicular east window. It has early C15 canopied stalls in the choir with exceptional misericordes. The reredos is the work of **George Jack** and dates from 1928 while the altar cross is by **Bainbridge Reynolds** 1909. The communion rail, with its carved text, 'Holy Holy Holy, Lord God' in pierced, rather Art Nouveau style, is said to have been wrought by a local craftsman in 1909. In the St Nicholas Chantry on the north side of the church is a two-light window by **Edward Woore** depicting St Giles and St Anthony. The window dates from the 1930s and is executed in a rather flat style which is far removed from the beauty and excitement of his earlier work. As if to make the point, not only is there a superb three-light window in the same Chapel (King Arthur, St George and St Nicholas) by **Trena M. Cox** dated 1926 but across the aisle is a splendid three-light window by Woore's mentor, **Christopher Whall** made after 1913. It shows Mary and the infant Jesus flanked by the archangels Gabriel and Raphael. In the next window towards the east 'The Good Shepherd' by **Burne-Jones** was made by **Morris & Co.** in 1893 and seems to have slipped past Morris's self-imposed embargo on putting 'modern' windows in ancient churches.

Access: Office Tel. 01254–823249.

Whalley Methodist Church in King St, (SD734364) has two of the best **Whall & Whall** windows in the region. They are fixed opposite each other in the north and south walls and were installed after 1926. On the north side the Virgin Mary sits cloaked in rich blues and purples with the infant Jesus sitting on her knee. A chorus of birds sing and rabbits and field-mice gambol at her feet. On the other side of the church St Francis, typically robed in brown, is preaching to an unusual selection of birds including a gorgeous peacock. The

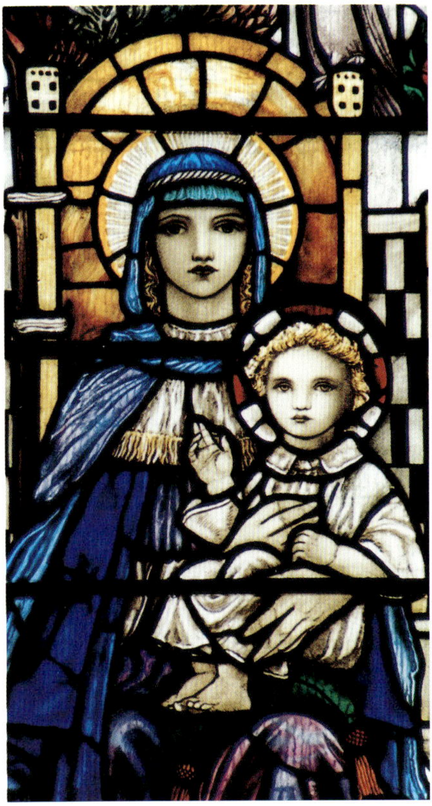

Methodist church, Whalley. Detail of the Virgin and Child by Veronica Whall, 1926.

remaining windows in the church are glazed with foliate designs. Might these have come out of the Whall & Whall Studio as well?

Access: Manse Tel. 01254–822130.

Whalley Abbey (SD730361) is in the centre of Whalley village. The Abbey ruins and gardens are open to the public. The Abbeyhouse built in the C16 is not, although it does have Open Days. It was restored in the latter part of the C19 but neither the date nor the architect is known. The large hall has many Arts and Crafts features with oak-panelled walls and a liberal amount of carving. There is a huge inglenook fireplace with **De Morgan** tiles. The elegant drawing room features another interesting fireplace which also has **De Morgan** tiles. The Abbey House is now a Retreat and Conference Centre belonging to the Blackburn Diocese. People looking for a quiet break may stay here and visits may be made by appointment. Currently it is closed for renovation but should be open by September 2005.

Access: Tel. 01254–828400.

WHITTINGTON is 2 or 3 miles south of Kirkby Lonsdale on the B6254.

St Michael's (SD600761) has some interesting windows attributed locally to James **Powell of Whitefriars** in 1875. In his *Reminiscences of my Life*, **Henry Holiday** tells how in 1883 he went first to stay at Whittington Hall with Colonel and Mrs Dawson Greene, for whom he had once designed some windows. He doesn't say whether the windows were for the Hall or the church. The west window has deteriorated badly but there are others here which are characteristic of Holiday's style.

Access: Vicarage Tel. 015242–21358.

WORSTHORNE is about 2 miles east of Burnley.

St John's stands in the centre of the village (SD876324). It was split in half in the early 1970s to provide the present church and a two-storey social centre complete with a licensed bar. The three-light east window 'St John', 'The light of the World' and 'St Mary' was made in 1935 by **George Wragge Ltd.** The tower window is by the same firm, post 1936, showing on the left Mary Magdalene washing Christ's feet and on the right, Christ welcoming the little children.

Access: Vicarage Tel. 01282–428478
Office Tel. 01282–453728.

GREATER MANCHESTER

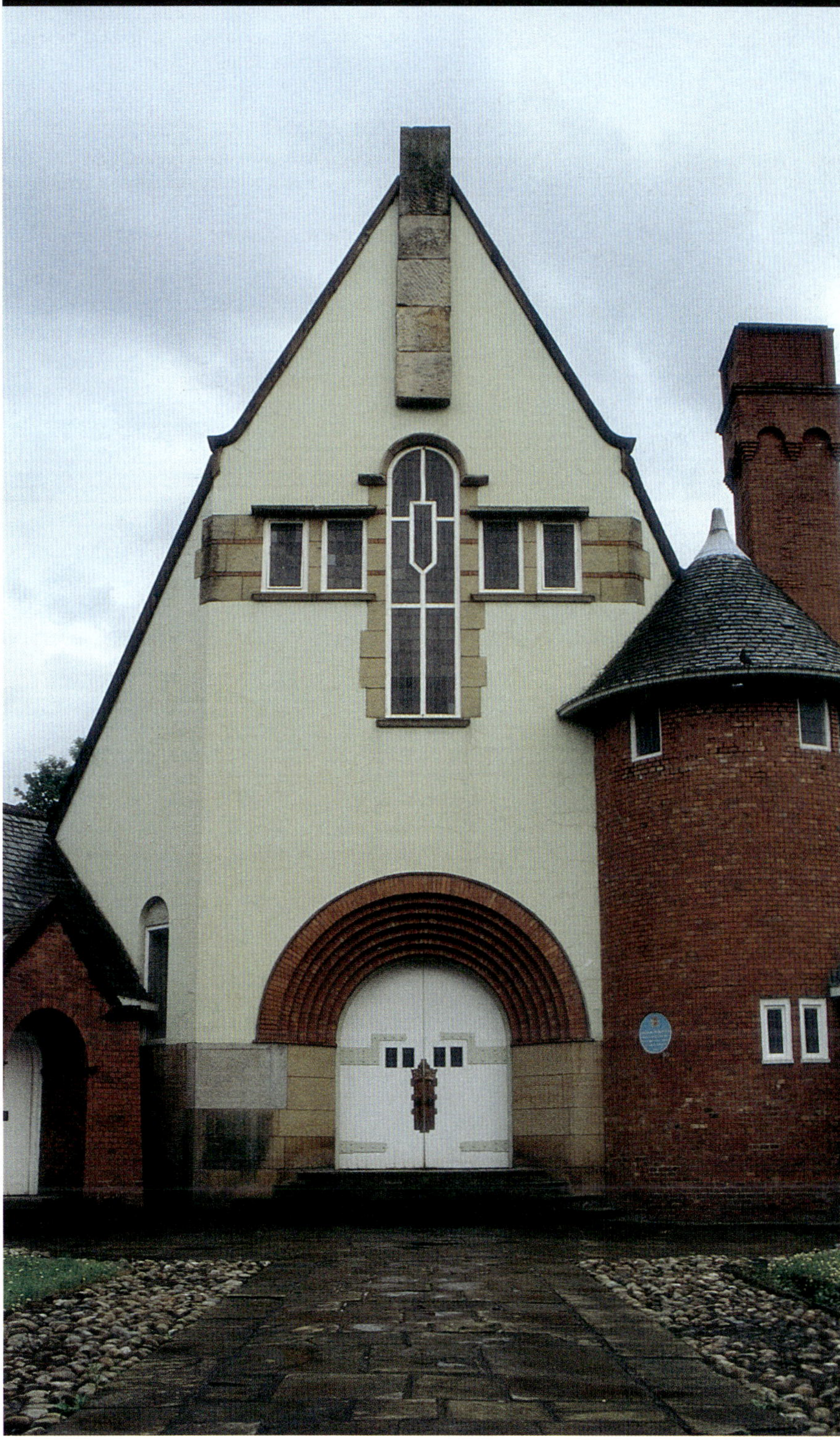

ALTRINCHAM lies on the southern edge of the Manchester conurbation north of Hale and south of Sale.

St George's, Church St (SJ767882) is a big and comfortable red brick building, originally Georgian but with alterations by **Paley & Austin**. On each side of the central three-light window in the apse is a tall lancet filled with stained glass by **Mary Lowndes**. On the left is 'St George' in pale but shining silvery-blues.

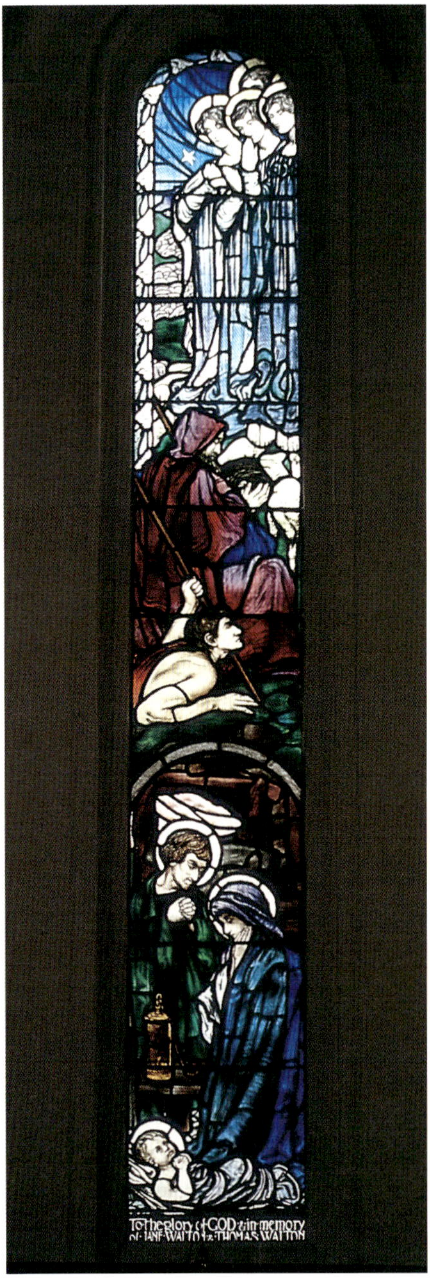

St George's, Altrincham. Nativity window by Mary Lowndes.

On the right is 'The Nativity' in darker tones with angels at the top of the window announcing the good news to two shepherds; meanwhile Mary and Joseph admire the infant in the stable below. There is an unsigned copper shield at the west end of the north wall which is a memorial to James Ernest Bytheway Hesketh who was killed in the Great War while serving in the Royal Flying Corps.

Access: Parish Office Tel. 0161–9414037.

The Altrincham & Dunham Massey War Memorial stands in a small garden of remembrance (SJ759877) off Dunham Rd. It was designed in 1919 by **George Faulkner Armitage**. At the centre of a raised platform stands a tall, white stone Celtic cross with a bronze flower trough around its base. It stands between two shorter, slender columns capped by electric lights. The platform is surrounded by a low stone parapet wall on top of which bronze plates are inset bearing the names of those killed in the war. On the wall's outer rim there is a band of entrelac decoration and carved text.

ASHTON in MAKERFIELD is close to the east side of the M6 motorway and is approached from junction 24 by the A58.

St Oswald and St Edmund's in Liverpool Rd (SJ576989) is a grey stone building, designed in 1930 by **J. S. Brocklesby** in a Romanesque style, complete with domes, apse and ambulatory. It is an interesting and pleasing building enlivened by a marvellous set of stained-glass windows made by the **Harry Clarke Studio**. The seven saints represented in the windows high in the apse were done by Clarke himself or under his direct supervision just one year before he died. Their colour, design and charisma make these windows absolutely stunning. When you have savoured the east end, preferably through binoculars, turn around and take a long look at 'Christ in Glory' in the west window. The windows in the aisles are from the same studio but were made after Clarke's death.

Access: Presbytery Tel. 01942–727249.

ASHTON under LYNE lies to the east of Junction 23 on the M60.

The Albion United Reformed Church, Stamford St (SJ944989) was built 1890–95 by John Brooke at the behest of local, wealthy Congregationalists. It stands within a bow shot of the largely rebuilt, mediaeval Parish Church and it is a real piece of nonconformist one-upmanship. The Albion is very long and wide with a high roof, a strong tower and a tall and elegant spire. Internally, the low narthex at the west end leads into the broad nave where the eye is immediately drawn to the east end of the church and a beautiful set of **Morris & Co.** windows. The east window was made in 1893

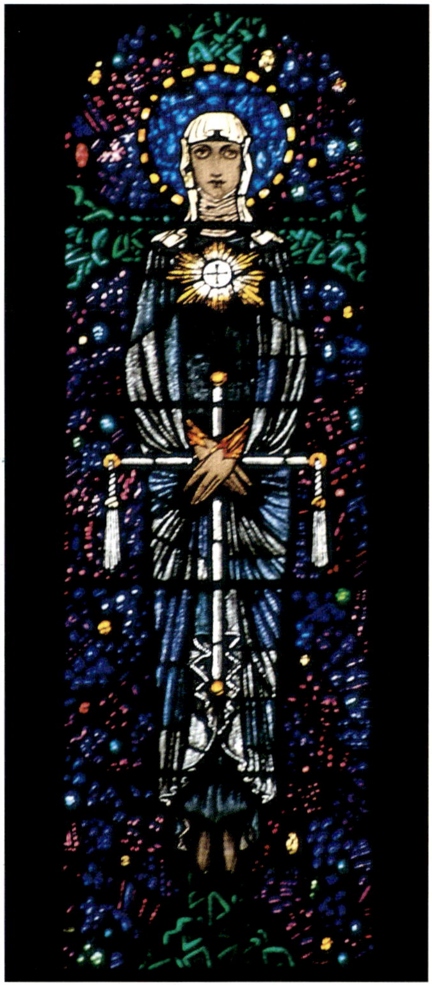

St Oswald's, Ashton in Makerfield. Apse window, 'St Juliana Falconieri' by Harry Clarke, c. 1930.

and has seven lights arranged in two tiers. Each of the fourteen panels has a **Burne-Jones** figure and all are surmounted by tracery containing a host of angels. The top tier of figures represents the virtues, while the lower figures represent their patron saints. Typically, **Morris** has chosen to place the figures to achieve the most balanced design rather than simply placing each saint under its particular virtue. The south transept window of 1895 shows ten New Testament figures, all designed by **Burne-Jones**. The window is made more remarkable because of the silvery-green effect of the tracery lights. There are smaller lights in the side walls of the transept at clerestory height. The major window in the north transept, installed in 1896, features ten Old Testament characters designed by **Burne-Jones**. The angels in the tracery on this side also have a silvery-green brilliance. There are clerestory lights in this transept also of 1896 and also by **Morris & Co.** According to Sewter the figures for both transept windows were specially designed for this location.

It is not unusual that the congregation should have decided to make their Great War Memorial in the form of a reredos. It was, however, a stroke of genius to commission the **Pilkington Tile Company** to produce it. The memorial, designed by **Gordon M. Forsyth**, comprises a set of ceramic panels showing Christ helping a fallen soldier to his reward in heaven. Panels on either side carry the names of fifty-seven men killed in the conflict and the reredos is completed by further panels representing St George on the left and St Michael on the right each with their attendant angels. **Forsyth** produced a work of great individuality and beauty which commands respect in its own right while contributing greatly to the artistic unity of the

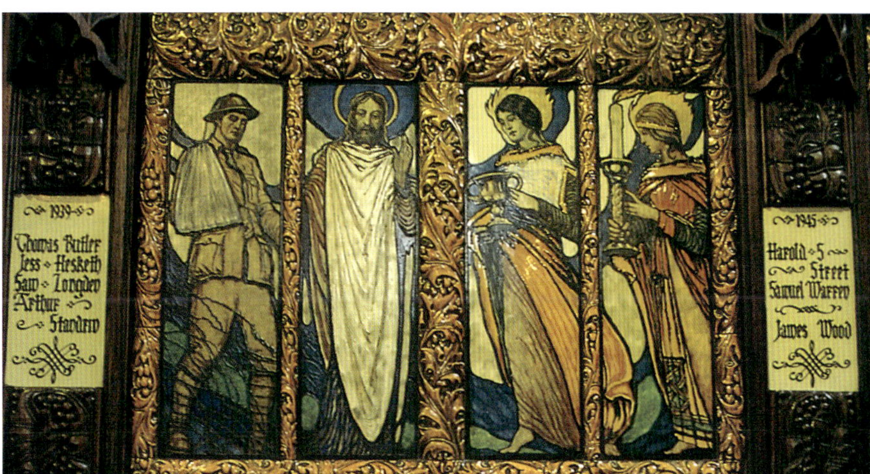

Congregation Church, Ashton under Lyne. Detail of the reredos designed by Gordon Forsyth, for Pilkington Tile Co., c. 1922.

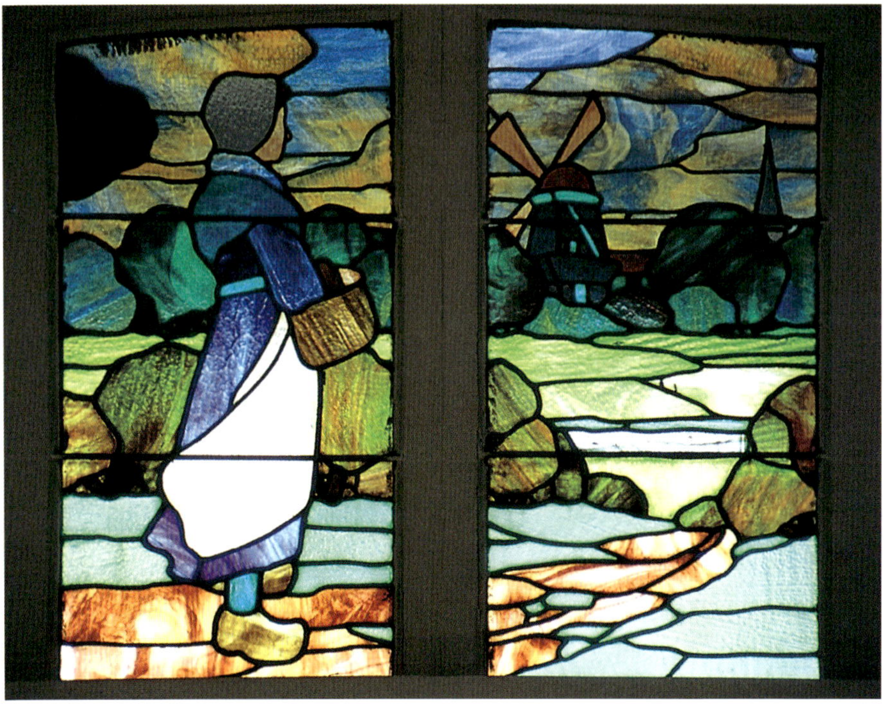

Tameside General Hospital. Stained glass panels by H. Fenton, c. 1909 for George Wragge Ltd.

chancel. The chapel in the south transept contains a much smaller, unattributed, but nevertheless beautiful memorial to members of the Hazelhurst Congregational Chapel who died in the Great War. It was brought here when that chapel closed.

The body of the church has a wide nave with very narrow aisles separated by arcades whose capitals, carved in various leafy designs, provide occasional surprises in the form of lurking birds or squirrels.

Access: Manse Tel. 0161–3390952.

Tameside General Hospital, (SJ954997) is situated to the north-east of the town centre off the A670, Mossley Rd. It was known as the Ashton Infirmary in 1908 when **George Wragge Ltd** of Salford was commissioned to supply decorative stained glass. This glass can still be seen. A very restful rural scene has been re-sited over a staircase in the main reception area of the Hartside Building, while another, in four panels, remains in situ over the entrance to the Darnton building. Two other panels have been re-leaded and re-fixed in this building but are obscured by false ceilings. *The Studio Year Book* for 1909 has an entry for **Harry Fenton** which refers to stained glass made for the infirmary and this is very probably it. The inner hall door at the Doctors' Home has stained glass incorporating the Glasgow rose device much loved by E. A. Taylor. He was Wragge's chief designer from 1906–10 but the windows are not quite in his style.

Access: The Fenton windows are in public reception areas of the hospital but the doctors' quarters are not accessible to the public.

ASHTON upon MERSEY is where the leafy southern fringe of Greater Manchester meets rural Cheshire.

St Martin's in Church Lane (SJ772929) is essentially a delicate C18 building which was given a sturdy but picturesque Jubilee tower by

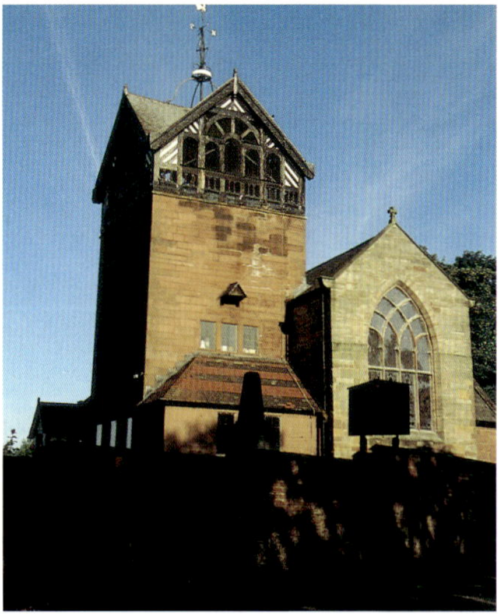

St Martin's, Ashton upon Mersey. Jubilee tower by George Truefitt, 1887.

George **Truefitt** in 1887. In the south porch there is a well-worked repoussé Great War Memorial made by **H. Webb** of Ashton upon Mersey. At the end of a list of some fifty men is the name of one woman.

Access: Vicarage Tel. 0161–9734204.

St Mary Magdalene's on Hamboro Rd (SJ775919) is an imposing stone building with an impressive spire. Internally it has an equally impressive three-light window by **Henry Holiday** at the east end of the north wall. It is the 'Presentation of the Holy Infant to Simeon' which dates from about 1890. There are two other windows in the same wall by **Powell of Whitefriars** who also made the glowing opus sectile figures in the chancel 1905–08. The ten saints in the chancel all have mother of pearl haloes and are set in sparkling gold mosaic. Looking down on this splendour from the north side of the chancel is one of **W. J. Pearce's** stained-glass Evangelists with rather Art Nouveau leading. On the west wall of the north transept is a bronze Great War Memorial made by **H. Webb** of Ashton upon Mersey.

Access: Parish Office Tel. 0161–2919283.

ATHERTON can be reached from Junction 4 or 5 on the M61 and a short ride on the A6 before heading south on the A579.

St John the Baptist, (SD676032) stands in Church St in the centre of Atherton proclaiming the town's late C19 affluence. It is an epic piece of **Paley & Austin** church building, executed in 1879 in two colours of stone with a massive tower on the south-west corner. The church was seriously damaged by fire in the early 1990s as a result of which the chancel screen now does duty as the reredos cutting off the east end of the church. The fire destroyed most of the stained glass in the church, but spared a two-light window made by **Edward Woore** in 1922. The window is now in the south aisle wall and has two angels looking down, one on Christ mistaken for the gardener by Mary Magdalene and the other on Jesus with the disciples on the road to Emmaus. It is a very engaging example of the artist's work.

Access: Rectory Tel. 01942–883359.

St Michael and All Angels, Howe Bridge, (SD665024) is a fine **Paley & Austin** church about ¾ mile south-west of Atherton centre on Leigh Rd. It was built in 1875 and is easily located by its flèche-cum-spirelet. Most of the stained glass is by Kempe but there is also an **Edward Woore** window. It appears in his entry in the *British Society of Master Glass Painters Catalogue of Work* (1929) as an east window at Howe Bridge made in 1922. The window is unmistakably by Edward Woore and the date is right but it is in the north transept. The colours are wonderful and show the boy Jesus working

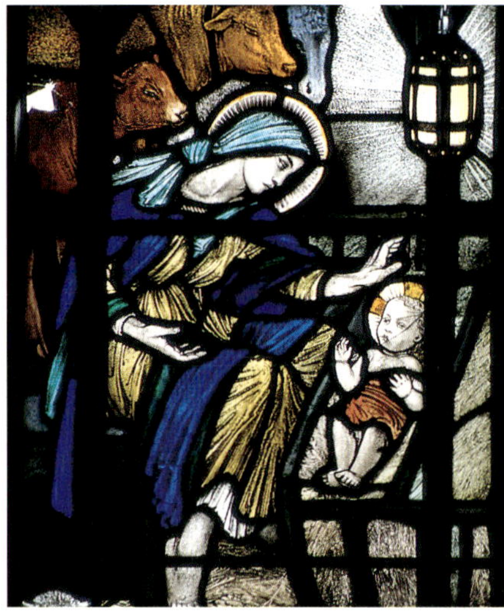

St Michael's, Howe Bridge, Atherton. Detail of 'Nativity' by Edward Woore, 1922.

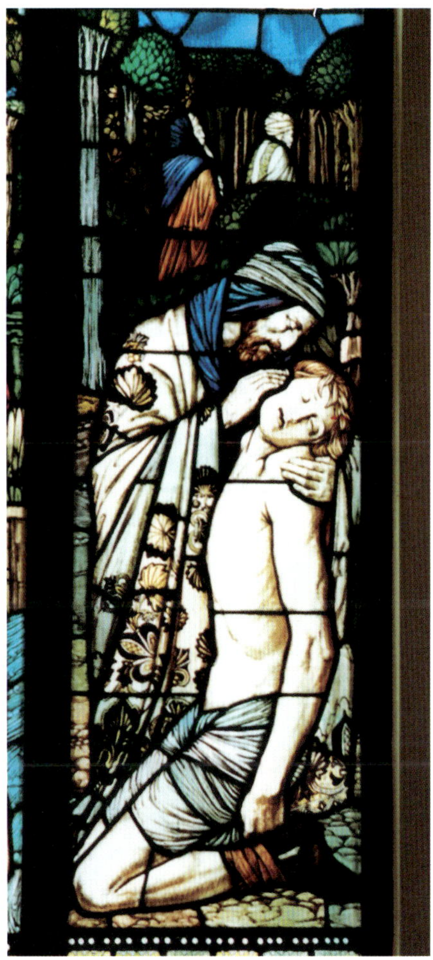

Baptist church, Atherton. Detail of the 'Good Samaritan' by R. A. Bell, 1904.

in the carpenter's shop on the left, a Nativity scene in the centre and Jesus arguing with the doctors of the law in the temple, on the right.

Access: Vicarage Tel. 01942–883359.

Atherton Baptist Church, Tyldsley Rd (SD684023) is a new building but the congregation had the perspicacity to bring a number of treasures with them when they moved in 1988. In addition to the finely carved pulpit, altar, sanctuary chairs and oak panelling which sit very well in the new building, they have saved and displayed a striking three-light window designed by **Robert Anning Bell**. The cartoon for the right hand panel, 'The Good Samaritan', was displayed at the Arts and Crafts Exhibition at the New Gallery, London in 1904 and reproduced in the Studio report of the exhibition. The central panel is the 'Baptism of Christ' while the left hand panel shows 'Dorcas' offering clothing to a naked child. In the tracery are three gorgeous, angelic musicians representing Faith, Hope and Charity. It is a very attractive window.

Access: Tel. church secretary 01942–883551.

BLACKLEY lies about 2 miles to the north of the Manchester city centre on the A664.

Most Holy Trinity in Cobden St (SD863019) was built in 1908 by **Basil Champneys** in red brick with lots of big, beefy buttresses. The chancel was never built and the open-keyed brickwork at the south-west corner is still waiting for the planned tower. Inside the church is tall, wide, light and airy and only slightly Gothic with five large five-light clerestory windows set above ten stone faced Gothic arches which stand, cloister like, along each side of the church and continue across the west end. The original stylish **Champneys** pulpit stands on the north side of the centre aisle. The altar is probably his too but the huge gilded and painted reredos came from the **Paley & Austin** church of St Lawrence in Morecambe. The priest's stall and the choir stalls look similar to those shown in a photograph dated 1909. However, another photograph taken in the 1950s shows obviously different furnishings from those in place today. Is Holy Trinity now on its third set of furnishings or have the Champneys originals been reinstalled?

Access: Vicarage Tel. 0161–2052879.

BLACKROD is about as far north as you get in Greater Manchester and sits either side of the B5408 about 2 miles south of Adlington, Lancashire.

St Katharine's in Black Horse St (SD613111) is an ancient church which was practically rebuilt, except for the tower, by **R. B. Preston** 1910. A more recent re-ordering of the interior has made substantial changes. The altar and reredos have been moved to convert the

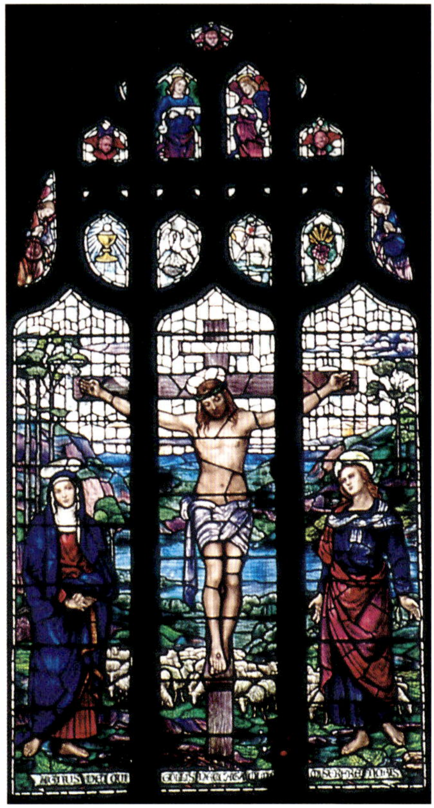

St Katherine's, Blackrod. East window by Mary Lowndes, 1914.

sanctuary to a Lady Chapel. The reredos has Arts and Crafts style painted and gilded panels which appear to have had some restoration, and the altar front has six painted-gesso saints. No information has yet come to light to suggest who executed them. 'The Crucifixion' in the east window is signed **M. Lowndes** and dated 1914. The 'St Cecilia' window in the south wall of the chancel is a superb piece made in the year 2000 by Linda Walton of Design Lights in a studio a quarter of a mile north-west of the church.

Access: Vicarage Tel. 01204–468150.

BOLTON straddles the A666 between Manchester and Blackburn. You need a good street map of Bolton and its surroundings. No churches are left open so you must telephone in advance.

St Thomas's, Eskrick St, off Halliwell Rd Halliwell, (SD708106) is a large impressive **Paley & Austin** basilica style church built in 1875. It is red brick inside and out with stone detailing. Its spare interior and the lightness created by the many clear-glass windows give a great sense of size and grandeur. The church has an interesting golden-oak altar made in the 1960s. It is set against the dark, Renaissance-style panelling carved in 1893 by **John Carlisle** of Barbon. The central panel over the altar recreates Leonardo da Vinci's 'The Last Supper' which is flanked on the north side by a panel showing Moses holding up the serpent of brass in the wilderness and on the south side by a panel representing Elijah fed by ravens. Beyond these panels are medallions bearing texts and beyond these are figures of the apostles and their symbols. Above the woodwork the east wall is decorated with raised panels of brickwork. At the centre of each panel is an encaustic tile decorated either with one of the Instruments of the Passion or with the emblem of one of the Evangelists. The very impressive east end is set off by the three-light east window which has clear glass in the side lights and Christ in Glory above a crucifixion in the centre. The window was made by **Powell of Whitefriars** in 1906.

Access: Vicarage Tel. 01204–387303.

St Simon and St Jude, Rishton Lane, Great Lever (SD717073) was built in 1901 by **R. K. Freeman** and has an impressive reredos designed by the architect and executed under his supervision by local craftsmen. The church has a good collection of marching banners including one for the Girls' Friendly Society by Miss **A. Burge** of London which is very attractive.

Access: Vicarage Tel. 01204–691539.

Christ Church is in Stitch mi' Lane, Harwood (SD748110). This small stone church built in 1840 is home to a three-light window designed

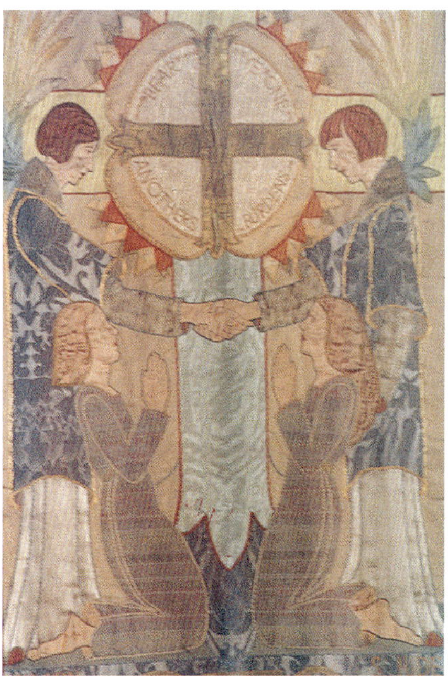

Ss Simon and Jude, Bolton. Girls Friendly Society Banner by Miss A. Burge, 1932.

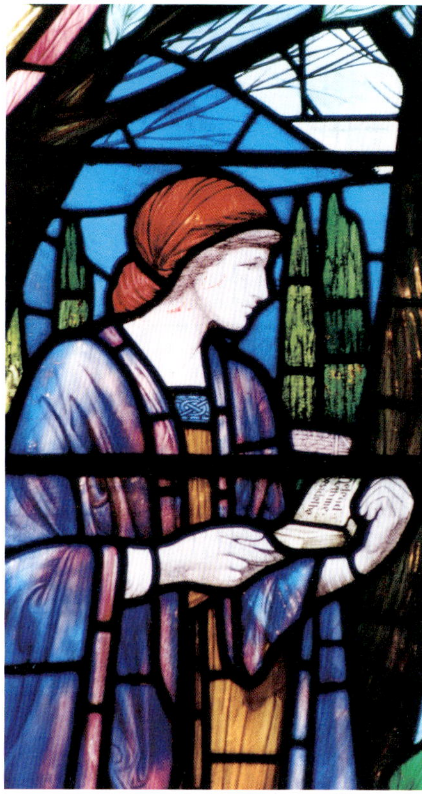

Christ Church, Harwood, Bolton. Detail of the east window by S. Meteyard, 1921.

by the painter **Sydney Meteyard**. It was made by **H. H. Martyn** in 1921 with rich colours and beautiful figures quoting from the 23rd Psalm.

Access: Vicarage Tel. 01204–525196.

St Stephen and all the Martyrs, Radcliffe Rd Leverbridge (SD733085) is the first of the two 'pot churches' designed by **Edmund Sharpe** in the 1840s. It is made of terracotta blocks which from a short distance look like pale, golden, Cotswold stone. Much of the interior is also unexpectedly made of baked clay, including the pew ends and the panels in the pew backs, all apparently beautifully carved and more deceiving now that the pews have been stripped and are all a golden pine. The dado is also of terracotta as is the crossing arch which is lined with hand painted tiles. The stained-glass windows all depict the lives of the Christian martyrs including the west-most in the north aisle which shows King Charles I about to be beheaded. But the best of the glass is the two-light window in the north aisle, not of an English Martyr, but of John the Baptist and Salome, designed by **Henry Holiday** in 1884. The pulpit is not 'pot' but really is made of wood and bears some Arts and Crafts influence.

Access: Vicarage Tel. 01204–528300.

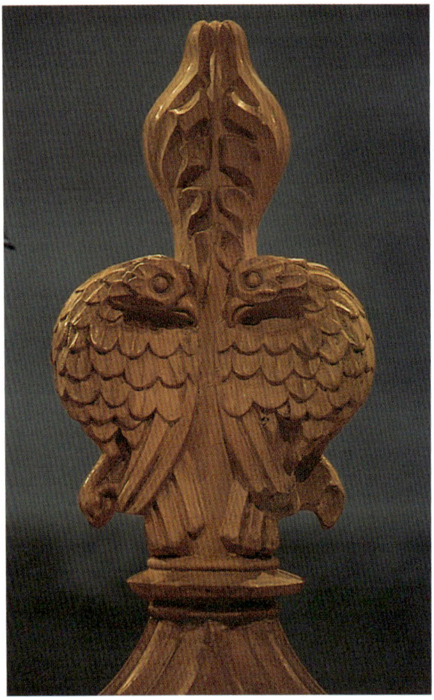

St Stephen and the Martyrs', Leverbridge, Bolton. Terracotta poppy head. E. Sharpe, c. 1845.

St Augustine of Canterbury, Thicketford Rd Tonge Moor, (SD729103) was built by **R. K. Freeman** 1880–86. It has a very elegant interior with a later and rather dominating gilded reredos. Above the reredos is the magnificent five-light east window designed by **Henry Holiday** and made in 1921. Binoculars are a decided advantage here in order to see the detail. **Holiday** had been designing windows for almost 60 years by 1921 and this window is as fresh as any of his work. Three of the small two-light windows in the south aisle were also designed by Holiday in 1921.

Access: Vicarage Tel. 01204–523899.

The Congregational Church and **Manse** in Blackburn Rd (SD716106) were built by **Jonathan Simpson** 1895. The church is now an antiques centre going under the name of '**The Iron Church**'. It still has stained glass in the apse at the east end in which three pairs of lights show 'The Nativity', 'The Crucifixion' and 'The Ascension'. A. L. Baldry's list of the work of **Henry Holiday** prepared in 1930 records three chancel windows with these topics made in 1899–1900 for 'a church at Bolton, Lancashire' and these are unmistakably **Holiday's**. At the opposite end of the church there is a five-light window with single lancets on either side made by **Reuben Bennett** *c.* 1895 and signed by **H. G. Hiller**.

Access: The centre is open seven days a week from 10.00 to 17.00. Tel. 01204–383616.

Smithills Hall off Smithills Hall Rd (SD700118) dates from the mid C14 since when it has undergone a series of additions and alterations. In 1870, the owners engaged **George Devey** to complete its transformation into a C19 country house. He remodelled the C16 west wing, increasing its height to provide servants' quarters, while making additions to the western and northern sides to produce a rambling 'been here for ever' look. Across the stream from the house he built the coach house and stable block which is now a restaurant. The tour of the Hall is very interesting in both the mediaeval and Victorian sections of the house. Note the reproduction **Morris & Co.** wallpapers and the genuine **William De Morgan** tiles.

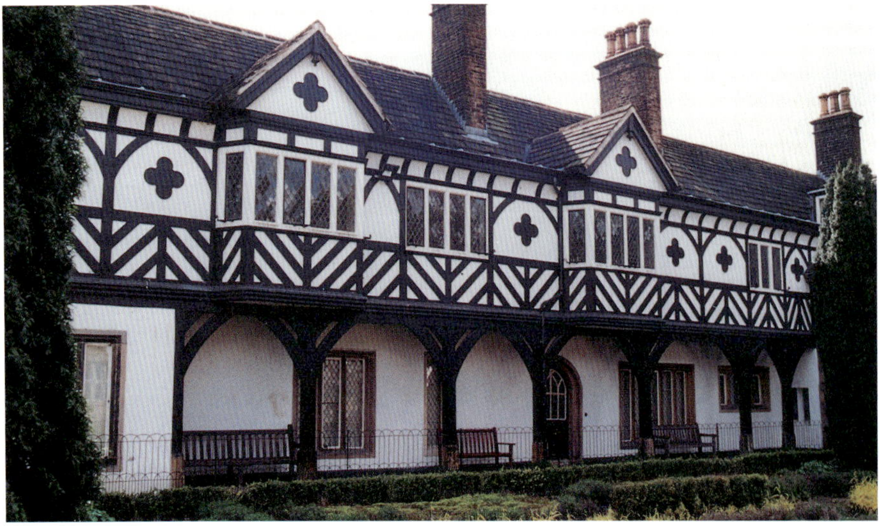

Smithills Hall. West wing remodelled by George Devey, c. 1872.

Access: 1 Apr–30 Sept, Tues–Sat 11.00 –17.00 and Sun 14.00–17.00. 1 Oct–31 Mar, Tues and Sat 13.00–17.00 and Sun 14.00–17.00. Open Bank Holiday Mondays. Admission charges. Tel. 01204–332377.

The Great War Memorial stands in front of the impressive Town Hall in **Victoria Square.** (SD717092) It takes the form of a small silver-grey granite arch set over a bronze cross overlaid with a sword. There is a bronze group on either side of the arch modelled by **Walter Marsden.** On the left is 'Peace' restraining the virile youth of the town anxious to rally to the flag. On the right 'Peace' cradles the body of a dead youth representing the sacrifice of those who were killed. The structure, by Gass and Hope, was unveiled in 1928 and Marsden's sculptured groups were added in 1932.

To the north of the Town Hall steps is the bronze statue of Lt Col Sir B. A. Dobson (1847–98) who was four times Mayor of Bolton. The sculptor was **John Cassidy** 1900.

Queen's Park, (SD707093) has a stone statue of Dr James Dorrian commemorating 'a life of usefulness'. It was made in 1898 by **John Cassidy** and is now placed in the bushes on the top terrace and is a little the worse for wear.

BOWDON is south of Altrincham and is reached via the A56 (when it is called Dunham Rd), or by the B5161 (turn up Stamford Rd).

The Church of St Mary the Virgin (SJ759868) is a large, historic, sandstone church rebuilt several times. The woodwork of the pulpit, choir and clergy stalls were designed by **Temple Lushington Moore.**

Access: Vicarage Tel. 0161–9282468.

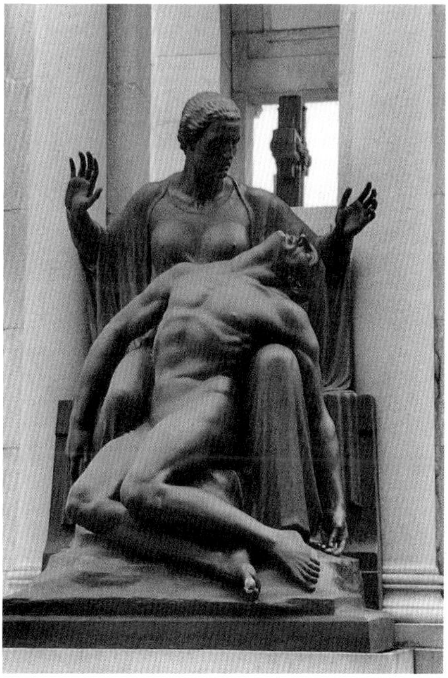

Bolton Great War Memorial. 'Peace and Sacrifice' by Walter Marsden, 1932.

BRAMHALL lies to the south of Stockport and to the east of Cheadle Hulme.

Bramall Hall, off Hall Rd (SJ890864) sits in its park as it has done since the C15. It was extended in the C16 and altered by the Victorians but it remains reputedly one of the best timber-framed buildings in England and there is much to enjoy in that respect. The house was in a poor state when **George Faulkner Armitage** was engaged by a new owner, Charles Nevill, to carry out repairs and to make some changes to the house. The December 1884 edition of the *Cabinet Maker & Art Furnisher* devoted six pages of highly complimentary text and illustrations to the work done at the Hall. **Armitage** designed the oak surround to the great fireplace in the hall and fitted the copper hood above the grate. He also designed the wrought-iron light brackets, bell pull and door furniture in the hall and throughout the house. The banqueting hall has a fireplace designed by **Armitage** but apparently incomplete in its decoration. The table and chairs in this room, designed by **A. W. N. Pugin** and made by Crace, were brought here from nearby Abney Hall. On the wall is a huge and well-framed painting by **Herbert Schmalz** which was commissioned for the house by Charles Nevill in 1886. It presents the poignant scene of a Viking queen meeting a group of warriors carrying her husband's cloak and helm on a litter. **Armitage** added a bay on the south side of the chapel where the west wall still has very faint but original pre-Reformation wall paintings and later black letter texts. The large painting on the north wall of the sanctuary 'Mary Magdalene and the Risen Christ in the Garden' is by **Herbert Schmalz** and dated 1896. The south staircase was designed by **Armitage** in 1887 and he continued the chapel bay upwards as an addition to what was then the main bedroom and later became a billiard room. The fireplace, panelling and wall lights are by **Armitage** while the inlaid tables and the credenza are by Crace after **A. W. N. Pugin's** designs. The credenza displays four Bernard Moore pots dated 1905–15, three **Pilkington Royal Lancastrian** pieces and one **Ruskin Pottery** bottle-vase. **Herbert Schmalz** painted the portrait in the south bay and he has three lithographs as well as two sketches in oils on the walls of the billiard room. These were done in the Holy Land, preparatory to undertaking paintings on Biblical themes. The brass firedogs in the drawing room are by **Armitage.** On the top floor of the house he created a boudoir for Mary Nevill, the chatelaine, in 1891 (if the date on the fireplace is to be believed). He also provided a built-in day-bed and extravagant

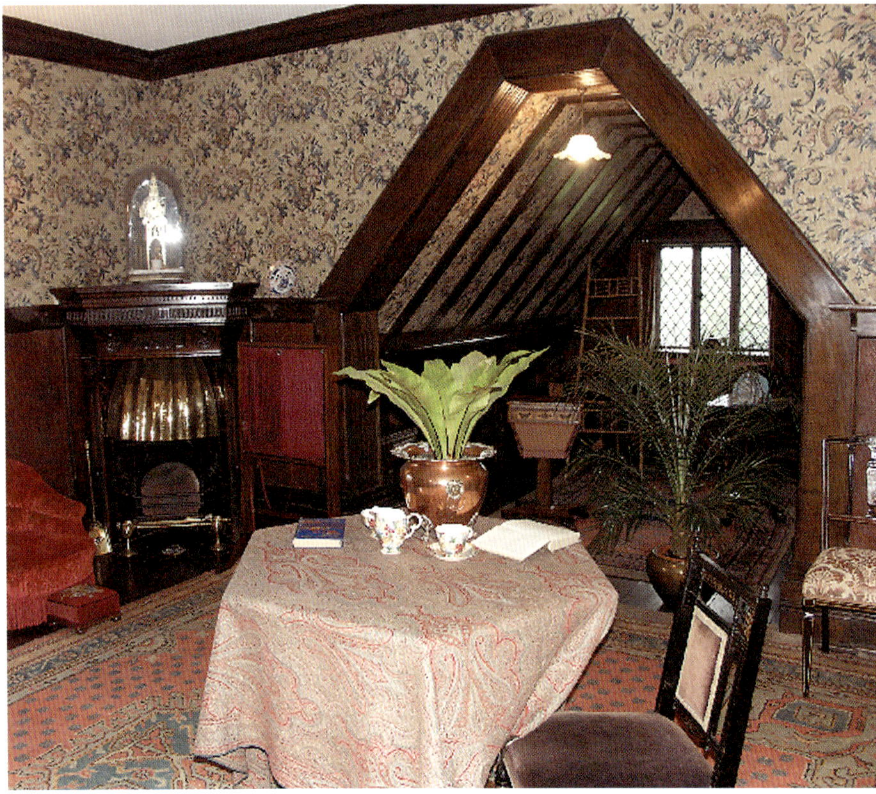

Bramall Hall, Bramhall. Mary Nevill's boudoir by G. F. Armitage, c. 1887. *Courtesy of Stockport MBC. Photo © Howard J. Green*

hinges for the door. The central staircase was reconstructed by Armitage and provided with very decorative wrought-iron rope brackets.

Access: Good Fri –30 Sept open daily 1.00–17.00 (11.00–17.00 on Bank Hols) 1 Oct–1 Jan open Tues–Sun 13.00–16.00 (Bank Hols 11.00–16.00). 2 Jan–Maundy Thurs open Sat and Sun only 13.00–16.00. Last visits should begin no later than an hour before closing time. Tel. 0161–4853708.

Holly Cottage, (SJ891842) is at the corner of Holly Rd, and Woodford Rd. It was built in 1905 by **Edgar Wood** for his friend and fellow member of the Northern Art Workers' Guild, the printer H. C. D. Chorlton and is still an attractive building although additions and alterations have been made.

Access: Private house.

BROOKLANDS is the residential area south of Manchester that lies between Sale and Timperley east of the Bridgewater Canal.

St John the Divine, Brooklands Rd (SJ789903) was built in 1864–68 by Alfred Waterhouse at the expense of Samuel Brooks, a Manchester banker. The church has a polychrome brick interior and a sparkling mosaic-tiled sanctuary. The window in the south wall, depicting Christ's Ascension accompanied by pink-winged angels, was made by **Morris & Co.** in 1897 using **Burne-Jones** cartoons. **Daniel Cottier's** 'Faith, Hope and Charity' window was unfortunately covered up when the organ was moved to its present position. The wrought-iron chancel screen was designed by **Henry Wilson** and installed by Jones and Willis in 1907.

Access: Vicarage Tel. 0161–9735947.

BURNAGE is about 3 miles south-east of Manchester city centre just to the east of the A34.

St Margaret's church in Burnage Lane (SJ866927) is a plain and simple building by **Paley & Austin** dating from 1875. There are three windows in the chancel, all made by **W. J. Pearce** as memorials of the Great War. It has to be said that they are not among his best work. The **Shrigley & Hunt** window in the south aisle and their painted reredos, on the other hand, are excellent. The decorative opus sectile panel on the north wall records the names of those killed in the Great War and was made by **W. J. Pearce**. There are interesting windows here designed by **Thomas Willford** of Brabyns Studio in Marple.

Access: Parish Office; open Tues and Fri. Tel. 0161–4324606.

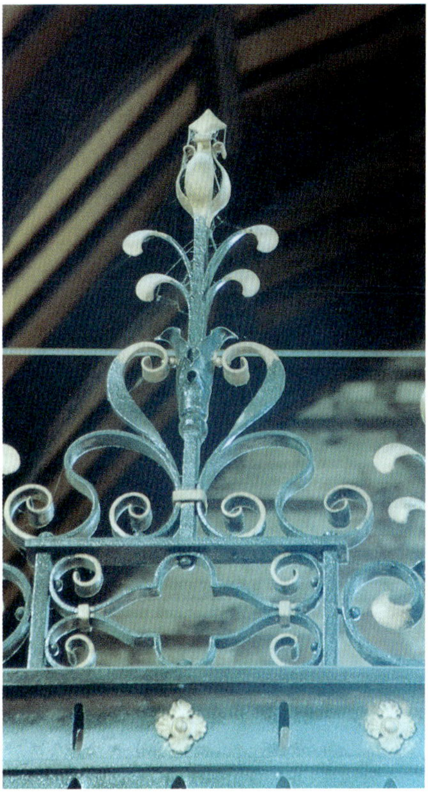

St John, Brooklands. Detail of the wrought-iron screen by Henry Wilson.

BURY stands at the junction of the A56 and the A58.

The Art Gallery, Museum and Library building is at the corner of Moss St and Manchester Rd (SD803106). It was built by **Woodhouse & Willoughby** 1899–1901. Decidedly 'artistic' says Pevsner, with excellent stained glass throughout the building by **W. J. Pearce**. The carving was done by **J. J. Millson** as was that on the building of the Technical School in Broad St. In the entrance hall of the Gallery is a maquette of a bronze of Charles S. Keene made by **George Frampton** in 1896. The gallery also has a collection of **Pilkington's Lancastrian Ware** and paintings by **G. F. Watts**, J. C. Horsley and E. A. Hornel as well as Turner and Lowry. The gallery is well known for its excellent and regular exhibitions.

Access: Open Tues–Fri. 10.00–17.00; Sat 10.00–16.30; Sun 13.00–16.00. Admission free, Tel. 0161–2535878.

The **Great War Memorial** in Market Place (SD804108) was designed by **Reginald Blomfield** and unveiled in 1924. It has two very large bronze reliefs by **Herman Cawthra** showing processions of military and civilian occupations. The **Lancashire Fusiliers Memorial** at Wellington Barracks (SD788102) was designed by **E. L. Lutyens** in 1922. It takes the form of an obelisk flanked by the colours of the Lancashire Fusiliers. The flags pass for fabric but are in fact painted and gilded stone. **George Frampton** was responsible for **The Lancashire Fusiliers South African War Memorial** in Whitehead Gardens (SD802104) which has the bronze figure of a Fusilier waving his busby. The gardens also house a whimsical **Clock Tower** designed by **Maxwell & Tuke**.

The John Kay Memorial stands near the bus station in Haymarket St (SD804106). It is an elaborate memorial to the inventor of the 'flying shuttle' who was born near Bury. It is an Italianate domed octagon with eight granite columns between which are bronze relief panels. One is a medallion of John Kay and two others depict looms. On the dome, a favourite haunt of pigeons, is the bronze figure of 'Fame' surrounded by smaller beautifully sculpted figures representing Agriculture, Engineering, Mining and Weaving. The sculpture is by **John Cassidy** and was unveiled in 1908.

CHADDERTON lies midway between Oldham and Middleton on the A669.

Manor Villas, at 1092–1104 Middleton Rd (SD894059) is a simple terrace of little houses designed by **Edgar Wood** in 1907. They have been much changed and are looking a bit ragged.

Access: Private dwellings.

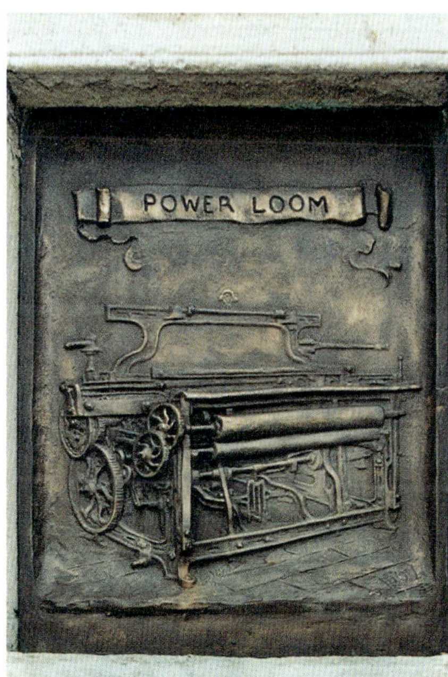

Kay Memorial, Haymarket St, Bury. Power loom panel by John Cassidy, 1908.

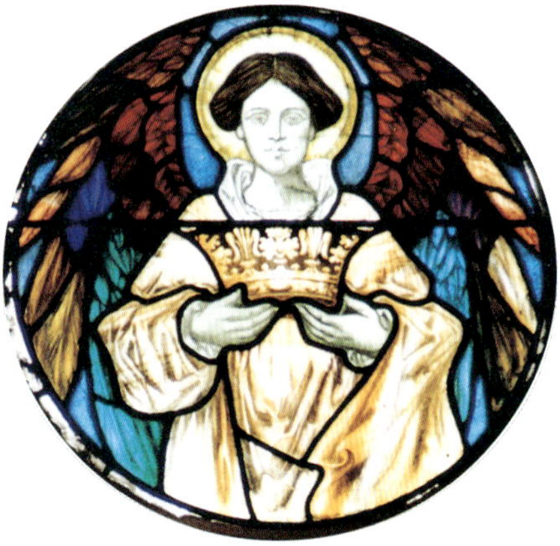

Christ Church, Chadderton. Detail of the 'Ainley memorial' window, c.1902.

Christ Church, on the corner of Washbrook and Block Lane, (SD908041) was built in 1870 by Henry Ainley. He died in 1902 and is commemorated in the choir stalls and in a stained-glass window at the west end of the church. The window is unsigned but its designer has a liking for sophisticated angels. There is a window by **W. J. Pearce** in the north wall depicting the parable of the talents. A picture of this window was reproduced in the report of his lecture to the Institute of British Decorators in London 1913.

Access: Vicarage Tel. 01616–242326 .

The **Great War Memorial** outside the Town Hall in Middleton Rd (SD910054) was designed by

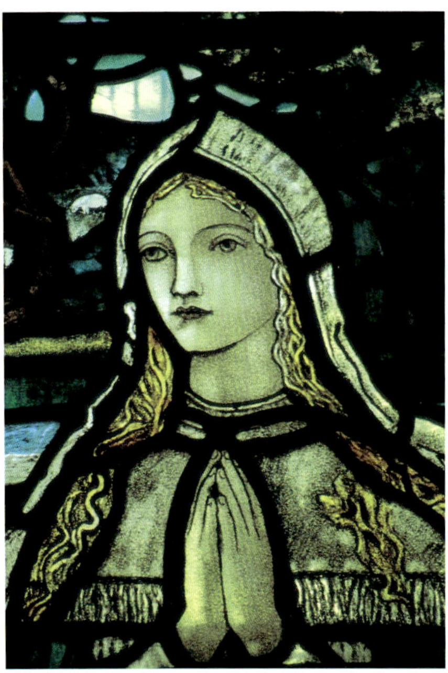

St Mary, Cheadle. Detail of the south transept south window. Veronica Whall, 1924.

the local architects Taylor & Simister and unveiled in 1921. A single soldier, executed in bronze by **Albert Toft** stands in mourning guarding the cenotaph.

CHEADLE lies just to the south of junction 3 of the M60.

St Mary's in High St (SJ856886) is a C16 church. The Brereton Chapel at the end of the south aisle has a beautiful five-light window made *c.* 1917 by **Christopher Whall** showing Christ as Salvator Mundi supported by Faith and Hope. In the south wall of the chapel is a very attractive window, made after 1921, by **Veronica Whall**. Its sparkle is somewhat dampened by the overgrown shrubs outside the window. The beautifully modelled bronze panel on the north wall is a memorial to those who died in the Great War and is unsigned.

Access: Parish Office Tel. 0161–4288050.

CHEADLE HULME is on the southern fringe of the Manchester conurbation west of Bramhall and east of the A34.

All Saints in Church Rd (SJ877856) was built and extended 1868–73 by **James Medland Taylor**. However, later additions and the collapse of the tower detract from the lines of Taylor's grey stone building. Internally he has been his eclectic self, showing little regard for the High Gothic vogue for adherence to 'style'. There are two two-light windows filled with the work of **H. G. Hiller**. David and Jonathan (dedication 1920) are in the third window from the east end of the south-aisle wall while St Michael and St George (dedication 1914) are in the west wall of the baptistery.

Access: Vicarage Tel. 0161–4853455.

The Great War Memorial was unveiled in 1921 and stands in its tiny but well-maintained garden at the busy junction of Manor Rd and Ravenoak Rd (SJ880861). It is a decorated red-sandstone cross bearing small bronze figures of a soldier and a sailor set in niches high on the shaft. Beneath them on three sides are bronze panels bearing the names of those who died. The panel on the fourth side bears the badge of Chester County Palatine. The monument was designed by **Arthur Beresford Pite** and the bronze figures were executed by Benjamin Clemens.

CLAYTON is about a mile west of Manchester city centre and lies between the River Medlock and the Ashton Canal.

St Cross, Ashton New Rd (SJ880985) was built by **William Butterfield** in 1863. It is one of only three examples of his work in the North West. It is a large dark-brick church with a tall slender tower with a pyramid roof. Inside, there is typical Butterfield polychrome brickwork, high clerestory windows and a well-decorated

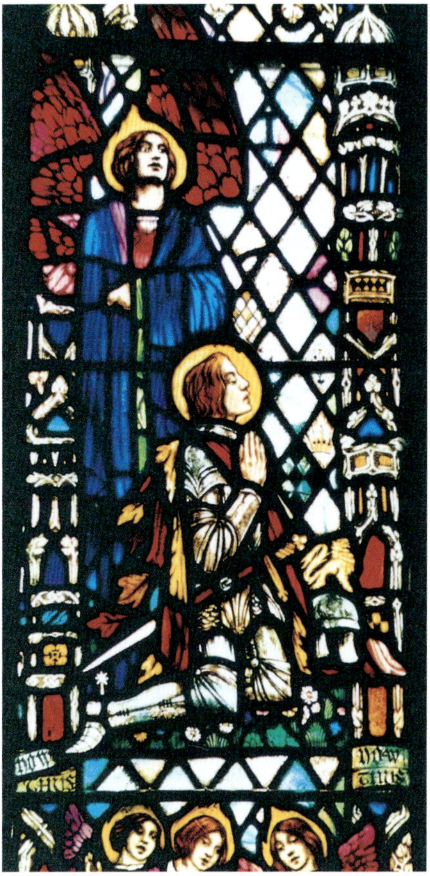

St Anne, Clifton. Pilkington memorial. Designed by G. Forsyth and executed by W. J. Pearce, 1916.

sanctuary which makes use of a variety of materials including many kinds of marble in the reredos and gilded and stencilled patterned work on the walls. The painted Stations of the Cross were brought here 'from a Liverpool church' – unsigned and undated but splendid.

Access: Rectory Tel. 0161–2230766.

CLIFTON village lies on the northern fringe of the Manchester conurbation and stretches out along the A666 south of the M60.

St Anne's Church, (SD776035) is just north of junction 16 of the M60 on the eastern side of Manchester Rd and was built in 1874 by E. M. Barry. It has a superb little two-light memorial window in the south wall of the nave which was designed and painted by **Gordon M. Forsyth** and made by **W. J. Pearce** in 1916. The window, dedicated to Captain Pilkington who was killed in the Dardenelles in 1915, is described in the March 1916 edition of *The Studio*. The design was carried out by Pearce using very small, very colourful and very knobbly pieces of Prior's glass. This combination produces wonderfully rich and varied colour effects which add to the emotional power of the window. In the north wall is another two-light memorial window, made this time by **George Wragge Ltd.** It is dedicated to another son of the village who was killed in the battle of the Somme in 1916. While it may be thought less beautiful than the Pilkington window it is nevertheless very powerful in its effect.

Access: Vicarage Tel. 0161–7941939.

DAISY HILL is about a mile south of Westhoughton on the B5235 (Lower Leigh Rd).

St James's (SD658043) is a big, red-brick, **Paley & Austin** church which is recognisable from a great distance by its extraordinary bell tower which is crowned with a golden cockerel. Internally, the simplicity of the church is an ideal setting for the huge and beautiful six-light east window made by **Morris and Co.** in 1897. The two central panels give **Burne-Jones's** version of an alfresco visit by the Magi to Mary, Joseph and the infant Jesus who are attended by four admiring young angels. The other panels show James, Peter, Paul and John topped and tailed by Morris's wonderful silvery-green intertwining foliage. Below the window and across the full width of the sanctuary are the nine painted panels of the reredos. The reredos case was designed by **Austin & Paley** in 1922 and apparently made in Leicestershire. William Waters in *Stained Glass from Shrigley & Hunt* credits A. C. Weatherstone of **Shrigley & Hunt** with the painting in 1924. It is painted in a Pre-Raphaelite manner with a central crucifixion scene flanked by angels and archangels. The muted colours of the figures are set off by the golden background of the panels. The reredos combined with the east window produces a glorious effect in the chancel.

Access: Vicarage Tel. 01942–813155.

DENSHAW is a village on the north-east rural fringe of the Manchester conurbation, about 3 miles east of Junction 21 on the M62 via the A640.

Christ Church, (SD976106) stands in the middle of the village and is blessed with a powerful west window made by **W. J. Pearce** *c.* 1911. It depicts 'Christ in Glory' surrounded by a wondrous throng of angels and saints.

Access: Vicarage Tel. 01457–874575.

DIDSBURY lies south of Manchester north of the M60 and west of the A34.

Emmanuel Church, Barlow Moor Rd (SJ846914) has been renowned for many years as the home of the BBC Radio 4 *Morning Service*. It was built in 1858 and has been much changed since then. In what used to be the south transept is a three-light **Morris & Co.** window showing

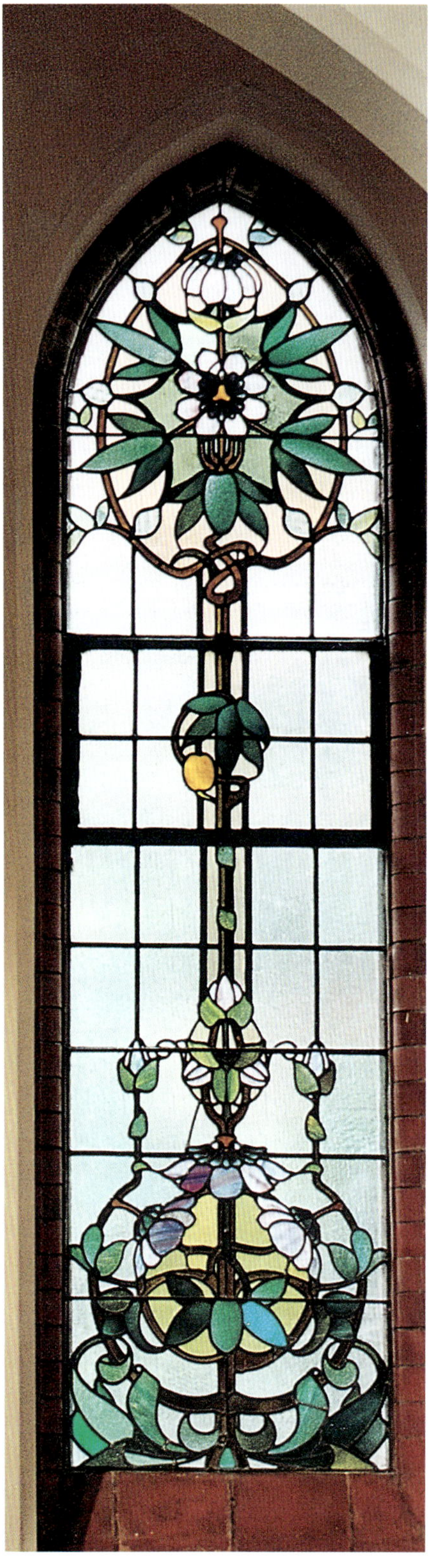

Grosvenor St Aidan, Didsbury. Floral design by W. J. Pearce, c. 1913.

'The Salvator Mundi' flanked by angels bearing scrolls. What used to be the Lady Chapel has been divided horizontally without a thought to the value of its stained glass. The lower part of the chapel has been converted to a kitchen and has the benefit of the bottom half of **W. J. Pearce's** 'Good Shepherd' window. The top half is in the loft and accessible by ladder.

Access: The Parish Office is at 6 Barlow Moor Rd. Tel. 0161–4457863.

Grosvenor St Aidan's (SJ842917) stands on the corner of Palatine Rd and Parkfield Rd South. It is a solid, rose-pink brick building which survived a very substantial fire in 1992. The miracle in that event was that despite considerable damage to the nave roof, the stained glass was substantially unaffected. The east window is post-1945 by Powell of Whitefriars but the remainder is vintage **W. J. Pearce** from 1913. The firm was at its best dealing with imaginative floral designs and this church surely has some of the best of them. The west window contains two panels moved from the east end of the church when the Powell windows were installed and have been reduced to fit the smaller window openings. They have portraits of St Aidan and St Columba in the central panels. The north and south transepts each have two tall two-light windows containing oak leaves and acorns, mistletoe and berries, ivy leaves and berries and date palms. The emblems of the four Evangelists appear in the tracery. The nave has four pairs of lancets on each side with remarkable plant and flower designs. A wide variety of colours, streaky and textured glass has been used to produce the most wonderful effects. All of the plant forms in the windows were chosen for their symbolism. For example, in the north aisle the panels are based on the daisy (innocence), the rose (martyrdom and purity), the periwinkle (eternal life) and the pansy (rememberance and meditation), while the south side is based on the Madonna lily (purity and chastity), the anemone (sorrow and death), the gentian (humility) and the iris (sword-lily symbol of the Virgin Mary).

There are two windows in the vestry containing panels which look as if they have been brought from elsewhere and set in new surrounds by **W. J. Pearce**. Among the memorials on the south wall of the south transept is a bronze tablet by **George Wragge Ltd** commemorating Peter Dunn, the first minister of the church, who died in 1916. The Great War memorial is a repoussé copper panel signed by **James Smithies** of Wilmslow. The pulpit is a later introduction to the church with an excellent carved frieze showing the Dove of the Spirit against the true vine.

Access: Open on Heritage open days. Church Secretary Tel. 0161–8605493.

ECCLES is on the A57 just south of the only junction on the M602.

The Great War Memorial stands in the square outside Eccles's fine library in Church St (SJ778985). It was designed by **John Cassidy** and unveiled in 1925. A bronze 'Victory' stands atop the Portland stone column holding out a palm in her right hand. On the front of the shaft is a bronze relief panel showing a soldier in mourning with reversed arms. Above him is the simple inscription 'Pax'.

FAIRFIELD is in north-east Manchester between Droylsden and Ashton under Lyne.

Fairfield Moravian Settlement (SJ904977) was founded in 1785 and stands between the Ashton canal and the A635. It is an unbelievably tranquil place. **Edgar Wood** and **Henry Sellers** were asked to add forty-six houses to the village in 1914. Their houses line the northern side of Broadway North in two series each numbered, confusingly enough, 1 to 23. While they show some allegiance to the Georgian style they also show how that style was susceptible to simple but effective development into a mild Art Deco.

Access: Private housing.

GATLEY lies south of the M60 and west of the A34.

St James Church, Church Rd, at Gatley Green (SJ843883) was built 1880–81 by **J. M. & H. Taylor**. They clearly did not have a big budget but managed to produce a picturesque brick and slate church on what at the time, would have been a rural village green. The church declares its personality with an elegant square tower with saddleback roof surmounted by a brilliant weather cock. There is an external staircase giving access to the tower and an apse at both the east and west ends. There is a long and flared slope to the roof and the relatively low lancet windows are separated by buttresses. It is said that the bricks were made locally from clay, excavated from the site and that the wood for the roof timbers was felled locally. Internally the church is very plain with the exposed red brickwork lightened by a double band of off-white bricks running around the nave and by the use of alternate white bricks in the arches. Typically for J. M. Taylor there is a liberal sprinkling of biblical quotations throughout the building.

Access: Vicarage Tel. 0161–4284764.

HALE is on the southern fringe of the conurbation, north of the M60 and south-east of Altrincham.

Royd House, number **224 Hale Rd**, (SJ784867) was built between 1914 and 1916 by **Edgar Wood** for himself. It has a concave two-storey front, a flat roof and a colourful but totally unexpected mosaic panel above the entrance door. 'Jazzy' said Pevsner and who can think of a more appropriate word? Royd House was his last project in this very leafy suburb where the hedges and shrubberies have seriously reduced the passer-by's view of the remainder of his work here. He began in 1891 with **Halecroft** on Hale Rd and followed that between 1901 and 1907 with **226 Hale Rd** and numbers **116, 117, 119**, and **121 Park Rd** together with **20** and **27 Plane Tree Rd**. Pevsner tells us on the advice of

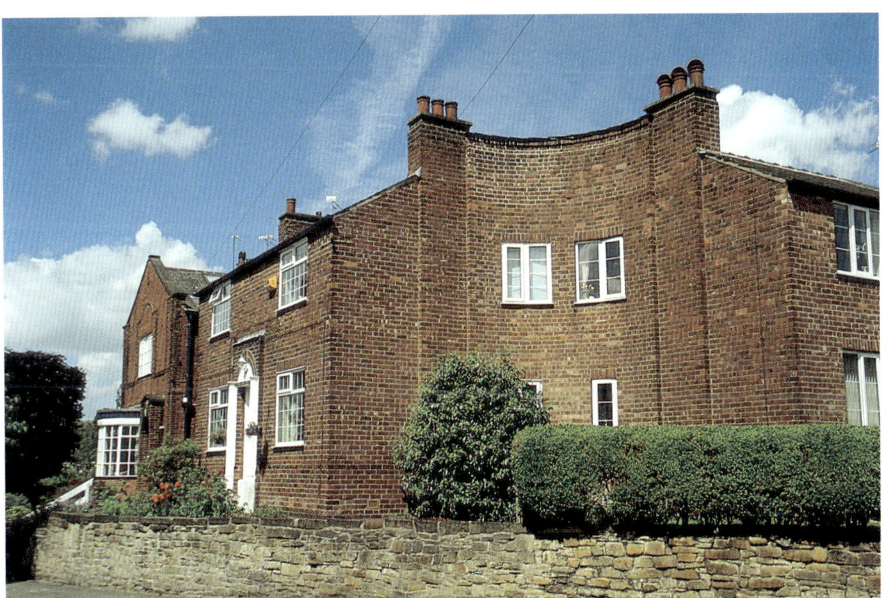

Fairfield Moravian Settlement. Houses in Broadway North by Wood and Sellers, c. 1914.

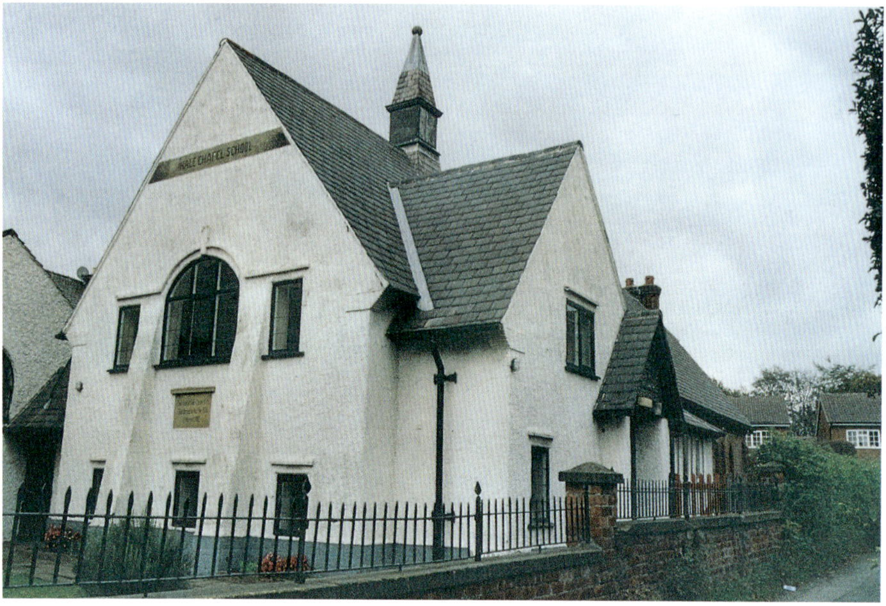

Hale Chapel School, Halebarns. Extended by F. B. Dunkerley, 1910.

John H. G. Archer that **John Cocker** of Timperley designed **223–233 Hale Rd** 1907–08. Just far enough away from all this activity, **Frank B. Dunkerley** built his own Tudoresque house, **Graythwaite**, in Barrow Lane in about 1910.

Access: All of these houses are private residences.

HALEBARNS lies on the A538 between Altrincham and Wilmslow.

Hale Unitarian Chapel, in Chapel Lane (SJ791854) is a delightful little C18 chapel which sits in its own tranquil garden and has the charm of simplicity with its polished oak and just one stained-glass window. This three-light east window was made in 1906 by **Morris & Co.** In the central light **Burne-Jones** has drawn a very curvaceous Charity mothering six cherubic children, four of whom are cavorting around her feet. She is accompanied in the lights on either side by two smaller, slighter, musical angels designed by **William Morris**.

Access: Tel. 01625–526445.

Hale Chapel School on Hale Rd (SJ794857) was greatly enlarged in 1910. The front extension, with its interesting roof-line, white harled walls, prominent buttresses and intriguing, decorative architectural detail, was designed by Frank B. Dunkerley.

Access: The building is used for community activities Tel. 01625–526445.

HAUGHTON lies between Denton and Hyde on the eastern side of the Manchester conurbation, overlooking the Tame valley.

St Anne's stands in St Anne's Drive (SJ934956) next to Junction 2 on the M67. The church is described in the Register of Listed Buildings as a 'Cruciform church without aisles. Organ chamber and vestry in eastern angles. Tower porch in southwest angle and a further south

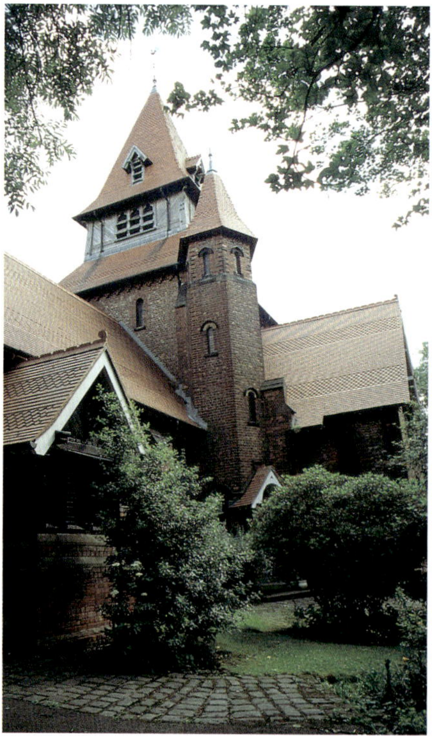

St Anne, Haughton by J. M. Taylor, 1882.

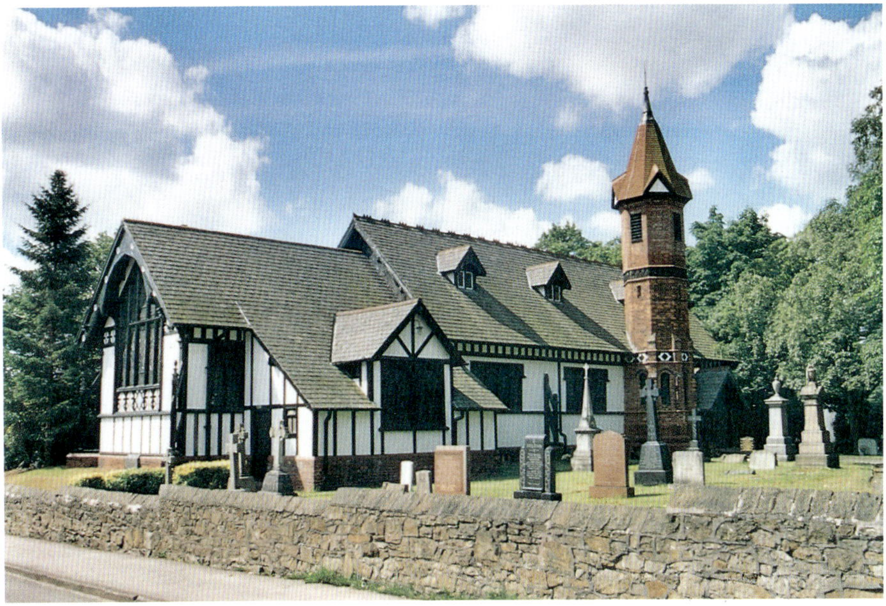

St Mary, Haughton Green by J. M. Taylor, 1876.

porch. Large crossing-tower, roofed in two stages, has a stepped-in, half-timbered bell stage and a square, swept spire with lucarnes. Banded, tiled roofs, walls of polychrome brickwork with stone dressings. Pointed, projecting baptistery at west end. Varied window forms and tracery.' By the nature of things there are no superlatives in this official description but this is, nevertheless, a splendid building. It was built in 1882 by **James Medland Taylor**. The client, Joseph Sidebotham, gave him £10,000 to work with and he produced a wonderful and original building of great interest and beauty inside and out. In addition to having deep pockets and an interest in John Ruskin, the patron was an excellent photographer and some of his 120 year old pictures appear to great effect in the very comprehensive guide book published in 1982 by the Rector and Churchwardens. It says in the guide that all the windows were made by **Heaton, Butler & Bayne** and installed as a complete set when the church was built. They seem more domestic than ecclesiastical filled with delicate, golden tree and flower motifs. The War Memorial Chapel in the south transept was designed by Isaac Taylor in 1919. A beautifully embroidered Mother and Child has been salvaged from an altar frontal and remounted to form a very attractive reredos in the chapel. The mosaics in the church are by Salviati and the stonework to the font and reredos was carved by Earp & Co. of Manchester. The nearby rectory was also designed by **J. M. & Henry Taylor**.

Access: Vicarage Tel. 0161–3362374.

HAUGHTON GREEN is on the edge of Denton just across the valley from Gee Cross.

St Mary the Virgin, Meadow Lane (SJ933937) is a stunning church by **James Medland Taylor & Henry Taylor** which was built 1874–76. This church is half timbered 'Tudoresque' and incorporates James Medland Taylor's characteristic brick tower, cross-gabled south aisle, complex roof timbers, baptistery apse and wide chancel arch. The south-aisle arches are supported by wooden pillars and there are the remnants of moulded plasterwork by the chancel arch (roses) and over the baptistery (pomegranates and apples). The reredos is carved oak with stained floral panels which are said to be the work of local craftsmen. The beautifully carved processional cross was made in 1954. The plain, diamond leaded-lights in the nave and south aisle have coloured roundels bearing symbolic devices. The west window has fading Renaissance-like silver-stained plant forms. The glass is similar to that at the nearby St Anne's, Haughton which is attributed to **Heaton, Butler & Bayne**. The baptistery is now a book store and a well-carved and decorative font has been installed at the east end of the south aisle.

Access: Vicarage Tel. 0161–3364529.

HEATON MOOR lies west of the A6 about a mile north-west of Stockport centre.

Methodist church, Stanley Rd (SJ877916) is a modern building which replaced a Gothic church built in 1873. The west wall of the foyer is almost filled with a huge five-light window saved from the original church. It is

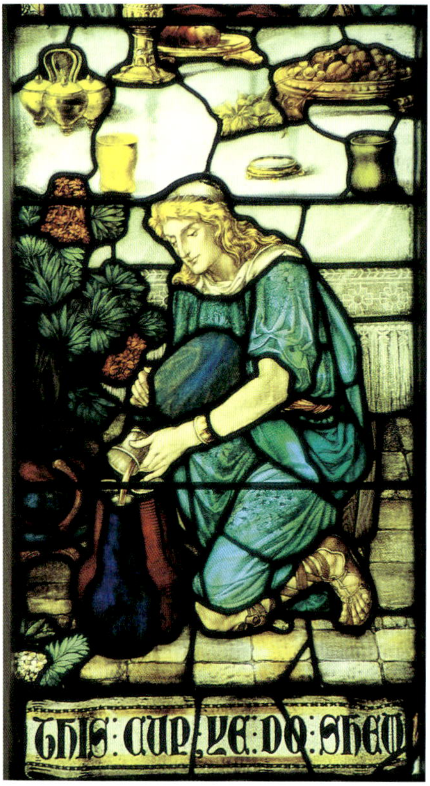

Methodist church, Heaton Moor. Detail of the foyer window by W. J. Pearce, Undated.

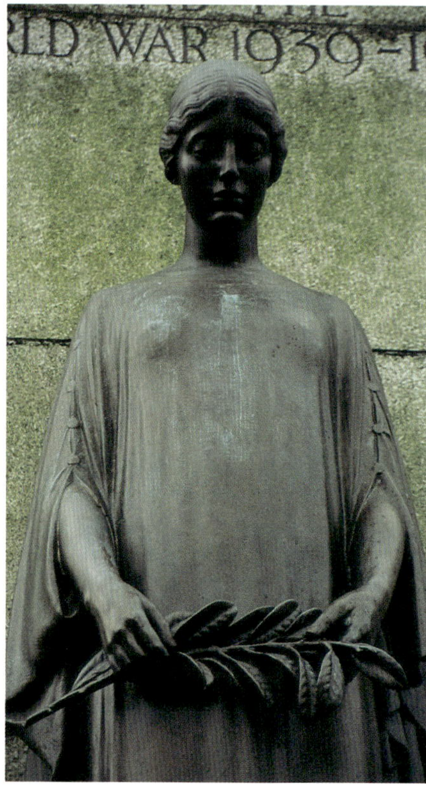

Heywood. Detail of Great War Memorial by Walter Marsden, 1925.

W. J. Pearce's wonderful 'Last Supper'. Some may think the green background a bit strident but the window is full of beautiful detail and the grapes in the lower panels look succulent. The first floor staircase and balcony provide a fine opportunity to get a good look at the window.

Access: Office open daily a.m. except Thur. Tel. 0161–4310262.

The Great War Memorial outside St Paul's on Heaton Moor Rd (SJ877917) was unveiled in 1921. It was designed by **J. H. Sellers** and the sculptor of the bronze soldier was **John Cassidy**.

HEYWOOD is just to the north of junction 19 on the M62.

Edgecroft, in Manchester Rd, was built by **Edgar Wood** in 1922 and is still a private dwelling. It was his last building before retiring to Italy.

Access: Private dwelling.

The Great War Memorial stands in a small park next to the Library in Rochdale Rd (SD857106) and was unveiled in 1925. The tall and elegant figure of 'Peace' by **Walter Marsden**, stands quietly with her head bowed in front of a simple Portland stone cenotaph. She holds an olive branch in her hand and seems to pose the eternal question; 'Why?' .

HORWICH is about 3 miles west of Bolton on the A673.

St Catherine's in Richmond St (SD635114) was built 1897–1902 by **R. K. Freeman**. The chancel was enlarged and the Lady Chapel and vestry were added 30 years later by his son. It is a very attractive red-brick church with sandstone dressings. The modern re-ordering has screened the two west-most bays and hidden an unusual memorial on the west wall. It was installed in 1918 and commemorates Catherine Ainsworth who helped found the church. The memorial takes the form of two beautiful tube-lined ceramic plaques, fixed either side of the oak panelling which had once been the background to the font. On the left is an idyllic sunlit cottage garden and on the right is a ruined building in a landscape consumed by flames. The work is brilliantly executed and thought to be by **Margaret Pilkington**. In the sanctuary the carving on the altar-front matches the rather Art Nouveau pomegranate motif on the back of the bishop's chair but it is unattributed. The woodwork in the choir, the communion rail, the priests stalls and the pulpit has a more Art Deco

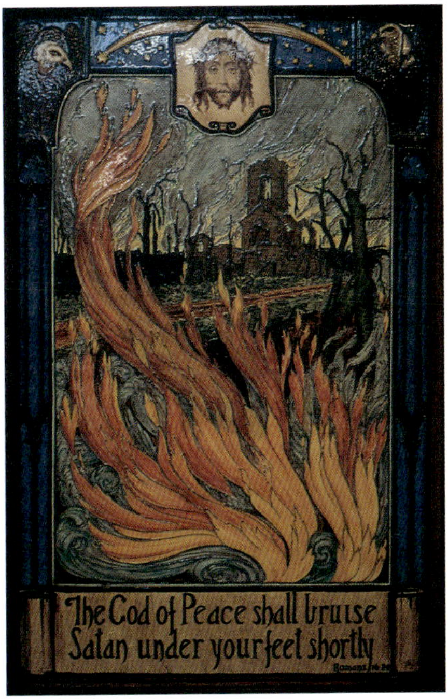

St Catherine's, Horwich. Ceramic Memorial attributed to M. Pilkington, 1918.

air about it and was designed 'free of charge' by **Mr Charles Cressey** of Horwich in 1902. He also designed the Caen-stone font with equal generosity, and it was made in 1903 by John Joshua Ware a joiner and builder in the town.

Access: Vicarage Tel. 01204–468263.

HULME is about a mile south of Manchester city centre.

St Wilfrid's off Royce Rd (SJ833969) was built in 1842 by A. W. N. Pugin and has recently been converted to commercial use. However, it retains three sparkling **Harry Clarke Studio** windows installed in the 1930s.

Access: Tel. 0161–2279889.

HYDE is on the extreme eastern edge of the Manchester conurbation, north of Stockport and south of Stalybridge.

Holy Trinity, Higham Lane, Gee Cross, (SJ958936) was built by **James Medland Taylor** and **Henry Taylor** 1873–74. It has been much changed. The tower, added by other hands in 1903 is a memorial to Queen Victoria. 'The Ascension' in the east window was made by **William Glasby** in 1927. Also by **Glasby**, is the two-light 'Good Shepherd' in the north aisle, installed in 1925.

Access: Vicarage Tel. 0161–3682337.

Hyde Chapel, Stockport Rd, Gee Cross, (SJ955935) has a two-light window in the south

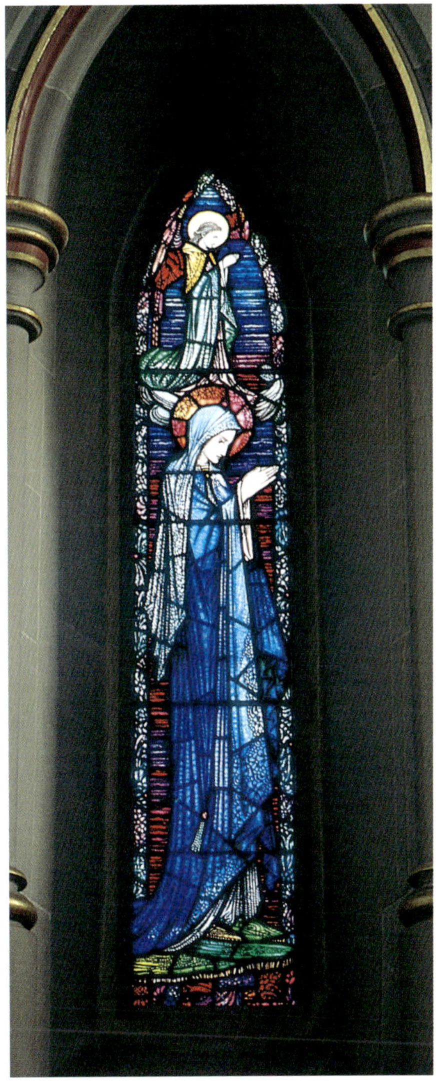

St Wilfrid, Hulme. Lancet window by the Harry Clarke Studio, c. 1935.

aisle with musical angels by **Morris & Co.** installed in 1915. There is another two-light window nearby which is said by A. C. Sewter to be by **Morris & Co.** It shows St Michael and St Raphael and according to Sewter was perhaps designed by **J. H. Dearle** *c.* 1925. However, Winifrid Holiday's list of her father's work includes a two-light window made for the Unitarian Church at Gee Cross with Ss Michael and Gabriel. In design terms it looks as if **Henry Holiday** won the commission but did **Morris & Co.** make the window for him? The five-light east window showing the risen Christ supported by angels and saints is a rare appearance in the North West of the work of **H. Victor Milner**.

Access: Archivist Tel. 0161–3683000.

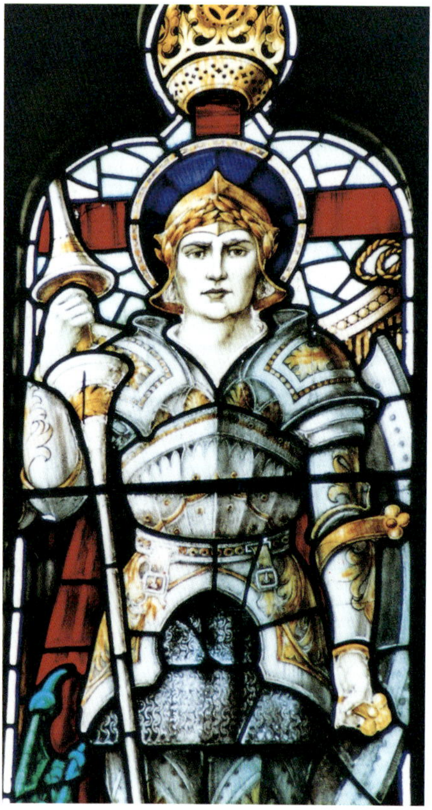

St Stephen, Kearsley. Detail of the Great War Memorial window by Reuben Bennett, c. 1920.

KEARSLEY is east of Farnworth on the A666.

St Stephen's on Bolton Rd (SD755046) was built 1871 by **James Medland Taylor**. It is stone built with a bell tower on the south-west corner (sinking a bit). The bright and impressive Great War Memorial window at the west end of the north aisle was made in 1920 by **Reuben Bennett** of Manchester.

Access: Vicarage Tel. 01204–572535.

LEIGH is on the western edge of the Manchester conurbation connected to Manchester by the Bridgewater canal and the A572.

St Thomas's in Chapel St, Bedford (SJ664999) is a big, red-brick church with a south-west tower. It was built 1906–10 by **R. B. Preston** and has an almost complete set of windows made by the **A. K. Nicholson** Studio. The east window is a fitting memorial to those who fell in the Great War. It has recently been cleaned and the grisaille now sparkles around the brilliant colours of the figures and entwined vegetation. The remainder of the windows provide a gallery of very well presented saints. The window that was not made by the Nicholson Studio is 'Christ Blessing the Children' in the north aisle, which was made by Powell of Whitefriars. While the carved oak war memorial on the west wall is very attractive, the work on the choir stalls at the other end of the church is exceptional. The sculptor has not yet been identified but it is brilliant work especially the bench ends which incorporate a very pert owl, two squirrels sharing a nut, a pelican feeding her chick and a pair of very graceful swans with intertwined necks. The archive of H. H. Martyn Ltd of Cheltenham records that they did work here but is not specific as to what or when!

Access: Vicarage Tel. 01942–673519.

LEVENSHULME is more or less bisected by the A6 as it heads north from Stockport to Manchester.

St Agnes's (SJ869948) stands on the corner of Slade Lane and St Agnes Rd. It was designed by **James Medland Taylor** 1884–85. The north aisle was added in 1895. The church is another brick and slate expression of Taylor's individuality, his love of the pointed arch and his refusal to be confined by the dogma of the Gothic styles. The building is full of interest inside and out. The two-light stained-glass window in what is now the vestry and was once the lady chapel, is undated and unsigned but its colouring, lead-lines and decorative borders suggest Geo. Wragge. The left panel is the Presentation in the Temple and the other shows the two Marys in the garden. The faculty for the window was granted in 1910.

Access: Rectory Tel. 0161–2242596 .

St Mark's is in Barlow Rd (SJ882944). The corner stone of the church was laid on 14 September 1907 by the Principal Grand Wizard of England attended by a procession of 400 fellow Masons 'bedecked with the regalia

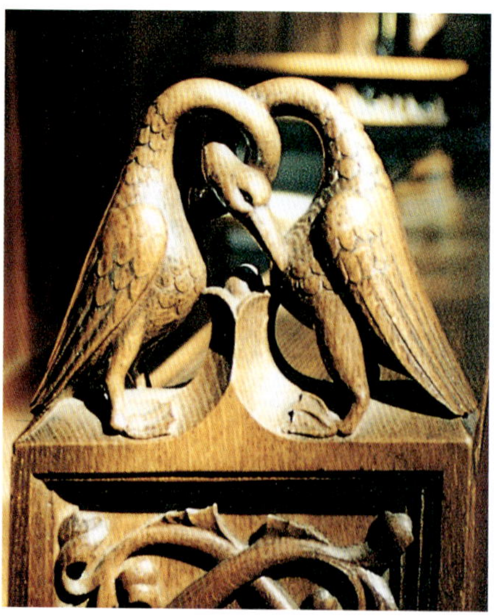

St Thomas, Bedford, Leigh. Woodwork detail. anon.

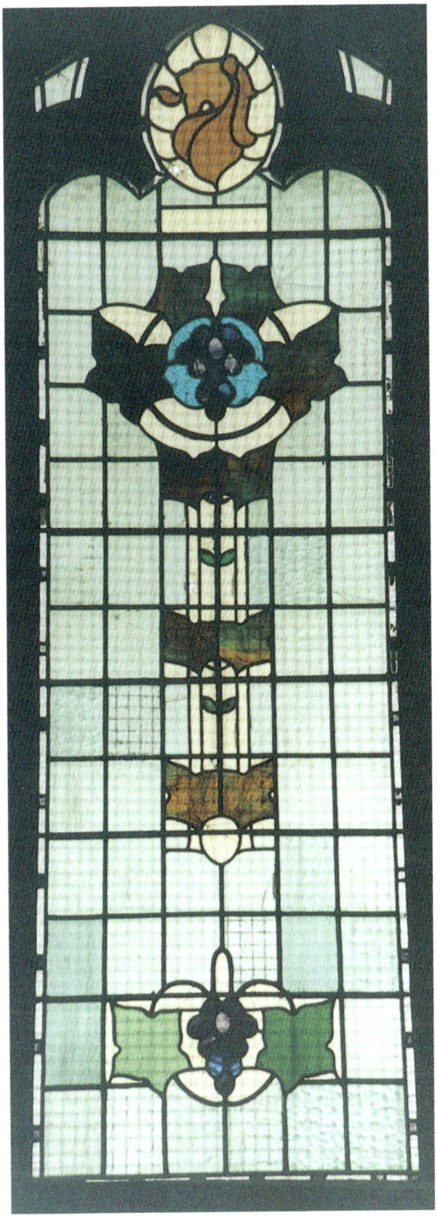

St Mark, Levenshulme. East window panel. Anon, c. 1908.

of their craft'. The church was consecrated on 13 July 1908 and despite the appearance of the Grand Wizard, there is nothing in the church by way of obvious Masonic symbolism. It was designed by **C. T. Taylor** and its red brick and white stone walls, stubby tower, triple gables and semicircular, single storey apse at the west end give it a very enticing appearance and while the exterior gives an impression of compactness it hides a surprisingly spacious interior. The view from the west door up the length of the church is wonderful. The great curves of the chancel arch span some 40 feet and despite the installation of the chancel screen in the 1930s, it still draws the eye into the sanctuary with its clear and bright east window set with conventionalised plant forms executed in a restrained Art Nouveau style. It is a much loved and highly polished church. The same design fills all the windows in the church except for the memorial window on the south side of the church which was made by **Thomas Willford** at Brabyns Brow Studio, Marple.

Access: Vicarage Tel. 0161–2249551.

LITTLEBOROUGH is about 3 miles north-east of Rochdale on the A58.

Holy Trinity on Church St (SD939164) has a carved reredos designed by **Percy Worthington**.

Access: Vicarage Tel. 01706–378334.

St Andrew's, Arm Rd, Dearnley (SD924159) was built in 1894. The chancel and chapel were added in 1912 by **Frank P. Oakley**. The east window is a definite-maybe for **W. J. Pearce**.

Access: Vicarage Tel. 01706–378466.

MANCHESTER CITY CENTRE

Manchester Town Hall in Albert Square (SJ839981) is an example of the Gothic Revival on the grand scale. It was designed in 1867 by Alfred Waterhouse. It took eleven years to complete the building which overlooks Albert Square and Thomas Worthington's Albert Memorial. Internally great attention has been paid to the decoration of the building. Waterhouse was at great pains to ensure that although different firms would be used to execute the work, a harmony and balance would be created through design and the control of materials. As well as the London-based firm of **Heaton, Butler & Bayne**, two local firms, Best & Lea and Pollitt & Coleman, won commissions for the internal decorations.

Busts and statues of local worthies are to be found in the entrance lobby and a purpose-built Sculpture Hall. On the right in the main vestibule is the seated figure of James Prescot Joule in dressing gown and slippers by **Alfred Gilbert** 1893 and in the Sculpture Hall on the window wall is a dark but interesting plaque commemorating Alcock and Brown by **John Cassidy** 1921. On the opposite side of the hall is a bust of Sir Charles Halle by **Onslow Ford** 1897. The most eye-catching statue however is the painted plaster figure of the 4th Duke of Lancaster made by **Farmer and Brindley**.

Waterhouse had hoped that there would be a series of murals linking the reception rooms through to the Great Hall but financial constraints made that impractical so that only the Council Chamber and Great Hall were completed. The Great Hall is a huge space seven bays long with an apse at the east end containing the organ and a platform. The waggon roof was decorated with a riotous

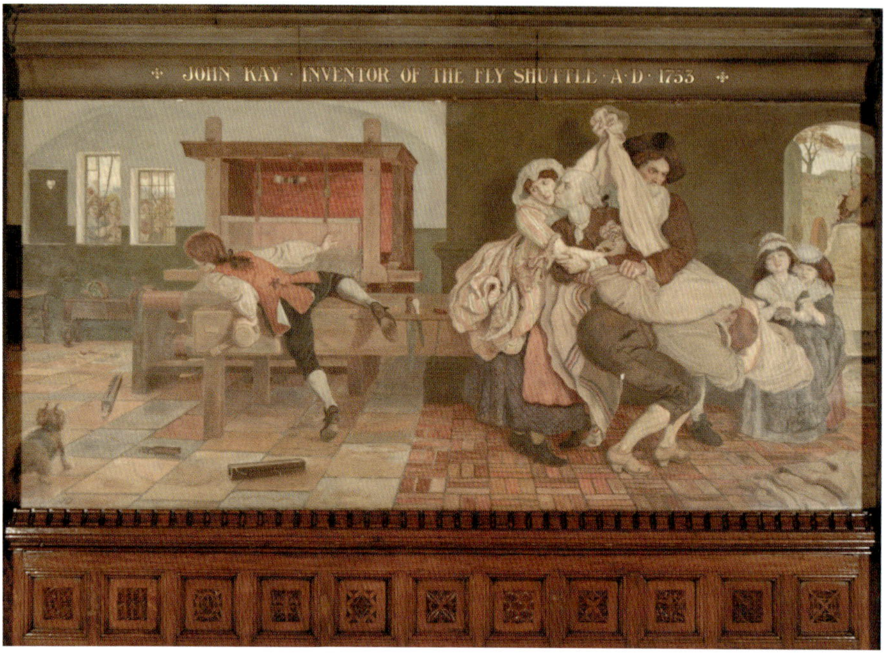

Manchester Town Hall. Mural. Maddox Brown. *Courtesy Manchester Town Hall. Photo © Stephen Yates/Manchester Metropolitan University*

display of civic pageantry and symbols by **Heaton, Butler & Bayne.** The walls are panelled with oak up to the dado and above this is a set of twelve paintings, six down each side of the room, which are among the greatest of Manchester's treasures though not greatly appreciated at the time of their completion. They are all the work of **Ford Madox Brown.** He started work in 1879 and did not finish until 1892. Although Manchester was slow to appreciate what it had in its midst, the art establishment in London acknowledged the achievement when Lord Leighton, President of the Royal Academy visited and gave it his seal of approval. **Ford Madox Brown** died six months after the murals were completed and did not see the reception his work received.

The following is the list of murals: The Romans building a fort at Mancunium A.D. 60; The Baptism of Edwin A.D. 627; The Expulsion of the Danes from Manchester A.D. 910; The Establishment of Flemish weavers in Manchester A.D. 1363; The Trial Of Wycliffe A.D. 1377; The Proclamation regarding Weights and Measures A.D. 1556; Crabtree watching the transit of Venus A.D. 1639; Chetham's Life dream A.D. 1640; Bradshaw's Defence of Manchester A.D. 1642; John Kay Inventor of the Fly shuttle A.D. 1753; The Opening of the Bridgewater Canal A.D. 1761; Dalton collecting marsh-fire gas.

The sculpture on the external south wall of the Town Hall extension was executed by **Herman Cawthra** in 1938.

Access: Visits can be arranged in advance by contacting the Town Hall to ensure that the Great Hall is not in use. Tel. 0161–2341792. In addition, the City's Blue Badge Guides do a tour of the Town Hall once a month on a Wednesday although access to the Murals is not guaranteed: Tel. 0161–2316928.

In **Albert Square**, in front of the Town Hall and looking into Cross St is a bronze statue by **Thomas Woolner** of Bishop James Fraser 1888. It is set on a granite base which has three bas-reliefs showing aspects of the bishop's work in the diocese.

The Central Library (SJ838979) next to the Town Hall was built 1930–34. It has a stained-glass window above the front door, with a number of small panels representing Shakespearean characters. The window was designed by **Robert Anning Bell**, and is a little more restrained than his earlier work. The library has over 700 titles printed by **Private Presses**, some of which were produced by the **Ashendene, Doves, Essex House, Kelmscott** and **Vale Presses**. There is a display case on the first floor corridor in inlaid wood by **J. H. Sellers.**

Access: Opening hours Tel 0161–2341971.

The Cenotaph (SJ839978) standing in St Peter's Square, outside the Central Library, is by **E. L. Lutyens**. It dates from 1924 and is a smaller version of the memorial in Whitehall. Behind the Cenotaph is **Temple Lushington Moore's** memorial to St Peter's church. The sculpture 'Humanity Adrift in the Sea of Life' 1907 by **John Cassidy** once stood in Piccadilly

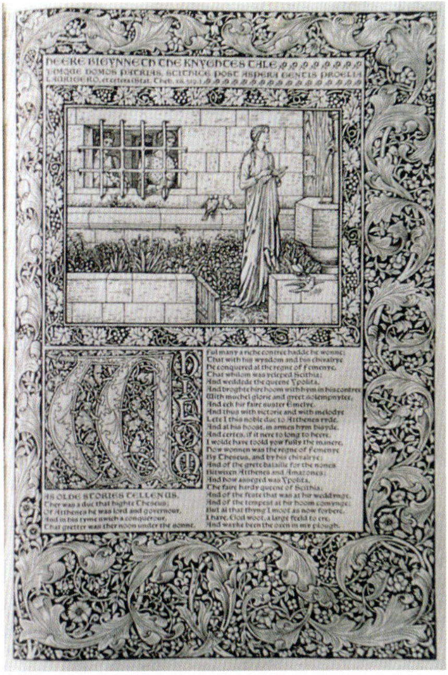

Central Library, Manchester. 'The Knyght's Tale', illustration from the Kelmscott Chaucer. *Courtesy of Manchester Libraries and Information Services*

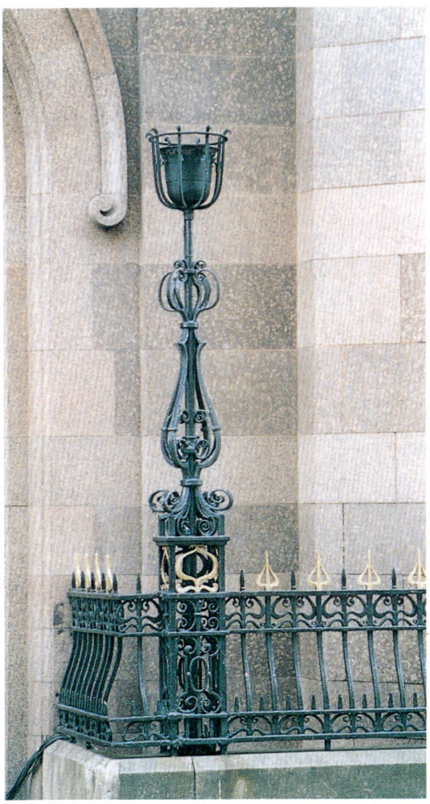

Midland Hotel, Manchester. Decorative ironwork by George Wragge Ltd, c. 1900.

Gardens and plans are afoot to re-erect it in St Peter's Square.

The Midland Hotel, (SJ838978) across the road from the Central Library was built in 1898 by Charles Trubshaw for the LMS railway and served the nearby Central Station (now converted to the G-Mex Exhibition Centre.) It is faced with **Burmantofts** glazed tiles and decorated with relief panels. The wrought ironwork surrounding the hotel was made by **George Wragge Ltd.** The interior is much changed but still retains one stained-glass window. It was made by **George Wragge Ltd** and shows a young woman dancing to the music of fairy pipers. Originally one of a series in the concert hall, it is now fixed in a light-well corridor on the mezzanine floor. It dates from the period in which **J. E. C. Carr** was Wragge's chief designer.

Access: Open all hours. Ask the concierge for directions to the stained glass.

Manchester Art Gallery in Moseley St (SJ841980) is housed in what was once the Athenaeum Club. When the Gallery's founding fathers bought the Club they also bought an adjoining plot of land to allow for future expansion. It took about 100 years for their foresight to pay off, but in 2002 the enlarged and improved Gallery was opened, to great acclaim. Today it has a splendid collection of paintings on the first floor interspersed with ceramics and sculpture. **Ford Madox Brown** is much in evidence. His famous epic 'Work' is here – a reminder that he toiled for ten years towards the end of his life to give Manchester Town Hall its mural masterpieces. All the Pre-Raphaelites and many of their followers are here. A recent acquisition is a lantern made for Holman Hunt in 1852 and held by his model for 'The Light of the World'. The ceramics on display include a striking collection of **William De Morgan** Isnik tiles and a huge ruby-lustre vase designed by **Halsey Ricardo**. Some of the best of **Pilkington** is on show, including lustre ware designed by **Walter Crane** as well as the firm's own designers. Much of the decorative art collection is on long term loan from the Manchester Metropolitan University's collection. There is furniture by influential architects and designers including a chest and an escritoire by **William Burges**, a chair by **E. W. Godwin**, the 'Four Seasons' cabinet by **Daniel Cottier** and Sussex chairs by **William Morris**. The Gallery also has a number of pieces of furniture by **J. H. Sellers** and some by **A. H. Mackmurdo**.

The Gallery of Craft and Design is housed in the former theatre of the Athenaeum and 'celebrates the role of craft and design across cultures and across time' Here, in a display of some 1,300 artefacts covering 3,000 years of development, are some splendid pieces of

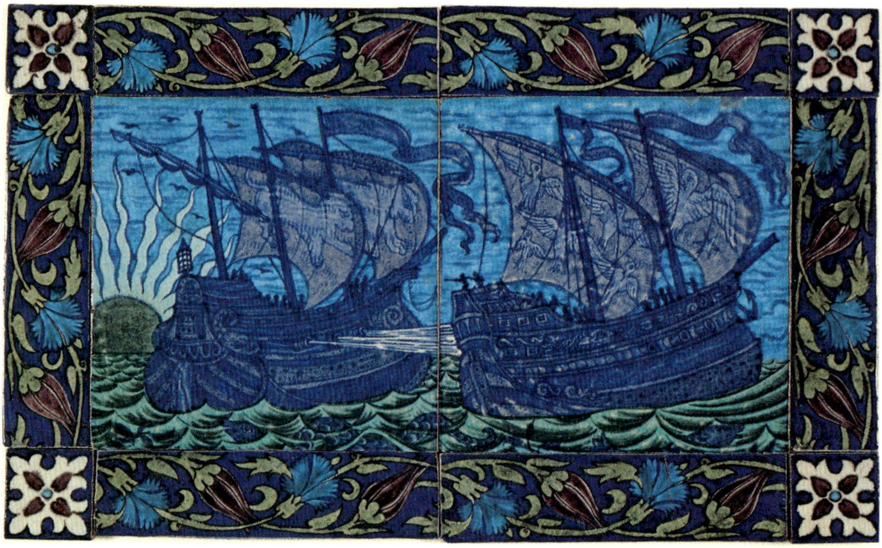

Manchester Art Gallery. William De Morgan tile panel in Persian colours, c. 1882. *© Manchester Art Gallery*

Whitefriar's glass, some art pottery and pieces of pewter and silver in Arts and Crafts styles.

Access: Open Tues–Sun 10.00–17.00.
Tel. 0161–235–8888.

The Midland Bank (SJ840983) building designed by **E. L. Lutyens** in 1929 stands on the corner of King St and Spring Gardens and is now occupied by HKSB.

Queen Victoria's Memorial Statue in Piccadilly (SJ844983) was made by **Onslow Ford** in 1901. In a mosaic-lined niche in the back of Victoria's pedestal is a very beautiful representation of 'Motherhood' by the same artist.

Britannia Hotel, Portland St. (SJ842980) was once the extravagantly splendid Watts warehouse and now has care of the firm's imposing Great War Memorial which stands guard in the porch. 'The Sentry' was sculpted by **C. S. Jagger**.

Asia House, 82 Princess St (SJ843976) is another of those formerly glorious packing and shipping warehouses as the ornate metal work decoration over the front entrance suggests. Now converted into apartments its is difficult to get in to see the former entrance hall lined with small windows with stained glass panels of stylised trees and the huge staircase lined with marble and faience with particularly eye-catching high-relief tiles of more but different, stylised trees at dado level.

Access: Private apartments.

The University of Manchester, The Sackville St building (SJ845977) was constructed 1895–1902. The Renaissance style terracotta panels on the exterior are by **Burmantofts**. Internally there is probably the largest collection of stained glass by

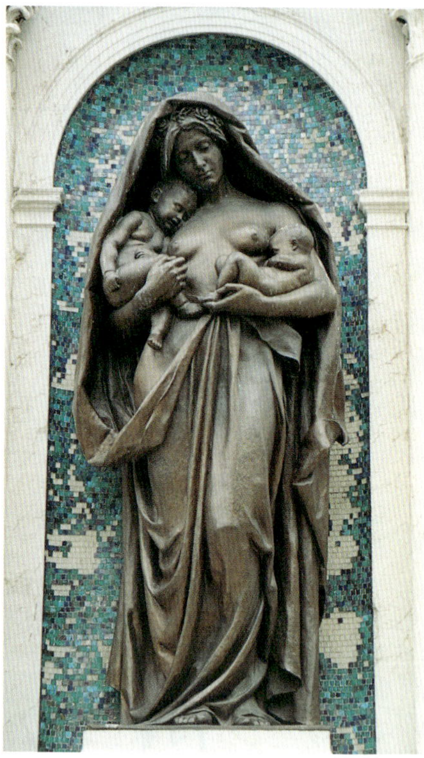

Piccadilly Gardens, Manchester. Motherhood by Onslow Ford, 1901.

W. J. Pearce gathered together in one place. It begins in the Sackville St entrance and carries on through the lower hall, up the main staircase and through the Great Hall. It comprises figurative, heraldic and plant-form designs. Some panels are purely decorative, such as the galleon in full sail over the main door. Others

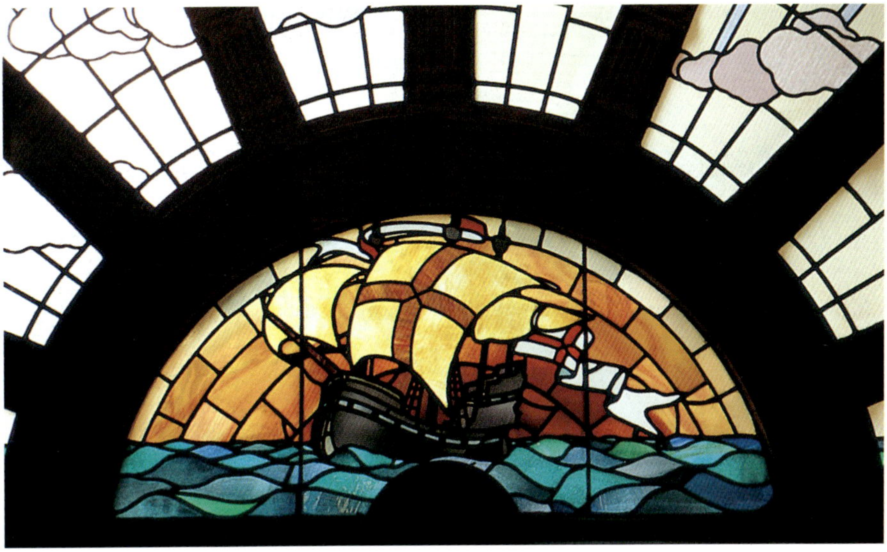

The University of Manchester, Sackville building, Manchester. Fan light by W. J. Pearce Ltd.

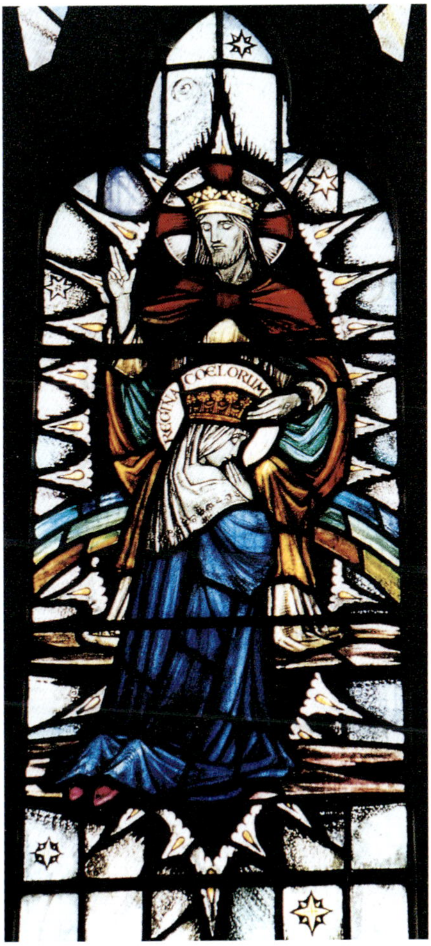

St Benedict, Ardwick. Detail of the east window by M. E. Rope, 1926.

commemorate individuals and institutions celebrated in the Sciences and Technology.

Access: Open to the public. (Groups should contact security Tel. 0161–3062444.)

Old Police and Fire Station, on the corner of London Rd and Whitworth St (SJ846978) was built 1901–06 by **Woodhouse, Willoughby** and Langham in a Neo-Baroque manner and in a durable, red Accrington Brick. It also has tawny and terracotta faience by **Burmantofts** which is used to decorate the building with statues and with especially striking relief panels of very elemental ladies representing fire and water.

St Benedict's in Bennett St, Ardwick (SJ866970) is a huge and impressive brick church built in 1880 by J. S. Crowther. The east window in the Lady Chapel and the St Francis in the south aisle are by **Margaret Edith Rope**, made in 1926 and 1935 respectively.

Access: The church is redundant and discussions are in hand to convert it into a climbing school.

The Picture House on the corner of Oxford St and Chepstow St (SJ840977) was one of the first purpose-built cinemas to be opened in Manchester. Built in 1911 of red brick and terracotta with much Edwardian detailing, today only the upper façade with its elegant lettering remains intact.

The offices of Tootal, Broadhurst, Lee & Co. in Oxford St (SJ840977) were built in red brick and terracotta 1896–98. Just off the entrance foyer on the half-landing is the stylish **Great War Memorial** which was designed by J. H. Sellers.

Access: Enquire at the reception desk during office hours.

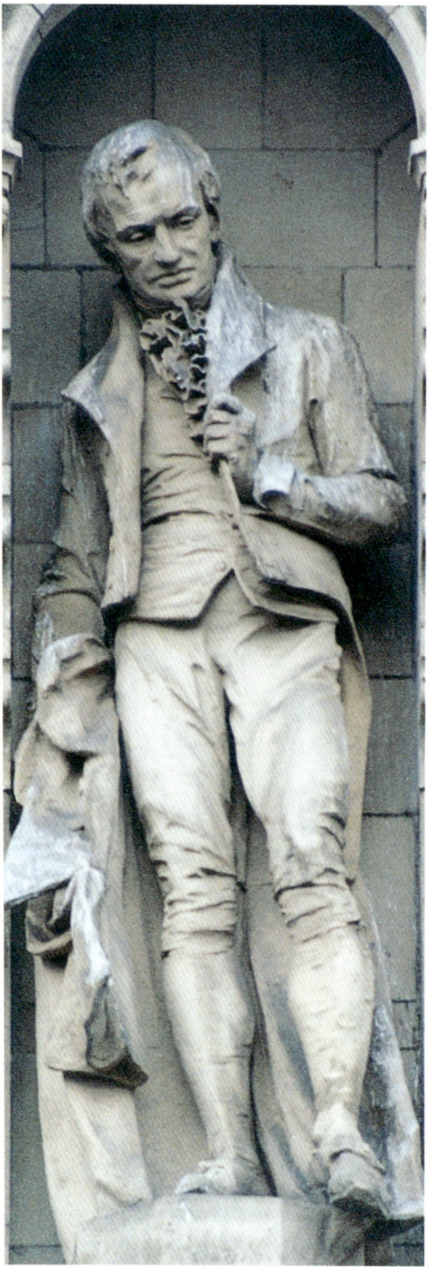

John Owens in niche above entrance to Whitworth Building, Manchester University, Oxford Road, by Harry Bates, 1886.

The Palace Hotel on Oxford Street (SJ841976) is the former Refuge Assurance building by **Alfred Waterhouse** 1891–95 extended by his son Paul 1910–12. **Doulton's** hard-wearing terracotta was used on the outside and **Burmantofts** supplied the faience for the interior. A welcome relief are the small statues of 'Thrift' and 'Industry' set into the metal work on either side of the main entrance gate.

Manchester Metropolitan University Library (SJ844972) is housed in the Sir Kenneth Green building in All Saints Square and contains some very Special Collections. In particular it has the **Arts and Crafts Collection** acquired by the Manchester School of Art which includes many wonderful items of glass, ceramics, metalwork and enamelling. Here is the work of **C. R. Ashbee, W. A. S. Benson, Walter Crane, Nelson and Edith Dawson, William De Morgan, Christopher Dresser, Alexander Fisher, Keswick School of Industrial Arts, William Morris** and **Richard Ll. Rathbone.** There are ceramics by **Della Robbia, Doulton, Pilkington, Ruskin Pottery** and glass by **James Powell** and **Tiffany** and much more. The early part of this collection was selected by **Walter Crane** with Charles Rowley who was chairman of the School of Art's management committee. The **Book Design Special Collection** comprises

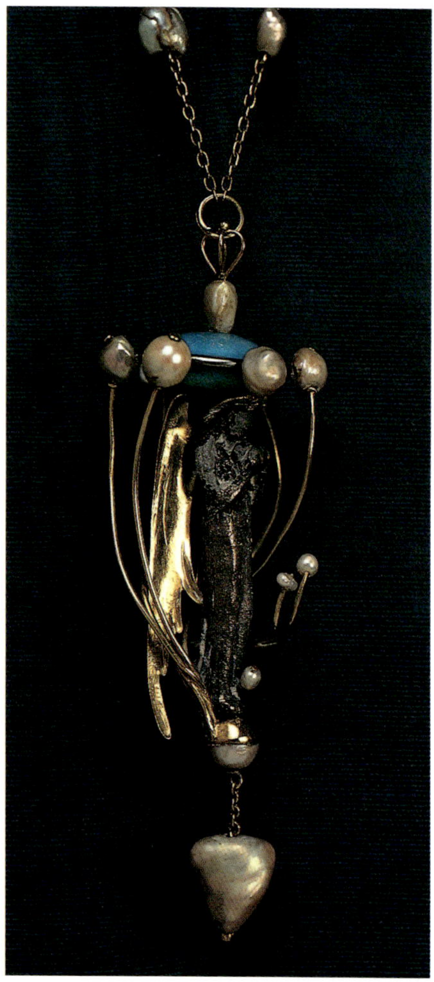

Manchester Metropolitan University Library. Pendant and chain by C. R. Ashbee, 1889. *Courtesy Manchester Metropolitan University Collection. Photo © Manchester Art Gallery*

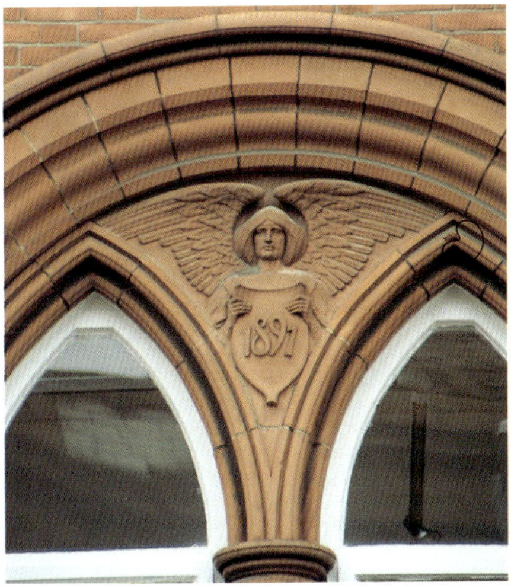

Manchester School of Art, Cavendish St, Manchester. Decorative terracotta by W. J. Neatby.

copies of children's illustrated books as well as examples of the work of the **Kelmscott, Essex House** and **Doves Presses** and many more books produced, written or illustrated by artists, designers and craftsmen of the Arts and Crafts movement. The library also owns the Laura Seddon Collection of greetings cards which includes designs by **Walter Crane** and Kate Greenaway. The library also holds the archive of the Manchester School of Art.

Access: The special collections are not on display but can be visited by appointment. Tel. 0161–2476610.

Manchester School of Art in Cavendish St, (SJ843970) was built in 1881 by George Redmayne and extended in 1897 on the Ormond St side. The terracotta angels in the tympana of the windows in the extension were designed by **W. J. Neatby** while he was head designer at Doulton.

The Church of the Holy Name of Jesus, on Oxford Rd (SJ848964), was built 1869–71 by J. A. Hansom & Son and is said to be one of their finest with a very imposing facade and an unexpectedly high, light and airy interior. The stained glass in the four tall lancets of the Great War Memorial in the south transept is by **Paul Woodroofe** while the nearby Chapel of the Madonna della Strada and its furnishings were designed by **J. F. Bentley**. The Reredos and altar frontal are beautifully carved and gilded as is the triptych frame which holds paintings by N. H. J. Westlake.

Access: Usually open. Presbytery Tel. 0161–2732435.

Manchester University's splendid Gothic buildings by **Alfred Waterhouse**, started in 1870 and completed thirty years later, are on Oxford Road (SJ845965). In a niche above the main entrance to the Whitworth building on Oxford Rd is a statue of John Owens the University's founder, by **Harry Bates**, 1886. **Bates** also did the marble relief of Socrates, 1886 in the oak gallery of the Council chamber.

Whitworth Art Gallery on Oxford Rd (SJ849960) was built in 1908 by J. W. Beaumont in red brick and terracotta. It houses the most comprehensive collection of textiles and wallpapers in the country after the Victoria & Albert Museum. Among the collection of several thousand wallpapers and fabrics are many designed by **Morris & Co.** and others by leading Arts and Crafts designers such as **Walter Crane, C. F. A. Voysey, John Dando Sedding, Heywood Sumner** and **Lewis F. Day**. The Pattern Books of Thomas Wardle of Leek are here and so is a panel copied from the Bayeaux tapestry by Alice Pattinson of the **Leek Embroidery Society**. There is a unique **Walter Crane** collection which includes designs for wall paper, metal work and pottery, watercolours and book illustrations. There is a large collection of drawings and watercolours by the Pre-Raphaelites and their circle, including ten drawings by **Ford Madox Brown** for his decorative panels for the Manchester Royal Jubilee Exhibition of 1887. The prolific Frank Brangwyn is well represented with some 70 of his drawings in a variety of media. The gallery also has a small collection of furniture including pieces by **C. F. A. Voysey, Edgar Wood** and **J. H. Sellers**. In the adjoining park there is a statue of King Edward VII by **John Cassidy** 1913.

Access: As only part of the collection is on show at any one time arrangements can be made to view works in store by appointment with the relevant curator Tel. 0161–2757450. Open Mon–Sat 10.00–17.00; Sun 14.00–17.00. Admission Free.

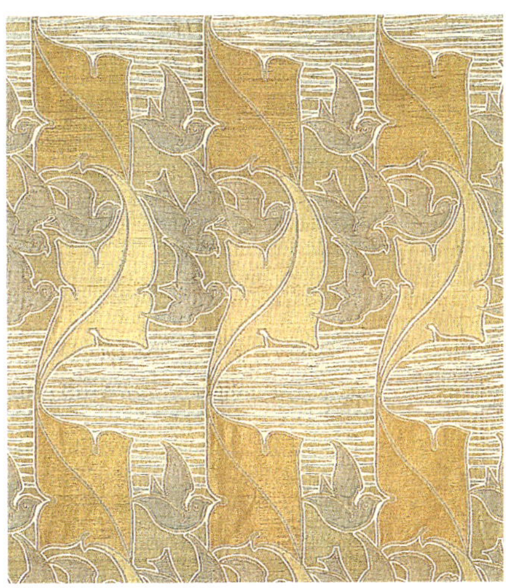

Whitworth Art Gallery. Silk and wool double cloth designed by C. F. A. Voysey and made by Alexander Morton, 1897. *© The Whitworth Art Gallery, University of Manchester*

Manchester Crown Court in Crown Square (SJ833984) is the modern repository of some of the figure sculptures which avoided Blitz damage and were salvaged when Waterhouse's Assize Courts building was demolished. The figures were by **Thomas Woolner** and were incorporated in the façade of the building in what has been described as 'part of a full blooded Ruskinian scheme'. There are nine life-sized representations of people prominent in the development of the English legal system. Five are ranged along a first floor corridor outside the courtrooms and four stand in a basement gallery.

Access: Arrangements can be made to visit. Tel. 0161–9541782.

The John Rylands Library in Deansgate (SJ836982) was hailed in its day by the *British Architects' Journal* as 'one of the finest buildings in England and a very welcome addition to the comparatively few pieces of good architecture which Manchester possesses.' The library was built 1900–09 by **Basil Champneys** who was commissioned by Mrs John Rylands after she had seen his work at Mansfield College, Oxford. It is a masterpiece of Neo-Gothic in a secular building and its front elevation is a mass of ornamentation. It is an inspirational building. The staircase with its vaulted ceiling and elaborate carving is an exhibition in itself of the best collaboration between an architect and his stone mason. The main library is an impressive space some 20 ft. wide, 120 ft. long and 30 ft. high with a vaulted ceiling. It has eight windowed bays on either side for storing books and there is a gallery right around the hall at first floor level giving access to reading rooms. Above the gallery there is a clerestory which contains panels filled with appropriate mottoes. Lower down above the shafts which support the gallery are a series of statues portraying famous writers, scientists and artists. At each end of the building there is a large window with fine tracery containing stained glass designed by Charles Kempe depicting philosophers and writers. Most of the stone sculpture, both figures and floral designs, was executed by **Bridgeman** of Lichfield and the plaster modelling was by **George Frampton.** The allegorical group representing Theology, Science and Art in the entrance lobby is by **John Cassidy** 1899 as are the statues on the first floor of John Rylands 1899 and Enriquetta Rylands 1907. The excellent decorative metalwork in the grills, rails, gates and light fitting are all by Singers of Frome.

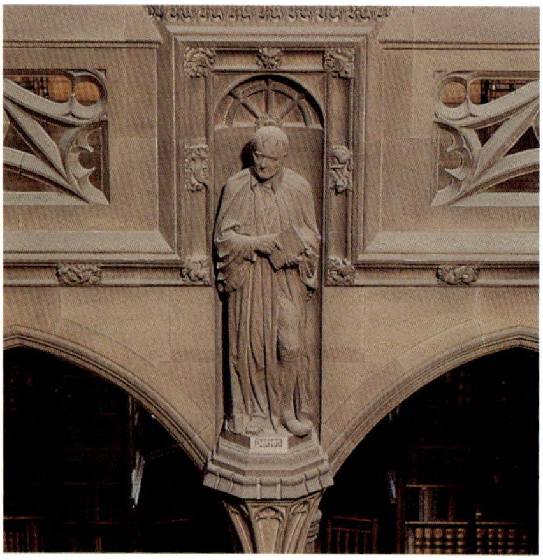

John Rylands Library, Manchester. Statue of John Dalton executed by J. Bridgeman of Lichfield, c. 1905.
© John Rylands University Library of Manchester

There are thousands of books in the Library so this is a good place to look for those illustrated by artists associated with the Arts and Crafts Movement such as **Anning Bell, Walter Crane,** Reginald Hallward, Stacy Marks, Joseph Pennell, Arthur Rackham, Charles Ricketts, **Heywood Sumner and Paul Woodroffe.** It also has a Private Press Collection which includes all the books published by the **Kelmscott Press**, the **Doves Press** and many by the **Essex House Press.**

Access: The building is part of the University of Manchester Library facilities but is open to the public who are welcome to become members of the library. At the time of going to print the building is closed due to major building work but an appointment to see particular books can be made with the counter staff Tel. 0161–2753764.

St Ann's (SJ838983) St Ann's Square, was built in 1709–12 and restored by Waterhouse in 1886–91. The stained glass in the apse was designed by **Frederic Shields** and made up by **Heaton, Butler & Bayne** 1887–89.

Access: Open during normal office hours.

The South African War Memorial (SJ838984) in St Ann's Square was sculpted by **Hamo Thorneycroft.**

Manchester Cathedral, (SJ838987) has been growing on this site since the C15. **Basil Champneys** built the west porch and vestry in 1898 and returned to build the south annex in 1902. There is a small but beautiful relief panel by **Eric Gill** over the entrance to the auxiliary buildings to the south of the church. It was sculpted in 1933 and shows the Christ Child with St Mary, St Denys and St George. *The Studio* (1905, vol. 37 p. 197) credits **George Bankart** with the lead rainwater heads. By the way, Edward Burne-Jones and Georgiana Macdonald were married here in 1860.

Access: Open every day.

Victoria Station (SJ841991) has a bronze memorial, thirty feet long and five feet high commemorating the men of the Lancashire and Yorkshire Railway who served in the Great War. It was made by **George Wragge Ltd** in 1922.

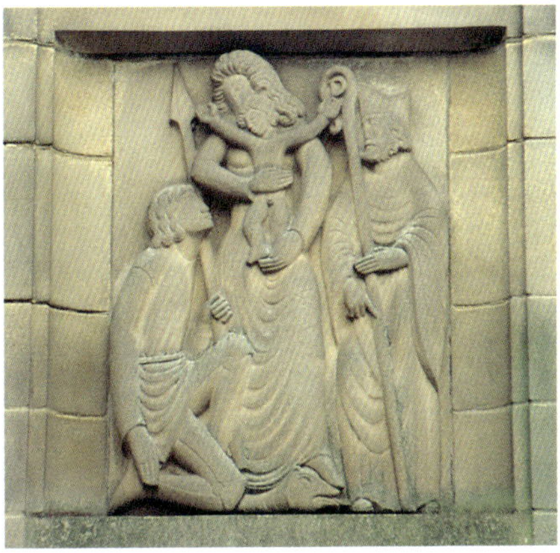

Manchester Cathedral. Bas relief by Eric Gill, 1933.

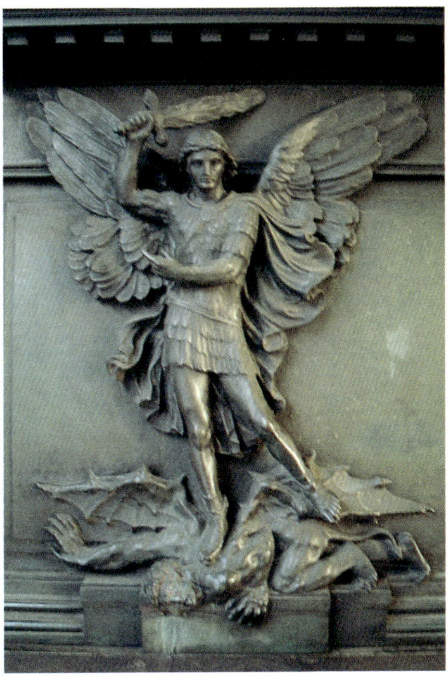

Victoria Station, Manchester. War memorial, detail executed by G. Wragge Ltd, c. 1920.

Ashton House, (SJ843992) stands on a wedge shaped site at the corner of Corporation St and Dantzic St. It was built by the City Architect 1908–10 as a women's lodging house. Externally the ironwork has mildly arts and crafts devices and the keystones and padstones of the ground floor brick arches are terracotta tiles laid on edge à la Lutyens.

Access: Private apartments.

MARPLE sits on the south-eastern edge of Greater Manchester about 4 miles east of junction 13 on the M60.

St Martin's Brabyns Brow, (SJ963894) was designed in 1869 by **John Dando Sedding** and built in stone as a simple nave and chancel church with a bellcôte and red-tiled roof. **Henry Wilson** added the north chapel 1895–96 and the north aisle in 1909. While Sedding's half-timbered south porch adds interest to the exterior the real joy of the church lies in its interior decoration. The sanctuary was designed by Sedding with a carved and gilded alabaster reredos and a painted ceiling both of which were restored in 1981. The chancel walls were also decorated but only three of Sedding's painted angels survive on the south side to hint at what must have been a glorious chancel. The stained glass in the five-light east window is by **Morris, Marshall, Faulkner & Co.** and was made 1869–70. It has since deteriorated and lost much of its detail. St Peter, St Thomas, St James the Greater, St Paul and St Bartholomew were all designed by **William Morris. Ford Madox Brown** designed St Andrew and **D. G. Rossetti** designed St Jude. All the other apostles and the central 'Crucifixion' and 'Nativity' panels were designed by **Burne-Jones.**

There are two two-light windows by the same firm which were placed in the south wall of the chancel in 1873. 'The Annunciation' in the east-most pair was designed by **William Morris.** In the second window the figure of Mary is by **Burne-Jones** and St Elizabeth and her son John are the work of **Ford Madox Brown. Morris** was responsible for the 'Presentation in the Temple' shown below the main figures.

The pulpit with bronze panels made by **Richard Ledward** was designed by **J. D. Sedding** while the stained-glass window nearest the pulpit was executed in the 1930s by **A. K. Nicholson.** The bronze war memorial on the south wall was designed for this church by **Henry Wilson** in 1925.

The stained-glass window east of the south porch 'Christ and his Disciples on the Sea of Tiberias' is by **Christopher Whall** as is the earlier west window showing St Martin as a bishop and a soldier. In the south-west corner is the font by **Sedding** which has an extravagant oak cover designed by **Henry Wilson.** The cover is inlaid with ebony and whitewood and has low-relief carving of fishes and wavelets. It is surmounted by a pierced golden globe adorned with apple blossom. The whole cover is suspended by a wrought iron chain which incorporates a symbolic crown of thorns, a more naturalistic gilded dove of the spirit and monograms of St Martin. Opposite the south door is another of **Wilson's** wonders in the form of a huge relief sculpture of St Christopher bearing the Christ Child on his shoulder. The white marble figure stands in a shallow apse in the north wall surrounded by green marble.

At the east end of the north aisle is the Lady Chapel designed and executed by **Henry Wilson**

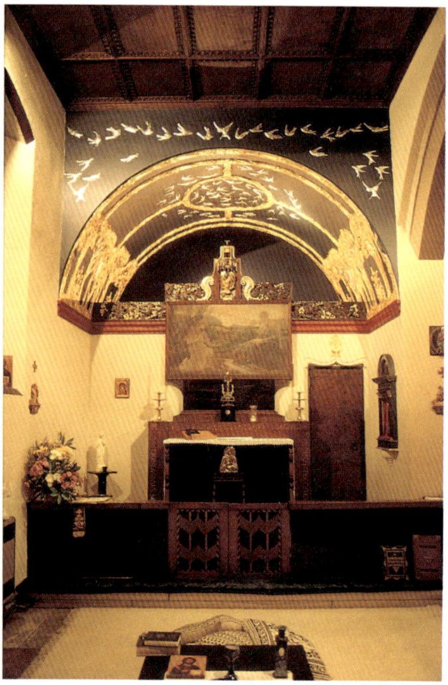

St Martin, Marple. Lady Chapel by Henry Wilson and Christopher Whall, 1895–96.

and **Christopher Whall**. The chapel has a barrel- vaulted roof and is decorated with a flock of silver moulded-plaster swallows and martins swirling above the altar in a deep blue sky. The sides of the chapel are covered with a gilded forest which almost hides the silver birds secreted in the branches. It is stunning decoration. The unusual reredos takes the form of a painting by **Whall** of 'The Annunciation' set in a Peak District landscape. **Wilson** was responsible for designing the woodwork on the altar and the communion rail and the beautiful brass head of Christ on the altar front. He also designed the altar furnishings including a beautiful cross and reliquary made of copper, brass, enamel and silver gilt.

Access: Vicarage Tel. 0161–4272736.

MIDDLETON is on the northern edge of the Greater Manchester conurbation north of Chadderton and east of Oldham. It was the home town of the architect **Edgar Wood** and many of his buildings are still standing. Most of these are small private houses not open to the public. However, the following route will pass most of his work in the town.

Leave the M60 at junction 19 and follow the A576 (Manchester Old Road) into town.

165 and **167 Manchester Old Road** (SD864056) stand on the right hand side of the road. They are a pair of semi-detached houses with an unmistakable triangular, dark-brick front elevation. The building raises eyebrows now, so what would have been the reaction in 1912?

Continue along Manchester Old Road to a roundabout where you should take the first exit into Kemp St, followed quickly by Archer Park and a left turn into Sefton Rd.

Westdeane, (SD863058) stands at the end of Sefton Rd. It was built in 1896 to an asymmetrical design demonstrating Wood's penchant for bays, canted or otherwise. Not the least of his quirks here is the tall, unsupported chimney on the gable end which rises, to the level of the main house chimneys. The back of the house can be seen from Sunny Bank Rd at the end of which stands Wood's family home which is now a nursery school.

Go back to the roundabout and take the second exit into Middleton Way. Go straight on at the next roundabout and turn left at the next into Assheton Way. There is yet another roundabout at the end of Assheton Way. Take the third exit into Long St.

Assheton Arms Hotel (SD871061) is on the right as you exit this huge roundabout. The hotel has recently been extended to incorporate **Williams & Glynn's Bank** which was built by Wood in 1889. It has a very innovative facade for its date but nothing is left of Wood's work inside.

Long St Methodist Church and School (SD870062) is on the left. It was designed in 1897 and built 1899–1901. This design pre-dates the more famous First Church of Christ Scientist in Victoria Park, Manchester by six years and it can be seen as a step in the development of the later design. The school and church are set around a courtyard and form a very attractive, well-proportioned group. The church itself is built in a sleek, undecorated Gothic style which produces a very restful interior with stock brick walls and sandstone pillars and arches. The only stained glass is to be found in small roundels in the porch doors and the whole decorative interest lies in the stone pulpit and font. The pulpit is an integral part of the low chancel-screen wall and is carved with a band of roses and a beautiful angel. The stone font incorporates a small bronze statuette of a mother carrying a baby in her arms while two small children clutch her skirts. The altar is flanked by two chairs designed by **Edgar Wood**, while his lectern, with its huge eagle and beautifully carved roses, languishes undeservedly in a corner at the back of the church. The mirrored glass 'windows' in the south wall are explained by the fact that this is a party wall with the building next door.

Access: The church is open on Saturday morning 10.30–12.00 otherwise Manse Tel. 0161–7988886.

The public library is almost opposite the Methodist Church and has a good collection of photographs of Wood's buildings. In the park behind the library are the marred and untended

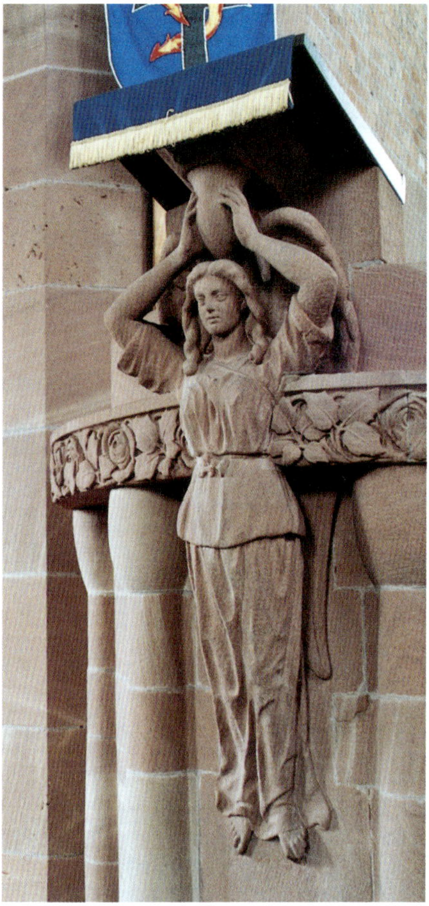

Long St Methodists, Middleton. Detail of the pulpit designed by Edgar Wood, 1901.

remains of a **memorial** (SD871063) designed by **Wood** in 1906.

A little way past the library on the left hand side is Mellalieu St. **36 Mellalieu St** (SD868064) is on the right hand side about half way down the street. It was built in 1910 and is said to be the first of **Wood's** houses to be built with a flat reinforced-concrete roof. It also has a very decorative and interesting doorway.

Turn around in Mellalieu St, go back and turn left into Long St where after a few hundred yards it becomes Rochdale Rd. There is a little cluster of Edgar Wood's houses here. **33** and **35 Rochdale Rd** (SD871066) are two houses named Redcroft and Fencegate built in 1891. Great pains have been taken in presenting the front elevation to disguise the fact that this is a pair of semi-detached houses. It has an asymmetrical front with a broad gable on the left, an off-centre doorway giving access to Fencegate which has a canted bay piercing the eaves on the right. The dormer window set in the roof above the bay helps to balance the mass of the left hand gable. Redcroft, entered from the side, was built as Wood's own home. **37** and **39 Rochdale Rd** (SD871067) were built in 1893 in red brick and their massive symmetry makes no attempt to disguise the fact that they are semi-detached. Very large 'semis' it must be said. The broad central bay is carried up through the eaves and topped by a gable above the third floor. It is flanked on either side by flat-topped canted bays set in front of broad dormer windows. **34** to **38 Rochdale Rd** (SD872066) are part of a short terrace and includes a corner shop and a pair of houses which were put up in 1898. They are much

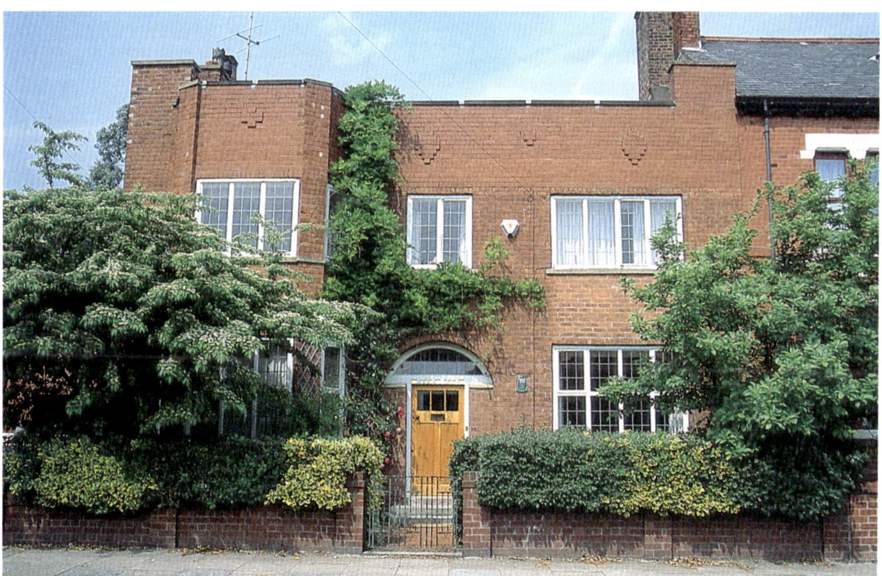

36 Mallelieu St, Middleton. Edgar Wood, 1910.

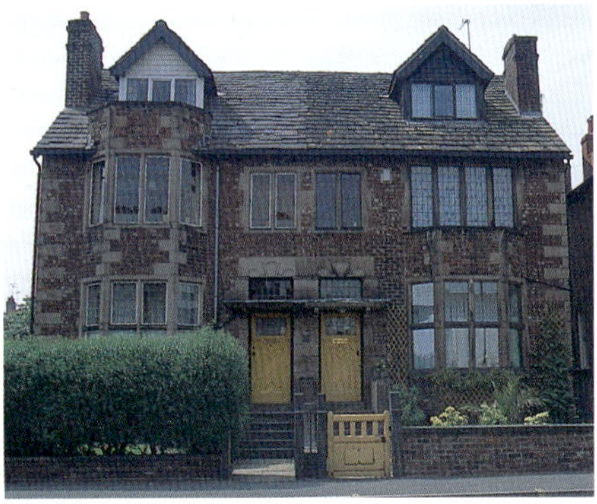

51 & 53 Rochdale Rd, Middleton. Edgar Wood.

changed and only the semicircular oriel at the corner attracts attention. **51** and **53 Rochdale Rd** (SD871067) are just a little bit further on, brick built with stone transoms and mullions in their bays. Were they designed to be asymmetrical or has 53 been altered?

Go on about ½ mile and then turn right out of Rochdale Rd into Stanycliffe Lane. This becomes Green Lane after a short distance and eventually, with another name change, becomes Hilton Fold Lane. **16–46 (evens) Hilton Fold Lane** (SD879061) comprise a terrace of small artisans' houses built between the wars in red brick with slate roofs, small front porches and gardens front and back.

Turn right from Hilton Fold Lane into Oldham Rd and right again into Temple St. **The Baptist Chapel** (SD878061) stands on the corner of Green Lane and Temple St and was built in 1889. It is very different in style from the Long St Methodist Chapel but sufficiently different from other contemporary examples of the genre to suggest individuality in the architect.

Access: N. W. Baptist Assoc. 01942–221595.

There are a lot of one-way streets here so do a loop back up Green St, right into Hilton Fold Lane and this time turn left into Oldham Rd. About a quarter mile later turn right into Elm St. **The Elm St School** (SD884059) is half way down the street on the right hand side. It is another product of the **Wood & Sellers** partnership built 1908–10 at the same time as the Durnford St School (demolished in 2003) and like Durnford St it was probably designed by **J. H. Sellers**. The Elm St school is built in red brick with stone trim and a flat, reinforced-concrete roof and as at Durnford St there are very strong vertical features in the composition. In keeping with the fashion of the day the boys and girls had separate playgrounds and entrances. In this case the entrances from the street are via covered ways separated by a small formal garden in front of a concave row of tall narrow windows.

Go back along Elm St and turn left into Oldham Rd follow the road towards the town centre and turn left into Towneley St This road forks left but go straight on into Kirkway and right again at the roundabout into the western end of Mount Rd. **22** and **24 Mount Rd** (SD870051) are semi-detached, dark-brick houses built in 1907 with canted flat-roofed bays extending above the eaves line.

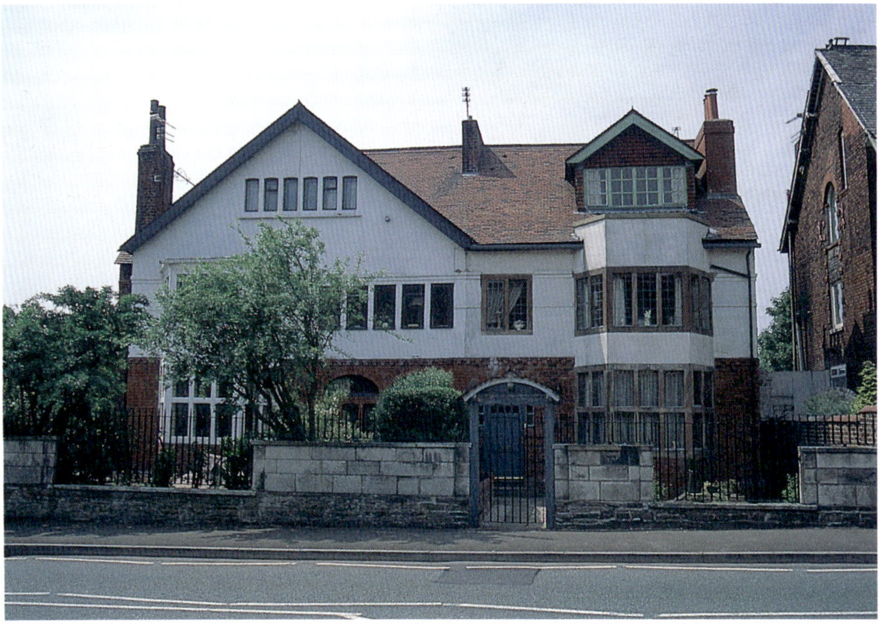

33 & 35 Rochdale Rd, Middleton. Edgar Wood, 1891.

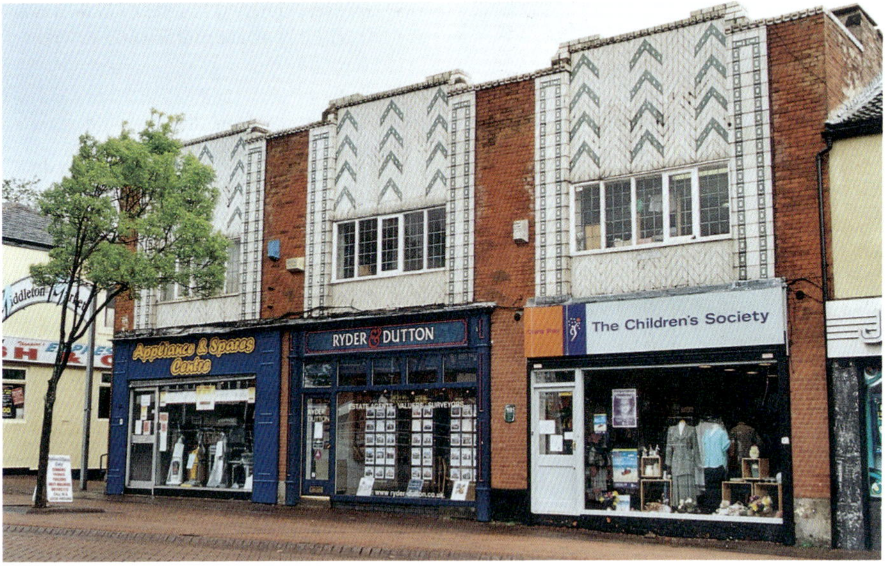

Middleton Gardens, Middleton. Shop fronts by Edgar Wood, 1908.

Mount Rd will deliver you to the A664 and, if you want the M60 turn right and head back to town. Go left at the first round about and left again onto Manchester Old Road and eventually to Junction 19. Otherwise, return to the town centre to look at the last of Wood's buildings. This is a block of three two-storey shops, **33**, **35** and **37 Middleton Gardens**, (SD869057), which have polychrome chevron brickwork at first floor level, designed in 1908.

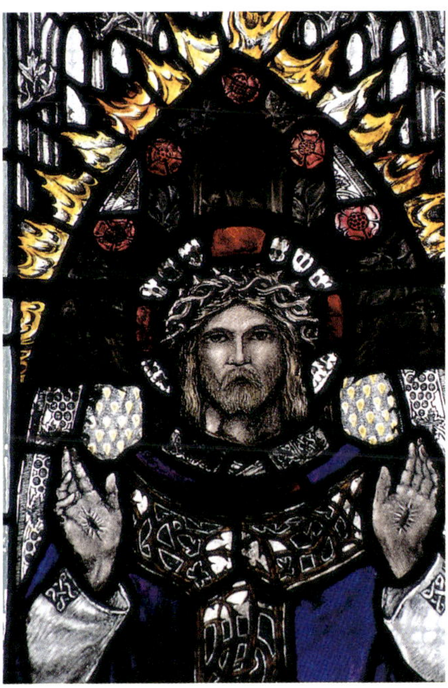

St Leonard, Middleton. Detail Christ Ascending, by Whall & Whall, 1924.

St Leonard's, in St Leonard's St (SD872063) is the ancient Parish Church of Middleton. It claims to have the oldest stained-glass war memorial in the country commemorating archers who fought at Flodden Field in 1513. It shows a row of archers each with his name inscribed above his figure. The tradition of stained-glass war memorials is continued in the window in the north wall commemorating the South African War. It was designed by **G. F. Bodley** and made by Burlison & Grylls. The Madonna and Child with four saints in the east window of the War Memorial Chapel are said to be by the **A. K. Nicholson Studio** although, unusually, the lights are not signed. In the east window of the Lady Chapel is a typically breathtaking five-light window made by **Whall & Whall** in 1924. It shows Christ ascending into heaven attended by his angels and watched by the disciples. The eye-catching window in the south wall showing Christ accompanied by Faith and Hope is by **Christopher Whall**. The copper repoussé plaque on the south side of the chancel arch was made by **James Smithies** of Wilmslow.

Access: The church is generally open from 11.00–15.00. Rectory Tel. 0161–6432693.

MONTON is near the western edge of the Greater Manchester conurbation and can be reached from Junction 13 of the M60 via the B5211 and the B5229.

The Unitarian Church at Monton Green (SJ765996) was built in C of E Gothic parish church style by Thomas Worthington 1875. Inside it has stone arches and white walls in the nave and an interesting unattributed series of stained-glass windows in the clerestories. It has

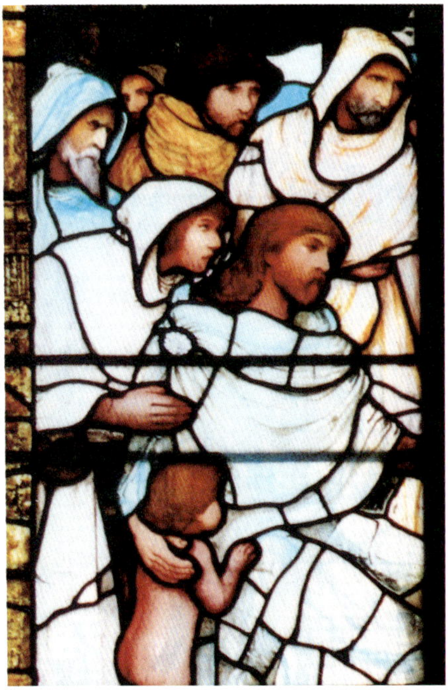

Unitarian Church, Monton. Detail of the north transept window by The Gateshead Glass Co, c.1892.

a couple of unusual features. The lectern is more of a mini stone pulpit than a reading stand and the canopied rear choir stalls would not be out of place in a grander church! There is a four-light window in the north transept made by **The Gateshead Glass Co.** in 1892. A central band across all four lights depicts Christ with a group of children on the left while on the right He is seen instructing Peter to feed his sheep. Above and below the picture panels are silver, crocketed pinnacles which produce a striking combination of silver and blue light. The designer was **Thomas Ralph Spence**. Few examples of Gateshead Glass are known in churches in the North West and this one is certainly worth visiting.

Access: Vestry Tel. 0161–7070779.

St Paul's, Egerton Rd, Monton (SJ768998), was built in 1911 by **R. B. Preston**. It is brick inside and out with lancet windows and a free approach to 'style'. Preston includes gables and porches and horizontal courses of red brick to create an interesting exterior. Inside, the church is furnished throughout in oak which has simple carved decoration. The main decorative feature of the church is the reredos on which the opus sectile panels, depicting Jesus and four saints, were designed by **William Aikman** and made by **Powell & Sons**. The chancel is enhanced by its mosaic floor in plain blue with a multi-coloured border.

Access: Vicarage Tel. 0161–7892420.

NORRIS BANK is at the Stockport end of the A5145, the Parrs Wood to Stockport Rd.

St Martin's Didsbury Rd (SJ880905) is one of those churches whose unfortunate sponsors ran out of cash leaving the church with a blank west end for the best part of ninety years awaiting the means to complete the building plan. In the meantime someone had the wherewithal to install an excellent stained-glass window in the Lady Chapel. It is unsigned but bears a dedication to members of the Pratt family suggesting that it is later than 1922. It shows Jesus and two disciples on the road to Emmaus and is a very intriguing window in terms of its style, colouring and particularly its potential authorship. The east window was made by **Reuben Bennett** after 1920.

Access: Rectory Tel. 0161–4421932.

NORTHENDEN is south of junction 5 on the M60.

St Wilfrid's in Church St (SD833901) was rebuilt in 1876 by J. C. Crowther and lives up to his reputation. There is an unsigned Great War Memorial here which is listed in the catalogue of the Church Craft League under the name of **Omar Ramsden**. It is a simple bronze panel in a polished wood frame and hangs on the north wall near the font. The wooden font cover was made in *c.* 1951 by **Robert Thompson** of Kilburn who was also responsible for the altar rail. The bishop's chair and the frontal chest are also attributed locally to Thompson but his

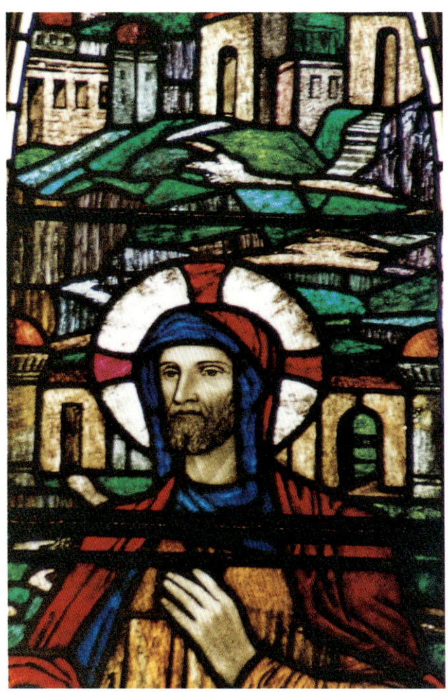

St Martin, Norris Bank. Detail of Pratt memorial window, c.1922 anon.

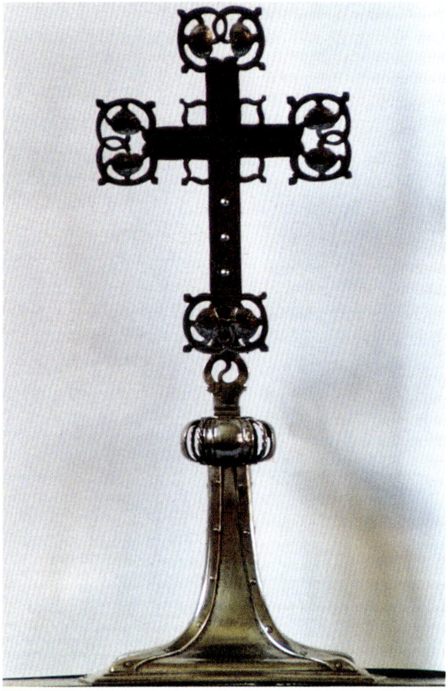

St Mary, Oldham. Altar Cross. Unsigned. Undated.

trademark mouse, if there, is not obvious. Were they made before 1919?

Access: Rectory Tel. 0161–9982615.

OLDHAM is 6 or 7 miles north-east of Manchester city centre just beyond M60 Junction 22.

St Mary's in Church St (SD928051) was built in the 1820s and was re-ordered in 1976 and re-decorated to match its earlier style. However, the two eye-catching triptychs painted by E. Stanley Watkins in 1908 survived the re-ordering. The larger work is behind the altar in the sanctuary and was described in the *Studio Year Book* for 1909 as 'containing upwards of seventy figures representative of the Church's history, dating from the Old Testament prophets to the present century and containing portraits of many celebrated personages.' The smaller triptych is in the Bishop Lake Chapel and commemorates Bishop Lake, who had been vicar of Oldham in the 1650s. He is shown with St Elizabeth standing to the left of a Pre-Raphaelite style 'Adoration of the Shepherds' while St Chad and Sir Ralph Langley stand on the other side. On the altar is an Arts and Crafts cross and candlestick set.

Access: Vicarage Tel. 0161–6786767.

St Margaret's in Chapel Rd, Hollinwood (SD911031) was re-built in 1880 by R. K. Freeman. It is a neat stone building with a slate roof. The tower was added in 1906 and it has slightly daring turrets and finials at each corner. Inside, the church is neat if unremarkable. The pew ends have carved decoration of different designs and the piers supporting the arches are each trimmed with a narrow marble column. Hovering where the arcade ends at the east end of the nave is a well-carved little stone angel. The tall candlesticks at the east end of the church, the credence table and the bishop's chair are all the work of Robert Thompson.

Access: Vicarage: 0161–6814541.

Dronsfield's Offices, in King St (SD924048) were built 1906–7 by J. H. Sellers and are usually glimpsed fleetingly as people whirl around the huge roundabout above the A68. The building was a pioneer of style in 1907 and is unmistakable with its dark green brick, the

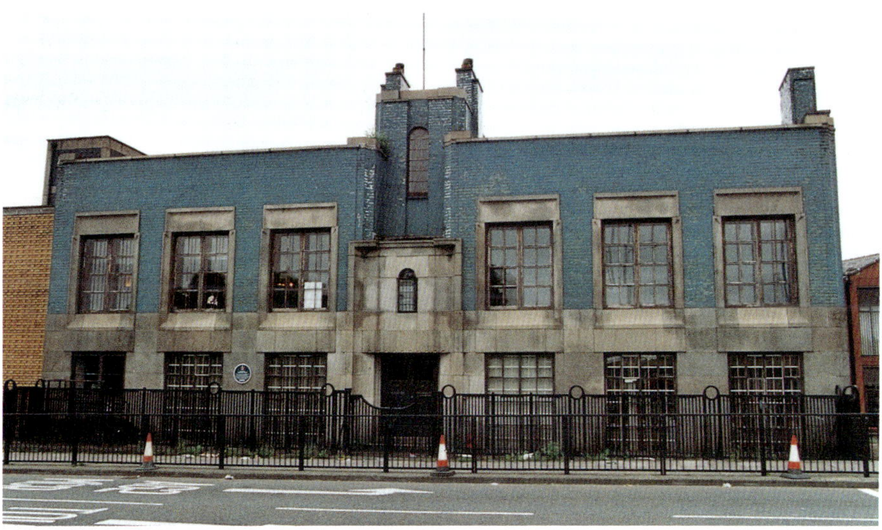

Dronsfield's Offices, Oldham. J. H. Sellers, 1907.

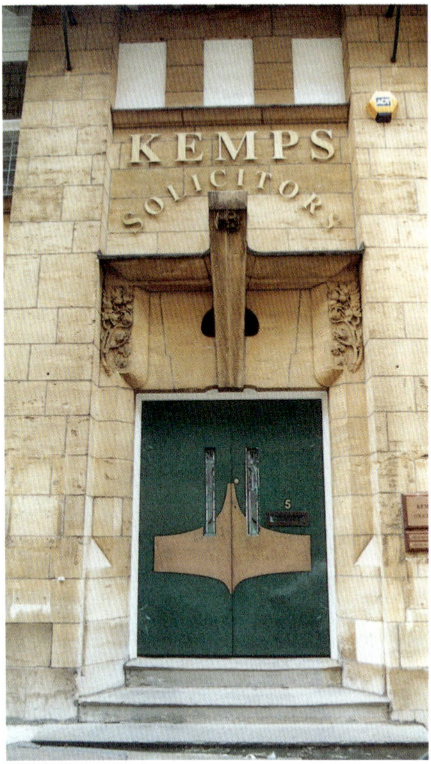

Greaves St, Oldham. Entrance to Kemps Solicitors. Edgar Wood, 1901.

angular decoration in the stonework around the entrance and windows, and of course, its flat roof and notional tower.

Access: Private Offices, not open to the public.

Greaves St, (SD928048) has a small office building designed by **Edgar Wood** in 1901. It is very stylish with curved brass panels and tiny slit-like stained-glass windows in the doors. The carved stone decoration is very evocative of the Art Deco style which had yet to develop.

Access: Private offices not open to the public.

Gallery Oldham in Greaves St (SD928049) is part of the new Cultural Quarter for Oldham. The gallery has changing exhibitions from its Decorative Arts and Social and Natural History collections as well as travelling exhibitions. Its collection of paintings includes a select few by Holman Hunt, Millais, **Rossetti**, Waterhouse, Leighton, **Ruskin** and **Crane**. The Gallery's interesting studio pottery collection dates from the 1930s except for two earlier pieces by **Martin Brothers**. It is planned that the old library, art gallery and museum will be part of another phase in the development of the Cultural Quarter.

Access: Open Mon–Sat 10.00–17.00. Little of the Decorative Arts collection is on permanent display but appointments can be made to view. Tel. 0161–9114653.

At the top end of **Alexander Park**, (SD934041) adjacent to Queens Rd, are two large bronze statues commemorating two of Oldham's MPs. The first was made in 1878 by **D. W. Stevenson** and is of John Platt with four elegant ladies at his feet. The second is of Robert Ashcroft *The Workers' Friend* who was MP from 1895–99. This statue was erected in 1903 and is the work of **F. W. Pomeroy**.

In **Church Terrace** (SD928052) below St Mary's church stands the town's Great War Memorial comprising a statue by **Albert Toft** of fighting men and a very long bronze casting with the names of the men of Oldham who fought in that and subsequent 'conflicts.'.

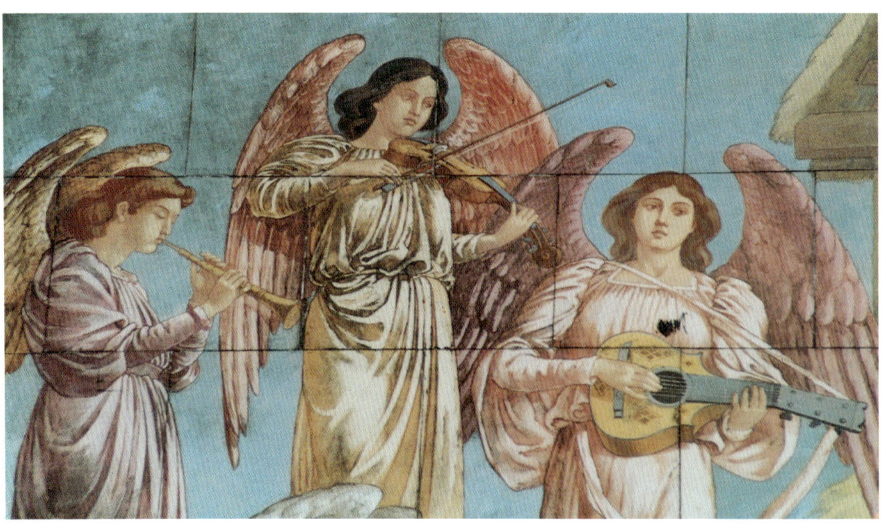

St Clement, Ordsall. Chancel decoration by Doulton, c. 1892.

ORDSALL lies on the western edge of Salford fragmented by redevelopment.

St Clement's in Hulton St (SJ817973) was built 1877–78 by **Paley & Austin**. It is a huge brick affair with a slate roof and flèche. The exterior is full of interest in the detailing. Internally it is very high with brick arcades supported on stone piers. The reredos is a gigantic ceramic representation of the crucifixion made by **Doulton** in 1892. The firm was also responsible for the unglazed, fired impasto tiles on the walls of the chancel with their floating musical angels. There are two opus sectile panels either side of the east window of St Clement and St John.

Access: Vicarage Tel. 0161–8720800.

PARTINGTON is the most south-westerly outpost of the Greater Manchester conurbation sitting astride the A6144 south of the Manchester Ship Canal.

St Mary's church in Manchester Rd (SJ718916) was listed Grade II in 2001 as a good example of an Arts and Crafts church. It was designed by **George Truefitt** and built in 1884 in Cheshire red-sandstone. It is not an exciting example of the genre but it has a degree of individuality in the bell stage of its tower, the long extension of the fall of the roof east of the tower and in the bluntness of the lancet windows in the east wall. Internally it is almost devoid of original fittings. The stained glass in the east window is by Percy Bacon.

Access: Vicarage Tel. 0161–7753542.

PATRICROFT lies on the western fringe of Eccles, on the A57 about a mile from Junction 11 on the M60.

Christ Church, on the corner of Liverpool Rd and Nelson St (SJ765985), was built by John Lowe 1868. The chapel in the south aisle has a two-light 'Crown of Life' window made in 1922 by **A. E. Child**. There are a number of windows here with the characteristics of **W. J. Pearce's** work but they are unsigned and undated. In the north aisle, beginning with the east-most window they are Hope and Charity, 'The Crown of Life', St John and St Nicholas and finally St George and St Martin. In the south transept there is another anonymous two-light window illustrating the Beatitudes. There are wall paintings in the chancel: St Paul, St Matthew, Mary, the Good Shepherd and St Peter. St Paul is slightly flawed anatomically and signed **Gustave Hiller** 1895. The Centenary History of the church written by J. R. Bleakley refers to the need to renovate the paintings *c.* 1939 when Hiller, then aged 75, came from Liverpool to do the work himself despite needing assistance to climb the ladders. The painted angel quatrefoils in the spandrels of the arcade are endowed with **Hiller's** unmistakable jaw-line.

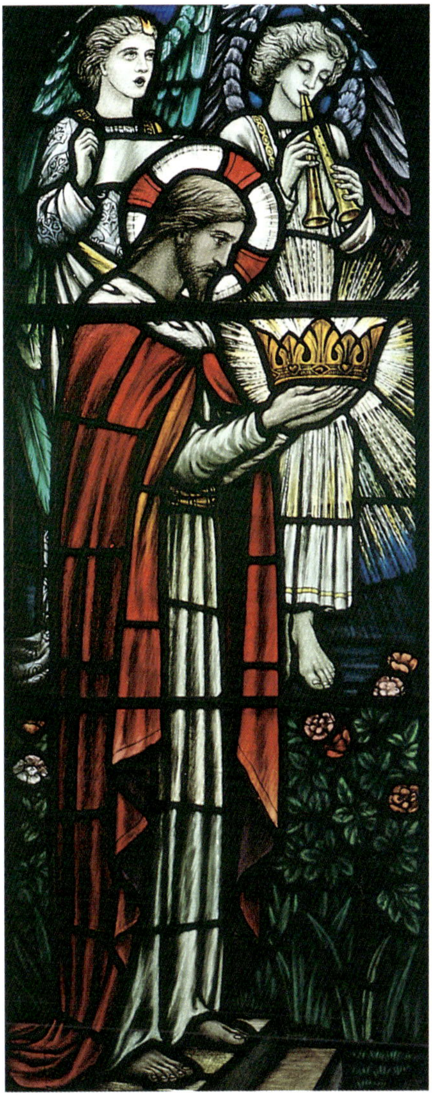

Christ Church, Patricroft. Detail of the 'Crown of Life' window by A. E. Child, 1922.

Access: Team Rector Tel. 0161–2815739.

PENDLEBURY is northwest of Salford on the A666 to Bolton.

St Augustine's in Bolton Rd (SD787016) is one of the most impressive of **Bodley's** churches. It was built 1871–74 as part of a group including the nearby school, gate house and lodge. It is a huge but elegant red brick building with stone-capped turreted buttresses and tall traceried windows. From the outside the church maintains its dignity in what are now rather bleak surroundings and raises high expectations of a beautiful interior. The whole building and all its fixtures, fittings, furnishings and stained glass were designed by **Bodley** and it lives up to the highest expectations. Inside it is a great uninterrupted space 80ft high and 159 ft long. There are no aisles other than the narrow passageways formed by piercing the internal buttresses and the floor space of the nave is unencumbered by pillars or pews. Intricate carving and pierced work characterise all the internal woodwork from the daring four tiered angel-topped font cover to the splendid and massive chancel screen with its walk way above. The restrained linen fold oak pulpit sits neatly against one of the sandstone buttresses and the choir stalls are carved with mythical animals and poppy heads. The view from the west end is dominated by the carved and painted reredos which was made by Watts & Co. The painter has not been identified but it is supposed to be 'someone in the firm'. There is a series of similarly anonymous paintings of saints on panels fixed on the internal buttresses. The stained glass was all made by Burlison & Grylls and installed in the mid 1870s.

Access: Parish Office Tel. 0161–7278175.

PRESTWICH is south of junction 17 on the M60.

St Margaret's in St Margaret's Rd (SD823045) is a Commissioners' church which has benefited greatly from the patronage of Edward Holt the Manchester brewer and other wealthy neighbours. The special joy of the church is its carved woodwork executed by **A. W. Simpson**. The choir stalls, made in 1899, were designed by **Dan Gibson** and are remarkable for the variety as well as the quality of the carving. The pulpit, made by **Simpson** in 1901, was also designed by **Gibson**. The copper preacher's lectern designed by Gibson was made by **Richard Rathbone** also in 1901. The altar and the reredos which extends across the whole width of the sanctuary were made by the

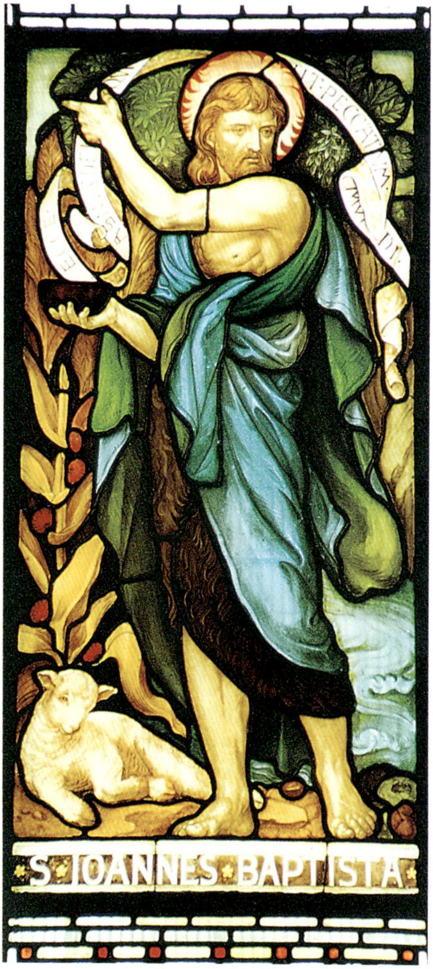

St Elizabeth, Reddish. John the Baptist designed by F. J. Shields, c. 1876–1880.

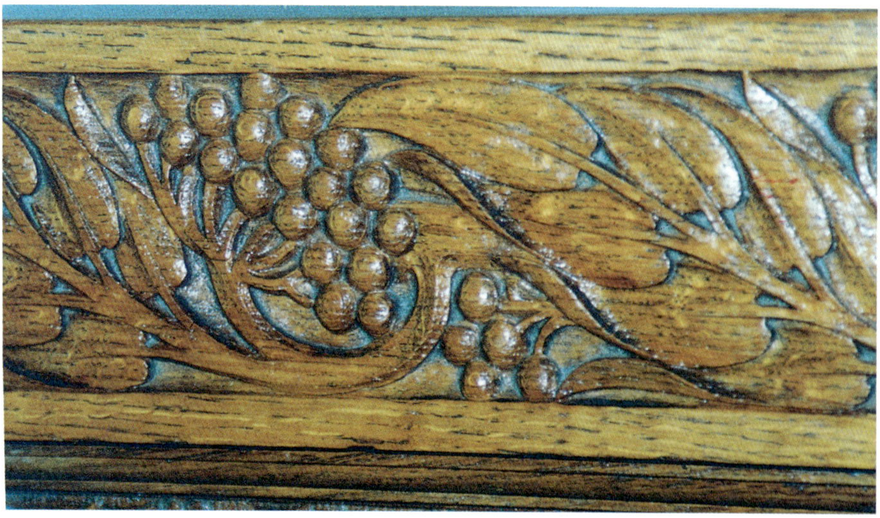

St Margaret, Prestwich. Detail of choir stall designed by Dan Gibson and carved by A. W. Simpson, 1899.

Gibson-Simpson partnership in 1902 and the altar rails, panelling, the bishop's chair and prie-dieu 1904–07. Dan Gibson died in 1907 but he had already designed the chancel screen which was not erected until 1920 after it had been adapted by **William Dolman** to serve as a memorial to Captain Joseph Holt who was killed at Gallipoli in 1915. The screen was carved by **Simpson** and the finely carved figures were executed by **William Aumonier**. The screen was subsequently moved to the west end of the nave. The parishioners' war memorial was designed by **William Dolman** and executed by **Simpson** and is now also fixed at the west end of the church. The English oak from which it is made came from Rydal Mount, the one time home of William Wordsworth.

R. B. Preston designed the elaborate credence-niche in the sanctuary and the 'Carver' memorial tablet above the choir stalls on the north wall. The east window is by Shrigley & Hunt 1895 and the opus sectile panels on either side of the east window and on the south wall of the chancel are by **Powell of Whitefriars** made in 1903. The church also has in safe keeping, an altar cross and vases by **Nelson Dawson**.

Access: Vicarage Tel. 0161–7732698.

REDDISH is about a mile north of Stockport centre, west of the meandering River Tame.

St Elisabeth's in Leamington Rd (SJ893935) was built by **Alfred Waterhouse** in 1883. It is a big church and as interesting and impressive inside as it is out. It is unusual in that it has no less than twenty-one stained-glass panels designed by **Frederic J. Shields** and made by **Heaton, Butler & Bayne**. Unfortunately eighteen of them are in clerestory windows and not easy to see. The others are at ground level at the east end of the north wall in a three-light window representing Melchizedek, the Crucifixion and John the Baptist. This group and ten of the clerestory lights were designed by Shields 1876–80 for Sir William Houldsworth's private chapel at Coodham near Falkirk in Ayreshire. How they came to be fixed here is an untold story. East of the three-light window is a beautiful bronze commemorative plaque dated 1911 and made by the **Keswick School of Industrial Arts**. In the Lady Chapel are three small stained-glass panels designed by **F. C. Eden**.

Access: Vicarage Tel. 0161–4323033.

ROCHDALE lies to the north of the M62 and can be approached from junction 20 or 21.

The Town Hall stands on The Esplanade (SD896133). 'We cannot have beauty without paying for it' Thus spake the Mayor of Rochdale in September 1871 when opening the new Town Hall and explaining why it cost eight times its original budget. Who would now quarrel with His Worship the Mayor? The building was designed in High Victorian Gothic by W. H. Crossland (1835–1908). The tower was destroyed by a fire in 1883 and **Alfred Waterhouse** designed its replacement. Otherwise the exterior is much as Crossland intended with interesting carved and gilded figures and a very colourful spirelet on the roof of the Great Hall. The internal decoration was

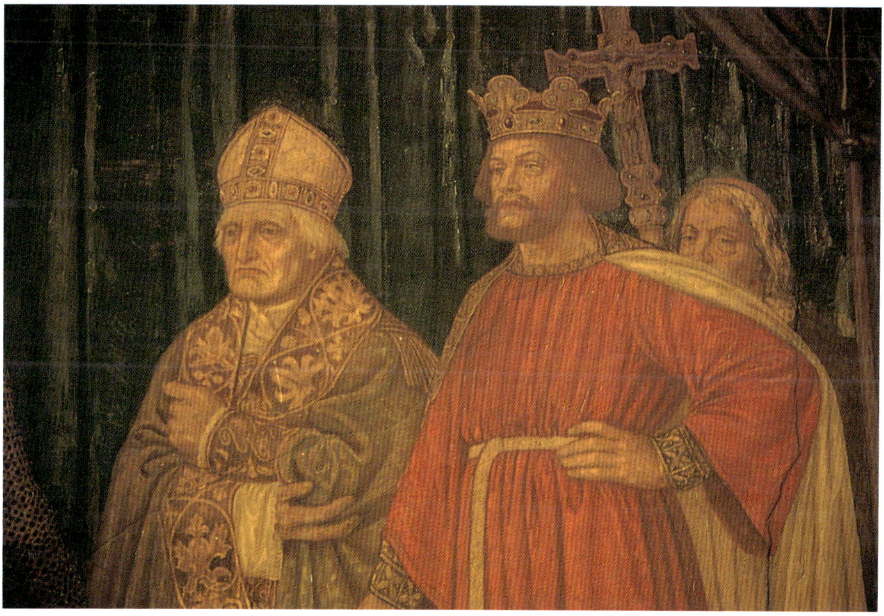

Rochdale Town Hall. Detail of the 'Magna Carta' mural. Henry Holiday, 1871. *Courtesy of Rochdale Town Hall*

supervised by **Heaton, Butler & Bayne** and it is very good. The main entrance floor is covered with **Minton's** encaustic tiles and there is a very grand staircase leading up to the Great Hall where, among other decorative delicacies, there is a mural by **Henry Holiday**. It was a huge undertaking, 35 ft long and 12 ft high which shows King John and his barons at the signing of the Magna Carta. Typically, Holiday took enormous pains over his research for the subject and in his memoirs recalls how he 'found an armourer who made me a complete suit of chain-mail to my pattern, with all the accoutrements.' He then surprised his five-year-old daughter, by stumping down the stairs to breakfast wearing the suit. Holiday was taken ill with a 'spinning of the brain' during the work and had to leave its completion to his friend Ellis Wooldridge. However, Holiday recovered in time to 'come back for a day or two at the close of the available period' to see to the final details – and no doubt to attend the grand unveiling. The stencilled wall decoration in the Hall has been restored and is a fitting foil to the magnificent stained glass by **Heaton, Butler and Bayne**, which shows all the monarchs and their coats of arms, from William I to William IV. Given a certain amount of 'bunking up' the artist has managed to get them all into fourteen windows, each with three-lights, while Victoria and Albert look down from the apex roundels at opposite ends of the Hall. The Council Chamber, reception rooms and the Mayoral suite are all highly decorated with stencilling, stained glass, paintings and carvings. In the former Council Chamber the frieze is made up of panels illustrating the inventions which revolutionised the textile industry. They are reminiscent of book illustrations by Walter Crane and are attributed to a Mr Allen – probably **James Milner Allen** who worked for **Heaton, Butler and Bayne**. In the Small Exchange room off the Mayor's Suite is an intricate frieze of foliage and wild animals attributed to Clement Heaton senior, who it is said made a speciality of drawing animals. To him too is attributed the design of the Minton floor tiles. While it is not quite Cardiff Castle, it is wonderful to see. The Council has produced a first-class illustrated guide.

Access: The Town Hall Keeper gives conducted tours every Friday or otherwise by prior arrangement. Tel. 01706–864773 to check availability and any admission charges.

The Great War Memorial stands across the Esplanade in front of the Town Hall. It is a large granite pier topped by a draped figure lying on a catafalque and is very reminiscent of the Whitehall Cenotaph. It was designed by the same architect, **E. L. Lutyens** 1919–22.

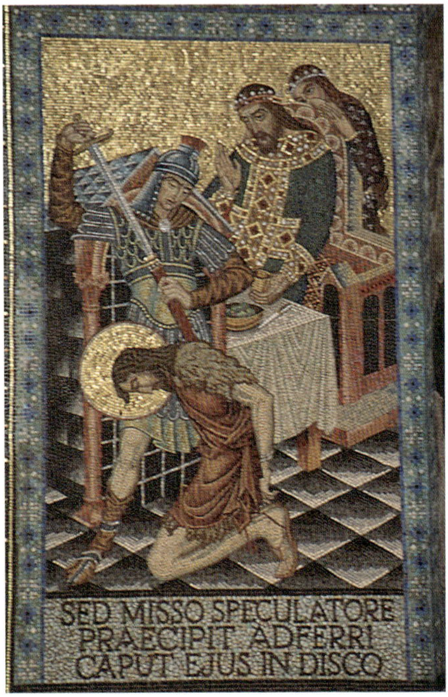

St John, Rochdale. Detail of the chancel mosaics.

St John the Baptist on the corner of McClure St and Dowling St (SD898128) was built in 1924 by the Manchester firm of Hill, Sandy & Norris. It is built on the Byzantine model with a very high central dome. It is simply furnished and decorated except for the chancel apse which is entirely covered in the most brilliant, glittering mosaic showing Christ in Glory with angels, saints and various scenes and symbols. According to the local leaflet, the work was undertaken by an unspecified firm of Italians working in Manchester in 1930.

Access: Presbytery Tel. 01706–646877.

St Chad, in Sparrow Hill and at the Top o't' Steps (SD896131) above the Town Hall square is the mediaeval Parish Church of Rochdale. It has seen great change in the past 800 years much of which has been to its advantage. The west window is set in the tower and contains three lights originally installed in 1873 by **Morris, Marshall, Faulkner & Co.** but repainted in 1882. There are two panels in each light the upper, larger ones each having a typically beautiful **Burne-Jones** figure, Hope, Charity and Faith while the smaller, lower panels show the much less frequently seen Despair, Envy and Folly.

Access: Vicarage Tel. 01706–645014.

St Peter's (SD907127) in St Peter's St, Newbold is a flight of fancy by **J. M. & H. Taylor**. It was built in 1868–71 of yellow stone laid like vertical crazy paving with red brick dressings. Red brick is also used as decoration in string

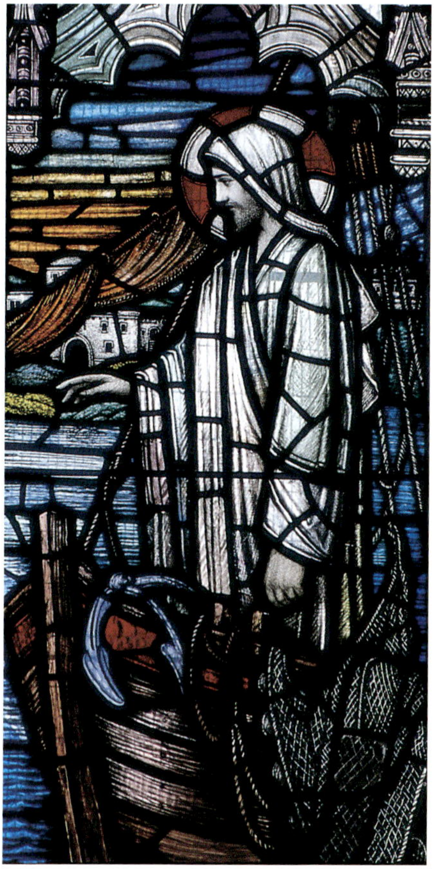

St Peter, Newbold, Rochdale. Detail of Christ calling Peter. Post 1914.

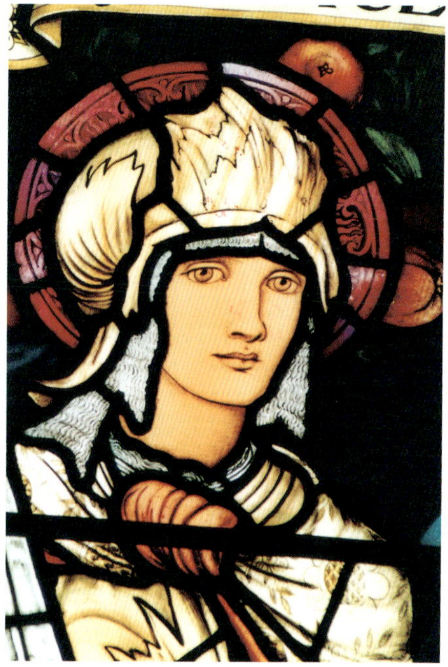

Unitarian Church, Rochdale. Details of 'Justice' by Morris & Co., 1902.

courses, gable end patterns and even in simulation of rainwater heads and down pipes. There is a small baptismal apse at the west end where one buttress flies over the west porch roof and another is carried through it. Internally the church has suffered from a rather utilitarian approach to reducing the size of the nave to create a parish room and offices in what was once the west end. There is the usual set of Medland Taylor's ceramic mottos. Totally unexpected in this church is a window in the north-east angle of the sanctuary apse. It was made some time after 1914 and shows Jesus calling Simon Peter. A brass plaque records the refurbishment of the window in 1989 and the mark 'Walmsley St Anne' appears in the bottom right hand corner of what seems to be its original setting. This and the style, would suggest the maker was **B. D. Walmsley**, of St Anne's Studio, Langdale but in the absence of a catalogue it is difficult to be sure whether or not this window belongs to the setting.

Access: Vicarage Tel. 01706–649886.

The Unitarian Church, in Clover St (SD894135) was built in the 1970s. Behind the altar is a row of eight superb stained-glass windows made by **Morris & Co.** for the predecessor church in Blackwater St. Clearly the apse was designed to accommodate the windows and the architect has produced a perfect setting. The stained-glass panels were made in 1902 from **Burne-Jones** cartoons and represent eight virtues: Truth, Justice, Liberty, Prudence, Knowledge, Love, Faith and Humility.

Access: Minister Tel. 01706–340465.

St Anne, Milnrow Rd, Belfield (SD916134) was built in 1912–13 by **R. B. Preston**. It is built of stone with a high south tower. Both the tower and the aisles have battered buttresses. The rather fussy exterior gives way to absolute simplicity and tranquillity inside the church. The walls of the nave, aisles and chancel are painted white in contrast to the soft grey of the stone arches and pillars of the aisle arcades. The pillars are of square section with rounded corners and at the top, have a gentle, slightly bulbous swelling in place of capitals. There is a small apse in the middle of the west end which holds the font and is lit by two small leaded windows with pale sea-green tinted glass which contributes much to the sense of peacefulness in the church.

Access: Vicarage Tel. 01706–646173.

St Aidan's, Manchester Rd, Sudden (SD883116) was built in 1914 by **Temple Moore**. The church has a stout west tower and rubble walling which gives it a rugged look reminiscent of the Northumbrian roots of its patron saint. There is an outdoor pulpit which was used until recently for preaching at Whitsun. The ruggedness of the exterior is not carried indoors. Like RB Preston's St Annes at the other end of town it is white with plain stone pointed-arches and square-sectioned pillars. Here the pillars are massive. This is Gothic, but not as the mediaevalists knew it. The ground-level wall niches, for instance, were built to house the radiators of the heating system! There is a painted and gilded reredos and the east window was made by Henry Grylls in 1946. The prayer desk, lectern and pulpit were designed by **T. L. Moore** and made by **Bridgeman** of Lichfield. Safely locked away are the silver paten and chalice which were also designed by Moore and made by the **Duchess of Sutherland's Cripples' Guild**.

Access: Vicarage Tel. 01706–631812.

Silver St Chapel, (SD888139) was built in 1893 by **Edgar Wood**. It is a very efficient and versatile building but the penetrating damp is the effect of Wood's penchant for difficult-to-reach valley gutters. Even so the gabling and the fenestration combine to produce a very attractive elevation to Edmund St. The decorative interest on the front lies in the modelled and painted Tree of Life in the apex of the gable.

Access: Church office Tel. 01706–657355 or 01706–522443.

Barcroft, 193 Bolton Rd (SD874117) was built by **Edgar Wood** in 1894 and remains a private house, not easily seen en route.

Access: Private dwelling.

Victoria Hotel, (SD890138) in Spotland Rd which was built by **Edgar Wood**, survives, just about, but not as a hotel.

Access: Private dwelling.

The George and Dragon public house (SD881106) in Manchester Rd, Castleton, was built by **Edgar Wood** in 1897. Its gabled, Tudoresque exterior remains pretty well unchanged, but it has been altered inside. The pub still has its **Edgar Wood** Inn sign.

Access: Normal licensing hours.

The Empire Hall, in Packer St (SD897133), off the Town Hall car park, has been converted to a pub but retains much of its decorative glass executed by **W. J. Pearce**.

Access: Normal opening hours.

Rochdale Museum and Art Gallery, Esplanade (SD894132) has recently undergone a scheme of refurbishment and re-opened in the autumn of 2002. **W. J. Pearce's** catalogue lays claim to the leaded windows in 'Art Gallery, &c., Rochdale'. **C. J. Allen** designed the stone frieze on the front of the building which was sculpted by the Manchester stone carver **John Jarvis Millson**. Among the Art Gallery's extensive collection are pictures by Frank Brangywn, **Eric Gill** and **Edgar Wood**. There is also a small bronze sculpture by **Albert Toft** entitled 'Cui Bono' (1937) .

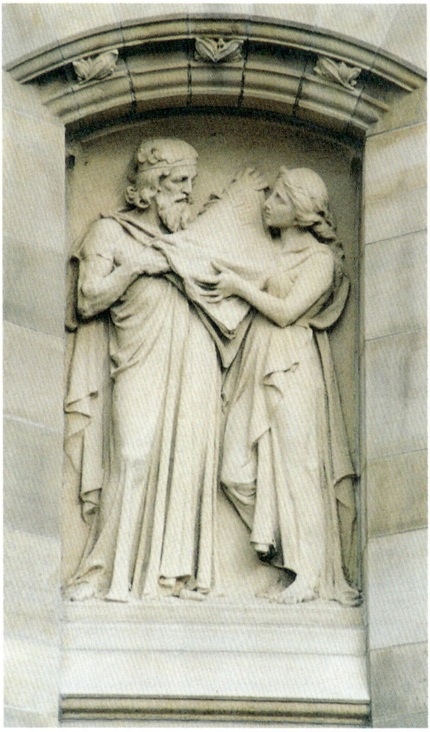

Rochdale Museum and Art Gallery. Sculpted panel. Designed by C. J. Allen. Executed by J. J. Millsom, 1913.

Access: Open Tues–Sat 10.00–16.30. Tel. 01706–342154.

Falinge Park lies within the curve of Falinge Rd (SD893140) in the north-west quarter of the town. It was designed in 1905 as a public park by **T. H. Mawson**. It is in the nature of things that parks and gardens will change over a 90 to 100 year period but this park, centred on the 'ruin' of the old house, has held its shape. The lawns and trees sweep up from the entrance on Falinge Rd towards the balustrades of the terrace, giving way behind the house to a wilder area. The two are separated on the east side by formal walled gardens with niches and arbours. Apart from the abundance of modern graffiti, Thomas would be very pleased to see his park 100 years on.

Access: Open 8.00 until dusk.

ROYTON is about 1½ miles north of Oldham town centre on the A671.

St Anne's between Broadway and St Anne's Avenue (SD920070) was re-built 1908–10 by **Temple Lushington Moore**. It is a large and interesting church with a huge, steep roof set off by the square south-east tower, added in

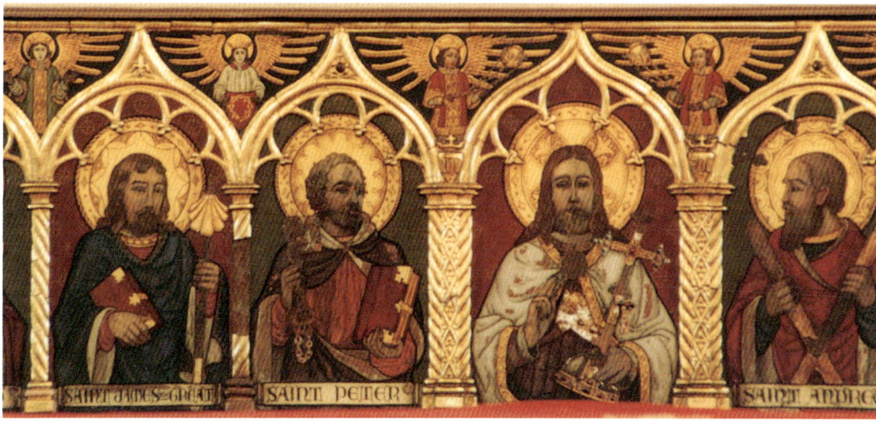

St Anne, Royton. Detail of the reredos designed by Mrs Temple Moore, c. 1910.

1926, and the lower, flat-roofed chapel built against the east end wall. The font, designed by **Temple Moore**, has been moved into the body of the church and the lean-to baptistery at the west end, has been separated from the nave by a glass screen. The stained glass in the west wall is by **G. E. R. Smith**. The rest of the interior has many interesting structural and decorative features, including the painted and gilded gesso saints, designed by Mrs T. L. Moore in 1910, for the reredos of the main altar. There are two school buildings adjacent to the church. The east-most building was designed by **Temple Moore** in 1916 while that nearest the church was designed in 1933 by his son-in-law Leslie Moore.

Access: Vicarage Tel. 0161–6242249.

RUSHOLME lies about a mile south-east of the Manchester city centre south of Longsight and east of Levenshulme.

Holy Trinity, Platt Lane, Fallowfield (SJ851948) was built 1845–46 by **Edmund Sharpe**. It is the second and the larger of his two 'pot' churches. The spire is very tall, very elegant and needle sharp and it is not until you get close that you will see that everything is not stone, but terracotta. There is a stained-glass window here depicting 'The Good Shepherd' which was designed by **Henry Holiday** for **Powell of Whitefriars**. There is also a beautiful but unsigned example of a WW1 roll of honour, and **W. J. Pearce** has two windows.

Access: Church Office Tel. 0161–2241123.

Gallery of Costume and Textiles, Platt Hall, Rusholme (SJ853948). The gallery contains one of the largest collections of costumes and accessories in Britain. However, only a few items relate to the Arts and Crafts period. A small part of the **Lewis Day** collection contains samples of embroidery of that period, one of which was commissioned for his book *Art in Needlework*, 1900. There is also a delightful dress by Jessie Newberry of the Glasgow School of Art and a child's dress and a collar inspired by the Glasgow School .

Access: Open on the last Saturday of the month from 10.00–17.00 or during weekdays by appointment. Tel. 0161–225217.

SALFORD is just to the west of its neighbouring city, Manchester, starting more or less, where the A6 crosses the Irwell.

Salford Museum, The Crescent, Peel Park (SJ820989) is better known for its splendid re-creation of a Victorian Street, its Victorian art collection and its local history displays, but it also has a large collection of **Pilkington** pottery and the archive of one of its most prolific artists, **Walter Mycock**.

Access: Open Mon–Fri 10.00–16.45, Sat & Sun 13.00–17.00. Tel. 0161–7362649.

SHAW straddles the A663 north of Oldham and south of junction 21 on the M62.

Crompton Great War Memorial in High St (SD937087) was unveiled in 1923. It shows a half-clad classical man wielding a sword to defend young children from wild beasts. It is a symbolic assertion that the sacrifice of those who fought and died in the war would secure the defense of future generations. This grand memorial is the work of **R. R. Goulden**.

St James's in St James St (SJ939094) has a secret in its garden. It has a large bronze sculpture by **William Hamo Thorneycroft** camouflaged in the undergrowth. It is of a seated woman with a book in her lap and a young boy standing by her side. At the boy's feet are a cricket bat and ball. The group represents 'Education' and is a copy in bronze of one the four supporting groups Thornycroft made for the Gladstone Memorial in London. It was cast in 1919 as a gift from local business

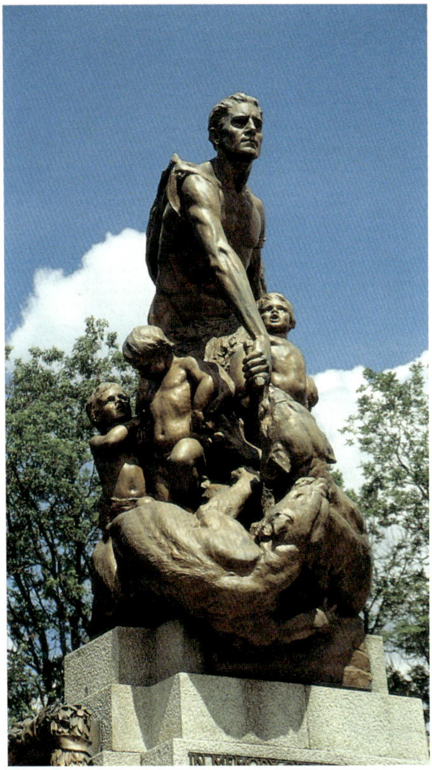

War Memorial, Shaw by R. R. Goulden. See p.109.

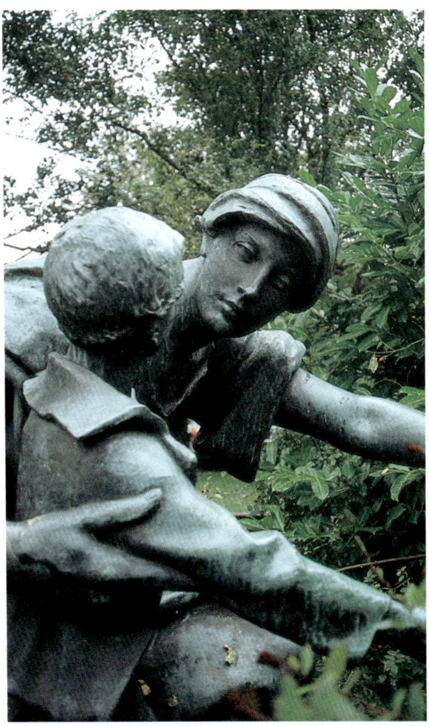

St James's churchyard, Shaw. 'Education' by W. Hamo Thorneycroft, 1919.

man James Cockcroft to adorn the town's Carnegie Library. However when the library needed more space in 1975 the statue lost its home and was consigned to the shrubbery at St James's. Shame!

STALYBRIDGE borders Ashton under Lyne on the eastern edge of the Manchester conurbation.

The War Memorial (SJ963985) is to be found by the river Tame at the southern end of the Trinity St Bridge. There are two concave walls, one each side of the bridge, which carry the panels inscribed with the names of the fallen while the end pillars of the bridge serve as pedestals for bronze sculptures by **F. V. Blundstone**. A fallen soldier lies on the eastern side and on the west rests a sailor, each supported by an angel.

STOCKPORT has grown up either side of the A6 south-west of Manchester.

St George's Church, Buxton Rd (SJ900890) is reputed to be the best work of **Paley & Austin**. It was built 1896–97 and is without doubt a beautiful building with a massive crossing tower supporting a high and elegant spire. Internally, the clerestory lights and the large amount of clear glazing give it a lightness which belies the great height of the nave and warms the pink Runcorn stone of the interior. The seven-light windows at the east and west ends were made by **Shrigley & Hunt** who have risen to the occasion, especially in the east window. The font and the reredos are of finely carved Derbyshire alabaster and the reredos at least was carved by **Bridgeman** of Lichfield. In addition to calling on the services of the Lancaster based stained-glass firm, the architects chose **James Hatch** of Lancaster to do the beautiful wood-carving in the choir. This is not an extravagantly decorated building but its detail repays close study.

Access: Usually attended between 9.00 and 12.00. Tel. 0161–4802453.

Our Lady & the Apostles (SJ894896) was built in 1905 by **Edmund Kirby** and stands near the Shaw Heath/Greek St roundabout. It is a huge church, bright red-brick and turbulent outside but high, light and restful inside. The smooth cream plaster is set off below the clerestory by a narrow band of dark brown quatrefoil brick panels. The exposed brick arches in the nave arcades have incised dog-tooth and zigzag decoration and stand on polished granite pillars, although it must be said that the join is less than elegant. The carved chancel screen is excellent but may be thought by some to suffer slightly from an over enthusiastic use of gold paint. The sanctuary sits in an apse with a very narrow but functional ambulatory. The altar is made of

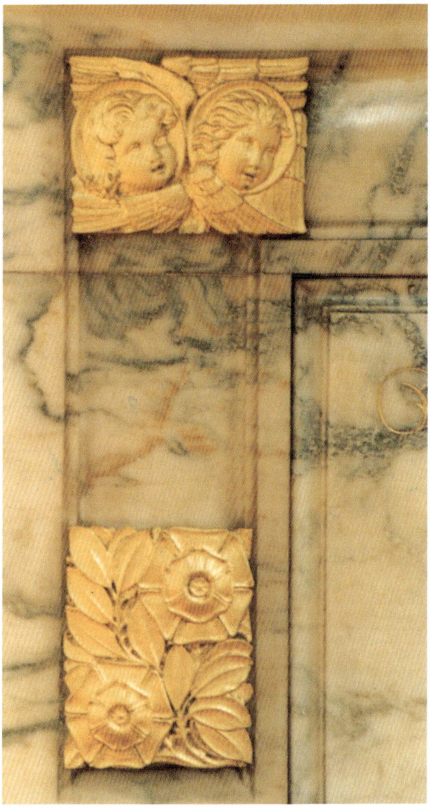

Our Lady and the Apostles, Stockport. Detail of the altar designed by Edmund Kirby, 1905.

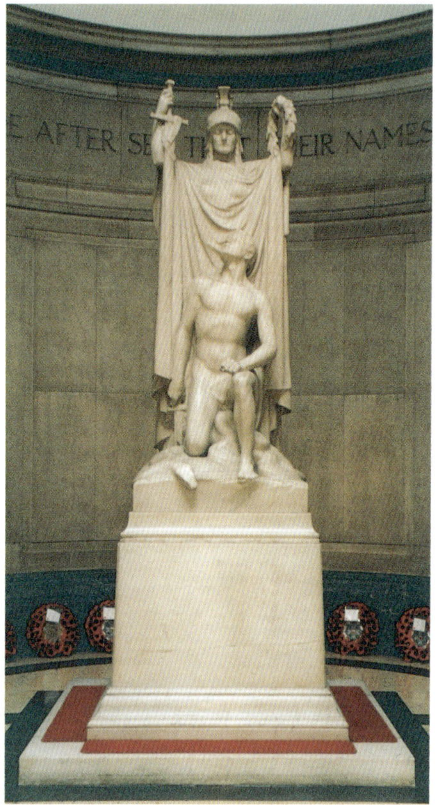

Great War Memorial, Stockport. Sculpture by Gilbert Ledward.

alabaster set with gilded plaques and is surmounted by a carved and pierced reredos backed by the colours of the three-light stained-glass window in the ambulatory wall. Made by **Margaret Agnes Rope** the window shows Mary, Joseph and the boy Jesus beautifully drawn and coloured. There is a huge and very decorative rose window in the west end of the church which, like the nave and clerestory windows, is patterned only by the lead lines.

Access: Presbytery Tel. 0161–4802489.

The Great War Memorial stands at the junction of Wellington Road and Greek St (SJ895898). It is a magnificent monument to the 2,200 men of the town who died in the Great War. It takes the form of a Memorial Hall and Art Gallery. Around the marble sides of the Memorial Hall are engraved the names of those who died in the Great War and the Second World War. The centre-piece of the memorial is a white marble sculpture by **Gilbert Ledward** in which a man kneels in front of Britannia, who holds the sword of honour in one hand and the laurel wreath of victory in the other. Crushed beneath the shield at the man's feet is a serpent symbolising victory over evil.

Access: Mon–Fri 11.00–17.00, Sat 10.00–17.00.

SWINTON lies on the north-west fringes of the Manchester conurbation, north of Pendlebury on the A6.

St Peter's (SD774017) stands at the corner of Chorley Rd and Partington Lane. It was built in 1869 by **G. E. Street** in his deft and distinguished C14 Gothic style. The stone lych-gate is unusual and looks as if it has been lifted from a C14 illustrated manuscript. Internally the church has Street's restful but grand proportions. In the south nave wall are three late Morris & Co. windows, full of good colours and details (look at the fishes in the basket). In the south transept is a window by **Joan Howson** dating from *c.* 1945. At the west end of the north aisle is a three-light window showing St Francis, St Hilda and St Columba which was made in 1932 by **Veronica Whall**. It stands next to one of her father's windows made in 1912, which is almost magical in the quality of the silver light it lets into the church. Next to this is an example of the work of **Edward Frampton** executed in his own studio *c.* 1886. The Lady Chapel appears to have been furnished by Watts & Co. while the chapel on the north side has a carved reredos moved here

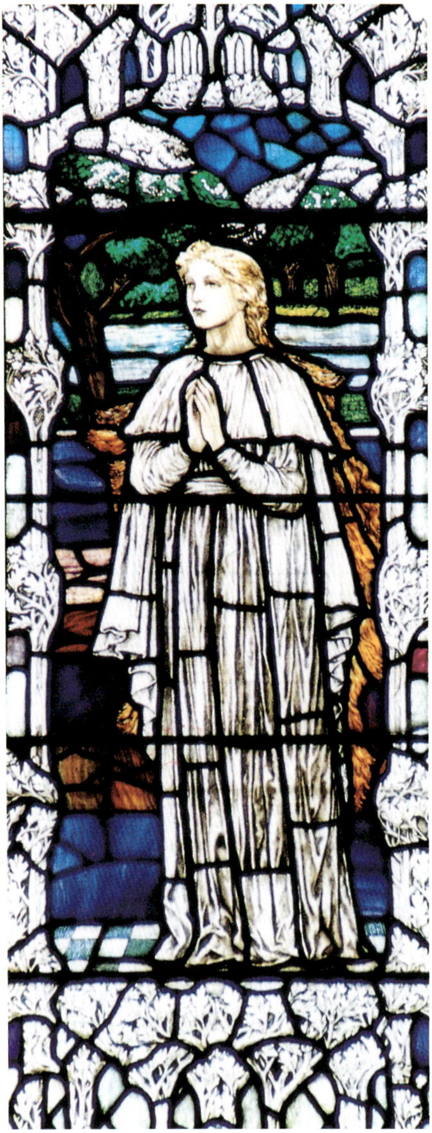

St Peter, Swinton. Detail, North aisle, C. W. Whall, 1912.

in the 1980s from St Peter's in Oldham. Its origins have not been researched.

Access: Parish Office 9.00–12.00 weekdays. Tel. 0161–7278175, Rectory Tel. 0161–7941578.

Holy Rood in Moorside Rd (SD765013) is a simple brick-built Early English church from the 1870s and a most unlikely spot to come upon a set of five windows by **J. E. Nuttgens.** The first, in the left hand side of a two-light window in the north wall, is a beautiful St Cecilia. The right hand light is occupied by another, no less beautiful, St Cecilia by a very different and so far unattributed hand. High up in the north transept is a small, round, brightly coloured window showing 'Christ in Glory'

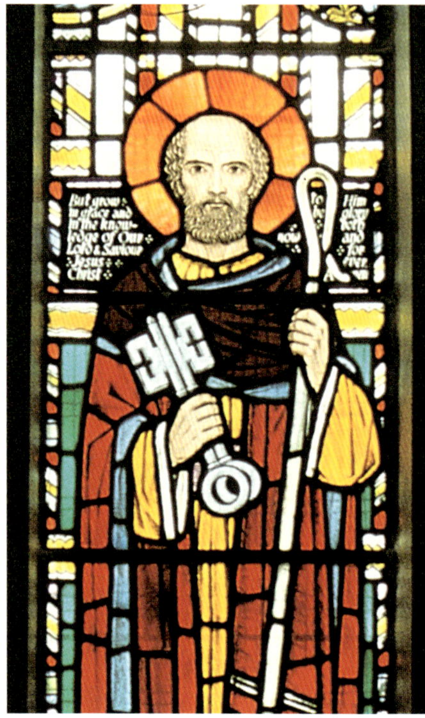

Holy Rood, Swinton. J. E. Nuttgens, 1976

which is signed and dated 1972 (when Nuttgens was 80). The Lady Chapel has four saints in two two-light windows; Helena and Elizabeth; Margaret of the Holy Rood (with a splendid dragon) and St Anne. The south aisle has an even later Nuttgens window signed and dated 1976 showing, Ss Michael, Peter and John the Baptist. Also in the south wall there is a St Joseph window by J. A. Nuttgens (son of J. E.) dated 1990. The east window of the Lady Chapel depicting St John, Virgin and Child and St Luke was made by Gilbert Sheedy who had been a student of Nuttgens.

Access: Vicarage Tel. 0161–7942464 .

The War Memorial (SD778016) in a garden bordering Chorley Rd is a short, squat cenotaph with a domed top, painted white and bearing a small and simple bronze cross with a spray of flowers. It was designed by **J. H. Sellers** and originally put up in Victoria Park, Swinton, in 1930. It was built with a niche containing a small bronze 'St George and the Dragon' made by **Henry Wilson.** The monument was damaged in the 1980s and St George was missing when it was re-erected on its present site. The paved area around the cenotaph and the four electric globe lamps on decorative iron supports are new work.

TIMPERLEY is east of Altrincham and north of Hale in the leafy southern borders of south Manchester.

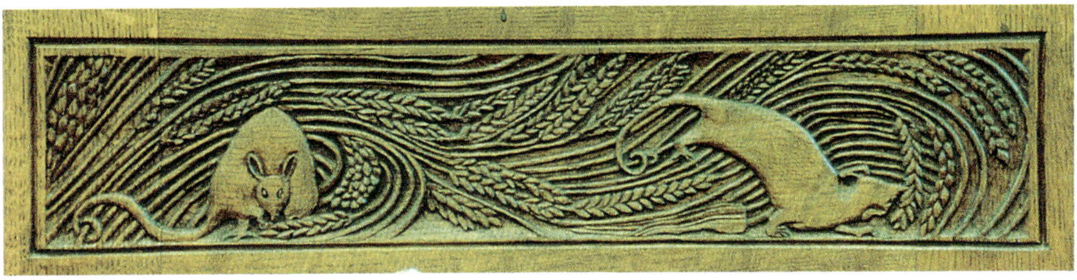

Christ Church, Timperley. Detail porch door. Timperley carving class.

Christ Church, Thorley Lane, Timperley (SD791882) was built of red sandstone in a Neo-Norman style by James Bayley of Altrincham in 1851 and enlarged by John Lowe in 1864. The church received a major face lift in the 1880s with the installation of stained glass in the east window by Heaton, Butler and Bayne in 1882 and the lining of the walls with terracotta tiles in 1887. Some of the later Arts and Crafts features of the church were the result of the appointment in 1905 of a practical, hands-on, woodworking vicar, the Reverend C. D. Wray. He served the parish until 1917 and made the carved internal doors of the north porch with the help of his woodworking class and a design by the architect **John Cocker**. **Edgar Wood** came to live just down the road at Hale and designed the reredos which was made by **George Wragge Ltd** in oak inlaid with walnut, ebony and box with a decorative inscription. The altar, altar rail and box pews are all attributed to **Edgar Wood** as is the cross of pewter, brass and enamel which was made in the **George Wragge Ltd** workshop in 1911. The **Wragge** studio made an almost complete set of windows for the church depicting some of the Virtues. 'Gentleness' was designed by **W. M. Anderson** but the other artists are unknown. The vignettes in the bottoms of the windows are particularly charming. The windows in the choir vestry have not been attributed.

Access: Vicarage Tel. 0161–9804330.

VICTORIA PARK is about 2 miles south east of Manchester city centre between Rusholme and Longsight.

Victoria Baths in Hathersage Rd (SJ857959) were completed in 1906 at a cost of over £59,000 and were described as the most 'splendid municipal bathing institution in the country'. The grand, red-brick building with its surfeit of stone dressings and terracotta friezes was designed by the first Manchester City Architect, Henry Price and provided bathing facilities for the residents of central Manchester. Three sets of swimming pools and slipper baths were provided. Two were for First and Second Class Males but there was only one Class for Females!

The building was lavish in its construction, provision and decoration. Everywhere was finished from floor to ceiling with tiles from the Manchester firm of **Pilkington Brothers** and the floors were finished with mosaics. There were beautiful stained-glass windows, most of which had floral motifs in brilliant colours and also a series of picture panels depicting various sports. Particularly splendid was the provision for the First Class Males with its screens, rails and balustrade made of polished baywood and pitch pine and with fine ornamental metalwork. The rest room of the Turkish Baths was as luxurious as it could be made. The stained-glass windows in this room show the Goddess of Purity hovering over blue water dotted with white water lilies. She is clothed in shades of purple and blue with brilliant

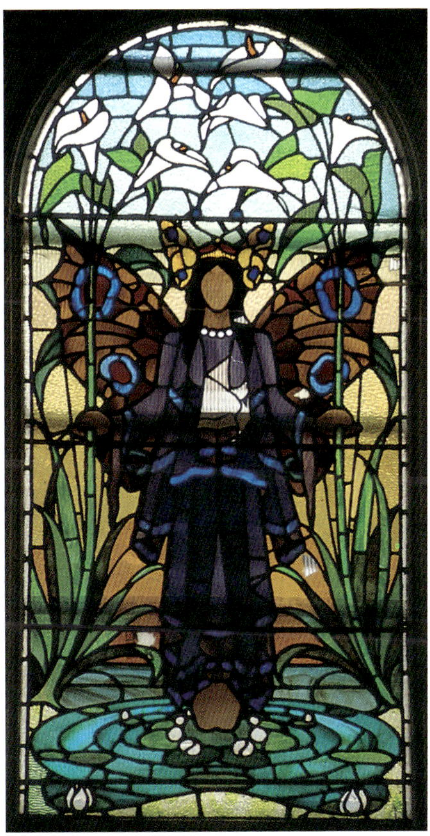

Victoria Baths, Manchester. Detail of the Goddess of Purity window. Anon.

butterfly wings and framed by tall arum lilies. Research is continuing into the provenance of the stained glass. There is a bronze panel in the main entrance hall commemorating the opening of the baths which has a border decorated with mosaic water lilies and irises. The panel is signed by **George Wragge Ltd.** Given this connection and the style of the glass it is tempting to suppose that much of it came from the Wragge Studio.

The Baths were in daily use until they were closed in 1993 and have since fallen into disrepair. A Trust has been formed to restore the building for alternative uses which will be of public benefit. Much needs to be done, including fund raising. Even in its current state it is well worth a visit to see a building which is not only a landmark in social history but which also contains some excellent decorative art of the period.

Access: The Friends of Victoria Baths arrange Open Days but for an appointment. Tel. 0161–2242020.

First Church of Christ Scientist, Daisy Bank Rd (SJ863957) is an exceptional building designed by **Edgar Wood** and built 1903–08. It is essentially Y-shaped in plan and set on a north-south access. The stem holds the body of the church while the arms contain the reading room on one side and the Sunday School on the other. These arms also define and enclose the paved forecourt. The forecourt is entered from Daisy Bank Rd through a quaint lych-gate which is exactly aligned to the axis of the church. Its form and style, including the steeply pitched roof, compliments that of the main building. It is from here that one can appreciate the originality of the building, seeing Wood at his most asymmetrical and picturesque.

It is built of common red brick with white rendering and stone copings on the central

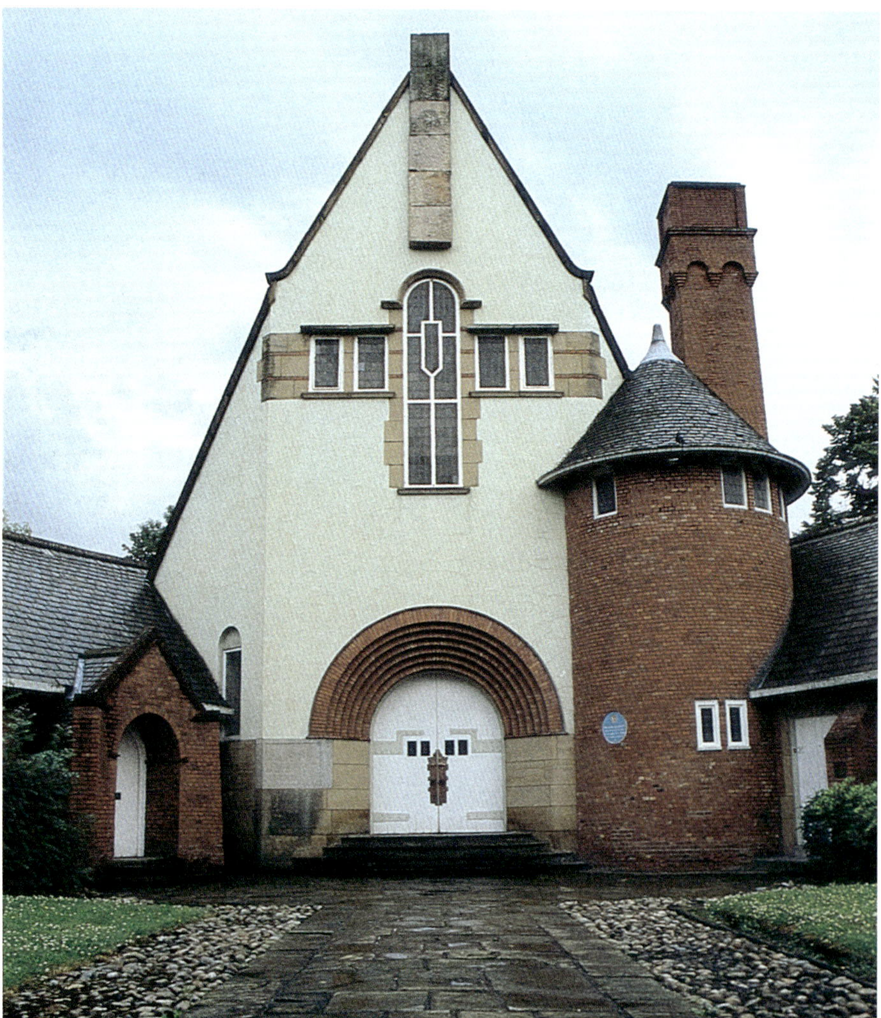

First Church of Christ Scientist. Victoria Park. Front elevation. Edgar Wood 1903–08.

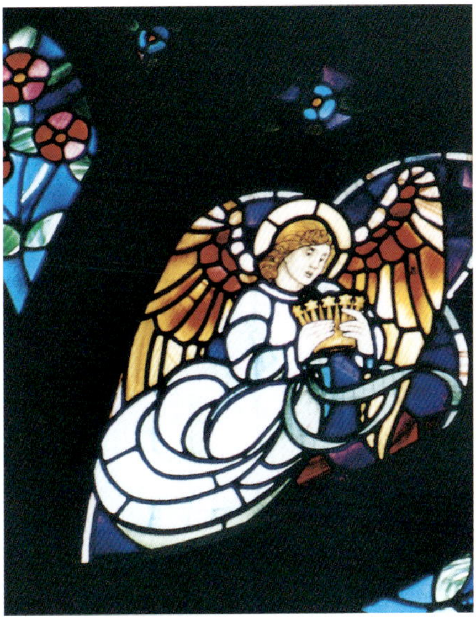

St Chrysostom, Victoria Park. Manchester. Tracery light. W. J. Pearce. Undated.

gable. This gable, with its steep sloping roof and white walls, is raked back with canted sides. Set into the wall is a long, round-headed window which extends left and right below the arch to create the shape of a cross. Below the window is the striking main entrance. Its wide arch is decorated by seven concentric brick arches complemented by the convex steps leading up to the doorway. The door itself is of solid oak, painted white and bearing spectacular repoussé brass lock plates made by **George Wragge Ltd.** To the right is a perfectly proportioned circular tower with a conical roof making the connection with the Sunday School wing and the entrance front, while behind that rises the slender, machicolated boiler chimney. To the left, the roof line is extended downward from the point of the gable, supported by a canted extension to the facade, until it meets the roof-line of the Reading Room wing. The canted bay of the Reading room extends upwards through the eaves in characteristic Edgar Wood fashion, complimenting the line of the main facade.

The building has undergone a number of changes of use since the 1970s. However the major internal features remain. Particularly striking is Wood's clever use of quartered marble in the main hall. This is used around the piers which support the arcades on either side of the hall, across most of the east wall creating a compelling quasi-reredos panel and on the south wall on either side of the entrance. On this wall too above the marble panels is Wood's extraordinary painted and gilded screen reminiscent of the mushrabiyyahs seen in North African buildings which fill unglazed window-openings to provide privacy, ventilation and shade. The main hall has an entrance on the west side which is reached by way of an unexpected domed 'porte cochère' while on the other side a door leads to the single-storey extension, which was added to the church in 1908 to provide vestries and a boardroom. In 2005 this Grade 1 listed building was empty and awaiting a suitable use which befits this unique Arts and Crafts building. It would make a superb North West Arts and Crafts Museum.

Access: JPS Real Estate Ltd, Altrincham
Tel. 0161–9297799 or caretaker 0161–2254655

St John Chrysostom, Anson Rd (SJ856956) has a three-light window in the Memorial Chapel made by **W. J. Pearce**, in memory of the men of the parish killed in the Great War. There is a round window in the west wall of the chapel with angels and flowers which is also the work of **W. J. Pearce**. Otherwise the glass is by Burlison & Grylls.

Access: Rectory Tel. 0161–2246971.

WALMSLEY is north of Bolton on the A666.

Christ Church, Blackburn Rd, Egerton (SD711143) was built in 1840 by **Edmund Sharpe**. It has two **Morris & Co.** windows both of which were made in 1889 using **Burne-Jones's** cartoons. In the north aisle is a two-light window showing Melchizedek on the left and Samuel on the right. The small panel

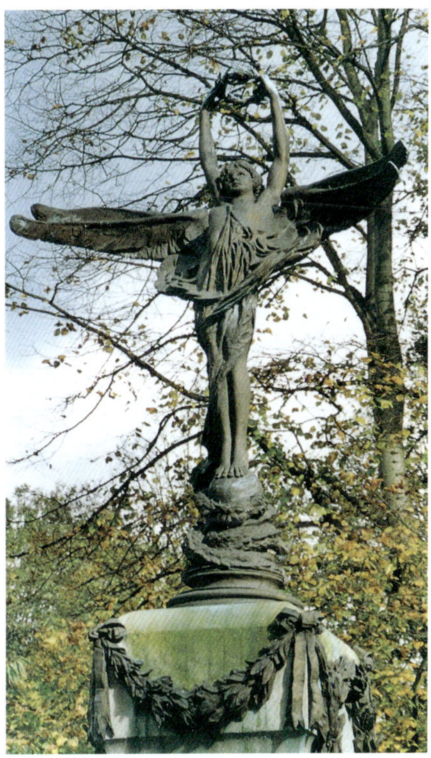

Whitefield War Memorial. Vernon March,1920.

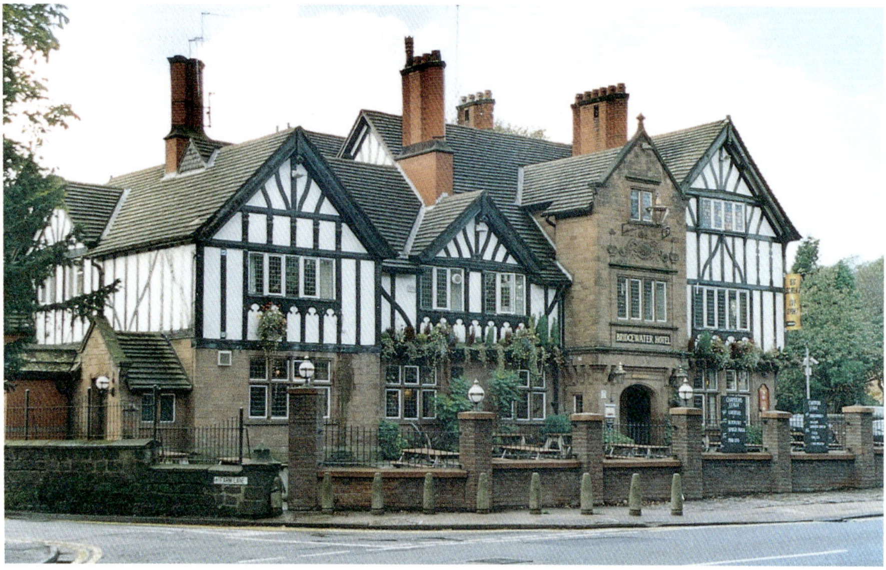

Worsley village. Bridgewater Hotel. John Douglas, 1902.

beneath Melchizedek represents 'The Last Supper' while 'Samuel and Eli' appear in another small panel below Samuel. In the south aisle Mary Virgin appears on the left above a stunning little panel 'The Adoration of the Magi'. In the right hand light St Elizabeth stands above 'The Annunciation'. Incidentally, the painted triptych in the Lady Chapel which looks very old is late C15.

Access: Vicarage Tel. 01204–304283.

WHITEFIELD is more or less due north of Manchester on the way to Bury close to Junction 17 on the M60.

The Whitefield War Memorial (SD803059) stands near the junction of the A667 and the A665 and takes the form of a beautifully sculpted bronze angel holding aloft the laurel wreath of victory while standing a-tiptoe on a coiled and defeated serpent or dragon. The pedestal is impressed with the name of **Vernon March** and the memorial was unveiled in 1920.

WIGAN is east of junction 26 of the M6.

St Andrew's (SD570065) stands on the corner of Woodhouse Lane and Beech Lane in the Springfield quarter of the town. It was built in 1888 and has an unpromising red brick exterior enlivened by a perky bellcôte. The east window is by **Abbott & Co.** 1917 and unusually for them it looks rather north European in style. There are many painted figures on the reredos, sanctuary walls and the pulpit all of which have suffered from over enthusiastic 'touching up'. But fortunately the carved woodwork in the chancel, particularly that of the reredos and the figures on the choir stalls, survive untouched. On either side of the chancel arch are opus sectile panels by **Powell of Whitefriars**. 'The Good Shepherd' on the right, designed in 1911 by **William Aikman**, and 'The Light of the World' on the left by James Hogan.

Access: Vicarage Tel. 01942–243514 .

All Saints Church, (SD582056) stands proudly feigning longevity in Wallgate in the middle of the town but in reality it is a Sharpe & Paley rebuild 1845–50 and no less imposing for that. The church boasts a three-light window in the north wall made in 1868 by **Morris, Marshall, Faulkner & Co. Edward Burne-Jones** was responsible for the central figure of St Christopher while the archangels Raphael and Gabriel on the left and Michael and Uriel on the right are by **Morris**. The pattern work is by **Phillip Webb**. The east window in the south chapel was made by **Heaton Butler & Bayne** but is not typical of them. It is in unusual shades and was designed by Lady Jane Evelyn Lindsey in *c.* 1910. It shows St Paul, St George, St Martin and St Oswald above small panels illustrating incidents from their lives. The splendid green and gilt Neo-Gothic chancel screen and the panelling in the chancel were designed by **W. D. Caröe** in 1903. The opus sectile panels showing David, Isaiah and Zaccharius were made by **Powell of Whitefriars** using cartoons designed by **George Parlby**.

Access: The church is usually open between 11.00 and 15.00 on Saturdays between May and September. Rectory Tel. 01942–244459.

St John's in Standishgate, (SD587060) was built in 1819. However in a store room, fixed in window openings boarded on the outside for safety's sake and therefore dark and dull, are five stained-glass panels which were brought from the convent school next door before it was demolished. The subjects of the panels are 'Mary Presented in the Temple', 'The Annunciation', 'The Nativity', 'Christ Disputing with the Elders' and a full length figure of 'The Virgin Mary' with two small angels at her feet. The inscription on this last panel records that they were presented by the pupils of Sister Edith of the Blessed Sacrament Headmistress 1906–47 in grateful esteem. The archives of the Provincial Office of the Sisters of Notre Dame confirm that the windows were made by the **Harry Clarke Studio** and installed in the convent in 1952.

Access: The panels are effectively 'in store' awaiting a decision as to what and where should be their long term home. Presbytery Tel. 01942–242325 .

WORSLEY huddles in a crook of the M60 on the western fringe of the Greater Manchester conurbation by the banks of the Bridgewater Canal.

St Mark's church (SD746007) was built in the 1840s by G. G. Scott and its very tall and slender spire is now an elegant landmark on the west side of the M60 near junction 13. It has a two-light window in the Ellesmere Chapel (south aisle) which was made in 1905 by **Morris & Co.** and uses the **Burne-Jones** cartoons for 'Fortitude' and 'Humility'. The most westerly window in the north wall is an undated two-light window by Alice Moore showing St Hilda and another Abbess whose name was either forgotten or too long for the cartouche. The lectern was designed by **John Douglas**.

Access: Rectory Tel. 0161–7902362
Church Tel. 0161–7905597.

Worsley Village (SD750003) is just to the east of junction 17 on the M60. It owes its picturesque existence to the first Duke of Bridgewater who built a canal in 1749 to connect his coal mines with central Manchester. The earliest houses here date from about 1764 but **The Green**, a crescent shaped access-road lined on one side by small groups of very attractive houses, dates from 1907. No two groups are the same and the mix of styles, black and white à la Douglas, large gables and buttresses à la Voysey, is all very interesting especially as nothing jars the eye. Not black and white but certainly by **John Douglas** is the **Bridgewater Hotel** built in 1902.

MERSEYSIDE

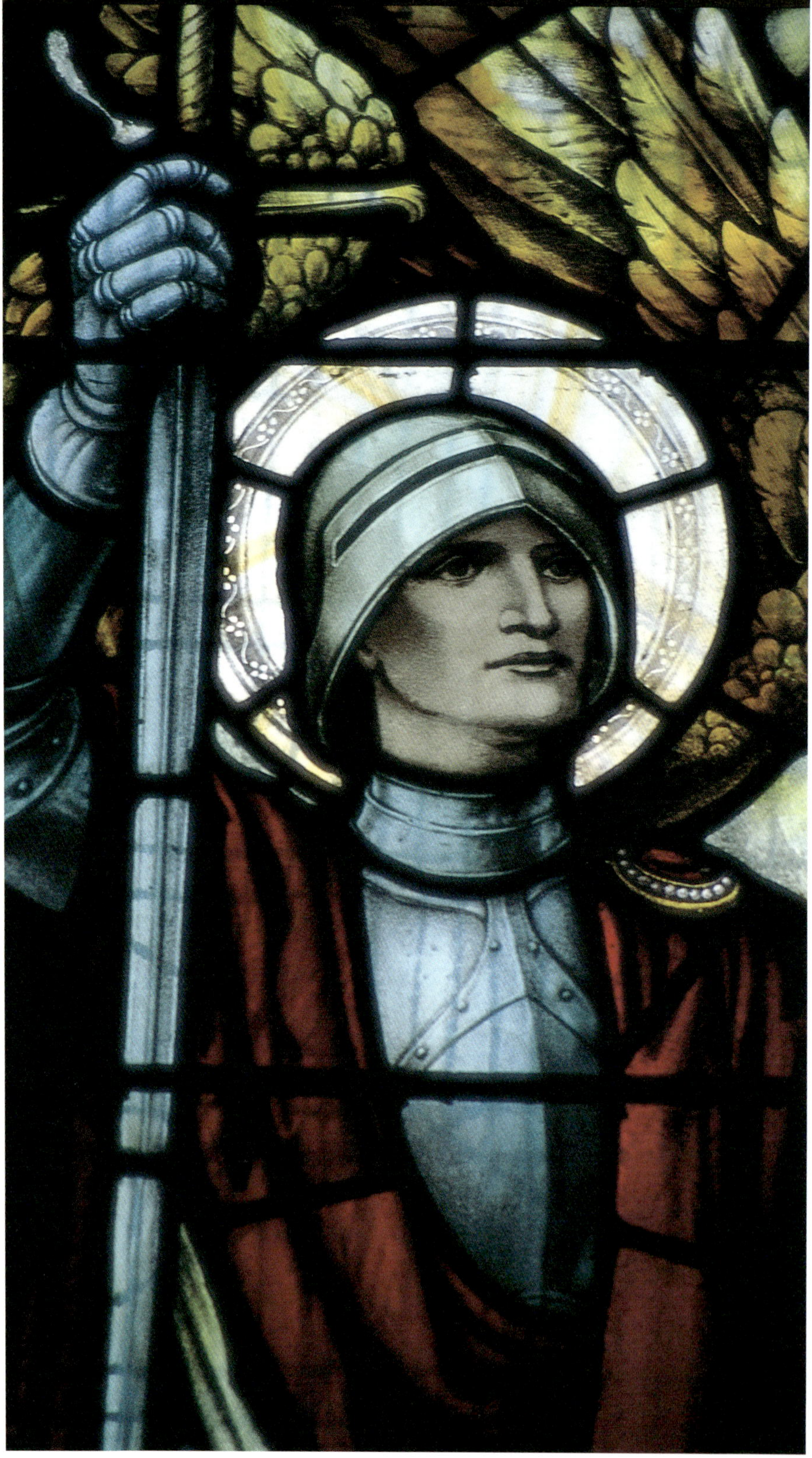

AIGBURTH is about 2 miles south-east of Liverpool City centre.

St Mary's in St Mary's Rd, Grassendale (SJ394851) has a seven-light west window designed by **J. E. Nuttgens** in 1953 providing an international view of 'Christ With the Children'. In the south-west corner is a pair of two-light windows, both attributed to the **Gateshead Stained Glass Co.** *c.* 1906 using designs by **James Eadie Reid**. In the south wall is 'The Baptism of Christ' and in the west is 'The Last Supper'.

Access: Vicarage Tel. 0151–4271474.

The Territorial Army Training Centre, on Aigburth Rd (SJ371870) has a large number of memorial plaques in the drill hall. On the wall of the stairwell lobby is a shining hammered copper memorial to the men of the 5th Irish Volunteer Brigade of the King's Liverpool Regiment who were killed in the Boer War. It was made by **Richard Ll. B. Rathbone**.

Access: Training Centre Tel. 0151–7274455.

Dark Horse Venture, previously The House of Providence at Kelton, Woodlands Road, Aigburth, (SJ385868) occupies the former convent chapel in which there are two lancets with stained glass made by **Paul Woodroffe** in 1925; 'Ecce Agnus Dei' on the left and 'Pulchra ut Luna' on the right. The apse walls have two unattributed lancets, 'The Annunciation' and 'The Resurrection', which are reminiscent of the **Earley Studio's** style. There is also a central Crucifixion window in which the vine decoration in the trefoils and the central crucified Christ are in the style of **Paul Woodfroffe** but John and Mary and the background look like the work of the **Earley Studio**. The site is due to be developed in 2005.

Access: Tel. 0151–7290092.

Sefton Park Library on Aigburth Rd (SJ370873) was built in a half-timbered style and is credited to the Liverpool City Architect **Thomas Shelmerdine** 1911. The repoussé copper commemorative plaque in the lobby was made by **Joseph Hodel**.

Access: Variable hours. Tel. 0151–7271559.

ALLERTON is about 4 miles south-east of Liverpool city centre.

All Hallows Church in Greenhill Rd, (SJ400875) at the north end of Calderstones Park, was built 1872–76 for the Liverpool merchant John Bibby by **G. E. Grayson**, of the Liverpool firm of Grayson & Ould. This beautiful red sandstone church is only one lancet short of a complete set of **Morris & Co.** windows. They were installed 1875–87 and are a wonderful sight. The earliest (1875) is a stunning east window which depicts 'The Adoration of the Lamb' and 'The Rivers of Paradise'. The north

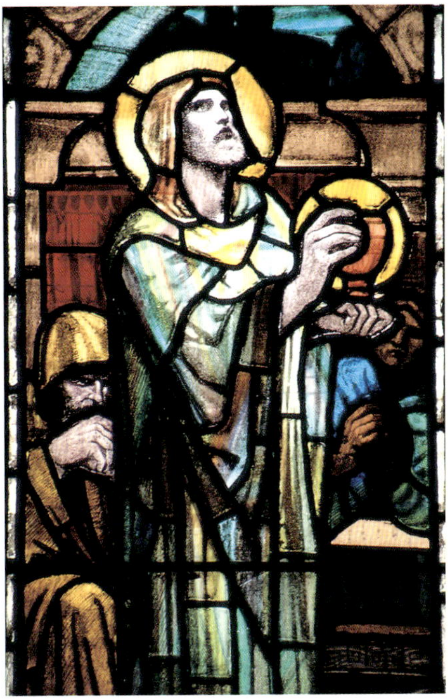

St Mary's, Grassendale. Detail, 'The Last Supper' attributed to Gateshead Glass Co.

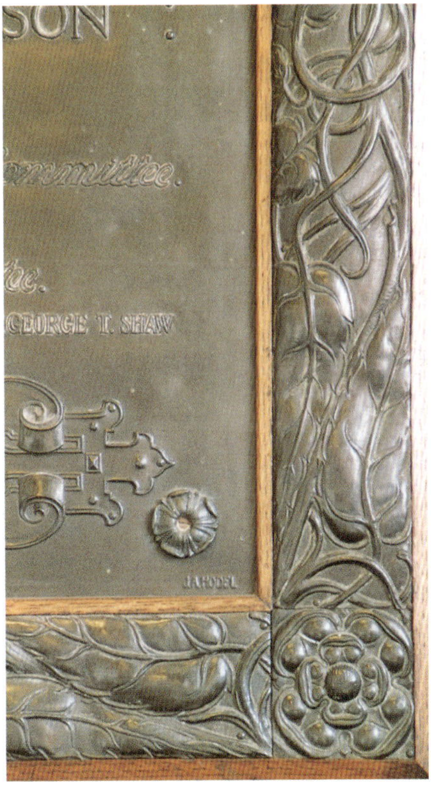

Sefton Park Library, Aigburth Rd. Detail of the commemorative plaque by J. A. Hodel, 1911.

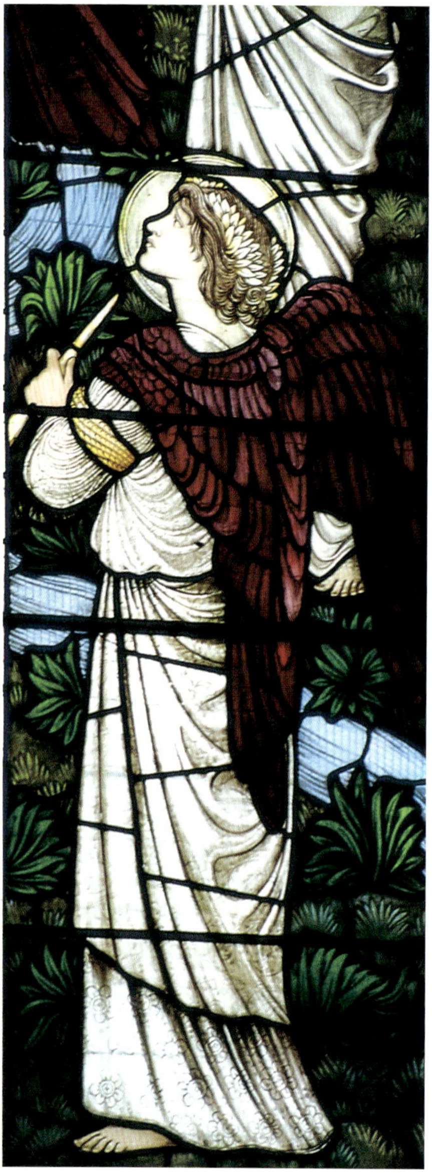

All Hallows, Allerton. Detail of the east window 'Rivers of Paradise'. Burne-Jones for Morris & Co., 1875.

and south transept windows are fine examples of **Morris's** decorative skill and his delight in nature. The foliage, fruit and flowers are exquisite and set off the **Burne-Jones** figures in the upper part of the windows and the four action-packed panels below the figures. The Magi led by the star and a guiding angel must be a favourite. In the nave there are some old friends, lots of good colours and also some less-often seen windows. These rarities include versions of 'The Nativity', 'The Baptism of Christ' and 'The Resurrection'. In the west-most window of the south aisle there is a ravishing Mary Magdalene in white with flowers in her hair, entering from the left to wash Christ's feet. Opposite, on the north side, is the last of the series (1887) which shows Jesus found by Mary in the Temple. The west window has the well-known versions of the four Evangelists. This is a beautiful church, well worth visiting for **Grayson's** architecture as well as for the windows.

Access: Parish Office Tel. 0151–2806388.

BARNSTON is on the A551 between Heswall and Woodchurch on the south-west fringe of Birkenhead.

Christ Church, (SJ281832) to the west of the main road was built 1870–71 by **G. E. Street**. It is a small church, aisleless but not artless. It is a simple and elegant example of a building 'fit for its purpose'.

Access: Parish Office Tel. 0151–6482404.

BEBINGTON lies west of Port Sunlight north of the B5137.

St Andrew's is on the corner of Church Rd and St Andrew's Rd (SJ332839). The history of the present church, which began with the Normans, is excellently told in great detail in the church guide written by Richard L Green whose family have lived here for most, if not all, of the intervening 900 years. There is much of the mediaeval to see but the Perpendicular Gothic windows on the south side contain stained glass designed by **Henry Holiday** and made by **Powell of Whitefriars**. On the nave side of the south chapel-screen are eight of **Holiday's** biblical women in a window made in 1880. In the top row are Sarah, Miriam, Ruth and Esther and below them The Virgin Mary, Elizabeth, Mary of Bethany and Dorcas. They are due for a careful cleaning in the near future and will then look even more spectacular. The window on the chapel side of the screen has eight of **Holiday's** biblical men. In the top row are Abraham, Moses, David and Elijah and below them are the New Testament set of Peter, Matthew, Andrew and John. All were made in 1886. The east window was made in 1953 by the **Brabyns Studio** at Marple to replace German glass blown out by a bomb in World War 2. The carved main altar was designed by **C. E. Deacon** and made by **Harry Hems of Exeter** in 1911. The reredos, designed by Bernard A. Millar was made by L. Brown & Sons of Wilmslow in 1951. **Deacon** and **Hems** were responsible for the altar, reredos and screens in the south chapel in 1908. There is a very plain and simple memorial plaque on the north wall made by **George Wragge Ltd**.

Access: Vicarage Tel. 0151–645648.

BIDSTON see Birkenhead.

BIRKENHEAD keeps its own counsel at the Wirral end of the Mersey Tunnel.

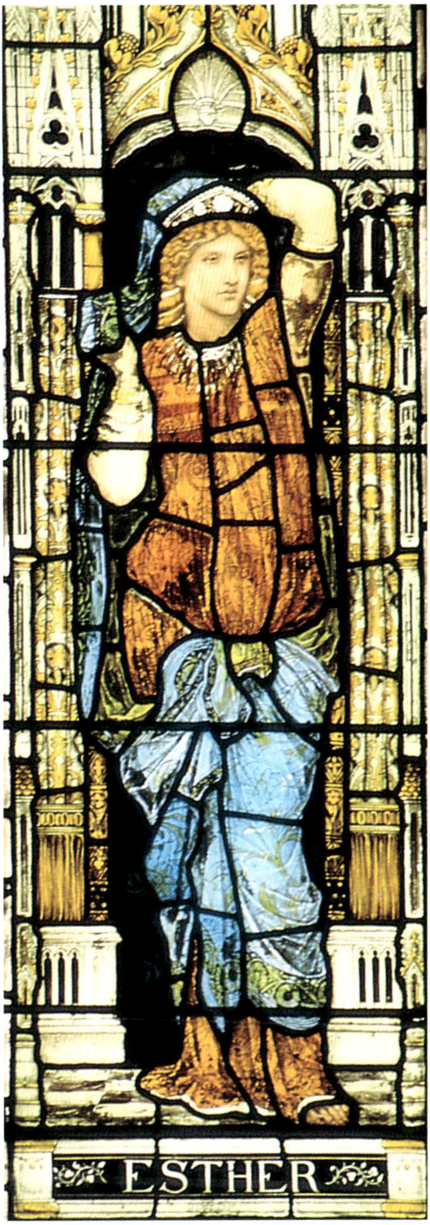

St Andrew, Bebington. 'Esther' by Henry Holiday, 1880.

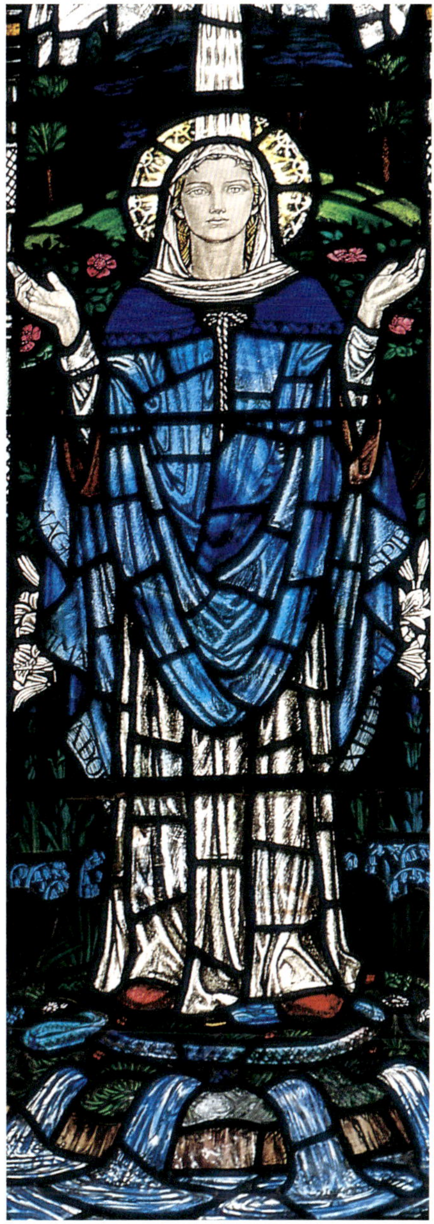

Holy Name of Jesus, Oxton, Birkenhead. Detail of the Lady Chapel window. M. A. Rope, 1916.

The Holy Name of Jesus in Beresford Road, Oxton (SJ302882) was built in 1899 by **Edmund Kirby** in the orchard attached to his own house. The church is quite domestic in scale and style and not, in itself, extraordinary. It does, however, have three exceptional stained-glass windows by **Margaret Agnes Rope**. The earliest, in the east wall of the Lady Chapel, is a three-light window made in 1916 which shows St Elizabeth, Our Lady, and John the Baptist. It is beautifully drawn with excellent colour. In the north wall of the same chapel is a window with twelve panels depicting Catholic martyrs and the manner of their martyrdom. It is not seen at its best being overshadowed outside and lit inside by the adjacent west window of the chapel. The third window, dated 1928, is on the south side of the church. It is a four-light window in which the two centre-lights contain images of St Winifrid and St Therèse of Lisieux.

Access: Presbytery: Tel. 0151–6523034.

St Saviour on the corner of Bidston Rd and Gerald Rd, Oxton (SJ301877) was built 1889–92. It has a huge gilded reredos by **G. F. Bodley** which is best admired from the back of the church. On the other hand, the chancel screen, the choir stalls and the altar and reredos in the south chapel bear very close examination. They were designed by Edward Rae, son of George Rae, who was a staunch patron of the Pre-Raphaëlite Brotherhood and who is commemorated in the west window. Edward Rae's designs were executed by the local firm of Edgar Gladstone Heath who, by the time they finished if not before, were expert in the technique of marquetry. The man-sized angels above the south chapel altar, attributed to **Hems of Exeter**, are beautifully sculpted. George Rae's five-light west window is by **Morris & Co.** 1903. In the top tier are Jesus, Deborah and three fiery-winged, lute-playing angels and in the bottom Mary the Virgin accompanied by Faith, Hope, Truth and Prayer. All the figures are from **Burne-Jones** cartoons and the colours especially in the early evening of a fine summer's day are radiant. The north transept contains a rose window depicting the 'Reception of Souls into Paradise' and two two-light windows which were all made from **Burne-Jones** cartoons in 1903. The church also has a collection of beautifully embroidered altar frontals designed by C. G. Hare and a rather nice **Della Robbia** plaque in the north chapel.

Access: Vicarage Tel. 0151–6521194.

St Stephen's in Prenton Lane, Prenton (SJ308864) is almost opposite '**Oriel Court**' which was built by **J. J. Talbot** in 1900. The church was built by **C. E. Deacon** in 1897 with the chancel added in 1909. It is an interesting approach to modernising the 'Gothic' with exceptional wood carving in the chancel and on the pulpit and lectern, all designed by **Deacon** and made by **Hems & Co.** of Exeter. There is a good collection of stained glass saints by **Trena M. Cox** dating from 1929 through to the 1960s. On the north wall of the chancel is a simple brass plaque bearing repoussé lettering by **Harold Stabler** which was made in 1907.

Access: Parish Office Mon–Fri 9.30–12.30. Tel. 0151–6083638.

St Oswald's Bidston Village Rd, Upper Bidston (SJ284903) has a C16 tower but the rest was substantially rebuilt in 1855–56 and extended at the east end in 1882 by **G. E. Grayson**. **Henry Holiday's** two-light window, 'Simeon and Anna', was made in 1882 for what was then the east end of the north aisle and is now in the office. The east-most window in the south aisle is by **Morris & Co.** It dates from 1912 and shows Veronica and the Virgin Mary, both in white and wearing red haloes. Both the figures and the dulcimer-playing angel in the tracery are from **Burne-Jones** cartoons. To the west of this is a window by **Robert Anning Bell** in which a young St Agnes, surrounded by a throng of angels, appears before a kneeling woman. In what was the west end of the church and is now the church hall there is a two-light window on the north wall by **Frank O. Salisbury**. **Trena Cox** has a two-light Nativity window in the north side of the west wall while at the west end of the south wall there is a two-light window by **H. G. Hiller** depicting St Cecilia backed by choristers and St Oswald leaning on his axe.

Access: Vicarage Tel. 0151–6524853 Office Tel. 0151–6534584.

Almshouses, Bidston Village Road, Bidston by **Woolfall & Eccles**, are just a few yards down the hill from St Oswald's and get a mention here because they were spotted in an article on 'Recent Designs for Domestic Architecture' in

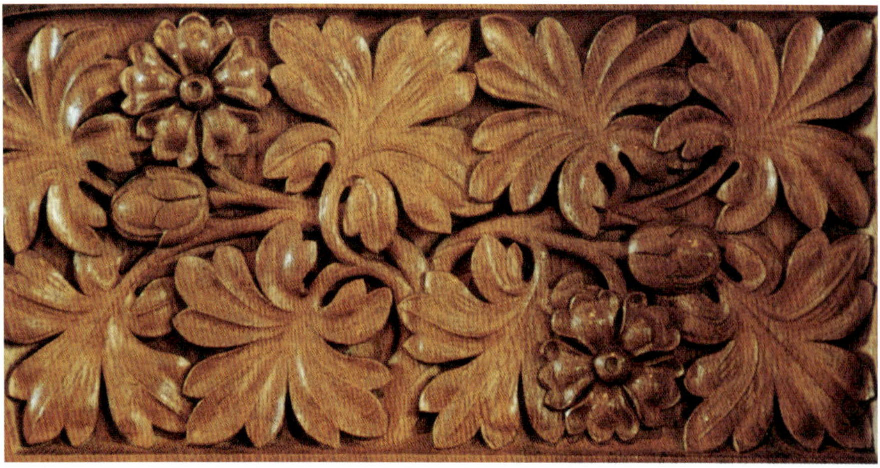

St Stephen, Prenton Lane, Birkenhead. Priest's stall decoration. Designed by C. E. Deacon, executed by Harry Hems, 1919.

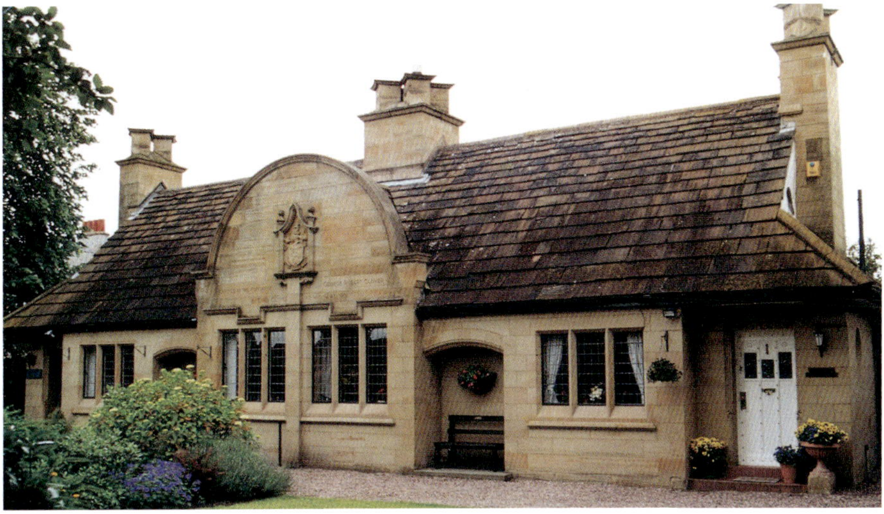

Almshouses, Bidston, Birkenhead. Woolfall and Eccles, c. 1905.

The Studio, vol 34, p. 336., which said 'It was intended that they should accord with the fine old church and with other buildings of the same period that adorn the village. The walls are of finely tooled Talacre stone and the roofs are covered with Yorkshire stone slabs with a very satisfactory result.' Small and no doubt very comfortable, nothing seems to have changed, except for a reduction in the height of the chimneys and an increase in the height of the hedge.

Access: Private dwellings.

Birkenhead Central Library, Borough Rd (SJ314882) is a large Neo-Georgian building with good parking available on the opposite side of the road. It has managed to retain three of the relatively few examples of *Della Robbia* pottery not in museums or private collections. Hung modestly in the library on the ground floor is a large plaque of a mythical young man with a stag on either side of him rearing up as if to leap away. It was presented by **Harold Rathbone** to Charles Gatehouse, deputy Chairman of the Libraries Committee 1898–1908. Two smaller plaques entitled 'The Sower' and 'The Reaper' are the work of **Conrad Dressler**. All three plaques were brought here from the original library when the new building was commissioned.

Access: Normal opening hours: Tel. 0151–6526106.

Williamson Art Gallery and Museum (SJ319881), Slatey Rd, with car park, has the largest collection of **Della Robbia** pottery in the world. There are over-sized pots and brightly coloured chargers which demonstrate the skills of local artists, mainly women such as Cassandia Annie Walker, Alice Louise Jones and Miss E. M. Wood. There are examples of the work of the firm's founder **Harold Rathbone** including his plaque based on **Ford Madox Brown's** 'Alfred the Great' and plaques by **Ellen Mary Rope** with her lovely cherubs and children. The museum has a collection of around 6000 paintings of which only a few can be displayed. They have some fine Pre-Raphaëlite pictures including work by **Edward Burne-Jones**, Evelyn De Morgan and Albert Moore to name but three. The gallery also displays some interesting New Sculpture.

Access: Open 9.00–13.00 and 14.00–17.00
Tel. 0151–6524177.

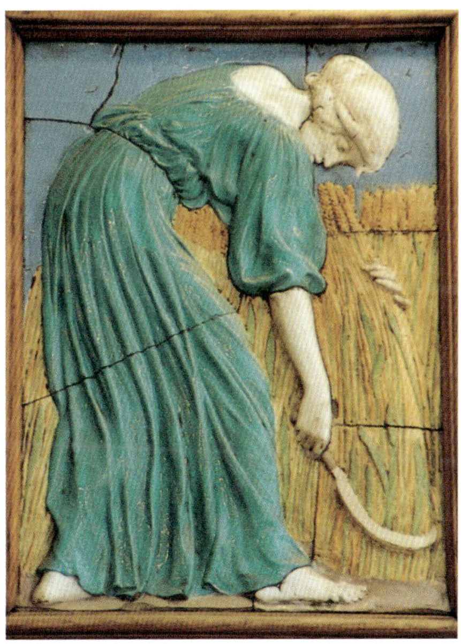

Central Library, Birkenhead. 'The Reaper'. Della Robbia designed by Conrad Dressler. *Courtesy of Birkenhead Library and Wirral Library Services*

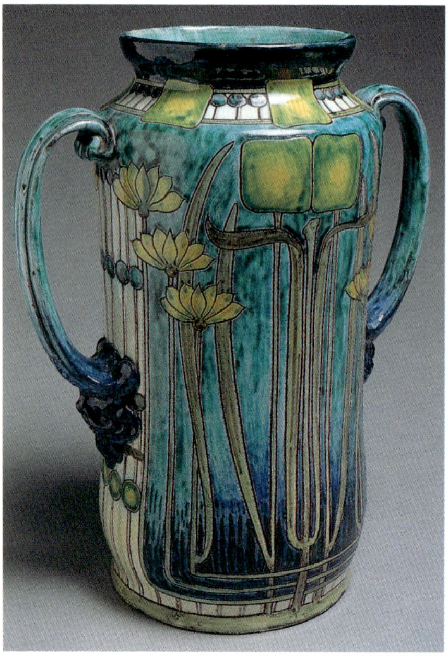

Williamson Art Gallery, two-handled vase decorated by Cassandia Walker for Della Robbia, 1904.
© Williamson Art Gallery and Museum, Birkenhead

The Wirral Museum, Hamilton Square (SJ326890) is located in the erstwhile Birkenhead Town Hall. The displays are mostly about life in Birkenhead but there is also a small and prestigious collection of **Della Robbia** work including **Harold Rathbone's** portrait plaque of William Morris, the gigantic commemorative vase presented to the Mayor of Birkenhead by the firm on the occasion of the visit of HRH Princess Louise in 1898, and some delightful plaques by **Ellen Mary Rope**. The second flight of the main staircase has a huge stained-glass window, 'The Visit to Chester of King Edward II' made by **G. P. Gamon**.

Access: Open Tues–Sun 10.00–17.00 Tel. 0151–6664010.

The Great War Memorial in Hamilton Square was designed by **Lional Budden** and has relief panels by **G. H. Tyson Smith**. It was unveiled in 1925.

41 and 43 Clifton Rd, Birkenhead (SJ319881) were built with **Della Robbia** terracotta plaques on their facades. The four panels, two on each house, have been painted white for many years. They were designed by **Ellen Rope** and depict children picking different fruits. It is a treat to see Della Robbia's architectural ceramics in situ in relatively modest houses.

BLUNDELLSANDS marks the northern limit of the stretch of coast occupied by the Liverpool conurbation about 6 miles from the city centre.

St Nicholas's, Bridge Rd (SJ311992) was built 1873–74 by T. D. Barry & Sons and extended in 1894 by **W. D. Caröe** who added the baptistery at the west end. Caröe's parents were members of the congregation here and their memorial plaque is fixed to the north side of the baptistery arcade. The stained glass in the apse is by Powell. The unattributed window second from the east in the north aisle is very interesting and unusual for 1888 – could it be **A. H. Marsh**?

Access: Vicarage Tel. 0151–9243551.

Mersey Road Methodist Church, (SJ314994) was built by **J. F. Doyle** 1891–92 and has a 'Resurrection' window made by **H. G. Hiller** as a memorial to the men of the congregation killed in the Great War. In the Sunday School room upstairs, there is a interesting window, 'Suffer Little Children to Come Unto Me' which is unsigned and undated and very much a window of two lights. The children on the right are delightful while Christ, on the left looks rather ungainly. Perhaps the window has been much repaired.

Access: Manse Tel. 0151–9283992.

BOOTLE is at the mouth of the Mersey about 3 miles north of Liverpool city centre.

St Matthew's, Stanley Road (SJ343960) has a stained-glass window by H. G. Hiller, *c.* 1920, depicting one of the most triumphant St Georges on Merseyside. He has clearly fought his dragon to a standstill and is savouring the plaudits of the congregation before applying the *coup de grace*.

Access: Parish Office Tel. 0151–9333366.

The Great War Memorial on the Stanley Rd frontage of South Park (SJ343947) is an imposing and beautifully sculpted monument made in bronze and stone. A Mother and Child stand on top of a triangular obelisk on the base of which are the finely sculpted figures of a soldier, a sailor and an airman. It is a fitting

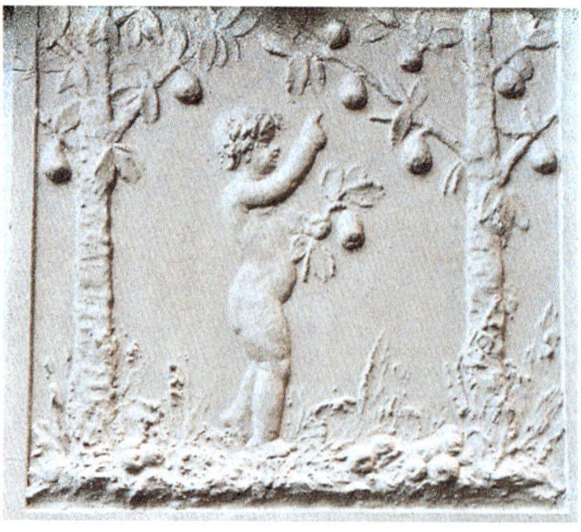

Clifton Rd, Birkenhead. Della Robbia terracotta plaque. Designed by Ellen Rope.

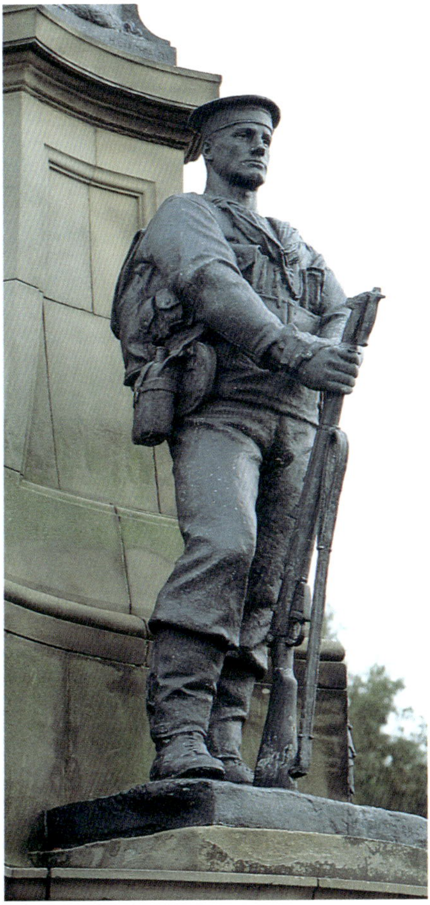

Great War Memorial, Bootle. 'Seaman' by Herman Cawthra, 1922.

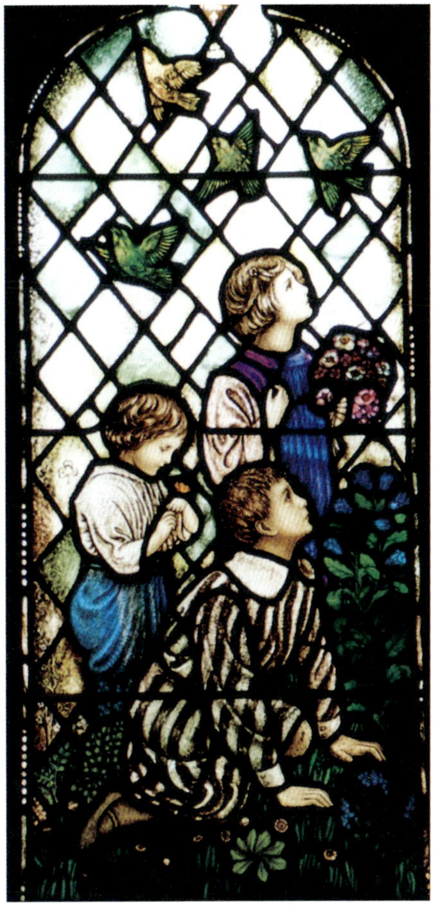

Church of the Resurrection and All Saints, Caldy. Detail of the Children's window. A. J. Davies for the Bromsgrove Guild, 1920.

memorial to more than one thousand men from Bootle who died in the war. It was unveiled in 1922 and the sculpture is the work of **Herman Cawthra**.

CALDY village is in the north-west corner of the Wirral peninsular between Heswall and West Kirby on the B5140.

The Church of the Resurrection and All Saints is in the centre of the village (SJ228851) and occupies the site of what was a school built by **G. E. Street** in 1868. There is little remaining of his work apart from a fireplace in the vestry. Today's church is largely the work of **Douglas & Minshull** carried out in 1906. The reredos, choir stalls and a small window in the south wall of the chancel came from C. E. Kempe's chapel in the very impressive Caldy Manor which is just up the road. The painted chancel screen fits a little awkwardly but there is nothing wrong with the suggestion of l'Art Nouveau in its angels. **William Aikman** was responsible for the cartoons of St Peter and St John in the small **Powell of Whitefriars** windows installed in the east wall in 1907. The delightful three-light window in the south aisle showing 'Christ with the Children' is by **A. J. Davies** for **The Bromsgrove Guild** in 1920. He uses slab glass for special effects such as making the girl's posy three-dimensional. The four-light window in the west end is by **Trena Cox** who completed the two middle panels in 1933 and the outer figures in 1946.

Access: Vicarage Tel. 0151–6255229.

CHILDWALL is about 4 miles east of Liverpool city centre just south of junction 5 on the M62.

All Saints on the corner of Well Lane and Score Lane (SJ415891) is, according to Pevsner, the only remaining mediaeval church in the whole of the metropolitan area of the City of Liverpool. It has however benefited from C18, C19 and C20 enlargements. The last was by **John Francis Doyle** in 1906. There is stained glass by Warrington, Kempe, Heaton Butler & Bayne and much excellent work by Percy Bacon. At the west end of the north aisle there is a three-light window made by **Mary Lowndes** in 1915 depicting 'The Supper at Emmaus'. Some of the chancel furnishings are said to have been designed by Scott and made for Liverpool Cathedral.

Access: Vicarage Tel. 0151–7372169.

EASTHAM is about ½ a mile north of Junction 5 on the M53.

The Village Great War Memorial stands in a small garden at the junction of Stanley Lane and Eastham Village Rd (SJ361800). Although it is small it is one of the finest of Merseyside's Great War Memorials. It takes the form of a stone stele on the top of which is the bronze figure of Christ. On the north side of the stele there is a poignant bas-relief of a soldier supporting his fallen comrade who looks up towards the bronze figure of Christ who offers him the Crown of Life. The west and east faces are carved with wreathes and the south side bears a crown of thorns. The sculpture is by **C. J. Allen** and the monument was unveiled in 1925.

ECCLESTON is on the western fringe of St Helens where it rubs shoulders with Knowsley Park.

Christ Church in Church Road, Eccleston (SJ485955) has three windows in the south wall. 'St Luke', 'Dorcas' and 'St George' all appear in the **Shrigley & Hunt** catalogue. 'St George' is a war memorial and typical of the firm's workaday style but 'St Luke' and especially 'Dorcas' are outstandingly different and look many years later than the commemorative date in the 1880s. Who designed them and when? The Arts and Crafts/Deco hybrid alabaster font is unattributed and equally puzzling.

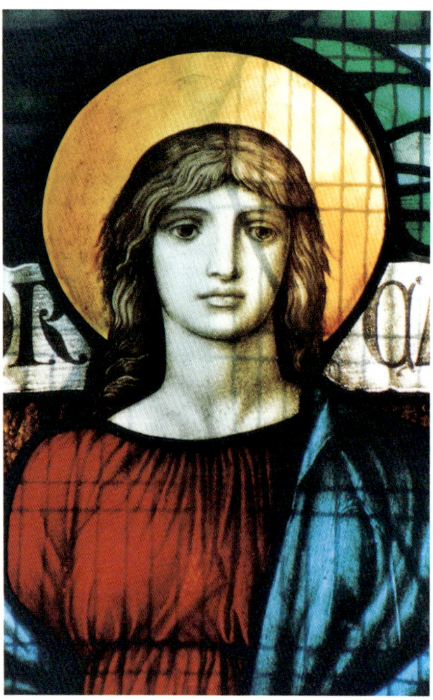

Christ Church, Eccleston. Detail of Dorcas by Shrigley & Hunt, No date.

Access: Parish Office Tel. 01744–451385.

EDGEHILL is the first railway station east of Lime St on the way to Manchester.

St Anne's church (SJ367900) in Overbury St, was built 1845–46 by Charles Hansom and the transepts were added by Pugin & Pugin some 40 years later. The central light in the apse is filled with a glowing 'St Anne and the Young Mary' and though unsigned it is very much in the style of the **Earley Studio.** The church used to have an altar piece 'The Girlhood of the Virgin Mary' painted by **May L. G. Cooksey** which was featured in the *Studio* (vol. 21) but it appears to have moved on.

Access: Presbytery Tel. 0151–7091713.

St Mary's, Irvine St (SJ365904) is an early C19 church with two **Morris** windows in the north wall. The west-most of these, made in 1873 by **Morris, Marshall, Faulkner & Co.** shows the 'Salvator Mundi' by **Burne-Jones** flanked by figures of the Virgin Mary and Martha both designed by **William Morris.** The second window is in the body of the church and has 'The Virgin and Child' flanked by 'Nathaniel' and 'Timothy'. All the figures are by **Burne-Jones** and the window was made in 1879. There is an unsigned window in the east end representing Mary Magdalene and the angels at the empty tomb. It was made after 1917 and has a hint of the Art Nouveau about it.

Access: Vicarage Tel. 0151–7096710.

FAZAKERLEY is on the north-east edge of the Liverpool conurbation west of junction 6 on the M57.

Emmanuel, Longmoor Lane (SJ374973) is a huge red-brick church built in 1908 by **W. H. Ward.** The east window shows Christ in the centre light with two Evangelists on each side and was made in 1929 by **Caroline Townshend** and **Joan Howson.** It is unusually large for them.

Access: Vicarage Tel. 0151–5252689.

FORMBY lies on the coast between Great Crosby and Southport.

Our Lady of Compassion, in School Lane, (SD301072) was built in 1864 by Henry Clutton. The circular baptistery was added in 1923 and boasts a set of six stained-glass windows made by **Paul Woodroffe.** They represent, 'The Healing of Naaman the Leper', 'The Baptism of Christ', 'The Martyrdom of

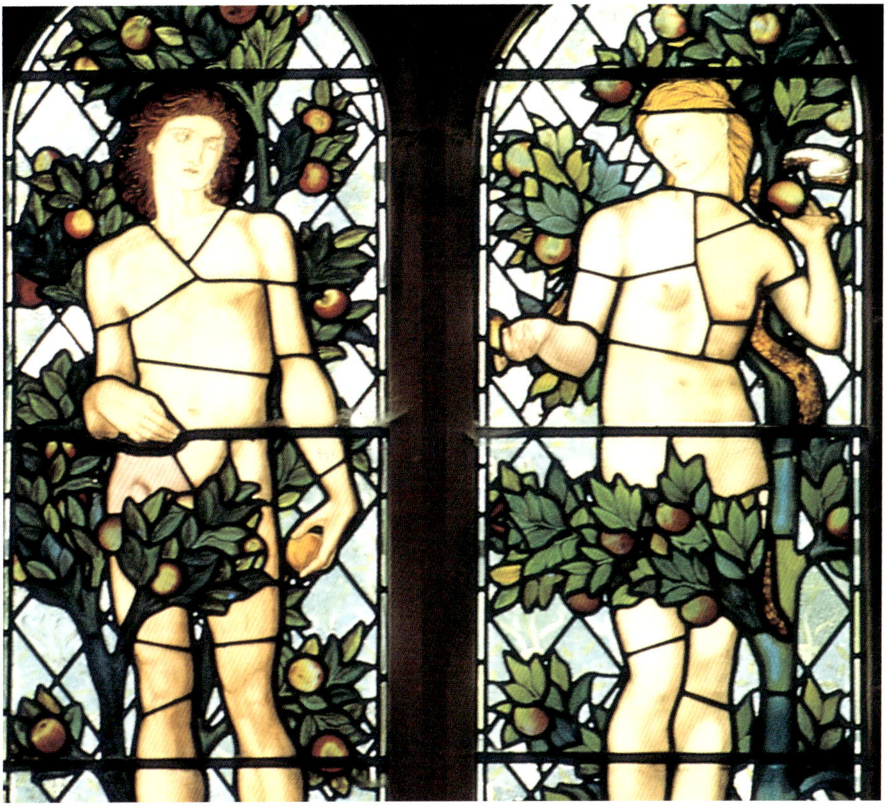

St John, Frankby. 'Adam and Eve' designed by Burne-Jones for Morris & Co., 1874.

St Alban', 'St Gregory and the English Slave Boys', 'St Paulinus Baptising in York' and a scene depicting 'The Open Gates of Heaven'. There is a small chapel in the south-west corner of the church with an unattributed, fine-wrought iron screen fixed to the wall behind the votive candle-rack. There is a life-like 'Mother and Child' in stone by **Alec Miller** and behind it a small vessica-shaped stained-glass window of 'God the Father with the Dove of the Holy Spirit' by **Paul Woodroffe**.

Access: Presbytery Tel. 01704–873230.

FRANKBY is at the Birkenhead end of the Wirral, west of the M53 and east of West Kirby on the B5139.

St John the Divine stands at the side of Frankby Road, (SJ247870) just to the north-east of the village. It was built in 1868 by W. J. Hey of Liverpool and has three pairs of windows in the north aisle, made in 1872 by **Morris, Marshall, Faulkner & Co.** The first pair show Adam and Eve naked, each standing in an apple tree with a seductive serpent whispering in Eve's ear. These cartoons were not used again until 1923 at All Saints Leek. Abel, Enoch, Abraham and Moses complete the set. All the figures were designed by **Burne-Jones**.

Access: Vicarage Tel. 0151–6786155 .

GARSTON lies just to the west of Liverpool's John Lennon Airport at Speke.

St Francis of Assisi, Earp Road, (SJ402848) is aglow with wonderful art work. The reredos has two opus sectile and golden mosaic panels each portraying episodes in the life of St Francis. In the side chapel on the north side, the reredos is decorated with painted saints and nearby on the north wall is a dramatic painting of the Crucifixion set in a gilt frame. The altar front in the south chapel is decorated with another painting showing the 'Descent From the Cross'. There are no stained glass windows in this church but it does have a frieze with fourteen paintings **May L. G. Cooksey** illustrating the Stations of the Cross.

Access: Presbytery Tel. 0151–4277518.

Garston Carnegie Library Bowdon Rd, (SJ397850) was built in 1909 by the City Architect **T. Shelmerdine** in a rather Voysey-like, rendered style. The commemorative plaque in the entrance lobby was worked by **C. E. Thompson**.

Access: Variable hours Tel. 0151–2332552.

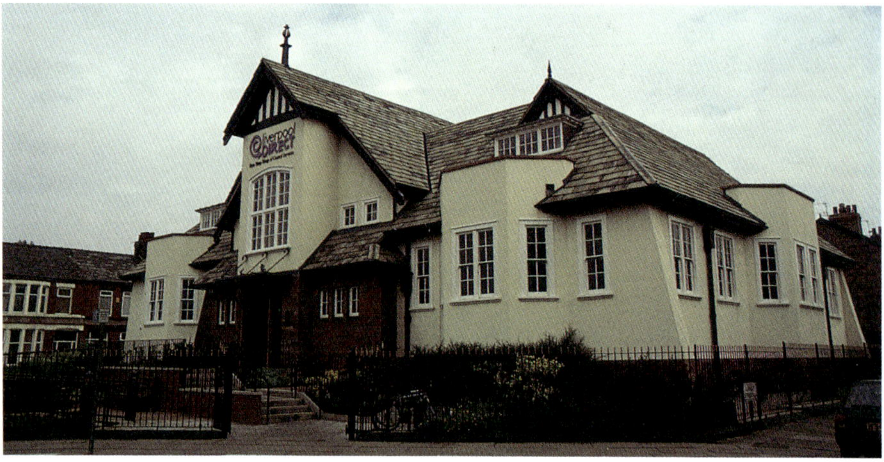

Garston Library by T. Sherlmardine, 1909. ***See p. 127.***

GATEACRE lies 6 miles east of Liverpool city centre on the eastern fringe of the city.

St Stephen's, Belle Vale Road, Gateacre, (SJ432881) was built 1872–74 by Cornelius Sherlock in red sandstone. The large, four-light west window made by Morris & Co. in 1883 is particularly striking. Each of the main lights has a central figure with a roundel above and below all set against Morris's pale green scrolled foliage. The figures are all based on Burne-Jones cartoons as are the scenes in the roundels. You will need binoculars to see the detail in the top row of 'Feeding the Hungry', 'Giving Drink to the Thirsty', 'Clothing the Naked' and 'Visiting Prisoners'. The lower roundels show 'Teaching the Ignorant', 'Visiting the Sick', 'Leading the Blind' and 'Christ Blessing the Children'. The nine tracery lights above the main panels each contain a golden-winged angel surveying the scene. On the south side of the chancel is a small, damaged, two-light window of St Roque and St Anna dedicated to an Anne C.... who died in 1912. Could this be the work of Townshend and Howson?

Access: Parish Office Tel. 0151–4879338.

GREAT CROSBY is north of Bootle and about 6 miles north of Liverpool city centre.

The Waterloo United Free Church, in Crosby Road North, (SJ322984) was built in 1891 by **George Baines** and was originally the Baptist Church. It is a rather dour-looking Gothic church on the outside but unexpectedly light, bright and airy inside, with large windows and very slender, steel columns supporting the exposed roof trusses. The windows and the glass screen beneath the west-end gallery contain very attractive plant-form stained glass which is not truly 'whiplash' Art Nouveau, but bends slightly in that direction. There is a satisfying unity in the design of what is more an auditorium than the nave of a church. This unity is exemplified by the happy juxtaposition of Gothic tracery on the wooden panels of the pulpit with the cut out 'Voysey Hearts' in the spandrels of its stairs and the wrought metal of the balusters.

Access: Manse Tel. 0151–9206132.

St Michael's in St Michael's Rd, Blundell Sands (SD309003) was built in 1930 by Quiggin & Gee of Liverpool. It is a large, brick church with the clean simplicity of line typical of its period. The east window and the north transept window were given by the Freemasons and made by F. C. Eden.

Access: Vicarage Tel. 0151–9249905.

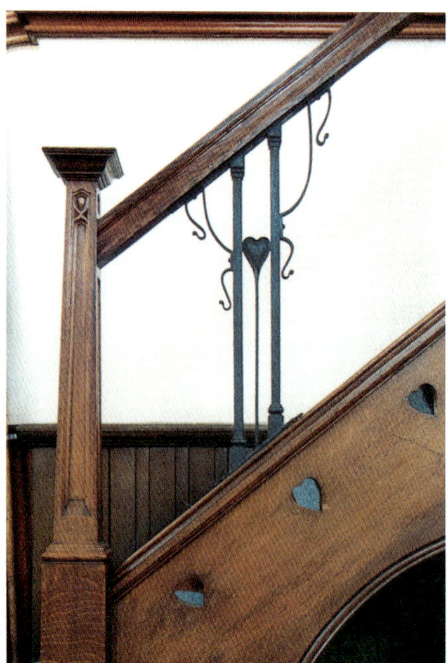

UFC, Great Crosby. Pulpit steps by G. Baines, 1891.

The United Reformed Church at the corner of Eshe Rd North and Mersey Rd (SJ314994) was designed by **Douglas & Fordham** 1891. It is a stone built church, with an elegant flèche. Internally the church is high, wide and handsomely-proportioned with narrow side-aisles and very attractive exposed roof-trusses. The walls are all plastered and painted with the exception of the sandstone arcades. The simplicity of the nave and the clear glass in the west window give added impact to the chancel. The five-light east window and the reredos beneath is a memorial to the people lost in the Great War. The window design is attributed locally to **Carl Almquist** and it was made by **Shrigley & Hunt**. **Almquist** would have been 70 when the window was designed at the end of the war and although his sight was fading he still did freelance work for **Shrigley & Hunt**. Beneath the window the sanctuary is panelled in light-oak on either side of the striking reredos. Its gesso panels are decorated and painted with symbols of valour and sacrifice while the central panel bears a cross set against a fruiting pomegranate tree. The brass cross is a later addition. The gesso work was executed in 1920 by **Joseph Lawton** of Liverpool. In the north aisle are two lancet windows by **Edward Frampton** and at the west end of the north aisle are two of **G. P. Hutchinson's** blue angels designed for **Powell of Whitefriars**.

Access: Open Sat 10.00–12.00; Fri 13.00–14.30 in school time. www.crosby-urc.org.uk or Tel. Mersey URC Synod 0151–7226590.

HALEWOOD lies north of Speke on the extreme south-eastern edge of the Liverpool conurbation.

St Nicholas's in Church Road, Halewood, (SJ450862) has seventeen lights filled with stained glass made by **Morris & Co**. The earliest windows, from 1874 are at the west-most end of the south aisle and show Timothy, St Paul and Melchizedek. In the chancel apse, three lancet windows containing two evangelists and an angel, sit either side of the east window in which St Nicholas is serenaded by two instrument-playing angels. All were designed by **Burne-Jones** except for the serenading angels which were designed by Morris. The north and south transepts each contain two single lights of female saints by **Burne-Jones** 1879 and 1881 respectively. Sadly many of these windows have deteriorated badly. At the west end of the north wall in an area now screened off from the nave there is an exquisite 'Adoration of the Magi' of 1881 by **Burne-Jones**.

Access: Rectory Tel. 0151–4875610.

HOYLAKE shares the north-west corner of Wirral with West Kirby.

Holylake Chapel in Station Rd, (SJ217889) was built as the Congregational Church by **Douglas & Minshull** in 1906. It lost its tower as a result of bomb damage in the Second World War. Fortunately its east window survived. This is a seven-light memorial to those who died in the Great War. It was made by **H. G. Hiller** and shows 'The Nativity', 'The Crucifixion' and 'The Ascension of Christ'. The Nativity scene is unusual as Mary is ensconced in a comfortable bed with a fluffy pillow and duvet. Two smaller windows at the east end of the north and south aisles also survived the bombs and show 'Christ and the Woman of Samaria' on the left and 'Christ Blessing the Children' on the right. Both windows are in the same style and the one on the left is signed **A. J. Davies** with a date which is difficult to read but is in the 1920s.

Access: Church office Tel. 0151–6320860 or 6326084.

St John's is on the corner of Birkenhead Road and Forest Road (SJ229901). It was built in red

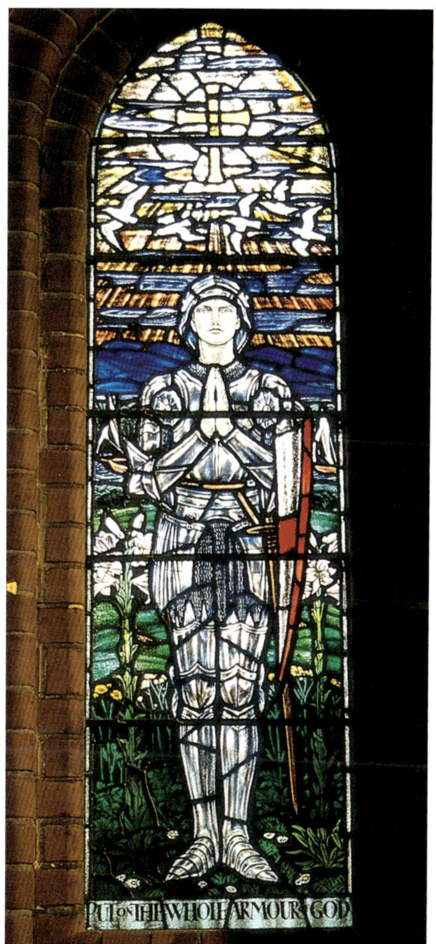

St Hildeburgh, Hoylake. Getty memorial window by M. A. Rope, 1919.

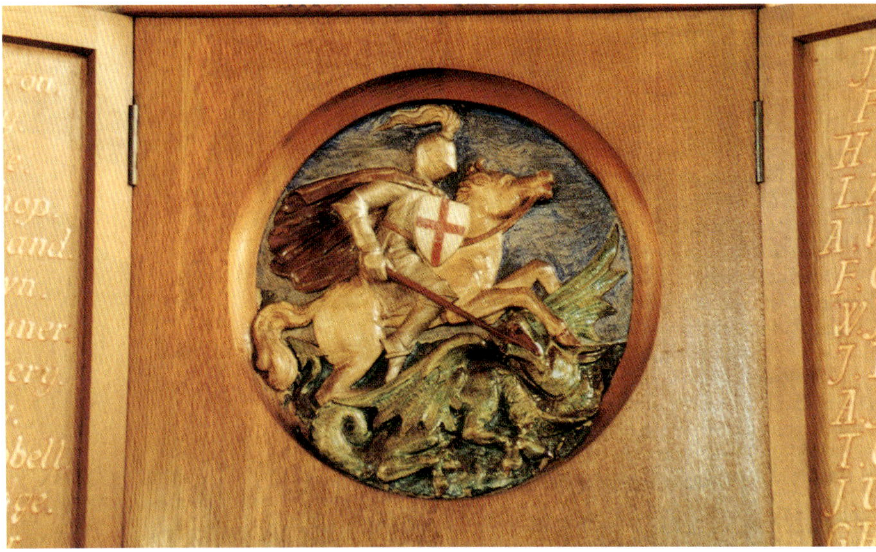

St Michael, Huyton. Detail of the War Memorial by P. A. Robson, c. 1920.

brick, inside and out, by **Edmund Kirby** 1911–13. There are three single-light windows in the baptistery by **H. G. Hiller** who also made the two-light 'Adoration of the Magi'.

Access: Vicarage Tel. 0151–6321661.

St Hildeburgh's (SJ215889) in Stanley Rd was built by **Edmund Kirby** 1897–99 in his red-brick style. The east window is by **Powell of Whitefriars** and dedicated to the members of the Royal Liverpool Golf Club who lost their lives in the Great War. The contemporary parish magazine credits Mrs Edmund Kirby with the design. Most of the stained glass in the nave and chancel is by Powell, except for the two three-light windows (third and fifth from the east on the north side) which were made in 1946 and 1947 by **William Aikman**. There is a very good mosaic and opus panel in the reredos. There is also a very handsome knight in shining armour in a single-light memorial window in the south wall. It was given in memory of James H. Getty in 1919 and designed and executed by **Margaret Agnes Rope**.

Access: Vicarage Tel. 0151–6323897.

HUNTS CROSS is about 6 miles east of Liverpool city centre with Speke to the south and Halewood to the north.

St Hilda's is just north of the railway station, and stands at the corner of Speke Rd and Stuart Avenue, (SJ432853). It is a small, attractive church built in 1898 in red brick with terracotta mullions and tracery. It has brick buttresses and gabled dormer-windows and is as good an Arts and Crafts mission church as you might find in Merseyside but the name of its architect remains a mystery. A broad chancel arch provides a perfect frame for the altar, reredos and east window. The oak reredos is fitted with five polished and glowing copper repoussé panels, none of which is signed. The east window is a memorial to the men of Hunts Cross who gave their lives in the Great War. It was made by **Joan Howson**, whose father was the Rector of Hunts Cross at that time.

Access: Parish Office Tues–Thur a.m. Tel. 0151–4864060.

HUYTON is about 7 miles east of Liverpool city centre, bounded on two of its three sides by the M62 and the M57.

St Michael's, Blue Bell Lane (SJ443911) is an ancient red-sandstone church with a long history of building and additions. Its stained glass is not so old however. **Henry Holiday** designed two two-light windows for **Powell of Whitefriars** during the 1880s. One shows 'Christ Summoning Lazarus From the Tomb' while the other is a bright and lively 'Suffer Little Children to Come Unto Me'. The oak triptych memorial-board on the east wall of the north aisle has some delightful painted reliefs with St George at the top and two angels at the bottom of the side panels. It is attributed in the National Inventory of War Memorials database to **Philip Appleby Robson**.

Access: Vicarage Tel. 0151–4493900.

Huyton Congregational church in Victoria Rd (SJ446909) was built by **W. D. Caröe** 1889–90 and supposedly derives from J. L. Pearson's Truro Cathedral. It is a large, heavy, stone church with an appropriately large tower and steeple. Internally it is remarkable for its lightness. Caröe has produced a forest of slender piers supporting pointed stone arches

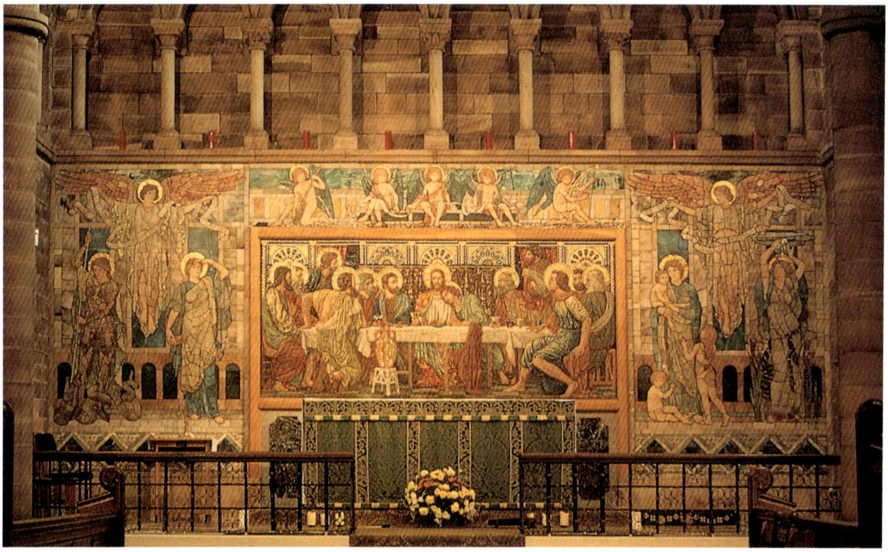

St Chad, Kirkby. East wall and reredos by Henry Holiday.

which run along the length of the nave and across the width of the building through the aisles and nave. The roof is supported on pierced stonework raised on these transverse arches. At floor level, there is a 'view' wherever you look. The east window is a superb Great War Memorial made by **Abbott & Co.** of Lancaster.

Access: Church Secretary Tel. 0151–4865324.

KIRKBY is beyond the urban fringe of Merseyside about a mile north of junction 2 on the M57.

St Chad's in Old Hall Lane (SJ409990) was built by **Paley & Austin** 1868–70 and is recognisable from a great distance by the saddleback roof of its rather slender tower. It is an excellent building, sturdy from the outside and very elegant inside. The church has an unrivalled collection of work by **Henry Holiday** covering the period 1872–97. Holiday designed all the stained-glass windows, bar one, as well as the fabulous *pièce de résistance* in the shape of the mosaic and opus sectile reredos. The earliest windows are the three lancets in the east wall above the reredos which were installed in 1872 and the latest, the three lancets in the lower part of the west wall were fixed in 1897. These windows show the development of Holiday's style over a twenty five year period. There are examples of his work in the intervening years in the aisle windows and the four magnificent archangels in the corners of the nave.

The reredos is not to be missed so don't visit during Lent, or it will be hidden from view. It covers the whole of the east wall from north to south and from the floor up to the blind arcade beneath the east window. Stunning angels, virtues, archangels and a particularly squirming serpent, all executed in opus sectile work, surround **Holiday's** brilliant mosaic of 'The Last Supper'. He has chosen to depict the moment when Judas, wearing a hat instead of a halo is seen slinking off through the curtained doorway. **Holiday** was never afraid of innovation and here he has been brave enough to introduce mirrored glass in appropriate parts of the mosaic. The effect could easily have run away with the design but the whole decorative arrangement, seen from the body of the church is highly successful. It is a major work and a wonderful sight. Not to be overlooked in the midst of all this work by Henry Holiday is the central light of the upper west window. It shows Jacob looking up at a host of angels ascending his ladder. It was made in 1930 and not signed but there is a great similarity between the angels and the purple robed figure here and those by **H. G. Hiller** in the Mersey Rd Methodist Church at Blundellsands.

Access: Rectory Tel. 0151–5472155.

KNOTTY ASH is north of the junction of the M62 and the Liverpool ring road.

St John Evangelist, Thomas Lane/Brookside Avenue (SJ408914) was built in the 1830s with later additions by **Aldridge & Deacon.** There are some Arts and Crafts treasures here. The figures of Samuel, Absolom and Timothy were installed in the third window from the east end of the north aisle in 1872 by **Morris, Marshall, Faulkner & Co.** while Enoch, Solomon and David were added in 1890 by **Morris & Co.** The east-most window in the north aisle was designed by **H. W. Lonsdale** as were the

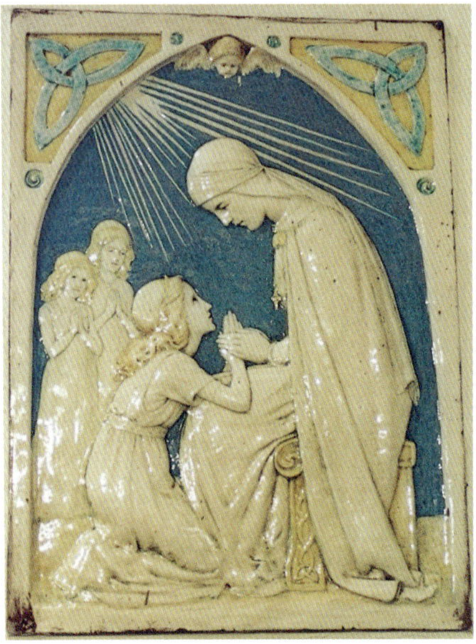

St John, Knotty Ash. Della Robbia Plaque.

windows in the north wall of the sanctuary, the east window of the Lady Chapel and the three windows in the south wall of the Lady Chapel. All of Lonsdale's windows were made up by **Heaton, Butler & Bayne**. Tucked away at the west end of the north aisle is a chapel full of memorial plaques by the **Della Robbia** studio. The wealth of angels in the relief panels is reminiscent of the work of **Ellen Mary Rope**. It is an unexpected pleasure to see this work in the location for which it was designed rather than in a museum. The church has good wood-carvings of prophets and saints on the furnishings and fittings, including the pulpit, two reredoses and a screen. Some of this carving is probably the work of local craftsmen. For example, there is an interesting chest in the south aisle which was presented to the church in 1893 by Anna Thompson of Thingwall, a patron of the church and a patron of the wood-carving class based in the nearby village hall. Inside the lid of the chest is a brass plaque with the names of those who made it. There are other small Arts and Crafts details to be seen in the church such as the chancel-gate hinges and other metal work.

Access: Vicarage Tel. 0151–2282396.

Knotty Ash Village Hall stands between the separate carriage ways of Prescot Rd (SJ410918). It was built *c.* 1895 by **C. E. Deacon** under the patronage of the Thompsons of Thingwall and provided the venue for exhibitions and Arts and Crafts classes attended by local people. The classes included wood-carving, leatherwork and repoussé metalwork. There was a gymnasium and a huge crown bowling green.

Access: Currently owned by Liverpool City Council and used as a Youth Centre.

LITTLE CROSBY is in the countryside just north of Blundellsands.

St Mary's is at the centre of this small village (SD320017). It was built in the mid-C19 and has much mid-C20 painted decoration especially the nave roof and the south transept. In the north-west porch, almost hidden behind the door, there is a small copper memorial plaque with unusual repoussé work. The inscription commemorates Agnes Blundell who died Jan 10 1890 and Nicholas Blundell who died July 12 1894. Their names and dates, recorded in stylised lettering, are separated by a central Art Nouveau plant form and enclosed

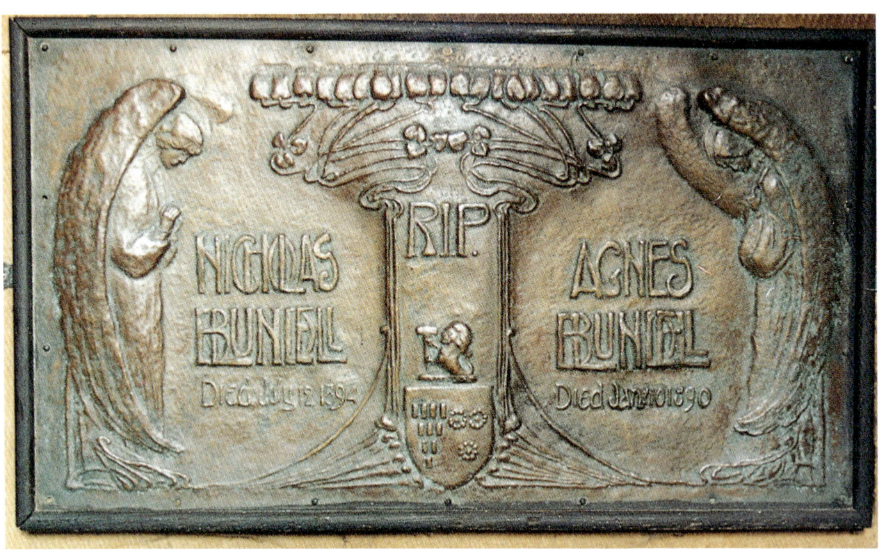

St Mary, Little Crosby. Memorial panel. Unsigned. Undated.

by the comforting curves of two angels' wings. The plaque is not signed or dated and prompts intriguing speculations as to its artistic provenance. There is more than a hint of the 'Glasgow School' in its design which adds to the intriguing possibilities.

There is an interesting decorative cross marking a grave at the eastern edge of the graveyard with carved plant forms climbing up the shaft and a leaden angel set in a roundel on the head of the cross.

Access: Presbytery Tel. 0151–9241783.

LIVERPOOL CITY CENTRE

The Royal Liver Building at the **Pier Head** (SJ338903) is the most familiar landmark in Liverpool. It was built by W. Aubrey Thomas 1908–10. The copper Liver Birds which top the cupolas of the building were made by George Cowper of **The Bromsgrove Guild** in 1911. The **Cunard Building**, designed by Arthur Davis with **Willink & Thickness** in 1916 has a carved frieze which features eagles modelled by **C. J. Allen**. In front of the main entrance is the **Cunard War Memorial** designed by Arthur Davis and executed by **Henry Alfred Pegram** in 1921. Its slender column is surmounted by a bronze nude male figure and pierced by the prow of a Roman ship. The mouldings and details were cast by **The Bromsgrove Guild**. The old **Mersey Docks and Harbour Board Building**, designed by Thornley, Briggs & Wolstenholme in 1907 has allegorical reliefs and free-standing figures by **C. J. Allen** on its west front. The decorative metalwork work both inside and out is by **George Wragge Ltd** as are the many colourful staircase windows, each representing one of the former British colonies.

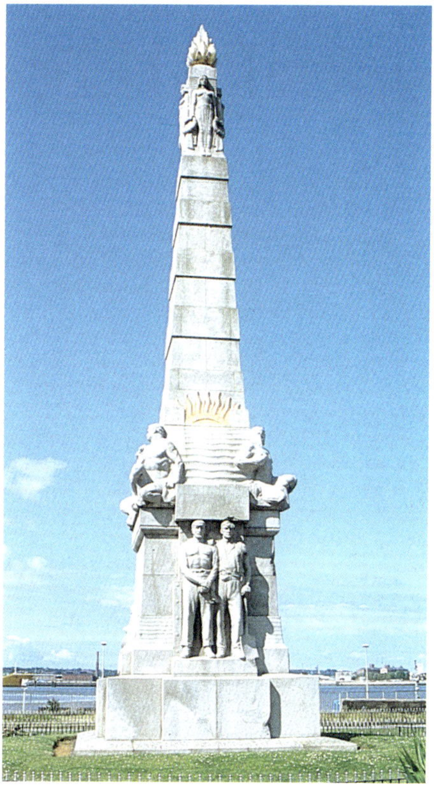

The Engine Room Heroes Memorial, Pier Head. W. Goscombe John, 1916.

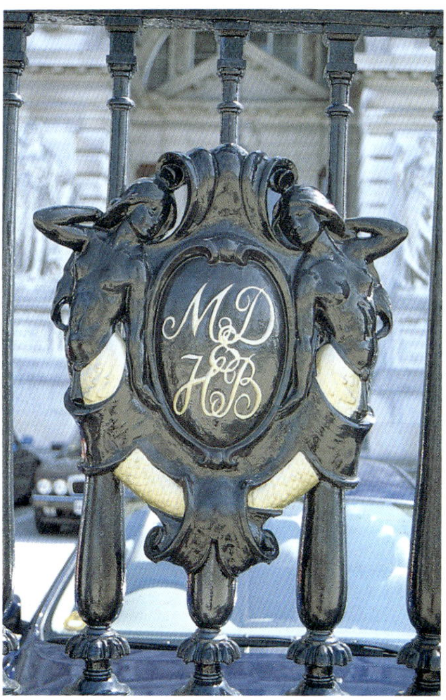

Mersey Docks and Harbour Board Building, Pier Head. Detail of the Gates. George Wragge Ltd, c. 1907.

In St Nicholas Place (SJ338904) is the magnificent memorial to the **'Engine Room Heroes'** designed by **W. Goscombe John** in 1916. It is a granite obelisk topped with a gilded torch-flame set above four sea maidens. On the pedestal base are high relief figures of the engine-room heroes. **Goscombe John** also sculpted the bronze equestrian **statue of King Edward VII** in front of the Cunard building in 1916. In front of the Mersey Docks & Harbour Board building is **George Frampton**'s allegorical **memorial in bronze** commemorating the Liverpool shipowner and philanthropist Sir Alfred Lewis Jones.

Across the Strand, on the corner of James St (SJ341902) is the striking **White Star Line** building designed by **Richard Norman Shaw**, 1895–98, in collaboration with J. F. Doyle and reminiscent of his New Scotland Yard offices.

The sumptuous **India Building** in Water St (SJ341904) has spikey, bronze, exterior lamps made by the **Bromsgrove Guild**.

The Town Hall in High St (SJ342905) was rebuilt in 1795 after a fire and still houses the Council

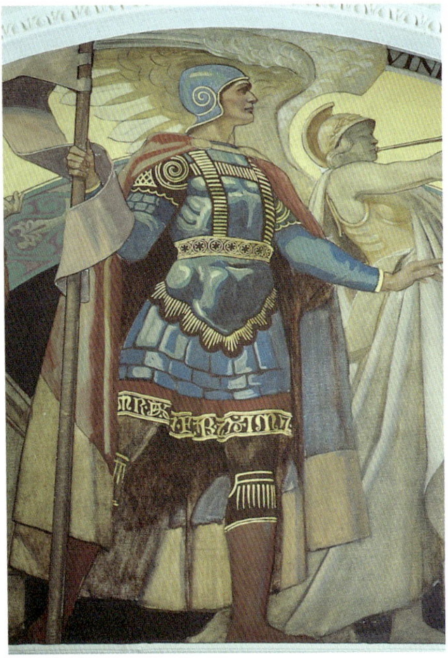

War Memorial, Liverpool Town Hall. Detail of mural by F. O. Salisbury, 1920.

Chamber, the Mayor's Parlour and the civic function suite. The superb wrought-iron work filling the arches in the portico is the work of **George Wragge Ltd.** The main entrance leads into a vestibule which has early Minton tiles on the floor, oak panelling designed by architect **F. M. Simpson** and door handles and finger plates by **R. Ll. B. Rathbone.** The four lunettes, painted in 1909 by **J. H. Amschewitz,** commemorate 700 years of Liverpool's history and represent 'King John Creating Liverpool a Free Port', 'Industry and Peace', 'Liverpool Centre of Commerce', and 'Education and Progress'. The titles of the pictures are listed on a small but beautifully-worked copper plaque at the side of the richly-carved fireplace. The case of Mayoral silver to the left of the grand staircase includes a lidded silver tazza made by the **Artificer's Guild.** Around the base of the huge dome above the stairwell are four paintings by **Charles W. Furse.** On the ground floor an anteroom to the council chamber was converted into a hugely impressive memorial to the 13,000 Liverpool men killed in the Great War. Apart from the panels listing the names of the fallen there are eight lunettes painted in 1920 by **Frank O. Salisbury.**

Access: Usually open to public but check for official functions which may limit access. Tel. 0151–2255532. Tours by appointment.

The Royal Insurance Building, on the corner of North John St and Dale St (SJ343905) was built in 1903 by **J. F. Doyle** and has a frieze at second-floor level sculpted by **C. J. Allen.**

14 Dale St, the former State Insurance Office (SJ343905) is by W. A. Thomas 1903–05. It has had a varied life in recent years. It was most recently a night club and currently there are plans to make it into a casino and restore its original, sumptuous, decorative scheme which includes a series of ten large, circular, coloured-plaster reliefs set in decorative marble surrounds. These roundels were executed by **Alfred Martin** and depict song titles such as 'Come Lasses and Lads', 'Black Eyed Susan' and 'The Gay Goshawk'.

Access: Managing Agents: Core Property Management and Consultancy Tel. 0151–2252500.

In Old Hall St stood the Cotton Exchange (SJ339908) by **Matear & Simon** which was demolished in 1967. The **War Memorial of the Cotton Association**, by **F. Derwent Wood**, was taken from the building and re-sited rather unceremoniously in a corner of the courtyard of the building which now occupies the site.

Castle St, (SJ343903) is the commercial centre of the city. Many of the banks and insurance offices here were designed by **Grayson & Ould** in styles as grand as their owners could afford. On the Brunswick St corner is the former **Adelphi Bank**, designed by **W. D. Caröe** 1894 and topped by green onion domes. It is now a coffee bar but the extravagant bronze doors remain. They were designed by **Caröe** and executed by **Stirling Lee** and illustrate the theme of brotherly love. On the other corner of Brunswick St is the **Nat West** formerly Parrs Bank, which was built 1898–1901 by **Richard Norman Shaw** in association with **Willink & Thicknesse.**

The Queen Victoria Memorial (SJ342902) in Derby Square was designed by **F. M. Simpson.** The sculpture is by **C. J. Allen** and was made 1902–06. It includes a very tall Queen Victoria surrounded by four allegorical groups. The groups represent 'Agriculture', 'Animal

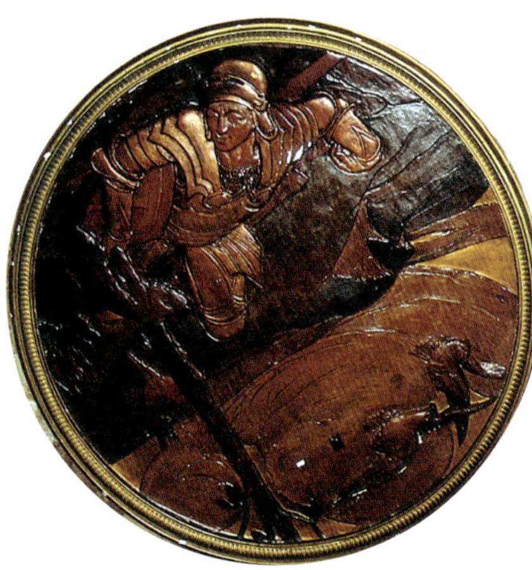

14 Dale St. Painted plasterwork by Alfred Martin c.1905.

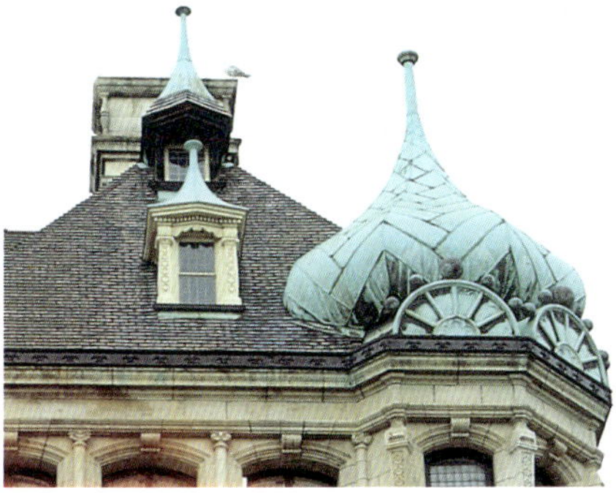

Former Adelphi Bank, Castle St. Onion domes by W. D. Caröe, 1894.

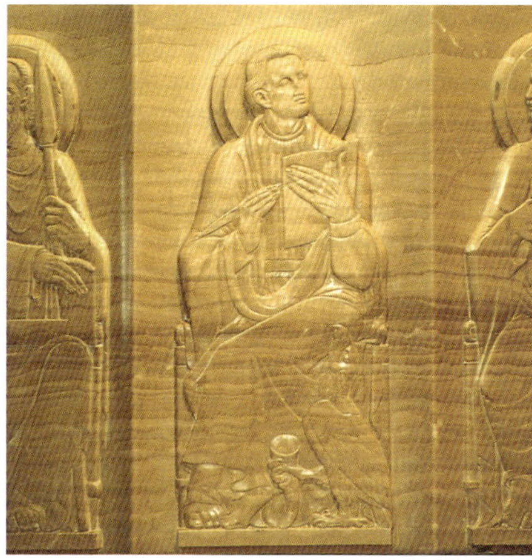

The Anglican Cathedral. Detail of the font by R. Carter Preston. Courtesy of the Dean and Chapter Liverpool Cathedral

Husbandry & Horticulture', 'Industry & Manufacturing' and 'Education and Commerce'.

Gustaf Adolfs Kyrken, also known as the Swedish Mission Church, at 138 Park Lane, (SJ347897) was designed by **W. D. Caröe** in 1883. It is built of red brick with stepped gables and an interesting bellcôte. The church was divided horizontally in the 1960s creating a small, simple octagonal chapel on the top floor. The remainder of the building now contains facilities for the social activities of the Mission. The reredos was dismantled during the alterations and the church has salvaged five beautiful, painted-gesso panels made in 1899 by **Robert Anning Bell**. They represent Christ the Good Shepherd flanked by Mary and John and two angels.

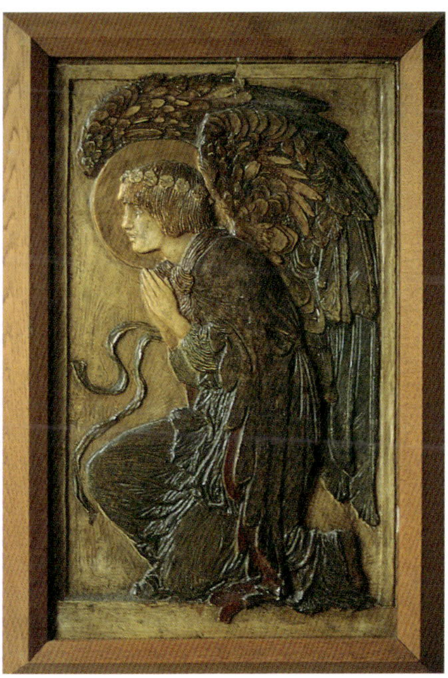

Gustaf Adolfs Kyrken, Park Lane. Painted Gesso panel. R. Anning Bell, 1899.

Access: Minister Tel. 0151–7097763.

The Anglican Cathedral (SJ353892), designed by G. G. Scott, is hugely impressive in an unconventional Gothic way and there are many interesting Arts and Crafts connections in its fittings and decorations. Entry is through a small door at the west end which leads into the Visitor Centre in the south-west transept. The nave walls are decorated with the 1930s sculpture of **Richard Carter Preston** with the Virtues and Vices represented on the north side and the Liberal Arts on the south side. His work can also be seen in the entrances to the Westford Porch where the theme is the Resurrection and again in the Rankin Porch where the Active Life is portrayed.

In the sanctuary, the main reredos, built in stone and partly gilded, was designed by **Walter Gilbert**, modelled by **Louis Weingartner** and made by craftsmen at **H. H. Martyn** of Cheltenham. **Gilbert** and **Weingartner** also designed the communion rail with its bronze figures representing the Ten Commandments. The bronze gates into the sanctuary were made by **The Bromsgrove Guild. Bainbridge Reynolds** was responsible for the door furniture, bronze grilles, the electric light-fittings in the Lady Chapel, the gate to the Bishop's stair and the processional cross made in 1927 in memory of the organist F. H. Burstall.

R. C. Preston has monuments to Sir Robert Jones, Bishop Ryle and Dean Dwelly in the south-choir aisle and one to A. J. M. Melly in the north-choir aisle. In the east transept on the north side is the War Memorial Chapel in which the sculpture of the reredos is attributed to **Gilbert** and **Weingartner**. In the south-east

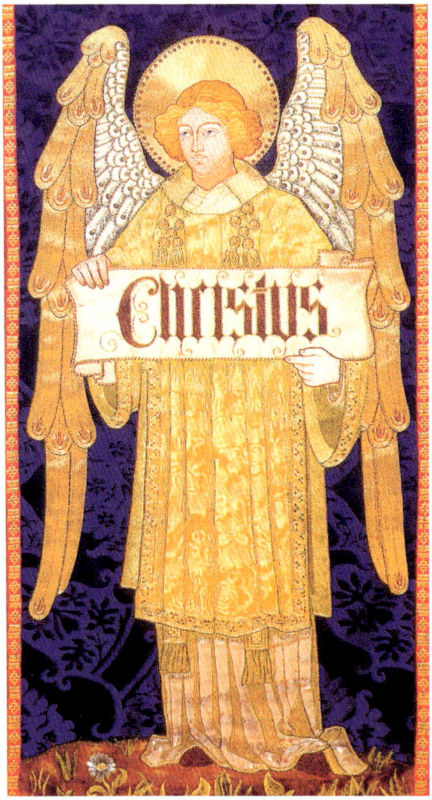

Anglican Cathedral: detail of the advent altar frontal, 1906–10, designed by G. F. Bodley for the Lady Chapel. The last of Bodley's designs and worked by Miss Comber. *Courtesy of the Dean and Chapter, Liverpool Cathedral*

transept at gallery level is the memorial of the 55th Lancashire Division which is also by **Gilbert** and **Wiengartner**. This transept houses the Lord Derby Memorial which was designed by G. G. Scott, and cast by **Farmer & Brindley**. There is also a statue made in 1957 by **Carter Preston** commemorating Max Horton. **Preston** was responsible for the relief figures on the font in the south-west transept.

The Chapter House windows, by **Morris & Co.**, were blown out during the war and remade *à la Morris* by **Powell of Whitefriars**. Those in the ambulatory are by Burlison & Grylls. All the stained glass in the choir, transepts, aisles, and Lady Chapel is by **Powell of Whitefriars** with **James Brown** having designed the great east window. The Lady Chapel, choir and transept windows were also rebuilt by Powell after bomb damage. Carl Edwards designed the later west window. The staircase to the Lady Chapel has an interesting window with the portraits of twenty one women who exemplify particular virtues. Christina Rossetti, for example, is fêted for her poetry and represents 'All Sweet Singers'. The Della Robbia statue of the Virgin in the Lady Chapel is C14 and from Italy, not from Harold Rathbone's studio in Birkenhead.

High up in the triforium of the cathedral is the **Elizabeth Hoare Embroidery Gallery**. Elizabeth Hoare was the niece of Giles Scott, architect of the cathedral and a director of Watts and Co. the clerical furnishers founded by Scott's father and his partners Bodley and Garner. She rescued many of the exhibits in the 1960s and 70s. The Gallery, which was opened in 1992, is the only one in Britain devoted entirely to the display and care of Victorian and Edwardian church embroidery. It contains examples of many of the major designers of the period from Pugin to Comper and shows the exquisite work done by embroiderers in convents, guilds or commercial workrooms. Not everything is on display. A room nearby contains the study collection which can be viewed by appointment.

Access: Open daily subject to services. For an appointment at the Elizabeth Hoare Gallery Tel. 0151–7096271.

The Philharmonic Dining Rooms at 36 Hope St, (SJ355898) designed in 1889 by W. W. Thomas, stand about half way between the city's two cathedrals. It is an Arts and Crafts treat. The swirling iron gates at the front door were designed by **H. Bloomfield Bare** who also made the repoussé panels depicting figures making music which decorate the inglenook in the main bar. In the Grandé Lounge (pronounced 'Grandee') the decorated plaster-relief over the

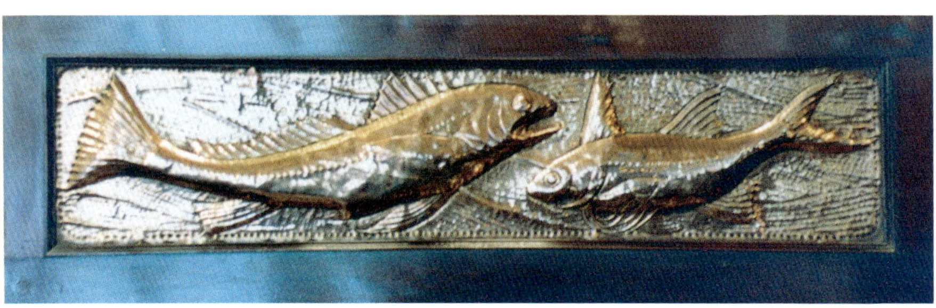

Grandé Lounge, Philharmonic Dining Rooms. Repoussé panel by H. Blomfield Bare, c. 1900.

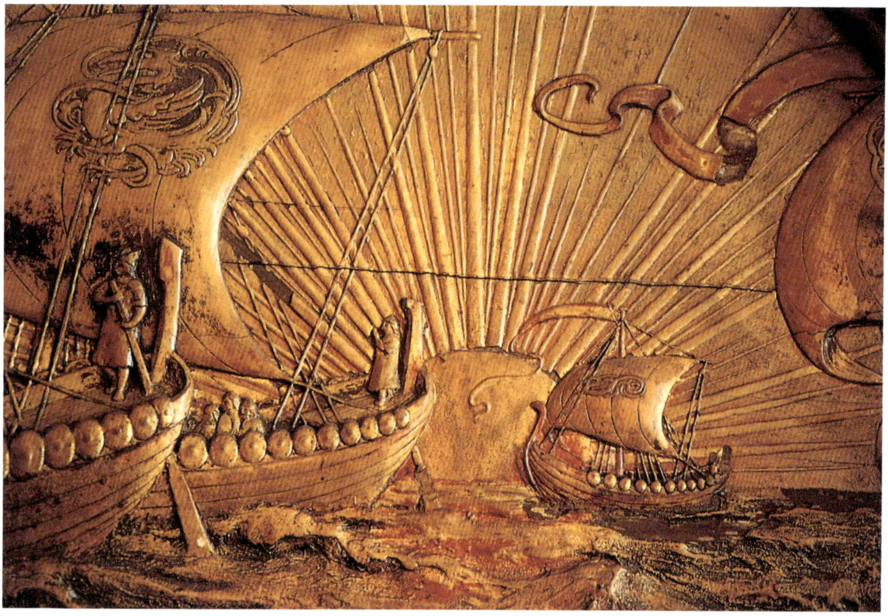

Vines Hotel, Lime St. Detail of gesso panel by H. G. Hiller.

doorway, 'Murmur over the Sea' and 'Apollo with Female Attendants', over the fireplace are by **C. J. Allen**. Of the 24 small rectangular repoussé copper panels set at dado level, the sixteen depicting animals, birds, fish, and floral motifs are by **H. Bloomfield Bare** and the eight scenes of the port of Liverpool are by **Thomas Huson**. All this work dates *c*. 1898–1900. The quality of the woodwork leaves nothing more to be desired but who did the stained glass? Coach loads arrive to ogle the marble and ceramics in the Gents' toilet. This is a working pub sometimes called **The Philharmonic Hotel**.

Access: Open daily. 0151–7072837.

On the opposite side of Hope St is the **Philharmonic Hall** built in 1932 by A. W. Rowse. In the entrance is a copper repoussé plaque by **Joseph Hodel** *c*. 1912 which is dedicated to the musicians who went down with the Titanic.

The Methodist Hall, (SJ351902) Renshaw St was built in red brick and yellow terracotta by **Bradshaw & Gass** 1904–05. It is now a night club but the building is still an arresting sight, a bizarre Byzantine pile with Art Nouveau flourishes.

The Vines Hotel in Lime St (SJ350902) is by Walter Thomas 1907. Externally it is more Edwardian Baroque than Arts and Crafts but inside it holds a feast of repoussée copper with woodwork worthy of the first class lounge of any early C20 ocean liner. Over the fireplace in the snug is a painted gesso panel by **H. G. Hiller** depicting Viking ships under full sail. The plaster relief frieze depicting puttis in rustic settings is by the **Bromsgrove Guild**.

Access: Open daily pub hours.

The Crown Hotel, at the railway station end of Lime St (SJ350903) has its name blazoned across the building in brash and distinctive gilded lettering. The window and door openings are framed in repoussée copper work and the boldness of the exterior stucco work is carried on inside by a riotous moulded-plaster ceiling. The most restrained decorative plant motif in the ceiling is picked up in the copper-work of the bar front.

Access: Open daily pub hours.

St George's Hall (SJ349906) is an icon of the city and typical of Liverpool's penchant for the Greco-Roman style of architecture. The sculpted panels either side of the portico were

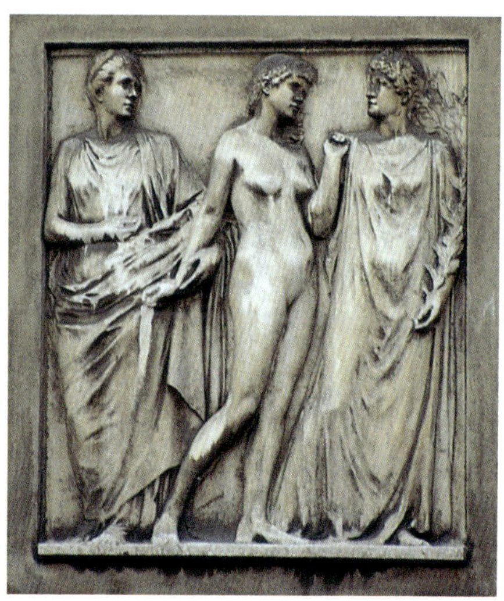

St George's Hall. Relief panel by T. Sterling Lee, 1887.

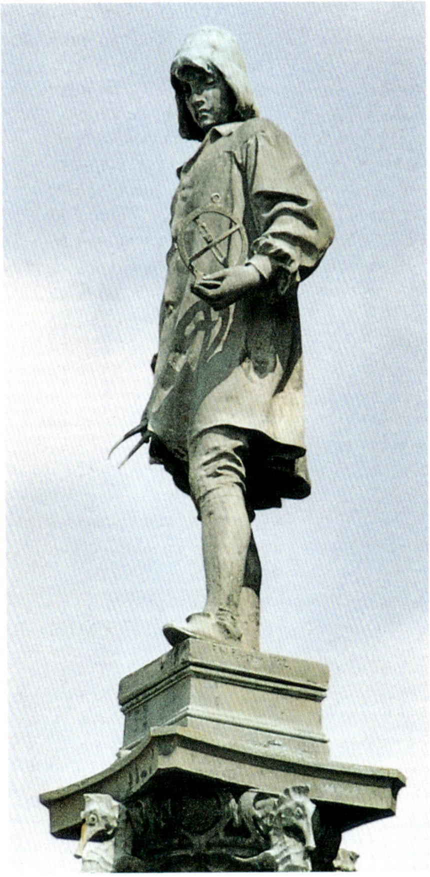

Liverpool Museum. Bronze figure, Byrom St entrance. F. W. Pomeroy.

executed by **T. Stirling Lee, Conrad Dressler** and **C. J. Allen**. The Council's Art Committee were so shocked by the naked and vulnerable figure of the young girl representing Justice in one of Stirling Lee's panels that the completion of the scheme was interrupted for several years and the remaining four panels in the series 'The Progress of Justice' were not completed by Stirling Lee until 1894.

In front of St George's Hall is the tomb-like **Great War Memorial** designed by **Lionel Budden** with bronze relief panels by **G. H. Tyson Smith**. It was unveiled in 1930. The long relief on the panel facing St George's Hall represents 'An Army on the March' and that on the side facing Lime St 'The Commemoration of Armistice Day'.

On the opposite side of the Hall is **St John's Garden** laid out by **T. Shelmerdine** in 1904 as a sculpture garden with work by **W. Goscombe John** (monument to the King's Liverpool Regiment, 1905) **George Frampton** (Wm. Rathbone 1899, Sir A. B. Forwood 1903 and Canon T Major Lester 1907) and **F. W. Pomeroy** (Mons. James Nugent 1905).

Liverpool Museum (SJ348908) was designed by E. W. Mountford 1896–1901. It faces William Brown St and incorporates the building which once housed the Liverpool Technical College. The external sculptures in the pediments and above the windows representing 'Commerce and Industry', 'Art and Science' and similar topics are all by **F. W. Pomeroy**. His too, are the delightful figures on the two ornate lamp-standards outside the original main entrance in Byrom St. The foyer in the Byrom St entrance has two large lunettes filled with reliefs modelled by **F. W. Pomeroy** and coloured by **Robert Anning Bell**. **Pomeroy** and **Bell** were also responsible for another, more highly-coloured lunette in what was the Examination Hall of the college. The central corridor from the Byrom St entrance to the Examination Hall has two overhead natural lighting bays, the surrounds of which are decorated with high-relief plaster panels by F. W. Pomeroy. There are no Arts and Crafts exhibits in the Museum collections.

Access: This part of the Museum is not normally open to the public. Arrangements can be made to visit by appointment. Keeper's office Tel. 0151–4784302.

The Liverpool Central Library (SJ349908) is situated between the Museum and the Art Gallery in William Brown St. In the east entrance to the Picton Reading Room, accessible only by walking through the main library, there is a beaten copper plaque inset with semi-precious stones made by **C. E. Thompson**, 1907, to commemorate the generous gift of the adjoining Hornby Library built by **T. Shelmerdine** 1906. The Library has a fine collection of private press books including all fifty-three books from **Kelmscott Press** and

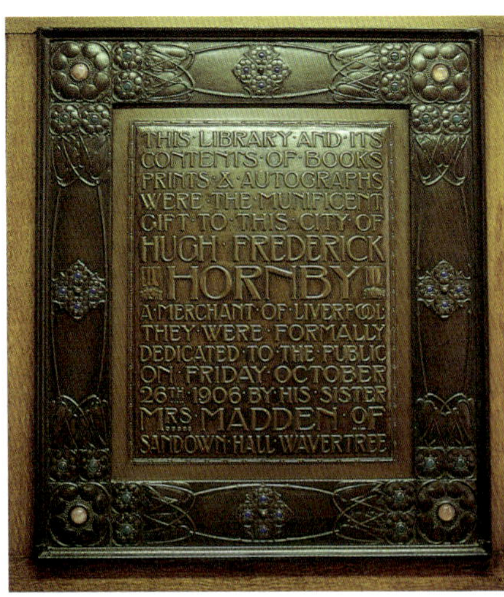

Central Library. Picton Library commemorative plaque. C. E. Thompson, 1906.

many also from the **Doves** and **Ashendene** Presses. There is also a collection of Special Bindings.

Access: Open Mon–Thurs 9.00–20.00; Fri 9.00–19.00; Sat 9.00–17.00; Sun 12.00–16.00. Tel. 0151–2335830.

The Walker Art Gallery in William Brown St (SJ349908) has a fine collection of Pre- and Post-Raphaelite paintings including **Henry Holiday's** 'Dante and Beatrice' Evelyn De Morgan's 'Life and Thought Emerging From the Tomb' **Ford Madox Brown's** 'The Coat of Many Colours' and 'Waiting'. There are works by Albert Moore, Spencer Stanhope, Alma Tadema, E. J. Poynter, Holman Hunt, Val Prinsep, **D. G. Rossetti, G. F. Watts** and **Edward Burne-Jones** .

There is work by well-known Arts and Crafts artists including **Walter Crane, Robert Anning Bell**, Byam Shaw, Charles M. Gere and Frank Brangwyn and that of many other fine, though less well-known painters who were also members of the Art-Workers Guild. The Gallery has a large collection of drawings and cartoons by **Henry Holiday** and archive material collected for its Exhibition of the Art Sheds in 1981. Its collection of 'New Sculpture' includes examples of the works of **C. J. Allen, Onslow Ford, Conrad Dressler, Albert Toft, Gilbert Bayes** and **George Frampton** to name but a few who were members of the Art-Workers' Guild.

The new **Craft and Design Gallery** on the ground floor is dedicated to showing the Gallery's extensive decorative arts collection. Among the choice Arts and Crafts pieces there is a silver altar-cross by **J. P. Cooper** 1907, a chalice and paten by **Robert Hilton**, a casket by **R. Ll. B. Rathbone** 1888–89 and another by **Joseph Hodel** 1906. **Hodel** also designed two beautiful gold pendants in the collection. **Christopher Dresser** has a brass candle-holder *c.* 1880, an electroplated kettle, burner and stand *c.* 1879 and a silver electroplated toast-rack *c.* 1880. There are examples of **James Powell's** Whitefriars glass with a decanter designed by **T. G. Jackson** and a pale green tumbler by **Philip Webb**. In the ceramics collection there are pots by **Doulton, Pilkington**, and **Martin Brothers** and a bowl and a clock by **Della Robbia**. More unusually there is a small piece 'Lavender Women' by **Phoebe Stabler** made for Carter, Stabler & Adams and a tile-panel 'Cinderella' designed by **Burne-Jones** and painted by **Lucy Faulkner** for **Morris Marshall Faulkner & Co.** 1863. The surrounding blue 'swan' tiles in the panel were designed by **Philip Webb**. Other later work by **Morris & Co.** on display includes an embroidered panel *c.* 1880 and a stained-glass window of 1909. There is another stained-glass window, this time by **Anning Bell** dated 1925. Most of the Gallery's furniture collection is at Sudley House but here there is a dining-room chair designed by **C. F. A. Voysey** for a house in Birkenhead *c.* 1902.

Access: Open Mon–Sat 10.00–17.00. Sun 12.00–17.00. Admission Free. Tel. 0151–4784199.

The Metropolitan Cathedral, Mount Pleasant, (SJ357902) is much smaller than the Church of England Cathedral but it is nonetheless impressive. This is not the Cathedral its sponsors set out to build. The intervention of the Second World War and a huge escalation of costs put paid to the building designed and started by **Edwin Lutyens**. All that remains of Lutyens's work is the huge crypt of what would have been his building. It now does duty as a concert venue and archivist's store.

Access: Open daily subject to services.

University of Liverpool, at Mount Pleasant was endowed in its early days by some of the wealthiest and most successful merchants in Liverpool. Today its fine collection of both architectural and portrait sculpture is largely a

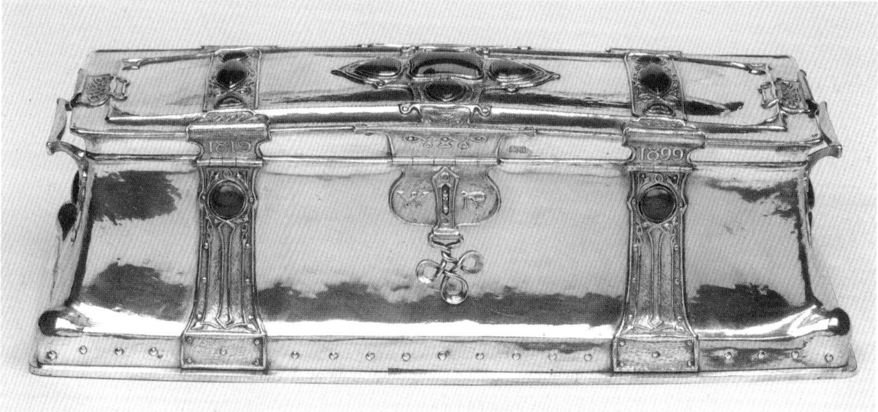

Walker Art Gallery, The Rathbone casket by R. Ll. B. Rathbone 1898–99. *© National Museums Liverpool*

tribute to them and their interest in decorative arts.

University Art Gallery is at 3 Abercrombie Square (SJ358900). The Gallery is relatively small and much of its collection is either on display elsewhere in the University or in store. Displayed in the Gallery itself are a number of portraits and reliefs of the benefactors or staff of the University by artists who include Augustus John and David Muirhead and sculptors like **C. J. Allen** and **George Frampton**. There are also four marvellous cartoons by **Edward Burne-Jones** prepared for the 'Joshua' window in St Giles, Edinburgh. Although not currently on display the Gallery has two treasured watercolours by the **MacNairs** – the one by **Francis (Macdonald) MacNair** is entitled 'Child in a Rose Bowl' 1899–1900 and the other by **Herbert MacNair** is 'Ysighlu' 1895. Much of the gallery's large collection of sculpture including medals by **C. J. Allen, George Frampton, Alfred Gilbert, E. C. Preston** and **G. H. Tyson Smith** is on display in Departments throughout the University.

Access: Open Mon–Fri 12.00–16.00.
Tel. 0151–7942348.

The ebullient red-brick **Victoria Building** on Brownlow Hill (SJ361903) was built 1889–92 by **Alfred Waterhouse** with terracotta reliefs executed by **Farmer & Brindley** on the tower façade. The imposing entrance hall, pillared and lined with **Burmantofts** tiles, houses the University's Great War Memorial. Made of stone and ivory-marble and partly gilded it was designed by **Gordon Hemm** and sculpted by **C. J. Allen** in 1926. On the first floor half-landing the triptych of coloured alabaster with a bas-relief portrait of Charles W. Jones is also by **C. J. Allen** 1910. On the next landing is the bronze bas-relief memorial on blue-grey marble to ship owner George Holt by **George Frampton** dated 1898.

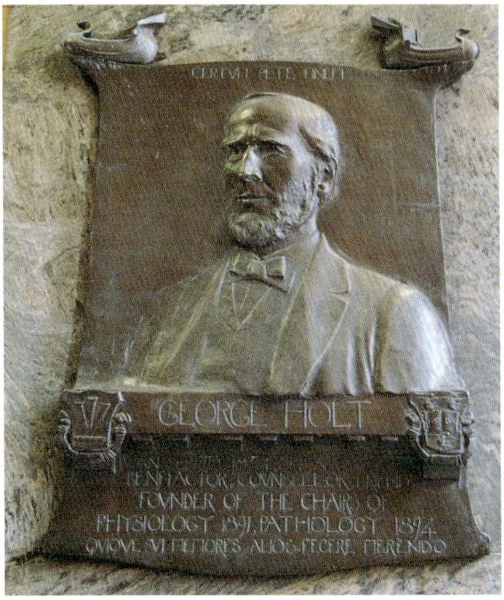

Victoria Building, University of Liverpool. George Holt memorial by George Frampton, 1898.

The adjacent **Ashton Building** was once the Faculty of Art. The façade of its quadrangle entrance is lavishly decorated above the pediment with two voluptuous ladies by **William Birnie Rhind**. His Sphinxes sit sedately in pairs on the parapet above the arched Ashton St entrance.

On the quadrangle side of the **Thompson Yates Building**, (SJ357904) designed by **Waterhouse** is a large terracotta panel by **C. J. Allen** depicting 'Physiology' and 'Pathology' as classical female figures (modelled, it is said, by the wives of the Department's Professors), 1896. **The Medical School** on the east side of Ashton St has a marble memorial plaque to Sir Rupert William Boyce executed by **C. J. Allen**, 1913.

In **Senate House**, on the Chatham St side of Abecrombie Sq (SJ360900) are bronze sculptures of two benefactors, Henry Tate by

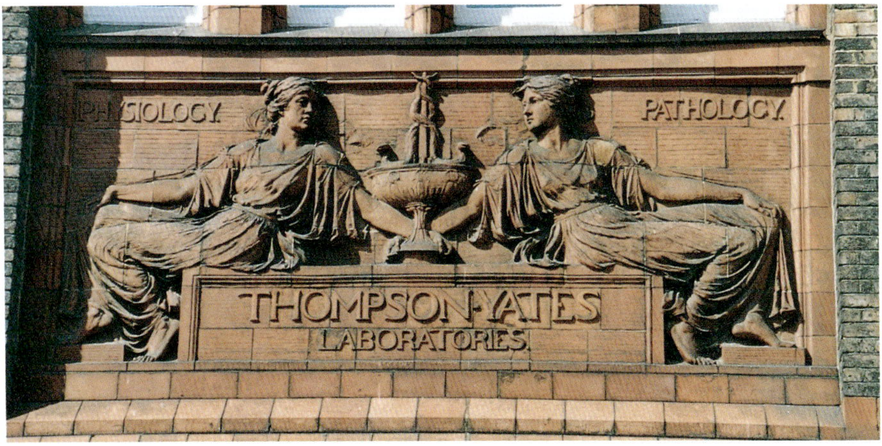

Thompson Yates Building, University of Liverpool. Terracotta panel. C. J. Allen 1896.
Courtesy of the University of Liverpool

Alfred Gilbert 1889–91 and William Rathbone VI by **C. J. Allen** *c.* 1901.

Access: Visits to University buildings must be cleared with the Press PR Department. Tel. 0151–7942247.

The Sidney Jones University Library off Chatham St (SJ360899) has a good collection of private press books mainly collected by William Noble (1838–1912) and Prof Walter Lyon Blease (1884–1914). The Noble Collection includes a complete set of William Morris's **Kelmscott Press** (1891–98), most of Lucien Pissarro's Eragny Press (1894–1914) as well as books by the **Ashendene**, Dun Emer, Cuala, **Doves**, and **Vale Presses**. There are also books and ephemera from the **Essex House Press** acquired from a different source. The publications from the presses of the inter-war years are in the Blease Collection. The University's Special Collections include the papers of sculptor **C. J. Allen** and copies of *Sphinx*, the magazine of the Guild of Undergraduates which was illustrated by the Applied Arts Department of the University.

Access: View by appointment. Tel. 0151–7942696.

St Francis Xavier, in Salisbury St (SJ356912) was built in 1848 by J. J. Scholes. The east end of the church was severely damaged during the Second World War when the stained glass, including a window by **Paul Woodroffe** was lost. However, **Woodroffe's** 'Francis Xavier Apostle of the Indies' made in 1907 survives in the Chapel of St Mary and the Angels. The chapel was added to the church in 1888 by **Edmund Kirby**. The altar has a tabernacle door by **Conrad Dressler** who also designed the wrought-iron screens on either side containing electrotype reliefs of 'The Holy Family' and the 'Presentation of the Virgin'. The church has a beautiful collection of vestments including an exquisite High Mass set made by the Benedictine Convent of Bergholt in 1898.

Access: Open for mass at 12 noon daily. Otherwise Tel. 0151–2981911.

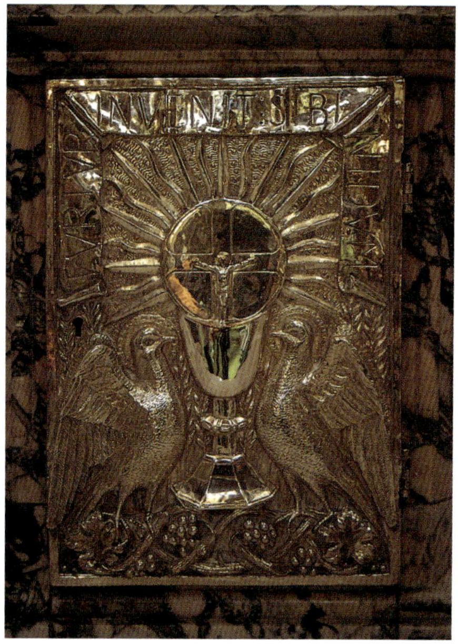

St Francis Xavier's, Salisbury St. Tabernacle door by C. Dressler.

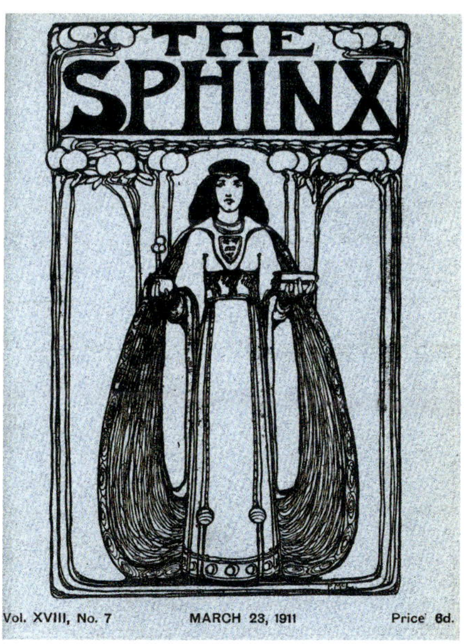

Sidney Jones Library. Front cover of 'Sphinx'.

MOSSLEY HILL lies to the east of Sefton Park about 3 miles south-east of Liverpool city centre.

St Barnabas, Allerton Road, (SJ392884) was built in 1914 by **J. F. Doyle**. Externally this is a very restrained church built of sombre, brown brick made in three or more sizes and bonded to give the appearance of stonework. Natural stone is used for the mullions and for decorative details. Inside it is all smooth, pale-grey stone with wide transepts and high, pointed arches. Polished limestone has been used to very good effect for the low chancel-screen, the pulpit and the octagonal font which has some finely carved panels. The east window was made by **H. G. Hiller** and is a Great War Memorial depicting heavenly and earthly forces. Hiller produced many inspired windows and this is among his best. In the narthex hangs a beautiful memorial to A. G. Moore who made the stained glass in the south wall. It is a lightly gilded painted-gesso panel depicting Christ giving his blessing. It was given by Moore's widow after 1941. Although it is unsigned and remains to be attributed, it is very reminiscent of similar work by **H. G. Hiller**.

Access: Parish Team Office. Open Mon–Fri 08.00–16.00

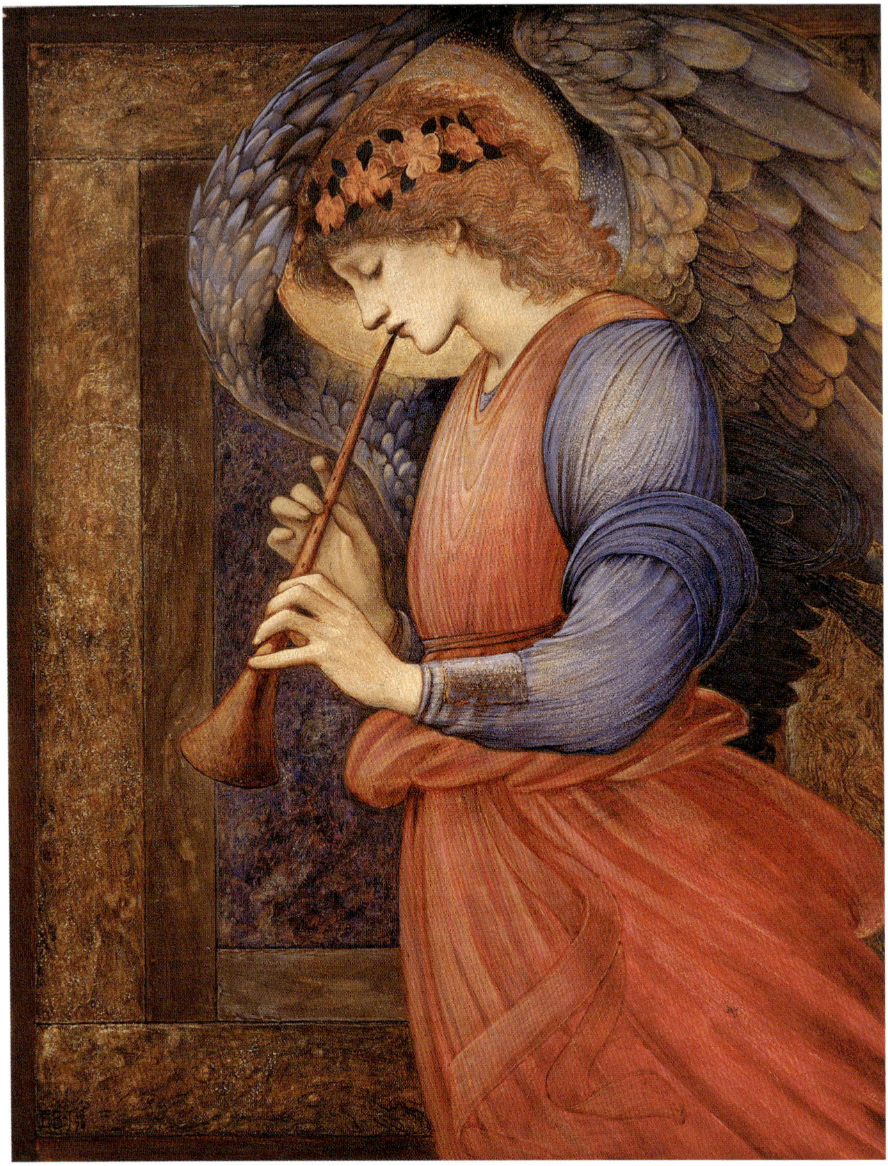

Sudley House, Mossley Hill. 'An angel playing a flageolet' by E. Burne-Jones, 1878. *© National Museums Liverpool*

Sudley House in Mossley Hill Rd (SJ387867) was once the home of George Holt the Liverpool ship owner, patron of the arts and the University. The house is now an art gallery housing his collection of paintings and sculpture. However, it also displays many of the City's Arts and Crafts treasures. The **MacNair Room** has four pieces of furniture designed by **Herbert** and **Frances MacNair**. The smallest piece, a table, was designed for the Turin exhibition 1902. The other three were made for their Liverpool home at 54 Oxford Rd (now demolished). There is a large cabinet from his studio, a wardrobe with three silvered, repoussé panels and a long, low dressing table. Above it hangs a repoussé panel, 'Cupid and Psyche' made in 1887 by **Harry Bates**. There are three framed panels of the 'King and Queen of Hearts' frieze made by **Robert Anning Bell** and his students for the University Club. He did the centre panel but that on the left was by student Fanny Hamel Lister and on the right by Enid Jackson. There is also a **Voysey** clock decorated by **Anning Bell** and two of his plaster reliefs 'Mother and Child' 1896 and 'Charity' 1901. A relief by **G. H. Tyson Smith** made in 1912 is of his own son Geoffrey.

There are several examples of **Conrad Dressler's** work with a collection of plaster maquettes and a panel 'Boy and Lantern' 1894. A painting by Liverpool artist **May Cooksey** 'The Marriage of St Catherine' hangs above the fireplace. Elsewhere in the house are a gong and a spider table by **E. W. Godwin** and paintings by **D. G. Rossetti, E. Burne-Jones**, Holman Hunt, Frederick Leighton, J. M. Strudwick and Stacey Marks. There is a fine collection of domestic sculpture including 'Eve' by **H. A. Pegram**, 'Love the Conqueror' by **F. W. Pomeroy**, 'The Shadow' by **Walter Marsden** and 'Grandmother and Child' by **Phoebe Stabler**.

Over recent years the rooms have been re-decorated in colours and style in keeping with the house. Some have wallpapers by Arts and Crafts designers. An 1883 design by **John D. Sedding** made by Sandersons is in the Holt room, while in the morning room the paper by an unknown designer for Heffer Scott & Sons was recently printed using the original blocks. Some of the rooms have the original wallpapers, chosen by George Holt when he moved into the house in 1884. All the rooms have interesting fireplaces, some with attractive tiles, which are contemporary with the house.

Access: From April 2005 the house is closed for major refurbishment. Tel. 0151–7243245 for progress reports.

St Matthew and St James at the corner of Mossley Hill Rd and Rose Lane, (SJ388870) is a classic **Paley & Austin** church (the best Victorian church in Liverpool according to Pevsner) built 1870–75. It suffered severe bomb damage in World War Two when it lost all its Morris & Co. and Henry Holiday windows. It has been carefully restored but some shrapnel damage, on the chancel arch for example, has been left as a reminder. The west window, renewed in 1951, depicts 'Paradise Lost' designed by Carl Edwards for **James Powell** and Sons. It uses bright and jewel-like colours and very small pieces of glass. The east window, executed in 1953 and also designed by Edwards, is in a slightly different style and magnificently illustrates scenes from the life of Christ.

A door at the south-west corner of the church leads to a connecting passage to the adjoining hall. The passage is glazed with two **Morris & Co.** windows which were brought here from Cheadle Congregational Church which was demolished in 1970. St Matthew and St Luke are both **Burne-Jones** figures. In the passage to the south vestry is a splendid, very decorative bronze memorial plaque to three young men, pupils at Greengate School, who were killed in the South African War. It is unsigned but can it be mere coincidence that **Francis Macdonald MacNair** had relatives who were managers of the Greengate School? The vicarage next door was built by **Paley & Austin** in 1873.

Access: Parish Office Tel. 0151–7246391.

NEW FERRY stands just to the north of Port Sunlight astride the B5136.

St Mark's stands on the corner of New Chester Rd and Earl St (SJ336856). It was built in the 1860s and the chancel was rebuilt in 1912 by Deacon & Horsburgh. The church has three three-light windows by **Morris & Co.** made in 1877 and six more by **Henry Holiday** which were added in 1880. The Morris windows second from the east in the south aisle, second from the west and second from the east on the north side each show an apostle in their outer lights and a related scene in the centre. All are badly in need of attention to remedy wear-and-tear and the effects of ageing. **Holiday's** windows, showing eighteen English saints, have been repaired but provide a very interesting collection. The church has a superb 'Benedicite' window in the west wall with a fascinating menagerie drawn in a band across all five lights. The window is unsigned, but quite Pre-Raphaelite in style and made in 1872. Could this be by **Henry Holiday** too? It doesn't appear in the list attached to Baldry's article in *Walkers Quarterly*, but then the list is not always accurate; it only refers to nine saints in

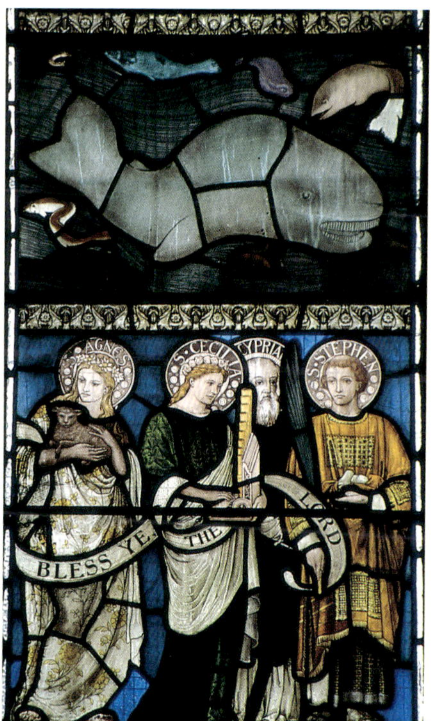

St Mark's, New Ferry. Detail of west window. Unsigned. Undated.

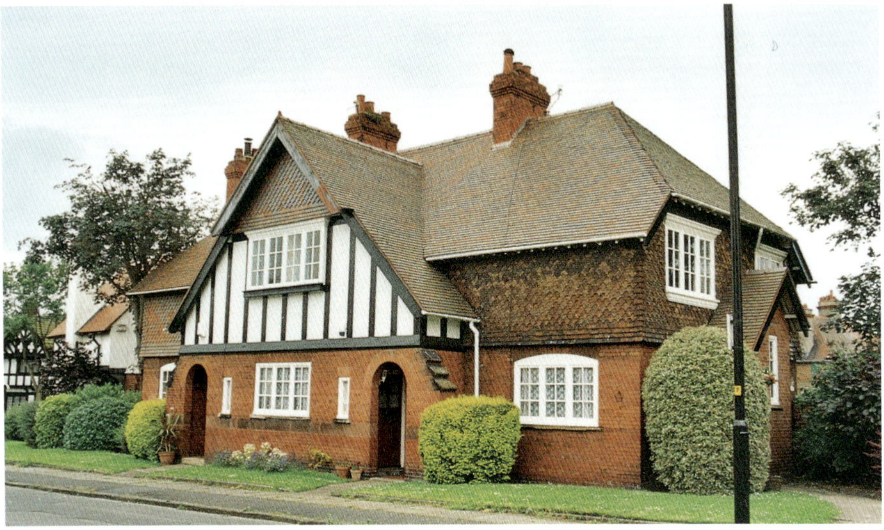

52–56 Primrose Hill, Port Sunlight by M. B. Adams, 1899.

this church when we can see there are eighteen. Binoculars will be worthwhile here.

Access: Vicarage Tel. 0151–6452638.

NEWTON le WILLOWS sits in the angle created by the M6 and the M62 north of Warrington and east of St Helens.

St Peter's, in Crow Lane (SJ581957) was built 1892–1901 by Demaine & Brierley of York and seems to be the only **Brierley** church in the region. It is a very large and elegant red-sandstone building with interesting *fin de siècle* curves in the tracery of the aisle windows. Internally it is graceful in its proportions and has broad arches supported on slender pillars. The church has an oak-panelled dado and the sanctuary is furnished with a painted altar-front and an intricately carved seven-panel reredos made and painted by **Shrigley & Hunt**. Most of the stained glass was also made by Shrigley & Hunt.

Access: Vicarage Tel. 01925–224815.

OXTON see Birkenhead.

PORT SUNLIGHT village lies east of the Birkenhead to Chester railway and west of the A41.

Port Sunlight (SJ337845) was conceived by William Hesketh Lever from the outset as the Sunlight Soap factory with a model village attached. He began the enterprise in 1886 and although new dwellings are currently being built, Lever's village was essentially constructed over a period of about 50 years before enemy action during World War Two created the need for some rebuilding. A total of about 850 houses were built together with the church, school, pub, girls' hostel, old boys' and pensioners' club, girls' club, theatre, community hall, village institute, swimming pool, bowling green, tennis courts and Lady Lever Art Gallery. The work involved more than two dozen architects with regional or national reputations, as follows:

Maurice B. Adams	
59–63 Greendale Rd	1899
52–56 Primrose Hill	1899
W. Naseby Adams	
5–13 Central Rd	1907
F. Barnish	
16–34 Central Rd	1911
H. Beswick	
156–66 New Chester Rd	1899
H. Blomfield	
36–44 Central Rd	1906
Bradshaw & Gass	
2–14 Central Rd	1906
11–21 Primrose Hill	1906
Deacon & Horsburgh	
1–3 Central Rd	1907
1–9 Primrose Hill	1907
Douglas & Fordham	
10–16 Boundary Rd	1905
Demolished and rebuilt	1947
1–9 Bridge St	1894
7–15 Corniche Rd	1898
128–32 New Chester Rd	1899
244–48 New Chester Rd	1898
284–86 New Chester Rd	1898
294–96 New Chester Rd	1898
19–23 Park Rd	1894
26 Park Rd	1895
17–23 Wood St	1894
49–55 Wood St	1895
Douglas & Minshull	
71–75 Bolton Rd	1898
268–74 New Chester Rd	1898

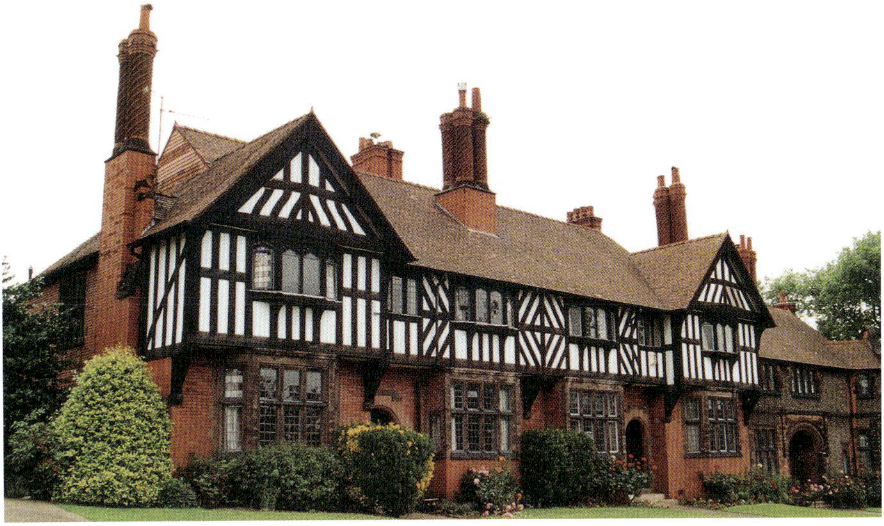

19–23 Park Rd, Port Sunlight. Douglas and Fordham, 1894.

6–14 Primrose Hill	1899
Garnet & Wright	
15–27 Central Rd	1907
E. George & Yeates	
25–29 Greendale Rd	1901
33–39 Greendale Rd	1901
178–90 New Chester Rd	1899
Grayson & Ould	
1 Bath St	1896
5–55 Bebbington Rd	1899
15 Bolton Rd	1890
20 Bolton Rd	1896
3–4 Brook St	1906
5–10 Brook St	1910
2–8 Boundary Rd	1899
13–31 Boundary Rd	1905
7–47 Boundary Rd	1905
1–4 The Causeway	1901
18–26 Circular Drive	1906
6–13 Church Drive	1905
55–59 Corniche Rd	1898
1–9 Cross St	1896
6k Greendale Rd	1901
7–10 Greendale Rd	1901
18–24 Greendale Rd	1899
30– 2 Greendale Rd	1901
40–43 Greendale Rd	1901
49–53 Greendale Rd	1901
83–87 Greendale Rd	1891
1–7 Lower Rd	1901
12–20 Lodge Lane	1899
192–98 New Chester Rd	1899
224–42 New Chester Rd	1898
288–92 New Chester Rd	1898
302–04 New Chester Rd	1898
310–26 New Chester Rd	1898
50–52 Park Rd	1895
2–8 Poets' Corner	1895
41–53 Pool Bank	1899
69–75 Pool Bank	1899
2–6 Pool Bank	1906
8–34 Pool Bank	1907
37–45 Primrose Hill	1901
1–8 Riverside	1895
7–9 Underley	1905
2–18 Windy Bank	1902
23–24 Windy Bank	1907
27–47 Wood St	1895
Bridge Inn Bridge St	1900
Schools, Church Drive	1903
E. Kirby	
49–53 Corniche Rd	1899
40–45 Primrose Hill	1899
T. M. Lockwood	
81–87 Bebbington Rd	1899
38–48 Park Rd	1895

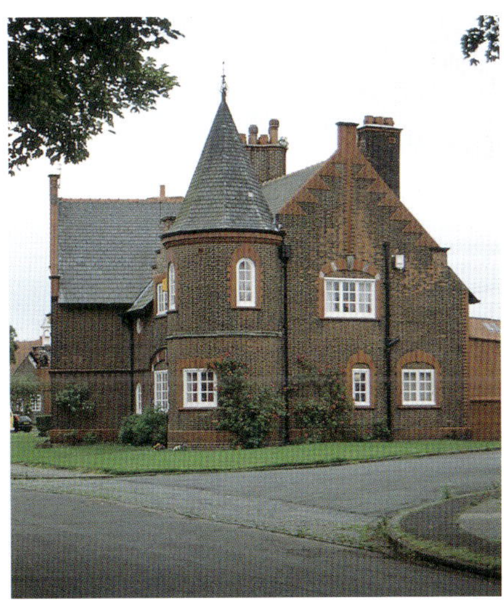

23–24 Windy Bank, Port Sunlight. Grayson & Ould, 1907.

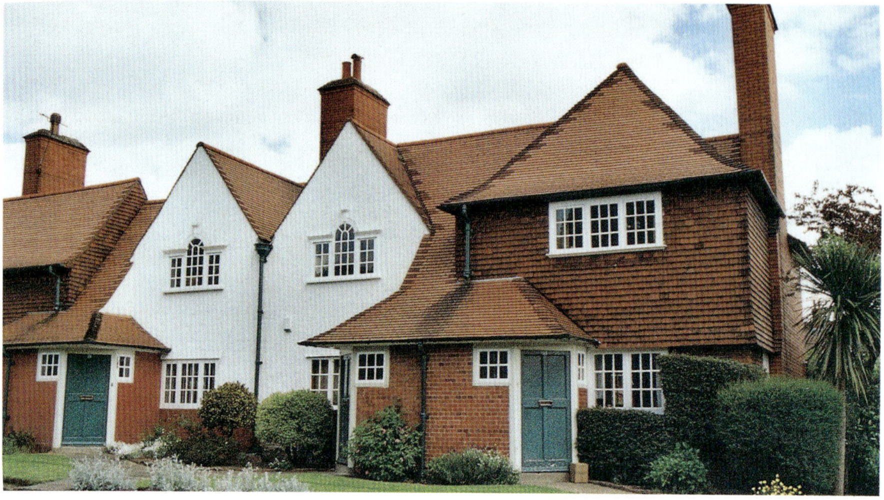

17–23 Corniche Rd, Port Sunlight. E. L. Lutyens, 1899.

E. L. Lutyens
17–23 Corniche Rd 1899

H. A. Matear
61–67 Corniche Rd 1898
148–56 New Chester Rd 1899
200–10 New Chester Rd 1899
21–25 Pool Bank 1899
16–28 Primrose Hill 1899

Maxwell & Tuke
Girls Hostel 1896
Now Bank & visitor centre

Ernest Newton
67–79 Bebbington Rd 1899
Ormrod & Pomeroy
23–35 Primrose Hill 1906

W. Owen
1–13 Bolton Rd 1889
2–12 Bolton Rd 1889
17–21 Bolton Rd 1890
for Minister, Doctor, School Teacher
57–65 Bebbington Rd 1899
22–42 Bolton Rd 1896
61–69 Bolton Rd 1898
1–Corniche Rd 1898
69 Corniche Rd 1898
71–78 Greendale Rd 1891
89–92 Greendale Rd 1894
170–76 New Chester Rd 1900
250–66 New Chester Rd 1898
276–84 New Chester Rd 1898
2–22 Park Rd 1894
28–36 Park Rd 1895
2–4 Primrose Hill 1899
1–7 Wood St 1894
Gladstone Hall 1891

W. & S. Owen
1–17 Park Rd 1892
64–78 Bolton Rd 1912
5–7 The Causeway 1901
2–16 Circular Drive 1899
28–38 Circular Drive 1899
1–5 Church Drive 1901
79–82 Greendale Rd 1891

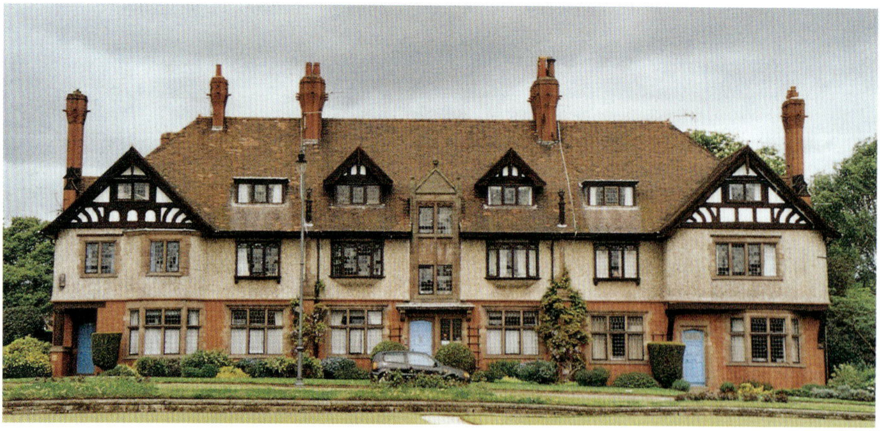

17–21 Bolton Rd, Port Sunlight by W. Owen, 1890.

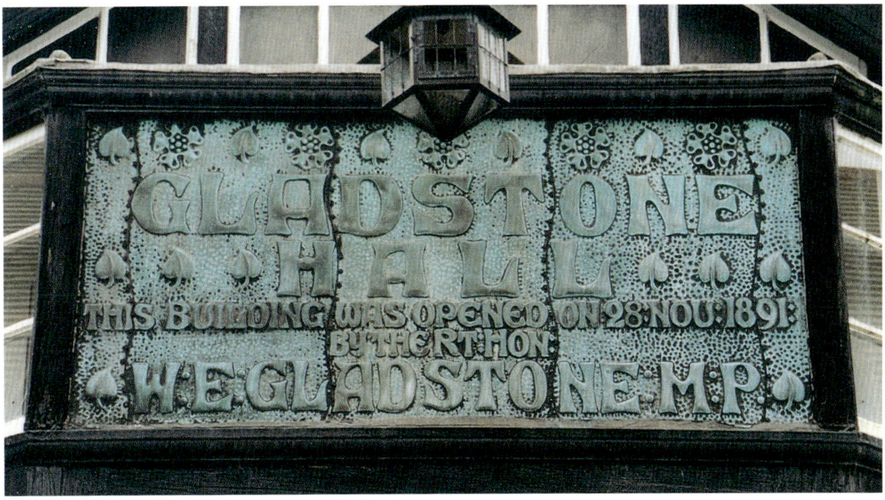

Gladstone Hall, Port Sunlight. Commemorative plaque by H. Bloomfield Bare, post 1891.

2–10 Lodge Lane	1900
212–22 New Chester Rd	1899
1–7 Pool Bank	1899
1–21 Water St	1912
Christ Church	1904
Fire Station	1902
Hulme Hall	1901
Lady Lever Art Gallery	1922
Pain & Blease	
54–58 Greendale Rd	1901
T. T. Rees	
43–47 Corniche Rd	1898
306–08 New Chester Rd	1898
C. H. Reilly	
15–27 Lower Rd	1906
J. Lomax Simpson	
60–62 Bolton Rd	1914
8–17 The Causeway	1913
46–72 Central Rd	1906
1–35 The Ginnel	1914
3–6 Greendale Rd	1925
6a–6h Greendale Rd	1926
1–18 Duke of York Cottages	1934
1–22 King George's Drive	1913
1–15 Jubilee Crescent	1938
29–3 Lower Rd	1907
35–59 Lower Rd	1907
47–57 Primrose Hill	1925
10–14 Queen Mary's Drive	1925
15–22 Queen Mary's Drive	1926
23–50 Queen Mary's Drive	1913
2–4 Water St	1914
1–5 Windy Bank	1926
Girls Club – now the Residents' club	1913

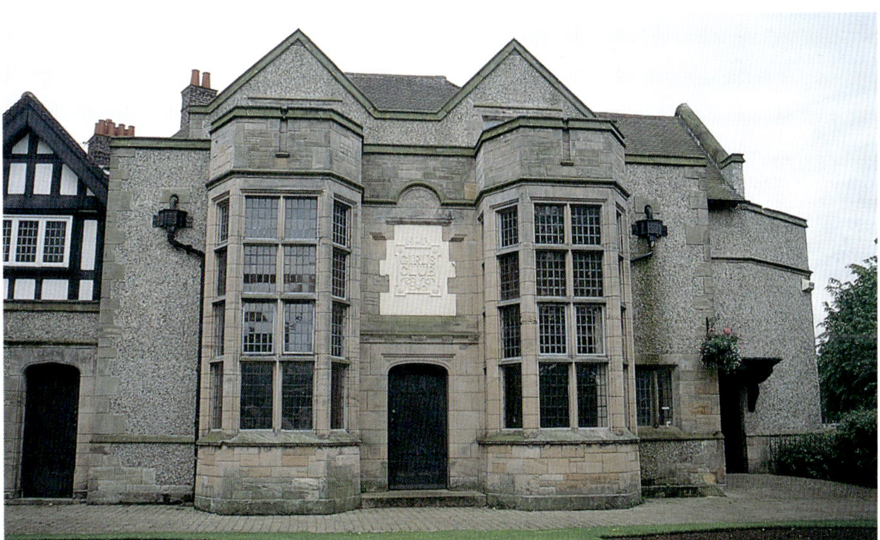

The Residents' Club, Port Sunlight by J. Lomax Simpson, 1913.

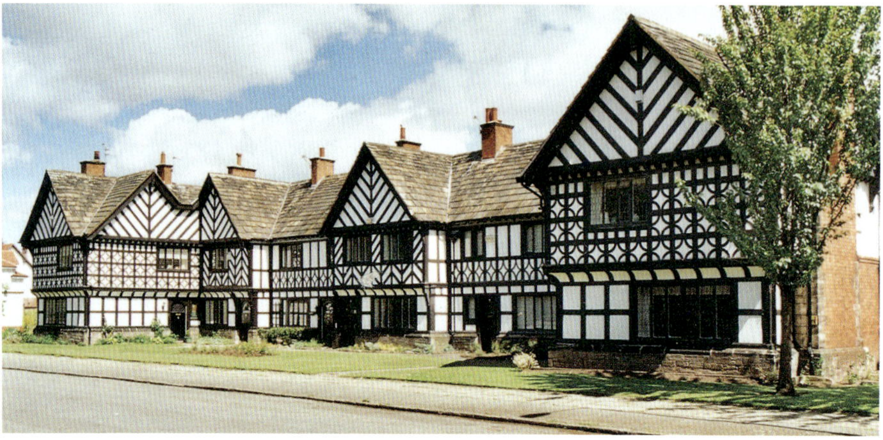

11–17 Greendale Rd, Port Sunlight. Wilson & Talbot, 1902.

John Simpson

31–35 Corniche Rd	1899
298–300 New Chester Rd	1898
30–38 Primrose Hill	1899

J. J. Talbot

3–33 Bath St	1897
89–97 Bebbington Rd	1899
9–10 Riverside	1897
25 Wood St	1894
Hesketh Hall	1903

Wilson & Talbot

16–22 Bridge St	1894
18–22 The Causeway	1901
25–29 Corniche Rd	1899
37–41 Corniche Rd	1898
11–17 Greendale Rd	1902
44–48 Greendale Rd	1901
64–70 Greendale Rd	1902
9–13 Lower Rd	1901
134–46 New Chester Rd	1900
24 Park Rd	1894
9–7 Pool Bank	1902
27–29 Pool Bank	1901
37–39 Pool Bank	1901

Christ Church in Church Rd (SJ338845) was built 1902–04 by **William & Segar Owen**. It was built as a non-denominational church and is aligned more or less north-south rather than east-west. Stylistically it nods to the Perpendicular but in a restrained and undemonstrative way. Internally the great timbers of the roof are an impressive decorative device, especially in the chancel. The unconventional mouldings of the arcades are allowed to fade into the piers without the intervention of capitals and the only decorative carving in the structure is on the padstones of the chancel arch. There is a high, wide and inviting nave with a relatively wide passage aisle on each side. The elaborate woodwork in the chancel is by **Messrs Hatch & Sons**, aided, so local tradition has it, by woodworking students at the nearby School for the Deaf and Dumb. The west window, by **Heaton, Butler & Bayne** (per Pevsner) is very effective – who designed it? In a loggia attached to the north wall of the church are the tombs of Lord and Lady Leverhulme with sculpture by **W. Goscombe John**.

Access: Volunteers try to keep the church open Apr–Oct Mon–Fri, late a.m.–mid-p.m. Open Sun p.m. Vicarage Tel. 0151–6454061

The Gladstone Hall (SJ336840)was built by **W. Owen** 1891 as a factory dining room but has since been converted to a theatre. There is a large repoussé panel over the entrance commemorating the opening of the hall in 1891. It was made by **H. Bloomfield Bare**.

The War Memorial, made 1916–22 by **W. Goscombe John**, is sited mid-way down the Causeway. (SJ336845) The tall granite cross stands proudly at the centre of a platform and is encircled by a group of bronze figures representing the defence of the home. On the outside of the surrounding parapet are more life-like and poignant groups representing the armed services and the Red Cross. Groups of children stand appealingly in panels placed on either side of the steps leading up to the platform. It is one of the most memorable of all war memorials.

The Lady Lever Art Gallery (SJ335848) was designed in 1913 by the firm of **William & Segar Owen** but not completed until 1922. It is a building in the grand Beaux Art style, a fitting memorial to Leverhulme's wife Elizabeth Ellen who died in July 1913. This large building with Ionic-columned entrances on all four sides is set apart from its village surroundings by its sheer scale and yet it fits happily into the central scheme of things and provides a magnificent closure to the view down the length of The Diamond, taking in **Goscombe John's** war memorial and Sir Charles Wheeler's fountain.

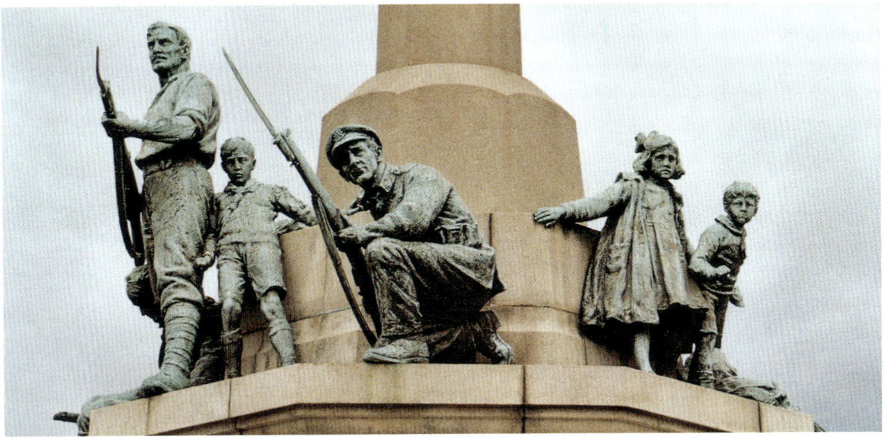

Great War Memorial, Port Sunlight. Detail by W. Goscombe John.

The building was constructed of reinforced concrete and faced with stone. Typically, the main contractors were Lever Brothers Works Department while the stone carving was done by Earp, Hobbs & Miller and by **J. J. Millson**. The gallery is basically a huge central rectangular space with a shallow dome at each end set over circular exhibition rooms. When it was completed Leverhulme moved in most of his huge private collection and other material he had especially acquired for the Gallery. He had the most eclectic of taste which started when he bought pictures which he could use for advertising his soap products. He went on to buy C18 art, furniture and ceramics and C17 and C18 Chinese pottery, enamels and jade. Much of his collection derived from the purchase of many pieces from other collectors. For visitors with a penchant for the Arts and Crafts this is the place to see New Sculpture and Pre-Raphaelite paintings. The collection of Pre-Raphaelite, and late C19 and early C20 paintings is in the huge main hall and so are many of the sculptures. This is a feast. It is hard to think of any other gallery that provides this range and quality of work and makes it so accessible. Everyone is here: Millais and Holman Hunt, Leighton and Tadema, Arthur Hughes and Frederick Sandys, **Rossetti** and **Burne-Jones** and many more. On either side of the gallery and in front of all these magnificent paintings there are beautiful sculptures. Mainly in marble and bronze, they are the work of **Gilbert Bayes, Onslow Ford, Goscombe John, Reynolds Stephens, Derwent Wood** and others. The picture on the far-end wall of the long gallery by Frederic Leighton is a show-stopper and not just because of its size. Magically, on the two adjoining walls is some of the best work of **Rossetti** and **Burne-Jones**. But even this is not all. In the little lobby to the left is **Ford Madox Brown's** 'Cordelia's Portion' and **Rossetti's** 'Pandora' In the next room is **Ford Madox Brown's** 'Cromwell on his Farm'.

Tucked away upstairs among the early C20 painters there is even a small picture by Eleanor Fortescue Brickdale and another by **Robert Anning Bell**. Downstairs there is a good café and an excellent well-stocked shop.

Access: Open every day 10.00–17.00
Tel. 0151–4784136.

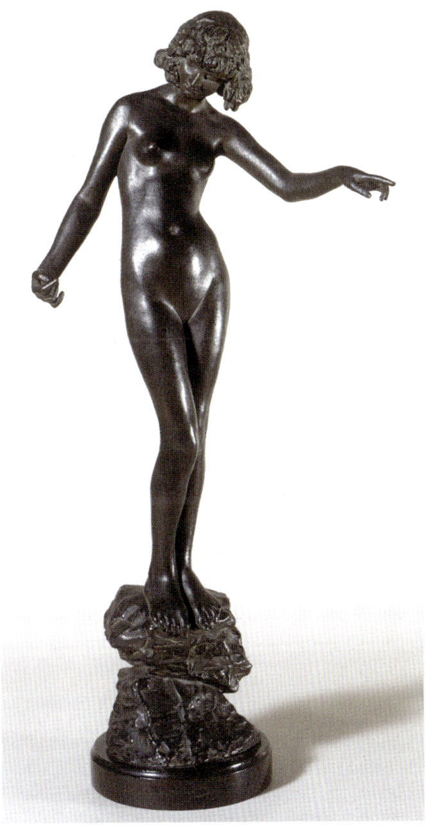

Lady Lever Art Gallery, Port Sunlight. 'Folly' by Edward Onslow Ford 1886. *© National Museums Liverpool*

The Lever Memorial, in front of the west entrance of the Lady Lever Art Gallery, was completed in 1930 and not surprisingly there is an Art Deco feel about the obelisk topped by the figure of 'Inspiration'. The four figures at ground level, representing 'Industry', 'Art', 'Education' and 'Charity' are more realistic. The monument was designed by **Lomax Simpson** and the sculptor was **William Reid Dick**.

More information can be obtained from the Port Sunlight Heritage Centre, 95 Greendale Rd. Open Apr–Oct weekdays 10.00–14.00. For other times Tel. 0151–6446466.

PRENTON see Birkenhead.

PRESCOT links St Helens to the eastern edge of the Liverpool conurbation.

St Mary's in Church St (SJ465927) is a C17 church built of red sandstone. The green and gold chancel screen was raised as a Great War Memorial. In the east wall of the south aisle there is a window by **Morris & Co.** installed in 1880 which shows Christ ascending accompanied by two angels all set in pale patterned quarries and designed by **Burne-Jones**. There are three splendid three-light windows made by **Edward Woore** 1922–38. The World War One memorial window in the south aisle was probably executed in collaboration with **Whall & Whall.** In the west wall of the north aisle his 'Christ Preaching on the Sea of Galilee' is set above 'The Parable of the Sower' while his 1938 window, at the west end of the north wall, is rendered in paler tones.

Access: Vicarage Tel. 0151–4260716.

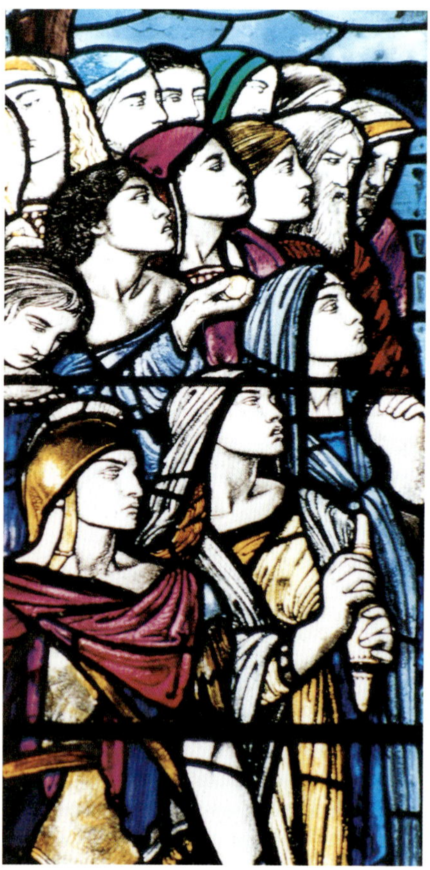

St Mary's, Prescott. Detail, west window by E. Woore, c. 1924.

Our Lady Immaculate and St Joseph in Vicarage Place, (SJ464927) was designed by J. Hansom. There is a two-light window in the north aisle made in 1903 by **Paul Woodroffe** showing a very wiry John the Baptist beside the Good Shepherd. Both figures are set against very interesting entrelac backgrounds.

Access: Presbytery Tel. 0151–4266462.

At the junction of the A58, St Helens Rd, and the B5201, Burrows Lane, is a **Great War Memorial** (SD473933). A soldier standing on a pedestal is offered the palm of victory by a young woman in civilian dress. It was sculpted by **Walter Gilbert** and **Louis Weingartner** and cast by **H. H. Martyn** of Cheltenham in 1922.

ST HELENS is an industrial town which keeps its distance from both Manchester in the east and Liverpool in the west.

St Helens World of Glass in Chalon Way (SJ511952) was opened in 1999 and exhibits some of the glass and pottery once displayed in the now defunct Pilkington Museum. These include a small amount of **Doulton Art Pottery**, Eccleston Pottery, and a teapot (1930) from the Midland Pottery Company's Old Teapot Works in Ravenhead. There is also an Art Nouveau copper plaque by **C. E. Thompson** marking the opening of the Sutton Carnegie Library.

Access: Open Tues–Sun 10.00–17.00. Admission charges. Tel. 08707–444777

The Victoria Memorial, in the paved square next to the Town Hall (SJ513955), is a bronze seated statue of a solemn Victoria RI holding an orb symbolising her royal power. It is remarkable how well the sculptor has captured the texture and flow of the material of her skirt. On the back of the statue is a small but beautiful figure of St George. Both large and small figures are the work of **George Frampton** 1906.

St Helen's in Church St (SJ513952) was built by **W. D. Caröe** 1920–26 on the site of the mediaeval church which was destroyed by fire in 1916. It is built of unassuming dark-red brick but it has striking external details and a stylish and novel tower. The interior is **Caröe** at his mature best – tall, slender stone arcades and white, rendered walls lightened by bright clerestory windows. The small but beautifully

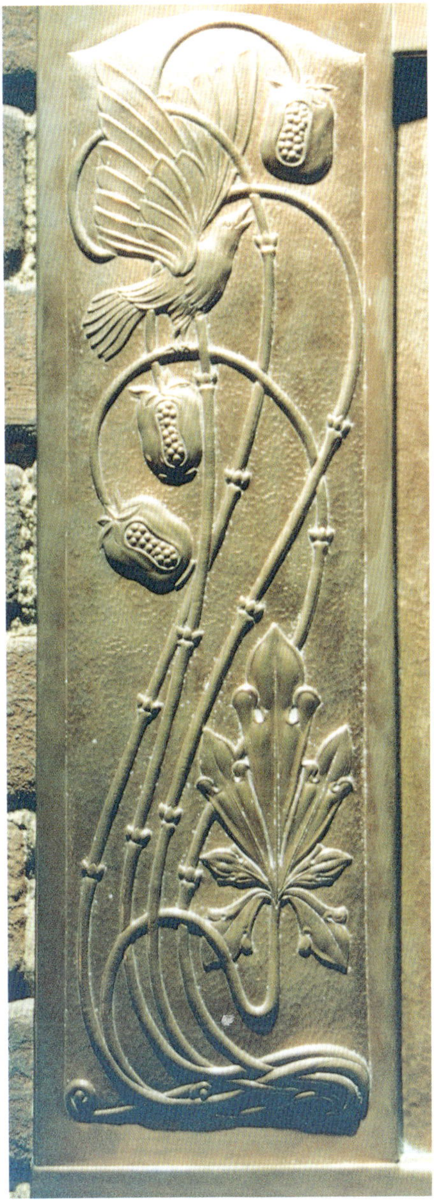

St Helens World of Glass. Detail of commemorative plaque by C. E. Thompson. *St Helens Metropolitan Borough Council Collection*

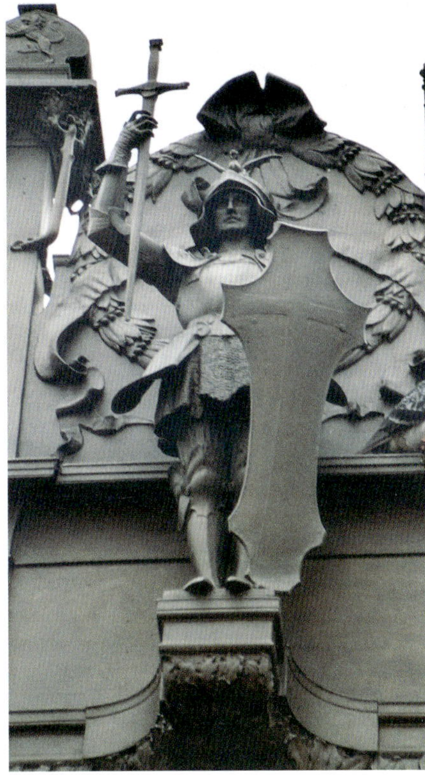

St George on the Victoria monument. St Helens by George Frampton, 1906.

made pulpit with its sounding board stands beside the chancel screen which has intricate, Neo-Renaissance carving. To the south of the chancel is the font which has a very elaborate and very tall, multi-tiered, carved oak font-cover topped off with a dove. The chancel and sanctuary provide a feast of the woodworker's art. The priest's chair, the choir stalls and the screens are all minutely and masterfully carved. In particular the screens behind the choir stalls could pass in parts for finely wrought ironwork. The reredos stretches across the

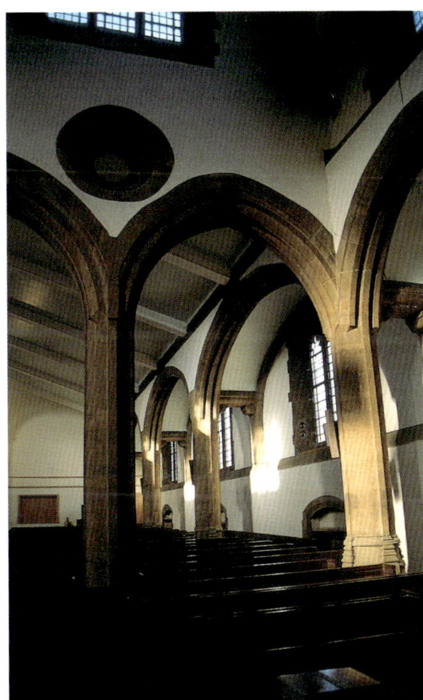

St Helen's, St Helens. Interior by W. D. Caröe, 1926.

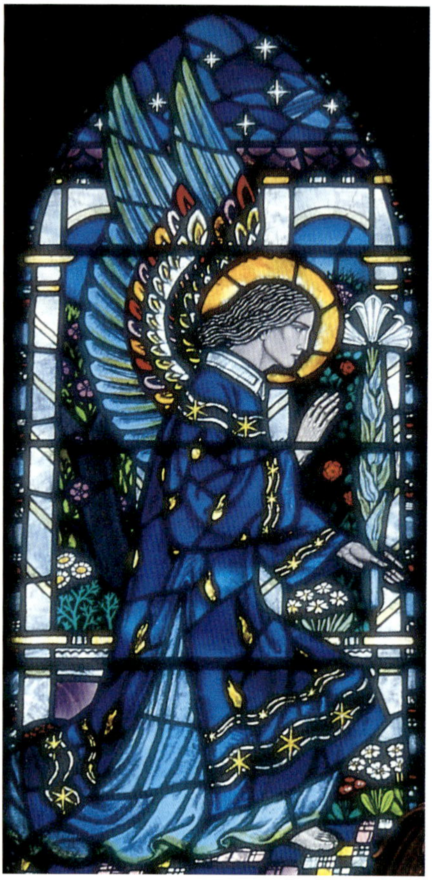

St Peter's Parr, St Helens East window by J. E. Nuttgens c. 1925.

whole width of the sanctuary and stands some twelve feet high. It depicts Christ accompanied by disciples and other notables with some smaller saints above. Although the wood is said to have come from a single oak tree it is not possible to say who carved it. The Lady Chapel is notable for another carved reredos depicting the 'Supper at Emmaus' given in 1929. This is a wonderful church and must be regarded as one of Caröe's finest.

Access: Parish Office open mornings Tel. 01744–813841.

St Thomas, Westfield St, (SJ506954) is a red-brick town church with a free style tower. The roof and furnishings were lost in a fire in the 1960s and little is left of the turn of the century architecture except for the chancel by **Aldridge & Deacon**. The post-1960 woodwork includes priest stalls, chairs, pulpit and lectern made in limed-oak by **Robert Thompson** of Kilburn Yorks.

Access: Vicarage Tel. 01744–22295.

St John the Evangelist, Crossley Road, Ravenhead, (SJ499941) was built by **J. M. Taylor** and **H. Taylor** in 1870. It is of stone, brick and ironstone slag – what could be more local? It has buttresses to its north and south walls, a decorative string course and a small bell tower set between the nave and chancel. The chancel screen is of intricate and finely-wrought ironwork. The nave roof is swept down to overhang the low side-walls suggesting the presence of aisles that are not there. The adjoining hall was built fifty years later as a Great War Memorial. Inside, the broad and spacious nave is dominated by the hammer-beam roof, the purlins of which are inscribed with many texts and symbols. There is a narthex at the west end with an excellent but anonymous, stained-glass window commemorating the death of Nurse Clara Evans in Bloemfontein during the South African War. There are Powell of Whitefriars windows in the Lady Chapel.

Access: Vicarage Tel. 01744–23601.

St Nicholas's in New St Sutton, (SJ522926) is a graceful, sandstone church which is not as old as it looks. It was built in 1848 by Sharpe and Paley although the tower was added in 1897 to commemorate the sixtieth year of Victoria's reign. The three-light east window is a typical early **Henry Holiday** design executed by **Powell of Whitefriars**. The central light shows a winsome, red-haired 'Charity' with babe in arms and a bonny little girl in a pink gown at her feet, while buxom 'Faith' to her right holds a rather heavy, wooden cross. 'Hope' casts her eyes up to heaven while trying to conceal a large anchor behind her skirts. The church has two beautiful old Mothers' Union banners, one of a Mother and Child and the other embroidered with a spray of lilies.

Access: Vicarage Tel. 01744–813841.

St Peter's, Broad Oak Rd, Parr, (SJ536955) was built 1864–65 by **James Medland Taylor** in three colours of stone and with a twin-gabled transept. The central pair of lights in the apse and the cusped roundel above them present an arresting representation of 'The Annunciation' in blue and although not signed or dated they are clearly the work of **Joseph Nuttgens**.

Access: Vicarage Tel. 01744–21213.

SEAFORTH is about 4 miles north of Liverpool city centre between Bootle and Crosby.

Our Lady Star of the Sea on Church Rd (SJ320979) is a big church. It was built in 1901 by Sinnott, Sinnott and Powell. Around the apse, more or less at what would be triforium height, are five large painted panels by **May L. G. Cooksey** which were illustrated in *The Studio* (vol . 45, p. 145) when it reviewed her solo exhibition held in 1909. The illustration shows a different and smaller reredos than that seen today. The five panels represent, (left to right) 'The Flight into Egypt', 'The Finding in the Temple', 'The Annunciation', 'The Presentation of Christ to Simeon' and 'The

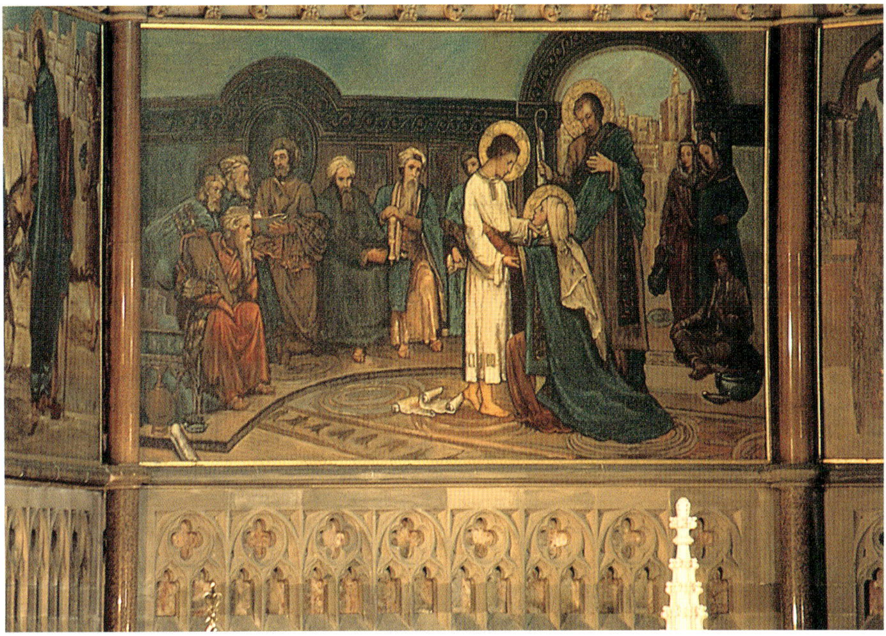

Our Lady Star of the Sea, Seaforth. 'Finding in the Temple' painted panel by M. L. G. Cooksey, c. 1908

Marriage Feast in Cana'. There is also a painted altar front which has not yet been attributed but is clearly present in *The Studio* illustration. The opus sectile work on the reredos in the south chapel is of the best quality, especially St Anne teaching Mary to read. The copper sanctuary lamp in this chapel takes the shape of a mediaeval galleon, beautifully made but by whom?

Access: Presbytery Tel. 0151–9282338.

SEFTON PARK lies 3 miles south-east of Liverpool city centre. The figure of Peter Pan (a replica of the statue in Kensington Gardens) sculpted by **George Frampton** and unveiled in 1926, has been restored and should be returned to Sefton Park in a new location in 2005.

St Agnes and St Pancras, Ullet Rd (SJ376885) was built by **J. L. Pearson** 1883–85. It was described by Pevsner as 'the noblest Victorian church in Liverpool erect, vigorous and not in the least humbled by being of red brick'. It was, nevertheless, given a stone interior. It is tall and sophisticated with slender piers and much rib-vaulting. There are transepts at both ends of the church and a noticeable French influence. The chancel has a very beautiful sculpted frieze running around the polygonal apse. The figures are handled in a very Pre-Raphaelite manner by **Nathaniel Hitch** who was also responsible for carving the reredos, the pulpit, the font and the baptistery. The stained glass windows fit perfectly the quiet and rather muted tranquillity of the interior. There are however touches of humour tucked away in the corbels where there are various grotesques and the two halves of the benefactor's wife's pet dog, one on each side of the nave. This is not an Arts and Crafts Church as such but Pearson was one of those who exerted a great influence on the younger generation of architects, such as W. D. Caröe. The reredos and the wrought-iron screen for the Lady Chapel were designed by **G. F. Bodley**.

Access: Vicarage Tel. 0151–7331742.

St Agnes vicarage and parish hall were added by **Richard Norman Shaw** 1887. The vicarage is one of the few remaining houses designed by Shaw in the North West. Like the church it is of red brick with stone dressings and it has interesting canted oriel windows.

The Unitarian Church (SJ377885) Ullet Rd, was commissioned by a number of wealthy and influential Liverpool Unitarians and designed and built 1896–99 by **Thomas and Percy Worthington**, who were themselves Unitarians. Most of the work on this church was done by Percy. He designed not just a church but a community complex including a hall, tea-cum-social room, kitchen, library and cloister, all set in laid-out gardens. Although it took three years to complete, there was always sufficient money for this enterprise to be carried out as planned, creating one of the few integrated public building projects of the Arts and Crafts period in the UK. The architects had considerable funds at their disposal and were able to employ the best of artists and craftsmen and the best of materials. Everything was of the highest quality. The metalwork of the front door and other metalwork fittings are by

Richard Ll. B. Rathbone. The light fittings down the nave are attributed to the **Birmingham Guild of Handicraft** and the woodwork including the sanctuary fittings were executed by **James Hatch** of Lancaster. The stonework was carved by **C. J. Allen. Morris & Co.** made most of the stained glass but perhaps most remarkable of all the decorative features are the painted ceilings in the vestry and library which are by **Gerald Moira.**

Access: Minister Tel. 0151–7331927 .

St Clare's, Arundel St, (SJ378887) was built by **Leonard Stokes** 1888–90. Pevsner describes it as 'a memorable building' and Goodhart-Rendel called it 'Probably Stokes's best work'. From the street, however, the dark coloured brick and stone dressings give the church and its integral presbytery, a rather sombre look disguising the splendid interior. The church was opened just five years after Pearson's rampantly Gothic St Agnes, just 200 yards away as the crow flies, and the contrast between the two must have been even more striking a hundred years ago than it is today. Inside, St Clare's is tall, bright and elegant with plain, smooth walls painted cream. It is lit largely by clerestory windows. Down the north side of the long nave a rounded arcade springs from what are internal buttresses pierced to form an access aisle. The south side is lined by confessionals which have just a hint of Art Nouveau in the mouldings on their stone door lintels and a lot of the Arts and Crafts in their fine metal hinges. The stone pulpit which sits on four unadorned legs has traditional tracery carving around its body but its shape was ahead of its day. The general restraint in decoration of the building itself is

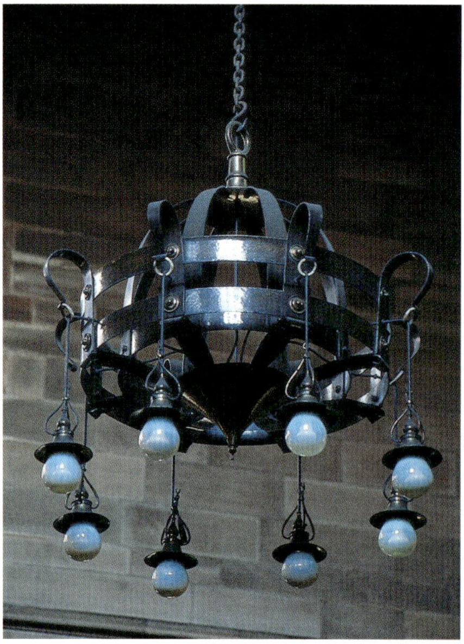

Unitarian Church, Ullet Rd, Sefton Park. Light fitting, Birmingham Guild of Handicraft, 1899.

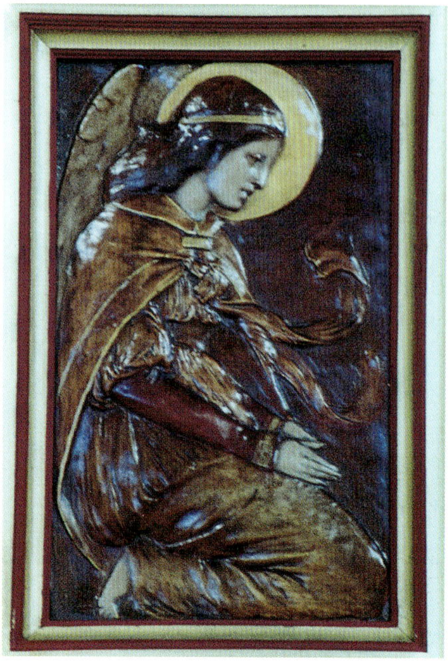

St Clare's, Sefton Park. Detail of the reredos. G. Frampton and R. A. Bell, 1892.

abandoned in the chancel which has a magnificent and riotously decorative reredos created by **George Frampton** and **Robert Anning Bell** who shared a studio in 1892 when the reredos was made. This brilliantly carved and gilded triptych stretches across almost the full width of the sanctuary and stands about fifteen feet high. It has five paintings and eight coloured gesso panels and is absolutely glorious whether seen from the sanctuary or from the far end of the nave.

Access: Presbytery Tel. 0151–7332374.

St Bedes in Harrington Road (SJ373887) was built originally by **J. E. K. Cutts** and **A. H. Mackmurdo** in 1883. The church was substantially damaged in a fire in 1919 and judging from a picture published before the pyrotechnics, there is little if anything left of the original building or its fittings and furnishing. However, this church has a nice two-light window by **H. G. Hiller** in the narthex, the subject is 'Christ and the Children'.

Access: Parish Office Tel. 0151–7343047.

Christ Church, Linnett Lane, (SJ370880) was built in 1871 by Culshaw & Sumners. Externally it is an attractive stone building with a slender spire, but like many others, it is showing its age. Internally it is tall and graceful and has three three-light windows made by **H. G. Hiller**. Two are in the south aisle dedicated around 1910 and 1922. The third is the west-most window in the north wall and was made after 1916 by **Hiller** from a design by

May Cooksey. It depicts Christ carrying the cross on the Via Dolorosa.

Access: Vicarage Tel. 0151–7272601.

SEFTON village is about a mile across the fields from the northern edge of the Liverpool conurbation on the B5422 to Maghull.

St Helen's, in the centre of the village (SD356014), is a large, essentially Perpendicular church with exceptional C16 screens. This church was a place of special interest for **W. D. Caröe** and he did restoration work here from 1907 into the 1920s. The aisle pews for instance are his work, as is the Great War Memorial on the north-aisle wall. At the west end of the south aisle is a four-light window with eight panels. The top four panels and the tracery were made as early as 1864 by **Powell of Whitefriars** and are among the first designs produced for them by **Henry Holiday**. They show 'Moses and the Brazen Serpent', 'The Crucifixion', 'The Ascension of Christ' and 'Elijah's Ascension'. The Sefton Chapel on the south side has a series of windows made by **H. G. Hiller** in 1936, with clerical figures set against clear quarries. Each side of the chancel arch stands an X-chair made by **Robert Thompson** in the 1930s and he has two later chairs in the sanctuary.

Access: Rectory Tel. 0151–9314676.

SOUTHPORT is where the A570 meets the Irish Sea.

Holy Trinity stands confidently on the corner of Manchester Rd and Hoghton St (SD342175) unabashed by the flamboyance of its red and white exterior. It was designed in 1897 by **Huon Matear**, consecrated in 1904 and given a new west front and tower in 1913. Even from a distance, the quirkerie at the top of this tower arouses curiosity and invites further investigation of the church. Curiosity is well rewarded here for this is the most comprehensive example in the North West of the work of the **Bromsgrove Guild**. They executed the chancel screen and pulpit, the bronze and gilt chancel gates, the clergy stall, choir stalls, the sanctuary rail and the oak altar-table. The huge reredos, designed by Matear and carved by the Guild, is adorned with a splendid painting by **Sydney Meteyard**. The Guild also made the narthex screen, the organ screens and four small but excellent stained-glass windows in the Lady Chapel. Some of the stained glass in the nave was recycled from a previous church on the site but two others, one in the centre of the south wall and the other in the north-transept are later and although they are currently un-attributed, they are very attractive. There is an unsuspected treasure hidden in the clerestory at

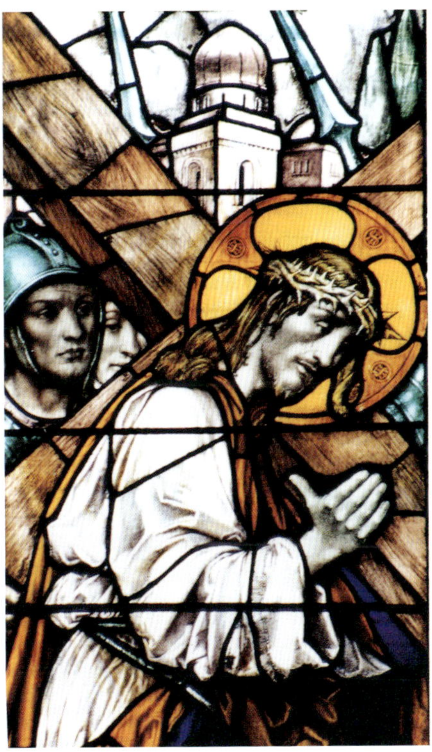

Christ Church, Sefton Park. Detail Molyneaux Cohan Memorial window. Cooksey & Hiller. No date.

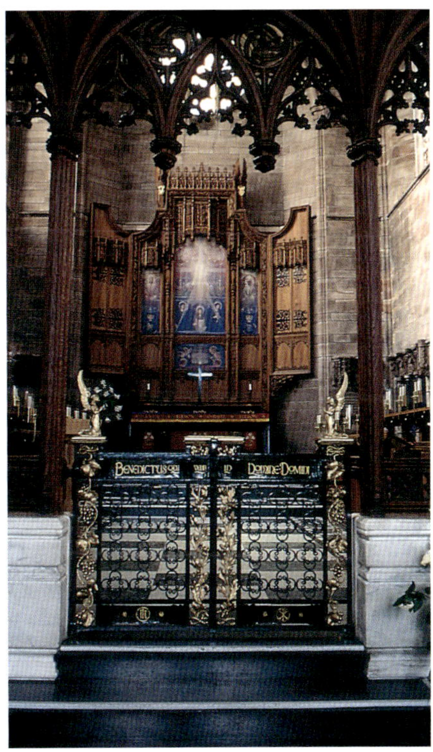

Holy Trinity, Southport. Sanctuary. Fittings by the Bromsgrove Guild, c. 1904.

the east end of the south wall of the chancel. It is 'The Annunciation' in a single window by **Wilhelmina Geddes**, a bit difficult to see but worth a crick in neck.

Access: Vicarage Tel. 01704–538560.

The Queen Victoria Memorial statue stands on the Promenade at the end of Neville St (SD336176). Somewhat aloof on its own traffic island, this is one of the most imposing and colossal statues of VRI. Her Majesty is looking out over the vast expanse of the sands searching in vain for the sea. The statue is by **George Frampton** and was unveiled in 1904.

THORNTON HOUGH is pretty well in the centre of the Wirral peninsular, about a mile west of junction 4 on the M53. W. H. Lever had a big hand in the creation of the village as it stands today, paying for the re-development of what he considered to be unfit houses and providing local amenities.

St George's in St George's way, (SJ305808) was designed by **J. Lomax Simpson** in 1907 for W. H. Lever. It is built of red sandstone in a simple Norman style and a non-conformist manner. It is of simple design but both inside and out it is a *tour de force* of the stone carver's art. No two corbels or arches are the same and the overall effect is one of great age, great peace and great beauty. There was no doubt a good reason the huge lych-gate.

Access: www.stgeorges-urc.com or Tel. Mersey URC Synod 0151 7226590.

All Saints (SJ305809) has a beautiful five-light window in the north transept featuring St Michael and a huge band of saints all made by **H. G. Hiller**. Opposite, in the south transept, is a sparkling window by **Powell of Whitefriars** showing Christ in Majesty accompanied by a band of saints. The cartoons were drawn by **J. W. Brown** in 1919. The Great War Memorial in the west window is unsigned but very striking in colour and design. It has an amazing St Michael with swirling red wings accompanied by two quieter but no less colourful and decorative angels.

Access: Parish Office Tues–Thurs 9.00–15.00. Tel. 0151–3361654.

Village Primary School in St George's way, (SJ305810) is by **J. Lomax Simpson** 1904. It is a long, low, pebble-dashed building enlivened by gables and unmoulded mullions and transoms in the Voysey manner. Much is hidden by the trees these days and it is difficult to get a real sense of the building.

West of the school and north of St George's church is a pair of semi-detached houses followed by a detached house called **Thicket Ford**. All three were built by **W. & S. Owen** in 1892. The nearby manse, now known as **Weald House**, was built in 1904 by **Grayson & Ould**.

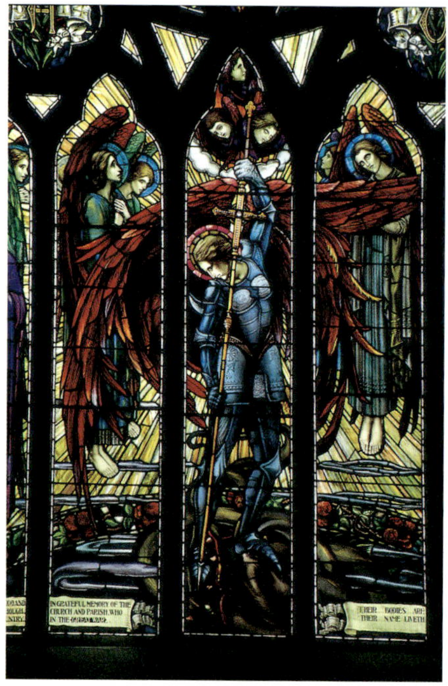

All Saints and St Michael, Thornton Hough. Detail of the west window. Unsigned, c. 1920.

In Manor Rd, west of the church, there is a picturesque row of houses numbered 1–6 by **W. & S. Owen** in a variety of styles. Just around the corner, numbers 1–7 Neston Rd were contributed by **Douglas & Fordham**. They built seven houses in almost as many styles which meld together to provide a picturesque view from the Green. At the corner of Neston Rd and Smithy Hill stands the **Village Smithy**, designed by **J. Lomax-Simpson** in 1905 complete with spreading chestnut tree. Turning south from the Smithy **The Folds** can be seen across the recreation field. This is a row of black and white, timber-framed houses, tile-hung and with tiled roofs. Numbers 7–11 were designed by **W. & S. Owen** and built in 1892 while the rest were designed by **Grayson & Ould**. On the south-west side of Raby Road are some black and white bungalows also by **Grayson & Ould**, followed by a short terrace of stone and roughcast houses built in 1906 by **Lomax-Simpson**. A walk up Church St in the shade of All Saints leads past Wilshaw Terrace built 1870 and on to the pub on the main road. After that down the hill is the **Village Club** (fronted by the Post Office and another shop) which was built as The Liberal Club by **Grayson & Ould** in 1904.

On the left, travelling north along Manor Rd is **Hesketh Grange** built in 1894 by **Grayson & Ould** to house Lever's father, followed by the High Victorian Copley House and then by **Thornton Manor**.

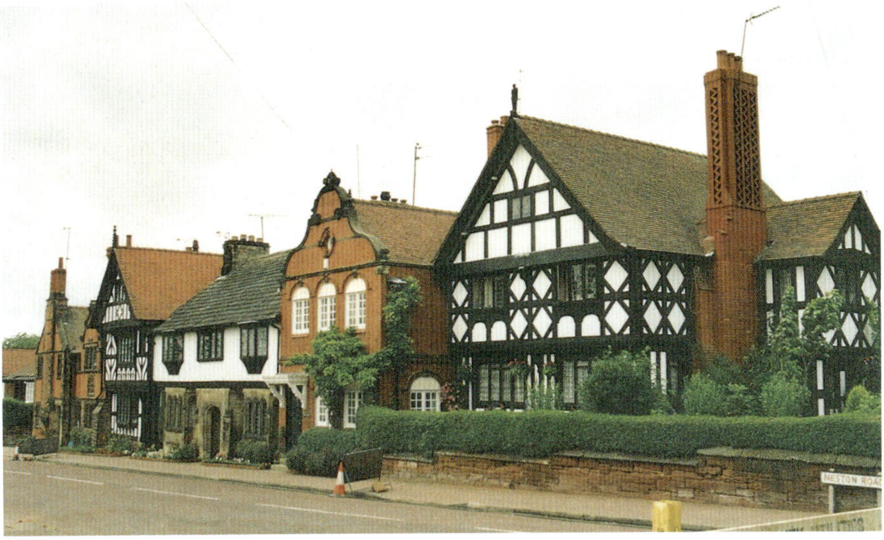

1-7 Neston Rd, Thornton Hough. Douglas & Fordham, 1893.

Thornton Manor (SJ300817) was in the hands of the Leverhulme family for over 110 years. It was bought in 1891 by entrepreneur and art collector William Hesketh Lever as his family home when he established his soap factory and model village in Port Sunlight. The house underwent constant alteration and addition in the first thirty years of his ownership at the hands of **Douglas & Fordham, Grayson & Ould, J. J. Talbot** and **Lomax Simpson** so that when he had finished, the house was no longer recognisable as the Victorian villa he had purchased. Each of the major rooms was decorated in a period style as a backdrop to his collection of works of art. The garden was an on-going development too. Lever had his own ideas about what he wanted and collaborated with **Thomas Mawson** to achieve his aims. He was not a man to sit about; he wanted a garden for walking and it was planned to allow for long walks around the estate. Flower beds, rose gardens and a two-acre kitchen-garden were a part of this scheme but so too were paths stretching down through lawns and woodlands and past the lake. This is not exactly an Arts and Crafts house in itself but the architects involved all had connections with the movement and designed many of the small houses in Port Sunlight.

Access: The house is privately owned.

THURSTASTON is west of the A540 midway between Heswall and Caldy.

St Bartholomew's in Church Lane (SJ248841) was built by **J. L. Pearson** in 1887, with a hefty tower and spire over the chancel. It is smaller inside than its outer appearance would suggest. It is a simple and elegantly proportioned nave and chancel church. It has two very good stained-glass windows by **Trena M. Cox**, one in the south wall made in 1934 and one in the north wall made in 1951. The remaining windows are thought to be by **Heaton, Butler & Bayne**. The organ-screen, with its highly decorative side panels painted by Richard Christie, was designed in 1905 by **Richard Norman Shaw** who built the nearby 'Dawpool' for the ship owner J. B. Ismay. Although Dawpool has now been demolished, **Shaw's** stables remain to the north of the church and have now been converted to housing.

Access: Vicarage Tel. 0151–6481816.

TOXTETH is just to the south of Liverpool city centre.

St James's in St James's Place, (SJ352891) is a redundant C18 church which is being restored. The work includes the refurbishment of the east window 'Christ and the Children' which was made in 1881 by **Henry Holiday**.

Access: Try the tourist information office for a progress report. Tel. 0151–7093631.

St Michael in the Hamlet, stands on the corner of St Michael's Church Road (SJ369871) and was built in 1815 by Rickman for John Cragg the local iron founder. Not surprisingly the roof is supported on slender cast-iron pillars and roof-trusses. Having seen St Michael's in its newly redecorated glory one wonders why the technology did not 'take off'. It is a remarkably airy and decorative church. The porch at the west end contains the Parish War Memorial which takes the form of a three-light stained-glass window designed by **H. G. Hiller**. It features a wonderfully vigorous St Michael in the centre panel and appropriate regimental badges in the side lights.

Access: Usually open on Heritage Open Days. Vicarage Tel. 0151–7272601.

Church of Our Lady of Mount Carmel, High Park St (SJ359882) is decorated with a series of paintings of the Stations of the Cross by **May Cooksey**.

Access: Presbytery Tel. 0151–7271463.

The Free Library on the corner of Upper Parliament St and Windsor St (SD354892) was built in 1902 by the city architect **Thomas Shelmerdine** in attractive red and white Edwardian style. Inside there is a painted lunette on the end wall of what is now the community room. It was painted in 1904 by **Alison Martin** and **Clinton Balmer** and was described in the *Studio* (vol. 30, p. 67) as showing Knowledge, 'supported on each side by figures symbolising Literature and the Arts; at the foot Labour is presenting the fruits of the earth and produce of the sea. On the extreme left under the Tree of Knowledge a well designed group of figures is instructing Innocence, and on the extreme right is Ignorance with his companions shrouded in gloom.' The lunette is about thirty feet wide and sixteen feet above the floor and ready for an overdue cleaning. Beneath the lunette, down at eye level, is a brightly polished repoussé copper panel commemorating the inauguration of the library. It is beautiful work incorporating roses with enamel cabochon centres and entrelac briars and was made by **C. E. Thompson** in 1902.

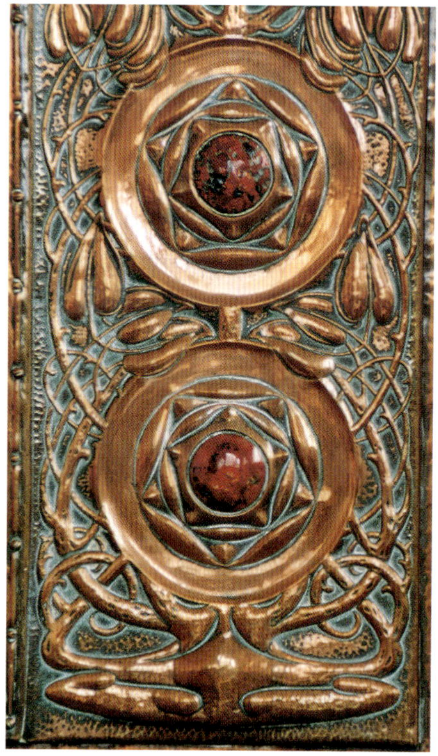

Detail, commemorative plaque, Toxteth Library. C. E. Thompson, 1902.

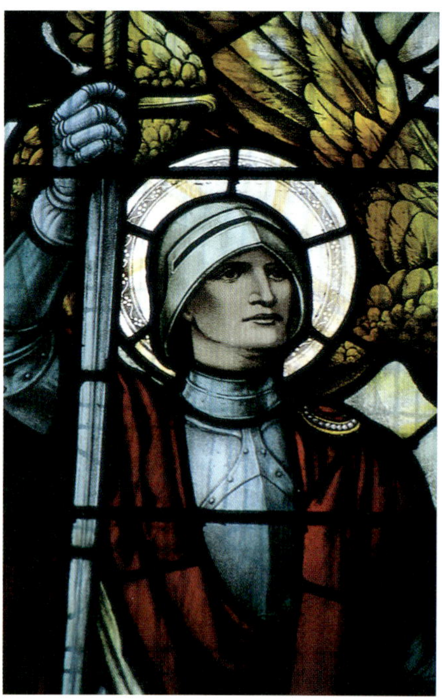

St Michael in the Hamlet, Toxteth. Detail of the war memorial window. H. G. Hiller, c. 1920.

Access: Opening hours variable. Tel. 0151–7097489.

On the corner of Princes Rd and Upper Parliament St is a damaged **memorial to Florence Nightingale** designed by **Willink and Thickness** and executed by **C. J. Allen**.

TUE BROOK is 2 miles up the A5049 north-east of the Liverpool city centre.

St John the Baptist, West Derby Rd (SJ380924) was built by **G. F. Bodley** 1868–70. Externally it is simpler in style than the High Victorian vogue and this leaves the visitor a little unprepared for the decorative 'orgy' inside. Not a wall or ceiling remains un-stencilled. The wall paintings on the east and west walls of the nave were executed by Kempe. Most of the fittings, including the pulpit, the font, the painted and gilded reredos and rood screen were made to **Bodley's** own designs. **William Morris's** angelic-musicians window was installed in the south wall of the chancel in 1868 and re-fixed in 2000 after a good and very worthwhile cleaning. The east window was also made by **Morris, Marshall, Faulkner & Co.** in 1868. It has five lights with ten subjects in two tiers. In the upper tier, Noah and Nehemiah are by **Ford**

Madox Brown and Moses, Christ on the Cross and David are by **Burne-Jones**. In the lower tier, St Peter and St Augustine, on the left, are by **Morris** while John the Baptist, St Alban and St Paul are all by **Burne-Jones**. St Ursula and St Nicholas in the west window in the south aisle are also by **Burne-Jones** 1868. The beautifully-embroidered church banners displayed here are on loan and were made by C. E. Kempe & Co. Pevsner suggests that the vicarage next door to the church may also have been built to **Bodley's** design.

Access: Vicarage Tel. 0151–2282023.

WALLASEY Leasowe, New Brighton, Liscard, Egremont, Seacombe and Poulton make up the township of Wallasey in the north-west corner of Wirral.

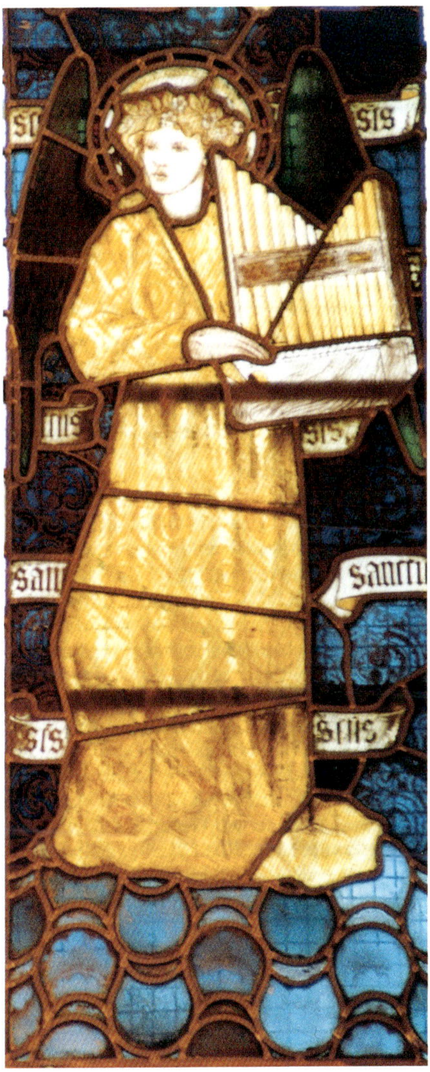

St John's, Tuebrook. Musical angel. William Morris, 1868.

St Nicholas's (SJ289931) was built in 1910 by **J. F. Doyle** and looks across Bayswater Rd to the first tee of the Wallasey Golf Course. It is a fairly standard Edwardian Gothic church. However it has a good set of Shrigley & Hunt windows, many of which have a maritime theme. The north chapel window has two very small golfers, hidden in the tracery, who caused something of a stir at their unveiling. There is an interesting but unsigned set of four beautiful paintings on the Great War Memorial at the back of the church. They show episodes from the life of Jesus which symbolise Enlistment, War, Death and Glory.

Access: Vicarage Tel. 0151–6393589.

St James's, Albion St (SJ307939) is a big, respectable building built by G. G. Scott in 1856. The reredos was painted by A. O. Hemmings in 1897 and he was also responsible, in 1899, for the figure painting on the walls and ceiling of the apse. The church has two windows by **H. G. Hiller**. In the north aisle a choir of angels announces the Nativity to the shepherds in two lights while Christ is seen blessing the children in the south aisle. The windows were made in 1923 and 1919 respectively.

Access: Vicarage Tel. 0151–6395844.

Opposite the Church is the Church Hall built by **Guy Dawber** in 1912–13.

Egremont Presbyterian Church on the corner of Seabank Rd and Manor Rd (SJ314924) is now known as the **URC Manor Church Centre**. It is a huge Neo-Gothic pile built in stone by Briggs, Wolstenholme & Thornley 1907–08. The church is aligned on a north-south axis but is described here by the liturgical points of the compass. The narthex, which has two windows made in 1926 by **Morris & Co.** opens into the vast nave of the church. Immediately on the left in the north wall is a very distinctive three-light window made in 1934 by **Wilhelmina Geddes** which depicts scenes from Psalm 100. This is followed by **Gilbert Gamon's** undated 'Faith Hope and Charity' and 'The Crucifixion' by **Morris & Co.** made in 1918. In the north transept are two huge three-light windows, 'The Sower' accompanied by a choir of sickle-bearing angels and 'The Good Shepherd' among his sheep. Both were designed by **William Aikman** in 1908 for **Powell of Whitefriars**. The five-light east window 'He is Risen' is by **H. G. Hiller** *c.* 1909. It is a little dark in the bottom third so it needs a bright day to show it to best effect. The window at the east end of the south aisle is by Percy Bacon. This is followed by an unusual window depicting scenes from the lives of Moses, Solomon and John the Divine. It is unsigned and undated and although commissioned from **The Artificers' Guild** it looks like the work of **John H. Bonnor**. The next window, 'The

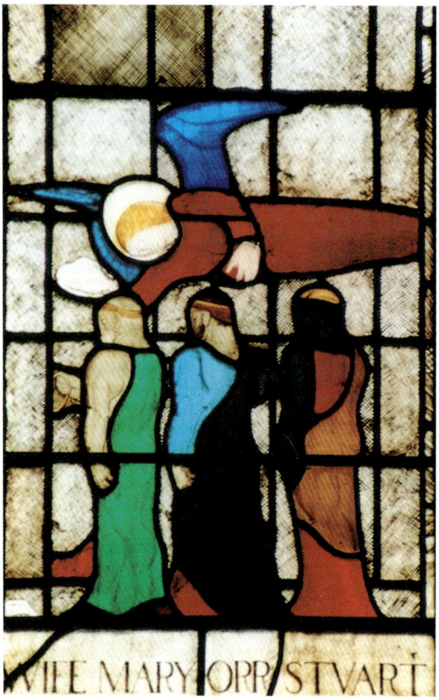

Manor Christian Centre, Wallasey. Detail of Psalm 100 window. Wilhelmina Geddes, 1934.

Transfiguration' is by **Morris & Co.** made in 1910 and based on **Burne-Jones's** cartoons. This is followed by another Percy Bacon window and by another window commissioned by the **Artificers' Guild** but designed and made this time by **Edward Woore** in 1922. It shows Jesus preaching on the shore of the Sea of Galilee and is very similar to Woore's window at Prescott. The west window is by Percy Bacon.

Access: Minister Tel. 0151–6382372.

Somewhere in Egremont are three small stained-glass windows made by **Mary Lowndes.** Have they been lost or are they lurking there still?

The Unitarian Church in Manor Rd, Liscard (SJ309922) was funded by Mrs Martha Elam, designed by the Liverpool architects **Edmund Ware** and **Edmund Rathbone** and decorated by the **Bromsgrove Guild.** When it opened in 1899 it was described by *The Studio* as 'very fresh, unconventional and fitting in design . . . producing an original and pleasing exterior for the front abutting on the main road.' Built of red brick and white stone, it defies traditional church building with its more domestic looking octagonal tower, pillared porch and stone mullioned windows. The church is entered through an imposing octagonal porch, which has white sandstone pillars the capitals of which are intricately carved with foliage. Above these are four figures representing Meditation, Eloquence, Devotion and Music. The carving was the work of **Benjamin Creswick.**

The church interior is simple in design but enhanced by the decoration of the chancel area and the striking light fittings in the nave which were designed by **Walter Gilbert.** There are still tell-tale signs on the pew backs which indicate that the woodwork was once stained green. The pulpit has three painted panels which portray the attributes of intellectual truth, moral goodness and spiritual beauty with well chosen texts clarifying the symbolism of the painting. The ends of the choir stalls are painted with the swirling figures of the elements Earth, Air, Fire and Water and the communion table is decorated with a frieze at the centre of which is Christ in Majesty with Faith and Charity set in stylised landscapes on either side. All the painting was the work of the artist and illustrator **Bernard Sleigh.**

Above the communion table are some beautiful ceramic panels glazed in blue, green and white, with figures set in a rural scene. A scroll conveys the text 'And what doth the Lord require of thee but to do justly and to love mercy and to walk humbly with God.' The tiles were produced by the **Della Robbia** Pottery of Birkenhead, which was owned by the architect's brother **Harold Rathbone.** In front of the choir stalls is the lectern, another piece of **Bromsgrove Guild** work designed by **Walter Gilbert,** which has formidably spikey metal palm leaves around the book rest. The text on its base 'The letter killeth but the spirit giveth

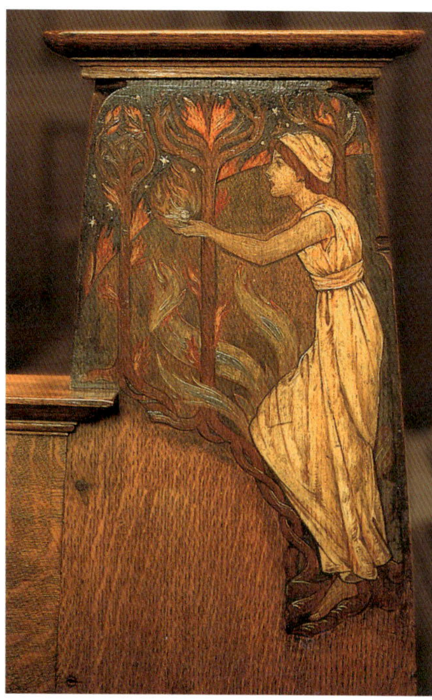

Unitarian Church, Manor Rd, Liscard. Bench end painted by Bernard Sleigh, 1899.

life' rewards contemplation. On the north wall of the nave is a memorial plaque worked by **Joseph Hodel** *c.* 1920. Attached to the church is a large hall built for the social and cultural activities of the church and for use by the community.

Access: The church has been restored by the Historic Chapels Trust and can now be hired by individuals or groups by contacting the Friends of Manor Road Tel. 0151–6399707.

The Great War Memorial (SJ314934) stands on the promenade just to the south of Magazine Lane. It is a Portland stone statue of three soldiers designed and executed by **W. Birnie Rhind**. It was unveiled in 1921.

WALTON is 2 miles north of Liverpool town centre.

The Church of the Blessed Sacrament, Walton Vale (SJ364965) was built in 1876 by **Edmund Kirby** but the east end had to be rebuilt after being destroyed during the Second World War. It remains a very attractive building and has a window by the Earley Studio at the west end of the south aisle. The wheel window at the east end seems to be from the same studio but of a later date.

Access: Presbytery Office Tel. 0151–4742682.

St John the Evangelist in Rice Lane (SJ363964) was started in 1875 by **Aldridge & Deacon** and completed in 1897 by Deacon alone. Pevsner tells us the reredos is signed by **Thomas Woolner** and is said to have been designed by

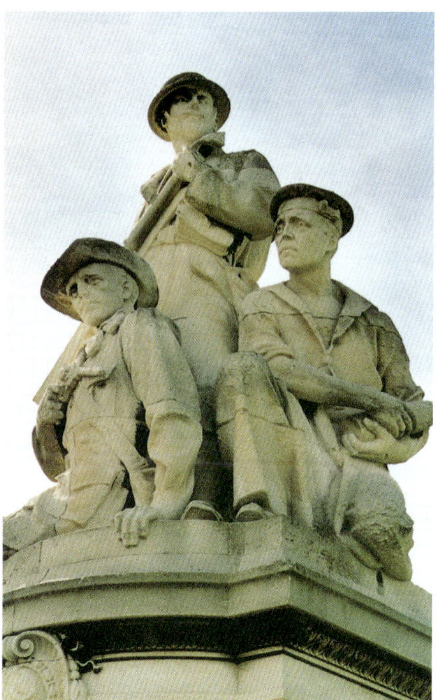

Great War Memorial, Wallasey. W. B. Rhind.

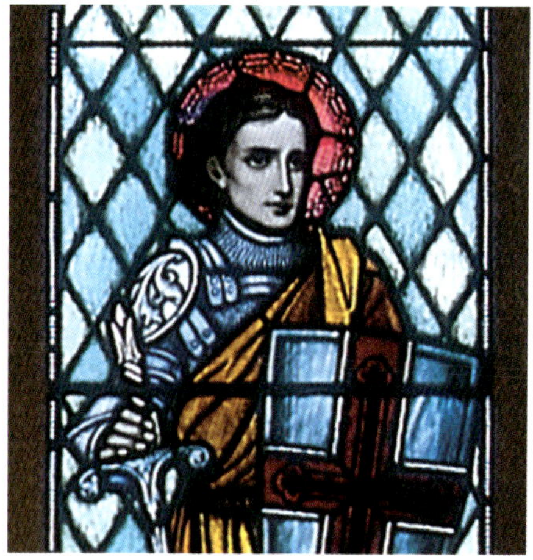

Blessed Sacrament, Walton. Detail of west window in the south aisle. Earley Studio. Undated.

G. E. Street. The altar front is painted with angels bearing the host and the wine. St Stephen and St Paul in the south nave windows are by **Henry Holiday** (1879) and there is a St John in the same wall which may also be by **Holiday** though it looks much restored. The west-most window in the north wall is a two-light 'Annunciation' designed by **H. G. Hiller** in 1918 using his 'autumn colours' palette. The pulpit has four sgraffito panels representing the Evangelists but nothing is published about their provenance.

Access: Vicarage Tel. 0151–5253458.

WATERLOO is 5 miles north of Liverpool city centre between Bootle and Crosby.

St John's, in St John's Road (SD317989) has a window with an unusual dedication 'To Roland Crawford Armour of Merchant Taylors' School, Crosby – released after a few hours illness from the Prison House of the Flesh 21st Dec 1884 aged 13 years 7 months, this window portraying the subject of his last scripture lesson is dedicated by his affectionate School Fellows'. The subject of the window is St Peter's delivery from prison by the Angel of the Lord and it was made in 1885 by **Henry Holiday**. Was the soldier's armour always so bright and brassy? It seems a bit out of balance for Holiday.

Access: Vicarage Tel. 0151–9207791.

The Great War Memorial at the junction of St Georges Rd and Great Crosby Rd (SJ323978) is a striking monument designed and executed by **F. W. Doyle Jones**. A winged Victory clad in a flowing but flimsy gown stands on a small globe on top of a stone plinth and purposefully holds up a symbolic laurel wreath in one hand and a palm leaf in the other. The memorial was unveiled in 1921 and moved to its present location in 1986.

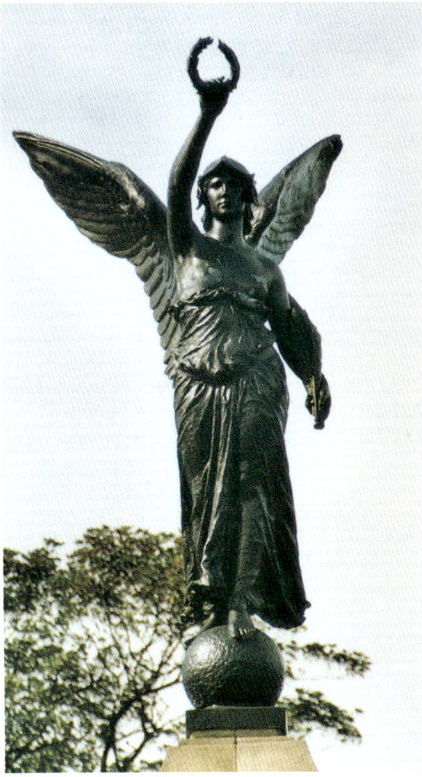

Great War Memorial, Waterloo. F. W. Doyle Jones.

WAVERTREE is about 3 miles east of Liverpool city centre, just north of Sefton Park.

St Bridget's in Bagot St (SJ379893) was built in the late 1860s and is recognisable from a distance by its very tall, elegant, brick campanile. It is a large and imposing dark-brick, basilica church and its gloomy exterior conceals a very bright and welcoming interior. It has a high, coffered and decorated ceiling and a large array of round-headed windows. Those at clerestory level have figures painted in the palest of hues. Laid in the plaster of the apse wall is a huge mosaic 'Last Supper' by Salviati 1886 and at the opposite end of the church, in the narthex screen and behind the font, is the Great War Memorial window by **H. G. Hiller**. It has three lights showing the crucified Christ flanked by John and Mary all set against a sinuous grape vine background.

Access: Vicarage Tel. 0151–7331117; Office Tel. 0151–7334313.

WEST DERBY VILLAGE is on the north-east fringe of the conurbation and on the edge of the Croxteth Country Park.

The **Village Cross** (SJ397934) near St Mary's church, now very weathered, was designed in 1870 by **E. W. Nesfield** who also designed the dairy at nearby **Croxteth Hall Home Farm** in the same year.

WEST KIRBY spreads itself serenely over the north-west corner of the Wirral Peninsular.

St Andrew's on the corner of Meols Drive and Graham Road, (SJ212873) was started by **Douglas & Fordham** in 1889 and completed by **Douglas & Minshull** in 1907. It lives up to expectations and even gives way to Douglas's penchant for the Teutonic with a slate-hung tower with pinnacles and spire all set diagonally between two cross gables. The church has a very small St George statue rendered in painted and gilded gesso on carved wood, presumably from someone's redundant reredos. It is unsigned, undated and undoubtedly beautiful. There is excellent woodwork in the choir, especially the discretely Art Nouveau angels on the bench ends of the priests' stalls.

Access: Vicarage Tel. 0151–6324728.

Meols Drive, which connects West Kirby with Hoylake is bordered by very desirable houses one of which, **Broad Eaves**, was designed by **Edmund Rathbone** *c.* 1901. Whether he designed any more of the houses in this area has not been researched. **Woolfall & Eccles** built **Ethan–Dune** in 1904.

The Great War Memorial at the top of Grange Hill (SJ219872) was erected in 1922 to honour the men of Hoylake and West Kirby. It is a colossal, granite obelisk bearing sculptures by **C. S. Jagger**. On the west face is the tall and slender figure of a woman endowed with a

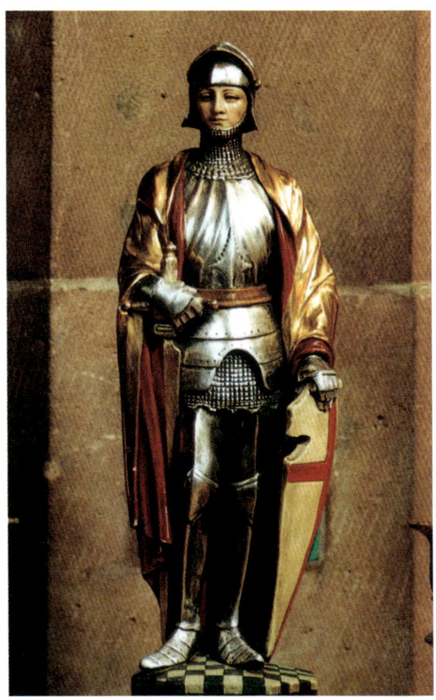

St Andrew's, West Kirkby. St George. Unsigned, undated.

wealth of symbolism in her dress, the chains hanging from her wrists, the wreath of twigs and poppies she holds out in front of her and the small figure of a baby clinging to her clothes which is visible through the wreath. On the east side stands a more than life-size soldier, legs astride, facing the world in full battle dress with his rifle held horizontally. It is a very emotive image. It appears Jagger was recommended for this commission by George Frampton and began the work in 1917 while recovering from his own war wounds.

WHISTON is in the north-east angle of the M62 and M57.

St Nicholas, Windy Arbor Rd, Whiston ((SJ467903) is a large but unassuming stone church by **G. E. Street** 1864–68. It is stone inside and out with substantial round pillared arcades and lancet windows. The west end has three windows provided by **Morris & Co.** in 1897. In the apex of the gable is a rose window showing 'Christ in Glory' surrounded by angels. Beneath this window are two tall, two-light windows which are also filled with angels.

The two lancets in the east wall of the south chapel were made in 1873 and contain six angelic musicians designed by **William Morris**. The three lancets in the south wall of the chapel were filled with **Burne-Jones's** languid lady saints and musical angels in 1898.

Access: Vicarage Tel. 0151–4266329.

WOODCHURCH is an area of principally post-war housing on the south-west fringe of Birkenhead.

Holy Cross (SJ276869) is an ancient, idyllic church which is hidden away in a post-war housing estate. In the midst of its mediaeval delights, the church has a three-light window by **Henry Holiday** in the south wall of the chancel. It features St Hilda, Christ and St Oswald and was made by **Powell of Whitefriars**. The east and west ends of the north nave, built in the 1960s, have stained glass by **Trena M. Cox**, made in the 1930s.

Access: Rectory Tel. 0151–6775352.

WOOLTON is 5 miles south-east of Liverpool city centre.

St Peter's, Church Road, (SD422869) is a large, stone, Neo-Gothic church built by **Grayson & Ould** 1886–87 to replace an earlier church. It has a typically ornate lych-gate by **Edward Ould**. Inside it is large and spacious with a hammer-beamed roof and elegant five-bay arcades. The five-panelled reredos is striking and was purchased for £200 from Boultons of Cheltenham. The panels were painted in 1905 in a charmingly Pre-Raphaelite style by Sigismund Goetze. A particularly delightful feature is the incorporation of mother of pearl and semi-precious stones in appropriate places in the painting. There is also a fine wrought-iron chancel screen. The stained glass is predominantly by Kemp. Two windows from the previous church have been re-used here. The three-light window at the east-most end of the south aisle showing the 'Nativity', 'Crucifixion' and 'Ascension' was made 1874 by **Morris, Marshall, Faulkner & Co.** using cartoons by **Burne-Jones**. The single panel of 'Noah Building the Ark' fixed in an internal window at the back of the nave was also designed by **Burne-Jones** and made in 1876 by **Morris & Co.**

Access: Parish Office Tel. 0151–4211191.

CHESHIRE

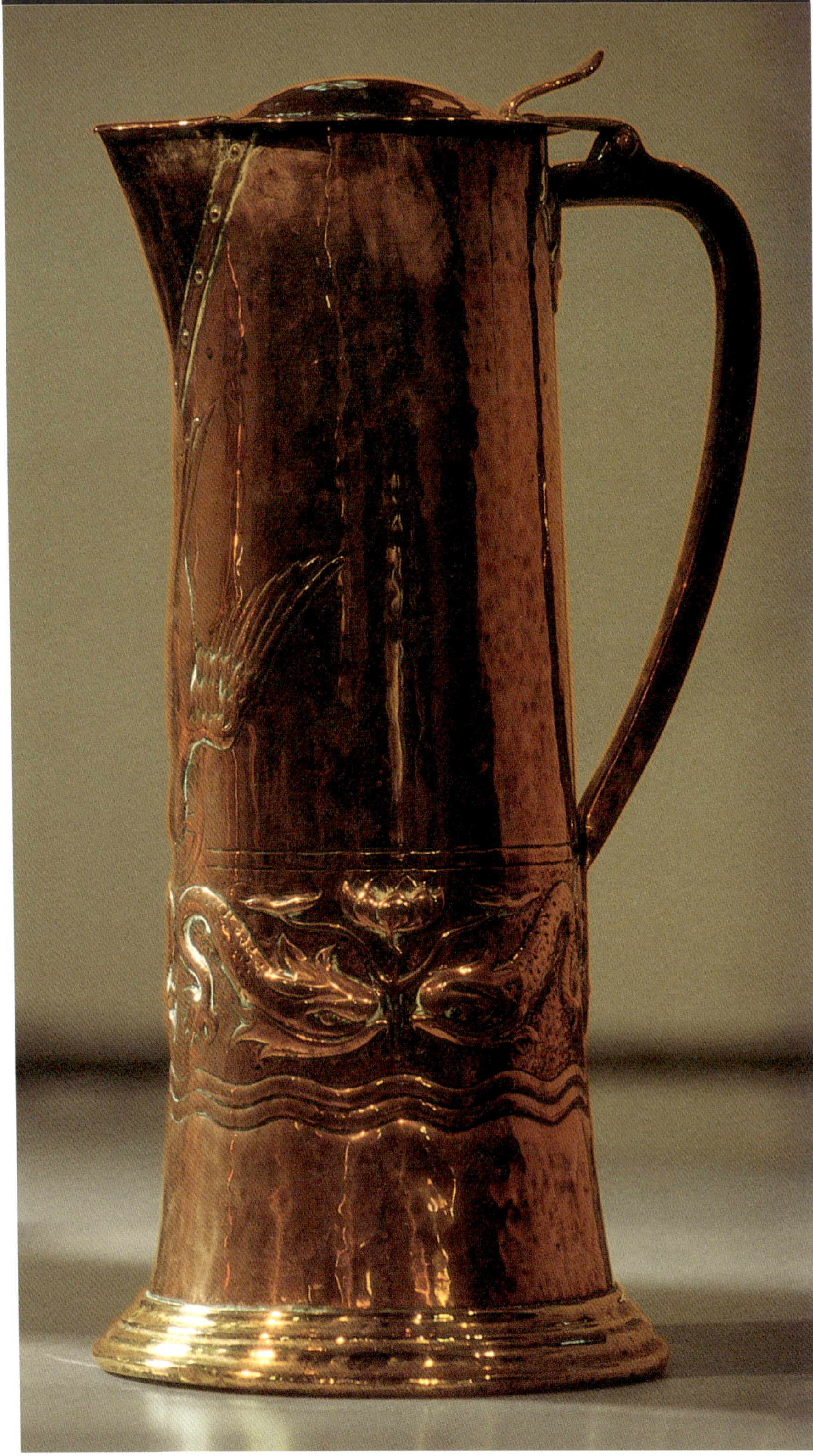

ALDERLEY EDGE is 14 miles south of Manchester on the A34.

St Philip's in Ryleys Lane (SJ842786) was built by J. S. Crowther in 1856. The chancel and its associated woodwork were added in 1907. The choir stalls, pulpit and organ screen are carved with vine motifs, angels, birds and animals all designed by **Percy Worthington**. **James Smithies** made the excellent memorial panel on the north wall. There is a two-light window in the south wall, made by **Morris, Marshall, Faulkner & Co.** in 1874 with figures of St Peter by **Burne-Jones** and St Andrew by **Ford Madox Brown**. Both lights have suffered deterioration.

Access: Parish Office open Mon, Wed, Fri 10.00–12.00. Tel. 01625 581477

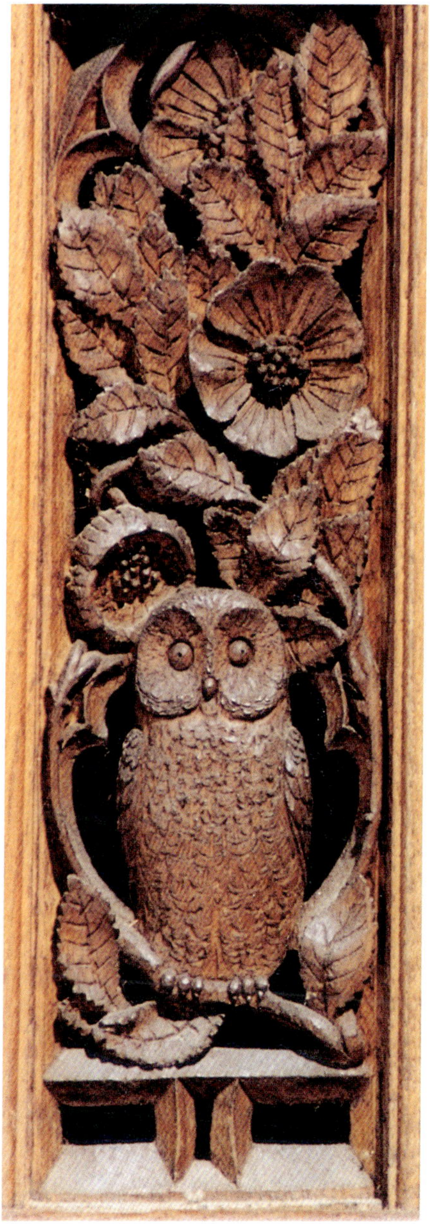

St Philip's, Alderley Edge. Detail of the organ screen. Designed by P. Worthington, c. 1907.

St Mary's Nether Alderley, (SJ842762) is essentially a C14 church with a mid C19 chancel. It was restored by **Paley & Austin** in the 1870s. The west-most two-light window on the south side of the chancel is by **Morris & Co.** dating from 1909. It shows the Archangels Gabriel on the left and Raphaël on the right. The dedication on the window sill is executed in repoussé work and signed **Js Smithies, Wilmslow**. The C14 font has an attractive cover which the National Association of Decorative and Fine Art Societies (NADFAS) attributes to **Harold Stabler**. The two-light window in the east wall of the north aisle, depicting a mother and child attended by musical cherubs and angels, was made in 1919 by **Irene Dunlop**. The dedication text is written in a deliberately naïve hand and is decorated with the most intricate entrelac designs. The finely carved chancel screen and pew ends are attributed to a local craftsman, **Mr Foden**.

Access: Vicarage Tel. 01625–583134.

The Union Bank now Barclays in London Road (SJ844783), was designed in 1904 by **Percy Worthington**. It is built in an interesting mix of red brick and local sandstone with curved bays on the front elevation and three rough-cast gables with bowed oriels on the north side. The lower panes of the ground floor windows have a rose motif in the stained glass. High up on the corner of the building a clock overhangs the pavement balanced on what appears to be a bowsprit, which is decorated with stone cherubs in relief, while a wise owl looks on from the adjoining frieze.

The Cricket Club pavilion off Moss Lane (SJ848784) was designed by **Percy Worthington** in 1899 but has since been much enlarged. The centre of the front facade is a reminder of how it once looked.

Woodbrook, Woodbrook Rd (SJ848782). **C. F. A. Voysey** undertook extensive alterations and additions to this house in 1905, 1908, 1915 and 1917–18 for Mr A. Heyworth.

Access: Private house.

Alderley Edge Cemetery Lodge is on Chelford Rd (SJ832781) and sits in the next parish. It was built *c.* 1907 by **Percy Worthington** in Cheshire brick and half timbering. The central arch, giving access to the cemetery, is decorated with a trailing vine and an appropriate text. There are angels carved on the heads of the wooden pilasters at the front corners.

Access: Private house.

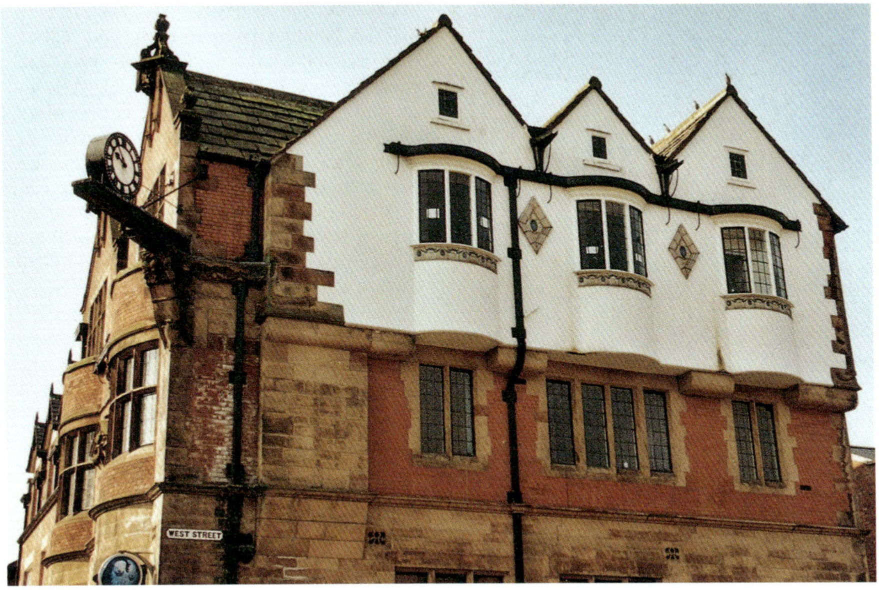

Barclays Bank, Alderley Edge by Percy Worthington, 1904.

ALDFORD is on the B5130 about 7 miles south of Chester.

St John the Baptist's (SJ419594) was built of red sandstone by **John Douglas** in 1866. The west tower and the turret staircase with its conical roof give it a very distinctive silhouette. Internally it has an especially attractive **Burne-Jones** angel playing a pipe in the **Morris & Co.** window fixed at the east end of the north aisle 1878. The choir stalls are quite simple but have appealing angels and dogs carved on their bench ends.

Access: Rectory Tel. 01244–620281.

Aldford is one of the Duke of Westminster's estate villages and most of its buildings were designed by **John Douglas** 1870–96. He was responsible for the school, reading room, smithy and Methodist church as well as most of the cottages and farmhouses. The Grosvenor Arms was remodelled by **Douglas's** firm in 1891.

ALSAGER is east of the M6 between junctions 16 and 17.

St Mary Magdalene's, on Crewe Rd (SJ796555) was built 1894–98 by **Austin & Paley** and has one of the most beautiful stained-glass windows in the North West. There can be no better description than that given in the Crewe and Nantwich Observer when the memorial window was unveiled in December 1926; it reported that the memorial 'is a most exquisite specimen of the work of **Mr Karl Parsons**, of Northwood, Middlesex. It is a lovely picture mostly in blues, violets and purples, very skilfully blended, pure and wonderfully rich in tone, and showing great attention to detail; the product of a masterly and conscientious artist. The chief places are occupied by the figures of St Michael, the Archangel of War and Justice, with his sword of flame and his scales; and St Gabriel, the Archangel of Peace and Purity, holding a lily, wreathed with roses, and with a diamond star on his breast. St Michael stands on the blue firmament studded with stars;

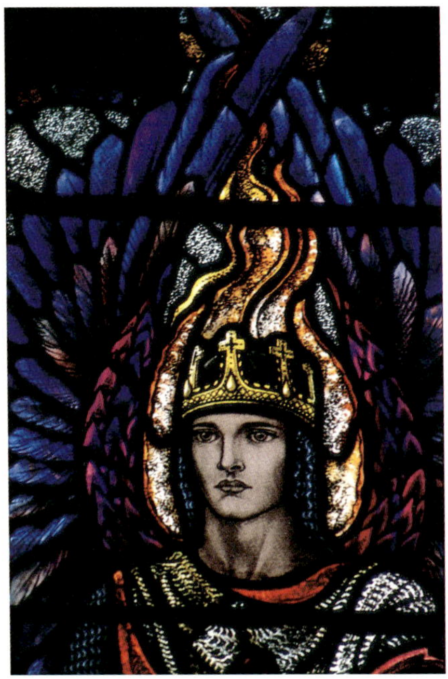

St Mary Magdalene's, Alsager. Detail memorial window by Karl Parsons, 1926.

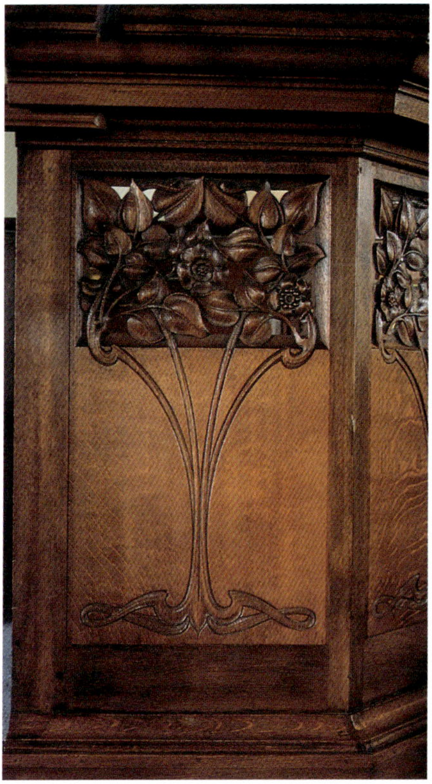

St John's, Ashton Heyes. Detail of the pulpit. F. H. Crossley. No date.

St Gabriel is on a green earth be-sprinkled with flowers ... The effect of the whole is very rich, beautiful and wonderful.' The six-light east window and the four-light west window were both designed by **Gerald Hutchinson** for **Powell of Whitefriars**.

Access: Vicarage Tel. 01270–875748.

APPLETON THORN is south-west of Warrington on the B5356.

St Cross, Stretton Rd (SJ637838) was built by **Edmund Kirby** in 1887 in local stone. It is a simple nave and chancel church with the tower over the choir. There is an interesting idiosyncrasy in the juxtaposition of the tower-buttresses and the roofs of the nave, chancel and vestry. Internally there is little decoration other than the interest created by the arches to the choir and the sanctuary, There is a small but almost theatrical arch giving access from the choir to the pulpit. The low baptistery at the west end has the comfortable feel of a country house ingle nook.

Access: Vicarage Tel. 01925–730276.

ASHLEY is to the south of Altrincham just beyond the M56.

St Elizabeth's in Ashley Rd (SJ772844) is a redbrick building dating from the mid 1880s. The altar and reredos are framed by tiled wall-panels in floral designs reminiscent in style and colours of **William De Morgan**. The position of the altar on the sanctuary floor is marked by a chain of golden doves set in the encaustic tiles. Above the reredos is a three-light window made by **W. J. Pearce** *c.* 1925. When viewed close up it appears that Pearce has sacrificed the quality of his drawing in favour of exploiting the qualities and colours of the glass. The window is best viewed from the back of the church where distance takes some of the heat from his colours and reveals the balance of his design. There is an unsigned repoussé panel on the south wall of the chancel dating from 1906.

Access: Vicarage Tel. 0161–9284182.

ASHTON HEYES is about 5 miles east of Chester on the B5393.

St John the Evangelist in Church Rd (SJ506698) was built in 1849 and **Douglas & Minshull** altered the chancel in 1900. The pulpit was designed in an Art Nouveau style by **F. H. Crossley** and there is a fine, gilded relief altar-front. The east window, showing the four evangelists, is signed by **A. K. Nicholson** but not dated. The small panels beneath the main figures have excellent pictures showing the Nativity, the Ascension, the Crucifixion and Resurrection of Christ. In the north chapel the two single-light windows 'The Baptism of Christ' and 'Mary and the Disciples Receiving the Holy Spirit' are also by **A. K. Nicholson**. The angels painted above the chancel arch are unsigned and undated .

Access: Vicarage Tel. 01829–751265 .

ASTBURY is just south of Congleton on the A34.

St Mary's (SJ846615) is big and beautiful and has all the accumulated furniture, fittings and atmosphere derived from a long life. In the South Chapel there are two two-light windows of more recent origin designed by **Irene Shakerley Dunlop**. In the east-most window, 'The Annunciation', the artist has given the Archangel Gabriel wonderful blue wings, a fiery halo around his head and a fiery cloud about his feet. The window is dedicated to her grandparents who died in 1907. In the second of Dunlop's windows, the Virgin Mary on the left and Christ on the right, each stand behind a small child. Both adult figures have very striking sunburst haloes. This window was made *c.* 1930 and commemorates members of the artist's family. The figure of 'Hope' in the tracery above this window was designed many years earlier by **Henry Holiday**. The painted roll of honour, dated 1919 and fixed on the north aisle wall, is signed by **Irene Shakerley**.

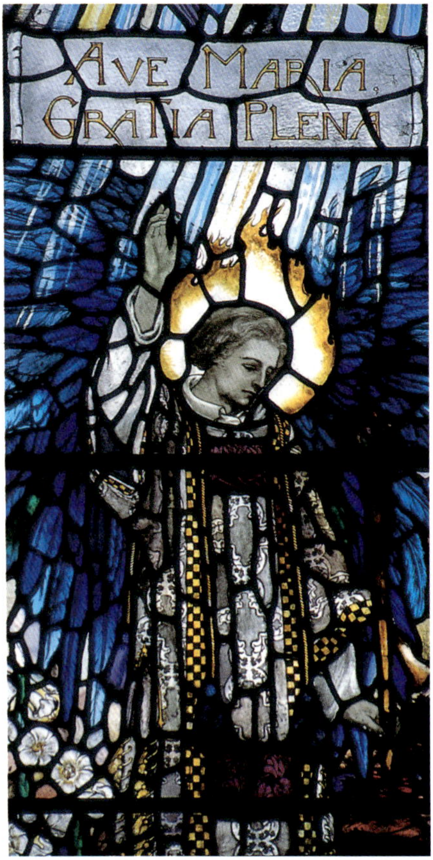

St Mary's, Astbury. Detail of the annunciation window by Irene Shakerley Dunlop. No date.

More local craftsmanship can be seen in the replacement coffered ceiling in the south aisle with its myriad of bosses executed by **Sam Frodsham**.

Access: Vicarage Tel. 01260–272625.

BICKLEY is about 4 miles north of Whitchurch just to the west of the A49.

St Wenefrede's (SJ537490) was built in 1892 by **Douglas & Fordham**. Internally much is made of the structural woodwork in the north arcade and the low, hammer-beam roof. There is a four-light window in the north wall by **J. E. Nuttgens** made in 1939 showing Wenefrede and Joan of Arc in the centre lights with Peter and Michael in roundels on either side. A three-light window in the north wall shows Ss Gabriel, Thomas and Michael. The church has an illuminated Role of Honour from the Great War executed in 1925 by **Jessie R. Furber**.

Access: Vicarage Tel. 01829–771225.

BOLLINGTON is about 12 miles south of Stockport off the A523.

St Oswald's on Henshall Rd (SJ921773) was built in 1908 by **F. P. Oakley**. It is stone outside with a brick interior. The nave and both aisles are under the same roof and the low positioning of the aisle windows together with the slender stone pillars of the arcades all contribute to the impression of great height and width. The three-light memorial window at the western end of the north wall is by **W. J. Pearce**.

Access: Vicarage Tel. 01625–573162.

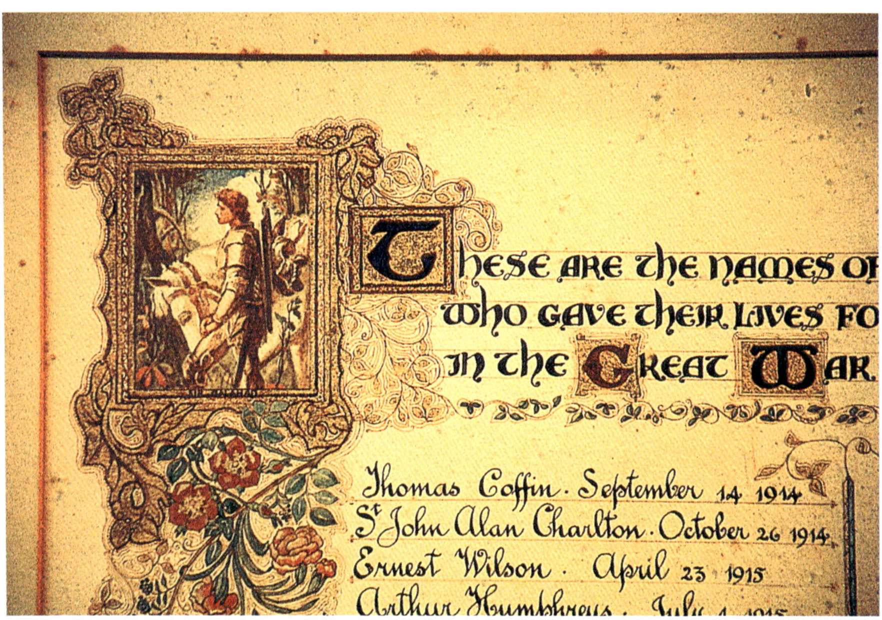

St Wenefrede's, Bickley. Detail of the Roll of the Honour by Jessie M. Furber, 1925.

St John's Vicarage in Shrigley Rd was designed by **Ernest Newton** in 1898.

Access: Private house.

BRUERA is something less than a hamlet about a mile north-east of Aldford along an unclassified road linking the B5130 with the A41.

St Mary's (SJ438606) has been standing at the side of this road since Norman times. The east window portrays a particularly agonising 'Crucifixion' by **Edward Frampton** who also made the west window. The faculty for the three-light window in the north wall was granted in 1898 but the artist's name is not known. The three lights are connected by the theme of water. The rivers of Paradise which rise on the left are crossed in the centre panel by St Christopher carrying the Christ child and flow on into the right panel beside the Path of Life. Each panel is bordered by Art Nouveau-style red rose bushes. Who made it?

Access: Vicarage. Tel. 01244–620281.

BURTON village is about 10 miles north-west of Chester.

Burton Manor (SJ315741) was built by **Charles Nicholson** 1904 on the site of a previous house for Henry Neville Gladstone, third son of Prime Minister Gladstone. It has some interesting features including an Italian style central courtyard which once boasted a fountain. Many of the ground floor rooms have flamboyant fireplaces and fine plaster-work ceilings. Of particular note is the Gladstone room, once the music room, where the floral motifs on the ceiling represent the symbols of Liberal Union. The orangery, now put to another use, was added by **Arthur Beresford Pite** who also did some of the garden design. These designs were later superseded by those of **Thomas Mawson**. Much of Mawson's work still remains and it is a delight to wander around the garden. The main garden with a terrace along the south side of the house looks out over clipped yew hedges which create compartments of flower beds and lawn with a rectangular pond in the centre. The garden to the east has a romantic approach with flights of stone steps and an ornamental gateway. Bounded by trees it is a charming sunken garden with grass filled parterres surrounded by informal herbaceous plants. The north garden, overlooked by the attractive old stable block, is raised out of sight and is reached by a flight of steps. It has a rectangular lily pond set in the centre of the lawn.

Access: Burton Manor is owned by Liverpool City Council and is a conference centre. It is open to visitors by appointment, including the restaurant. Tel. 0151–3365172.

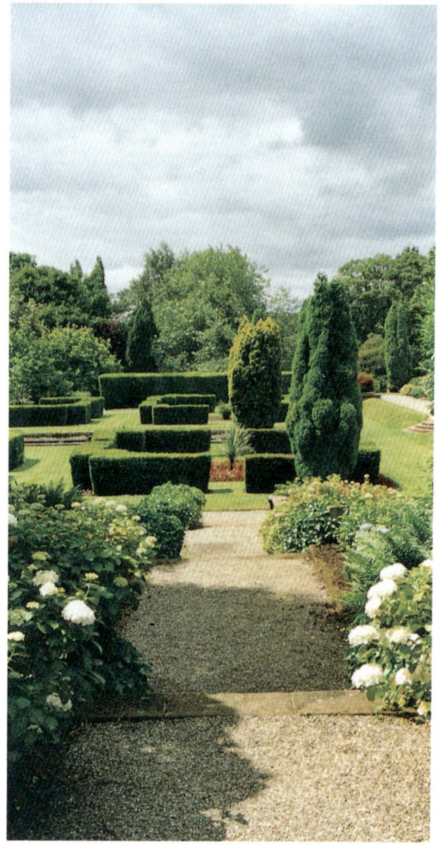

Burton Manor, Burton. Detail of the Garden by T. H. Mawson, 1906.

Estate houses (SJ319744) **H. S. Goodhart-Rendel** designed the gardener's cottage for Burton Manor in 1904. At the eastern end of the village he built two pairs of quaint cottages in 1910 and another pair in 1913 for the H. N. Gladstone estate.

The Vicarage (SJ316746) in Vicarage Lane was designed by **Charles Nicholson**.

CAPESTHORNE HALL (SJ841728) is a mile south of the junction of the A34 and the A537.

The chapel was refurbished 1888–89 when the oak panelling was removed from the apse and replaced by a Salviati mosaic. At the same time the chapel received a set of five unsigned stained-glass windows and four large white terracotta relief panels designed by **George Tinworth** for **Doulton**. In one of these Eve is seen standing on an elephant to pick the forbidden fruit.

Access: The Hall, chapel, park and gardens are open to the public from Easter to Oct on Sun, Wed and Bank Holidays. The Garden and Chapel from 12.00–17.00 and the Hall from 13.30–16.00. Admission charges apply. Tel. 01625–861221.

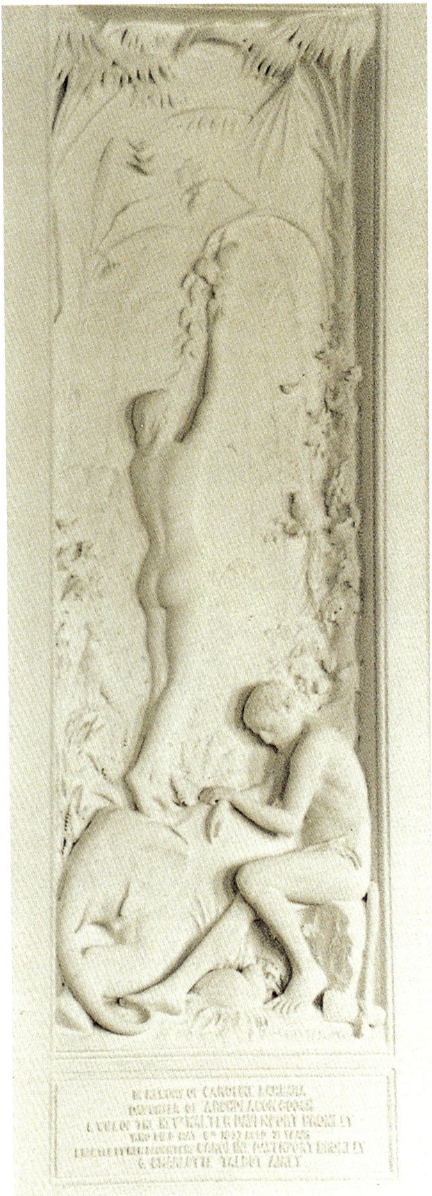

The Chapel, Capesthorne Hall. Terracotta panel by George Tinworth, 1889. *Courtesy of Mr and Mrs Bromley Davenport*

CHELFORD is about 6 miles west of Macclesfield where the A537 crosses the A535.

St John the Evangelist on Holmes Chapel Rd (SJ819740) is an C18 church with two late **Morris & Co.** Great War Memorial-windows designed by **J. H. Dearle** in 1920 and 1921. On the south side of the chancel are three small lancets, 'Hope', 'Charity' and 'Faith' made in 1934 and based on **Burne-Jones's** cartoons. The finely carved pulpit was designed by **Percy Worthington** who is said locally to have been responsible for the altar rail with its beautiful angels.

Access: Vicarage Tel. 01625–861231.

CHESTER, the Roman city of Deva, rests in a curve of the river Dee just a ballistae shot from Wales.

In the city centre the half-timbered black and white architecture known as The Rows, is a mixture of Restoration survivals and late Victorian renewals. Nothing substantial remains of the work of T. M. Penson, who started Chester's black and white revival in the 1850s and much of the later work is down to **T. M. Lockwood** and **John Douglas**.

Examples of **Lockwood's** contribution include: Nos 9–13 on the north side of **Eastgate St** built in 1900; the erstwhile Williams Deacons Bank at **The Barrs** 1893; **Blossoms Hotel** 1896 and the very decorative **Old Bank Chambers** 1895 in **Foregate St** and **1**, **2** and **4 Bridge St**. His Plane Tree Inn at **20 Bridge St** 1873 had become a fast-food restaurant by 2002.

John Douglas was something of a speculator and developer in the city but did not build exclusively on his own land. He was responsible for the half- timbered work on the east side of **St Werburgh St** 1895–99 including **St Oswald's Chambers** at the northern end. He also designed what was **Martin's Bank** on the corner

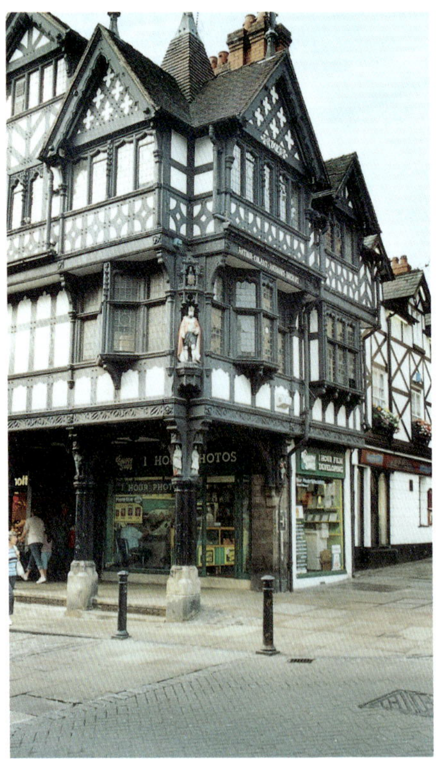

31 Shoemakers' Row, Chester by John Douglas, 1902.

of **St Werburgh St** and **Eastgate St** where after his death his past students and assistants fixed a plaque commemorating his life and work. In 1883–84 the partnership of Douglas & Fordham built the turreted **Midland Bank** in **Eastgate** next to the city wall and in 1897 Douglas designed the nearby **Jubilee Clock** which has pride of place above the East Gate, The supporting decorative iron work for the clock was executed by James Swindley. Douglas had proprietary rights in **Shoemakers' Row** in **Northgate St** but the whole Row is not all his own work. His firm, Douglas & Minshull, rebuilt **5–9**, **11–13**, probably **19** in 1900 and certainly **27–31** in 1902. The corner of **31** is decorated with carved figures, including King Edward VII. Douglas built the barrack-like **Parker's Buildings** in **Foregate St** in 1889 as model tenements for retired Eaton Hall Estate workers. He also built the nearby shop at **117 Foregate St** and at **142** he built the erstwhile police headquarters in red brick and terracotta.

Douglas built the **Baptist Church** in **Grosvenor Park Rd** 1879 and the beautifully mixed-and-matched terrace of houses numbered **6–11**. He designed the half-timbered lodge for **Grosvenor Park** 1865 and 1898–1901 did the **Public Baths** with their two storied half-timbered entrance on **Union St**. Internally, the baths are very utilitarian with no decoration. There are two pools which are still called 'Atlantic' and 'Pacific'. Eccentrically, the 'Atlantic' is larger than the 'Pacific'. What used to be the **Lombard Insurance** building on the corner of **Foregate St**, together with **1–11 Bath St** were built by Douglas in 1903, in red sandstone with ingenious turrets. **Number 13**, larger, detached from the terrace and built in red brick and tile, is of the same date. There is a short terrace of seven small, brick cottages in **Lumley Place** attributed to Douglas who also rebuilt **38 Bridge St** in 1897.

The Bull & Stirrup in Upper Northgate St, built in 1889, has a ceramic tile panel in the side entrance hall which shows the arrival in Chester, by boat, of Edgar the Pacific. Unsigned and undated but a splendid survival.

Access: Normal Pub hours.

Chester Cathedral, stands between St Werburgh St and Abbey St (SJ406665). The church of St Paul was given cathedral status by Henry VIII in 1541 since when it has had many restorations and alterations including work by G. G. Scott and after 1882 by Arthur Blomfield. Inside the building revels in the peaceful co-existence of the old and relatively new. In the north aisle of the chancel are huge mosaic panels, illustrating Old Testament stories, designed by J. R. Clayton of Clayton & Bell using soft, muted colours. The panels were made by Burke and Co. in 1886. Some of the church regalia is displayed in the north choir aisle including a beautifully crafted crosier designed by G. F. Bodley and made by Carl Krall. The staircase to the nave pulpit was designed by Harry Beswick and the handrail was made by James Swindley.

George Faulkner Armitage was responsible for the carving on the High Altar and for a number of misericords on the north side of the choir: Nos 5, 7, 8, 10 from the west end; No 9 is by Bridgeman who did much of the other carving in the stalls.

There are two four-light windows in the west wall of the south transept made by James Powell & Sons. The most northerly of these,

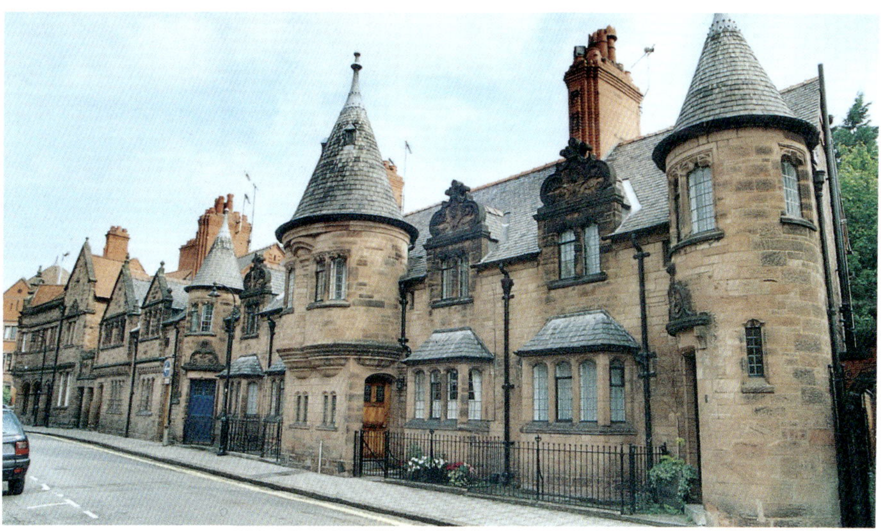

1–11 Bath Street, Chester by John Douglas, 1903.

the 'Chancellor Raikes' window, was designed in 1892 by Charles Hardgrave while at the other end of the wall **J. W. Brown** designed the splendid 'Arnold House School War Memorial' in 1921. Also in the south transept is the first Duke of Westminster's memorial sculpted by **F. W. Pomeroy** in 1902. The surrounding metalwork was designed by C. J. Blomfield and executed by Hart & Son, Peared & Co. Against the south wall of the transept is a display case holding the hearse cloth designed by Christopher R. Webb and made in 1929 by the Sisters of Bethany. Webb also designed the St Werburgh Banner made by the **Warham Guild** in 1929 but it is not always displayed. The Lady Chapel has the Mothers' Union banner which was also designed by Webb and executed by Mary Ozanne of Sawbridgeworth, Herts in 1949.

In the cloisters **A. K. Nicholson, F. C. Eden, G. P. Gamon** and **Trena Cox** have installed some two dozen stained-glass panels made between 1921 and 1927 which illustrate the Anglican Calendar of Saints.

A. K. Nicholson contributed the sequence from 30 Nov–2 Feb in the east cloister, the 19 Mar–23 Apr in the north cloister and 18 Oct–25 Nov in the south cloister. This latter window, (St Catherine) has an inscription to the effect that it was the gift of **A. K. Nicholson** and bears the initials of all the craftsmen involved in making his series of windows. **Nicholson's** 'St Menthon' window in the south cloister is dedicated to George Mallory who died on Mount Everest. He has a later window

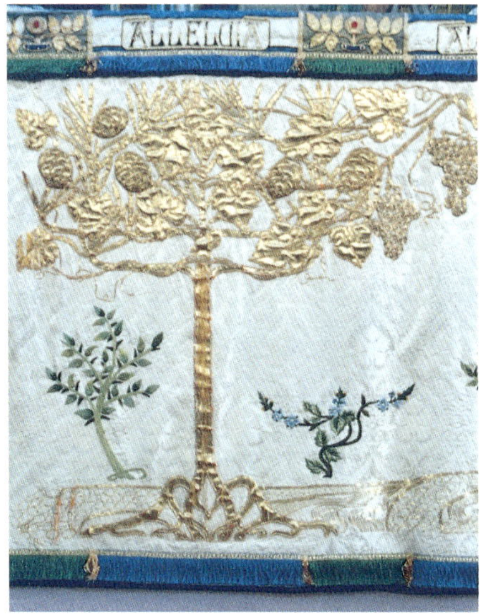

Chester Cathedral. DEtail of the white festal altar-frontal designed by Robert Hilton, 1903. *Courtesy of the Dean and Chapter of Chester Cathedral*

(1932) in the east cloister which shows a Prior at his desk instructing two monks and a 'St Andrew' window which was fixed in the Sacristy in 1936.

G. P. Gamon added the 24 Feb–7 Mar to the series 1921–26. **F. C. Eden's** windows were installed 1923–27 in the north cloister and represent the 25 Apr–2 July and in the west cloister 15 July–15 Oct. His 'Nativity of the Virgin Mary', 8 Sept, was not installed until 1932. **Eden** made the 'Ranulf Higden' window in the Slype in 1931.

Also in the Slype is **Trena Cox's** 'St Christopher' 1927. Back in the cloister, **Cox** provided two four-light windows in the south-west corner. In 1926, on the west side, she installed Hugh Lupus, St Ermengild, St Thomas of Canterbury and King Henry II. King Alfred, St Plegmund, Simon de Whitchurch and Ranulf Higden were installed on the south side in 1925. This latter window is dedicated to two sisters, Bellamira and Albinia Payne. Both were artists in needlework and are credited by Dean Addleshaw with working the Cathedral's beautiful gold and white Festal altar frontal designed in 1903 by **Robert Hilton**.

The refectory has a huge window with a tree of life peopled by St Werburgh and a pantheon of early English Saints. The window was made by **James Powell & Son** of Whitefriars and Dean Addleshaw attributes the design to **J. W. Brown**. The roof timbering in the refectory was designed in 1939 by **F. H. Crossley** who also designed the **Chester War Memorial** on Cathedral Green in 1922.

Access: The Cathedral is open daily but access may be curtailed during services.

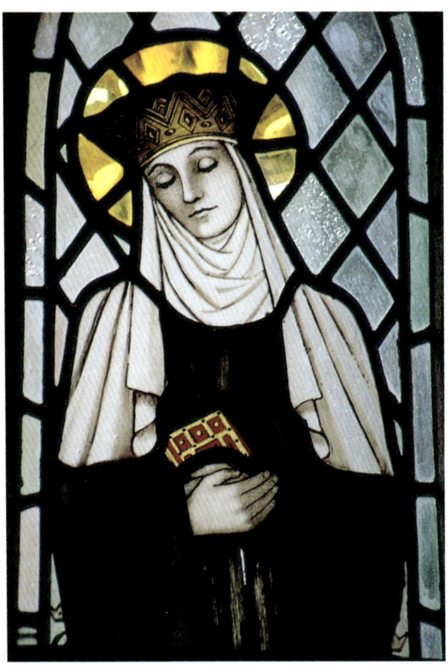

Chester Cathedral. St Ermengild by Trena Cox, 1926. *Courtesy of the Dean and Chapter of Chester Cathedral*

St Mary Without the Walls, in Overleigh Rd, Handbridge (SJ 407655) was built 1885–87 by F. B. Wade for the Duke of Westminster. It is large and grand in a Gothic way. The reredos is very impressive and intriguing. It was designed in 1888 by **Frederic Shields** and made in cloisonné by **Clement Heaton**. This is not cloisonné enamel but cloisonné coloured plaster, an unusual technique which gives the impression of mural painting. The archangels on either side of the reredos, were made using the same technique, 'but later, 1896' says Pevsner '. . . and somewhat different in style – more Burne-Jonesish'. There is a letter in the Cheshire Record Office, written by Clement Heaton from his studio in Neuchatel, Switzerland, to the Vicar of St Mary's on 16 December 1895 which confirms that Shields provided the designs which were adjusted by **Heaton**.

The east window was made by **Edward Frampton** in 1887. St George and St Alban occupy the side lancets while the three centre lights show Christ on the Cross supported by Mary and John. Beneath them three smaller panels show 'The Annunciation' (with the signature 'EF87' in the scroll), 'The Nativity' and 'The Magnificat'. The church's centenary booklet credits **Frampton** with all the stained glass in the church.

Access: Vicarage Tel. 01244–671202.

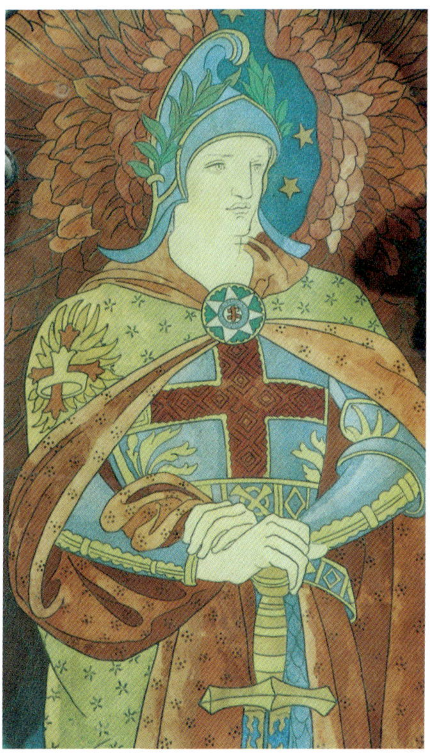

St Mary Without the Walls, Chester. Detail of reredos by F. J. Shields and Clement Heaton, 1895.

St John The Baptist is across the road from the Tourist Information Centre in Little St John St (SJ409661) next to the Roman amphitheatre. The present building was started in 1075 by the first Norman Bishop of Chester. Inside its massive round pillars and undecorated nave arches are stolidly Norman while the triforium and the clerestory above it represent later Gothic developments. The north porch was destroyed when the upper part of the tower fell down in 1881 but both were rebuilt by **John Douglas** 1882. The great west window was made by **Edward Frampton** 1887–90. It has three lights, each with three transoms giving twelve panels which illustrate events from the first 1000 years of the history of the church in Chester. They read from left to right, beginning in the top left with the 'Massacre of the Monks in Bangor Iscoed in 613 AD' and ending in the bottom right with 'The Arrival in the City of the Restoration Bishop, Bryan Walton, in 1660'. Binoculars are a decided advantage here. There is a single-light window by **A. K. Nicholson** in the north aisle.

The reredos in the chancel was designed by **John Douglas** 1876 with a painting of 'The Last Supper' by **Heaton Butler & Bayne**. The magnificent organ case was designed in 1895 by **T. M. Lockwood**. The organ rises in two towers of gleaming silver pipes encased in finely-carved mellowed oak. In the centre the organist sits in his own oriel balcony and the screen is crowned with two trumpeting angels. **Lockwood's** own memorial window, by Shrigley & Hunt, is the east-most window in the north aisle.

Access: Vicarage Tel. 01244–683585.

Methodist Church on the west side of St John St (SJ408663) was given a new front in 1906 but essentially the body of the church dates from 1811. Inside, the east end has a glorious Great War Memorial window by **H. G. Hiller**. In the centre light a kneeling knight receives his heavenly crown from a pair of angels while the outer lights are filled with more angels bearing his shield and helm.

Access: The adjoining church centre is open 10.00–16.00 Mon–Sat. Tel. 01244–323037.

The Queen Victoria Memorial (SJ404658) stands almost in the centre of the imposing courtyard of what was once the site of William the Conqueror's castle but is now the Cheshire County Council HQ. The bronze statue, by **F. W. Pomeroy** 1903, portrays a benign Queen Victoria, enthroned with her orb and sceptre.

Christ Church in Gloucester St (SJ407670) was rebuilt in stages by **John Douglas** 1876–1900. However the chancel fittings were designed and decorated 1900–10 by **Charles Nicholson**. His work includes the reredos, the organ casing and the screen between the choir and Lady Chapel and the reredos and screen in the Lady Chapel.

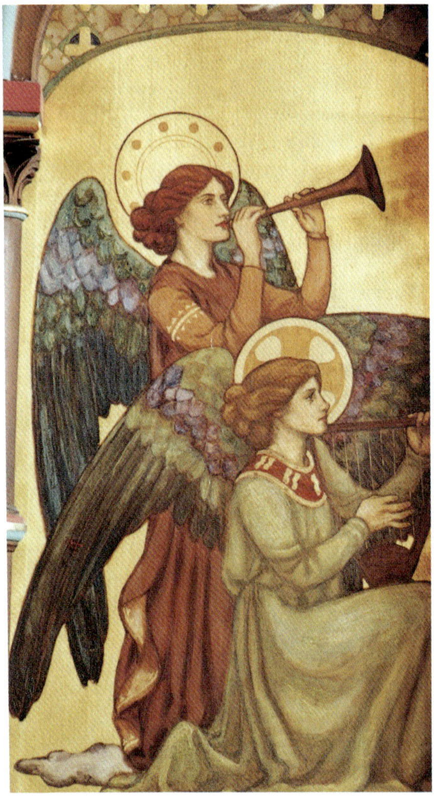

Christ Church, Chester. Detail of the organ screen by Gertrude M. Siddall, c. 1911.

All are well carved and brightly coloured and gilded. On the nave side the organ screen has four panels painted with elegant music-making angels by **Gertrude Siddall** to commemorate the reign of Edward VII.

On the south side of the chancel arch hangs an unusual and decorative oak prayer-board which was illustrated in *The Studio* (Vol. 30, p. 164) in a review of an exhibition of the work of **Robert Hilton** held in Chester in 1903. Also by **Hilton** are the Bishop's chair and prie dieu in the sanctuary. Repoussé copper panels set in the sides of the chair contain brightly-enamelled alpha and omega symbols and a tooled leather picture is set into the hood. The chair was illustrated in *The Studio* (1902 Vol. 25, p. 55) and is listed with the prie dieu in the Church Craft League Catalogue. The gleaming copper and be-jewelled hymn board on the north side of the chancel arch remains unattributed.

The centrepiece of the baptistery is an alabaster font with mother of pearl inlaid at the base, but it is unattributed. One of the decorated copper baptismal jugs is signed by **James Smithies** of Wilmslow. The font is overlooked by three single-light windows by **A. K. Nicholson** illustrating the Nicene Creed. Nearby the single-light window in the west wall depicting an angel swinging a sensor, is signed **A. Hilton**, one of Robert Hilton's talented artistic daughters.

By-the-way, the Vicar of Christ Church up to 1906, Rev. Frank Howson who inspired all this Arts and Crafts work, was the uncle of Joan Howson the stained-glass artist.

Access: Vicarage Tel. 01244–382217.

St Paul's Boughton (SJ418664) was restored 1875–76 by **John Douglas** when he was a member of the congregation. His 'restoration' amounted to the total conversion of the 1830 Georgian styled building into the present day red brick Neo-Gothic. He added the black and white half-timbered south aisle in 1900 and the spirelet in 1905. The body of the church is very wide with the north aisle, the nave and the original south aisle all under one roof and supported on tall, slender, wooden pillars. The nave walls are brightly painted and decorated with stylised trees. The total effect is quite theatrical. The fine wrought-iron chancel screen was designed by **Douglas**. The panelling in the sanctuary including the War Memorial reredos was installed in 1920. Its painted gesso panels are signed by **H. G. Hiller**. The woodwork in the choir dates from the 1930s.

Above the reredos is the three-light east window filled with glorious stained glass made by **Morris & Co.** in 1881. The three major figures, Anna, St Paul and St Elizabeth are all by **Burne-Jones** as are the wonderful panels beneath them representing 'The Annunciation', 'The Nativity' and 'The Adoration of the Magi'. The walls of the apse are painted with

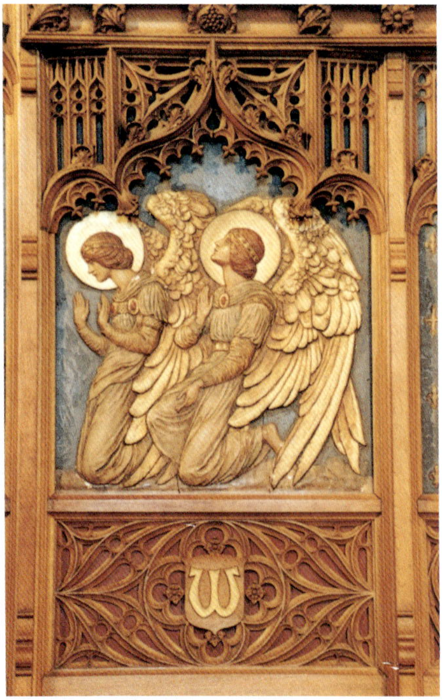

St Paul's, Chester. Detail of the reredos by H. G. Hiller.

flowers on a pale blue ground and the ceiling above bears golden stars. The run of four windows on the north-west side containing musical angels were all designed by **William Morris**. The east-most pair were made in 1881 and the other two in 1887. The three-light east window of the St Giles Chapel was made by **Morris & Co.** in 1899 using **Burne-Jones's** cartoons for the figures of Martha, The Salvator Mundi and Mary Virgin. The altar front in this chapel carries a small, painted gesso panel, a little the worse for wear, unsigned but very cleverly crafted and attributable to **H. G. Hiller**. The chapel was created in 1930 but the gesso panel may be a little older.

There are three more **Morris & Co.** windows in the south aisle wall dating from 1925 and 1927 each with ten lights in two tiers of five. The top tier in each case crowded with angels set above New and Old Testament figures. The baptistery at the south-west corner of the building was created by Douglas out of the original porch and contains six single-light windows which were made by **Edward Frampton**.

Access: Vicarage Tel. 01244–351377.

Chester College Chapel on Parkgate Rd (SJ402673) was built in the 1840s by Rickman and the east window is attributed by Pevsner to the pupils and staff of the College, who, he tells us, also executed the woodwork. The two east-most windows on the south side of the church are by **Trena Cox**. St Francis and St Anselm are dated *c.* 1933 while St Werburgh and St Chad, are stylistically later but undated. The fourth window from the east, 'The Adern Memorial Window', dates from 1923 and bears **Cox's** logo which also appears on two small lights in the porch.

Access: Chaplaincy Tel. 01244–375444 ext 3083.

The Grosvenor Museum at 27 Grosvenor St (SJ405660) is most noted for its displays of all things Roman and for its silver, but it has many other attractions among which is a small collection of Art pottery including **Doulton** and **Pilkington** ware and **Minton** tiles. There are three spoons by the **Keswick School of Industrial Arts** in the silver collection.

Access: Open 10.30–17.00 Mon–Sat. 13.00–16.00 Sun Tel. 01244–402008.

CHRISTLETON is just outside the eastern boundary of Chester bounded along its southern edge by the Shropshire Union Canal.

St James's, on the corner of Pepper St and Little Heath Rd (SJ441657), is the only example in Cheshire of the work of **William Butterfield**. While the lower portion of the tower is C15, the remainder including its pyramid roof, the aisles, nave, chancel and vestries are all **Butterfield's** 1875–77. The exterior is not remarkable, but **Butterfield** makes his presence felt inside with soft red and white sandstone throughout and chequer patterns in the sanctuary. There is a glowing repoussé copper memorial plaque on the south wall made at the **Keswick School of Industrial Arts** in 1911.

Access: Vicarage Tel. 01244–335663.

CONGLETON is 6 miles south of Macclesfield by the A536.

St James's in West Rd (SJ854630) is a simple 1840s Commissioners' church. The carving on the altar, reredos, pulpit sounding-board and font cover was executed by **Samuel Frodsham** of Congleton. The three-light east window of Christ in Majesty with all his saints is by **G. P. Hutchinson** for **Powell of Whitefriars**.

Access: Vicarage Tel. 01260–273722.

Holy Trinity, at the junction of Biddulph Rd and Reades Lane, Mossley (SJ879618) has a three-light east window made by **Morris & Co.** in 1889. It shows the Crucifixion with Mary and John on either side of the cross in the upper tier of panels and St Peter, John the Baptist and St Paul below them. In the south aisle is a two-light 'St Christopher' with a diamond cut inscription 'By Florence, Robert and Walter **Camm** for William Thomas Camm, the Studio, Smethwick, assisted by Violet Allreidge and Eve Fell' The window was dedicated in 1948. The carving and lettering on the choir stalls have a particular Arts and Crafts flavour but the craftsman is unknown.

Access: Vicarage Tel. 01260–273182.

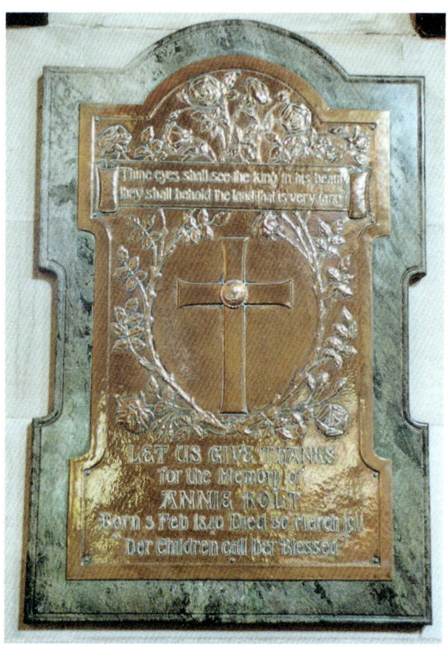

St James's, Christleton. Memorial Plaque. KSIA, 1911.

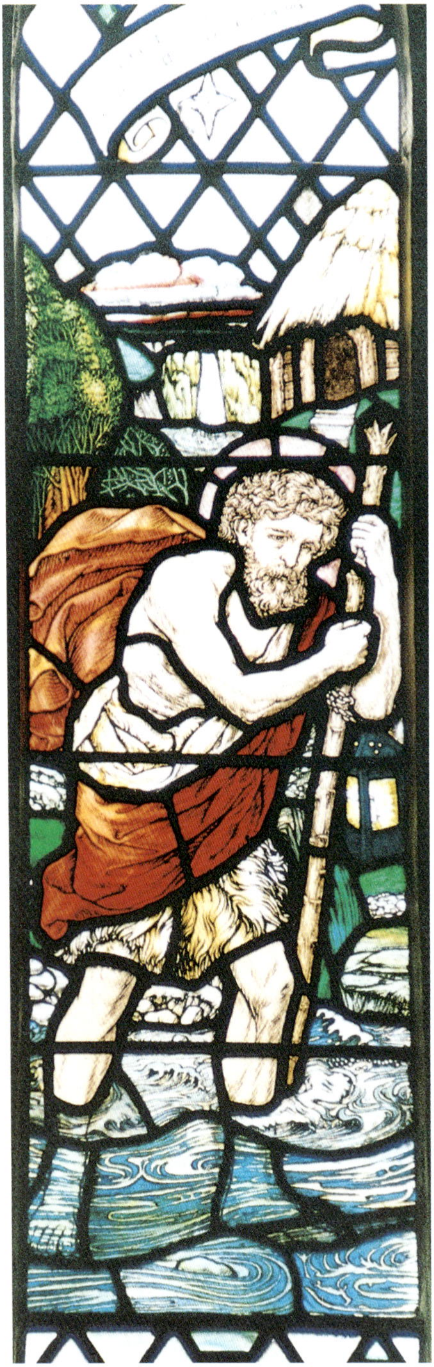

Holy Trinity, Congleton. Detail of St Christopher. Camm Studio, 1948.

Congleton Town Hall, (SJ860629) is squashed in the middle of a terrace in High St and was designed by **E. W. Godwin** following his success with the Neo-Gothic Northampton Town Hall. It was built 1864–66 in his Neo-Gothic style and finished in rough stone both inside and out but with good carved decoration. Not surprisingly, it is much changed from Godwin's day but it still displays great municipal pride and gravitas. The Assembly Rooms at the rear of the building take the form of a galleried hall with a further small stone gallery on the end wall. The remarkable feature here is the range of huge circular windows in the gallery walls which provide all the natural light for the hall.

Access: The building houses the Tourist Information Office where arrangements can be made to visit. Tel. 01260–271095.

CRANAGE is about a mile north of Holmes Chapel on the A50 Knutsford Rd.

Cranage Village Club (SJ752685) was designed in a Voysey-like style in 1907 by **Percy Worthington**. The main hall has a glowing repoussé copper fireplace.

Access: The Hall is not generally open to visitors but it is available for hire. Tel. 01477–537619.

CREWE is 10 miles north-west of Stoke on Trent.

The Municipal Building in Earle St (SJ706558) can be located by the steam-engine-shaped weather vane on its cupola. It was designed by **Henry T. Hare** in free Neo-Baroque style 1902–05. Its main Arts and Crafts interest is the stone relief work on the façade, where three pairs of over-sized reclining ladies represent aspects of commerce and industry. They were sculpted by **Frederick E. E. Schenk**.

St Andrew's in Bedford St (SJ704544) has four stained-glass panels which were taken from the redundant St John's in Stalbridge Rd and fixed here in 1999. High up in the west wall is the magnificent circular 'Ascension' window designed by **A. J. Davies** 1929 for **The Bromsgrove Guild**. His too is the single-light of 'St Christopher' on the west wall while the single light on the south wall 'The Baptism of Christ' is by **Ida Kay** of Birmingham, 1907. The 'St George' was made by Percy Bacon & Bros in 1919 as part of the St John's Great War Memorial.

Access: Vicarage Tel. 01270–569000.

St Paul's on West St (SJ702560) is now the operational centre of a charitable trust, known as 'Christian Concern'. The building has retained its west window, 'Suffer Little Children to Come Unto Me' and a two-light 'Presentation of the Infant Jesus' in the east wall of the north transept. Both are attributed locally to Lucy N. L. Wright and were made in 1912 and 1913 respectively. However 'The Presentation' in particular, shows many of the characteristics of **H. G. Hiller**.

Access: St Paul's Centre Tel. 01270–586186.

St Mary Virgin in Church Lane, Wistaston (SJ681535) is a Georgian building, brick built in a simple manner. It has a **Morris & Co.** 'Virgin

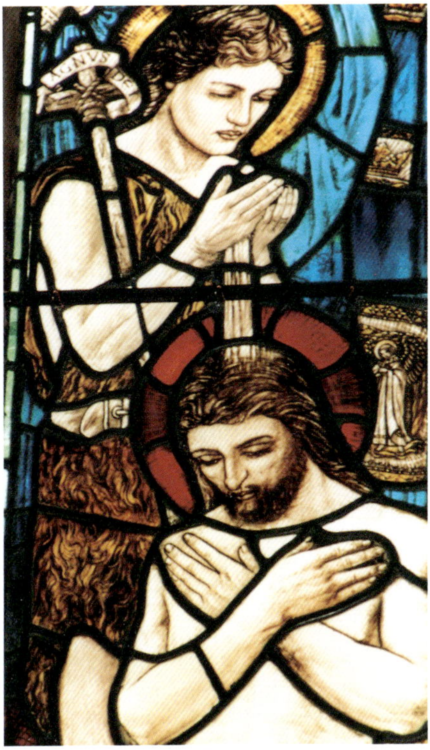

St Andrew's, Crewe. Detail of 'John the Baptist' window by Ida Kay, 1903.

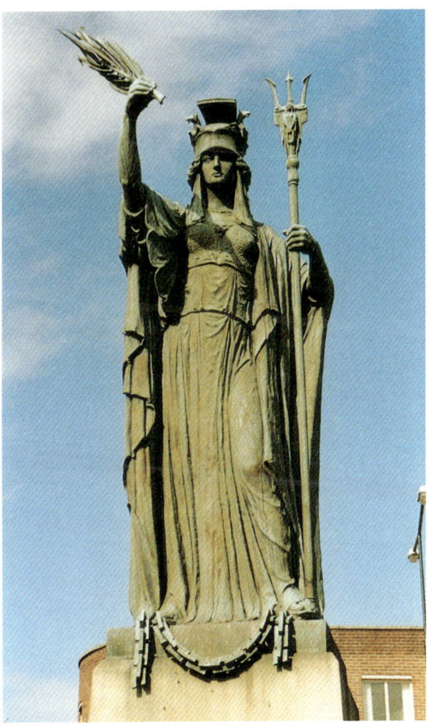

Great War Memorial, Crewe by W. Gilbert and L. Weingartener, 1920.

Mary' on the south side of the chancel and on the north side are two windows by **G. P. Gamon** showing 'Faith' and 'Charity'. They are undated but marked with his logo. 'Hope', standing between the Gamon figures, is altogether a more modern interpretation. In the north wall of the nave, second from the west end, is an interesting round-headed window with a version of the 'Good Samaritan'. It is unsigned and commemorates a death in 1906.

Access: Vicarage Tel. 01270–665742.

The Great War Memorial, in Market Sq. (SJ706558) is an imposing bronze statue of a very feminine Britannia with trident and palm of victory. It was modelled by **Walter Gilbert** and **Louis Weingartner** for **H. H. Martyn** of Cheltenham *c.* 1920.

CREWE HALL is about a mile west of Crewe, off the A5020.

The house itself, despite its Jacobean look, is essentially a rebuild by E. M. Barrie following a disastrous fire in the 1860s. The gardens of the house were laid out by W. A. Nesfield but have changed over time. Lord Crewe chose Nesfield's son, **W. E. Nesfield** to design some estate cottages. **Weston Lodge** on Weston Rd built in Elizabethan style, is said to be by **Nesfield**. **Stowford Cottages** (SJ732534) on the other hand, just to the east of the lodge and built in 1864–65, certainly are his and must be among the earliest examples of the 'Old English' style.

DAVENHAM is about 2 miles south of Northwich off the A556.

St Wilfrid's in Church Lane (SJ663713) has a very tall and slender spire designed by **Edmund Sharpe** *c.* 1850 which is visible for miles around. Half way along the south aisle is the Great War Memorial by **Robert Lorimer** designed in 1929, the year of his death. It takes the space of three pews and is separated from its neighbours by low, intricately carved wooden screens, There are high riddle posts at the four corners on top of which stand small carved angels. On the altar two carved figures stand on either side of the casket containing the Book of Remembrance and above is the marble memorial-tablet decorated with a small, gilded wreath inset with an exquisitely painted miniature of St George and the Dragon. The wood carving in this elaborate memorial is of the finest quality. The stained-glass windows on either side of it are by **J. C. Bewsey** 1932.

In the church yard, about 50 yards north-east of the north-west corner of the church is the Russell Allen family tomb also designed by **Lorimer** and executed in stone by the **Clow Brothers** with a small angel kneeling at each corner.

Access: Vicarage Tel. 01606–42450.

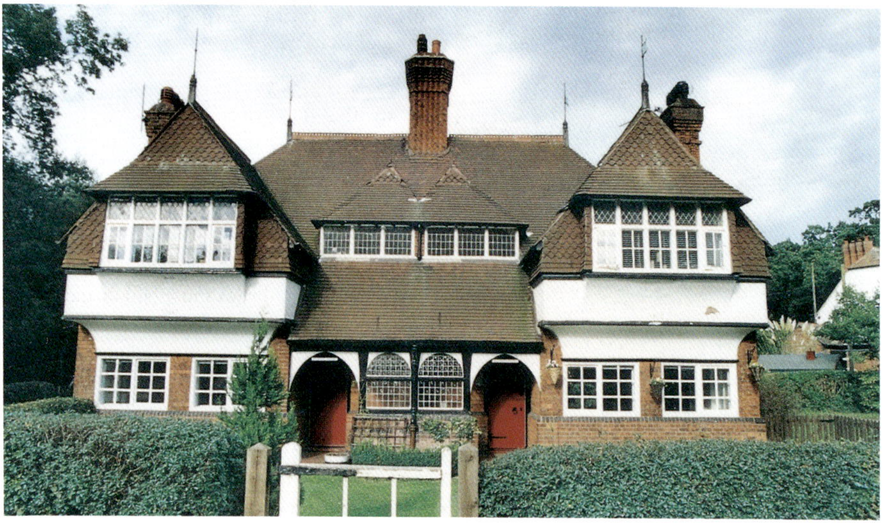

Stowford Cottages by Crewe Hall by E. W. Nesfield, 1865.

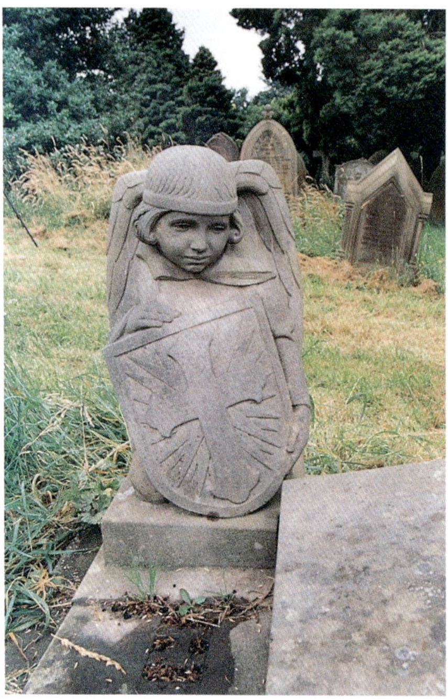

St Laurence, Davenham. Detail Russell Allen Tomb. Designed by R. S. Lorimer, Executed by Clow Bros.

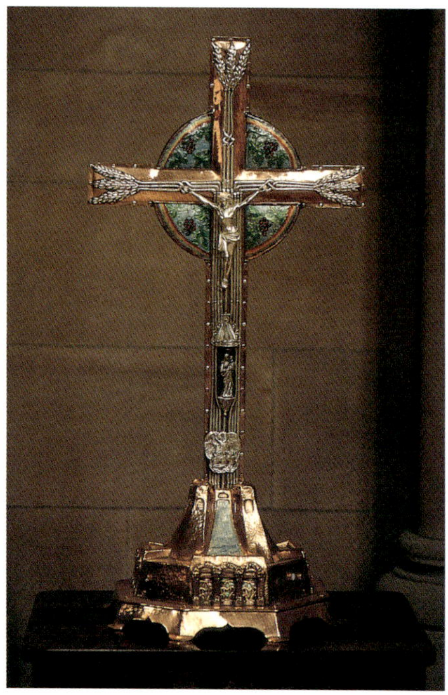

Eaton Hall Chapel. Altar cross by R. Hilton, 1903.

EATON HALL, comprising the hall, gardens and park lies south-west of Chester to the south of the A55 and the east of the B5445. In the forecourt of the House is an equestrian statue of Hugh Lupus by **G. F. Watts**.

Eaton Hall Chapel, (SJ415609) was built in the 1870s by **Alfred Waterhouse** as part of the first Duke's huge Neo-Gothic palace which was demolished and replaced with a modern house in 1961. However, the chapel and the adjoining stable court were retained. Externally the chapel is remarkable for its tall and massive tower. Internally there is a wealth of decorative art. The chapel has an exquisite copper, silver, abalone and enamel altar-cross made in 1903 by **Robert Hilton** and a set of painted gesso panels in the apse arcade made by **Morris & Co.** in 1894. The carved alabaster in the low screen wall and the pulpit is attributed to the skilled craftsmen on the estate. One of the chapel's glories is the outstanding set of stained-glass windows designed, in a rather muscular Pre-Raphaelite style, by **Frederic**

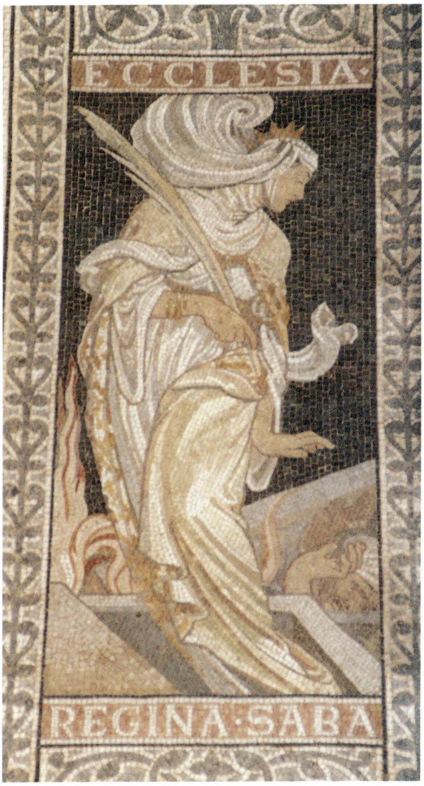

Eaton Hall Chapel. Mosaic panel by F. J. Shields, c. 1880.

Shields who also supervised their manufacture by **Heaton Butler & Bayne**. The other glory is the eighteen mosaic panels in the blind arcades on the north wall also designed by **Shields** and made in France. Here his figures are expressed in a more swirling Burne-Jonesian fashion. This must be the most complete example of the decorative art of **Frederic Shields** to survive unspoilt. The theme of the windows and the mosaics is the *Te Deum*. It is to be expected, in the light of **Shields's** great piety that they should be full of erudite symbolism which is matched in equal measure by his imaginative and beautifully contrived designs. There are no less than forty-two stained-glass panels containing scenes or figures. It is a phenomenal and wonderful sight. The panels showing St Andrew and St Philip in the north wall of the gallery bear **Shields's** monogram and the date 1879.

The chapel is approached through what was the stable court, designed by **Waterhouse** but in a very different and contrasting style – red brick, pink Cheshire stone, half timbering, red tiles, loggias and arcades. He seems to out-Douglas John Douglas who was also working on the Estate at this time.

In his book, *The Work of John Douglas* Edward Hubbard estimates that over a period of some twenty years the first Duke was responsible, for securing the building, remodelling or enlargement of four churches and chapels, eight parsonages and large houses, about fifteen schools and institutions, fifty farms either in whole or part, three hundred cottages, lodges, smithies, gamekeepers' houses, two factories, two inns and about a dozen commercial buildings on the Eaton Estate and in Chester. This catalogue of Douglas's work cannot be dealt with in full but reference is made to some of his buildings elsewhere in the gazetteer.

In the park itself the **Aldford Approach Lodge** is, in fact, a pair of semi-detached cottages on the edge of Aldford village, which were designed in 1877. The Approach crosses the River Dee by way of a decorative iron bridge where the **Bridge Lodge**, designed in

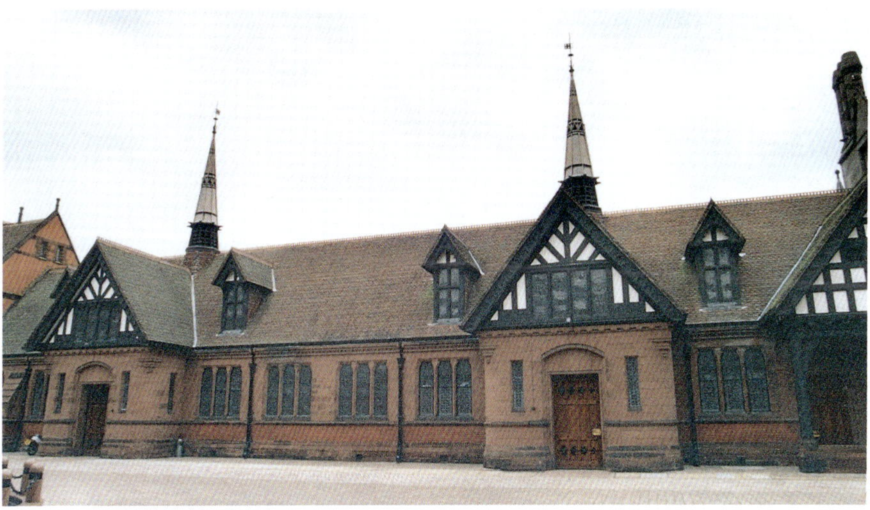

Eaton Hall, Stable wing by Waterhouse, c. 1870-83.

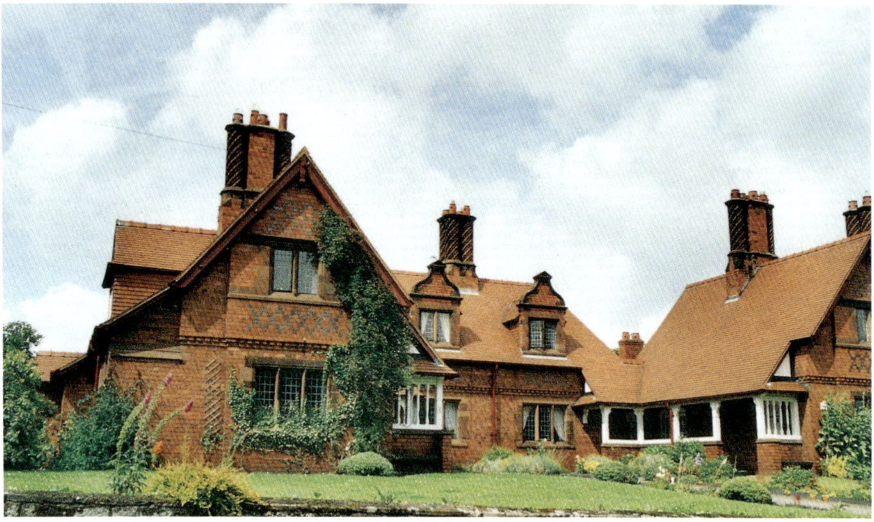

Grosvenor Estate houses by John Douglas, c. 1885.

1894, nestles in the nearby greenery. The **Eccleston Approach Lodge** and gates were designed in 1894. Behind the Lodge is the **Park Keeper's Cottage** of 1873. It is now known as Deer Park Cottage and is half-timbered, tile-hung and decorated with pargetting à la Nesfield. The **Stud Lodge** east of the drive is also by **Douglas** (1883) and in similar style to the Keeper's Cottage. The Stud itself is by **Waterhouse** as is the Laundry (now the Estate Office) which was extended and repaired by **Douglas** after a fire in 1907.

Chester Approach began as far away as Overleigh in Chester but the section from there to Eccleston is now disused. Just beyond Eccleston village is the iconic **Eccleston Hill Lodge** which was built by **Douglas** 1881–82. Edward Hubbard describes it as 'the marvellous Eccleston Hill Lodge. . . . so intense in the concentration of Germanic and other characteristic forms and details that it appears almost as a Douglas self-parody.' North of the Lodge is **Eccleston Hill**, designed in 1881–82 as a large house suited to the dignity of His Grace's Secretary. To the east of the lodge stands **The Paddocks** built in the following year at the Duke's expense for his nephew and agent The Hon. C. T. Parker. The house as it stands now is huge, despite some demolition in 1960, and has more than a passing resemblance to a small French Chateau. Both houses are placed strategically just outside His Grace's Park and just outside the workers' village.

About ½ mile south of Eccleston Hill Lodge and to the east of the drive is Eaton Lodge built in 1870–71 as the **Gamekeeper's Cottage and Kennels**. It has a stone ground-floor with half-timbering above and another 'flight of fancy' in the roof forms and chimney stacks. The Chester Approach meets the Pulford Approach and Belgrave Avenue at the site of an obelisk designed by **Douglas & Fordham** in 1890. The Pulford Approach Lodges pre-date Douglas but the **Black and White Cottages** on the Approach, just off the south-west corner of the disused airfield, are his and were built in 1885–86. They feature in **M. B. Adams's** *Modern Cottage Architecture*, 1904.

The gardens at Eaton Hall have undergone considerable change, nevertheless much still remains of the Arts & Crafts period. **Edwin Lutyens** designed the Italian garden which can be seen in a simplified form, with its magnificent stone Dragon fountain in the centre of the pool. The gates at its south end are attributed to Lutyens as are the impressive gates at the entrance to the walled kitchen garden. **Detmar Blow's** design for the south-terrace is there in outline but the planting plan has changed. In the Dutch Tea-Garden designed by **C. E. Mallows**, stands **John Douglas's** Tea House but it is without the original tiles designed by Stacy Marks. In **Mallows's** day the Dutch garden was filled with bulbs instead of today's herbs and bedding plants. However the garden still displays many of his hard landscape characteristics such as decorative brick paths and mill wheels.

Access: Eaton Hall is the country seat of the Duke of Westminster but the chapel, park and gardens are open to visitors for a limited period on the Easter, May and August Bank Holidays each year. Ring the Chester Tourist Information Centre 01244–402111 for dates and times.

ECCLESTON is about 2 miles south of Chester city centre on what was the Roman road.

This is one of the most attractive of the Eaton Estate villages and is a virtual catalogue of John Douglas's range of domestic architecture. 1870–99 he built on no less than 20 sites in the village including: Church Cottages and the

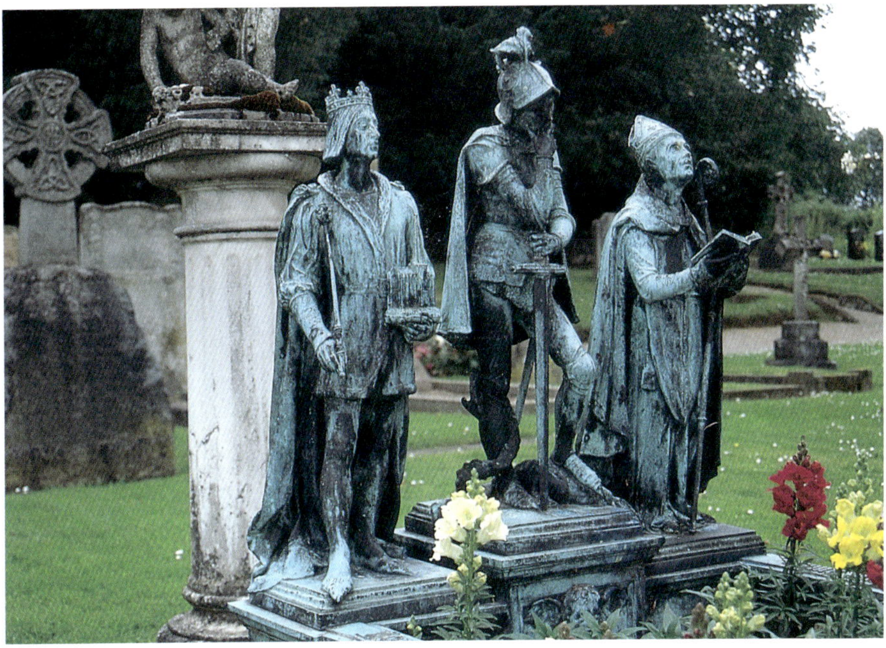

Eccleston churchyard. Detail of the tomb of Hugh Earl Grosvenor by D. Blow and E. Madeline, 1909.

coach house by the cemetery gate (now offices); a pair of cottages south-west of the church; the school and the school house; Morris Oak, which was built as the upper servants' house; four cottages 1–4 Eaton Rd; a pair of houses east of the back gate of the Paddocks; the Smithy; the stables incorporated into the village hall and last but not least the police house.

St Mary's (SJ412628) was built by **G. F. Bodley** in 1898. It has a carved, painted and gilded reredos but otherwise it is not much decorated. The stained glass is by Burlison & Grylls in a Kempe-ish sort of style and was presumably designed by Bodley.

Access: Vicarage Tel. 01244–674703 .

In the detached graveyard to the north-east of the church is the small **tomb of Hugh Earl Grosvenor** who died in 1909 aged four. It takes the form of a low enclosure with alternate panels of portcullis and roses and at the west end there are three sculpted figures, Edward I, St George and St Hugh all in bronze. It was designed by **Detmar Blow** and sculpted by Emil Madeline.

ELLESMERE PORT is south of the river Mersey and separated from the Stanlow oil refining complex by the M53.

C. R. Ashbee designed a small estate of 52 cottages 1906–09 for the Wolverhampton Corrugated Iron Company in **Dudley Rd**, **Penn Gardens**, **Stafford Gardens** and at **21–25 Enfield Rd** (SJ 398764). Changes have been made to the external appearance of most of them but enough remains to ensure they continue to excite interest.

FRODSHAM is just south-west of Runcorn on the A 56.

St Laurence's in Church Rd (SJ521773) is essentially by **Bodley & Garner** 1880–83. It has three good **A. K. Nicholson** windows: the west-most three-light clerestory window on the south side of the chancel shows Ss Alban, Augustine of Canterbury and Aldam, 1936; his undated four-light window 'Blessed be God in His Angels and his Saints' is in the north chapel. It shows the calling of St Peter on the left, St Francis with the animals and birds on the right and a host of archangels, angels and seraphims between them set against a dark blue starry sky. In the south chapel his 'The Tree of Life' is dated 1938. It depicts Adam and Eve at the foot of the tree and Christ in Majesty in the centre top. Pairs of figures are spread out on the branches of the tree: Handel and St Cecilia, Lister and St Luke, Wren and St Barbara, Galileo and St Catherine, Livingstone and St Paul, Newton and Euclid. The last pair appears to be the odd one out and specialist knowledge is needed to pair up Queen Matilda with Mary of Bethany.

Access: Vicarage Tel. 01928–733378.

HARTHILL is a picturesque hamlet about a mile north-east of the junction of the A41 and A534.

All Saints (SJ500552) is a C17 church with a C20 window in the north wall of the sanctuary

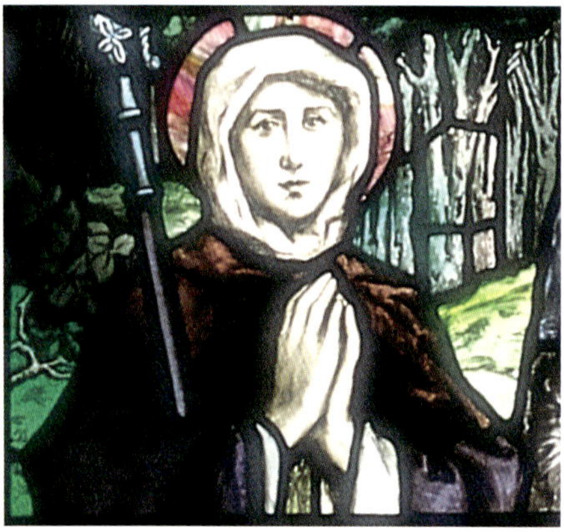

All Saints', Harthill. Nativity with saints by Mary Lowndes, 1908.

made by **Mary Lowndes** in 1908. The three lights show St Werburge, the Virgin and Child and St Augustine. The four-light window in the south wall east of the porch was made in 1930, surprisingly enough, by Clayton & Bell. The church is now closed but there are plans for future use.

Access: Vicarage Tel. 01829–771225.

HELSBY is on the A56 south-west of Frodsham and Ellesmere Port close to junction 14 on the M56.

St Paul's (SJ492759) was started by **John Douglas** in 1868 and extended by the addition of the chancel and south aisle in 1909 when the firm was known as **Douglas & Minshull**. The short, slated bell tower and spirelet are recognisably Douglas's. Internally, the nave and chancel have a High Victorian feel which is lightened by the relatively slender arcade of the 1909 work.

Access: Vicarage Tel. 01928–722151.

HIGH LEGH is about 3 miles east of junction 20 on the M6 on the A50.

St John's (SJ700841) was built in 1883 by **Edmund Kirby** and is a successful, picturesque indulgence. The half-timbered tower in particular with its transomed and mullioned bay-window halfway up the tower, stands on one red tiled gable and is topped by another which points ever upwards to the bell stage and its red-tiled pyramid roof. It all amounts to attention-seeking of the first order. The black and white exterior walls turn out to be red brick inside and have deep window reveals and stepped brick sills.

Access: Parish Office Tel. 01925–759132.

KNUTSFORD lies about 2½ miles east of the M6 junction 19 and in addition to being the home of the Victorian novelist Mrs Gaskell it was also home to the eccentric Richard Harding Watt who caused the town to be endowed with some very attractive and eccentric buildings.

St Cross on Mobberley Road (SJ756786) was built by **Paley & Austin** 1880–81. It is built of red brick and terracotta with an imposing crossing tower. The stained glass includes two windows by **Morris & Co.** The west window made in 1894 has six lights all based on **Burne-Jones** cartoons. 'The Adoration of the Magi' occupies the two centre lights and is supported by Isaiah and John the Evangelist on the left and by Peter and Jeremiah on the right. The east-most window in the south aisle was also made from **Burne-Jones's** cartoons in 1899 and shows 'The Good Samaritan', 'Christ is Love' and 'Dorcas'.

Access: Vicarage Tel. 01565–632389.

Bexton Croft (SJ755776) in Toft Road is the first house built in England by **M. H. Baillie Scott**. Set in a well-treed garden, it is a relatively small country house dating from 1895–96, which contains many of his characteristic features, such as half-timbering, a double height hall and an inglenook.

Access: Private house.

The Ruskin Recreation and Reading Rooms (SJ753790) and the adjoining terraces of cottages and towers in Drury Lane are the work of **Richard Harding Watt** and his architect Walter Aston and date from 1899–1902. They look very exotic in this setting.

Access: The Ruskin Rooms are currently private offices and not available to visitors.

The Gaskell Memorial Tower and King's Coffee House in King St (SJ753786) are now the Belle

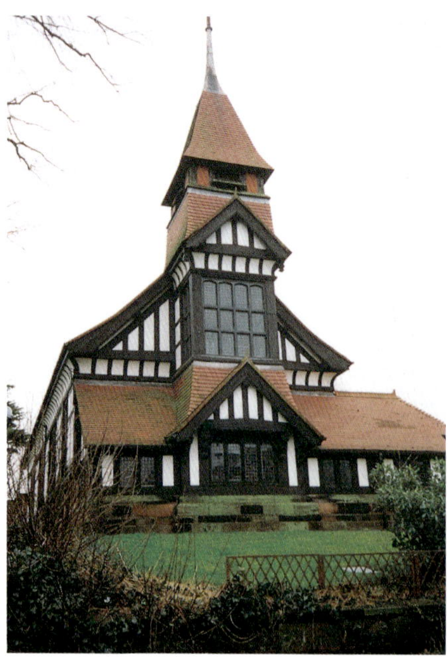

St John's, High Legh by Edmund Kirby, 1883.

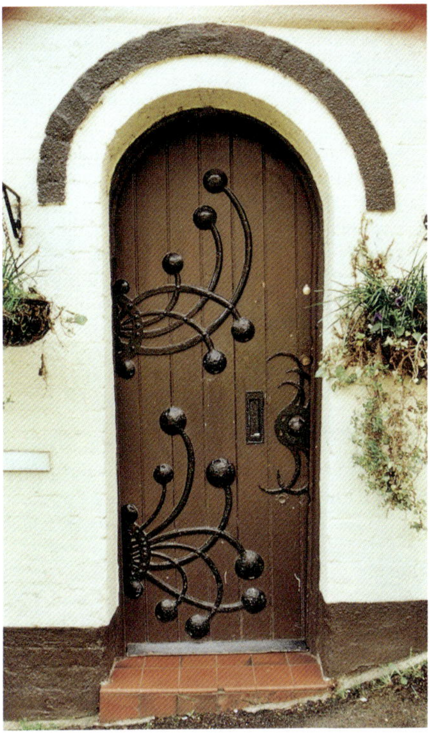

Drury Lane, Knutsford. Door furniture by Richard Harding Watt.

Époque Restaurant. They were built by **Richard Harding Watt** 1907–08 with the help of his architect W. Longworth. It is an unexpected building in a Georgian street with its stone tower. The pillars supporting the porch are carved with the names of all the Kings and Queens of England. Internally the restaurant is decorated in a mixture of Belle Époque and Art Nouveau styles with the odd Arts and Crafts artefact for good measure.

Access: Tel. 01565–633060.

Leigh Road (SJ758776) can, according to Pevsner, boast the maddest sequence of villas in all England. They are here as a result of the extraordinary endeavours of **Richard Harding Watt** and his architects. They are outrageously Italianate, hugely satisfying and 90 years on, highly decorative.

Access: The villas are all private houses.

Wood Garth on Leycester Rd (SJ759775) was built in 1903 by **Percy Worthington** for **George Wragge**. It is a large L-shaped, roughcast house.

Access: Private house.

Knutsford Memorial Hospital, on Northwich Rd (SJ744786) was built 1921 by public subscription as a memorial to those men of Knutsford and the surrounding district who were killed in the Great War. It was designed by **Percy Worthington** in a slightly Georgian style. It is now the Cheshire Headquarters of the British Red Cross. The statue of a soldier standing on a plinth in front of the building was sculpted by **Hamo Thorneycroft** and cast by the Albion Art Foundry, Fulham in 1918. It predates the hospital and was commissioned by the parents of Lt. Baronian who was killed in Mesopotamia in 1917. It was originally sited in the family's garden in Leigh Rd and brought here in 1946.

Access: The statue stands outside the hospital's front door.

MACCLESFIELD is about 10 miles south of Stockport via the A523. From the late C18 it was home to the silk industry and its history is retold in the Heritage Silk Museum in Roe St.

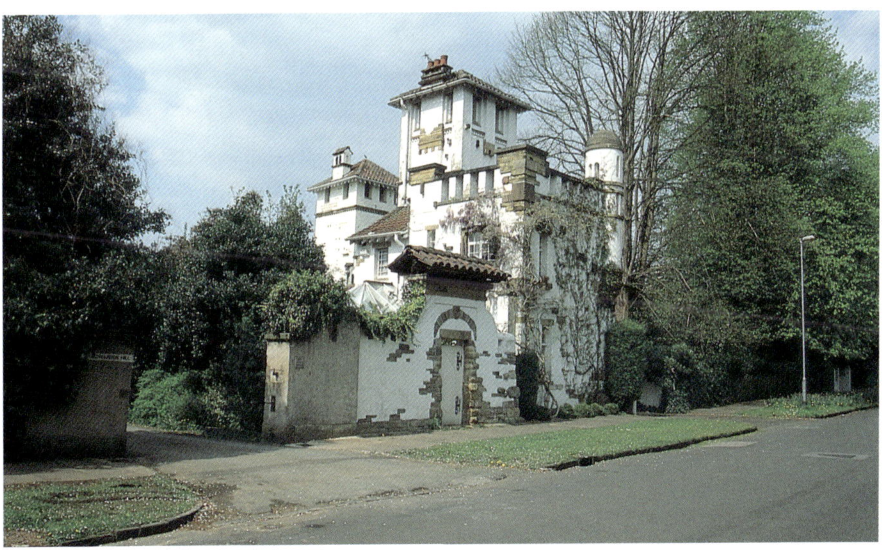

Leigh Rd, Knutsford. A villa lodge by Richard Harding Watt.

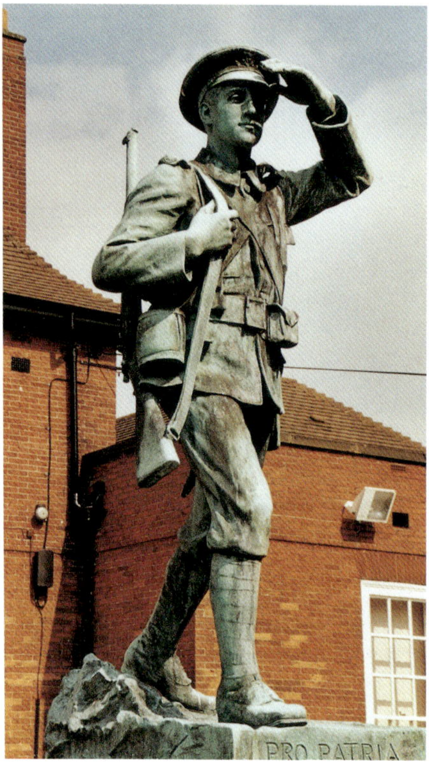

Knutsford Cottage Hospital. War Memorial by Hamo Thorneycroft.

Like Leek, Macclesfield had a School of Embroidery established in 1882 by Joshua Nicholson in his Hope St mill. The Park Lane **Silk Industry Museum** (SJ917733), in the former School of Art, holds the School archive. It has a small display of the work of the School of Embroidery as well as examples of the design work of the Art School's students. Almost next door the Paradise Mill, containing restored jacquard handlooms, is part of the museum's exhibition

Access: Open Mon–Sat 11.00–5.00. Check winter opening times. Admission charge. Tel. 01625 612045

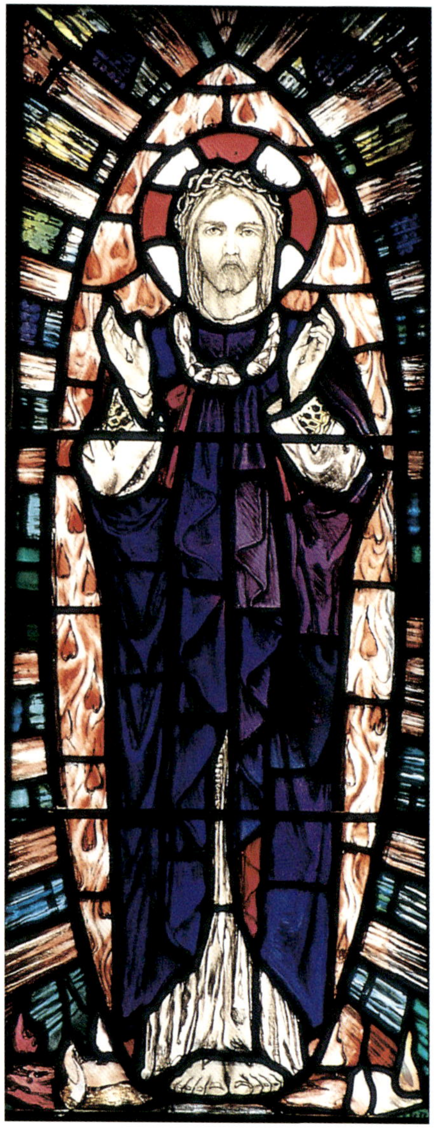

St Michael's, Macclesfield. Detail north aisle window by C. Whall, 1910.

St Michael's in Market St (SJ918737) was first consecrated in 1278 but apart from the tower, the Savage Chapel (1501–07) and the huge array of the monuments of knights and their ladies, much of today's church is the work of Arthur Blomfield 1898–1901. The reredos, altar table and communion rail were designed by **Charles Nicholson** in 1946. The east window above it and the 'Queen Victoria Memorial' window at the west end are really wonderful work by **Powell of Whitefriars.**

In the Savage Chapel there are three excellent windows by **Morris & Co.** They are 'late' as Pevsner puts it, but very impressive. The small window on the south side, 'Faith, Love & Charity' was made in 1901. The east window is **J. H. Dearle's** 'Ascension' 1907. On either side of the east window, also made in 1907, are Archbishop Savage and St Chad on the left and St Werburgh and Queen Eleanor on the right. In the south wall are two three-light windows, both made in 1918: 'The Adoration of the Magi', adapted from the **Burne-Jones** design for the 'Star of Bethlehem' tapestry and 'The Crucifixion with Mary and John'.

Back in the body of the church, the north aisle west-most window depicting 'Valour', 'Fortitude' and 'Victory' was made by **Morris & Co.** in 1918 as were the five-light War Memorial window high up above the south door and the small two-light 'Justice' and 'Humility' opposite the belfry. Almost hidden at the east-most position on the south wall and behind the organ is a three-light window by **Christopher Whall** made *c.* 1910. It features St Peter in jewelled green, Christ in a fiery mandora and a beautiful Mary Magdelene accompanied by a cherubic chorister. Lastly in the parish room is a three-light 'Holy Family' window by **Paul Woodroffe**. It shows Joseph on the left working in the carpenters' shop, the young Jesus in the centre sweeping up the shavings while Mary sits spinning wool in the third light.

Access: Parish Office open Tues–Fri 9.30–12.30. Tel. 01625–421984.

St Alban's in Chester Rd (SJ912736) was built by **A. W. N. Pugin** 1839–41 in the Perpendicular style. Still without its spire, for want of cash, the church is nevertheless huge, impressive and because there is much clear glass in the windows, it is very light. Behind the north door, in the cloister is a cartoon for a single-light window drawn by **Margaret Agnes Rope** showing scenes of the death of two English Martyrs. Where is the window? Was it ever made? Why is the cartoon here?

Access: Presbytery Tel. 01625–423446.

The Great War Memorial in Park Green (SJ920732) was unveiled in 1921. It is an explicit and poignant reminder of the sacrifice made in that war. On a square stone plinth at the base of a pedestal a soldier lies dead on the battlefield apparently unable to fit his gas mask in time. Brittannia leans over him offering the honour of a laurel crown. On top of the pedestal stands the bronze figure of womanhood holding a wreath of remembrance in her hand. The sculptor was **John Millard**.

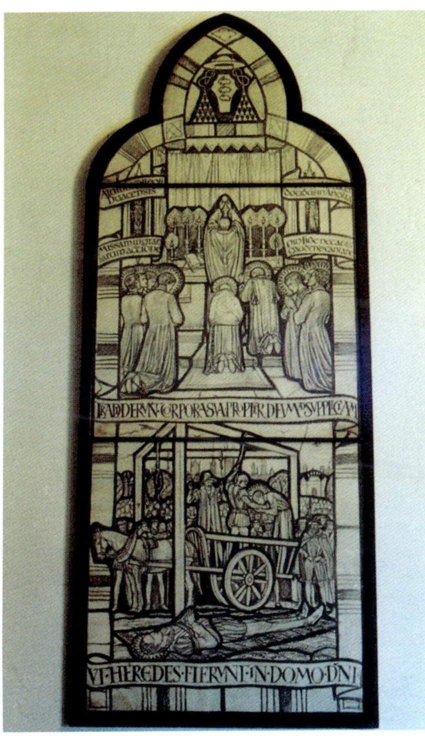

St Alban's, Macclesfield. Cartoon by M. A. Rope, no date.

MALPAS is in the bottom left hand corner of Cheshire on the B5395 about 5 miles north-west of Whitchurch.

St Oswald's (SJ486473) stands in its Perpendicular glory on top of the hill at the centre of the town. On the north side of the chancel is a four-light window by **A. K. Nicholson**. In the north wall is an excellent four-light window illustrating the Nativity with the adoration of the shepherds and the three wise men. It was made in 1928 and has been attributed to Ballantines of Edinburgh.

Access: Vicarage Tel. 01948–860209.

MERE is a dispersed rural parish to the north-west of Knutsford.

The Great War Memorial (SJ728818) was erected in honour of the Mere Estate workers killed in the war. It is sited on land at the junction of the A556 and the A50 and takes the form of a short but slender stone pillar of an octagonal section decorated on four sides with narrow ceramic tiles bearing chevron patterns. The designer was **J. H. Sellers**.

MOBBERLEY is about 2 miles north-east of Knutsford town centre and 1½ miles from the end of the runway at Manchester airport .

St Wilfrid's (SJ790801) is a mediaeval church with a chancel screen made in 1500 which Pevsner describes as the best in Cheshire. Mobberley was the home of George Mallory the mountaineer who died on Mount Everest and his life is celebrated here in a memorial window in the north wall made by **A. K. Nicholson** in 1924. There is a later window commemorating other members of the family in the south wall of the chancel which was made by Nicholson's partner **G. E. R. Smith** in 1950. On the south wall of the nave is a beautiful brass and copper memorial to the men killed in the Great War. The quality of the work is very fine. The central panel at the top of the frame worked to represent the celestial city. The decoration incorporates a small roundel showing St George slaying the dragon and the whole plaque is decorated with cabochons, enamel and abalone. The ceiling of the south aisle was designed by **W. D. Caröe**.

Access: Vicarage Tel. 01565–873218.

MOTTRAM ST ANDREW is 3 miles east of Wilmslow just off the A538.

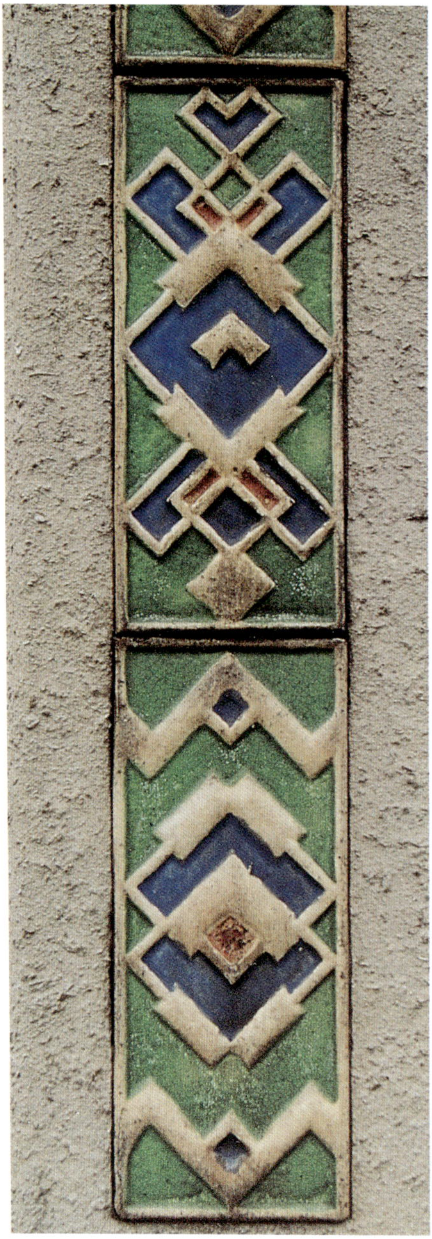

Mere. Detail Great War Memorial by J. H. Sellers. See p. 185.

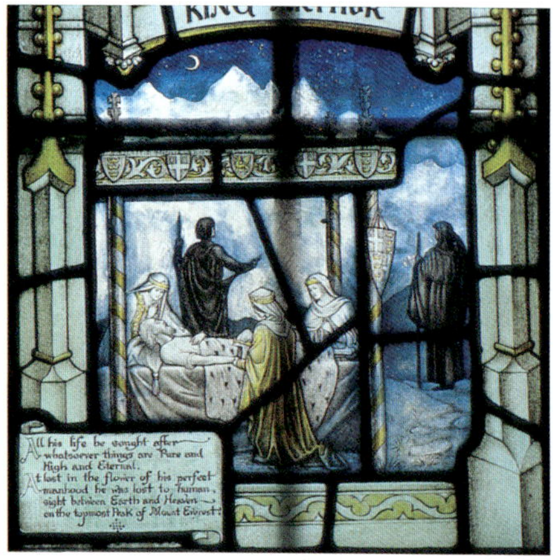

St Wilfrid's, Mobberley. Detail of the Mallory Memorial by A. K. Nicholson, 1924.

The **Village School** in Priest Lane has a single window, suitably protected but not easily seen, which was made in 1909 by **Morris & Co.** It is **Burne-Jones's** 'St Christopher' with the Christ-child on his shoulder.

MOULTON is between Northwich and Winsford 'twixt the Weaver Navigation and the A533.

St Stephen's in Church St (SJ655697) was designed by **John Douglas** in 1876. It has a stone exterior with big slate roof and a spirelet which was once slated but is now covered in lead. Internally it is red brick to dado level and yellow brick above and it has huge exposed roof-timbers. The woodwork is restrained for **John Douglas** but nevertheless elegant. The three-light east window is by **J. C. Bewsey**. Otherwise there is much of **Trena M. Cox**, especially a striking pair of lancets in the west end which are at the same time a Second World War memorial and a commemoration of the Coronation in 1953.

Access: Vicarage Tel. 01606–42450.

NANTWICH is about 20 miles south-west of Chester via the A51.

St Mary's off Church Lane (SJ653523) is a C14 church, restored in the 1850s by G. G. Scott, retaining the splendid choir canopies and about twenty carved misericordes. More recently, in 1920, a three-light memorial window was installed by **Harry Clarke** in his unmistakable style and rich jewel-like colours. The centre light is the 'Madonna and Child' flanked by 'St Cecilia' and 'Richard the Lion Heart'. It is difficult to conceive of a more wonderful memorial. Opposite, on the north wall, is a three-light window made by **Reuben Bennett** of Manchester and designed by **H. G. Hiller** in 1901. It shows 'The Light of the World' accompanied by David with his harp and Miriam beating her timbrel.

Access: The church is attended and open daily (Mar–Dec) from 10.00 a.m. but it is as well to check for weddings, funerals and baptisms. Vicarage Tel. 01270–625268.

NESTON is on the western edge of the Wirral hanging off the A540 about 15 miles north-west of Chester.

St Mary and St Helen's is in High St (SJ 291774). Only the C14 tower survived the

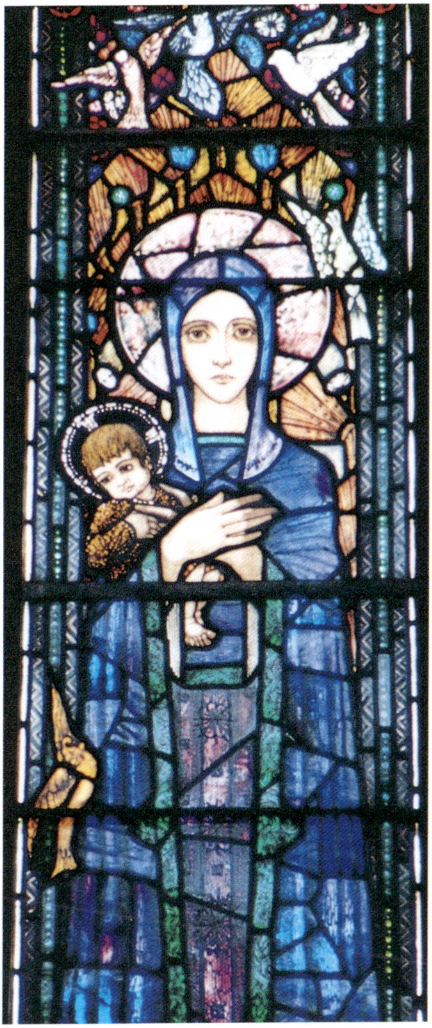

St Mary's, Nantwich. Knowles memorial window by Harry Clarke, 1920.

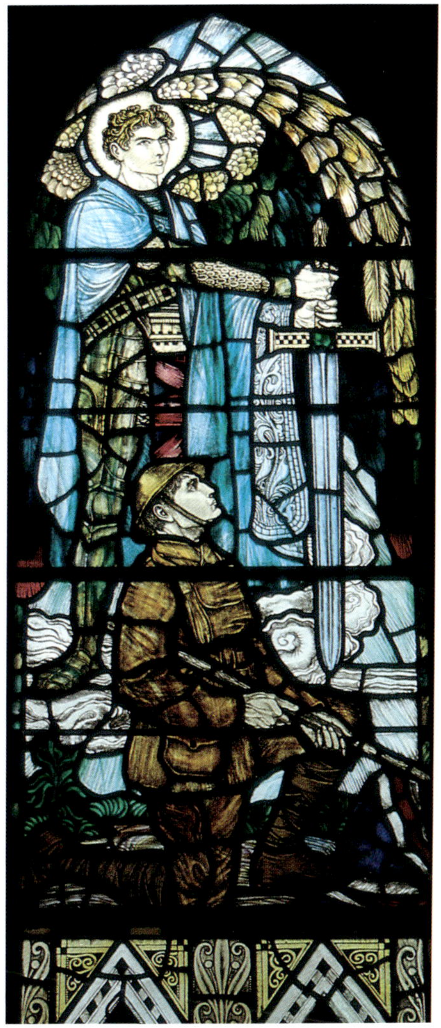

St Mary and St Helen's, Neston. Detail of the War memorial window designed by Bernard Rice.

re-building by **J. F. Doyle** in the 1870s but the church retains a sense of age and continuity. There are five windows by **Morris & Co.**: in the south aisle, second from the east are 'Justice and Humility'; in the north aisle in the east-most window is 'Enoch, David and Elijah' 1894; the third window from the east in the north aisle is 'Mary Virgin and St John' 1901 and the second from the east 'St Paul and St Thomas' 1906. All the figures in these windows were designed by **Burne-Jones**. The fifth **Morris & Co.** window is in the east end of the north aisle and shows 'The Empty Sepulchre' by **J. H. Dearle** 1928. Also in the north aisle fourth from the east end is a striking two-light Great War memorial-window designed by **Bernard Rice** and made by **Williams & Gamon** in 1920. There is an elegant set of wrought-iron gates on the inside of the west door of the church commemorating Reginald Bushell who died in 1904 and on the wall between the south porch and the west wall, is an unsigned repoussé brass cross with enamelled cabochons.

Access: Vicarage Tel. 0151–3531000.

PARKGATE is on the west side of the Wirral Peninsular between Neston and Heswall.

Mostyn House School Chapel (SJ280780). There has been a Mostyn House School in Parkgate since 1855. The Headmaster in 1895 was A. G. Grenfell and it was he who designed the school chapel using his friend the architect Frederick Fraser to design the furnishings and act as consultant when necessary. The chapel is of special interest because of its windows. Originally only the three three-light windows in the apse were to be of 'painted glass' (i.e. pictures painted on glass rather than canvas) in

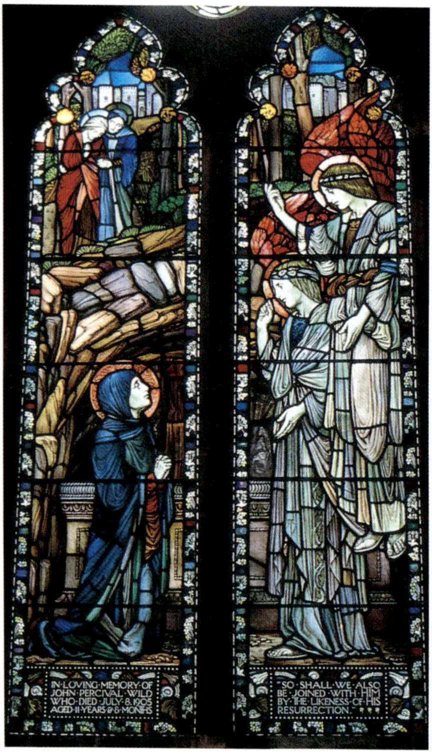

Mostyn House School Chapel, Parkgate. J. P. Wild memorial window by R. Anning Bell, c. 1906.

the style of the Joshua Reynolds window at New College Oxford, A fourth was produced in the same style based on **Frederic Shields's** painting of 'Christ Teaching Peter to Walk on the Water'. It is exciting to be able to compare these windows with the work of **Robert Anning Bell** who over a period of twenty-two years from 1899 designed seven two-light windows for the chapel in a very different style. Virtually all were paid for privately by the families of the boys they commemorate. They fill most of the north and south walls with magical images; some are poignant and gently sentimental, others are bold and exotic. All use colour, light and detail to create a unique and masterful display of the art and craft of stained-glass window making. The excellent guidebook, produced by the school, describes them all in detail. There are other interesting features in the chapel including fine wrought iron work in the front pews down the centre aisle, a variety of well preserved Puginesque Minton floor tiles and a two-light window by **G. P. Gamon** depicting Sir Philip Sydney and Sir Richard Grenville.

Access: The chapel can only be visited by appointment. Tel. 0151–3361010.

PLEMSTALL is a farm and a church at the end of a lane just east of the village of Mickle Trafford which in turn is about 3 miles north-east of Chester city centre on the A56.

St Peter's Church, at the end of Plemstall Lane (SJ457701) (past St Plegmund's well) is a Perpendicular church with a Georgian tower. The incumbent 1907–46 was the **Revd J. H. Toogood** who carved his way around the church for thirty-nine years leaving an amazing legacy behind him. The rood screen for instance has seventeen figures in addition to the crucified Christ, Mary and John. He also carved the top of the parclose screen, the altar, reredos and surrounding figures, choir stalls, the lectern, the baptistery screen, sculpted panel in the baptistery, the pulpit, the figures added to the Great War Memorial and not least, the contributions box by the door. It is a prodigious oeuvre. There is no local knowledge as to whether or not the reverend gentleman held classes for his parishioners.

Access: Vicarage Tel. 01244–300306.

PRESTBURY is about 2 miles north-west of Macclesfield on the A538.

St Peter's Church (SJ900769) is a C13 foundation with some C19 restoration by G. G. Scott. The tower is late C15 and there are Jacobean and early Georgian furnishings and fittings. The paintings in the spandrels of the arcade were done by an itinerant in 1719. The five-light east window is by **A. K. Nicholson**. It shows Christ crucified on a cross which is the living 'tree of life which bare twelve manner of fruits' Rev 22 v2.

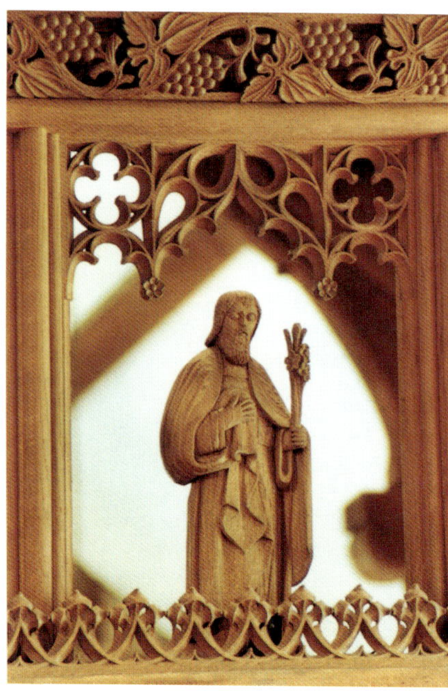

St Peter's, Plemstall. Detail of the chancel screen by the Revd J. H. Toogood. No date.

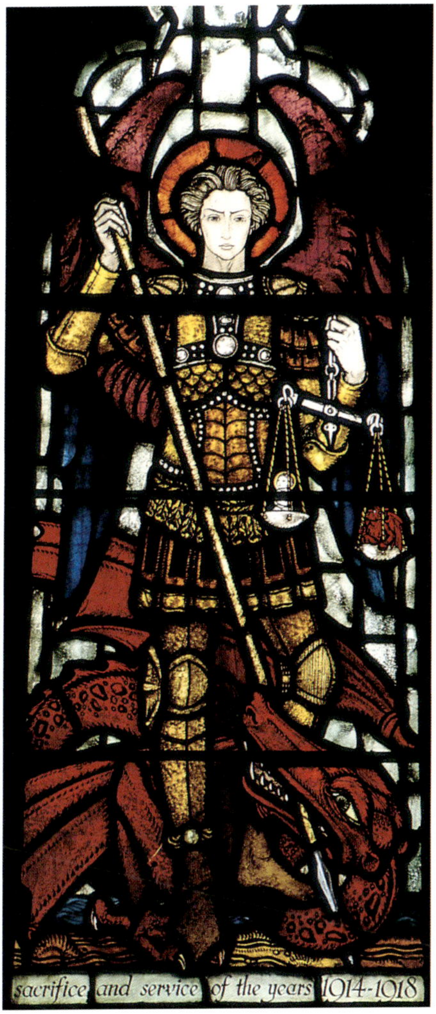

St Michael's, Runcorn. St Michael by Martin Travers, 1921.

Access: Open daily 9.00–17.30. Tel. 01625–829288 / 827625.

St Peter's Vicarage, across the road from the church, down a lane and hidden among the trees, is by **Ernest Newton**, built in 1893.

Access: Private house.

PULFORD is to be found on the B5445 about half way between Chester and Wrexham and just on the Cheshire side of the border with Wales.

St Mary's (SJ375588) is set back a little from the road opposite the Grosvenor Arms. It was built in 1881 by **John Douglas** in red sandstone with a tower topped with a shingle covered spire and pinnacles, replacements for those lost in a fire in 1991. The church has a narrow nave and chancel with a north transept off the choir. There is nothing extravagant but it is typical of the elegance and quality of design and execution expected of the architect. The painted reredos is the work of **Shrigley & Hunt**.

Access: Vicarage Tel. 01244–674703.

RUNCORN is on the southern end of the iconic Runcorn-Widnes Bridge and can be approached from Junction 11 or 12 of the M56.

St Michael's in Greenway Rd (SJ511826) was built 1884–92 by T. D. Barry. It has two two-light stained-glass windows in the south wall made by **Martin Travers** in 1921. The east-most shows St George and St Nicholas and the second shows Joan of Arc and St Michael. Both windows commemorate people killed in the Great War.

Access: Vicarage Tel. 01928–572417.

St Mary's off Castle Rd, Halton (SJ537819), was built by G. G. Scott 1851–52 and occupies an excellent hill top location. Winifrid Holiday's list of her father's work, attached to A. L. Baldry's article on **Henry Holiday** in *Walker's Quarterly Magazine* 1930, includes an entry, for St Mary's, Halton, of a window of 'Christ Blessing the Children' *c.* 1880. There is just such a light in the north wall of this church twinned with another showing Moses watching the Egyptians drown in the Red Sea but it was made after 1893. Baldry makes the point that Winifrid's list is neither complete nor accurate as to subject, place or date but if these lights *were* made from Holiday's cartoons they were not made by one of his regulars. The next window to the east is signed by **George Wragge Ltd** of Salford and was made after 1912. It shows 'Christ Healing a Lame Man' in the left light and the 'Good Samaritan' on the right. Both have been repaired and have lost some of their appeal.

Access: Vicarage 01928–563636.

SAIGHTON village is about 3 miles south-west of Chester on an unclassified road linking the A41 to the B5130.

Saighton Grange, (SJ444618) at the southern end of the village, was once the principal country seat of the Abbots of Chester but is now **Abbey Gate College**. The C15 gate house remains but the rest of the house is from the 1860s and 70s. The chapel is very small but it houses two single-light windows by **Morris & Co.**, St Francis 1897 and St Veronica 1901. Between these is a window attributed to **Henry Payne** showing St Agnes in flowing yellow robes with the Dove of the Holy Spirit.

Access: By appointment only. Tel. 01244–332077.

SANDBACH is just to the west of junction 17 on the M6.

St John the Evangelist, Church Lane, Sandbach Heath (SJ775616) is out of town on the eastern

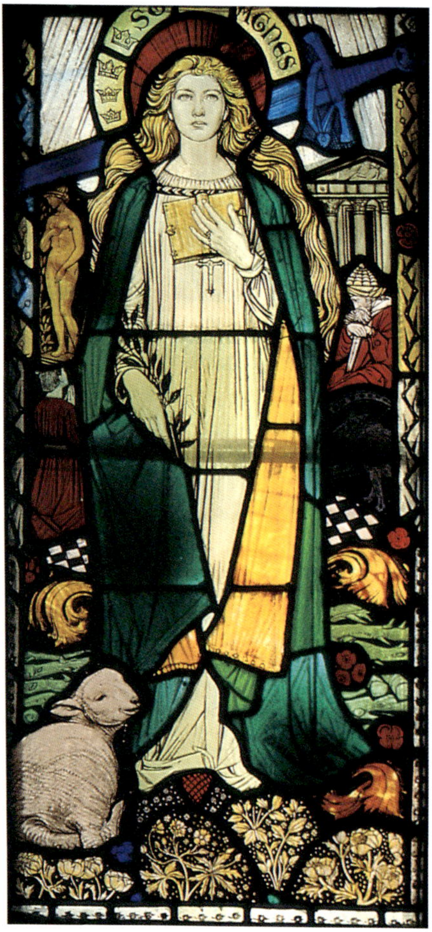

Abbey Gate College Chapel, Saighton. St Agnes. Attributed to Henry Payne.

side of the M6. It is a large G. G. Scott Gothic church built 1861, solid and spacious with fine stone carved capitals. There is spectacular carving on the wooden reredos and the panels lining the sanctuary. A foxglove, a lily, horse chestnuts and their leaves, a passion flower, vine, irises and bull-rushes are carved with such depth and undercutting they could be real. The work was obviously executed by an artist with a Ruskinian regard for nature. The artist in this case was **Jessie B. Kennedy** who spent nineteen years after the death of her first husband, Mr Twemlow, doing this work as his memorial.

Access: Vicarage Tel. 01270–768826.

SANDIWAY is just to the north of the A556 about 11 miles east of Chester.

St John's Church in Norley Road (SJ608712) was built 1902 by **John Douglas** who was born in the village. He donated the land and contributed to the cost. His interior woodwork is superb as ever both in his furnishings (note the low- relief carving on the choir stalls on the

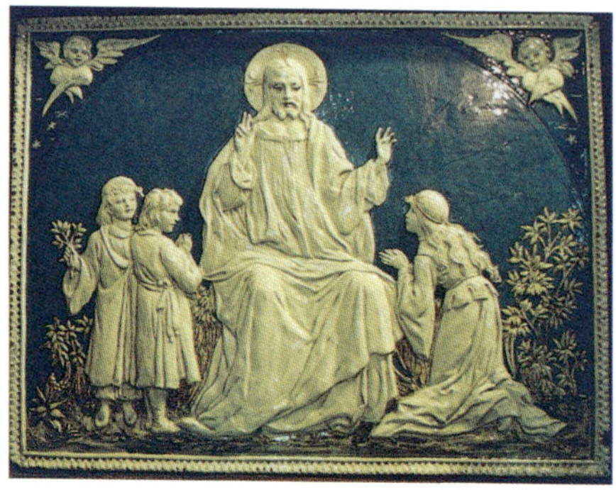

St John's Sandiway. Della Robbia plaque, no date.

north side of the chancel and the Bishop's chair) and in the exposed structural timbers of the roof. The baptistery has a window signed by **G. P. Gamon** and a **Della Robbia** plaque 'Suffer Little Children to Come Unto Me'. It is signed with the sailing boat symbol on the right and with **Harold Rathbone's** initials on the left.

Access: Office Tel. 01606–301505. Vicarage Tel. 01606–883286.

SAUGHALL village lies about 4 miles north-west of Chester city centre between the A540 and the Welsh border.

All Saints in Church Road (SJ363705) was designed by **J. M. & Henry Taylor** and built in phases 1895–1910. The church is a good example of Taylor's ability to use the structure as decoration. The arcades, for example, are supported on square brick piers with smooth, flush, stone capitals. They are undecorated, yet inherently decorative. The sanctuary has an opus sectile reredos and stained glass by **Powell of Whitefriars**. The painting on the apse ceiling by Herman Salomon *c.* 1911 shows the Angel of the Lord announcing the Nativity to the shepherds.

Access: Vicarage Tel. 01244–880213.

STYAL village lies to the east of Manchester Airport off the B5166.

The Norcliffe Unitarian Chapel, near Oak Cottages off Altrincham Rd (SJ835835) was built in the C18 by the Greg's of nearby Quarry Bank Mill and enlarged in 1867. The west window holds two of **Henry Holiday's** early stained-glass panels designed for **Powell of Whitefriars** in 1866. They have deteriorated a little but show 'Christ Blessing the Children' on the left and 'The Wise and Foolish Virgins' on the right. Is there an insight into Henry Holiday's psyche here in the fact that all the wise virgins appear to be brunettes and all the foolish virgins appear to be blonde?

Access: Open Sun (Easter to end Sept) 14.30–17.00. Services weekly Sun 6.00 p.m.

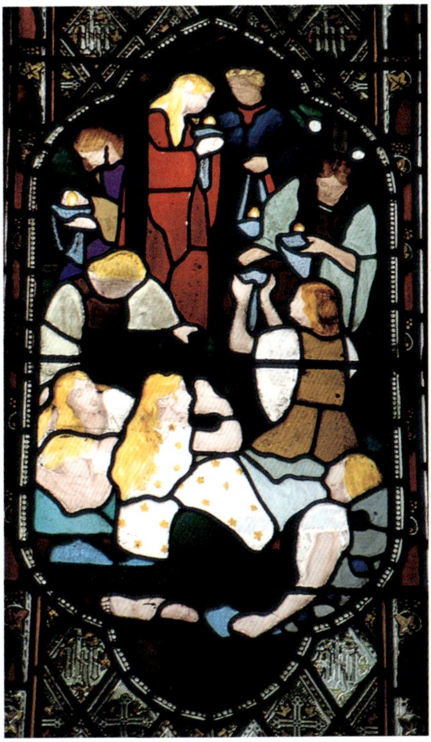

Norcliffe Unitarian Chapel, Styal. 'The Wise and Foolish Virgins' by Henry Holiday, 1867.

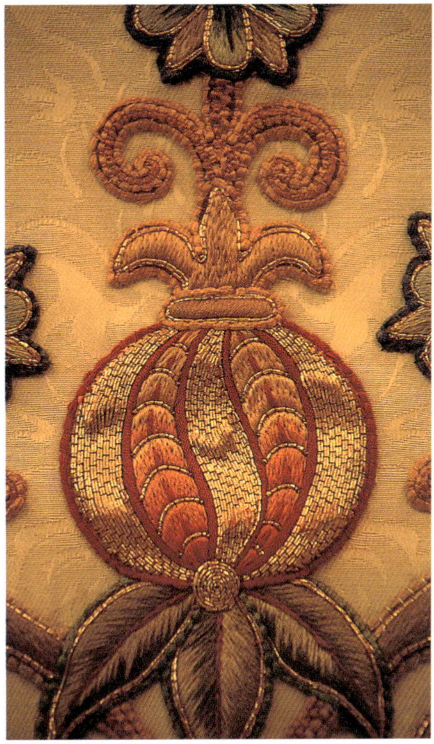

St James's, Sutton. Detail of pulpit fall. Worked by Mrs Wise from a Leek Embroidery Society pattern, no date.

SUTTON is about 2 miles south-west of Macclesfield town centre.

St James's (SJ930712) off Church Lane is an 1840s church with a fine wrought-iron screen. The west-most window in the north wall is **Henry Holiday's** version of 'I am the Light of the World'. The smaller panel below shows 'Christ Healing the Blind Man'. This is the window that greets you as you enter the church and it is very impressive. On the south side, in the window nearest the chancel is an anonymous 'Dorothea' surrounded by flowers and made in 1912. Opposite in the east-most window on the north side stands a **Burne-Jones** 'Dorcas' 1910 by **Morris & Co.** and in a panel below is 'The Good Samaritan'. The church has, along with other church embroidery, three altar-frontals, red, green and white, which Anne Jacques records in *Leek Embroidery* as having been made by Mrs Wise from patterns supplied by the **Leek Embroidery Society**. They are beautifully kept and it is a joy to see the quality and fineness of the needlework.

Access: Vicarage Tel. 01260–252228.

TABLEY is a sparsely populated parish to the west of Knutsford more or less surrounding Junction 19 on the M6.

Tabley House off the A5033 between the M6 and the A556 (SJ725778) is an C18 house which was the ancestral home of the Leicester family. The C17 chapel which now stands to the west of the house originally stood next to Tabley Old Hall, on an island in Tabley Mere. The Old Hall became ruinous and the chapel was taken down and re-built on its present site in the 1920s. It has a **Morris & Co.** window with six lights arranged in two rows of three which are filled with **Burne-Jones** figures commemorating the children of Sir George and Lady Catherine Warren. The figures represent St John, St Catherine and The Virgin Mary in the top row and St Helen, St Francis and St Margaret below. St Francis is the namesake of a son of the house who died aged three and he is accompanied in the window by two cherubs in remembrance of two daughters who also died very young. Curiously, the window was installed in 1897 when two of the sisters, Eleanor (represented by St Helen) and Margaret were still alive. The daughters were gifted artistically and the east window and the reredos above the altar are both attributed to them together with an embroidered altar cloth designed by **Burne-Jones**.

Access: Tabley House is owned by the University of Manchester. The first floor is a collection of the works of British water colour painters. The House and the Chapel are open April–Oct on Thurs–Sun 14.00–17.00. Admission charges. Tel. 01565–750151.

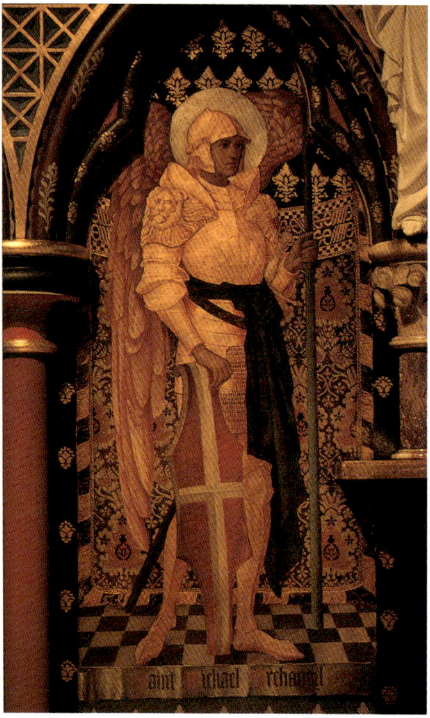

All Saints, Thelwall. Detail of the sanctuary painting by Shrigley & Hunt.

St Paul's (SJ723800) stands to the west of the A556 just north of junction 19 on the M6. It is a small Salvin church built 1855–56 which has not one but two glorious stained-glass windows by **Christopher Whall**. At the east end of the south aisle is his two-light window 'Christ's Charge to Peter' and 'Paul Bidding Farewell to the Elders at Ephesus' made in 1908. At the west end is his two-light 'Peter and Paul'. The east window is by **Frank O. Salisbury** and the carving of the chancel screen, the pulpit hood and the altar rail are attributed to **Fred Crossley** 1890–1910. Outside, in the church yard is a tombstone to H. L. B. Langford Brooke (ob.1909) by **Eric** and **Macdonald Gill**.

Access: High Legh Vicarage Tel. 01925–759132.

THELWALL is the most eastern finger of Warrington tucked between the Manchester Ship Canal and the A56.

All Saints stands at the junction of All Saints Road and Bell Lane (SJ649872) and has been expanding steadily since it was founded in 1843. The most recent extension, the north aisle, was added by **William Owen** in 1890. Thelwall was founded in 923 A.D. by King Edward the Elder and there is a triptych fixed to the south wall which commemorates his coronation in 902 A.D. and that of Edward VII in 1902. It was designed by **F. C. Eden** and made in 1907 by Heifer Bros of London. The script on the memorial was executed by **Eric Gill**. The sanctuary, baptistery and chancel arch have very attractive wall paintings by **Shrigley & Hunt**. Also in the sanctuary is a fine two-light leaded window in a design incorporating Edward the elder's crown and a floral motif. Unsigned and undated, local tradition attributes them to **Christopher Whall** but the experts disagree.

Access: Vicarage Tel. 01925–261166.

WARRINGTON is 21 miles east of Manchester and 18 miles west of Liverpool and is more or less bounded by the M56 in the south, the M6 to the east and the M62 in the north.

St Elphins in Church Lane (SJ615884) is a mediaeval foundation but, everything bar the chancel, was built 1859–67. The carved wooden organ-screen at the west end with its two wonderful trumpet-playing angels was made by **James Hatch & Co.** of Lancaster in 1908 to designs by **William & Segar Owen**. The War Memorial Chapel has a very fine C15 alabaster

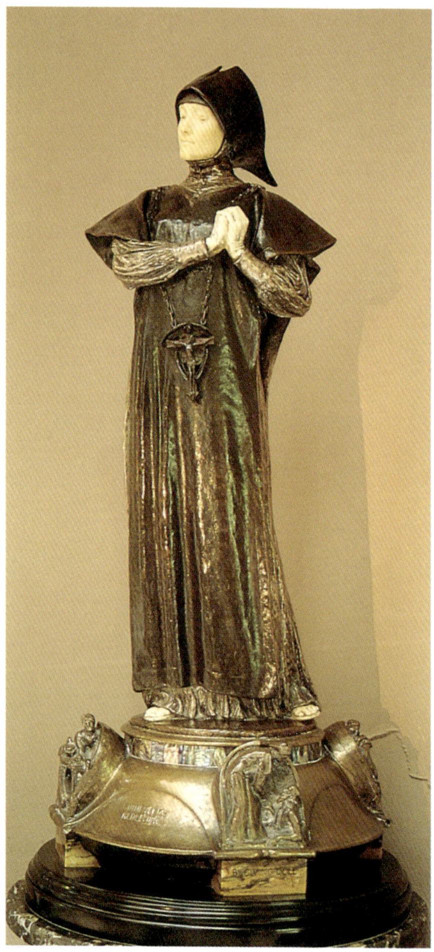

Warrington Museum and Art Gallery. 'Guinevere's Redeeming' by W. Reynolds Stephens. *Courtesy of Warrington Library, Museum and Archive Service*

tomb with a knight and his lady and a very cheerful dog. On the opposite side of the church is the effigy of Lord Winmarleigh carved in 1892 by **H. H. Armstead**. At the west end of the nave is the skilfully embroidered banner of the St Elphin's branch of the Girls' Friendly Society.

Access: Vicarage 0161–9620062.

St Mary's, in Buttermarket (SJ609883) was built by Pugin and Pugin in 1877. It has three beautiful stained-glass windows by **Harry Clarke Stained Glass**. The earliest, in the north chapel, was blessed by the Bishop of Liverpool on All Saints Day 1931. The four lights show 'The Visitation' and 'The Annunciation'. The windows are typical of Clarke's very individual style but because of their position, they need a really bright day to show them at their best. At the other end of the north wall are two three-light windows from the same studio. The central light of the most westerly of them depicts the Blessed James Bell of Warrington, who was martyred for his faith in the C16, with panels in each of the other lights showing scenes from the lives and deaths of other saints. While this window is mainly blue, the window next to it is mainly red and shows 'Christ the King' in its central light with scenes from his life in the adjoining lights. The dedication of this window dates from 1934 although it is not clear when either of the windows was made.

Access: Presbytery Tel. 01925–635664.

Our Lady's is in St Mary's St Latchford (SJ613876). It was originally called St Mary's when it was built 1901–02. The parclose screen in the sanctuary and the sedilia were designed by **John Douglas** in 1907 while the apse contains stained glass made by **Margaret Agnes Rope** in 1932 and 1937. The earlier window on the north side shows the figures of Blessed James Bell and Blessed James Finch above panels depicting their martyrdom. On the south side are the figures of St Thomas More and St John Fisher above similar scenes.

Access: Presbytery Tel. 01925–634849.

Warrington Museum, in Museum St (SJ605880) gives pride of place, in a niche on the first floor landing, to the stunning little bronze sculpture of 'Guinevere's Redeeming' made by **W. Reynolds Stephens**. It was exhibited at the Royal Academy in 1905 and illustrated in *The Studio* (1905 Volume 35 p. 41).

Access: Open Mon–Fri 9.00–17.00; Sat 9.00–16.30. Tel. 01925–442392.

Just around the corner from the Museum, in the Queen's Gardens, Palmyra Square is a **monument** to the soldiers killed in the South African war. It was sculpted by **Alfred Drury** as was the bronze plaque on the plinth which records the names of the fallen.

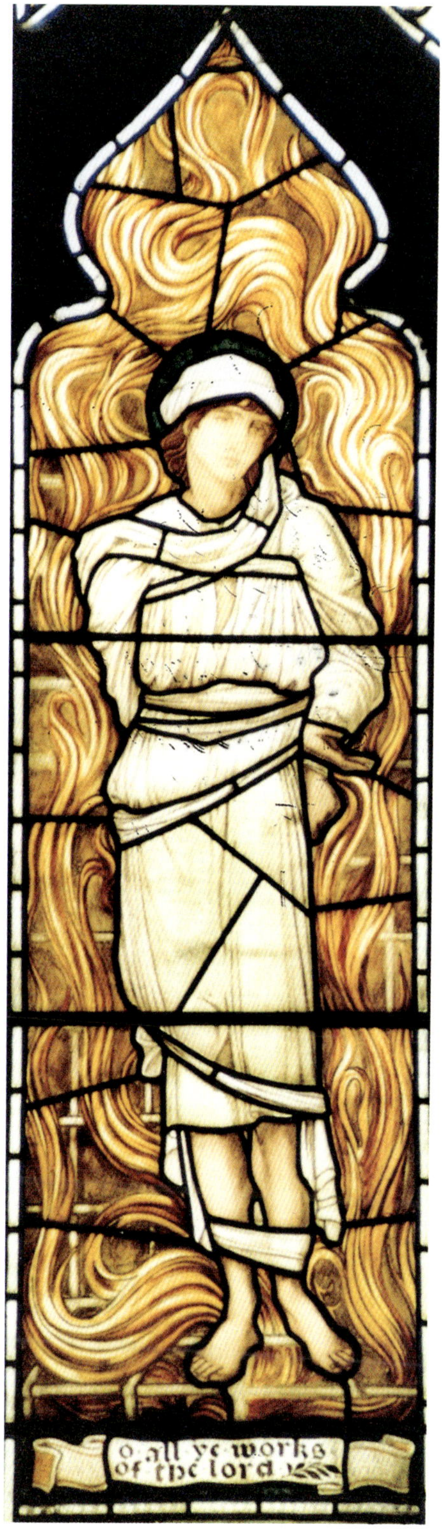

St Luke, Farnworth, Widnes. Detail of the 'Fiery Furnace' window by E. Burne-Jones for Morris & Co., 1876.

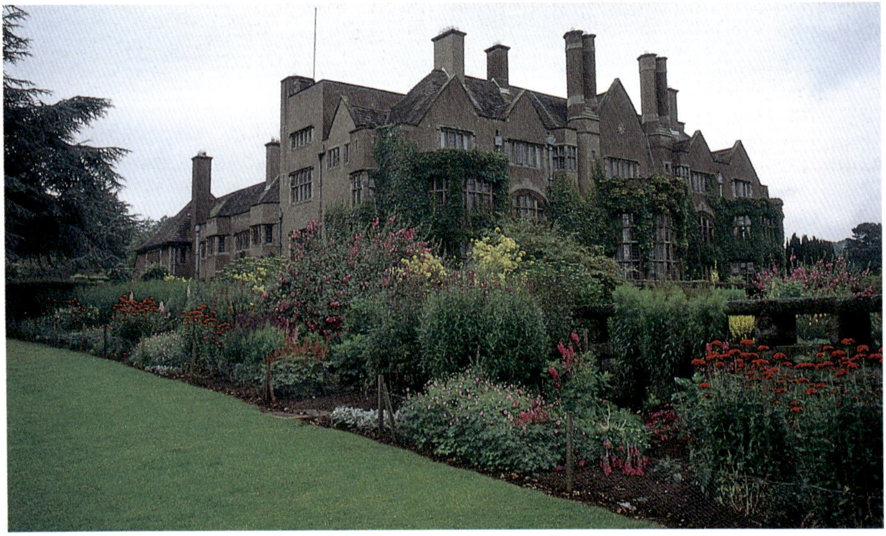

Tirley Garth, Willington by C. E. Mallows, 1906–12.

WHITEGATE is about 2½ miles north-west of Winsford at the end of Grange Lane.

St Mary's (SJ629693) was built by **John Douglas** in 1874 using the C14 wooden pillars of the original church to support his hammer-beam roof. In the north aisle there is a three-light window 'Christ in Glory' with musical angels made by **Edward Frampton**, to commemorate Queen Victoria's Diamond Jubilee. It was designed by his pupil Bernard Youard in 1902.

Access: Vicarage Tel. 01606–882151.

WIDNES is built on the banks of the river Mersey 19 miles east of Liverpool at the northern end of the iconic Runcorn-Widnes Bridge.

St Luke's church on the corner of Pit Lane and Dragon Yard Farnworth (SD517877) is a mediaeval church which has accumulated much to interest visitors over the seven hundred years of its development. From the Arts and Crafts period it has a very interesting and rare window made by **Morris & Co.** in 1876. It is a three-light window at the western end of the north wall showing Shedrak, Meshak and Abednego in the fiery furnace. **Burne-Jones** has managed to give them an intriguing air of nonchalance amidst his writhing yellow and orange flames. The faces of Meshak and Abednego have deteriorated a little but this remains an outstanding window. Sewter records only one other use of these cartoons and that was in 1870 at Middleton Cheyney in Northants.

Access: Vicarage Tel. 0151–4242735.

St Ambrose's church, in Halton View Road, (SD528864) is a huge red-brick building by **J. F. Doyle** 1883. It has a rather dark and looming exterior which is transformed into a soaring cheerful lightness on the inside. Internally it remains a simple building with a minimal amount of decoration in the exposed brickwork. The apse has a painted reredos and altar front and there are two stained-glass windows made by **H. G. Hiller**. St George in the north-east angle and St Ambrose in the south-east both date from about 1919. The three-light west window is undated and unsigned but is claimed by Caroline Townshend and Joan Howson in their entry in the BSMGP Catalogue for 1929. The pulpit, designed by Doyle, is of terracotta with alabaster pilasters and sculpted sandstone figures.

Access: Vicarage Tel. 0151–420804.

St Mary's in St Mary's Road (SD514838) was built by **Austin & Paley** 1908–10. It is a magnificent building with a huge tower set in the centre of the west wall and stained glass by **Shrigley & Hunt** including the great five-light east window. **H. G. Hiller** has a single light window of the 'Good Shepherd' in the south chapel.

Access: Vicarage Tel. 0151–4204963.

WILLINGTON is not so much a hamlet, more a house or two about 1½ miles south-west of Kelsall.

Tirley Garth south of Tirley Lane (SJ545664) is the largest country house built by **C. E. Mallows** who, with **Thomas Mawson,** also designed the gardens. Work began in 1906 for J. W. Leesmith, and was completed in 1912 for R. A. Prestwich. It is rendered and has stone facings and stone flagged roofs. Each elevation presents a different but interesting face with spectacular use of windows, chimneys and gables. The plans provided for inspiring views from the south garden front to Beeston and Peckforton Castles and beyond them to no less

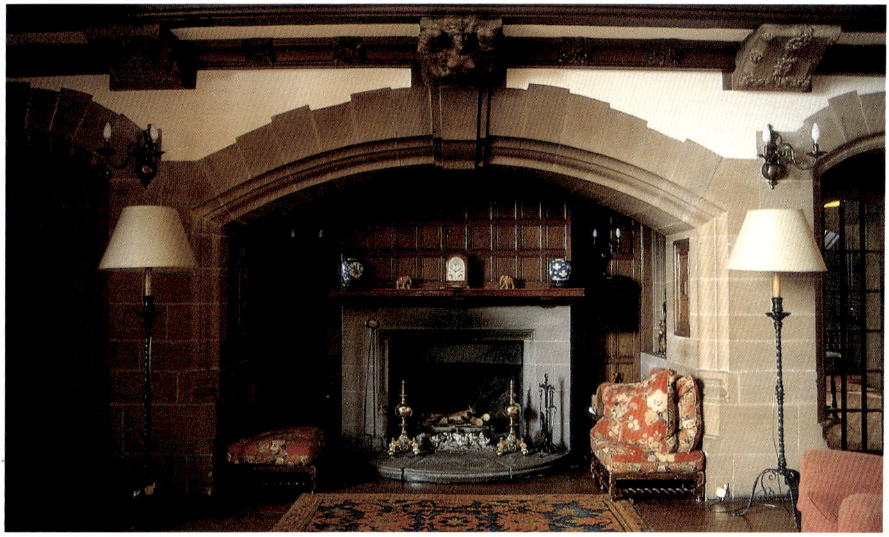

Tirley Garth, Willington. Fireplace in the Great Hall designed by C. E. Mallows, 1906–12. *Courtesy of MRA*

than five counties. The substantial growth of many trees over the past 90 years has limited the view today. The garden planting scheme has changed over the years but the structure remains substantially as **Mallows** and **Mawson** left it.

The main entrance to the house from the carriage court leads through a tunnel-vaulted passage into a square central court, or garth, which is surrounded on all sides by a cloister walk and has a circular pond at its centre. The lead fountain in the pond was made by the **Bromsgrove Guild**. The small entrance hall in the south-east corner of the garth opens on to two main rooms and to a corridor, which runs the full length of the house leading to other principal rooms and to the domestic facilities in the east wing. The main living room is the Great Hall which is two storeys high and has a large inglenook fireplace at one end and a gallery on three sides at first floor level. The room is flooded with light flowing through the tall, stone mullioned and transomed bay window. In the Great Hall as in so much of the house, the use of oak for the panelling and in the floors gives it an unmistakable stamp of quality. There is a white drawing room which is more classical than spectacular and a family sized, oak- panelled dining room. The rest of the house is given over to bedrooms and domestic offices. There are wonderful views from the principal bedrooms many of which have fireplaces decorated with **Pilkington** tiles.

Access: Private house. The gardens are open every Sunday in May. Tel. 01829–732301.

WILMSLOW is about 12 miles south of Manchester on the A34.

St Bartholomew's in Chancel Lane (SJ848815) has three three-light windows by **Morris & Co.** made in 1920 from **J. H. Dearle's** cartoons representing 'War', 'Victory' and 'Peace'. There is a shining copper memorial on the north wall of the north chapel by **James Smithies**. In the south chapel is the **Shrigley & Hunt** stained-glass memorial to Henry Boddington of Pownall Hall, brewer, painter and patron of the arts who died in 1925. It was designed by **E. Holmes Jewitt**.

Access: Parish Office open Mon–Fri 10.00–12.00. Tel. 01625–520309.

Pownall Hall (SJ836819) is situated on the western edge of Wilmslow at the end of Carrwood Road. There has been a house on this site since 1300 but its claim to Arts and Crafts fame began when the brewer, **Henry Boddington** the second, bought the house in 1886. He employed **Ball & Elce** to redesign its interior and the architects used many of the trappings of the Arts and Crafts in the house with inglenooks and bays, wainscoting and half-timbering and not least mottoes for which Henry Boddington had a great penchant. They re-styled the large entrance hall in half- timbered black and white in the tradition of Tudor Cheshire farm houses with oak panelling and sturdy oak beams. The carving on the huge stone fireplace of emblems and Saxon names for the days of the week was the work of Manchester craftsman J. J. Millson, who was commissioned to do all the stone carving both inside and outside the house. On the upper floors with the exception of the master bedroom which is decorated in Liberty's Mauresque fashion, the rooms reflect the Cheshire Tudor styling of the entrance hall with quaint Arts and Crafts details.

However it was Boddington's use of the **Century Guild** to help him decorate and furnish the main downstairs rooms which gives

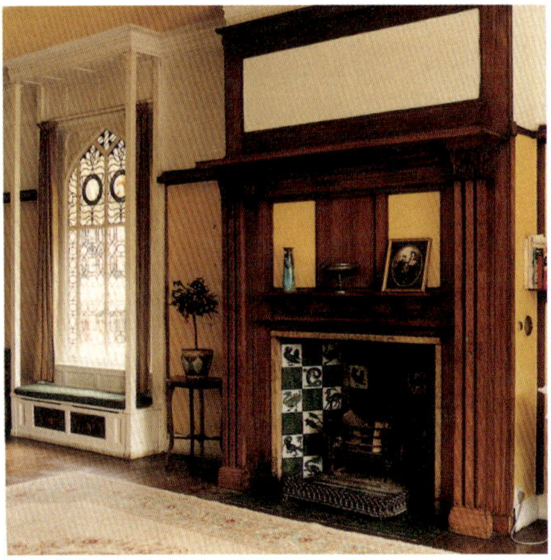

Pownall Hall, Wilmslow. Drawing room fireplace. Century Guild, c. 1887. *Courtesy of Pownall Hall School. © Boswell Photography*

the house its particular Arts and Crafts interest. Although much has gone this remains the only known example of the Guild's work in its original setting. The decoration was considered to be fashionably avant-garde. The sitting room was furnished and decorated in shades of lemon with satinwood furniture and fittings. To-day it retains its stained glass, much of its woodwork and the elegant fireplace with De Morgan tiles set in a satinwood surround and over mantel. The dining room, decorated in more sombre style, still has part of the plasterwork frieze of foliage and hounds and the fireplace designed by **Mackmurdo**. Two guilded stooping figures carved by **Benjamin Creswick** support the mantelshelf beneath which is a small picture painted by **Selwyn Image**. The tiles are by **De Morgan** and the cast iron work by **Charles Winstanley**. Boddington owned many pieces of furniture by the Century Guild some of which are now part of the Manchester Art Gallery collection. Some fine examples of the Guild's metal work can be seen in the front entrance porch with its wrought iron bell-pull in the shape of an arum lily and the sturdy, oak door decorated with sprawling, Art Nouveau hinges. Elsewhere in the house there are wall sconces, door plates, hinges, knobs and handles all works of art in themselves.

The house's other treasure of the Arts and Crafts period is its stained glass made by **Shrigley & Hunt**, although no information has come to light to identify the designers. Every room is blessed with quite remarkable windows from coats of arms and tulips in the hall and scenes from Greek myths in the morning room to the magnificent four-light staircase window depicting the Spirits of the Four Winds. The figures are set against a background which reflects the changing seasons with beautifully crafted birds, butterflies and flowers

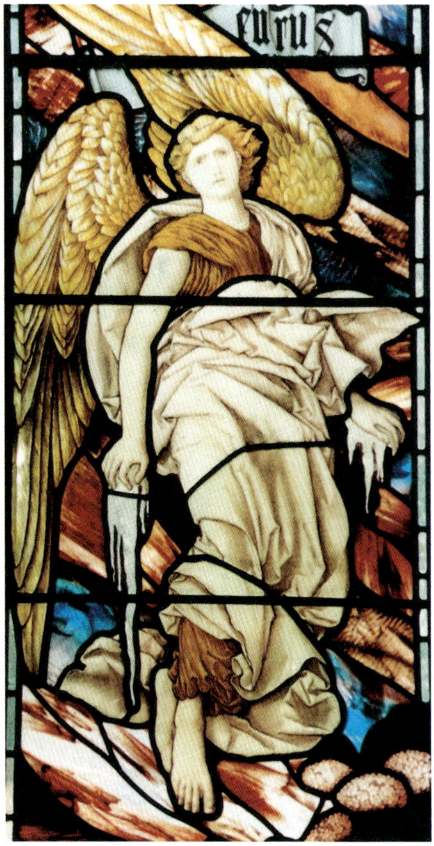

Pownall Hall, Wilmslow. Detail of the staircase window. Shrigley & Hunt, c. 1887. *Courtesy of Pownall Hall School.*

demonstrating a masterly use of streaky glass. Upstairs in what were the children's nurseries and schoolroom there is more glass but here the style changes to portray more appealing subjects. There are owls, bats and poppies, toadstools around an oak tree, St George with his dragon and illustrated nursery rhymes. There is another interesting window. A. C. Sewter's Catalogue of the Stained Glass of William Morris and his Circle records a window depicting Chaucer and Dante ordered by Mackmurdo and Horne for an unspecified location. Here it is, at the end of the corridor between the library and the morning room, readily recognisable as the work of **Morris & Co.**

Access: Pownall Hall is now a private school. Visits may be made by appointment. Tel. 01625-523141.

The Croft, Adlington Rd (SJ864812), is a large surburban Arts and Crafts house built *c.* 1902 by **Edmund Rathbone** for a relative Mrs Alice Briggs. Further along on the other side of the road is **Rosegarth** (SJ865812) built for Alice's daughter Dorothy in an Arts and Craft style by Hubert Worthington in 1924.

Access: private houses.

NORTH STAFFORDSHIRE

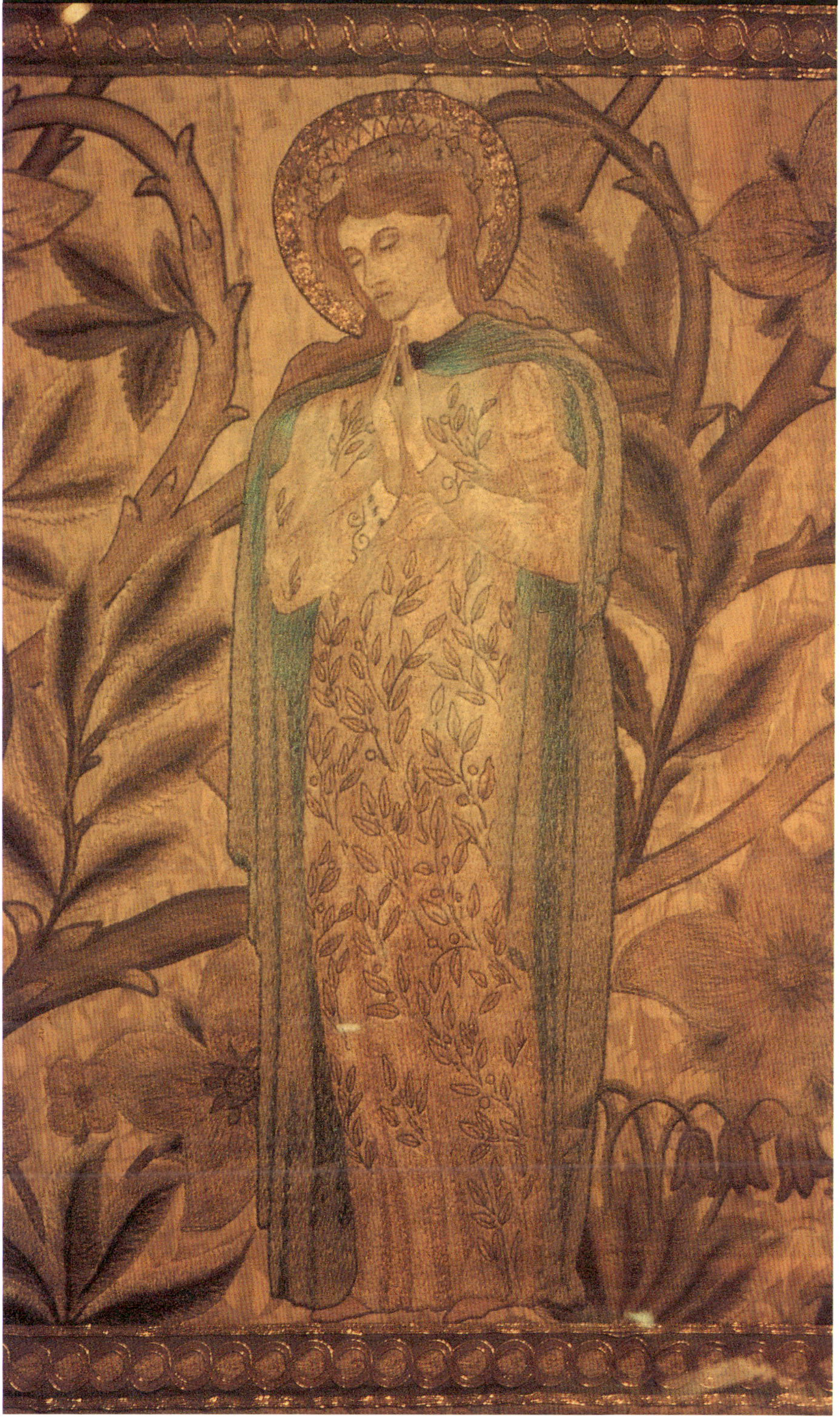

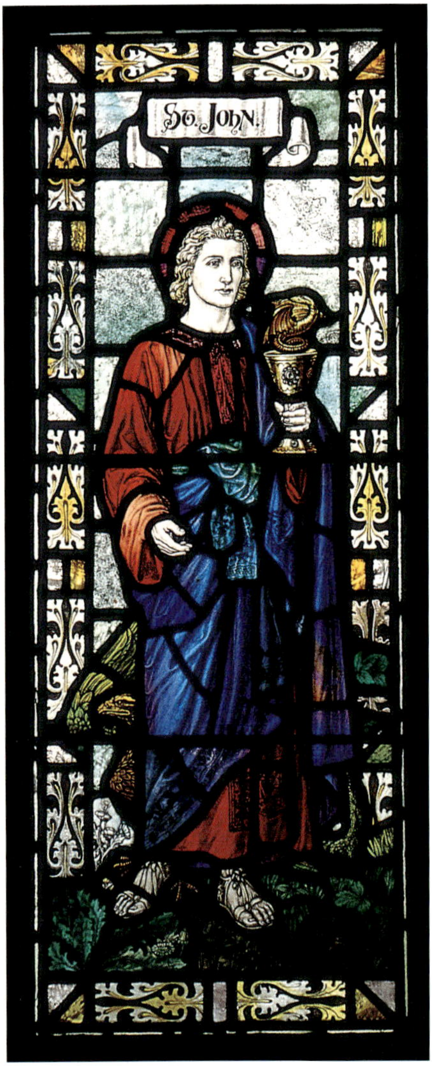

St Mary and St John Berkhamstych. St John by Florence Camm, 1916.

BERKHAMSTYCH is about 6 miles east of Leek on the A52.

The Chapel of **St Mary and St John** on the south side of the A52 (SK046525) is less than ½ mile east of the turning for Ipstones. 'The Crucifixion' window at the east end was made by **Morris & Co.** in 1908 using **Burne-Jones's** figures set against a leafy background. At the west end of the south wall is a two-light window of 'St John and St Barnabas' made by **Florence Camm** in 1916.

Access: Vicarage Tel. 01538–266313.

BROWN EDGE is about a mile across the fields from the north-east corner of the Potteries conurbation and 1½ miles west of the A53 at Endon.

St Anne's (SJ908541) was built in 1844 but the three-light east window 'The Ascension' dates from 1874, the latter days of **Morris, Marshall, Faulkner & Co.** Christ ascends into heaven supported by angels and watched by Mary, Peter, John and Andrew. The figures are set against **Morris**'s scrolled-foliage background. Andrew was designed by **Ford Madox Brown** and the other figures were drawn from **Burne-Jones**'s cartoons. The glass has weathered badly and the window has lost much of its detail.

Access: Vicarage Tel. 01782–513323.

BURSLEM is between Hanley and Tunstall on the A50.

St Joseph's in Hall St (SJ866498) was built 1925–27 by **J. S. Brocklesby**. It is a large, brick church built in a Romanesque style enlivened by a tall, square campanile and a shorter round tower. Internally, the apse is crowned by a stylised 'Christ Pantocrator' painted on a golden background and supported by swirling angels. It is by Moira Forsyth who assisted her

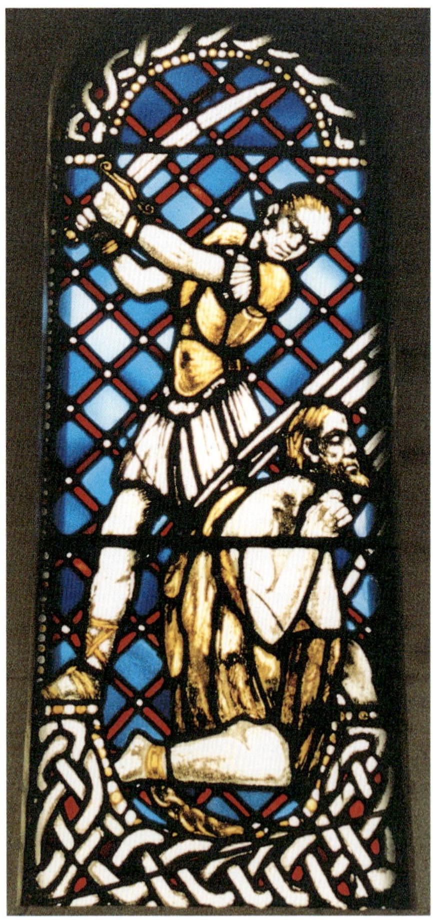

St Joseph, Burslem. Baptistery, 'Beheading of John the Baptist' by Gordon Forsyth.

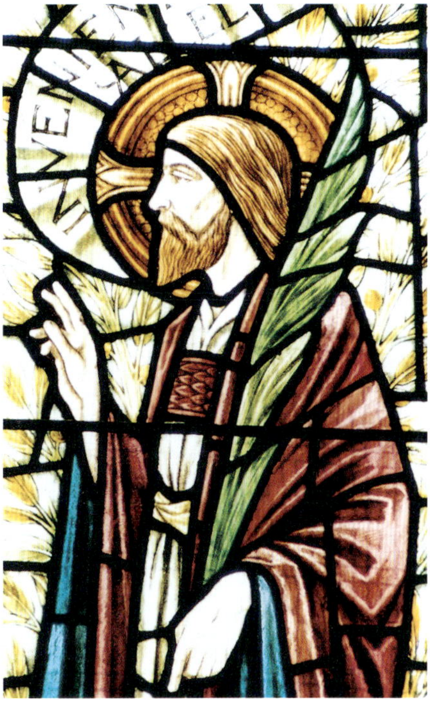

St Peter's, Caverswall. Detail of the 'Mary and Jesus' window by Selwyn Image, c. 1905.

father, **Gordon Forsyth** with the twenty-eight marvellous stained-glass panels in the apse, nave, transepts, west end and baptistery. It is not clear whether the paintings on the wall and reredos in the south transept are the work of the father or the daughter, or if they were a collaboration. The panelled ceilings of the nave, transepts and gallery are also painted.

Access: Presbytery Tel. 01782–837602.

CAVERSWALL village lies to the west of Stoke on Trent in rural North Staffordshire.

It is approached by a narrow winding lane from either the A521 or the A520.

St Peter's (SJ952428) was founded in the C12 and has C17 and C19 additions and alterations. Most of the stained glass was installed by Kempe in 1880 but the two light window at the east end of the north aisle was designed by **Henry Holiday** for **Powell of Whitefriars** in 1884. It shows St Longinus and St Peter. The two-light east window of the south aisle, showing Mary and Jesus, is a rarity in the North West. It was designed in rather muted shades by **Selwyn Image** *c.* 1905.

Access: Vicarage Tel. 01782–388037.

CHEDDLETON is some 5 miles south of Leek on the A520 .

St Edward the Confessor (SJ971524) is an ancient church which was restored 1863–64 by G. G. Scott and decorated with some of the earliest work of **Morris, Marshall, Faulkner & Co.** In the chancel are eight stained-glass panels designed in 1864 by **Ford Madox Brown** with canopies, pattern work and borders by **Philip Webb**. The subjects on the north side are: Edward the Confessor and King Alfred, Constantine and St Helen and on the south side, St Louis and Charlemagne and Penda King of Mercia and King Ethelbert. Seven of these panels are unique and the eighth, Edward the Confessor, can only be found here and at All Saints, Cambridge.

The altar piece is a triptych made up by **Morris, Marshall, Faulkner & Co.** who added two painted wings to a carved C15 Flemish panel showing 'The Deposition From the Cross'. The painted decoration on the wing panels was designed by **William Morris**. The fabric on the sedilia in the south wall of the sanctuary is the original material supplied by **Morris & Co.**

In the south wall of the nave is the stunning 'Three Angels' window made in 1869 from **Burne-Jones's** splendid cartoons and enlivened by **Morris's** sense of colour including his particularly brave and effective use of the hottest of reds for the angels' wings. In contrast, in the south-west corner is a two-light window of 'The Baptism of Christ' and 'The Cleansing of Naaman'. It is much less flamboyant and uses muted colours but it was also designed by **Burne-Jones**.

In the north aisle, fixed behind glass on the west wall, is an altar frontal made by the **Leek Embroidery Society** in 1890 using a design by **Gerald Horsley** of 'The Three Marys'. The church has other beautiful frontals and several smaller church embroideries by the **Leek Embroidery** Society. Above this frontal is a two-light window made in 1866. Three of its

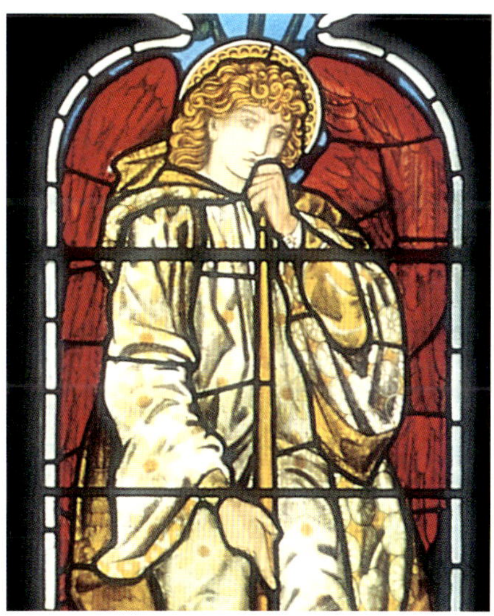

St Edward's, Cheddleton. Red-winged angel by Burne-Jones, 1869.

four panels, the 'Sacrifice of Cain and Abel', the 'Sacrifice of Zacharias' and 'Abraham Blessed by Melchisedek' were drawn by **Ford Madox Brown**. The fourth panel is 'The Last Supper' designed by **William Morris**. The panels in the east-most window in the north wall were also designed by **William Morris** in 1868 and show Boaz and Ruth – is there a hint of Mr & Mrs Morris in these faces? The three panels of the east window in the north aisle are based on **Burne-Jones** cartoons. St Cecilia occupies the centre light with the small panels, 'Christ Found in the Temple' on the left and 'Christ Blessing the Children' on the right. The window was made in 1892.

Thomas Wardle the dye-master was a church warden here in the early 1860s and his brother in law, George Young Wardle, was already working for Morris in 1864. This would account for the profusion of early work by 'The Firm' in the church.

Access: Usually open. Vicarage Tel. 01538–360226.

CHESTERTON is about 3 miles north-east of Newcastle under Lyne on the B6500.

Holy Trinity (SJ832495) has a row of apostles by different stained-glass firms in its south wall. St John was made by **Morris, Marshall, Faulkner & Co.** in 1874 using a **Burne-Jones** cartoon. It is badly preserved and has suffered some physical damage. The east window of the south aisle has also been damaged and subsequently repaired. It is unsigned and undated but the style and colouring suggest the work of **James Eadie Reid** for the **Gateshead Glass Company**.

Access: Vicarage Tel. 01782–562479.

COBRIDGE is east of Hanley and south of Burslem on the A53.

The Moorcroft Factory, shop and Museum is on Sandbach Rd (SJ877492) and has a historical landmark in the shape of its last remaining bottle kiln. The one room museum is a treasure house of the very best of the firm's pottery, tracing its development from 1897 when William Moorcroft started work for James MacIntyre up to the present day.

Access: Open Mon–Sat 10.30–17.00 and Sun 13.00–16.00. Tel 01782–214345.

DENSTONE is on the B5032 between Ashbourne and Uttoxeter.

All Saints, (SK100409) was built 1860–62 by **G. E. Street** who was also responsible for the village school, the vicarage, the churchyard cross and the lych-gate. Inside the church he designed the font, the pulpit, reredos, organ screen, choir stalls and the ironwork to the door. The stained glass is an exceptional and early set of windows by Clayton & Bell and contemporary with the building of the church. It is a rare treat to see an altar frontal in use that was designed by **G. E. Street**.

Access: Vicarage Tel. 01889–590263.

Denstone College (SK090403) has a huge chapel approached by a narthex-like lobby in which there is a three-light window by **Christopher Whall.** It was donated in 1916 by the mothers of Old Denstonians killed in the Great War. The design describes the mothers' sacrifice of their sons through the representation of Mary gathering children about her while she contemplates the broken body of Christ. He is tended by angels and His crown of thorns lies on the ground. To Mary's left Christ is seen in glory, riding on a white horse, his helmet surrounded by a crown of thorns which is

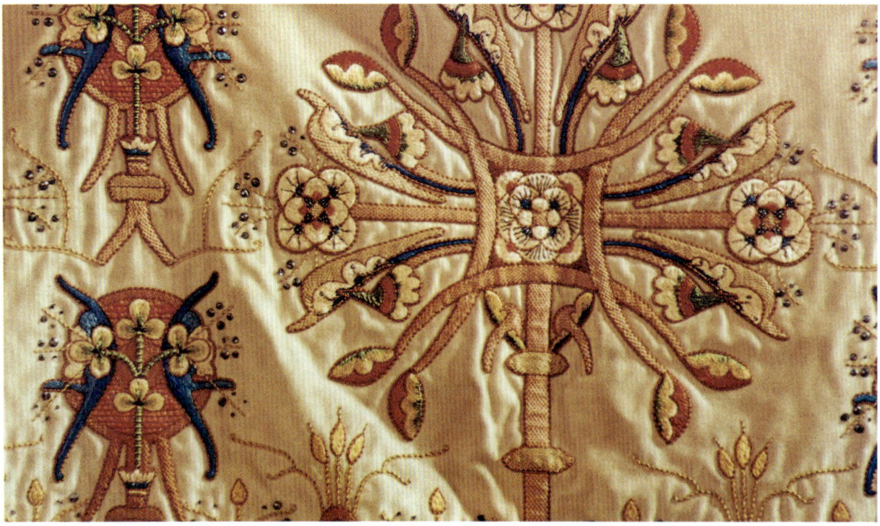

All Saints, Denstone. Detail of Altar frontal designed by G. E. Street.

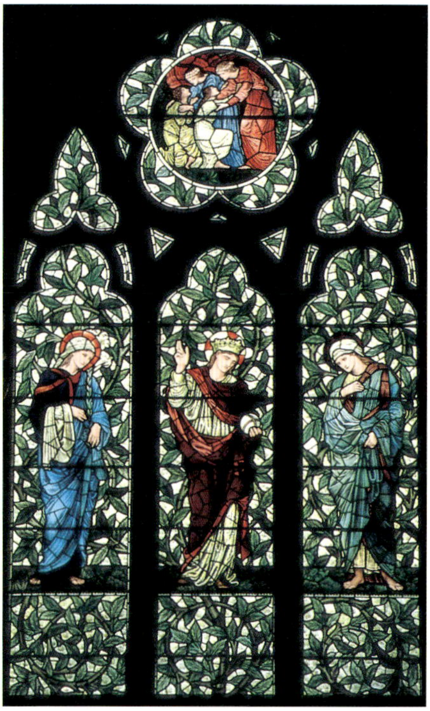

St Luke's, Endon. East window by Morris & Co., 1893.

seen bursting into flower. It is a beautiful, hugely emotional and powerful window.

Access: By appointment with the Chaplain. Tel. 01889–590484 or 01889–591164 (weekends).

ENDON is some 5 miles south west of Leek on the A53.

St Luke's (SJ928538), almost at the top of Endon Bank was restored in the 1870s and provided with a three-light **Morris & Co.** east window in 1893. It shows Christ in the centre light with Mary and John on either side. All the figures, designed by **Burne-Jones**, are set against the varied greens of **Morris's** scrolled foliage background. In a roundel in the tracery **Burne-Jones's** angels are seen welcoming souls into paradise. At 10.30 on a sunny September morning the total effect is amazing.

Access: Vicarage Tel. 01782–502166.

HANLEY is more or less at the centre of the Five Towns astride the A520.

All Saints in Leek Rd (SJ889467) is a huge brick box designed in 1910 by **Gerald Horsley**. It has an outdoor pulpit on the west end and an ornamented surround to the west door. Internally it has a high, wide nave and a north aisle separated by a five bay arcade. The chancel has a low, stone screen-wall with an integral pulpit which is worked with a finely carved and decorated cross. The woodwork in the choir is very simple but not in the least 'ordinary'. The beautiful triptych reredos was painted by **James Eadie Reid**. The centre panel shows the Risen Christ standing with his arms outstretched in front of a cross, surrounded by soldiers and sailors, nurses and civilians. On the left wing is 'The Nativity' and on the right, 'The Supper at Emmaus'.

The east window shows Christ sitting in shining glory with his angels in the top portion of all five lights. In the lower portion, wearing the richest of reds, the four Evangelists surround a central panel in which a soldier and a sailor look up to Christ sitting above them. The window is unsigned but, given the **Eadie Reid** connection here, it is tempting to attribute the window to **The Gateshead Stained Glass Co.**

On the west wall are two display cabinets containing altar frontals designed by **Horsley** for **The Leek Embroidery Society**, one of which is still used during advent. The brass font-ewer was made by the **Keswick School of Industrial Arts**.

Access: Vicarage Tel. 01782–205713.

The Potteries Museum and Art Gallery in Bethesda St (SJ882476) has an exceptionally good collection of ceramics. The display, on virtually the whole of the first floor of the museum, leads visitors through the earlier centuries and later decades of ceramic development. There is a feast of ceramics allied

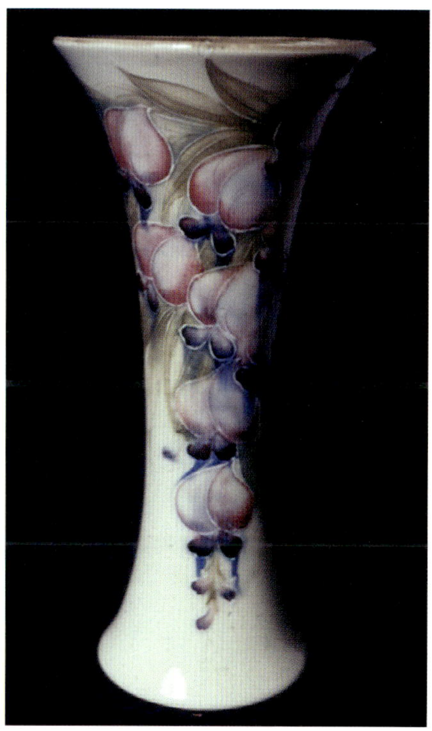

Hanley Potteries Museum. 'Wisteria', vase by Moorcroft c. 1912. © The Potteries Museum and Art Gallery, Hanley.

to the Arts and Crafts period with examples of the work of **Doulton, Minton, Pilkington,** Maw & Co, **Martinware, Moorcroft, Ruskin Pottery,** Bernard Moore, Watcombe, Elton, Linthorpe, Buller and **Della Robbia**. The work of **William De Morgan** is cleverly juxtaposed with tiles and pots from Iznic Turkey and Moorish Tunisia. There is an extremely large, two-handled **De Morgan** jar, made in two sections and decorated with fabulous beasts which were hand painted in ruby lustre. There is a display of **Minton** tiles beginning with framed decorative wall-panels from the 1880s, passing through the Art Nouveau and Art Deco periods and into the 1940s.

In the Fine Art Department there are pictures by G. Clausen, Walter Russell, W. J. Sickert, **Eric Gill, Gordon Forsyth** and Moira Forsyth. The New Sculpture is represented by the bronzes 'Comedy and Tragedy' by **Alfred Gilbert** and 'Boy with Catapult' by **William Reid Dick**. The large white stone sculpture at the entrance to the cafeteria is by **Gilbert Ledward**.

Access: Mon–Sat 10.00–17.00, Sun 14.00–17.00, closed Christmas and New Year. Admission free. Tel. 01782–232323.

HARTSHILL lies between Newcastle under Lyme and Stoke on Trent.

Holy Trinity in Hartshill Rd (SJ866458) was built in 1852 by G. G. Scott for Herbert Minton and is very solid and impressive. Internally, it appears to have been viewed both as the family chapel and as an annex to Minton's ecclesiastical products showroom. There is a great variety of encaustic tiles all over the floors while glazed tiles with chevron or diaper patterns cover the walls up to the dado which takes the form of a frieze of commemorative quatrefoil plaques. The three-light window in the west wall of the bell tower was made in 1936 by **Leonard Walker**. Local tradition has it that the central figure is an unusual St Chad supported by St Elizabeth of Hungary on his right, strewing flowers before her and St Fina of Gemignano on his left, bearing fruit. It is a very striking window and demonstrates Walker's ability to use the qualities of the glass and lead lines to create form in his work.

Access: Vicarage Tel. 01782–616969.

HOLLINGTON village is on an unclassified road leading from the B5030 south of Rocester to the A522.

St John's (SK060389) was built 1859–61 by **G. E. Street** who also designed the stone pulpit and screen as well as the choir stalls. The apse window, installed in 1861, is very early Clayton & Bell. The fabric displayed on the west wall was designed by **G. E. Street**.

Access: Vicarage Tel. 01889–590424.

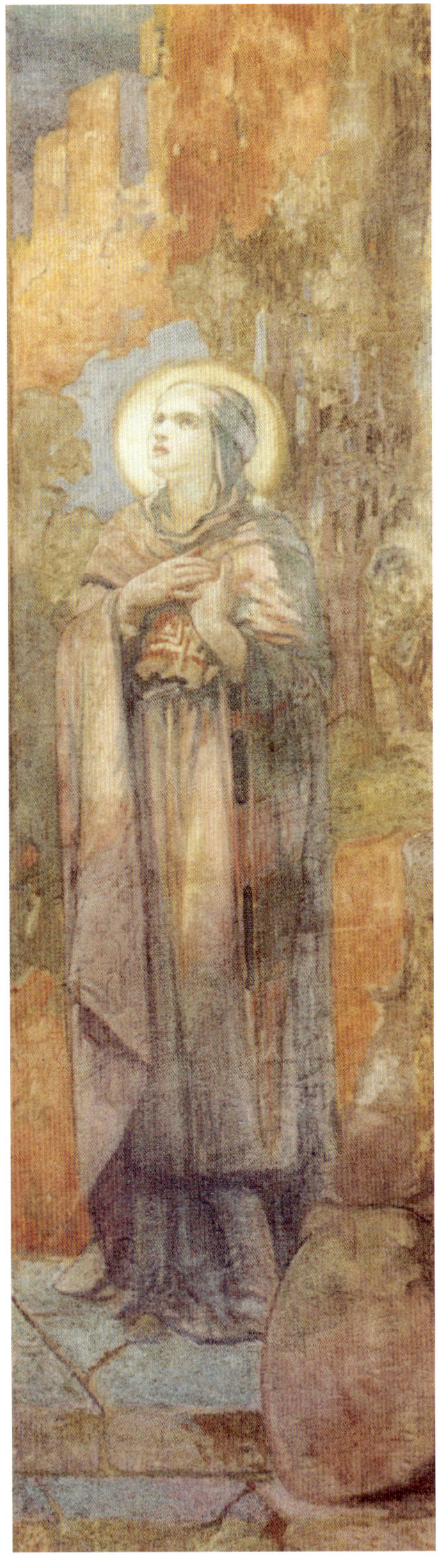

St Leonard's Ipstones. Detail of 'The Annunciation' by James Eadie Reid, 1917.

IPSTONES is on the B5053, about 2 miles south of its junction with the A52, the Leek to Ashbourne road, .

St Leonard's (SK018502) was built in the C18, restored by G. G. Scott in 1877 and given a new chancel designed by **Gerald Horsley** 1902–03. His design for the rood screen is very much of its time but it does not clash with its C18 setting. This setting is enhanced by wall paintings above the chancel arch and on the east wall of the sanctuary. The latter is signed **J. Eadie Reid** 1917 and represents 'The Annunciation' with Gabriel to the left of the east window and Mary to the right. The work above the chancel arch shows 'Christ in Glory' surrounded by his disciples. This is also thought to have been painted by James Eadie Reid. The provenance of the striking stencilled angels filling the space either side of the chancel screen is not known. The church has a number of church embroideries by the **Leek Embroidery Society** some of which were designed by G. G. Scott. Outside, there is a stone crucifix carved above the east window which is also attributed to 'anon'.

Access: Vicarage Tel. 01538–266313.

LEEK is some 9 miles north east of Stoke on Trent on the A53.

All Saints, Compton, (SJ985561) stands at the side of the A520 proclaiming its individuality in a rather solid way. It was built 1885–87 by **Richard Norman Shaw** who declared this to be his best church. It is stone built, with a huge tiled roof and a massive, stubby, central tower. This heavy exterior gives way to a light and bright interior in which the architecture is enhanced by a cornucopia of decorative art.

The seven-leafed reredos, designed by **William Lethaby**, was painted by **F. Hamilton Jackson**. The figures are set against a plain, gilded background and in another place might overwhelm the rest of the chancel decoration. Not so here. Above the reredos is a nine-light east window, by **Morris & Co.** installed in 1923, some 35 years after the reredos, but so appropriate in this setting. The walls and ceiling of the chancel and sanctuary are covered with painted decoration designed and executed by **Gerald Horsley** who also designed and decorated the Bishop's chair and the Credence table. The painting 'Benedicite Omnia Opera', high up on the organ screen, is by **John Edgar Platt** who also painted 'Venantius of Ravenna' hanging on the wall above the steps down to the vestry.

The Lady Chapel has a three-light window by **Morris & Co.** installed in 1887 (Faith, Hope and Charity by Burne-Jones) and a wall painting of 'The Annunciation' by **Gerald Horsley** who also designed the three-light window in the chapel depicting Ss Stephen,

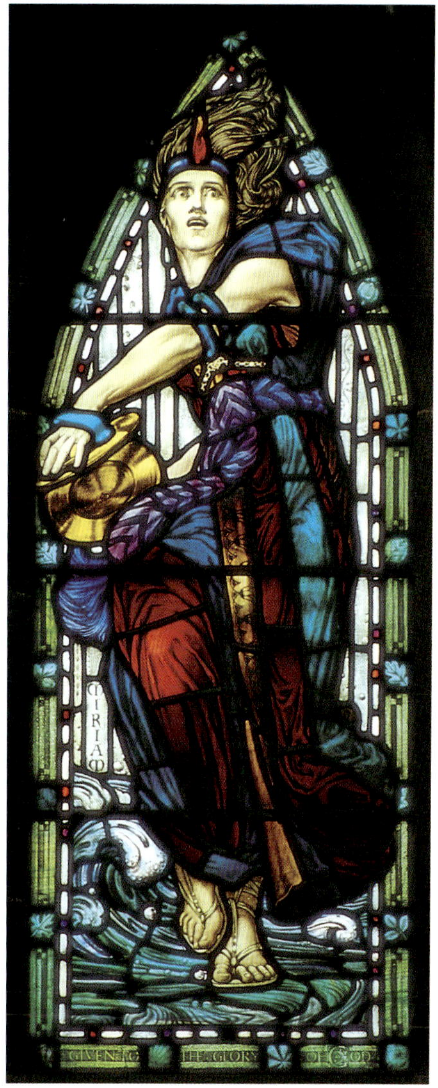

All Saints Leek, 'Miriam' designed by John E. Platt, c. 1912.

Catherine and Alban. The wall painting of St Francis and dozens of birds and animals is by **Edgar and Phoebe Platt** as are 'Adam and Eve', and 'Noah's Ark'. **Edgar Platt** was also responsible for designing the 'Saints of Anglo-Saxon Staffordshire' window in the chapel and the spirited 'Miriam, Esther and Ruth' window in the north aisle which was made at Lowndes and Drury.

The pulpit and font were both designed by **Lethaby** but there is some doubt as to whether he or **Shaw** designed the lectern. The west organ-screen and the woodwork in the Lady Chapel were executed by the local man **William Galton**. The ceramic plaque of St Peter on the south wall and a small stained-glass window in the porch were contributed by **Wooliscroft**. The remaining stained glass in the church is very

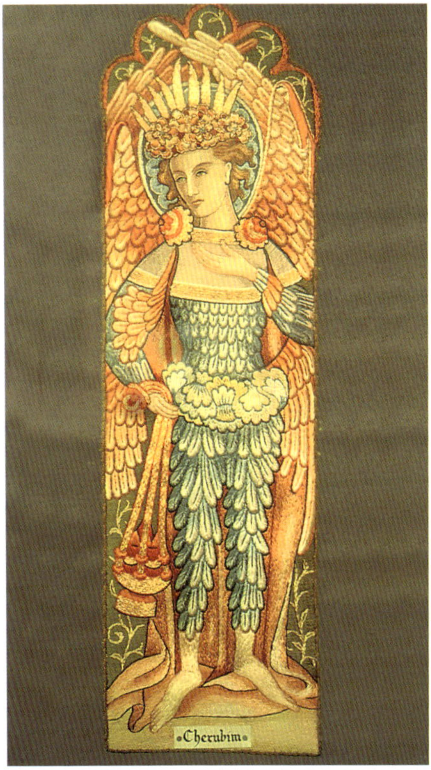

St Edward the Confessor's, Leek. 'Cherubim' Leek Embroidery Society.

late **Morris & Co.** 1934 and 1938. The four-light window in the south aisle is by Duncan Dearle made in 1948 using Burne-Jones's cartoons. This being the home of the **Leek Embroidery Society**, the church has wonderful embroidery including altar frontals designed by **R. N. Shaw** and a funeral pall by **Gerald Horsley**.

Access: Open Wed and Sat 09.00–12.00. Vicarage Tel. 01538–382588.

St Edward the Confessor in Church St (SJ983567) is the ancient Parish Church of Leek and was rebuilt after a fire in 1297. Its Victorian restoration was done 1865–67 by **G. E. Street** who also added a new chancel. He designed the choir stalls, pulpit, lectern, low chancel-screen, the wrought-iron organ-screen and say local sources, the east window. There is much **Morris & Co.** glass in the north and south transepts dated 1902–03 and another three-light window in the south aisle made in 1930. Sewter credits **Bodley** with the design of the stained-glass rose window in the north transept, 1903.

The church has a large collection of the **Leek Embroidery Society's** work and has a permanent display which includes copes, altar frontals, collection bags and other ecclesiastical accoutrements. There are occasional special displays.

Access: Open on Wed, Fri, Sat 9.00–16.00. Parish Office open 10.00–12.00 Mon, Tues, Thurs and Fri. Tel. 01538–388134. Vicarage Tel. 01538–382515.

St Luke's, Queen St (SJ988566) was built in 1847 and the chancel was lengthened in 1873. It has an admirable reredos by **J. D. Sedding** and a well-carved organ screen. The wooden chancel-screen is of an unusual design and has been variously attributed to **Richard Norman Shaw** and **William Lethaby**. The east-most window in the south wall is by **Henry Holiday**. The church has some magnificent work by the **Leek Embroidery Society** designed by **J. D. Sedding** including several altar frontals, pulpit and lectern falls, book marks and alms bags.

Access: Parish Office Tel. 01538–373306 Mon–Fri. 9.00–12.00. Vicarage Tel. 01538–386109.

St John's Mill St (SJ978569) is a red brick, slate roofed church by **W. L. Sugden**. It was built as a small mission church in a freestyle manner in 1875 and enlarged in 1881.

Access: Parish Office Tel. 01538–388134. Mon, Tues, Thurs and Fri 10.00–12.00. Vicarage Tel. 01538–382515.

The Friends' Meeting House, in Overton Bank, (SJ982565) dates from 1694. It was used by the Leek branch of the Socialist League and from 1896, the year in which William Morris died, it was known as 'The William Morris Labour Church'. The interior was decorated with stencilled designs by **Walter Crane**. In 1930 the building reverted to being a Quaker Meeting House and the stencil work was white washed over. A very small portion of Crane's design has been exposed to give an indication of how it used to be.

Access: Tel. 01538–384662.

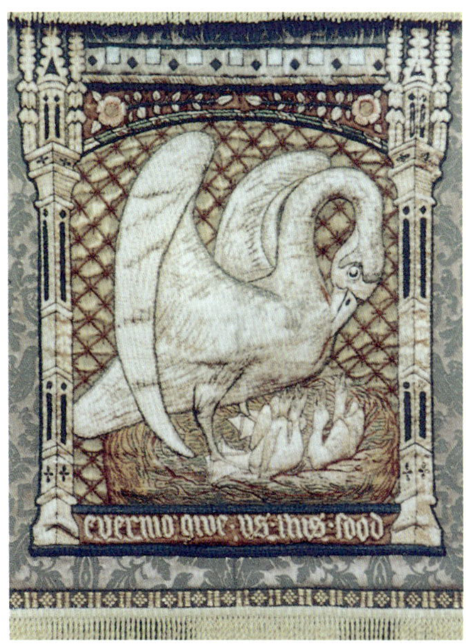

St Luke's, Leek, Detail of an altar frontal designed by J. D. Sedding.

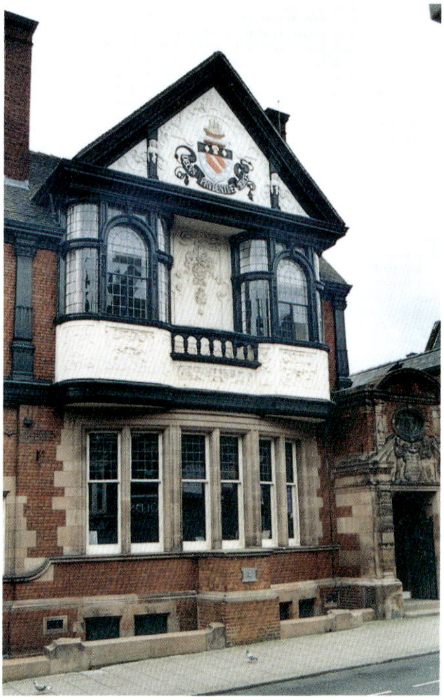

Derby St Leek, Natwest Bank. W. L. Sugden, 1877.

Spout Hall, at 66/68 St Edward St (SJ983564) was built by **Richard Norman Shaw** in 1873 while Nos 58–60 (**Les Hêtres**) also half-timbered, was built ten years later, probably by **William Sugden** of Leek. 54 and 56 St Edward St were home to Thomas and Elizabeth Wardle and the Leek Embroidery Society respectively.

Nicholson Institute, Off Stockwell St (SJ985567) is by **Sugden** 1882–84. It has a domed square tower at the front and relief panels on the walls of the court. The Institute has a small museum featuring examples of the work of the **Leek Embroidery Society**.

The Natwest Bank, once the District Bank, in Derby St (SJ984565) was built by **Sugden** in 1882. Its staircase has a magnificent, unattributed stained-glass window.

The houses **Ferne–Lea, Cranford** and **High Barn** in Fynney St were designed by Reginald Longden, a pupil of **R. N. Shaw** and **33** and **35 Bath St** were built by **William & Larner Sugden**. There is some doubt as to whether **Sugden** or **Shaw** built the **Condlyffe Alms Houses** (SJ984559) near the cemetery off Cheddleton Rd. **Little Hales** out on Buxton Rd 1880 is an example of **W. L. Sugden's** 'picturesque' domestic style.

At the bottom of Derby St is the town's **Great War Memorial** (SJ986565) which takes the form of a clock tower. The Architect was **Percy Worthington** and the decoration was undertaken by the **Birmingham Guild**.

LONGSDON is about 3 miles south west of Leek on the A53.

St Chad's (SJ959547) was built in 1903–05 by **Gerald Horsley** using local stone. It has a rugged exterior and a massive tower. This external ruggedness is transformed into lightness inside by a sureness of touch in the proportions and a willingness to allow the quality of the materials, stone and wood, to speak for themselves. There is little applied decoration. This was not Horsley's intention as can be seen in *Architectural Review* (1906), p. 258 which reproduces his 'Suggested Decoration in Tempera Painting for St Chad's'. The 'suggestion' is reminiscent of his work at Ipstones and at All Saints, Leek. There is some excellent decorative ironwork on the organ shutters and good, if minimal, carving on the organ screen and pulpit. Was it Horsley or his client who chose Comper to provide the stained glass for the east window?

Access: Vicarage Tel. 01538–385318.

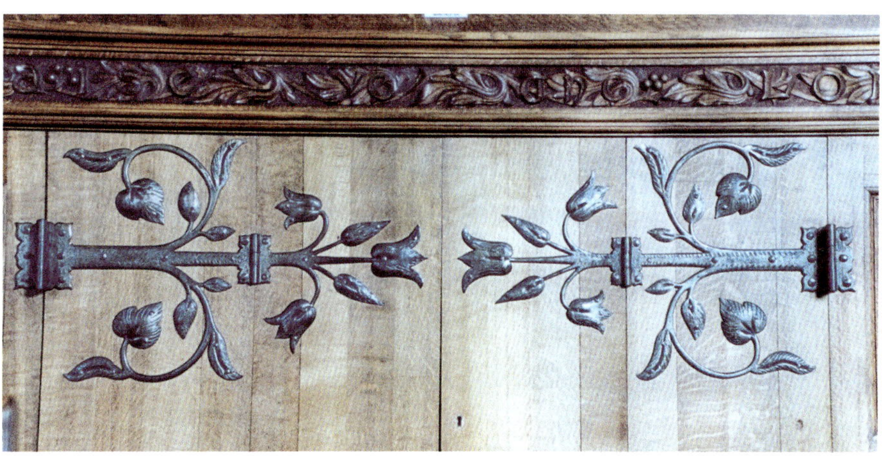

St Chad's, Longsdon. Organ door hinges. Designed by G. Horsley.

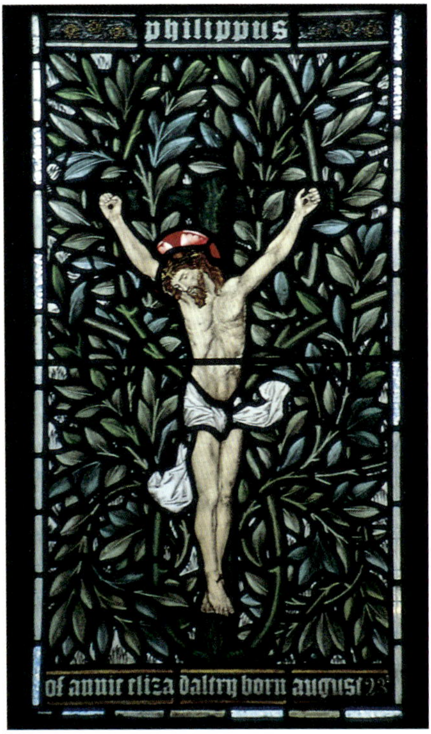

All Saints, Madeley. 'Crucifixion' panel. Morris, Marshall, Faulkner & Co., 1872.

MADELEY lies 5 miles to the west of Newcastle under Lyme on the A525.

All Saints (SJ773444) has been here, subject to enlargement and restoration, since the C12. The three-light window in the west wall at the end of the south aisle is the work of **Morris, Marshall, Faulkner & Co.** from 1872. Noah and Philip by **Madox Brown** and Peter by **Morris**, occupy the upper two thirds of each light. A Crucifixion scene, designed by **Burne-Jones**, occupies the space below St Philip. All the figures are set against a foliage background designed by **William Morris** in sombre shades of green.

Access: Vicarage Tel. 01782–750205.

MEERBROOK is near Tittesworth Reservoir and is signposted off the A523 (2 miles from Leek) and the A53 (3 miles from Leek) .

St Matthew's (SJ989608) was built by **Richard Norman Shaw** 1868–73. The church has less of the originality of All Saints, Leek and looks to **G. E. Street** for its inspiration. The stone pulpit was designed by **Shaw** as was the chancel ironwork, organ case and reredos. The east window is by **Heaton, Butler & Bayne** 1870 and it is said locally that **Shaw** had a hand in its design as he did in the design of the church embroideries.

Access: Vicarage Tel. 01538–382588.

ONECOTE is about 5 miles east of Leek as the crow flies and 2 miles north of the A52 on the B5053.

St Luke's (SK048552) is a small and simple C18 church much enhanced by the gift of a set of secular stained-glass panels. They were made in 1863 by **Morris, Marshall, Faulkner & Co.** for Onecote vicarage and were moved here in the mid 1970s. The three panels, 'Ploughing, Reaping and Sowing' now in the east window, came from the dining room and were designed by **Burne-Jones, Morris** and **Madox Brown** respectively. A. C. Sewter suggests they were adapted from designs made in 1862–63 for a set of twelve tiles, each representing a month of the year. There are, in addition, five roundels from the vicarage drawing-room windows which show the heads of King David, Homer, Chaucer, St Cecilia and Queen Penelope. They were all made from cartoons by **Burne-Jones** and were fixed here in their original surrounding quarries. The King David roundel and the three panels in the east window are unique.

Access: Vicarage Tel. 01538–266313.

ROCESTER is on the B5030 about 4 miles north of Uttoxeter.

St Michael's (SK112394) is one of only five churches with stained-glass windows by **William De Morgan**. The east window was made in 1872, and is currently attributed by the Church to De Morgan. It is a large window with two panels in each of its five lights. The bottom row shows, from left to right, 'The Annunciation', 'The Visit to Elizabeth', 'The Nativity', 'The Flight into Egypt' and 'The

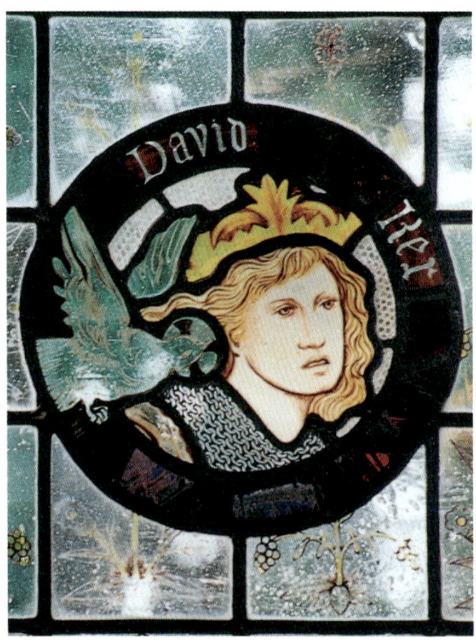

St Luke's Onecot. 'David Rex' designed by Burne-Jones for Morris, Marshall, Faulkner & Co., 1863.

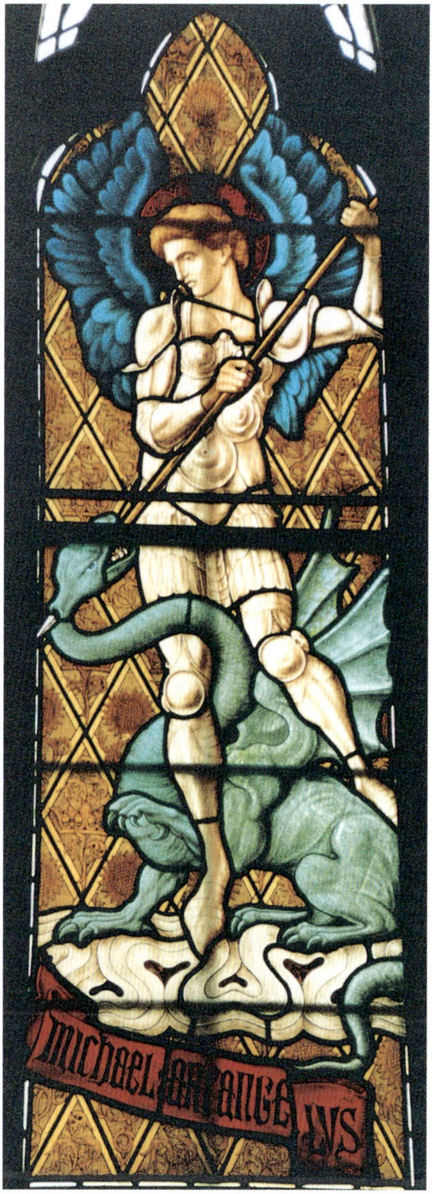

St Michael's, Rocester. Detail 'St Michael' window. William De Morgan, c. 1872.

Presentation in the Temple'. The top row begins on the left with 'Christ in the Garden of Gethsemane', 'The Presentation of Christ to the Crowd', 'The Crucifixion', 'The Deposition from the Cross' and 'The Resurrection'.

In the vestry is a magnificent single-light window, which is more recognisably by De Morgan. It shows St Michael slaying his dragon against a background of diamond shaped quarries bearing stylised sunflowers and other plant forms. It is unsigned and undated but the dragon in particular is so fantastic it could have walked off a De Morgan tile or charger.

The west-most window in the south wall, depicting 'Christ in Glory', was made in 1935 by Rope & Parr of Northampton. On the north side, third from the west end is a two-light window depicting Mary of Bethany and Lazarus. It is signed DN, or is it DM and yet another **De Morgan** window? Unlikely we think.

Access: Vicarage Tel. 01889–590357.

TUNSTALL is in the north-west corner of the Potteries centred, more or less, on the junction of the A50 and the A527.

Sacred Heart in Queen's Avenue, (SJ864513) was built 1925–30 by **J. S. Brocklesby** in the Romanesque manner with three and a half green copper domes. The domes and the church's two towers, one large and square the other small and round, catch the eye from miles away. Internally it has a nave, two aisles, an apse and an ambulatory and all is brightness and light. There are many windows but little stained glass. Such stained glass as there is, apart from one light by **Abbott & Co.** of Lancaster, is by **Gordon Forsyth**. The Lady Chapel has a small apse on the north side of which is a tall, narrow lancet window which has a slender Gabriel appearing to the Virgin Mary who is seen kneeling in another lancet on the opposite side of the apse.

The main apse has five attractive stained-glass windows high up above the ambulatory. The central light shows a pelican, symbol of self sacrifice, with an angel in each of the lights on either side. Forsyth has used very small pieces of glass and given his angels elongated figures with large hands and small heads. The first and fifth lights show the symbols of the Evangelists surrounded by entrelac work.

The quality of the woodwork in the pews, the nave and the choir is exceptional as is the carved decoration to the pew ends and the choir stall fronts. This work was also designed by **Forsyth** and, it is said, executed by volunteers during the 'Depression'.

Access: Presbytery Tel. 01782–838357.

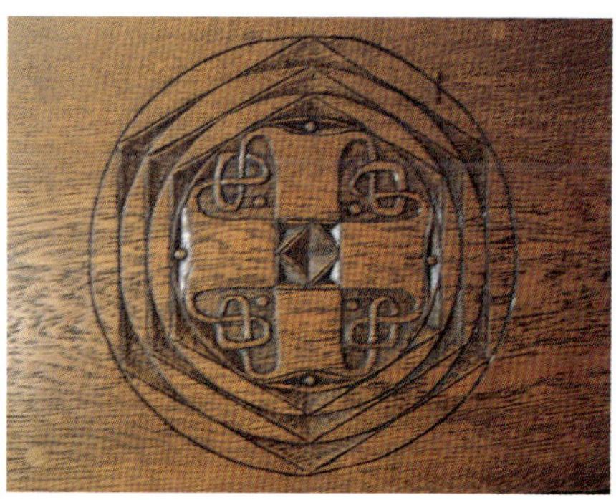

Sacred Heart, Tunstall. Bench end decoration, c. 1930.

WHO'S WHO

In this biographical index are all the artists and craftsmen who have links with the Arts and Crafts Movement and whose work is identified in the gazetteer. Because of space constraints we have only been able to include those fine-art artists who have also executed decorative art in the North West.

KEY

AG	Art Gallery & Museum
CU	Cumbria
GM	Greater Manchester
JRLib	John Rylands Library
LA	Lancashire
Lib	Library
L'pool C	Central Liverpool
M/cc	Central Manchester
MS	Merseyside
Mus	Museum only
NS	North Staffordshire
TH	Town Hall
WAG	The Walker, Liverpool
WhAG	Whitworth Art Gallery
MMULib	Manchester Metropolitan University Library
UMIST	University of Manchester Institute of Science & Technology
Uni	University

ABBREVIATIONS

AA	Architectural Association
ARA	Associate of the Royal Academy
AR	Architectural Review
ARIBA	Associate of Royal Institute of Architects
AWG	Art Workers Guild
BSMGP	British Society of Master Glass Painters
FRIBA	Fellow of the Royal Institute of Architects
JBSMGP	Journal of the British Society of Master Glass Painters
PRO	Public Records Office
RA	Royal Academy
RCA	Royal College of Art
RIBAJ	Royal Institute of British Architects Journal
RSA	Royal Scottish Academy

Abbott & Co. of Lancaster
Stained-glass makers. Little has been published about the activities of the firm but some of its records are held at the PRO at Preston. A firm of this name was established in Lancaster in 1860 but it is not clear when it started making stained glass. They are first recorded as stained glass and leaded-light manufacturers in *Bulmer's Directory* of 1913. The style and quality of their work like many another with Arts and Crafts affiliations, appears to have varied in proportion to their patrons' demands, but at their best they produced splendid windows particularly in the years leading up to the Great War and in the immediate post-war years.

See: **CU:** Tebay **LA:** Blackpool, Lytham St Annes **GM:** Wigan **MS:** Huyton **NS:** Tunstall.

Ref: Edwards, Margaret, *The Studios of Lancaster's Artists in Stained Glass* (Lancaster Museums 1983)

Adams, Maurice Bingham (1849–1933)
Architect & writer. He trained in Brighton where he was for a time architect to the Borough Council. In 1872, aged 23, he was appointed editor of the *Building News* which was owned by the philanthropist, J. Passmore Edwards. Adams went on to design a number of Free Libraries for Passmore Edwards and Carnegie. From 1875 he lived in Bedford Park where he designed some houses, the Church Hall and the School of Art. He also supervised the building of R. N. Shaw's (qv) St Michael and All Angels church. He designed fireplaces for the Coalbrookdale Company and architectural terracotta and faience for Burmantofts (qv).

See: **MS:** Port Sunlight (2)

Ref: Obit. *Builder* (25.08.33), pp. 295–300; *RIBAJ* (9.9.33), pp. 814–15

Adams, W. Naseby (1887–1952)
Architect. Born in Liverpool he was the eldest son of the Vicar of St Augustine's, Everton. He studied at the Liverpool School of Architecture under C. H. Reilly (qv) and began his career with Briggs and Wolstenholme, moving on to Hobbs and Thornley before setting up in partnership with Duncan Campbell in about 1912. He saw action in WW1 and was wounded but was able to resume his career. By 1920 he was working in London as chief assistant to E. L. Lutyens (qv).

See: **MS:** Port Sunlight

Ref: *Who's Who in Architecture*, 1926; Obit. *Builder*, 183, (1952), p. 134; *RIBAJ* (Sept 1952), p. 425

Aikman, William (1868–1959)
Stained-glass worker. Aikman was born in Edinburgh into a family of artists and craftsmen. His father was George Aikman the landscape painter. After an apprenticeship at Ballantine's, a major stained-glass firm in Edinburgh, he travelled to London in 1892 and joined James Powell & Son. There, he worked in close collaboration with James Powell and J. W. Brown (qv) and assisted Sir William Richmond with his mosaics in St Paul's Cathedral. In 1913 he left Powell to set up his own studio at 7 Camden Square, London NW1. Aikman taught stained-glass work for a number of years at the Camberwell School of Art after WW1 and in 1934 he moved to Sutton, Surrey where he worked until his death aged 91. He exhibited designs for stained glass at the RA on nineteen occasions 1893–1941. He was a founder member of the BSMGP and was elected to the AWG in 1931.

See: **CU** Mealsgate, Watermillock
GM: Monton, Wigan **MS :** Caldy, Hoylake, Wallasey

Ref: Obit. *JBSMGP*, 13, no. 1 (1959–60)

Allen, Charles John (1862–1956)
Figure sculptor. Born at Greenford, Middlesex and educated at Palace School, Enfield. He was apprenticed to Farmer and Brindley (qv) in 1887 and studied at Lambeth School of Art and the RA Schools. He was employed as a carver in stone and wood at Farmer and Brindley until 1889 when he left to become chief assistant to Hamo Thorneycroft (qv) and George Frampton (qv). From 1894 he taught sculpture at Liverpool University's School of Architecture and Applied Art, and from 1905 he was Vice-Principal of the Liverpool Municipal School of Art. Much of Allen's work was executed in Liverpool. He was elected to the AWG in 1894 and won the Gold medal for Sculpture at the Paris Exhibition in 1900.

See: **LA:** Rochdale AG **MS:** Eastham, L'pool C(4) + WAG + Uni.AG, Uni.Lib,+ campus(5) Sefton Park, Toxteth

Ref: Cavanagh, Terry, *Public Sculpture of Liverpool*, 1997; Clough, Matthew H, ed., *C. J. Allen 1862–1956, Sculptor and Teacher*, 2003

Allen, James Milner (fl. 1861–1900)
Stained-glass artist. He was chief designer for the stained-glass firm Lavers and Barraud *c.* 1861–*c.* 1867. His work is described by Martin Harrison as 'distinctive' being 'robust, romantic medieval in character'. He is known to have worked as a free-lance artist for Heaton Butler & Bayne and for Shrigley & Hunt (qv) 1875–83.

See: **CU:** Broughton in Furness **GM:** Rochdale TH

Ref: Harrison, *Victorian Stained Glass*, 1980; Walters, *Stained Glass from Shrigley & Hunt*, 2003

Almquist, Carl (1848–1924)
Stained-glass artist. Almquist was born in Sweden and came to London in 1870 to study stained-glass work before setting up a studio in Stockholm. He never returned to Sweden and after four years working in London, as assistant to Henry Holiday (qv), he joined the newly-formed Lancaster firm of Shrigley and Hunt (qv). He spent the next forty years as their chief designer. He lived in Lancaster until 1878 but returned to London when the firm opened an office and showroom there. His style, particularly in the early part of his career shows the influence of his mentor, Henry Holiday. Inevitably though, his designs were often a reflection of the stylistic demands of the firm's clients. By 1920, losing his sight, he had moved from London to Hove where he died in 1924.

See: **CU:** Barbon, Bardsea, Kirkby Lonsdale
LA: Garstang, Lancaster, Over Wyredale
MS: Great Crosby

Ref: Lövgren, B. R. 'Carl Almquist His Life & Work', *JBSMGP*, 21, no. 10, 1997

Amschewitz, Jacob/John Henry (1882–1943)
Portrait painter, muralist, etcher, illustrator and cartoonist. He was born at Ramsgate of Polish parents. He studied at the RA Schools and won a prize for mural decoration. He exhibited at the RA from 1904. In 1908 he won first and second place in the Liverpool Pageant Memorial Competition. He worked in South Africa (1916–22) then returned to London for some years before returning to Johannesburg. He was elected to the AWG in 1925.

See: **MS:** L'pool C, TH

Ref: Waters, *Dictionary of British Artists*, 1975

Anderson, W. M. (fl. *c.* 1910)
Designer. He is credited with the design of one of the George Wragge Ltd windows at Timperley Church.

See: **GM:** Timperley

Ref: Salford Library archives, *Local contemporary Press*

Armitage, George Faulkner (1849–1937)
Woodworker, designer, architect. He was born at Longsight into the nonconformist family of one of Manchester's Cotton Kings. When he was three, his family moved to Altrincham and he was educated privately in Bowdon and Manchester. He travelled widely, studying and working in woodworking shops and studios in England, France, Switzerland and Italy. By 1873 he had returned to Altrincham where he started his business in his parents' house. By 1878 he had entered into partnership with his brother Joseph and a cousin, John Rigby, setting up the Stamford workshop and studio in Church St, Altrincham. The firm provided a comprehensive decoration and furnishing service, much on the lines of Morris & Co. The business was very successful in executing Armitage's designs in wood, metal, plasterwork and embroidered textiles. They exhibited widely and undertook commissions in England and on the Continent. There were showrooms in Manchester and London. In 1887 Armitage was commissioned to design and decorate the central dome and nave of the Manchester Jubilee Exhibition Hall; in which connection he must have worked closely with Ford Madox Brown (qv). The firm survived beyond Armitage's retirement in 1911. Arthur Simpson (qv) of Kendal spent 3 years 1882–85 in Armitage's studio and workshop and architect Barry Parker was articled to Armitage from 1889 to 1893. The Isle of Man architect, Armitage Rigby was the brother-in-law of G. F. Armitage and managed the Altrincham Office 1887–89. Armitage's chief recreations were said to be golf and cycling and he had a bowling green in his own back garden.

See: **CU:** Hawkshead **GM:** Altrincham, Bramhall **CH:** Chester

Ref: Allwood, Rosamond, *George Faulkner Armitage, Furniture History* 23, 1987; Collingwood, Gillian 'George Faulkner Armitage–Cumbrian Connections', *Quarto*, April 1996; Obit. *Altrincham Guardian* (12 Nov 1937), p. 10

Armstead, Henry Hugh (1828–1905)
Sculptor. Trained at the Royal College of Art and became chief designer for the gold and silversmiths Hunt and Roskell. He then changed tack and concentrated on portrait and figure sculptor, funerary monuments and memorials working in marble, bronze and wood. He contributed a frieze to the Albert Memorial in London and amongst many other commissions executed the beautiful angel lectern at Holy Trinity, Sloane St, London.

See: **CU:** Carlisle **MS:** Warrington

Ref: Waters, *Dictionary of British Artists*, 1975

Arnold, Hugh (1872–1915)
Stained-glass artist. He studied at the Slade School of Art in the 1890s and moved to the Central School where he was trained by Christopher Whall (qv). He set up his own studio but had his windows made-up in collaboration with Lowndes and Drury. His work tended to be restrained but he enjoyed using thick slab glass. He was elected to the AWG in 1902 and in 1913 published *Mediaeval Glass in England and France* which was illustrated by L. B. Saint. Arnold volunteered for active service in the Great War and was killed at Gallipoli at the age of 43.

See: **CU:** Kirkby-in-Furness, Millom, Wythburn

Ref: *Hugh Arnold: An account of the special meeting held March 31 1916, by the Art Workers' Guild.* Ely Stained-Glass Museum, Display information

Artificers' Guild (fl. 1901–42)
Metalworkers. The Guild was founded in Chiswick, London in 1901 by Nelson Dawson and Edward Spencer who worked in Dawson's workshop. They produced a wide range of metalwork: forged and wrought iron, silver, brass and bronze. In 1903 the Guild was bought by Montague Fordham, who had been a director of the Birmingham Guild of Handicraft but was by this date running his own Fordham Gallery in Maddox St, London. Dawson left the Guild and Edward Spencer became its chief designer. Many leading artists were represented at this very successful Gallery, including John Paul Cooper and Henry Wilson, who exerted some influence on the Guild's designers. The Gallery was moved later to Conduit St and continued in business until 1942.

See: **LA:** Downham **MS:** L'pool C TH, Wallasey

Ref: Karlin, E. Z., *Jewelry and Metalwork in the Arts and Crafts Tradition* (1993)

Ashbee, Charles R. (1863–1942)
Architect, designer, educator, social reformer and a huge influence on the development of the Arts and Crafts movement. Ashbee trained as an architect with G. F. Bodley (qv) and at the same time established the Guild of Handicraft in the east end of London. He designed and built a small number of houses, the most notable being in Cheyne Walk, Chelsea, where he began his practice in 1890. He lived at No. 37 Cheyne Walk which he built for his mother. In 1898 he set up the Essex Press with men and equipment from the defunct Kelmscott Press and added the production of fine printing and binding to his accomplishments. In 1906–09 he designed model cottages in Ellesmere Port having previously done work for the same client at Dudley. He wrote extensively on design-related topics, travelled to America on lecture tours and worked as a planner and conservationist in Jerusalem 1919–22, under the British Mandate. Ashbee was elected to the AWG in 1897 and became Master in 1929.

See **LA**: Turton Tower **GM:** M/cc MMULib. **MS:** Ellesmere Port

Ref: Crawford, Alan, *C. R. Ashbee*, 1985; Obit. *RIBAJ* (June 1942), p. 134; *Builder* (29.5.1942), p. 476

Ashendene Press (1894–1935)
C. H. St John Hornby, a director of W. H. Smith set up a hand press in his home in Ashendene, Hertfordshire inspired by Morris's Kelmscott Press. It moved to Shelley House in Chelsea in 1900. The Press produced forty titles in total many of which were printed using 'Subiaco', a type designed by Emery Walker and Sydney Cockerell. Many books were decorated with woodcut initials designed by Eric Gill (qv), Graily Hewitt or Louise Powell.

See: **GM:** M/cc Libs, **MS:** L'pool C Lib, Uni Lib

Ref: Cave, R., *The Private Presses* 1983

Aumonier, William & Sons
Architectural carvers. The family firm was established by William Aumonier senior (1839–1914). He trained with Alfred Stevens at Colman & Davis in George St, London W1 and then studied in Paris and worked for Viollet le Duc on the restoration of Amiens Cathedral. He did the carving at the Horniman Museum, Forest Hill for C. Harrison Townsend and the sedilias and faldstools for St Paul's Cathedral. He became a member of the AWG in 1895. His son William (b. 1870) attended the West London School of Art after which he joined the family firm and took over the reins in 1913. Father and son worked on many prestigious modelling and carving projects including the Birmingham Law Courts, Bath Municipal Buildings and Oxford Town Hall. William junior joined the AWG in 1913 and wrote *Modern Architectural Sculpture* 1930.

See: **CU:** Crosby on Eden **GM:** Prestwich

Ref: Gray, A. S., *Edwardian Architecture*, 1985; Spalding, F., *Dictionary of British Art* 6, 1990; *Census 1901*; Obit. *RIBAJ* (14.2.1914), p. 239; *Builder* (30.1.1914), p. 143

Baines, George (1852–1934)
Architect. Articled to J. Bottle and Henry Olley of Yarmouth, he was assistant to W. G. Habershon and to Alfred Robert Pite for a year. He set up his own practice at Post Office Chambers, Accrington, Lancs. in 1871 and specialised in non-conformist churches. He had an office in London from 1884. In 1901 his son, Reginald, joined him in the practice, and together they were responsible for some 200 nonconformist commissions, which they executed in a wide variety of styles.

See: **MS:** Great Crosby

Ref: Obit. *RIBAJ*, 41 (1934), p. 659; *Builder*, 146 (23.03.1934), p. 494

Ball, Joseph Lancaster (1852–1933)
Architect. Born in Maltby Yorkshire, he was articled to W. W. Pocock in London and established his practice in Birmingham, where he is best known for his collaboration with W. R. Lethaby on the former Eagle Star Insurance Building 122–24 Colmore Row, 1900. He was Director of the Birmingham School of Architecture 1909–16.

See: **Cu:** Windermere

Ref: Gray, A. S., *Edwardian Architecture*, 1985; Obit. *RIBAJ*, 41 (24.2.1924), pp. 418–19; *Builder* 145 (15.12.1933), p. 958

W. Ball & T. B. Elce (fl. 1886)
Architects. William Ball and his partner Thomas B. Elce were both born in Manchester in 1856 and 1853, respectively. No information has come to light about their training or early careers. They built the first stage of the Manchester Corn Exchange in 1897 and T. B. Elce designed Mynshull's House in Cateaton St, Manchester. Some of their work, including St John's Church at Silverdale, Black Friars pub in Salford and the alterations at Pownall Hall, Wilmslow, was commissioned by Boddingtons, the Manchester brewing family.

See: **LA:** Silverdale **CH:** Wilmslow

Ref: *PRO archive material* M/c Central Library; Hartwell, C., *Pevsner Architectural Guide on Manchester*, 2001; S. Evans 'A. H. Mackmurdo and the Century Guild', Thesis, 1986; *Census 1901*.

Balmer, Clinton (fl. 1901–1909)
Artist and book Illustrator. He trained at the Municipal School of Art in Mount Street, Liverpool and studied figure drawing under Augustus John at the Liverpool University College. He exhibited at the Walker Art Gallery in Liverpool 1901–09 but lived in London in the early years of the C20. He later moved to New York where he became an illustrator.

See: **CU:** Carlisle AG **MS:** Toxteth

Ref: *The Studio*, 30 (1904), p. 68; Tullie House *Pre-Raphaelites & Beyond*, Catalogue, 2001

Bankart George Percy (1866–1929)
Architect and artist in ornamental plaster and lead work. Born in Leicester where he attended Wyggeston Grammar School and Leicester School of Art and Technical College. In 1883, still in Leicester, he was articled to the architect Isaac Barradale where Ernest Gimson was a fellow pupil. He then worked in various architects' offices. In 1897 he returned to Leicester to work as an instructor in plaster work at Leicester School of Art and in 1899 he joined the Bromsgrove Guild in Worcestershire. He modelled, designed and executed all the plaster and lead work for the Guild until 1907. By 1908 he had set up his own very successful workshop in Gray's Inn Road WC1 from where he promoted his special style of plasterwork (based on the C17 and C18 work at places like Haddon Hall). His largest commission was for all the decorative plasterwork at the Victoria &

Albert Museum for Aston Webb but his services were much sought after and he worked for most of the leading architects of the day up to the time of the Great War. He was elected to the AWG in 1900. He published *The Art of the Plasterer* in 1908 and three other works 1926–27.

See: **GM:** M/c Cath.

Ref: Gray, A. S., *Edwardian Architecture*, 1985; Watt, Q., ed. *The Bromsgrove Guild*, 1999; Obit, *Builder*, (19.4.1929), p. 719

Banks, Thomas Lewis (1842–1920)
Architect. Born in Cockermouth, Cumbria and articled to James Glode Stapleton from 1860. He travelled on the continent 1869–70 before setting up his own practice in London and Whitehaven in 1871. He was in partnership with Charles Harrison Townsend 1884–88.

See: **CU:** Egremont, Eskdale

Ref: *RIBA Directory* 2001; Obit. *Builder*, 214 (3.5.1968), p. 76; *RIBAJ* 27 (1920), p. 391

Bare, Henry Bloomfield (ob.1912)
Architect and metal worker. He was a pupil of C. E Giles 1861–63 and assistant to Thomas J. Willson and Samuel J. Nichol. He subsequently worked for William Baker, railway engineer on the L&NWR 1866–76, after which he established his own practice in Liverpool designing, altering and decorating many houses in the Merseyside area. He was in partnership with Henry Langton Beckwith from *c.* 1886 and was made FRIBA in 1888 – proposed by G. E. Grayson (qv). In 1891 he went to Philadelphia where he developed a residential practice and returned in 1895 to resume his practice in Liverpool. He also took up designing and executing repoussé metalwork, attending evening classes at the School of Applied Art under R. Ll. Rathbone (qv) *c.* 1900. He and his wife were members of the Positivist Church of Humanity, which had opened in 1883 in Falkland St, Liverpool. It is said that he had a metalwork studio in Port Sunlight village. Bloomfield Bare was a founder of the Liverpool Architectural Society and was an occasional Liverpool correspondent of *The Studio*.

See: **MS:** L'pool C, Port Sunlight

Ref: Obit. *Builder*, 102 (26.1.1912), p. 108; FRIBA nomination papers

Barkentin and Krall
Art metalworkers and goldsmiths. Jes Barkentin, of Danish descent, was already established in Regent St when he was joined *c.* 1873 by German born Carl Christopher Krall (*c.* 1844–1924). Barkentin and then Barkentin and Krall produced a number of remarkable silver and silver-mounted objects usually richly decorated with gems and enamels which had been designed by William Burges (qv). They also executed much of J. D. Sedding's (qv) and Henry Wilson's (qv) church metal work during the 1870s and 80s. Krall was elected to the AWG in 1885.

See: **CH:** Chester Cath.

Ref: Culme, J., *Directory of Gold and Silversmiths*, 1987

Barnish, Frederick Jardine (b. 1879)
Architect. Trained at Liverpool University School of Architecture. Fellow of the Liverpool Architectural Society. He was working in Warrington in 1926.

See: **MS:** Port Sunlight

Ref: RIBA *Directory*, 2001

Barrowclough and Sanders (fl. *c.*1920)
Stained-glass artists. The firm operated from Greaves Studios in Lancaster. Allen Barrowclough was born in Althorpe, Essex in 1881 and by 1901 he was living and working in Lancaster where he trained with Shrigley & Hunt. It is not known how he came to meet and enter into business with Joseph Newbold Sanders, who was born in Birmingham in 1886. Sanders was trained in stained-glass work at the Birmingham School of Art under Henry Payne (qv) with whom he worked at Madresfield Court. By 1906 he had joined A. J. Davies (qv) at the Bromsgrove Guild (qv) stained-glass workshop and worked there until 1914 when he joined up with the Artists Rifles and went off to the Great War. Post-war, he set up his studio in Lancaster and by 1920 was in partnership with Allen Barrowclough. They produced a curious but satisfying amalgam of the styles of Henry Payne, A. J. Davies and Shrigley & Hunt. Their work is not catalogued and nothing has been published on the history of the firm.

See: **LA:** Lancaster, Longton, Nelson

Ref: Edwards, M., *The Studios of Lancaster's Artists in Stained Glass*; *1901 Census*; Watt, Q., *The Bromsgrove Guild*, 1999

Bates, Harry (1850–99)
Sculptor. Born in Stevenage, Herts. He began work as an architect's clerk then 1869–*c.* 1879 he was first apprenticed to and then worked as a stone carver at Brindley & Farmer (qv). He attended the Lambeth School of Art, where he was taught briefly by Jules Dalou before progressing to the RA Schools in 1881. He won a travelling scholarship in 1883 and spent two years in Paris where he met up again with Dalou and with Rodin who is said to have influenced his work. He became a leading light in the New Sculpture movement and worked in London for the remainder of his career, producing both statues and relief panels. He exhibited widely in England and at the Glasgow Institute of Fine Art. He was elected to the AWG in 1887.

See: **MS:** Mossley Hill AG

Ref: Beattie, S., *The New Sculpture*, 1983

Bayes, Gilbert (1872–1933)
Sculptor. Born in London he was the son of an artist. From 1891–95 he attended evening classes at the City and Guilds School in Finsbury. In 1896 he attended the RA Schools where he was taught by some of the most prestigious sculptors of the day. His mentor, George Frampton, had a great influence on his work. He was a successful student winning numerous medals and a travelling scholarship which took him to Italy and Paris. Bayes was at the centre of the New Sculpture movement. His work had great diversity in style, materials, techniques and subject matter. It was often highly decorative and incorporated both symbolism and naturalism. He produced a vast range of work, not only figures, groups and war memorials but applied work which included anything from presentation cups to door fittings and stained glass. He worked in an equally wide range of materials including metals, stone, wood, plaster and ceramics. During the 1920s and 30s he used Doulton's polychrome stoneware for many of his most dramatic pieces. He was a member of the AWG and its Master in 1925.

See: **LA:** Preston AG **MS:** L'pool WAG, Port Sunlight

Ref: Irvine & Atterbury, *Gilbert Bayes Sculptor*, 1998

Bell, Robert Anning (1863–1933)
Painter of figure subjects, portraits, landscapes and religious works in oil and water colour. He was also a book illustrator and designed book plates, mosaics, stained glass and coloured bas-reliefs. Born in Soho, he was educated at University College School, London and then articled for two years in the London office of his architect uncle. In 1881 he entered the RA Schools and went on to study at the Westminster School of Art and in Paris under Aimé Morot. His mosaics adorn the main porch of Westminster Cathedral, the House of Lords, the front of the Horniman Museum, Forest Hill and the north front of Birmingham University. He designed fabrics for Morris & Co. and wallpapers for Essex and Co. while his stained glass and painted gesso-work is to be found up and down the country. He was an instructor in painting and drawing at the Department of Architecture and Applied Art at Liverpool University 1894–98 and Professor of Decorative Art at Glasgow School of Art from 1911. He became Professor of Design at the RCA 1918–24. He was elected to the AWG in 1891 and was Master in 1921. In *Who's Who* he gave his hobbies as 'gardening and conversations with C. F. Annesley Voysey'(qv).

See: **GM:** Atherton, M/cc AGs & Libs **MS:** Bidston, L'pool C WAG +(2), Mossley Hill AG, Port Sunlight AG, Sefton Park **CH:** Parkgate

Ref: Rose, P., *The Coloured Relief Decoration of Robert Anning Bell, DASJ*, no. 14, 1990; Obit. *RIBA* (29.12.1933), pp. 201–02; *Builder* (1.12.33), p. 857. Obit. *JBSMGP*, 5 (1934)

Bennett, Reuben (b1849)
Decorator and stained-glass artist. By 1894 Bennett was advertising his firm as painters and decorators of churches, residences and public buildings, with premises at 53 South King St Manchester. By 1898 he had added stained glass to the firm's services and taken additional premises at 20 South King St. In 1899 the stained-glass business moved to Mount Clifton. This development of the business appears to coincide with the arrival in the firm of H. G. Hiller (qv). The firm's work has not been catalogued.

See: **GM:** Bolton, Kearsley, Norris Bank
CH: Nantwich

Ref: *Slater's Manchester, Salford and Suburban Directory*, 1894, 1898, 1899

Benson, William Arthur Smith (1854–1924)
Architect, designer and metalworker. Born in London and educated at Winchester and New College Oxford. He was articled to Basil Champneys (qv) until 1880 when, encouraged by William Morris (qv), he set up a metalworking shop at Chiswick. He opened showrooms at 82–83 New Bond St where he displayed a range of domestic utensils, mainly in copper and brass. His innovative designs for the new electric light fittings earned him a great reputation. He supplied not only the domestic market but colleges, cathedrals and churches. Standen in East Grinstead, Sussex designed by Philip Webb (qv) contains the original electric lighting designed and supplied by Benson. He also designed furniture for Morris & Co. and Henry & Co., wall papers for Morris and grates and fireplaces for Coalbrookedale and the Falkirk Iron Co. However he designed few houses one of which was his own house, Windleshawe in Withyam, Sussex. Benson was a founder member of the Arts and Crafts Exhibition Society in 1888 and a member of the AWG from 1894. He was also involved with the Home Arts and Industries Association.

See: **GM:** M/c City AG & MMU Lib.

Ref: Gray, A. S., *Edwardian Architecture*, 1985; Rose, P., 'William Arthur Smith Benson: a pioneer designer of light fittings', in *DASJ*, no. 9, 1985.

Bentley John Francis (1840–1902)
Architect and designer of stained glass, church furnishings and fittings, wallpapers and textiles. Born in Doncaster and educated privately he had a practical early training with engineering and building firms. Bentley became an improver in the office of Henry Clutton until 1860. The same year he converted to Catholicism and in 1862 set up his own practice at 14 Southampton St, Strand. He received many commissions for churches, church fittings and furnishings including the Church of the Holy Rood,

Watford. His major work was Westminster Cathedral. He was elected to the AWG in 1889. His career is documented in two volumes by his daughter Winifrid de l'Hôpital in her book *Westminster Cathedral and its Architect*, which was published in 1919.

See: **CU:** Kirkbride, Shap **GM:** M/cc

Ref: Gray, A. S., *Edwardian Architecture*, 1985; Anson, P., *Fashion in Church Furnishings*, 1960; Obit. *RIBAJ* (8.3.1902), p. 219 and *RIBAJ* (26.7.1902), pp. 437–41; *Builder* (8.3.1902), pp. 228–29, 243–44 and *Builder* (15.3.1902), p. 258

Beswick, Henry (1856–1926)
Architect. Chester born and bred. He was articled to T. M. Lockwood (qv) in 1871 and later returned to his office as an assistant. He commenced independent practice 1889 and was Cheshire County Architect from 1896.

See: **MS:** Port Sunlight **CH:** Chester Cath.

Ref: RIBA *Directory of British Architects*, 2001

Bewsey, John C. (ob. 3.2.1940)
Architect and stained-glass artist who trained in the Kempe Studios and was associated with Shrigley & Hunt 1904–09. He exhibited at the RA on nine occasions and three times at the RSA 1906–22 He often worked in association with Robert Lorimer after the Great War.

See: **LA:** Fleetwood **CH:** Davenham, Moulton

Ref: Waters, W., *Stained Glass from Shrigley & Hunt*, p. 57

Birkett, J. (fl. 1880)
Metalworker. Birkett was a jeweller in Keswick who became an instructor in metalwork at the Keswick School of Industrial Arts in 1886. He was responsible for executing many of the School's commissions and exhibition pieces.

See: **CU:** Keswick

Ref: PRO Carlisle, *Keswick School of Industrial Arts archive*, Minutes of Committee Meetings 12 Nov 1887.

Birmingham Guild of Handicraft
The Birmingham Guild grew out of the Kyrle Society founded c1880 to better the lot of working people by laying out parks and encouraging house decoration and garden craft. The Birmingham Guild of Handicraft was set up *c.* 1890 as a separate organisation to establish craft classes in Birmingham run on Ruskinian lines to 'supply handmade articles superior in beauty and soundness of workmanship to those made by machinery and to make only such as shall give just pleasure both to the craftsman and to the buyer of them' (*The Quest*, 1 (1894), p. 3). The Guild was directed by local professional men interested in the arts. These included Montague Fordham, a solicitor, who later set up his own gallery in London, architect W. H. Bidlake and the architect, designer and craftsman Arthur Stanfield Dixon. By 1895 the Guild, which had some 18 members had become a self-supporting Limited Company with a managing director, Claude Napier Clavering who had been a student at Birmingham School of Art. Its motto was 'By Hammer and Hand'. The Guild ran several classes including a furniture work shop, a print shop under the supervision of Arthur Gaskin where they produced a monthly magazine *The Quest* and a very successful metalwork shop in which designs by A. S. Dixon and C. N. Clavering were made up in beaten copper, brass and silver. By 1910 the Guild had merged with E. & R. Gittins & Co. makers of jewellery and architectural metalwork.

See: **MS:** Sefton Park **NS:** Leek

Ref: Crawford A. 'The Birmingham Setting,' pp. 30–32 in *By Hammer & Hand*, 1984; Karlin, *Jewelry and Metalwork*, 1993

Black, George (1846–1929)
Born and educated in Carlisle, George Black was apprenticed to his father's joinery business in Catholic St and later in Lorne St, Carlisle. He took over the firm on his father's death developing it into a highly successful and respected wood-working business, working particularly in hard woods. His reputation was such that he was C. J. Ferguson's preferred wood-working firm for his many prestigious commissions including Bamburgh Castle, Naworth Castle, Dalston Hall and St Aidan's Church, Carlisle but his work in these places has not been identified.

His obituary informs us that Black did work in over fifty churches in the Carlisle Diocese and for some years employed around a hundred joiners to complete his commissions all over the country. He retired in 1917.

See: **CU:** Kirkbride

Ref: Obit. *Cumberland News (26.10.1929)*, p. 10

Blomfield, Reginald Theodore (1856–1942)
Architect. Born in Devon, he was brought up in Kent and educated at Haileybury College, Herts and Exeter College, Oxford. In 1881 he entered his uncle Arthur Blomfield's office and the RA Schools. In 1883 he set up his own office in the same building as E. S. Prior and through him met Macartney (qv), Newton (qv) and Horsley (qv) – the Richard Norman Shaw (qv) coterie. He was a member of the AWG 1887–1903 and 1921–23. He was a partner in the short-lived furniture-making venture Kenton & Co. 1890–92. He wrote extensively on architecture and his *History of Renaissance Architecture in England* was extremely influential.

See: **GM:** Bury

Ref: Gray, A. S., *Edwardian Architecture*, 1985; *RIBAJ* (Jan, 1943), pp. 65–67, and *RIBAJ* (Feb, 1943), pp. 88–89; *Builder (8.1.1943), pp. 39–40.*

Blow, Detmar (1867–1938)
Architect. Born in London, he was educated at Hawtreys and articled to Wilson and Aldwinckle in 1883. He attended the South Kensington Schools winning the AA Travelling Scholarship in 1888. He accompanied John Ruskin (qv) on a trip to Italy in 1889. On his return, he apprenticed himself to a builder in Newcastle upon Tyne where he learnt the craft of a stone mason and by 1891 he was laying stone for Philip Webb (qv) during the repairs to East Knoyle church. Blow also did the stonework for cottages designed by Ernest Gimson in Leicestershire. He saw himself as an artist-craftsman designing cottages and reconstructing old country houses. He joined the AWG in 1892–93 and rejoined in 1904. By 1906, after what might be described as an itinerant practice, he was joined by Ferdinand Billerey and concentrated thereafter on more substantial work in London's West end and among the country houses of England. Detmar Blow lived his later life near Painswick in Gloucesteshire.

See: **CH:** Eaton Hall, Eccleston

Ref: Gray, A. S., *Edwardian Architecture*, 1985; Obit. *RIBAJ* (3.4.1939), p. 571; *Builder* (10.2.1939), p. 305; Drury, M, *Wandering Architects*, 2000

Blundstone, Ferdinand Victor (1882–1951)
Sculptor. Born in Switzerland to an English father, he studied in England at the South London Technical Art School and at the RA Schools. After WW1 he received some notable commissions for memorials, including one for the Prudential Assurance Co. office in London. He spent some time living in Heaton Norris, Stockport in 1908, but lived most of his life in London. He assisted Gilbert Bayes (qv) in the modelling department at the Sir John Cass School during the 1920s. Blundstone was elected to the AWG in 1924.

See: **GM:** Stalybridge

Ref: Ward-Jackson, *Public Sculpture in the City of London 2003*

Bodley, George Frederick (1827–1907)
Architect. One of the great Victorian Gothic Church builders. He trained under Sir George Scott (1811–78) from 1845–49 and set up his own practice in the 1850s going into partnership with Thomas Garner in 1869. Bodley gave Morris, Marshall, Faulkner and Co. their first contracts for stained-glass windows in his early churches, notably St Michael's, Selsey 1859–62 and St Martins on the Hill, Scarborough 1861–63. Bodley was himself a great decorator of churches and in 1870 founded the church furnishing firm of Watts & Co. with the younger George Gilbert Scott and Thomas Garner. (There was no 'Watts' in the firm. The name is said to have arisen from the old tag 'What's in a name?')

See: **GM:** Pendlebury, Middleton **MS:** Oxton, Sefton Park, Tuebrook **CH:** Chester Cath, Eccleston, Frodsham **NS:** Leek

Ref: Gray, A. S., *Edwardian Architecture*, 1985

Bonnor, John H. (1876–1916)
All round craftsman and stained-glass artist. His family were Welsh gentry in Denbighshire. He was a member of the Junior AWG and trained as an architect but later he became a metalworker and jeweller. He went on to teach himself woodwork and the art of stained glass. He taught at Camberwell School of Art.

See: **CU:** St Bees **MS:** Wallasey

Ref: Green, Romney, 'John Houghton Bonnor', *The Studio*, 1920

Bradshaw and Gass
Architects. John Bradshaw Gass (1855–1939) attended Bolton School of Art and studied engineering at Owen's College, Manchester. He went to the RA Schools in 1880 and was articled to his uncle, J. J. Bradshaw in Bolton. He spent a period as an assistant to Ernest George (qv) before returning to Bolton and entering into partnership with his uncle. The firm specialised in the design of cotton mills and public buildings in Lancashire. A. J. Hope joined the partnership in 1903.

See: **MS:** L'pool C, Port Sunlight

Ref: RIBA *Directory*, 2001; Obit. Bradshaw: *RIBAJ* (11.5.1912), p. 492; *Builder* (3.5.1912), p. 528. Gass: *RIBAJ*, 46 (1939), pp. 952–53; *Builder* (7.7.1939), p. 5

Bridgeman R. & Sons
Robert Bridgeman was born 1844/45 in Birwell Cambridge. He worked first at Birwell Engine Works, Thetford before taking up an apprenticeship in woodwork and carving at Rattees in Cambridge. In 1872 he was a journeyman at the building firm of John Thompson of Peterborough where he worked on Peterborough Cathedral as a sculptor. He continued with that firm working on Chester Cathedral 1874, Bridlington Priory 1876 and Lichfield Cathedral 1878 by which time he was head sculptor. In 1879 he set up on his own at Stone Yard, Lichfield, moving to Quonians in 1882. He took an active part in the life of Lichfield being its sheriff in 1907 and its mayor on two occasions 1913 and 1914. The firm continues today under the name of Linford Bridgeman.

See: **CU:** Ambleside **GM:** Rochdale, M/cc JR Lib, Stockport **CH:** Chester Cath

Ref: Keyte Owen, *The Annals of a Century, Bridgemans of Lichfield* 1993

Brierley Walter Henry (1862–1926)
Architect. Brierley was articled to his father in York and then worked in practices in Warrington and Liverpool. In 1885 he joined the firm of James Demaine of York. He was architect to North Riding County Council

1901–23 and Consultant to the Diocese of York 1908–21 His domestic work shows him to be an exponent of early 17C vernacular style. The bulk of his work is to be found in Yorkshire.

See: **LA:** Accrington (2) **MS:** Newton le Willows

Ref: Gray, A. S., *Edwardian Architecture*, 1985; Obit. *RIBAJ* (18.9.26), p. 575; *Builder* (3.9.26), p. 365

Brocklesby, John Sydney (1879–1955)
Architect. Trained with Frank E. Smee 1896–1901 and remained with him as an assistant until 1902. He then spent a year in the Housing Department of the London County Council and went on to J. T. Pieditch in 1903. He set up on his own in 1906.

See: **GM:** Ashton in Makerfield **NS:** Burslem, Tunstall

Ref: RIBA, *Directory of British Architects*, 2001; Spence, C. and Wilson, G., *Elbow Room*, 1984

Bromsgrove Guild (1890–1966)
The Guild was founded by Walter Gilbert (qv) *c.* 1890 and continued until 1966. It began as a loose association of designers and craftsmen, who worked together, on commissions arranged by Gilbert. In the beginning, individuals worked from their own workshops, free to take on other commissions. Later, as work expanded and the Guild's reputation grew, many craftsmen were fully employed including Bankart, (qv) Weingartner (qv) and A. J. Davis (qv). The Guild produced metal work, lead and plaster work, stained glass, jewellery and embroidery. The metalwork, for which the firm is best known, ranged from church lamps to the gates and railings of Buckingham Palace.

See: **LA:** Lancaster, Rawtenstall, Tarleton **MS:** Caldy, L'pool C Cath + (4), Southport, Wallasey **CH:** Crewe, Willington

Ref: Watt, Quintin, *The Bromsgrove Guild*, 1999

Brown, Ford Madox (1821–92)
Artist. Born in Calais and trained in art at Bruges, Ghent and Antwerp Academy 1837–39, he worked in Paris 1840–43 and settled in London in 1844. He sent work to the RA from 1840. Although he was not a member of the Pre-Raphaelite Brotherhood he was a close friend and mentor of Rossetti (qv) who introduced him to William Morris (qv). Madox Brown was a founding partner of Morris, Marshall, Faulkner & Co., for whom he designed stained glass and furniture. His major public commission in the north of England was the painting of 12 murals in the great hall of Manchester Town Hall. His work is on display in most major galleries.

See: **CU:** Troutbeck **LS:** Cockerham **GM:** M/cc TH + 2AGs, Marple **MS:** Birkenhead AG, L'pool C WAG, Tuebrook, Port Sunlight AG **CH:** Alderley Edge **NS:** Brown Edge, Cheddleton, Madeley, Onecote

Ref: Waters, *Dictionary of British Artists*, 1975; Surtees. V., ed., *The Diary of Ford Madox Brown*, 1981; Newman, T., *Ford Madox Brown and the Pre-Raphaelite Circle*, 1991; Ford, F. Madox, *Ford Madox Brown, A Record of his Life and Work*, 1972

Brown, James W. (1842–1928)
Stained-glass designer. J. W. Brown was born in Newcastle upon Tyne and received his early training under William Scott Bell at the Government School of Design where he later served as a teacher. In 1866 he went to London where he is said to have 'formed a close association with William Morris' and where, by the mid-1870s, he was designing stained glass for Powell and Sons. He later left Powell and opened his own studio in Stoke Newington. He continued as a freelance designer and produced further designs for Powell well into the C20.

See: **LA:** Blackburn **MS:** L'pool Cath, Thornton Hough **CH:** Chester Cath

Ref: Hall, Marshall, *Artists of Northumbria*, 1982

Budden, Lionel (1887–1956)
Architect. Born in London and educated at Merchant Taylors School in Crosby and the Liverpool School of Architecture. He graduated in 1909 winning travelling scholarships which enabled him to spend a year at the British School in Athens. He taught at the School of Architecture from 1911 and succeeded C. H. Reilly as Roscoe Professor of Architecture from 1933.

See: **LA:** Blackpool **MS:** Birkenhead, L'pool C

Ref: Cavanagh, T., *Public Sculpture in Liverpool*, 1997; Obit. *Builder*, 191 (27.7.1956), p. 149

Burge Miss A.
An embroiderer. She is reputed to have lived in London and was working *c.* 1930

See **GM:** Bolton

Burges, William (1827–81)
Architect and designer. The son of a civil engineer, he trained first as an engineer and then as an architect with Edward Blore and M. D. Wyatt. He was an ardent and eccentric mediaevalist. With the Marquis of Bute he 'mediaevalised' Cardiff Castle 1868–81 and created the fairy-tale Castell Coch 1875–81. His house in Melbury Rd, London, was a smaller version of these Gothic palaces. He also built churches including St Finn Bar's Anglican Cathedral in Cork begun 1863 and the small church at Studley Royal in Yorkshire 1871–78. His major interest was in decoration. His rooms were highly and lavishly decorated and his furniture though simple and solid in style was uniquely decorated. He shared with his friend E. W. Godwin (qv) an interest in Japanese Art and was a collector of Japanese Prints.

See: **GM:** M/c City AG

Ref: Dixon and Muthesius, *Victorian Architecture*, 1995; Smart, *Muscular Churches*, 1989

Burmantofts

Ceramic manufacturer. The firm started *c.*1845 using the clay extracted from sinking shafts at the Rock Colliery in the Burmantofts district of Leeds and was known as Willocks and Co. In 1879 a wealthy Leeds businessman John Holdroyd took over the business and increased the production of architectural salt-glazed bricks, terracotta, ceramic tiles and pottery. During the 1880s the firm became well known and rivalled Doulton with its fashionable tile-cladding for the exteriors and interiors of buildings. Its Art pottery, produced impasto, partie-coloured and lustre ware during the 1880s and in 1888 the firm became known as The Burmantofts Company. It was however merged along with several other potteries in 1889 to become part of the Leeds Fireclay Company. Art Pottery production ceased in 1904 but the architectural ware continued until after WW2 when the luxury housing and office market had all but disappeared. The firm closed in 1957.

See: **GM**: M/cc (2) + UMIST. **MS:** L'pool Uni.

Ref: Bradford Art Galleries and Museums, *Burmantofts Pottery* (Bradford, 1983); Garlick, A., *Burmmantofts Pottery*, *c.* 1991

Burne-Jones, Edward Coley (1834–98)

Artist, stained-glass designer. He was born in Birmingham and attended Birmingham Grammar School before he went up to Exeter College Oxford in 1853. There he met William Morris (qv) and started a life-long friendship and collaboration. Both men exchanged their plans to enter the church for careers in art and design and became fascinated with the medieval golden age of chivalry, art and craftsmanship. Ned Jones, as he was then known, took painting lessons from Rossetti (qv) and worked in a Pre-Raphaelite style throughout his career. He became not just a fine-art painter but also a decorative artist painting furniture and tiles, designing embroidery, illustrating books and designing stained glass. His first commission for the latter was in 1856 when he was asked to design windows for James Powell and Sons (qv). He worked for Powell until 1861 when he joined Morris, Marshall Faulkner and Co. From 1875 he was responsible for almost all of the stained-glass figure work for the newly formed Morris & Co. He also designed a fabulous series of tapestries for the firm and did illustrations for books published by the Kelmscott Press. He was elected to the AWG in 1891 and was knighted in 1894. Examples of his work are to be seen in galleries throughout the country and around the world.

See: **CU:** Brampton, Broughton in Furness, Carlisle AG + (1), Irton, Kirkbampton, Lanercost, Plumpton, Ponsonby, Staveley, Troutbeck **LA:** Blackburn (2), Calder Vale,Cockerham, Lytham, Mellor, Oswaldtwhistle, Preston, Whalley **GM:** Ashton under Lyne, Brooklands, Daisy Hill, Hale Barns, M/cc, Marple, Rochdale (2), Walmsley, Wigan, Worsley **MS:** Allerton, Bidston, Birkenhead AG + (1), Edgehill, Frankby, Gateacre, Halewood, Knotty Ash, L'pool C, WAG, UniAG, Mossley Hill AG + (1), Port Sunlight AG, Prescot, Tuebrook, Wallasey, Whiston, Woolton **CH:** Alderley Edge, Aldford, Chelford, Chester, Eaton Hall, Knutsford, Macclesfield, Mottram St Andrew, Neston, Sutton, Tabley, Widnes **NS:** Berkhamstych, Brown Edge, Cheddleton, Chesterton, Endon, Leek (2), Madeley, Onecote

Ref: Wildman and Christian, *Edward Burne-Jones Victorian Artist-Dreamer*, 1998; Fitzgerald, P., *Edward Burne Jones*, 2003

Butterfield, William (1814–1900)

Architect. He was apprenticed to a builder and then articled to E. L. Blackburn 1833–37, restorer of ancient churches. He joined a Worcester practice before setting up on his own in London in 1840. He worked almost exclusively on churches – he designed approximately one hundred of them. He was an un-conventional Gothic revivalist who had the realism to make Gothic conform to the necessities of the age abandoning Pugin's nostalgia for the middle ages and in this respect may be seen as a fore-runner of the Arts and Crafts Movement. Other work included buildings for Keble College Oxford, Rugby School and the Royal Hampshire Hospital. He became a champion of the Anglo-Catholic movement becoming a member of the Cambridge Camden Society in 1842 and of the Ecclesiological Society in 1848. He is probably best known for his use of colour built into the structure of his churches mostly through the use of polychrome brickwork. Butterfield was a loner and did not publicise his work, nevertheless, he had great influence on W. H. Lethaby and on generations of young architects of the Arts and Crafts Movement.

See: **CU:** Lamplugh **GM:** Clayton **CH:** Christleton

Ref: Thompson, *William Butterfield*, 1971; Smart, *Muscular Churches*, 1989; Obit. *AR*, 7 (1900), p. 260

Camm, Florence (1874–1960)

Stained-glass artist. Florence Camm was the daughter of Thomas W. Camm who founded his stained-glass studio in Smethwick in 1855. Florence trained at the Birmingham School of Art and subsequently taught there until, in 1912, her father died and she joined her two brothers in the family business. The style of the firm's windows changed almost over-night reflecting Florence's own style which had developed under the influence of Henry Payne (qv). Most of her work is to be found in the West Midlands but the firm sent windows to the USA, New Zealand, India and Spain. Miss Camm exhibited her designs at the RA, almost on an annual basis from 1905 and was still designing for the firm in the 1950s.

See: **CH:** Congleton **NS:** Berkhamstych

Ref: Obit. *JBSMGP,* 13, no. 2 (1960–61), p. 445

Campbell, Smith & Co. (1873–)
Charles Campbell, the founder of the firm trained in the school of Art and Architecture run by William Burges and Edward Poynter and spent sixteen years apprenticeship in the arts and decorative trade. In 1873 Campbell set up in partnership with Frederick Smith and then with his younger brother Henry Alexander when Frederick retired. He was employed by Burges (qv) to decorate his restoration work at Cardiff Castle, Castell Coch and then Burges' London home in Melbury Road. In its early years certainly c 1884 the firm designed and probably made stained-glass windows but many records were lost in the blitz during WW2. Members of the Campbell family continue to run what is still a small art-decoration business, which relies on the skills in design and hand craft of its artists and craftsmen. Examples of its work which include prestigious buildings like Westmister Abbey, Buckingham Palace and the Halls of many Worshipful Companies as well as theatres, hotels, clubs, smaller churches and cathedrals can be seen around the country.

See: **CU:** Vale of Lune

Ref: Campbell, *Campbell Smith & Co,* London, 1989

Carlisle, John (b. 1850)
Born in Middleton, Westmorland John Carlisle lived in Barbon where he was a joiner, cabinet maker and a very fine woodcarver. His work is unrecorded but he must have worked across the North West given that it is known he did the reredos at St Thomas's Bolton.

See: **CU:** Barbon **GM:** Bolton

Ref: *1901 Census*; St Thomas, Bolton *church records.*

Caröe, William Douglas (1857–1938)
Architect. Caröe was born in Liverpool where his father was the Danish Consul and a corn merchant. He gained a degree in mathematics at Trinity College, Cambridge and then spent a year in Liverpool in the office of Edmund Kirby (qv) in 1879 before going to the London office of J. L. Pearson (qv). He assisted with the drawings for Truro Cathedral and he was with Pearson while the practice worked on St Agnes Church in Liverpool. Caröe crossed swords with William Morris(qv), Phillip Webb(qv) and the redoubtable Society for the Preservation of Ancient Buildings, over Pearson's restoration work at Westminster Abbey. Nevertheless, he learned much from Webb and was influenced by Sedding (qv) and Wilson (qv). He joined the AWG in 1890 sharing the Guild's preoccupation with craft work. He resigned in 1910 but rejoined in 1933 when Lutyens(qv) became Master. He established a very large practice in London which was extended in 1895 when he became architect to the Ecclesiastical Commissioners. He was Secretary to the RIBA Art Standing Committee from 1891 to 1895 and subsequently became a member of the RIBA Council. He had many assistants and delegated work but it is said that he insisted on supervising all work done in his office until the end of his life. He did many repairs and restorations to cathedrals and abbeys but he also designed a number of country houses including extensions to his own home, Vann in Chiddingfold Surrey, where the gardens are occasionally open to the public.

See: **CU:** Broughton Moor, Egremont
GM: Wigan **MS:** Blundellsands, Huyton, L'pool C (2), Sefton Village, St Helens
CH: Mobberley

Ref: Freeman, W. D. *Caröe: His Architectural Achievement*, 1990; Obit. *RIBAJ* (7.3.1938), p. 459; (11.4.1938), p. 558; (9.5.1938), p. 669; *Builder* (4.3.1938), p. 435.

Carr, John E. C. (b. 1869)
Designer. Born in Dumbarton and started his career in 1892 in the Decorative Art Department of William Denny & Co. the Clydeside ship builders. In 1894 he moved to the Glasgow-based stained-glass firm of William Meikle & Co. where he was joined, a year later, by J. T. Stewart. Meikle sent both men to visit the Morris & Co. studios at Merton and they returned to Glasgow full of ideas and inspired by what they had seen and the people they had met including Morris (qv), Burne-Jones (qv) and Walter Crane(qv). Some time before 1898 Carr left Glasgow and moved south with his wife and two young children to live and work in Manchester. He joined the firm of George Wragge Ltd of Salford. A number of pieces of his metalwork and stained glass were displayed at the Northern Artworkers' Guild Exhibition, held in Manchester in 1898. His role at George Wragge Ltd. was to design metalwork and to establish a stained-glass studio. Little of his stained glass has been identified but his work is well illustrated in *The Studio* in 1898 and 1904. It is not clear when Carr left Wragge. The 1901 census shows that he was living in Willesden and his family included a two year-old daughter born in Manchester. He describes himself to the Census enumerator as a designer/craftsman working on his own account. Why he moved to Willesden, whether or not he continued to design for George Wragge Ltd and what became of him thereafter has yet to be researched.

See: **LA:** Blackpool TH **GM:** M/cc

Ref: Donnelly, M., *Glasgow Stained Glass – a preliminary study* 1981; *The Studio*, 14 (1898) and *The Studio*, 30 (1904)

Carrick, Alex (1882–1966)
Sculptor. Born in Musselburgh, he trained as a stone carver in the studio of Birnie Rhind in Edinburgh. He attended Edinburgh School of Art and the RCA in London. He returned to teach sculpture at the Edinburgh School of Art 1914–42, with a break for service in the Great War. He became head of the School of Sculpture and in that context, as well as more widely through his work, exerted great influence. He provided sculptures for several war memorials in the 1920s including the Scottish National War Memorial in Edinburgh.

See: **CU:** Workington

Ref: Spalding, *Dictionary of British Art 6, 1990*

Cassidy, John (1860–1939)
Born Slane, County Meath, Ireland. Studied at Manchester School of Art, winning four National medals and several Queens's prizes. He took up sculpture full-time in 1887 and produced many portraits and several statues. He was elected a member of the Cambrian Society (1912) and a Fellow of the Royal Society of British Sculptors (1914). His home was in Ashton upon Mersey and he was Vice President of Manchester Academy of Fine Arts and President of Manchester Sculpture Society.

See: **GM***:* Bolton, Bury, Eccles, Heaton Moor, M/cc TH, JR Lib +(2),

Ref: Waters, *Dictionary of British Artists*, 1975

Cawthra, Hermon (1886–1971)
Sculptor. Born in Yorkshire and apprenticed to a monumental mason for seven years from the age of 14. He began studying in the evenings in 1904 at the Salts Art School, York. He attended Leeds School of Art 1907–09, the RCA 1909–11 and the RA Schools 1912–16. He was declared unfit for service during the war and did his bit carving wooden propellers for the RFC. After the war he worked on his own account based in London until, in 1939 he went to teach at Brighton School of Art. In 1941 he moved to Hull as Head of Sculpture at the School of Art. At the end of the Second World War he returned to London and later took up a teaching post at Bournemouth Municipal College of Art. He retired in 1956 aged 70. Cawthra was elected to the AWG in 1927.

See: **GM:** Bury, M/ccTH **MS:** Bootle

Ref: Waters, *Dictionary of British Artists*, 1975

Century Guild (1882–1888)
Design Studio. Founded by A. H. Mackmurdo (qv) and Herbert Horne who co-operated with a number of other artists, designers and craftsmen including close friend and colleague Selwyn Image (qv), in carrying out interior design projects and the production of furniture, metal ware and other associated decorative ware. The 'firm' seems to have lacked the commercial acumen or drive of Morris & Co. and was consequently relatively short-lived. Nevertheless it was very influential. Its equally influential mouth-piece *The Hobby Horse* was founded in 1884.

See: **CH:** Wilmslow

Ref: Stansky, Peter, *Re-defining the World, Chap. 2*, 1996; Evans, S., 'The Century Guild of Artists at the International Inventions Exhibition, London, 1885', *DAGJ*, 1997

Champneys, Basil (1842–1935)
Architect. Educated at Charterhouse and Trinity College Cambridge, he was articled to John Prichard of Llandaff and set up his own practice in 1867. Much of his work was in Oxford and Cambridge for schools, churches and colleges. This included the Indian Institute at Oxford 1883–96 and Newnham College Cambridge 1874–75. He built Bedford College, London in 1910. He was Surveyor to St Mary's Manchester, which later became the cathedral and he designed a number of additions to the building. His work extended to the building of schools and houses including a house for Henry Holiday (qv) in Hampstead and his own home in Frognal, Hampstead 1881. He was a founder member of the AWG.

See: **LA:** Haslingden(2) **GM:** Blackley, M/cc Cath + JRLib

Ref: Gray, A. S., *Edwardian Architecture*, 1985; Obit. *RIBAJ*, 27.4.1935, p. 737; *Builder*, 12.4.1935, p. 682; Jones S., 'Champneys, an under rated Victorian' in the *Victorian* 2003; Watkin, D., *The Architecture of Basil Champneys*, 1989

Chant, Arthur Guy (1887–1959)
Architect. Born at Atherstone in Warwickshire. He attended Kingsdown School in Bath. He was architect to Shropshire County Council 1930–51 and for them he remodelled Shire Hall at Shrewsbury, built Shropshire Technical College, the Priory Grammar School and Grammar Schools at Whitchurch and Wellington. He was a musician, playwright and poet and a devout Methodist. He was one of the founders in 1942 of the County Architects' Society, its secretary for 8 years and its president 1950–51

See: **LA:** Lancaster

Ref: Obit. *Builder* (21.08.1959), p. 61; *Methodist Recorder* (8.10.1959)

Child, Alfred Ernest (1875–1939)
Stained-glass artist. Child was born in London and at the age of sixteen he gave up a future in accountancy to take up a scholarship at the Goldsmith's Institute, London c1891 where he studied stained-glass work. He was a pupil of Christopher Whall (qv) and became his paid

assistant. In 1901 he married and moved to Dublin to teach in the Metropolitan School of Art where he became a major influence on the development of Irish stained glass. In 1903 his influence was extended when he became the first manager of Sarah Purser's 'AnTúr Gloine' (The Tower of Glass) stained-glass studios in the city.

See: **GM:** Patricroft

Ref: Bowe, Caron and Wynne, *Gazetteer of Irish Stained Glass*, 1988

Chilton, Margaret Isabel (1875–1962)
Painter and stained-glass artist. Born in Bristol she attended the RCA in London at the turn of the century, where she was trained in stained-glass work by Christopher Whall (qv) and Alfred Drury. Around 1906 she returned to Bristol to establish her own stained-glass studio and to teach privately. Some of her windows were made in collaboration with Lowndes & Drury. In 1918 she moved to Glasgow to work as a designer at the Abbey Studio and four years later she set up a studio at 13a George St, Edinburgh in partnership with Marjorie Kemp (qv), a graduate of the Glasgow School of Art. They moved to 8 Fettes Row, Edinburgh at the end of the Second World War. Most of their work is in Scotland but a fine series of windows can be seen at St Andrew's, Leytonstone 1922–46

See: **CU:** Milburn

Ref: William Morris Gallery, *Women Stained-Glass Artists of the Arts and Crafts Movement*, 1985; Armitage, E. L., *Stained Glass*, 1960

Clarke, Harry (1889–1931)
Stained-glass artist and book illustrator. Harry Clarke was born in Dublin where his father had established a stained-glass business. He left school at the age of fourteen, when his mother died and set to work in the family business. He attended evening classes at the Dublin School of Art prior to winning a scholarship in 1910 which enabled him to attend as a full-time student. He won the National Gold Medal Competition in three consecutive years. He developed his own exceptional and beautiful style out of the Christopher Whall (qv) inspired techniques taught by A. E. Child (qv) and a sideways look at the work of Aubrey Beardsley, the Symbolists, Art Nouveau and Byzantium. When his father died in 1924 he took on the management of the Dublin Studio while continuing his own commissions and working on book illustrations. He made visits to London and in particular to the Glass House in Fulham where he met Karl Parsons (qv). In January 1926, he suffered serious injuries when he fell off his bicycle in Dublin. He developed meningitis and this precipitated a gradual decline in his state of health which he disregarded in his passion to get on with his work. He also contracted pulmonary TB and died in Davos, Switzerland in 1931. The firm was registered as Harry Clarke Stained Glass Ltd in 1930 and continued production until it closed down in 1973. He left only nine sets of his own windows in England. In addition to stained glass he designed textiles for Seftons Fabrics and illustrated a number of books and magazines *Fairy Tales of Perrault* and *Tales of Mystery and Imagination* by Edgar Alan Poe are but two extremes of his subject range.

See: **GM:** Ashton in Makerfield, M/cc Hulme, Wigan **CH:** Nantwich, Warrington

Ref: Bowe, N. G., *The Life and Work of Harry Clarke*, 1989

Clark, James (1858–1943)
Painter in oil and water colour of portraits, landscapes, flower and religious subjects; book illustrator and designer of stained glass. Clark studied art at Hartlepool, at the RCA, London and at L'Ecole des Beaux Arts in Paris before settling in London. He was elected to the AWG in 1903. He travelled extensively in the Holy Land to add to his authority as an artist developing religious themes. One of Clark's windows for the now defunct St John's in Windermere was featured in *The Studio* 27 (1903), p. 56. There is another article on his painting in *The Studio* Volume 14, (1898) pp. 152–61. There is some inconsistency in the sources as to whether or not there is an 'e' on the end of Clark.

See: **CU:** Barrow, Casterton, Kirkby Stephen

Ref: Waters, *Dictionary of British Artists*, 1975; *The Studio*, 14 (1898)

Clow, W. & A.
Woodworkers. The two brothers were in business in Edinburgh from 1891. They first worked for architect Robert Lorimer in 1909 and worked more or less exclusively for him thereafter. They executed the stalls in the Thistle Chapel in St Giles, Edinburgh for Lorimer in 1892. They were superb craftsmen.

See: **LA:** Fleetwood **CH:** Davenham

Ref: Savage, P., *Lorimer and Edinbugth Craftsmen*, 1980

Cocker, John
Architects. John N. Cocker (ob. 1926) and his son worked in partnership at 7 Market St, Altrincham from *c*. 1905. John Cocker junior (1883–1960) was articled to J. T. Ashton 1899–1904 and attended the municipal Schools of Art and Techology, Manchester. He was assistant to Goulder and Ashton 1904–05 and qualified in 1905. Most of his work was local and included the extension to Altrincham public library and a number of church halls and houses. His work has been described as 'in the style of Edgar Wood'.

See: **GM:** Timperley, Hale

Ref: RIBA *Directory*, 2001; Obit. *Builder*, 199 (2.9.1960)

Collingwood, W. G. (1854–1932)
Artist, designer, writer. William Gershom Collingwood was born in 1854 and educated at Liverpool College, University College Oxford and the Slade School of Art. He had a studio in London and made his living as an artist, although he was also a university extension lecturer. Later he became Professor of Fine Art at University College Reading. In 1880, he became John Ruskin's secretary, assisting in the publication of Ruskin's prolific writings. He was an able scholar in his own right with a great interest in archaeology particularly in Northumbrian Crosses and in the Viking Age. He wrote many books related to these subjects as well as those about Ruskin's life. After the Great War, during which he was an intelligence officer, he returned to the Lake District, where he continued his interest in archaeology giving it practical form in the neo-Celtic War Memorials he designed. His wife Edith was a painter with a considerable reputation as a miniaturist His three daughters were also gifted artists. Barbara (1887–1951) was a talented sculptor and Dorothy (1886–1964) was a water colour artist. Ursula was a painter of flowers and miniatures. She taught art at Blackwell School during WW2.

See: **CU:** Ambleside AG, Coniston Mus + (2), Grasmere, Hawkshead, Kendal(3), Keswick

Ref: Armitt Library *Archives* & Armitt Gallery *Website*

Cooksey, May Louise Greville (1878–1943)
Painter of figures and landscapes in watercolour and oil, ecclesiastical artist and etcher. She was the daughter of the architect Harry Smith Cooksey and was born in Birmingham. She was sent to a private school at Leamington and took lessons at the Leamington School of Art before studying at the Mount Street School of Art in Liverpool under Mr F. Burridge. She won the Liverpool Travelling Studentship, went to Italy and devoted a year to the study of the early Italian masters, whose spirit is an influence in her work. She taught at South Kensington School before returning to Liverpool. In addition to painting she was an etcher and designed at least one stained-glass window made by H. G. Hiller (qv).

See: **MS:** Garston, Edgehill, Mossley Hill AG, Seaforth, Sefton Park, Toxteth

Ref: *Census 1901; The Studio* 19 (1900) and 45 (1909)

Cooper, John Paul (1869–1933)
Architect, metalworker and jeweller. Born in Leicester into a wealthy family, Cooper attended Old Hall School in Shropshire and Bradfield College, Herts. In 1888 he was articled to John D. Sedding when Henry Wilson was Sedding's chief assistant. He and Wilson became good friends spending many sketching holidays together and attending drawing classes at the Royal Architectural Association Museum in Tufton St and at Heatherleys. After Sedding's death in 1891 Cooper helped Wilson complete outstanding commissions but like Wilson turned his attention to the decorative arts becoming a talented craftsmen in plaster work, gesso, metalwork and jewellery. He had completed his articles as an architect by 1894 and set up his own studio in London. He first exhibited at the Arts and Crafts Exhibition Society in 1893. In 1901 he became a teacher of metalwork and enamelling at the progressive Birmingham Municipal School of Art. In 1906 he moved to Kent and set up his own workshop, exhibiting the finest jewellery, shagreen, gesso and metalwork nationally and internationally. His work was also sold through the Artificer's Guild in Maddox St, London. During the 1920s he received many important public commissions particularly from cathedrals, churches and chapels for crosses and other liturgical plate. He was a member of the AWG from 1908.

See: **MS:** L'pool CWAG

Ref: Kuzmanovic, *John Paul Cooper*, 1999

Cottier Daniel (1838–91)
A pioneering interior designer and stained-glass artist. Born in Glasgow, he was apprenticed to local painter David Kier (1802–64) who was master glazier at Glasgow Cathedral 1859–64. In 1862 Cottier moved to Edinburgh as chief designer for Field and Allan but in 1864 moved back to Glasgow to set up on his own as an interior designer. His first commission was the painted decoration for Townhead Church Glasgow 1865–66 where the East window was provided by Morris & Co. He was influenced by Burne-Jones (qv) but his later work was to move well away from the Morris style. He moved to London and set up his interior design business in 1869. By 1873 he had opened branches in New York and Sydney selling furniture and decoration, much of it in Aesthetic movement style. In England he opened up the Aesthetic market with his friend, art dealer, Angus Crabbe.

See: **CU:** Ravenstonedale **GM:** Brooklands, M/cc AG

Ref: Donnelly, M., *Glasgow Stained Glass, 1981*

Cox, Trena M. (1895–1977)
Stained-glass artist. Nothing has been published about the long and productive life of this individual and stylish stained-glass artist. Born in Camberwell 1895 she worked for Williams and Gamon (qv) in Chester and set up her first studio in Birkenhead from 1916. In 1923 she moved to Victoria Rd, Chester and then in 1929 to 96 Watergate. She was a Fellow of the British Society of Master Glass Painters and exhibited 1916–29 mainly at the Walker

Art Gallery but also at the RA. Some sources give her name as Trina M Cox.

See: **LA:** Fleetwood, Whalley **MS:** Bidston, Birkenhead, Caldy,Thurstaston, Woodchurch **CH:** Chester Cath + College, Moulton

Ref: *Census 1901;* Johnson and Greutzner, *British Artists 1880–1940*, 1999

Crane, Walter (1845–1915)
Artist, designer, illustrator. He was born in Liverpool but by the age of fourteen he was working in London, producing drawings on wood for W. J. Linton's wood engraving firm. He was largely a self-taught artist and exhibited his first picture at the RA in 1862. He was elected to the AWG by the Committee in May 1884, holding office as Master in 1888 and in 1889. He was also a Founder Member of the Arts and Crafts Exhibition Society. Perhaps best known as a book illustrator, he also painted landscapes, portraits and figure subjects. In addition he was an interior decorator and designed plasterwork friezes, wallpapers, carpets, ceramics and textiles. He designed Morris & Co's first tapestry. He was part-time Director of Design at the Manchester School of Art 1893–96 and was a founder member of the Northern Art Worker's Guild. In addition to doing his own readily identifiable work he exerted an enormous beneficial influence on the movement as an educator and publicist.

See: **LA:** Calder Vale **GM:** M/c 2AGs, JRLib, MMULib, Oldham AG. **MS:** L'pool C WAG. **NS:** Leek

Ref: Crane, Walter, *An Artist's Reminiscences*, 2nd edn 1907; Smith & Hyde, eds, *Walter Crane 1845–1915*, 1989

Cressey, Charles (b. 1876)
Architect. Born Lancs. He was part of the practice of Cressey & Keighley which had offices at 65 Chorley New Road, Horwich and at Morecambe. His family had a joinery business in Horwich, Nr Bolton.

See: **GM:** Horwich

Ref: *1901 Census; Local Trade Directories.*

Creswick Benjamin (1853–1946)
Sculptor and metalworker. Born in Sheffield, he was apprenticed to a knife grinder in Sheffield but gave this up due to ill health. In the 1880s he worked under Ruskin's supervision at Coniston and Oxford and opened a studio in London in 1884. He met A. H. Mackmurdo and became part of that loose association known as the Century Guild. He taught at Birmingham School of Art from 1889 and was a member of the Bromsgrove Guild. He produced a lot of architectural sculpture for Birmingham buildings.

See: **MS:** Wallasey **CH:** Wilmslow

Ref: Ward-Jackson, *Public Sculpture of the City of London* 2003; T. Raffles Davison, 'An English Sculptor', *British Architect*, 27 (1887), p. 303

Cripples' Guild of Handicraft, Duchess of Sutherland's
Millicent, Duchess of Sutherland (1867–1955) of Trentham created 'The Potteries and Newcastle Cripples Guild' *c.* 1900 with the aim of ensuring that every disabled child in the Potteries received proper medical treatment and learned a useful trade or craft. Classes were established making artificial flowers, baskets and photo frames but by 1902 the skills of printing and metalwork had been added to classes for boys. Frank Arthur Edwardes, a skilled artist and enameller became chief instructor of metalwork. He and the Duchess collected designs from art galleries and museums all over the world which were simplified and reproduced in silver or silvered copper.

In 1907 the Guild became a limited company known as the Duchess of Sutherland's Cripples' Guild of Handicraft. It had workshops employing twelve disabled boys at the Providence Works, Wilson St, Hanley, a shop at 13–14 New Bond St London and a registered assay mark at Birmingham. The Guild flourished until the outbreak of WW1 when the workshops were moved to Trentham and later employed disabled adults. The workshops closed in 1922

See: **GM:** Rochdale

Ref: Stuart, D., *Dear Duchess*, 1982

Crossley, Frank Herbert (?–1955)
Architect, designer and woodworker. Born in Yorkshire, he moved to Cheshire in 1887 where he started work as a farm hand in Knutsford. He attended a wood-carving class run by the vicar's wife at Over Tabley and developed such expertise that he ended up running the class. He went on to study part-time at Manchester School of Art. In 1898 he became a part-time peripatic teacher of drawing and wood-carving with Cheshire County Council during the winter months. He studied and drew buildings all over England and later amassed a vast collection of photographs which are now in the Courtauld Institute. Of his architecture there is little evidence but his beautiful woodwork can be seen in several churches in Cheshire and not least the roof in Chester Cathedral refectory. He wrote many books on churches and woodwork including *English Church Craftsmanship* (1941) *The English Abbey* (1943) and as part of the County Book Series, *Cheshire* (1949). He was a member of the Chester Archaeological Society and wrote for its journal.

See: **CH:** Ashton Heyes, Chester, Tabley

Ref: Obit. *Chester Archaeological Society Journal*, 42 (1955), pp. 50–51

Crouch, Butler & Savage
Architects. Joseph Crouch (1859–1936) was born in Birmingham and educated in the city and at the South Kensington Schools. Crouch began his practise in Birmingham in 1882 and was joined by Edmund Butler in 1886 and by Rupert Savage in 1911. For some years, after about 1896, the firm was closely involved with the Arts and Crafts, designing houses in Birmingham suburbs and especially in Four Oaks, Sutton Coldfield, which were decorated by the artists and craftsmen who made up the Bromsgrove Guild.

See: **LA:** Rawtenstall

Ref: Granelli, Remo, 'Architecture, All the World and Time Enough' pp. 41–47 in *By Hammer and Hand*, ed by Crawford, A., 1984

Curwen, John Flavel (1860–1932)
Architect. Born in London 1860 and educated at Mill Hill School. Articled to a firm of architects in London, he set up his own practice in Kendal in 1886, which his son took over in 1928. His work was mainly within Cumbria. His chief interest was in restoring old buildings but he also built a number of houses locally. He was surveyor of the southern area of the Diocese of Carlisle for 13 years. He was also a considerable archaeologist and writer on local history. He was a member of the Society of Antiquaries and the Cumberland and Westmoreland Antiquarian and Archaeological Society for whom he wrote.

See: **CU:** Kendal

Ref: Kendal PRO, archives; *Builder*, 143 (12.8.1932), p. 247; Obit. *RIBAJ*, 40 (1933), p. 27

Cutts, John Edward Knight (1847–1938)
Architect. He was articled to Ewan Christian 1865–70 and remained his assistant for 5 years. He set up his own practice in 1878, working from Bedford Chambers, 28 Southampton Row. He was a partner of A. H. Mackmurdo for a short time in the early 1880s when they designed the ill-fated St Bede's Toxteth. He was in partnership with John Preston Cutts his brother c. 1880 and was Diocesan surveyor to St Albans 1881–87.

See: **LA:** Longton **MS:** Sefton Park

Ref: RIBA *Directory*, 2001

Davies, Archibald John (1877–1953)
Stained-glass artist. From 1893 he trained to become a portrait painter at the Birmingham School of Art but turned to stained-glass work He set up his own studio in Moseley while teaching at the Bournville branch of Birmingham School of Art. In 1906 he moved to Bromsgrove to join the Bromsgrove Guild (qv) with whom he worked for the remainder of his life. He designed his windows, drew the cartoons, selected the glass, painted them, fired them and leaded them. He was an archetypal Arts and Crafts practitioner. His windows can be found in cathedrals and churches all over the world. In addition he designed and executed glass for luxury liners, public buildings and commercial premises illustrating secular rather than religious themes.

See: **LA:** Tarleton **MS:** Caldy, Hoylake **CH:** Crewe

Ref: Watt, *The Bromsgrove Guild*, 1999; Obit. *JBSMGP*, 11, no. 3 (1953–54)

Davis, Louis (1861–1941)
Painter, book illustrator and stained-glass artist. Educated at Abingdon School, Oxfordshire, he was a student, assistant and friend of Christopher Whall (qv) in the 1890s and shared lodgings with him near Dorking in 1892. Davis was elected to the AWG in 1891. His window designs were probably made-up by Lowndes and Drury 1897–1901; after that by Powell of Whitefriars and later still by Thomas Cowell who had been a foreman at Powell's before his retirement. He worked with Henry Wilson (qv) and also with Robert Lorimer (qv) who described him in 1896 as '. . . a ripper, a chap of about 40 but as keen as a boy. Such a lovable chap, he and I became great pals at Oxford last year.' He was commissioned by Lorimer to do major stained-glass work in Scotland including Dunblane Cathedral and Paisley Abbey.

See: **LA:** Fleetwood

Ref: Savage, *Lorimer*, 1980; Ely Museum display information; St Mary & St Nicholas Church, Littlemore, Oxford *Website*; *Census 1901*

Dawber, E. Guy (1861–1938)
Dawber was the son of a merchant from Kings Lynn in Norfolk. He trained as an architect in Norfolk, and worked in Dublin before moving to London in 1882 where he entered the offices of George and Peto working in London and the Cotswolds. He set up on his own in 1890 in a room in the village institute at Bourton-on-the-Hill. The following year he moved his base to London and established a long-running and expert practice in the design of smaller country houses. He married Mary Eccles of Roby, Liverpool, sister of the architect Thomas Edgar Eccles (qv). Dawber was elected to the AWG 1897 and later became President of the RIBA.

See: **MS:** Wallasey

Ref: Gray, A. S., *Edwardian Architecture*, 1985; Obit. *RIBAJ* (9.5.1938), pp. 631, 633, 666–68 and *RIBAJ* (23.5.1938), p. 770; *Builder* (29.4.1938), pp. 824, 827

Dawson, Nelson (1854–1942)
Metalworker and jeweller. He trained as an architect and then studied painting at South Kensington School. In 1891 he began working in metals and studied enamelling under Alexander Fisher (qv). He married the water colourist, Edith Robinson in 1893. They set up a studio in Chiswick which became one of the

best known husband and wife studios producing beautiful enamelled work often illustrated in *The Studio*. Nelson Dawson founded the *Artificers' Guild* (qv) in 1901.

See: **GM:** M/cc MMULib., Prestwich

Ref: Karlin, *Jewelry and Metalwork*, 1993

Day, Lewis Foreman (1845–1910)
Decorative artist and designer of textiles and glass. He was educated in Brighton and then spent time in France and Germany. At the age of twenty he returned to England to work for Lavers & Barraud, as a stained-glass artist where he stayed for five years. He also taught on a part-time basis. In 1870 he became a freelance designer of textiles, wallpapers, stained glass, embroidery, carpets, tiles, pottery and book covers. He sold designs to many textile manufacturers including Thomas Wardle, A. H. Lee, Alexander Morton, Turnbull and Stockdale (for whom he was Artistic director for a time) and Brinton's carpets. He was among the first members of the AWG and was Master in 1897. He was a frequent exhibitor at international and national shows. He lectured on design and was an examiner in painting and ornament for the Board of Education. He was a considerable author. As an honorary member of the Northern Art Workers Guild he exhibited at their exhibitions in 1898 and 1903. He designed a stained-glass window in Martlesham church in Suffolk which was executed in Manchester by Walter J. Pearce Ltd.

See: **GM:** M/cc CityAG, WhAG + Costume AG.

Ref: D. M. Ross, 'Lewis Foreman Day, Designer and Writer on Stained Glass', *JBSMGP*, 3, no. 1 (1929–30); Rycroft, Elizabeth, 'Lewis Foreman Day, 1845–1910', in *DASJ*, no. 13 (1989)

Deacon, Charles E. (1844–1927)
Architect. A North-West man. He was articled to Sir James Allanson Picton 1862–68 and worked in several offices in London, including that of Sir William Emerson, before setting up in partnership with Charles Aldridge in 1872 in Liverpool and later with his son. He designed many churches in the North West. He was a Neo-Gothicist but with occasional Arts and Crafts and Art Nouveau flourishes. Deacon (son) & Horsburgh designed 2 blocks of houses in Port Sunlight.

See: **MS:** Bebington, Birkenhead, Knotty Ash (2), New Ferry, St Helens, Port Sunlight, Walton

Ref: RIBA *Directory*, 2001; Obit. *Builder*, 133 (15.7.1927), and *Builder*, 133 (19.8.1927); *RIBAJ*, 34 (1927), p. 639

Dearle, John Henry (1860–1932)
Designer and craftsman. He is remembered almost entirely for his work for Morris & Co. and is therefore often under-rated. He started work for Morris & Co. in 1878 as an assistant in the Oxford St shop but when his artistic talents were discovered he worked first in the stained-glass painting workshop and then he was trained as a tapestry weaver. By 1890 he was the firm's chief textile designer. He designed tapestries, carpets, embroideries, fabrics and supervised most of the textile production. He also designed stained glass. After Morris's death he became Art Director and ran Merton Abbey Works up to his own death in 1932

See: **LA:** Blackburn, Calder Vale **GM:** Hyde **CH:** Chelford, Macclesfield, Neston, Wilmslow

Ref: Proctor, H., *The Holy Grail Tapestries*, 1997

Delahunt, Jennie (b. 1877)
Sculptor and modeller. Born in Hanley, Staffs the third of the four children of Charles Dalahunt, an excise officer, and his wife Jane. In 1901, Jennie was a student at Manchester Municipal College of Art where she was a medallist and scholarship winner. She exhibited a statuette at the RA in 1908 whilst living in Lancaster where she was an art teacher at the Lancaster School of Art and the Girls' Grammar School.

See: **LA:** Lancaster

Ref: *Census 1901*; *RA Exhibitions 1905–1970*

Della Robbia Pottery (1894–1906)
The pottery was founded in Birkenhead in 1894 by the painter, designer and poet Harold Rathbone (qv) and sculptor Conrad Dressler (qv). The style was based on the work of the C15 Della Robbia family, who produced coloured, glazed terracotta plaques in Italy. The new enterprise, which was set up to specialise in architectural ceramics had royal patrons and was supported by leading artists including Holman Hunt, Alma Tadema, William Morris (qv), Walter Crane (qv) and Lord Leighton. From 1897 when Carlo Manzini took over from Dressler, the firm increasingly produced domestic hollow-ware inspired by Italian majolica and decorated with sgraffito patterns and painted decoration. Designers included Robert Anning Bell (qv), Carlo Manzoni and Ellen Mary Rope (qv) as well as, students from local Schools of Art and local 'untutored' people. The pottery was sold by such shops as Morris & Co. and Liberty's.

See: **MS:** Birkenhead 2AGs, Lib + (1), Knotty Ash, L'pool C WAG, Mossley Hill AG, Oxton, Wallasey **CH:** Sandiway **NS:** Hanley AG

Ref: Williamson Art Gallery and Museum, *Della Robbia Pottery*, 1980

De Morgan, William Frend (1839–1917)
Artist, stained-glass artist, potter, inventor, novelist. He trained for four years at the RA Schools as a painter in the Pre-Raphaelite manner but later turned to stained glass, tiles and pottery, in pursuit of which he managed to

set fire to his house in Fitzroy Square in 1869. He re-established the pottery in 1872 at his mother's house in Cheyne Walk, Chelsea moving his workshop and show room to the Orange House in Cheyne Row and then to a larger site at Merton Abbey 1882–88. He rediscovered many lost arts of firing pots and obtaining lustre glazes and invented new equipment to enable him do this. He was a member of the Rossetti (qv), Burne-Jones (qv), Morris circle and worked with A. H. Mackmurdo's (qv) *Century Guild* (qv) in the 1880s. After his marriage in 1887 he moved to The Vale, Chelsea and with Halsey Ricardo he opened a new and initially successful factory at Sands End, Fulham 1889–98. For health reasons he spent his winters in Florence. He became better known in later life as a novelist and during the Great War applied his inventive genius to submarine and aerial warfare.

See: **CU:** Bowness, CarlisleAG, Dalston, Hutton in the Forest, Windermere **LA:** Padiham, Whalley **GM:** Bolton, M/ccAG, MMULib. **CH:** Ashley, Wilmslow **NS:** Hanley AG, Rocester

Ref: Greenwood, *The Designs of William De Morgan*, 1989

Devey, George (1820–1886)
Architect. Country house man but his use of vernacular style in repairing and reproducing small cottages was seen by Nesfield and Shaw in 1862 and inspired the 'Old English Style'. Most of his work was in southern England especially at Penshurst in Kent.

See: **GM:** Bolton

Ref: Dixon and Muthesius, *Victorian Architecture*, 1985; *RIBA* Proceedings, NS 3 (1887), p. 46–47; *Builder*, 51 (20 Nov 1886), p. 728

Dick, William Reid (1879–1961)
Sculptor. Born in Glasgow and trained at Glasgow School of Art until 1907. He then attended the City and Guilds College at Lambeth and first exhibited at the RA in 1908. He did military service in France and Palestine during WW1 and post-war was a distinguished sculptor of memorials including the huge Lion crowning the Menin Gate at Ypres and the sculpture in the Kitchener Memorial Chapel in St Paul's Cathedral. He was President of the Royal Society of British Sculptors 1933–38 and in 1938 became the King's, later Queen's sculptor. One of his memorable works is the equestrian Lady Godiva in Coventry *c.* 1950. He was elected to the AWG in 1922.

See: **MS:** Port Sunlight **NS:** Hanley AG

Ref: Waters, *Dictionary of British Artists*, 1975; Ward-Jackson, *Public Sculpture of the City of London*, 2003

Dix, Arthur J. (b. 1861)
Stained-glass artist. Born in High Wycombe but working in London, he made windows on his own account and for other artists including Arthur Orr, James Clark and Alice Mary Gordon. He exhibited at the RA 1898–1915.

See: **CU:** Holme, Kirkby Stephen, Windermere

Ref: *Census 1901. RA Exhibitions 1905–1970*

Dodgshun, Edward John (1854–1927)
Architect. He was articled *c.* 1870 to Thomas Ambler in Leeds. He worked for a year with G. E. Street (qv) and then spent another year with William Burges (qv) where he met W. F. Unsworth. They set up in practice together in 1875 and in the same year won the competition for the Shakespeare Memorial Theatre, Stratford on Avon. By 1898, Dodgshun was in partnership with G. Dale Oliver (qv) of Carlisle, whom he had met first in Street's office. Much of their work was done in Leeds. They also rebuilt Silcoates School, Wakefield and did a number of churches in Surrey, some in collaboration with Axel Haig, the celebrated etcher and friend to Carl Almquist (qv).

See: **CU:** Carlisle, Kirkbride

Ref: Gray, A. S., *Edwardian Architecture*, 1985; Obit. *RIBAJ*, 34 (2.4.1927), p. 377

Dolman, William Ledsham (b. 1875)
Architect. He was assistant to Joseph Dolman, a builder in Repton 1892–1902 before becoming assistant to Dan Gibson (qv) of Windermere 1902–07. He took over Dan Gibson's practice when he died in 1907.

See: **GM:** Prestwich

Ref: RIBA *Directory*, 2001

Douglas, John (1829–1911)
Architect. Invariably known as John Douglas of Chester. He was born at nearby Sandiway where his father was a building contractor. Douglas learnt his woodwork skills from his father and after finishing his schooling, travelled to Lancaster in the late 1840s where he trained as an architect with E. G. Paley. He returned to Chester *c.* 1859 where he set up his own practice. He undertook the study of Cheshire's vernacular black and white half-timbered architecture and for almost fifty years used this and other vernacular styles across Cheshire and elsewhere in the country. He was an operational contemporary of Shaw (qv) and Nesfield (qv) and may well have rubbed shoulders with Nesfield whilst working on the aristocratic estates of Cheshire and neighbouring Staffordshire. He was in partnership as Douglas and Fordham 1884–97 and as Douglas and Minshull 1897–1911.

See: **LA:** Great Altcar, Over Wyresdale(2) **GM:** Worsley **MS:** Caldy, Great Crosby, Hoylake, Port Sunlight, Thornton Hough(2), West Kirby **CH:** Aldford(6), Ashton Heyes, Bickley, Chester(14), Eaton Hall, Eccleston(20), Helsby, Moulton, Pulford, Sandiway(2), Warrington, Whitegate

Ref: Hubbard, E, *The Work of John Douglas*, 1991; *RIBAJ*, 18 (1911), pp. 589–90; *Builder*, 100 (2 .6.1911), p. 697

Doulton
The firm of Doulton and Watts was set up in Lambeth in the 1820s making salt-glazed stone ware and decorative Toby jugs. It was not until the 1860s that the firm, by now Doulton & Co. linked up with John Sparkes, the progressive head of the nearby Lambeth School of Art to provide for the practical application of the students' art in a commercial setting. It took several years for the Lambeth Studio to become well established as they introduced new materials, techniques, designs and motifs. George Tinworth (qv) was one of the first students in 1866. Hannah and Arthur Barlow arrived in 1871 and Frank Butler in 1872. By 1873 demand had grown for Doulton's Lambeth Ware and the studio expanded. Among the new set of students were Florence Barlow, Emily J. Edwards, Eliza S. Banks, Louisa Davis and Eliza Simmance; all people whose pots are now coveted by collectors. At Doulton the artists had the freedom to design their own pieces and each piece was unique, at least until the beginning of the 1880s, when a cheaper range of 'artist designed' ware was introduced. The Studio went on to produce other pottery than stoneware, including faience, impasto and majolica and with these developments came a growing range of glazes, shapes, styles and decorative devices. Alongside all this, Doulton continued to produce their architectural and garden wares. In addition to terracotta, they produced carraware, vitreous fresco and faience tiles which were used for facing smart buildings like Harrods, Debenhams, the Savoy Hotel and Doulton House in London. By the turn of the century the firm had developed Polychrome Stoneware, a material which became popular for ceramic sculpture in the 1920s and 30s and was used particularly by Gilbert Bayes (qv). During WW2 what remained of the Lambeth Art Studios was turned over to making supplies for the war effort and post-war the market had declined to the extent that the Lambeth works closed down in 1956.

See: **LA:** Blackpool, PrestonAG **GM:** MMULib + campus, Ordsall, St Helens **MS:** L'pool C WAG **CH:** Capesthorne, Chester Mus. **NS:** Hanley AG

Ref: Eyles & Irvine, *Doulton Lambeth Wares*, 2002; Werner, A., 'John Charles Lewis Sparkes', *DADJ*, 13, 1989

Doves Press (1900–1916)
Established at No. 1 The Terrace Hammersmith by Thomas James Cobden-Sanderson and Emery Walker. Walker left the partnership in 1909 and the Press moved to 15 Upper Mall Hammersmith. Fifty-seven titles were published. The Dove typeface was designed by Emery Walker and the books were devoid of decoration except for the occasional hand-drawn initials in colour. The Press's reputation relied on the clarity of type and quality of composition and materials.

See: **LA:** Blackburn AG, Preston Lib **GM:** M/cc Libs(2), MMULib; **MS:** L'pool C Lib, Uni Lib

Ref: Cave, R., *The Private Presses*, 1983

Doyle, James Francis (1840–1913)
Architect. Born in Liverpool, he is well-known for his collaboration with Richard Norman Shaw (qv) in that city. His own work was mainly in and around Liverpool and included churches and some of the more prestigious houses in the Birkenhead suburbs.

See: **MS:** Blundell Sands, Childwall, L'pool C (2), Mossley Hill, Neston, Wallasey
CH: Neston, Widnes

Ref: Gray, *Edwardian Architecture* 1985; Obit. *Builder* (21.2.1913), pp. 235, 253

Doyle-Jones, Francis William (1873–1938)
Sculptor. He was born in West Hartlepool and trained at South Kensington School under Lanteri. He first exhibited at the RA in 1903. He was commissioned to make a number of Boer War memorials including those at Middlesbrough 1904, West Hartlepool 1905 and Gateshead 1905. He also executed a number of WW1 memorials including Gravesend and Sutton Coldfield 1922. His exhibition work was largely portrait busts. He exhibited widely with the Royal Hibernian Society, the Glasgow Institute, the Walker Art Gallery Liverpool and other galleries.

See: **CU:** Cockermouth, Penrith **MS:** Waterloo

Ref: Ward Jackson, *Public Sculpture in the City of London*, 2003

Dresser, Christopher (1834–1904)
Born in Glasgow of Yorkshire parents, he went to the Government School of Design in London 1847–54. He was a lecturer and writer on Botany, but soon turned his attention to design and the theory of art. During the 1860s he was engaged as a designer by some of the most prestigious names in art and industry including Minton, Wedgwood and Coalbrookedale. Later he produced avant garde designs in silver, made by Elkington, while John Couper & Sons of Glasgow used his designs for Clutha Glass. In the 1870s he wrote and lectured on the 'Principles of Decorative Design' and on Japanese ornament. He became an authority on the Japanese Art Industry and a promoter of Japonism in Britain, setting up a company to import Japanese goods. In 1879 he set up the Linthorpe Art Pottery at Middlesbrough and in 1880 established the short-lived Art Furnishers' Alliance covering all fields of interior design. For the remainder of his life he continued to be

at the forefront of design and was one of the most radical and prolific designers of the 19C believing not only that design should be simple and functional with appropriate ornmentation but that machine production did not rule out good design.

See: **GM:** M/ccAG + MMULib **MS:** L'pool C WAG

Ref: Halen, *Christopher Dresser*, 1990

Dressler, Conrad (1856–1940)
Sculptor and Designer. Born in London of German parents, he studied at the National Art Training School under Edward Lanteri and later in France. He exhibited at the RA from 1883. He worked as a sculptor and set up a foundry in Chelsea. In 1886 he stayed with John Ruskin (qv) at Coniston, who influenced the development of his style and later met William De Morgan (qv) who furthered his interest in pottery. 1893–95 he set up the Della Robbia Pottery (qv) with Harold Rathbone (qv) and in 1897 set up his own pottery at Medenham in Bucks where he produced tiles and architectural ceramics. He invented the tunnel kiln. Dressler went to live in Paris in 1920 and from there went to the USA.

See: **MS** L'pool C WAG + (2), Mossley Hill AG, B'head AG

Ref: Spalding, *20th Century Painters and Sculptors;* Cavanagh, *Public Sculpture of Liverpool*, 1997; Walker, R. P., 'Conrad Dressler and the Medenham Pottery' in *DASJ*, 18 (1994)

Drury, Edward Alfred Briscoe (1856–1944)
Sculptor. Born in London. He studied at Oxford School of Art and at South Kensington under Dalou and Lanteri, working in Dalou's studio in France 1881–85. He returned to England in 1886 where he worked for Sir Joseph Boehm. He became a member of the AWG in 1899. Drury developed his own recognisable style for his romantic bronze pieces involving the female figure. He had many large architectural commissions including the allegorical groups on the War Office in Whitehall 1904 and with F. W. Pomeroy he modelled the monumental figures on the piers of Vauxhall Bridge *c.* 1906. He executed a number of WWI memorials and many public statues.

See: **LA:** Preston **MS:** Warrington

Ref: Ward-Jackson, *Public Sculpture of the City of London 2003*; Gray, A. S., *Edwardian Architecture*, 1985

Dunkerley, Frank Brookhouse (1868–1951)
Architect. Born in Timperley, Cheshire and educated at Marlborough College. He was articled to Messrs Potts & Dixon of Manchester and became an improver and draughtsman with John Douglas (qv) of Chester 1890–94. He was an assistant to Roger Smith after he qualified. He then spent some time in Italy before setting up independent practice in Manchester in 1897. He was in partnership with Waddington and Son and later with Isaac Taylor with whom he built the Sanatorium Children's Village in Belmont, Cheadle in 1927.

See: **CU:** Windermere **GM:** Halebarns

Ref: RIBA *Directory*, 2001; Obit *RIBAJ*, 58 (1951), p. 482

Dunlop, Irene née Shakerley (b. 1893)
Stained-glass artist and portraitist. Marguerite Irene Shakerley was born at Somerford Park near Congleton. She is described as a stained-glass artist in *British Artists 1880–1940* and is recorded there as exhibiting at the RA in 1920 and 1922. The same publication records Mrs Irene Dunlop as a miniature portrait painter exhibiting in 1927 and living in London and again in 1939 while living at Lane End, Bucks.

See: **CH:** Alderley Edge, Astbury

Ref: *Census 1901*; *RA Exhibitions 1905–1970.*

Earley Studio
Irish stained-glass studio. Established in 1852 and known first as Earley and Powell, the firm produced ecclesiastical furniture and were painters and decorators, suppliers of 'architectural and sculptural decorations' and makers of stained glass. Members of the Earley family were involved in the artistic side of the Earley business for over 100 years. In 1902 the firm worked with A. E. Child(qv), on a stained-glass window of St Elizabeth in the church at Ardrahnn in Laban Co. Galway but it was not a regular connection. The firm was still in business in the early 1970s but little has been published about it.

See: **CU:** Cleator **MS:** Aigburth, Edgehill, Walton

Ref: *The Industries of Dublin*, 1887/88; Wynne, M., *Irish Stained Glass*, 1977

Eden, Frederick Charles (1864–1944)
Architect and stained-glass designer. F. C. Eden was born in Northamptonshire and educated at Wellington School and Keble College, Oxford. He spent a few months in the office of William Butterfield (qv) before going to G. F. Bodley (qv). After ten years with Bodley he set up his own practice where he dealt mostly with ecclesiastical work designing stained glass as well as other decorative features in his buildings. In 1910, having become frustrated that his stained-glass ideas were not adequately executed, he began making his own windows and went on to make over 200 in the course of the next twenty-five years.

See: **GM:** Reddish **MS:** Great Crosby
CH: Chester Cath., Thelwall

Ref: Croome,W. I., 'Frederick Charles Eden' *JBSMGP*, 13, no. 4 (1962–63); Gray, A. S., *Edwardian Architecture*, 1985

Essex House Press – see **Guild of Handicraft**

See: **GM**: Mc/c 2 Libs, MMULib **MS:** L'pool Lib + Uni Lib

Farmer and Brindley (1850–1930)
Wood and stone carvers, monumental masons, sculptors, decorative craftsmen and church furnishers. William Farmer (1823–79) and William Brindley (1832–1919) both came from Derbyshire. Initially Farmer set up his business in London and employed Brindley as a stonecarver. Their partnership was formed in the 1860s. The first known example of their work was Wooland Parish Church, Dorset for George Gilbert Scott. During the 1870s many of their commissions came from Scott and Alfred Waterhouse (qv). After Farmer's death the firm expanded its work to include not only Gothic but Byzantine, Renaissance, Jacobean and Arts and Crafts styles in order to meet the designs of many well-known architects of the day including Bodley (qv), T. G. Jackson (qv) and W. R. Lethaby (qv). Eminent sculptors such as Harry Bates (qv) and C. J. Allen (qv) trained with the firm. The firm's work can be seen all over the country in churches and public buildings, some of the most celebrated of which are the Albert Memorial, the Natural History Museum, South Kensington and Manchester Town Hall.

See: **GM:** M/c TH(2), **MS:** L'pool Cath, L'pool Uni. campus

Ref: Cavanagh, Public Sculpture of Liverpool, 1997; Hardy, E., *Farmer & Brindley*, Victorian Society Annual (1993)

Faulkner, Lucy (1839–1910) and **Kate** (1841–98)
Artists. Sisters of C. J. Faulkner, partner in Morris, Marshall, Faulkner & Co. and next door neighbours of William Morris (qv) in the 1860s. Lucy became Morris's principal tile painter and Kate, in addition to painting tiles, executed painted decoration and gesso work for Philip Webb and decorated the famous Stanmore Hall piano 1891–94.

See: **CU**: Brampton **MS**: L'pool WAG.

Ref: Cormack, P., 'Decoration and Applied Art', in *Pre-Raphaelites and Other Masters*, 2003

Fell Robert
Woodcarver Applethwaite

See: **CU**: Ings

Ref: Leaflet in Ings Church, Cumbria

Fendley, George Herbert (1885–1945)
Born in Lincolnshire, he came to Carlisle as a child and was apprenticed to Mr W. Little of Castle St as a wood carver. He set up his own wood-working business at Lowther St and in 1905 was advertising his Wood Carving School. He taught at Carlisle Art School and at the Keswick School of Industrial Arts. He later moved to Warwick Road and in the 1910 Trade Directory his firm described itself as being 'architects and contractors'. When W. Little retired Fendley and his wife Elizabeth set up an antique business in his Castle Street shop and later they established a hand-tufted carpet factory at Newtown.

See: **CU:** Calthwaite.

Ref: Obit. *Cumberland News* 6.10.1945, p. 6; *Carlisle Directories* 1905–11; Carlisle PRO, *K.S.I.A archive*; *Calthwaite Church Guide*

Fenton, Harry (b. 1887)
Designer. Born in Salford one of the four sons of John Fenton, a box manufacturer, and his wife Annie. Nothing is known of his education but he is described in the *Studio Year Book* for 1909 as a designer of stained glass, ecclesiastical decoration, gesso, mosaics, wallpapers and textile fabrics and as a craftsman in stained glass and gesso. Many of his designs were carried out by Messrs Wragge Ltd of Manchester. Was Fenton a free-lance artist craftsman or on the staff of George Wragge Ltd?

See: **GM:** Ashton under Lyne

Ref: *1901 Census*; *Studio Year Book* (1909)

Ferguson, Charles. J. (1840–1904)
Architect. He completed his studies with G. Cory in Carlisle before joining G. G. Scott's office for a period in London in the mid-1860s. In 1868 he returned to Carlisle and was taken into partnership by Cory, who, apart from being in private practice, was also the County Architect. It is said that subsequently Cory did the engineering work and Ferguson did the architecture. He built up a large ecclesiastical and country house practice, was a diocesan architect and architect to the Grosvenor Estate in Cumbria. Most of his work was done in Cumberland from his Carlisle office, although he also had a London office *c.* 1886–1901. He worked with the architectural styles but was far from being a copyist and whilst not an innovator of the first rank, his work shows originality and individuality, especially in his fonts and bellcôtes. He restored Bamburgh Castle for Lord Armstrong and did restoration work on Muncaster and Naworth castles. He was a guarantor of the first Arts and Crafts Exhibition Society in 1888 and was elected to the AWG in 1893. He died at his home, Caldew Lodge in Cumdivock, in 1904.

See: **CU:** Bassenthwaite, Brampton, Bridekirk, Burneside, Carlisle(2), Cumdivock, Dalston (2), Eaglesfield, Gamblesby, Gosforth, Keswick (2), Mealsgate, Nether Denton, Plumbland, Seascale, Silloth, Tebay, Watermillock

Ref: Kendal Record Office; Obit. *Carlisle Journal* (2 December 1904); Smith, Leslie 'Charles J. Ferguson, a North Country Ecclesiastical Architect', *Abbot Hall Quarto*; Magazine, n.d.

Fisher, Alexander (1864–1936)
Silversmith and enameller. He studied at South Kensington School and in Italy and Paris. He taught for four years at the Central School of Arts and Crafts from 1896 and founded his own school of enamelling in Kensington in 1904. He was largely responsible for the revival of enamelling in England and taught many students who later excelled in this craft: Nelson Dawson (qv), Ernestine Mills, Hon Madeline Wyndham and Lady Mary Carmichael (who in turn taught Phoebe Traquair). He wrote frequently for *The Studio* and exhibited internationally as well as at the Arts and Crafts Exhibition Society. Among the wide range of items he made were exquisite plaques, sconces, caskets, church crosses, triptychs and jewellery. He also did designs for needlework which were embroidered by his wife and by the Royal School of Needlework. He was a member of the AWG from 1904. His daughter Kate was also a fine jeweller and silversmith designing for Hutton & Co.

See: **LA:** PrestonAG, **GM:** M/cc MMULib.

Ref: Karlin, E. Z., *Jewelry and Metalwork*, 1993; Fisher, A., *The Art of Enamelling upon Metal*, 1906

Fitzroy Picture Society (fl. 1893)
The Fitzroy Picture Society was established in 1893 by the group of artists who frequently met at 20 Fitzroy Square, the home of A. H. Mackmurdo. Their aim was to provide good quality prints at prices that schools, Sunday schools, churches and other institutions could afford. They used colour lithography, this being the only way that large prints could be produced without huge expense. It is known that pictures were provided by Selwyn Image (qv), Haywood Sumner (qv), Christopher Whall (qv) and Louis Davis (qv). Volume one of *The Studio* (1893) describes the pictures as 'drawn in bold black lines and printed in simple flat colours, but yet are brilliant and rich besides being distinguished by a certain originality we have learned to expect from the artists. Therefore they are not only excellent pictures in themselves, but adorn a room to an unusual degree.'

See: **CU:** Croglin

Ref: *The Studio*, 1 (1893), pp. 28–29

Foden, Joseph (fl 1920)
Carpenter, woodcarver. He worked for the Stanley Estate in Nether Alderley and lived at Monks Heath when he executed the carving on the chancel screen in St Mary's, Nether Alderley. He later set up his own business based in Mottram, Cheshire.

See: **CH:** Alderley Edge

Ref: NADFAS church recording: Research by Mr B. Hobson

Ford, Edward Onslow (1852–1901)
Sculptor. Born in Islington North London, he trained as a painter in Antwerp 1870 and in Munich 1871–72 but returned to England in 1872 determined to become a portrait sculptor. He was influenced by Alfred Gilbert (qv) and became a leader in the New Sculpture Movement producing portraits and allegorical figures. He exhibited regularly at the RA and received many commissions for public sculpture. He was a life-long and founding member of the AWG and Master in 1895.

See: **GM:** M/cc. **MS:** L'pool C WAG, Port Sunlight AG

Ref: Ward-Jackson, *Public Sculpture of the City of London*, 2003

Forsyth, Gordon (1879–1952)
Artist and designer. He was born in Fraserburgh the son of a journeyman cooper. He attended Gray's School of Art in Aberdeen and moved to London and the RCA in 1901. He was the Art Director at Minton Hollins & Co. 1903–06 before becoming Art Director for the Pilkington Tile Co. at Clifton Junction near Manchester. He spent the years 1916–19 in the RFC where he designed mechanical targets. He returned to Pilkington's in 1919 but moved the next year to Stoke-on-Trent where he became Superintendent of Art Instruction until 1944. He was a water- colourist and designer of stained glass, church metalwork and furnishings. He exerted a great influence on the development of the ceramic arts in the North West.

See: **GM:** Ashton under Lyne, Clifton **NS:** Burslem, Hanley, Tunstall

Ref: Eatwell, A., 'Gordon Mitchell Forsyth, *Journal of the Decorative Arts Society*, No. 13, 1989; Potteries Museum & Art Gallery Hanley, *Forsyth Archive*

Frampton, Edward (1850–1929)
Stained-glass artist. He was articled to a lawyer but was allowed to give up the law and to study art on condition that it was ecclesiastical art. He trained with Clayton & Bell and attended Langham School of Art before setting up his own studio in Buckingham Palace Rd, London *c*. 1881. One of his first commissions was the east window of Denver Cathedral, Colorado later destroyed by fire. Outside the North West his work can be seen in St Margaret's Westminster, Hawarden Parish Church, St James Church, West Hampstead and Sutton Parish Church, Surrey.

See: **CU:** Ings **LA:** Gt Altcar **GM:** Swinton **MS:** Gt Crosby **CH:** Bruera, Chester (3), Whitegate

Ref: *JBSMGP*, 11, no. 2 (1952–53)

Frampton, George James (1860–1928)
Sculptor of portrait and figure subjects, memorials and reliefs in a wide range of

materials. He attended Lambeth School of Art and the RA from 1882, where he was an outstanding pupil winning the Gold medal in 1887. He taught modelling at the Slade School of Art and in 1894 became joint Director with W. H. Lethaby of the LCC Central School of Arts and Crafts. He was elected to the AWG in 1887 and was Master in 1902. He was knighted in 1908. Perhaps his best known work is Peter Pan in Kensington Gardens 1912. He designed many memorials including: Edith Cavell near the National Gallery, and the St George and Dragon war memorial in High Holborn.

See: **MS:** L'pool C WAG,Uni AG + campus + (2), Sefton Park, Southport **GM:** Bury(2), M/cc JRLib

Ref: Gray, A. S., *Edwardian Architecture*, 1985; Jezzard Andrew, *The Sculpture of George Frampton*, 1999; Fine Art Society, *Peter Pan and Eros, Sir George Frampton & Sir Alfred Gilbert*, 2002

Freeman, Richard Knill (*c.* 1838–1904)
Architect. Articled to George Rake of Portsea 1854–60 and worked in various offices in Portsmouth, Manchester and Bolton 1860–63. He was in partnership with George Cunliffe, 1865–71 and then practiced on his own. He exhibited at the RA on seven occasions between 1882 and 1894.

See: **CU:** Greythwaite **LA:** Blackpool, Horwich, Turton **GM:** Bolton (2), Oldham

Ref: RIBA *Directory*, 2001; Obits: *RIBAJ*, 11 (1904), p. 484; *Builder*, 87 (9.7.1904), pp. 46–47

Frodsham, Sam b. 1890
Woodworker and carver, working in Congleton where he and his father ran a joinery business. He learnt cabinet making from an Italian firm in London, and also went to art school. He did restoration work on old furniture as well as new work mainly in Cheshire churches. During WW1 he ran evening woodwork classes at the senior school in Congleton attended by adults as well as pupils of the school.

See: **CH:** Astbury, Congleton.

Ref: *Cheshire Life*, 40, No. 5 (May 1974)

Furber, Jessie R. (b. 1880)
Artist. Living at 25 Heath Road Whitchurch, Cheshire in 1901, she was still living in Whitchurch when she exhibited at the Royal Academy in 1938.

See: **CH:** Bickley

Ref: *RA Exhibitions 1905–70*

Furse, Charles Wellington (1868–1904)
Portrait and figure painter. Born at Staines the son of the Archdeacon of Westminster. He attended the Slade School of Art 1884, winning the Slade scholarship in 1885 and completing his art education at Julian's Atelier in Paris. He exhibited at the New English Art Club and from 1888, at the RA. He was elected to the AWG in 1892 and became an ARA in 1903.

See: **MS:** L'pool C TH

Ref: http//74.1911encyclopedia.org/F/FU/FURSE_CHARLES_WELLINGTON.htm

Galton, William (fl. 1904)
Cabinet maker. In the 1904 Kelly's Directory he had a workshop at 30 King St, Leek.

See: **NS:** Leek

Ref: Staffs PRO *All Saints Leek archives*; *Kellys 1904*

Gamon, Gilbert (1871–1941)
Stained-glass worker. The son of a wealthy Chester solicitor, he was apprenticed to Shrigley & Hunt *c.* 1888 and became a member of the design team in 1891. He worked for Carl Almquist in their London office for about ten years and set up his own business in Chester. He worked in partnership with G. W. Humphry *c.* 1903 and later as Gamon and Williams.

See: **CU:** Colton **MS:** Birkenhead AG, Wallasey **CH:** Chester Cath, Crewe, Neston, Parkgate

Ref: Walters, *Stained Glass from Shrigley and Hunt*, 2003; *Census 1901*

Garnett, Annie (1864–1942)
Needlewoman. Born at Bowness on Windermere where her father was a land-agent and owner of the Crown Hotel in Bowness. The family lived at 'Fairfield', a large house nearby. Annie received no formal education but she had artistic talent and was blessed with a keen sense of colour, a good eye and a great love of nature. She was a good embroiderer and put her skills to good use when she established the Windermere Industry in 1890. The business soon outgrew its space in a village hall and moved to the stables of her home, re-christened 'The Spinnery'. She taught women to use the spinning wheel and handloom and to embroider material with what were often her own designs. Some of these designs were sold at Liberty's shop in London. The Spinnery's cloth, beautiful in texture and colour and the desirable things made from it, won prizes at national exhibitions all over the country. The business foundered in the 1920s when she became ill and had no one to whom she could pass it on.

See: **CU:** Bowness, Kendal AG

Ref: Abbot Hall, Kendal, *Annie Garnett archives*; Brunton, J., *The Arts and Crafts Movement in the Lake District*, 2001

Garnett & Wright (fl. 1907)
John Garnett, architect, was born 1851 in Ramsbottom, Greater Manchester. No information has come to light about the practice.

See: **MS:** Port Sunlight

Ref: *Census 1901*

Gateshead Stained Glass (1879–1926)
Stained-glass manufacturers. The Gateshead Stained-Glass Studio was established in 1879 at Sowerby's Ellison Works, Gateshead by John George Sowerby (1850–1914) and Thomas Ralph Spence (qv). Much of the early design work was carried out by Spence and A. H. Marsh. Their designs show the influence of the Aesthetic Movement and Morris & Co. The firm's logo was an owl perched on a tree branch with a sun rising behind it. Production was of a high quality and the costs were high as they incorporated a variety of processes and types of glass. In 1882, Spence moved to London and Marsh became chief designer and in the same year the stained-glass department was incorporated with an art pottery. Both Spence and Marsh became free-lance designers in the later 1880s. By 1887 the firm was in financial difficulties and was taken over by Henry Gordon Drummond a former draughtsman at the works. The firm continued to use Sowerby's patents and kept the name of Gateshead Stained Glass. From 1900 the chief designer was James Eadie Reid (qv) who introduced a more direct Arts and Crafts style to the studio's work. The firm closed in 1926.

See: **GM:** Monton **MS:** Aigburth **NS:** Chesterton, Hanley

Ref: Cottle, Simon, *Sowerby Gateshead Glass*, Tyne & Wear Museums Service, 1986.

Geddes, Wilhelmina (1887–1955)
Stained-glass artist. She received her schooling at the Methodist College in Belfast and from 1903 attended the Belfast Art School. In 1910 she moved to the Metropolitan School of Art in Dublin. There she met Sarah Purser and joined the Tower of Glass Studio where she soon developed her own individual style. She moved to London in 1922 where she rented a studio at The Glass House in Lettice St, Fulham. She was described by Joan Howson (qv) as 'the finest stained-glass artist of our time.'

See: **CU:** Bardsea **LA:** Southport **MS:** Wallasey

Ref: Bowe, N. G., 'W. Geddes 1887–1955' *JBSMGP* (1988)

Geldart, Ernest Martin (1848–1929)
Designer. Trained as an architect with Alfred Waterhouse but did not practice and instead was ordained a deacon in 1873 anda priest in 1878. Ill health caused his retirement from the church in 1900 and he took up design, working in stained glass, embroidery and furnishings. He wrote on the subjects of church decoration and symbolism.

See: **CU:** Brathay

Ref: V&A Museum, *Victorian Church Art*, 1971

George, Ernest, & Yeates (1893–1919)
Architects. Previously George and Peto, this was one of the major architectural practices of the period. Alfred Yeates had started as a pupil, became an assistant and eventually a partner when Peto retired through ill health in 1893. The practice was well known for its country houses. Ernest George was elected to the AWG in 1889.

See: **MS:** Port Sunlight (3)

Ref: Gray, A. S., *Edwardian Architecture*, 1985; Obit. *RIBAJ* (23.12.1922), pp. 106–07; *Builder* (15.12.1922), pp. 900, 903

Gibson, Dan (1866–1907)
Architect and designer. Dan Gibson's life and work is under-researched. He was born at Bassingthorpe in Lincolnshire but it is not known where he trained or how he came to settle at Bowness on Windermere. He spent a short time collaborating with T. H. Mawson on architectural gardening projects in the late 1880s before going up to London to work in the offices of Ernest George & Peto. He returned to Windermere to recuperate from an illness and in 1898 rejoined T. H. Mawson as a junior partner. He brought his architectural and design skills to the partnership, which only lasted two years after which Gibson directed his talents to domestic architecture, design of book bindings, jewellery and interior design. He died unexpectedly at the age of 41.

See: **CU:** Ambleside, Bowness(3), Graythwaite, Windermere (2), Winster **LA:** Hest Bank **GM:** Prestwich

Ref: *Census 1901*; T. H. Mawson, *The Life and Work of an English Landscape Architect*, 1927; 'The Lesser Country Houses of To-day' *Country Life supp.* 13.4.1912

Gilbert, Alfred (1854–1934)
Sculptor. He discovered his vocation for sculpture whilst waiting for a scholarship to attend medical school at the Middlesex Hospital. He entered the RA Schools in 1874, worked in the studio of Sir J. E. Boehm and then went to study and work in Paris and Rome. In 1893 he completed the Shaftsbury memorial in Piccadilly Circus followed by a host of extremely prestigious monuments, memorials and busts and, on a smaller scale, the Preston Mayoral chain. He suffered a financial failure in 1901 and lived and worked abroad until 1926. He was a member of the AWG 1888–91, 1901–04 and 1932–34.

See: **LA:** Preston AG **GM:** M/cc TH **MS:** L'pool Uni (2) **NS:** Hanley AG

Ref: Dorment, R., *Alfred Gilbert, Sculptor and Goldsmith*, 1986

Gilbert, Walter (1871–1946)
Designer, metal worker. Gilbert studied at Birmingham School of Art under Benjamin Creswick (qv). He worked as an instructor at Rugby Technical School, from 1893 and at an unspecified work place in Harrow before becoming headmaster of Bromsgrove School of

Art *c.* 1898. Gilbert founded the Bromsgrove Guild (qv) *c.* 1898. In 1918 he left the Guild to become managing director of the Art Department of H. H. Martyn of Cheltenham where, in collaboration with Louis Weingartner (qv) he was responsible for much of the firm's most prestigious work. Gilbert's best known work is the screen and gates of Buckingham Palace, designed while with the Bromsgrove Guild.

See **LA:** Burnley **MS:** L'pool Cath, Prescot, Wallasey **CH:** Crewe

Ref: Watt, Q., *The Bromsgrove Guild*, 1999

Gill, Arthur Eric Rowton (1882–1940)
Sculptor and designer of cut letter and print fonts. Gill was articled to W. D. Caröe (qv) and attended the Central School of Arts and Crafts. He discovered his skills lay in the design and carving of inscriptions on wood and stone. He originated the script *Gill Sans* and introduced WH Smith shop fascias to elegant Roman lettering. He did much memorial work including low reliefs and post WW1 turned his interest to scuplture. He did Prospero and Ariel on Broadcasting House Langham Place London. He was a member of the AWG 1904–09.

See: **LA:** Fleetwood, Morecambe **GM:** M/cc Cath, Rochdale AG **CH:** Tabley, Thelwall **NS:** Hanley AG

Ref: Yorke, Malcolm, *Eric Gill, Man of Flesh and Spirit*, 1981; Collins, Judith, *Eric Gill, The Sculpture*, 1998

Gill, Macdonald (1884–1947)
Architect, mural painter and cartographer, brother of Eric. Born at Brighton and educated at the Royal Naval Academy, Bognor, Chichester School of Art and the Central School of Arts and Crafts. In 1901 he was articled to L. Pilkington and in 1903 became assistant to Charles Nicholson (qv) and H. C. Corlette. Like his brother Eric Gill (qv) he played a major part in the revival of lettering based on Roman and medieval standards. He was a skilled cartographer and is best known for his picture maps which appeared as advertisements in books, on posters and as mural decoration in shops and public buildings. These included his map of the London Underground (1913) and murals like his brilliant depiction on tiles of Windsor Castle at the Windsor branch of Boots the Chemists. He also carried out decoration at Lincoln Cathedral, the House of Commons, and the Guildhall Cambridge. He was a member of the AWG and the Guild of Memorial Craftsmen. He worked for some years for the Imperial War Graves Commission.

See: **CH:** Tabley

Ref: Waters, *Dictionary of British Artists*, 1975; Obit. *RIBAJ* (Mar. 1947), p. 286; *Builder* (17.01.1947), p. 93

Glasby, William (b. 1864)
Stained-glass Artist. Born in Bloomsbury, London little is known of him until Henry Holiday chose him to be his chief painter and foreman when he set up his own stained-glass studio in Hampstead in 1890. Holiday closed his studio in 1906 and Glasby is then recorded as painting for Morris & Co. from 1909 until 1923. He may well have worked elsewhere in this period and by 1925 was signing his own windows, presumably made in his own studio.

See: **LA:** Foulridge **GM:** Hyde

Ref: *1901 Census*; Sewter, A. C. *The Stained Glass Of Willaim Morris & His Circle*, 1975; Holiday, H., *Reminisences*, 1914

Godwin, Edward William (1833–86)
Architect and designer. Born in Bristol, the son of a builder, he was articled to the City Surveyor, Architect and Engineer, William Armstrong. In 1854 he opened his own office in Bristol. He adopted the Neo-Gothic style and inspired by John Ruskin's 'The Stones of Venice' won the competitions for Northampton and Congleton Town Halls in 1861 and 1864 respectively. In 1865 he moved his office to 23 Baker St, London. He began to design furniture and developed his well-known Anglo-Japanese style. While continuing his architectural work he wrote for the architectural press and developed his interest in design for the theatre. He also designed wallpapers and fabrics. He formed life-long friendships with architect William Burges and writer Oscar Wilde. He led an eccentric and bohemian life becoming a major figure in the Aesthetic Movement.

See: **CH:** Congleton **GM:** M/cc AG **MS:** Mossley AG

Ref: Lambourne, *The Aesthetic Movement*, 1996; Soros, S. W., ed., *E. W. Godwin: Aesthetic Movement architect and designer*, 1999

Goodhart-Rendel, Harry Stuart (1888–1959)
Architect and writer. Educated at Eton and Trinity College, Cambridge. He began by studying music but turned to architecture and set up his own practice in 1911. He served with the Grenadier Guards in both World Wars. His architectural output was not great but he was a prolific writer and in that sense influential. He was a member of the RIBA Council from 1926 and its President from 1937–39. He was Slade Professor of Fine Art at Oxford 1933–39.

See: **CH:** Burton

Ref: RIBA *Directory of British Architects*, 2001; Obit. *Builder* (1.8.1959)

Gordon, Alice Mary (b. 1888)
Artist. Christened Marian Alice she was born *c.* 1888 the daughter of E. W. Wakefield and his wife Mary. She attended the Art School in Kendal but her career was interrupted by marriage until she moved to Glasgow where her son was studying at the university. There, she

resumed her interest in sculpture and took up stained-glass work. When she returned to Kendal she designed three stained-glass windows and wrote *A Short History of Kendal* which was published in 1952.

See: **CU:** Holme, Kendal

Ref: Slowe, V., 'Alice Mary Gordon', *Quarto Magazine*, Jan. 1970

Goulden, Richard Reginald (1877–1932)
Sculptor. Born at Dover. He studied at the RCA and exhibited at the RA 1903–32 from a studio in Fulham. He became art adviser to the Carnegie Dumferline Trust and produced bronze reliefs for the Carnegie Centre at Dunfermline. He also made a statue of Carnegie and a fountain for the local park. He contributed the high relief portrait of G. F. Watts for the façade of the V&A. In WW1 he enlisted in the Royal Engineers but was invalided out in 1916. He made many war memorials. He was a Fellow of the Royal Society of Sculptors and a member of the AWG 1912–32.

See: **LA:** Shaw

Ref: Ward-Jackson, *Public Sculpture in the City of London*, 2003

Grasmere Hermit (fl. 1892)
Woodworker referred to with reference to the Langdale Chase Hotel. He is said to have lived on the island in the middle of Grasmere and to have done his carving in Easedale but he remains an elusive figure with no proper name.

See **CU:** Windermere

Grayson, George Enoch (1834–1912) and **Ould, Edward Augustus** (1852–1909)
Architects. Grayson was responsible for much of the office and warehouse building in Liverpool during the 1870s and 80s The partnership with Ould was established in Liverpool in 1886. Ould was born in Cheshire where his father was the Rector of Tattenhall. He was a pupil of John Douglas (qv) and gained from him a superb understanding of traditional half-timbering techniques. The partnership ran a large country house practice making use of Cheshire half-timbering but in other respects following Shaw and Nesfield. Their output included Wightwick Manor three miles west of Wolverhampton which now belongs to the National Trust and is well known for its Arts and Crafts furniture and fittings. They also did buildings at Trinity College and Selwyn College, Cambridge. George Hastwell Grayson became a partner in 1897.

See: **MS:** Allerton, Bidston, L'pool C, Port Sunlight, Thornton Hough (6), Woolton
CH: Chester

Ref: Gray, A. S., *Edwardian Architecture*, 1985; Obits: Grayson, *RIBAJ*, 20 (1913) p. 61; *Builder*, 103 (15.11.1912), p. 593 and *Builder*, 104 (24.1.1913) p. 132; Ould, *RIBAJ*, 16 (1909) p. 292; *Builder*, 96 (6.2.1909), p. 157

Griggs, Frederick Landseer Maur (1876–1938)
Architect, etcher and illustrator of architectural subjects and landscapes. Born at Hitchin, Herts. He was articled to architect Walter Millard at Hitchin who taught him to draw in what became his distinctive style. He was a member of the Council for the Preservation of Rural England and the Society for the Protection of Ancient Buildings. Some of his work involved the restoration of buildings in the Cotswolds where he lived. With Norman Jewson, he designed a house in Chipping Camden and he also designed the WW1 Memorial Crosses at Biddenham and Chipping Campden. He is best known for his black and white drawings and etchings. He frequently worked on architectural drawings with C. E. Mallows (qv). He did the illustrations for Macmillan's popular series of *Highways and Byways* and contributed illustrations to several books including Old *Cottages in Oxford* and *The Life of G. F. Watts*. He joined the AWG in 1910.

See: **CU:** Carlisle

Ref: Gray, A. S., *Edwardian Architecture*, 1985; Obit. *Builder* (10.6.1938), p. 1127; Moore, J. N., *F. L. Griggs, the Architecture of Dreams*, 1999

The Guild of Handicraft (*c.* 1886–1914)
The Guild was set up in the late 1880s, by C. R. Ashbee (qv) in the east end of London. It was initially a training school which developed into a craft workshop designing and making furniture, metalwork and jewellery. It was a Ruskinian community-venture promoting the joy and satisfaction to be derived from well executed hand-work.

In 1898 an additional activity was added to the Guilds craft's when Ashbee purchased the plant (but not the type and blocks) used by William Morris (qv) in his Kelmscott Press. He also employed Morris's compositors and pressmen. The first type used was 'caslon' but in 1901 Ashbee designed his own type 'Endeavour'. The press, named Essex House, remained under Ashbeee's control until *c.* 1907 when Dr A. K. Coomaraswamy took over the direction. Ninety titles were printed 1898–1910.

In 1902 the lease on the East End premises expired and Ashbee moved the whole operation to Chipping Campden in the Cotswolds; finding accommodation and workshops for some 50 workers and their families. It was a democratic community but it was Ashbee who established the community rules and its philosophy. Practicing artists and craftsmen such as Alec Miller (qv), Paul Woodroffe (qv) and F. L. Griggs (qv), who also lived in Chipping Campden helped with the training of the Guild members. Despite being able to produce work of an excellent quality, the Guild ran into financial trouble in 1908 and the business was carried on as a Trust until 1914 when it was eventually wound up.

See: **CU:** Urswick **GM:** M/cc MMULib

Ref: Crawford, A., *Ashbee*, 1987

Hare, Henry Thomas (1861–1921)
Born at Scarborough, Yorkshire. He was articled to C. A. Bury of Harrogate and worked in London for Z. King & R. H. Hill. He studied in Paris before setting up on his own in London. He was master of the Edwardian municipal building, designing mostly in a Neo-Baroque style. He was President of the RIBA 1917–19.

See: **CH:** Crewe

Ref: Gray, A. S., *Edwardian Architecture*, 1985; *Builder* (14.1.1921), pp. 59, 67 and (21.1.21), pp. 90, 93–94

Hatch, James & Co. (1841–*c.* 1924)
Woodworkers. The firm, described as Millwrights and Joiners, was founded by James Hatch in Lancaster in the 1840s and by 1851 had moved its permanent address to Queens Place, King St. In 1913 it was listed in Bulmer's Directory as 'Builders and Contractors, Quarry Owners, Church furniture makers and carvers, Steam Saw and Machinery Works'. When James retired, the firm was run by his sons, John and William with the assistance of an uncle. The firm produced an extremely high standard of craftsmanship and frequently did the woodwork for Paley & Austin. The firm was last recorded in the Kelly's directory for 1924.

See: **LA:** Silverdale GM: Stockport MS: Port Sunlight, Sefton Park, Warrington

Ref: Lancaster Museum archives: *Trade Directories 1841–1924*

Healy, Michael (1873–1941)
Stained-glass Artist. Born in Dublin where despite early recognition of his drawing talents, he did not attend the Dublin School of Art until 1896. After further study at the Royal Hibernian Academy Schools he spent eighteen months in Italy and after his return to Dublin he joined Sarah Purser at the Tower of Glass in 1903. He worked there until his death in 1941. Healy's windows occur in only one church in England and that is St Peter's at Wallsend. He made up the Wilhelmina Geddes windows at Bardsea during her illness.

See: **CU:** Bardsea

Ref: Bowe, N. G., *Gazetteer of Irish Stained Glass*, 1988

Heaton, Butler & Bayne (1860–1953)
Firm of decorators working with stained glass, mosaics, etc. In 1852 Clement James Heaton set up a stained-glass studio. He was influenced by the work of AWN Pugin and Charles Winston whose research into glass production led to the rediscovery of some fine medieval colours. Heaton undertook research into pigments and created a wide range of 'new' colours. In 1860 he joined up with James Butler, a manufacturer of leaded glass. They collaborated for design purposes with Clayton and Bell. In 1862, Robert Turnill Bayne, a designer from Clayton and Bell joined the firm. Bayne's style owed much to the influence of Rossetti's early painting and has been compared to some of Morris & Co.'s early work. The other great influence on the style of the firm up to the end of the 1880s was the work of Henry Holiday who is known to have designed for them. The firm continued to survive into the next century by adapting to meet popular taste. They enjoyed success in the USA where for a short time Garham Manufacturing Co. was their stained-glass agent. The firm was dissolved on the death of Basil Richard Bayne, grandson of one of the firm's founders.

See: **CU:** Walton **LA:** Gt Altcar, Melling **GM:** Haughton, Haughton Green, M/cc, Reddish, RochdaleTH, Wigan **MS:** Knotty Ash, Port Sunlight **CH:** Chester, Eaton Hall **NS:** Meerbrook

Ref: Bayne, S. B. N., *Heaton, Butler & Bayne: c. 1986*

Heaton, Clement John (1861–1940)
Decorative artist. He was the son of the stained-glass manufacturer and was apprenticed to Burlisson and Grylls. He was a partner in the family firm for a short time but resigned in 1886. He was a contributor to the Century Guild, designing metal work and light fittings. He became a specialist in cloisonné enamelling. He set up his own business, 'Heaton's Cloisonné Mosaics Ltd' and did design work for Liberty and Co. He went to Switzerland and collaborated with Paul Robert on the internal decoration of the Musée des Beaux Arts in Neuchâtel. He also designed stained-glass windows for Swiss churches. He later lived in the United States and had a studio in New York around 1912.

See: **CH:** Chester

Ref: Ceresole, A., 'The Work in Cloisonné of Clement Heaton', *DASJ*, 20 (1996), pp. 34–42

Hemm, Gordon (?1891–1956)
Architect. Born at Stockport and trained at Liverpool School of Architecture under Reilly. He was a partner in the firm of Foden, Hemm & Williams of Liverpool and Manchester. He wrote books on and painted Liverpool subjects occasionally exhibiting at the RA.

See: **MS:** L'pool Uni

Ref: Cavanagh T., *Public Sculpture in Liverpool*, 1997; Obit. *Builder*, 191 (23.11.1956), p. 897

Hems, Harry & Sons
Carver and ecclesiastical furnisher. Born 1843 in London, Hems moved to Exeter *c.* 1866

where he established a successful business as a stone mason, ecclesiastical sculptor and church furnisher. The firm carried out repairs to many medieval churches as well as filling commissions for work in new churches and public buildings all over the country. By 1881 he employed some 70 men and had worked on over 400 churches and 100 public buildings. Later his three sons, Grevil b. 1870, Harry T. b. 1874 and William b. 1878 joined him in the business. In 1897 the firm was known as Harrry Hems & Sons. Harry senior died in 1916. His son Harry T. went to work with George Percy Bankart in the Lead shop at the Bromsgrove Guild around 1900.

See: **MS:** Bebington, Oxton **CH:** Bollington

Ref: Exeter CC web site: *www.exeter.gov.uk/ time trail, The Victorian City*; Watt, *The Bromsgrove Guild*, 1999; Obit. *Builder*, 110 (14 Jan.1916), p. 57; *Builder*, 110 (14 Apr.1916), p. 280

Hill, Oliver Francis (1887–1968)
Architect. Born in London, educated at Uppingham School and a neighbour of Edwin Lutyens (qv), who recommended he took a job in a builder's yard on leaving school. He was then articled to William Flockhart and spent two years at the Architectural Association's evening Drawing School. He set up his practice at Dover St London and built his first house in 1910. He went on to design luxury houses and gardens in southern England and chic London houses and flats throughout the 1920s and 30s To his domestic work he added pubs, new towns, tube stations and schools in a successful and high-flying career. This came to an end with the end of the Second World War when his style was out of favour. He turned to painting in the Cotwsolds and took on the lease of Daneway House in Sapperton, continuing to design for his old clients and friends.

See: **LA:** Morecambe

Ref: *Country Life*, 190 (14.11.1996) pp. 50–53; Powers, A., *Oliver Hill, architect and lover of Life*, 1989; Obit. *RIBAJ*, 75 (June 1968), p. 277; *Building*, 214 (3.5.1968), p. 76

Hiller, Henry Gustave (1864–1946)
An artist, designer, craftsman who worked in stained glass, gesso, metalwork, painted panels and decoration. He was born at Moss Side, Manchester and despite showing early artistic talent he left school to go, initially, into the wholesale warehouse trade. However he changed direction and began designing and executing work in the stained-glass section of a Manchester firm, probably Reuben Bennett (qv). He attended classes at the Manchester Technical Art School, at Owens's College and finally at Manchester School of Art, where he was influenced by Walter Crane (qv). He moved to Liverpool *c.* 1904 and set up his own very successful stained-glass studio and workshop in Seel St. He worked there for the next thirty-six years, apparently on his own, before retiring to spend his last years in Anglesey. Hiller had a great interest in natural history and devoted his spare time and artistic talents to scientific drawings of microscopic plants and gnats. A number of these beautiful water colours were bought for the Liverpool Museum.

See: **CU:** New Hutton **LA:** Accrington, Foulridge, Silverdale **GM:** Bolton, Cheadle Hulme, Patricroft **MS:** Bidston, Blundellsands, Bootle, Hoylake (2), Kirby, L'pool C Mus.+ (1), Mossley Hill, Sefton Park (2), Sefton Village, Thornton Hough, Toxteth, Wallasey(2), Walton, Wavertree **CH:** Chester (2), Crewe, Nantwich, Widnes(2)

Ref: Obit. *North Western Naturalist*, 21 (Sept–Dec 1946), pp. 258–60; Dolman, B., *A Dictionary of Contemporary Artists*, 1929; *Census 1901*

Hilton, Agnes Aubrey (b. 1879)
Born in Chester in 1879, the elder daughter of Robert Hilton (qv). She trained at Birmingham Municipal School of Art 1897–99 under Henry Payne and worked with him at Madresfield Court 1902. She exhibited with the Chester Guild of Arts and Crafts. Her working life is unresearched. *Circa* 1920 she was living with her father in Beetham, Cumbria, where she wrote and illustrated books, one of which was *The Hermit of Eskdale*, 1930.

See: **CU:** Beetham **CH:** Chester

Ref: *1901 Census*; Chester PRO *Christ Church archive; B'ham School of Art archives; The Studio*, 25 (1902) & 30 (1904)

Hilton, Robert (1853–*c.* 1935)
Metalworker. Born in Chester, he was a talented artist and a craftsman in wood and metalwork. He specialised in enamelling and silversmithing. He lived and worked in Alresford in Devon for some years before moving to Rhyl *c.* 1896. He returned to Chester a few years later and set up his own studio in his house in Overbridge Rd, Handbridge. He had a business address in Northgate St, Chester. His silverwork from 1896 has Chester assay marks. He was an active member of the Chester Guild of Arts and Crafts and of the Northern Art Workers Guild. He wrote an article about the art of enamelling for the catalogue of the Northern Art Workers Guild's Exhibition of 1903. He exhibited his work nationally and his work was illustrated in *The Studio* magazine. In 1904 he had a one-man exhibition of his ecclesiastical work in the old Chapter House in Chester. In 1905 he was appointed Director of the Keswick School of Industrial Arts and stayed there until 1920. During his retirement he lived at Hale Nr Milnthorpe and wrote a history of Beetham Parish Church 1933.

See: **MS:** L'pool C WAG **CH:** Chester Cath.+(1), Eaton Hall

Ref: Chester PRO, *Christ Church archives*; PRO Carlisle, *KSIA archives*; *Catalogue of Northern Art Worker's Guild Exhibition 1903; The Studio*, Nos 14, 25, 27, 30, 34; Bruce, Ian, *The Loving Eye and Skilful Hand*, 2001

Hitch, Nathaniel (1841–1938)
Sculptor. Born in Ware, Herts he was apprenticed to Farmer and Brindley, attending evening class at Borough Polytechnic. As a journeyman sculptor he worked all over the country mainly on churches but also on Cardiff Castle. He worked in wood, stone and marble and his reputation was such that he had regular commissions from architects who valued his work including W. D. Caröe and in particular J. L. Pearson with whom he worked on Truro Cathedral and Westminster Abbey.

See: **MS:** Sefton Park

Ref: Parish Magazine Feb 2004 All Saints Church, St Andrews, Fife

Hodel, Joseph Anton (1873–1930)
Metalworker and Jeweller. Born in Switzerland, married to an English woman, he established a jewellery and art metalworking studio at Hanway St, London in partnership with Louis Weingartner (qv) in the mid-1890s. By 1901 Hodel had moved to Bromsgrove to work with the Bromsgrove Guild. In 1902 Hodel and Weingartner collaborated with the Guild in producing a gilt, embellished silver trowel and a bronze and silver casket for the use of King Edward VII laying the foundation stone at the Royal College Dartmouth. This was followed by the production of several other 'royal' trowels, mallets and caskets. In 1909 Hodel went to Liverpool to be an instructor in metalwork and jewellery at the Liverpool Municipal School of Art and was a regular exhibitor at the Arts and Crafts Exhibition Society and at the Walker Art Gallery. Some of his finest work was beautiful pieces of Art Nouveau-style jewellery.

See: **MS:** Aigburth, L'pool C WAG, Wallasey

Ref: *Census 1901*; Watts, *Bromsgrove Guild 1999*; Zarlin, *Jewelry and Metalwork*; *The Studio*, 37 (1906)

Hodgson, Thomas (1833–1905)
Architect, builder and artist. There is little information about Thomas Hodgson. Hodgson is a local name so it is likely he was born in Keswick where his family were in the building trade and that his practice was in Keswick. He had a close association with the town being involved in the establishment of Fitz Park. He was a Trustee and Hon Secretary of the Fitz Park Trust for many years.

See: **CU:** Keswick

Ref: Keswick Museum archives

Holiday, Henry George Alexander (1839–1927)
Painter of genre and historical subjects, mural painter, designer of stained glass and illustrator. Educated at home by his father and aunt, he went to Leigh's Art School 1854 and to the RA Schools 1855. His early interest was in painting and in 1857 he started to teach painting and drawing at a private academy. He exhibited several pictures at the RA and came into contact with Rossetti (qv), Madox Brown (qv) and Burne-Jones (qv) who influenced his work. He later became interested in mosaic work, stained glass and sculpture. In 1862 he succeeded Edward Burne-Jones as chief designer at Powell of Whitefriars but did not work exclusively for them. He founded his own stained-glass studio in Hampstead in 1890 and ten years later was making his own pot glass. He closed his own workshop in 1906 and had his windows executed by Lowndes and Drury at the Glass House and by E. L. Armitage after *c.* 1920. He was elected to the AWG in Jan 1884.

See: **CU:** Ambleside(3), Barrow, Bootle, Bridekirk, Buttermere, Calder Bridge, Casterton, Cotehill, Finsthwaite, Grasmere, Keswick, Kirkby Lonsdale, Muncaster, Ponsonby, Rydal, Soulby, Walton, Warwick on Eden, Winster, Wythburn **LA:** Accrington, Baxenden, Blackburn, Edgeworth, Great Harwood, Leck, Melling, Ormskirk, PrestonAG, Upholland, Whittington **GM:** Ashton upon Mersey, Bolton(3), Hyde, Rochdale TH, Rusholme **MS:** Bebbington, Birkenhead, Huyton, Kirkby, L'pool WAG, New Ferry, Sefton, St Helens, Toxteth, Walton, Waterloo, Woodchurch **CH:** Astbury, Styal, Sutton, Runcorn **NS:** Caverswall, Leek

Ref: Holiday, H., *Reminiscences of my Life*, 1914; *Stained Glass as an Art*, 1896; *JBSMGP*, 2, no. 2 (1927) and 29, no. 1 (1989–90)

Horsley, Gerald Callcott (1862–1917)
Architect, artist, designer. He was educated at Cranbrook School, Kent and Kensington Grammar School and articled to Norman Shaw (qv) in 1879. There he met William Lethaby (qv), E. S. Prior and Mervyn Macartney (qv) and with them became a founder member of the AWG in 1884. Much of his best known work was painted decoration but his major architectural design was St Paul's School for Girls, Brook Green, Hammersmith in 1901. Later he designed station buildings for the London North Western Railway including Harrow & Wealdstone and Hatch End.

See: **NS:** Cheddleton, Hanley, Ipstones; Leek, Longdon

Ref: Gray, A. S., *Edwardian Architecture*, 1985; Obit. *RIBAJ*, 24 (1917), pp. 220–21, 240–41, *Builder*, 113 (13.7.1917), p. 23: AR, 42 (Aug. 1917), p. 44

Howson, Joan (1885–1964)
Stained-glass artist. Joan Howson was born near Wrexham at Overton on Dee, the only daughter among four children of an Archdeacon. She studied music in Paris but had to return to England when her mother became ill to help her father in his Manchester parish. When he was transferred to Hunts Cross she was able to study textile design and stained glass at the Liverpool School of Art 1910–13. In 1913 she moved to London to become the first pupil of Caroline Townshend (qv) at the Glass House in Lettice St Fulham becoming her partner and life-long friend, sharing an interest in socialism and promoting women's suffrage. During the Great War, Joan Howson worked in a French Hospital and stayed afterwards to run an embroidery business for French women until she returned to England in 1920. She carried out many stained-glass windows between the wars with Caroline Townshend and devoted much of her time to the repair of old windows. Townshend and Howson set up their own studio in Deodar Rd, Putney and during the Second World War lived in North Wales where they ran a home for evacuees from Fulham and Liverpool. Howson continued to work on new windows and on repairing war damage after Townshend's death in 1945.

See: **CU:** Burneside, Eskdale Green, Mosser Mains, Skelsmergh **GM:** Swinton
MS: Fazakerley, Gateacre, Hunts Cross
CH: Widnes

Ref: Obit. *JBSMGP*, 14, no. 2 (1965); William Morris Gallery, *Women Stained-Glass Artists*, 1985

Huddart, Arthur (1865–1951)
Architect. Born in May 1865 in Windermere he was the first son of Joseph and Elizabeth Huddart. As a child he lived in the Lake District and had private education until he was sent to the Moravian School in Fairfield, Manchester. From there he went to Manchester College of Art and South Kensington School of Art (1883–86) His architectural training was with T. L. Banks (qv) who had offices in London and Whitehaven. He would have been training at the time that Charles H. Townsend (qv) was with the practice and is thought to have worked with him on St Bega's Chapel at Eskdale Green. He set up on his own in Lowther St, Whitehaven *c.* 1892. All Huddart's work is in the north west of England and his major work was in Eskdale where he lived for many years.

See: **CU:** Eskdale Green(2)

Ref: Whitehaven PRO *archives*.

Huson, Thomas (1844–1920)
Artist, landscape and genre painter and engraver. Born in Liverpool. He worked first as a chemist doing art in his spare time. He exhibited regularly at the WAG from 1871 as well as at the RA. He was a member of the Royal Society of Painters-Etchers and Engravers from 1881 and of the Royal Institute of Painters in Water Colours from 1883.

See: **MS:** L'pool C

Ref: Cavanagh T., *Public Sculpture in Liverpool*, 1997

Hutchinson, Gerald P. (b. 1867)
Stained-glass artist. Born in Rugby. Nothing is published about his early life. He worked for James Powell of Whitefriars becoming head of the stained-glass studio. He was elected to the AWG in 1895. By 1901 he and his wife and two children had moved out of Chelsea and were living at Chislehurst in Kent with a governess and two maids. Hutchinson contributed to the list of work executed by members of the BSMGP in 1929, submitting the work of the James Powell Studio under his name as Director of the studio.

See: **CU:** Bridekirk, Keswick, Pennington, Temple Sowerby **LA:** Lytham St Annes
MS: Gt Crosby **CH:** Alsager, Congleton

Ref: *Census 1901*. BSMGP, *Directory*, 1929.

Image, Selwyn (1849–1930)
Artist and decorator. He was educated at Marlborough College and New College, Oxford. He was ordained in 1872 but gave up the church in 1880 to devote his life to art and literature. He was closely associated with the Century Guild (qv) and *The Hobby Horse* which was launched in 1884. He was an artist, a designer of embroidery, stained glass and other church decoration and a published poet. He was a member of the AWG from 1887 and its Master in 1900. In 1910 he became Slade Professor of Fine Art at Oxford.

See: **CU:** Croglin **CH:** Wilmslow
NS: Caverswall.

Ref: Obit. *JBSMGP*, 3, no. 4 (1930)

Jack, George Washington Henry (1855–1931)
Architect. Born in the USA of British parents, he moved to London in 1875 after a short stay in Glasgow. In 1880 he entered the office of Philip Webb (qv), continuing the practice when Webb retired in 1900. Jack became skilled in modelling and wood carving and by 1890 had become the chief furniture designer for Morris & Co. He taught carving at the Central School of Arts and Crafts and after 1900 at the RCA under William Lethaby (qv). George Jack also designed mosaics and wrote about woodwork and carving. He was elected to the AWG in 1906 and was granted honorary membership in 1925.

See: **CU:** Brampton **LA:** Whalley

Ref: Gray, A. S., *Edwardian Architecture*, 1985; Obit. *Builder* (15.1.1932), p. 133

Jackson, Frederick Hamilton (1848–1923)
Painter in oil and water colour of landscapes, coastal scenes and genre. He studied art at the

RA Schools and exhibited at the major London galleries from 1870. He was master of the Antique School at the Slade under Poynter and Legros. In 1880 he founded the Chiswick School of Art with E. S. Burchett. He became a member of the AWG 1887. He wrote 'Intarsia and Marquetry' in the series *Handbooks for the Designer Craftsman*. 1903.

See: **NS:** Leek

Ref: Waters, *Dictionary of British Artists*, 1975

Jackson, Thomas Graham (1835–1924)
Architect, artist and writer. Born at Hampstead London he was educated at Brighton College and at Oxford. He was articled to George Gilbert Scott 1858 and set up his own practice in 1862.

Jackson is best known for his work in Oxford where he designed many colleges and other buildings in his own free style of the late C16 and early C17 which came to be known as 'Jacksonobethan'. He also designed stained glass windows and glass table-ware for James Powell & Son. He was a member of the AWG from 1889 and its master in 1896.

It was Jackson and R. N. Shaw who wrote *Architecture a Profession or an* Art in 1892 advocating the need for training which provided a common foundation course (including practical work) for architects, artists and craftsmen including builders but without examinations and giving an opportunity for individuals to return to education in mid-career. In his later career he wrote many notable books on architecture.

See: **GM** : M/cc City AG

Ref: A. S. Gray, *Edwardian Architecture*, 1985; Rudoe, J. & Coutts, H., 'The table glass designs of Philip Webb and T. G. Jackson for James Powell & Sons' in *DASJ*, 16, 1992,

Jagger, Charles Sargeant (1885–1934)
Sculptor, war artist. Born at Kilnhurst, Yorkshire, he studied at Sheffield School of Art and at the RCA 1903–10 under Lanteri. He won a travelling scholarship and worked for a time in Venice and Rome, winning the Rome Scholarship in Sculpture. At the outbreak of WW1 he joined the Artists' Rifles and served in Gallipoli, France and Flanders where he was wounded. He was awarded the Military Cross. After the war he resumed his career and not surprisingly some of his best work was inspired by his war-time experiences. His best known works are the Royal Artillery memorial at Hyde Park and the Great Western Railway Memorial at Paddington station. He was a regular exhibitor at the RA.

See: **GM**: M/cc **MS:** West Kirby

Ref: Waters, *Dictionary of British Artists*, 1975; Compton, A., *The Sculpture of C. S. Jagger*, 2004

Jewitt, Edward Holmes (1849–1929)
Born in Headington, Oxford in 1847, Edward Holmes Jewitt grew up in a family of book engravers and became an artist and stained-glass designer. His early life is unresearched. In 1877, aged twenty-nine, he joined Shrigley & Hunt. When Carl Almquist (qv) moved to London in 1874 Jewitt became head of Design at Lancaster and he and Almquist co-ordinated the bulk of the design work for the firm for over 40 years. Like all those who worked for Shrigley & Hunt his work is not publicly attributed and information about a small part of the work he did can be found in Mrs Fisher's Account book held in the Lancaster Museum. His last recorded work was in 1919.

See: **CU:** Bardsea **LA:** Lancaster **CH:** Wilmslow

Ref: Walters, *Stained Glass from Shrigley and Hunt*, 2003

John, W Goscombe (1860–1952)
Sculptor. Born in Cardiff the son of a stone carver and sculptor who worked on Cardiff Castle with William Burges (qv). John attended Cardiff School of Art and went to London in 1882 as assistant in the Lambeth workshop of Thomas Nicholls while attending Lambeth School of Art. He then worked for Charles Bell Birch and went on to the RA schools in 1884. He studied in Paris 1890–91 and became sculptor to the upper-crust producing many beautiful monuments and portrait busts. He did the statues of King Edward VII and Queen Alexandra outside the main entrance to the Victoria & Albert Museum. He was a member of the AWG 1891–1900 and was knighted in 1911. He gave many of his own works to the National Museum of Wales.

See: **LA:** Preston AG **MS:** L'pool C (2), Port Sunlight (3)

Ref: Gray, A. S., *Edwardian Architecture*, 1985; Pearson, Fiona, *Goscombe John at the National Museum of Wales*, 1979

Kay, Ida Lillian (b. 1881)
Sculptor and stained-glass artist. Born in Stafford. By 1901 her family was living in Edgebaston and Ida was a student at Birminghan School of Art. Her stained-glass work was shown in *The Studio* 1902. She exhibited portrait busts at the RA in 1910 and 1911

See: **CH:** Crewe

Ref: *Census 1901*

Kay-Shuttleworth, Rachel Beatrice (1886–1967)
Embroiderer, lacemaker, collector, teacher. Born at Gawthorpe Hall near Burnley she was educated at home until at the age of fifteen she was sent to a boarding school which specialised in music. She gave up music in favour of needlework and lacemaking which became her

major interests. She was presented at court as a 'debutante' and moved in the highest court circles. She travelled widely through Europe, North Africa and the USA always examining, studying and collecting examples of needlework and textiles which she used in her lectures. She devoted her life to the care of her ageing parents and to serious and effective involvement in important projects aimed at reducing social deprivation, encouraging youth and establishing the importance of the art of needlework. In 1912 she conceived the idea of establishing a 'Craft House' in which teachers and students of textile crafts could meet and work. It was not until the 1950s that she was able to install her textile collection in Gawthorpe Hall and establish her 'Craft House' there.

See: **LA:** Padiham.

Ref: Williams, Canon G. A., *Rachel Kay-Shuttleworth*, 1968; Johnson, J. & Greutzner, *A Dictionary of British Art*, 1999; *Census 1901*

Kelmscott Press see **William Morris**

See: **LA:** Blackburn AG, M/cc Central, JR Libs + MMULib, Preston Lib **MS:** L'pool C Lib +UniLib

Kemp, Marjorie Boyce (1888–1975)
Stained-glass artist. She was born in Blairgowrie, Perthshire and studied at the Glasgow School of Art. She went into partnership with Margaret Chilton (qv) in 1922 sharing a studio at 13a George St, Edinburgh moving later to 12 Queen St and after the Second World War to 8 Fettes Row. After her partner's death in *c.* 1962 Marjorie retired from stained-glass work.

See: **CU:** Milburn

Ref: William Morris Gallery, *Women Stained- Glass Artists*, 1985

Kennedy, Jessie B.
Wood-carver. Mrs Kennedy lived at the Hill, Sandbach Heath. Little else is known.

See: **CH:** Sandbach

Ref: St John's Church, Sandbach Heath, Cheshire

The Keswick School of Industrial Arts (1884–1984)
The School was started in the Crosthwaite Parish Hall by Canon and Mrs Rawnsley (qv) to provide education, training and work for local people. Following an increase in numbers and activities, funds were raised for a purpose-made school which was built by Paley & Austin at Greta Bridge in 1894. The KSIA produced hand-made work in metal – copper, brass, pewter & silver – as well as enamelling, leather-work and woodwork. For a time the Ruskin Linen Industry (qv) operated in association with the School. The School employed skilled artists and craftsmen as instructors, including Arthur Simpson (qv), Harold Stabler (qv), Herbert Maryon and Robert Hilton (qv). The School's wares were displayed at many national and international exhibitions.

See: **CU:** Barrow, Brampton, Brathay, Carlisle, Crosby on Eden, Hutton in th' Forest, Kendal, Kentmere, Keswick Mus.+(3), Seascale
LA: Burnley **GM:** Reddish **CH:** Christleton
NS: Hanley

Ref: Ian Bruce, *The Loving Eye and Skilful Hand*, 2001; Carlisle PRO *KSIA archives*

Kilbride Joseph M. (1857–1936)
Wood-worker. Born in Watermillock he started work as an apprentice wood carver with Messrs Joseph James of Penrith and later worked in Newcastle, Liverpool, Manchester, Lancaster Preston, Carlisle, Barrow and Bolton. He started up on his own in Barbon in 1900 and remained there until he retired. His work can be seen in many churches in Cumbria.

See: **CU:** Barbon, Bowness, Crosby Ravensworth, Kirby Stephen, Shap

Ref: Obit. in St Bartholomew's Church, Barbon, Cumbria

Kirby, Edmund (1838–1920)
Architect. Born in Liverpool, and educated at Sedgely Park School and Oscott College. He attended the RA Schools and was articled to E. W. Pugin. He worked for Hardman and Co., ecclesiastical designers, and later became an assistant to John Douglas (qv). He set up his own practice in Liverpool in 1867 and worked there for the next forty years. Much of his work was in the North West and covered the whole range of public, commercial and domestic building. It was a hugely successful practice.

See: **GM:** Stockport **MS:** Hoylake, L'pool C (2),Oxton, Port Sunlight (2),Walton
CH: Appleton Thorn, High Leigh

Ref: Liverpool PRO, *Kirby archive*

Krall see **Barkentin & Krall**

Langdale Linen Industry (fl. 1884–*c.*1919)
Set up in 1884 by Albert Fleming, a philanthropic solicitor and a supporter of Ruskin's ideals, to restore the crafts of hand spinning and weaving to Cumberland. It was managed by his housekeeper **Marian Twelves**, who taught herself to spin and weave and passed these skills on to local people. They were then able to earn money for the thread they spun and the linen that was woven and made into useful items for sale. The industry was based at a cottage in Elterwater, Langdale. It went on to exhibit its wares at exhibitions all over the country. When Marian Twelves left Langdale for Keswick, her place as manager was taken by Elizabeth Pepper one of her brightest students and a farmer's wife. She ran it for many years developing a wider range of handicrafts. The business thrived until the First World War when demand dropped and

post-war markets changed. The business gradually petered out.

See: **CU:** Ambleside AG + (1), Coniston Mus., Kendal AG.

Ref: Coniston Museum, *archives;* Brunton, J., *The Arts and Crafts Movement in the Lake District*, 2001; Haslam, S., *John Ruskin and the Lakelands Arts Revival*, 2004

Lawton, Joseph (1885–?)
Artist. He was educated at a Board of Education School in Manchester and Manchester School of Art which he entered on an internal scholarship. In 1910 he was living in Anfield, Liverpool and working as a designer for stained glass and decoration. He attended the Liverpool City School of Art 1910–13 and exhibited at the Walker Art Gallery 1911–16.

See: **MS:** Gt Crosby

Ref: Johnson & Greutzner, *Dictionary of British Art 5*, 1999; Aldham Robarts Resource Centre John Moore's University, *City Art School Attendance Register No 1*

Ledward, Gilbert (1888–1960)
Sculptor. Born in Chelsea, the son of R. A. Ledward (qv). He studied at the Chelsea Polytechnic, Goldsmith's College and the RA Schools. He worked in marble, stone and bronze executing portraits, figures and monuments in the New Sculpture style. He served in the Great War and afterwards designed a number of war memorials including the Guards' Division memorial facing Horseguards' Parade. He was Professor of Sculpture at the RCA 1927–29. He set up an organisation called Sculptured Memorials and Headstones with a number of other craftsmen including Eric Gill (qv) and moved to Gill's workshop in Berkshire during WW2. A major work from 1936–38 was the giant male nude *Inspiration* on the Adelphi building, Victoria Embankment, London. He was elected to the AWG in 1933.

See: **LA:** Blackpool, Stonyhurst **GM:** Stockport **NS:** Hanley

Ref: Johnson & Greutzner, *Dictionary of British Art 5*, 1999; Ward-Jackson, *Public Sculpture in the City of London*, 2003; Moriarty, C., *The Sculpture of Gilbert Ledward*, 2003

Ledward, Richard A. (1857–90)
Sculptor. Born in Burslem he studied at the Art School there while working as a modeller for Pinder Bourne & Co. He won a scholarship which enabled him to attend the National Training School at South Kensington where he spent some time as an instructor. He later taught at Westminster and Blackheath Schools of Art. He exhibited regularly at the RA from 1882. He specialised in terracotta reliefs and made the busts of a number of well-known figures including Rt Hon W. E. Gladstone MP. He was elected to the AWG in 1888.

See: **CH:** Marple

Ref: *Dictionary of National Biography*, vol. XI, 1993

Lee, Thomas Stirling (1857–1916)
Sculptor. Born in London. Sterling Lee was apprenticed to J. Birnie Philip and attended the RA Schools when he won a gold medal 1877 and a travelling scholarship 1879. He studied in Paris and Rome 1881–83 and returned to England to help Alfred Gilbert with his lost–wax casting experiments. He exhibited widely and contributed architectural sculpture to many buildings. He was elected to the AWG in 1889 and was Master in 1898.

See: **MS:** 'L'pool C (2)

Ref: Cavanagh, *Public Sculpture in Liverpool*, 1997; Beattie, *New Sculpture*, 1983; Obit. *The Studio*, 68 (1916)

Leek Embroidery Society (*c.* 1880–*c.* 1912)
The Leek Embroidery Society was started *c.* 1880 by Mrs Elizabeth Wardle the wife of the silk dyer and manufacturer, Thomas Wardle of Leek. Wardle tutored William Morris (qv) in the use of vegetable dyes at his works in Leek and Morris inspired Mrs Wardle to create the Leek Embroidery Society out of what had been a very skilful leisure pursuit. Over twenty years, the Society became a successful and nationally acclaimed organisation which specialised in using tussur silk thread and fabrics dyed by Thomas Wardle. Under Elizabeth Wardle's supervision, the Society taught the art of embroidery and made many items for sale, including very popular embroidery kits. Many of their designs were created by well-known designers and architects including Walter Crane (qv), William Morris (qv), Norman Shaw (qv), John Sedding (qv), Gerald Horsley (qv) and G. G. Scott. After Elizabeth Wardle's death in 1902 her daughter Lydia and Mrs Clara Bill continued running the Society which continued for at least another 10 years.

See: **GM:** M/cc Whitworth AG **CH:** Sutton **NS:** Cheddleton, Hanley, Ipstones, Leek (4), Longsdon, Merebrook

Ref: Jacques, Anne G, *Leek Embroidery*, 1990; Jacques, Anne, *The Wardle Story: A Victorian Enterprise*

Lethaby, William Richard (1857–1931)
Architect, writer and educator. He was educated at Barnstaple School and articled to local architect Alexander Lauder who designed Wesleyan chapels and set up the Devon Art pottery. He was employed as assistant in offices in Derbyshire and Leicester until 1879 when he won a travelling scholarship to France where he sketched some thirty cathedrals. He joined Norman Shaw's (qv) office and entered the RA Schools 1880 where he won a Silver Medal and the RIBA Pugin prize. In 1879 he became chief assistant to Shaw and with his colleagues in the office founded the AWG in 1884, becoming its Master in 1911. He set up his own practice in Hart St in 1889 and founded a furniture company, Kenton and Co. with architect

friends. He designed furniture and fireplaces, wood and stone carving, leadwork, embroidery and pottery for a number of firms to augment his income. He admired and was influenced by Ruskin (qv), Morris (qv) and Philip Webb (qv) and like Webb he tried to build from first principles. His work included large country houses like Melsetter House on the Isle of Hoy in Orkney and Avon Tyrell, Hampshire. He was responsible for The Eagle Insurance Company's offices in Birmingham with J. L. Ball and he designed All Saints, Brockhampton, Herefordshire. Lethaby was an inspiring teacher and strove to promote the teachings of Webb and Morris. He was appointed first art adviser to the new LCC in 1892 and helped found the Central School of Arts and Crafts. He taught at the RCA, South Kensington where he became first Professor of Design from 1900–18. He wrote many books related to architecture.

See: **NS:** Leek

Ref: Gray, A. S., *Edwardian Architecture*, 1985; RIBA Library, *William Richard Lethaby 1857–1931: a bibliography of his literary works* (London, The Library, 1950); Obit. *RIBAJ* (8.8.1931), pp. 696, 737 & *RIBAJ* (19.9), p. 738 & *RIBAJ* (17.10), p. 770; *Builder* (24.7.1931), pp. 134, 138–39, 179

Lockwood, Thomas M. (1830–1900)
Architect. He was articled to Philip Carston Lockwood surveyor of Brighton from 1851 and was a draughtsman in various offices from 1855–62 including those of T. M. Penson and George Woodhouse. He set up independent practice in Chester in 1862 and was later joined by his sons William Thomas and Philip H. Lockwood. He is best known for black and white work in Chester during the 1880s.

See: **CH:** Chester Centre (8), Boughton, and Port Sunlight (2)

Ref: RIBA, *Directory*, 2001; Obit. *Builder*, 79 (21.7.1900), p. 60, *RIBAJ* (July 1900), p. 450

Lonsdale, Horatio Walter (1844–1919)
Decorative painter, illustrator and stained-glass artist. Lonsdale was born in Mexico of English parents and sent to school in England. He travelled in France and Germany to complete his education. He had a great flair for languages and in later years added Spanish and Italian to his French and German. In 1865 he attended the RA School of Architecture and in 1868 became assistant to William Burges (qv). He designed stained glass and mural decoration for Burges's great projects at St Finn Barr Cathedral in Cork, St Mary Studley Royal, Skelton Church, Cardiff Castle and Castell Coch. He also worked on Burges's own 'Tower House' in Kensington. When Burges died in 1881, Lonsdale continued to enjoy some patronage from the Marquis of Bute but beyond that his work is not well researched. He was elected to the AWG in 1887 and was a founder member of the Arts and Crafts Exhibition Society. He was an expert on perspective and published two books on the subject; *Perspective of Shadows* in 1912 and *Inverse Perspective* in 1915.

See: **CU:** Hawkshead, Rusland **MS:** Knotty Ash

Ref: Gallery Lingard, *Horatio Walter Lonsdale, Architectural Artist*, 1984; Obits: *RIBAJ*, 26 (1919), pp. 261, 273, *Builder*, 117 (26.9.1919), p. 327

Lorimer, Robert Stoddart (1864–1929)
Architect. Educated at Edinburgh Academy and University, he was articled to Rowand Anderson in 1885. In 1889 he joined G. F. Bodley's office in London and went to James MacLaren in 1890. McLaren died shortly afterwards but was a great influence on Lorimer. In 1893 he set up his own practice in Edinburgh. He did much prestigious restoration work and additions to castles and country houses but also designed simple churches and small houses. In 1901–03 he designed the Thistle Chapel in St Giles Cathedral, Edinburgh but his greatest work is considered to be the Scottish National War Memorial Chapel on Castle Rock, Edinburgh. Lorimer gathered around him a talented group of artists and craftsmen including Phoebe Traquair, Louis Davis (qv), Douglas Strachan, Maurice and Alice Meredith Williams (qv) and the Clow brothers (qv). He was elected to the AWG in 1922.

See: **CU:** Carlisle (2), Dalston, Plumpton (2), Workington **LA:** Fleetwood **CH:** Davenham

Ref: Savage, P., *Lorimer and the Edinburgh Craft Designers*, 1980; Obit. *RIBAJ*, 36 (1929), p. 771, 792; *Builder*, 137 (20.9.1929), pp. 458, 460, 478; *AR* 66, (Oct.1929), pp. 16, 206–07

Losh Sarah (1785–1853)
Amateur architect and designer. By rights this lady and her church should not appear in this book, but if she had been born fifty years later her inclusion would have been unquestioned although she would still have been viewed as something of an eccentric. She was born into a wealthy family, who lived at Woodside in Wreay. She had a wide-ranging private education and travelled extensively. Losh must have been a woman of exceptional ability given that she not only designed and arranged for the building of the church but also chose the exotic materials and employed many classical and religious allusions in her decoration of it. The church was built towards the end of her life in memory of her younger sister Catherine, her parents and great friend, William Thain who was killed by an arrow while serving in India. She went on to restore St John's Church at Newton Arlosh, Cumbria.

See: **CU:** Wreay

Ref: Wreay church leaflet; website: www.visitcumbria.com

Lowndes, Mary (1856–1929)
Stained-glass artist. She was born at Poole Keynes, now in Gloucestershire. Her family moved to Sturminster Newton in 1862 where her father was the vicar. The church there has her first ever stained-glass window. Lowndes attended the Slade School of Fine Art in London 1883–86. She became a pupil of Henry Holiday (qv) for whom she worked on cartoons, drawing figures from life as was Holiday's way. By the 1890s she had taught herself the techniques of glass painting as well as designing and was working in the studio of Britten and Gilson taking full advantage of that firm's introduction of Prior's Glass. Christopher Whall (qv) was also using Britten and Gilson at this time and influenced her not only in terms of her stained-glass techniques but also to the extent that in 1897 she joined with Alfred Drury, a craftsman at Britten and Gilson, to set up the Lowndes and Drury studio and workshop. They offered facilities for independent artists to have their windows made up by skilled craftsmen under their own supervision or indeed to paint and glaze their stained-glass work themselves. The project was so successful that in 1906 the operation moved to purpose-built premises in Lettice St, Fulham known as 'The Glass House'. Mary Lowndes made over one hundred windows on her own account from the mid-1890s up to her retirement in the 1920s. She was involved in the Women's Suffrage Movement.

See: **GM:** Altrincham, Blackrod **MS:** Childwall, Wallasey **CH:** Harthill **NS:** Leek

Ref: O'Donoghue, Mary Lowndes; *JBSMGP*, 24 (2001); William Morris Gallery, *Women Stained-Glass Artists*, 1985.

Lucchesi, Andrea Carlo (1860–1925)
Sculptor. He was educated at Euston College and the West London School of Art before attending the RA Schools. He was assistant to H. H. Armstead (qv) and Edward Onslow Ford (qv), before going on to work for two silversmith firms, Garrard's and Elkington's and eventually setting up his own studio. He exhibited work at the RA almost every year 1881–1925. Lucchesi's best known work is the memorial to Onslow Ford of 1903 at the corner of Abbey Road and Grove End Rd, NW8. He was elected to the AWG in 1907.

See: **CU:** Carlisle Cath, Kendal, Keswick(2)

Ref: Waters, *Dictionary of British Artists*, 1975; *Royal Academy Exhibitions* 1905–70; Johnson & Greutzner, *Dictionary of British Art* 5, 1999

Lutyens, Edwin Landseer (1869–1944)
Architect. Born in London and educated at home because of poor health. In 1885 he studied architecture at South Kensington Schools and later joined George and Peto's office. Early commissions led him to set up on his own, aged twenty, at 6 Gray's Inn Square. He benefited from the advice and encouragement given by Gertrude Jekyll and her new approach to gardens. He greatly admired the work of Philip Webb (qv) and Norman Shaw (qv) and developed his own free Arts and Crafts style. He moved into Shaw's old offices in Bloomsbury Square and built up a large practice and a reputation for superior houses, which stood out among their contemporaries. His output included Tigbourne Court Witley (1899), Goddards at Abinger (1900), Grey Walls, Gullane, East Lothian (1901) and Deanery Garden, Sonning (1901) with gardens by Jekyll. In 1903 he refurbished Lindisfarne Castle. He was involved in the planning and development of the centre of Hampstead Garden Suburb. He was elected to the AWG in 1903 and was Master in 1933. As the new century progressed and architectural fashions changed, Lutyens adapted his designs and his work began to feature classical forms. 1912–31 he spent time in India building the Viceroy's house and other major government buildings in New Delhi. Post-war, Lutyens was asked to design many cenotaphs and other memorials and to assist with the rebuilding in the City of London. He was knighted in 1918 and was President of the RA from 1938.

See: **CU:** Barrow in Furness, Muncaster **GM:** Bury, M/cc (2), Rochdale **MS:** L'pool Cath, Port Sunlight **CH:** Eaton Hall

Ref: Gray, A. S., *Edwardian Architecture*, 1985; Brown, J., *Lutyens and the Edwardians*, 1996; Ridley, J., *Edwin Lutyens, his Life, his Wife, his Work*, 2003; Hussey, C., *The Life of Sir Edwin Lutyens*, 1984; Weaver, L., *Houses and Gardens by E. L. Lutyens*, 2001

Macbeth, Ann (1875–1948)
Needlework artist and teacher. She was born in Bolton, Lancs but trained and taught at the Glasgow School of Art. In 1901 she became an assistant to Jessie Newberry in embroidery classes. She was a prolific and original designer. She extended her teaching to bookbinding metalwork and ceramic decoration and became chief instructress *c.* 1907. She designed some pieces of jewellery for Peter Wylie, carpets for Alexander Morton and embroidery items etc. for Liberty's, Knox Linen Thread Co., and Donalds of Dundee. She received commissions from Glasgow Cathedral. Her designs sprang from natural forms and she came to believe that though they must be decorative and beautiful, the items made should be useful. Her work was shown at many international exhibitions. She was active in developing the skills of teachers and in ensuring effective teaching methods for all ages from school children upwards. She wrote a number of books collaboratively to this end. In 1920 she moved to Patterdale where she set up

embroidery classes and other practical craft classes organised by the Women's Institute.

See: **CU:** Patterdale **LA:** Padiham

Ref: Ives, Marjorie, *The Life of Ann Macbeth of Patterdale*, nd; Arthur, E., 'Ann Macbeth 1875–1948' in *Glasgow Girls*, 1990

Macartney, Mervin Edmund (1853–1932)
Architect. He grew up in Co. Armagh and went to Lincoln College Oxford 1873–77. He entered the office of Norman Shaw (qv) in 1877 and set up his own practice in 1882. In 1884 he helped to found the AWG and became its Master in 1899. He was also a founding member of the short-lived furniture firm of Kenton & Co. His practice was mainly domestic and his particular interest was in C17 & C18 architectural styles. Between 1898 and 1901 he co-authored with John Belcher, two volumes of *Later Renaissance Architecture* and he was editor of *The Architectural Review 1906–20*. He was surveyor to St Paul's Cathedral 1906–1931 and collaborated with Detmar Blow (qv) on the design of the Earl Kitchener of Khartoum Memorial Chapel in St Paul's Cathedral crypt. He was also consulting architect for Durham Cathedral. He was knighted in 1930.

See: **LA:** Downham

Ref: Gray, A. S., *Edwardian Architecture*, 1985; Obits: *RIBAJ* (12.11.1932), pp. 25–26; *Builder* (4.11.1932), pp. 760 –765 (18.11.32), p. 846.

Mackmurdo, Arthur Heygate (1850–1942)
Architect, designer and political sociologist. He attended Felsted School in Essex and was articled to Chatfield Clarke in 1869, going as an improver to James Brooks round about 1870. He attended Ruskin's drawing classes at Oxford and had close association with Ruskin for some years and claimed to have travelled with him in Italy. He was greatly influenced by Ruskin and helped establish Ruskin Societies around the country. His first house was designed for his mother in 1873 in Enfield. In 1875 he set up his own practice in Southampton Row but moved in 1880 to 20 Fitzroy St, W1. He kept an open and hospitable house where many visitors interested in art and design congregated. He went on to design a few houses around Enfield and Chelsea and a church in Liverpool with T. E. Cutts (qv). In 1883 he took Herbert Horne into his practice as a pupil making him a partner in 1885. In 1882 Ruskin (qv) recommended Mackmurdo for the post of Art Professor at Liverpool University but he was unsuccessful in the competition. Also in 1882 Mackmurdo and Herbert Horne founded The Century Guild (qv) – a co-operative for ensuring co-ordination and quality of design in the decorative arts. Many talented artists and designers were involved. In 1884, he also founded and co-produced *The Hobby Horse* a quality magazine on the arts. Both projects were very influential but short-lived. Mackmurdo is recorded as being a pioneer of Art Nouveau design. Early examples of this style can be seen in Walthamstow Museum where the 'whiplash curve' is evident in his design of a chair and in the frontispiece of his book *Wrens City Churches* published in 1883. He was a member of the AWG 1888–93. By 1904 Mackmurdo had moved to Great Ruffins, the house he built for himself and his wife in Essex and virtually retired from architecture, switching his interests to plans for social and currency reform. His political philosophy is described in his book *The Human Hive* written 1926.

See: **GM:** M/cc CAG **MS:** L'pool C, Sefton Park **CH:** Wilmslow

Ref: William Morris Art Gallery archives; *The Studio*, 16 (1899); Evans, S., 'Arthur Heygate, Mackmurdo and the Century Guild' (unpub. thesis, 1976)

MacNair, James Herbert (1868–1955)
Designer. He was born in Glasgow into a well-off military family and educated at the Collegiate School in Greenock. He spent a year studying water-colour painting in France and in 1888 was apprenticed to John Honeyman, a Glasgow architect. It was here he met Charles Rennie Macintosh. They both attended evening classes at the Glasgow School of Art, where they met Margaret and Frances Macdonald. The foursome worked together on a number of projects in graphic art, furniture and architecture. MacNair set up independently as a designer at 227 West George St, Glasgow in 1895, producing designs for furniture, book illustrations, bookplates watercolours and posters. An office fire destroyed much of his work in 1897. In 1898 he took up the post of Instructor in Decorative Design at the School of Architecture and Applied Art in Liverpool, where he was a popular and innovative teacher and undertook several commissions in the city. He married Frances MacDonald (1873–1921) in 1899. She gave private embroidery lessons and collaborated with her husband in the design of jewellery, furniture and silver. Together they designed a writing room for the Scottish Section of the Turin International Exhibition in 1902. For the University, MacNair designed two medals in collaboration with C. J. Allen (qv), book-covers for the School of Tropical Medicine and, with his wife, costumes for the production of Greek Plays. He was elected a member of the Liverpool Academy in 1899. In 1905 when the Liverpool School of Applied Art was merged with the Liverpool School of Art, MacNair set up independent studios with artist Gerard Chowne at Sandon Terrace to teach drawing and painting. He was a founder member of the Sandon Society of Artists in 1908. In that year he lost his private income when the family shipping business went

bankrupt and as he had no commissions, the couple returned to Glasgow, where they lived in straightened circumstances. After Frances's death in 1921 MacNair never painted again and destroyed much of his own and his wife's work.

See: **MS:** L'pool C WAG, UniAG, Mossley Hill AG

Ref: *victorianweb.org/art/design/macnair*; Landow, Prof. George P., 'James Herbert MacNair 1868–1955, A Brief Biography' and Billicliffe, Roger, 'James Herbert MacNair, 1868–1955 An Evaluation', *The Studio*, 26 (1902)

Mallows Charles Edward (1864–1915)
Architect. Born in Chelsea. The family moved to Bedford where he attended Bedford Art School and was articled to T. Mercer of Bedford in 1879. In 1882 he joined the London office of Salamans and Wornum going to the RA Schools in 1883. Later he worked for H. H. Bridgman and Wallace & Flockhart. He won the Pugin Prize in 1889 and set up his own practice in Bedford in 1892. He designed garden ornaments for John P. White's Pyghtle works. 1887–91 he did a series of pencil drawings of Cathedrals of England for the *Century* magazine and spent 6 months each year travelling and sketching. Mallows' special skill was as a draughtsman and perspective artist and he was constantly asked to prepare drawings for architectural competitions and frequently invited to join partnerships which were often temporary. He drew for the *Architectural Review* and *The Studio*. He was also a designer of beautiful houses and gardens, the earliest being at Biddenham, Bedfordshire.

See: **CH:** Eaton, Willington

Ref: Gray, A. S., *Edwardian Architecture*, 1985; Obit. *RIBAJ* (12.6.1915), p. 403, & *RIBAJ* (26.6.1915), p. 407 & (31.7.1915), p. 458; *Builder* (4.6.1915), p. 528; *The Studio*, 44 (1908)–46 (1909)

March, Vernon (1891–1926)
Sculptor. Born in Hull one of nine children in the family of George and Elizabeth March. By 1901 the family had moved from Hull to Battersea where five of March's older brothers were recorded in the census as designers or art craftsmen or art students all working on their own account and all working from home. Little is known of March's life or training. He exhibited at the RA in 1907 whilst living at 64 Glebe St, Chelsea and from 1909 he sent exhibits from Goddendene, Farnborough in Kent. He won the competition for the Canadian National War Memorial in 1925 but died at the age of thirty-five in 1926. His design was executed by his six brothers and sisters.

See: **GM:** Whitefield.

Ref: *1901 Census*; Johnson & Guertzner, *British Artists* 1999

Marsden, Walter (b. 1883)
Sculptor. Born at Church near Accrington Lancs where his father was a blacksmith. He is described in the 1901 census as an 'apprentice terra cotta' and fourteen years later he was living in Chelsea and exhibiting a bronze bust at the RA. In 1916 and 1919 he sent work to the RA from The Artists Rifles' OTC, Hare Hall Camp, Gidea Park near Romford. In the meantime, he had been awarded the Military Cross. In 1923 he exhibited parts of the Lytham St Anne's war memorial at the RA. He was elected to the AWG in 1930.

See: **LA:** Church, Lytham St Anne's (2) **GM:** Bolton, Heywood **MS:** Mossley AG

Ref: *Census 1901*; *RA Exhibitions* 1905–70

Marsh, A. H. see **Gateshead Glass**

Martin, Alfred, (1872–1938)
Art decorator and sculptor. He lived in Liverpool and attended the Liverpool University School of Architecture and Applied Art evening classes in Painting and Drawing 1902–04. He exhibited at the WAG and at the RA. He emigrated to South Africa *c.* 1905.

See: **MS:** L'pool C

Ref: Cavanagh *Public Sculpture in Liverpool*, 1997; *The Studio*, 36 (1906); Aldham Robarts Centre archives *Art Sheds Registers 1901–04*

Martin, William Alison (b. 1879)
Artist and art decorator. Painter in oil and watercolour of figure subjects and landscapes, etcher and lithographer. He trained at the Municipal School of Art in Mount St, Liverpool and at Julian's and Calorossi's studios in Paris. He also spent time in Italy before returning to England. Back in Liverpool, he attended evening classes in life drawing and painting 1901–04 at The Liverpool University School of Architecture and Applied Art. He exhibited at the RA in 1902 and on many occasions at the WAG in Liverpool. He was featured in *The Studio* (vol. 30, p. 69) with Clinton Balmer in a review of their lunette at the Toxteth Library.

See: **MS:** Toxteth

Ref: *The Studio*, 30 (1904), p. 69; Frances Spalding, *Dictionary of British Art*, 6, 1990; Aldham Robarts Centre archives *Arts Sheds Registers 1901–04*

Martin Brothers
Potters. Four brothers: Robert Wallace born 1843, Charles Douglas 1846, Walter Fraser 1857 and Edwin Bruce 1860 founded the Martin Pottery in Fulham in 1873. Three of the brothers had worked at Doulton's in Lambeth. In 1877 they moved their studio to Southall, which was where their successful 'wally' bird tobacco jars and caricature jugs were made in the 1880s. During the 1890s the firm also made a range of domestic wares including fountains and tiles for dados and fireplaces. The firm

closed in 1915. A large collection of their work can be seen at Southall Public Library.

See: **CU:** Carlisle AG **GM:** Oldham AG **MS:** L'pool WAG **NS:** Hanley AG

Ref: Southall Local History Society, *The Martin Brothers*, booklet, 1995; Haslam, M., *The Martin Brothers: Potters*, *c.* 1978

Martindale, James Henry (1855–1931)
Architect. Trained in Kendal 1872–77 with David Brade then moved to Leeds to be assistant to George Cosen 1877–80. He returned to Carlisle in 1881 where he joined C. J. Ferguson (qv), becoming his chief assistant. He set up his own practice in Carlisle 1898.

See: **CU:** Calthwaite, Seascale.

Ref: RIBA, *Directory of British Architects*, 2001.

Martyn H. H. & Co. (1888–1971)
Founded by H. H. Martyn in Sunningend, Cheltenham, the firm was initially known for its ecclesiastical wood, stone and marble carving. By 1900 it had become a limited company and had diversified into decorative plasterwork, joinery, cabinet making, wrought ironwork and castings in bronze and gun-metal. Later the firm produced stained glass and pressed steel. It had many orders from the shipbuilding industry to fit out new luxury liners including the ill-fated Lusitania.
H. H. Martyn prided itself on the quality of its work and the skill of its employees creating what they described in their brochure as 'an Association of Arts Craftsmen'. Walter Gilbert (qv), former founder and director of the Bromsgrove Guild became the firm's Art Director from 1918 and worked closely with colleague Louis Weingartner (qv) who also came from the Bromsgrove Guild, to produce some of the most notable of Martyn's sculpture work including war memorials. In 1934 the firm was acquired by Maples.

See: **GM:** Bolton, Leigh **MS**: Eccleston, L'pool Cath, Prescott **CH:** Crewe

Ref: Gloucestershire PRO *H. H. Martyn archives*, D5922

Mason, William Lovell (1865–1916)
Architect. He attended Manchester School of Art and was articled to G. H. Bibby of Manchester 1881–83. He spent two years as an improver with Paul Ogden before joining his father's practice in Ambleside. He was killed in a motorcycle accident at the age of 51.

See: **CU:** Ambleside.

Ref: Obit. *RIBAJ* (26.6.1915), pp. 404, 427

Matear, Huon Arthur (1856–1945)
Architect. Educated at Dr Sauls School, Rock Ferry, he was articled to J. F. Doyle (qv) in Liverpool and was assistant to him 1876–82 entering into practice in 1887. He designed the Courts of Justice, Fire and Police Stations in York in 1889, the Liverpool Cotton Exchange with F. W. Simon 1906 and 250 cottages in the village of Hadly, Salop. He also designed large generating stations and other engineering works.

See: **MS:** Southport, Port Sunlight

Ref: RIBA, *Directory*, 2001; *Who's Who in Architecture*, 1914.

Mawson, Thomas H. (1861–1933)
Landscape gardener. He was born in Scorton, south of Lancaster. In 1877 he went to London to work with the landscape gardener John Willis. By 1885 he had moved to Windermere and established his landscaping business at Lakeland Nurseries. He designed many gardens around Windermere and a number of houses, mainly for members of his family. In 1898 he went briefly into partnership with the architect Dan Gibson (qv). Later he was greatly in demand throughout the country, where his work was often connected with parks and town-planning. His book, *The Art and Craft of Garden Making*, 1900, ran to many editions and set out his belief that house and garden should be designed as an architectural unity. He was elected a member of the AWG in 1902. During the Great War he promoted the concept of helping disabled ex-servicemen to maintain independence by establishing purpose made villages with appropriate industrial or craft workshops for their employment.

See: **CU:** Bowness, Cockermouth, Eskdale Green, Graythwaite, Rydal, Windermere (3) **LA:** Blackpool, Hest Bank (4), Lancaster(2) **GM:** Rochdale **MS:** Thornton Hough **CH:** Burton, Willington

Ref: Kendal PRO, *Mawson archive;* Mawson, T. H., *The Life and Work of an English Landscape Architect*, 1927; Mawson, T. H., *The Art and Craft of Garden-making*, 1926

Mawson, William Henry
Metalworker. He attended night classes at the Keswick School of Industrial Arts (qv) in the 1890s and won the School Prize in 1898. He was employed as a craftsman at the KSIA from *c.* 1899 and set up on his own some time after 1904.

See: **CU:** Keswick Mus., Hutton in the Forest

Ref: *Keswick Museum archive*; Carlisle PRO, *KSIA archive*.

Maxwell & Tuke (fl. 1867–1894)
James Maxwell was articled to Thomas Holmes of Bury and set up his own practice when he was 21 years old. William James Tuke was articled to William Tuke, architect and surveyor in Bradford 1857–61 and left him to spend time in a builder's office in Chester to learn practical construction. He then moved to Wolverhampton as an assistant to George

Bidlake before joining Mills and Murgatroyd in Manchester. In 1865 he joined James Maxwell's practice and two years later they created the Maxwell & Tuke partnership which lasted twenty-six years until both men died in 1893. They developed a large practice which built on the grand scale, witness Blackpool Tower and the plans for the creation of St Anne's on Sea.

See: **LA:** Blackpool, Bury **MS:** Port Sunlight

Ref: RIBA, *Directory*, 2001; Obit. *RIBAJ*, 1 (1894), p. 116.

Medcalf, William J. (fl. 1901–21)
Painter and stained-glass artist. Born in 1879 at Aughton, Lancs one of five children of the architect Thomas Medcalf. He trained at the Department of Architecture and Applied Art at the University of Liverpool and was then Drawing Instructor at the University's Day Training College from 1909–11. He exhibited at the WAG 1901–21. His stained-glass windows at Aughton church are the only ones so far identified.

See: **LA:** Aughton

Ref: *Census 1901*; Morris Colin, *History of Liverpool Regional College of Art*, 1985

Meteyard, Sydney Harold (1868–1947)
Painter of portraits and figure subjects, decorative painter and stained-glass designer. He was born at Stourbridge and studied at Birmingham School of Art where he became a teacher. He worked on stained glass and other decorative commissions for the Bromsgrove Guild (qv).

See: **GM:** Bolton **MS:** Southport

Ref: Waters, *Dictionary of British Artists*, 1975

Miles, Harvey Thomas (1837–?1904)
An architectural sculptor, monumental and general mason in marble, wood and stone. Born in Norwich, he is first noted in business as a monumental mason at Church Walk Ulverston with a Mr Affleck, a partnership that continued for some years. Miles was living in Cark in Cartmel about 12 miles from Ulverston in the 1880s and in the 1901 Census he had moved to Greenodd some three miles from Ulverston. By 1894 he was working on his own and does not appear in records after 1904.

See: **CU:** Coniston

Ref: Cartmel and Furness Directories

Millard, John (b. 1874)
Portrait sculptor. Born in Wigan Lancs . He studied at Warrington and Manchester Schools of Art, then studied and taught at L'Ecole des Beaux Arts in Paris. He later settled in Wigan and taught at Manchester Municipal School of Art from 1913.

See: **CH:** Macclesfield

Ref: Waters, *Dictionary of British Artists*, 1975

Miller, Alec (1879–1961)
Wood carver and teacher. Born and trained in Glasgow, he studied at Glasgow School of Art 1900–02 and went to Florence in 1908. He exhibited widely at the RA and in the USA. He moved to Chipping Campden in 1902 to join C. R. Ashbee (qv) and the Guild of Handicraft (qv) where he taught drawing and sculpture 1902–14. He taught at the Oxford School of Art 1912–23. He provided carving for the Guild's commissions and later worked on his own account.

See: **CU:** Urswick **MS:** Formby

Ref: Waters, *Dictionary of British Artists*, 1975; Wilgress, J., *Alec Miller: Guildsman and Sculptor in Chipping Campden*, 1987

Millson, John Jarvis (b. 1851)
Stone carver. He was born at Donington in Lincolnshire. Nothing is known of his early life. By 1886 he had established himself in Manchester executing architectural sculpture.

See: **LA:** Bury AG +(1), Rochdale, Silverdale
GM: M/cc **MS:** Port Sunlight AG
CH: Wilmslow

Ref: *Census 1901*

Milner, Henry Victor (ob. 1944)
Stained-glass artist. His life and work have not been well documented. He lived in Havistock Hill, Hampstead and had a workshop attached to his house. He made three stained-glass windows for his local church of St Silas. He had worked with Burlison and Grylls but his main commissions came from Temple Lushington Moore (qv) who frequently used him 1887–1908

See: **CU:** Wythburn. **GM:** Hyde

Ref: *St Silas Church, Kentish Town website: saintsilas.org.uk/section/118*

Minton Ltd
Potters. The Pottery was founded by Thomas Minton in 1793. Herbert Minton who took over when his father died in 1836 was responsible for introducing bone china and new products such as encaustic tiles, parian ware and majolica. He developed links with the Art world being closely associated with Henry Cole (the industrial designer, writer and first director of the South Kensington Museum) and architect, A. W. N. Pugin. His later partner Colin Minton Campbell was responsible for the establishment in 1871 of Minton's Art Studio Pottery, employing well known freelance artists including the radical Christopher Dresser (qv). The Studio was ended by a disastrous fire in 1875. At the turn of the century Minton had a new art director in Léon Solon. He and his assistant John Wadsworth, based in Stoke, developed the Secessionist wares, which interpreted the Art Nouveau style and sold successfully up to WW1. Minton was a major

innovator in the production of tiles for which they commissioned designs from well-known artists.

See: **GM:** Rochdale **MS:** L'pool TH **CH:** Chester AG, Parkgate **NS:** Hanley AG, Hartshill

Ref: Atterbury & Batkin, *The Dictionary of Minton*, 1990; Jones, J., *Minton the First 200 years of Production*, 1993

Moira, Gerald (1867–1959)
Decorative artist. He was educated privately before attending the RA Schools in 1888. His early work included flamboyant decorative painting for restaurants such as Lyons Trocadero 1896. In the New Sessions House at the Old Bailey he painted *Moses and the Tablets of the Law* and a number of lunettes whose subjects also related to Law. He was a landscape and still-life painter and did some miniature paintings for the Queen's Doll House in 1924. He was Principal of the Edinburgh College of Art 1924–31 and a member of the AWG from 1898.

See: **MS:** Sefton Park

Ref: *The Studio*, 20 (1900); *The Studio*, 40 (1907); Obit. *RIBAJ* (Nov 1959), p. 30; *Builder* (14.8.1959), pp. 17–18

Moorcroft, William (1872–1945)
Potter. His early schooling was in Burslem where he later attended evening Art classes at the Wedgwood Institute. In 1895 he went to the South Kensington School of Art where he obtained his Art Master's Certificate in 1897. He joined James Macintyre & Co. in Burslem as a designer in their Art Pottery studio and introduced a new range of pottery with highly stylised transfer-printed decoration enriched with enamels and gilding, which was sold as Aurelian Ware. By 1898 he had become manager of the ornamental ware department and developed a new range of decorative slip-trailed pots known as Florian Ware which was sold by Liberty's of London. Many of these designs show his interest in organic form and his belief that decoration should not be for its own sake but should add to the beauty of the form or shape of the piece. It was his name, rather than Macintyre's, that became internationally renowned. In 1913 he set up on his own in a new factory at Cobridge where the firm is still producing Moorcroft pottery.

See: **NS:** Cobridge, Hanley AG

Ref: Atterbury, P., *Moorcroft*, 1990

Moore, Temple Lushington (1856–1920)
Architect. He attended the RA Schools in 1877 and was articled 1875–78 to George Gilbert Scott junior and continued as an assistant until 1885. He was a Gothic designer with the lightest touch and a penchant also for the Renaissance styles. His main body of work was in the building of churches particularly in the north of England, though he did some alterations to a number of large country houses including Allerton Hall, Leeds. He also designed stained glass.

See: **CU:** Kirkandrews on Esk, Wythburn **LA:** Preston **GM:** Bowdon, M/cc, Rochdale, Royton

Ref: Obit. *RIBAJ* (31.7.1920), p. 429; *Builder* (9.7.1920), p. 37; Gray, *Edwardian Architecture*, 1985; Brandwood, G. K., *Temple Moore*

Morris, William (1834–96)
Artist, designer, writer, socialist, capitalist! He was educated at home in Waltham Forest before being sent to Marlborough College. In 1853 he went up to Exeter College, Oxford to train for the priesthood. There he met Edward Burne-Jones (qv) and so began a life-long friendship and working relationship. Disappointed by a lack of religious fervour but inspired by the writings of Carlyle, Ruskin, Tennyson etc, Morris and Jones turned to art, particularly the work of the Pre-Raphaelite Brotherhood which appealed to their appreciation of all things mediaeval. In 1856, having rejected the church as a career, Morris was apprenticed to G. E. Street (qv) in his Oxford office. There he met Philip Webb (qv) and began another lifelong friendship. However, the practice of architecture did not attract him and he decided to take up the decorative arts. He married Jane Burden in 1859 and by 1861, with Burne-Jones (qv), Rossetti (qv), Madox Brown (qv), Charles Faulkner and Peter Paul Marshall he set up the business of Morris, Marshall, Faulkner & Co. in Red Lion Square, London to supply everything needed for the best quality 'hand made' interior design. They described themselves as 'Fine Art Workmen in Painting, Carving and the Metals' They produced furnishings and household wares and from the beginning they were also involved in designing and making stained glass. Their objective was to bring artistic influences to bear on the process of design and to ensure a high quality of craftsmanship in the firm's products. The firm looked back to historical precedents but gave them a modern interpretation rather than taking the copyist approach preferred by their rivals in business. The workshops and showrooms were moved to 26 Queen Square Bloomsbury in 1865 by which time Rossetti, Marshall and Faulkner had left the business. Madox Brown left in 1875 the year in which the business was reorganised and placed on a more business-like footing as Morris & Co.

The firm continued to provide specialist services in interior decoration and in the design and making of tapestries, fabrics, wallpapers, furniture, carpets and last but not least, stained-glass windows. The firm's stained-glass work was exceptional in part because of the quality of its designers; Rossetti, Madox Brown, Burne-Jones, Morris and Webb who worked for the firm up to 1875. By that time there had evolved a very powerful collaborative team of Webb, Burne-Jones and Morris, with Morris taking principal responsibility and especially overseeing colour and production. In 1877 the showroom and offices were moved to 449 Oxford St and in 1881 the firm bought Merton Abbey to house its studios and workshops. The firm was revolutionary in its beginnings and extremely influential in terms of design and quality throughout the C19.

In 1890 Morris established the Kelmscott Press publishing in the six years of its existence some fifty-five titles, many of which were his own writings. The books were printed either on hand-made paper or vellum in type faces of his own design. Many of the books had elaborate wood-block illustrations by leading artists, particularly Edward Burne-Jones. Morris designed all the other ornamentation from 'glorified full-stops' to borders and titles. His achievement in this field encouraged others to establish their own private presses.

Morris was much more than just a decorative artist and designer. He was a poet and writer, a political activist, a traveller and a conservationist. He founded The Society for the Protection of Ancient Buildings in 1877. Morris died in 1896 and Burne-Jones followed him in 1898. Thereafter the firm was run by J. H. Dearle (qv) and the business began the slide towards its eventual demise in 1947.

[Morris & Co. should not be confused with the firm of William Morris of Westminster Ltd which was established by another William Morris in the early 20C]

See: **CU:** Brampton, Broughton in Furness, CarlisleAG + (1), Hutton in the Forest, Irton. Kirkbampton, Lanercost Priory, Ponsonby, Staveley, Troutbeck **LA:** Adlington, Blackburn (3), Calderdale, Church, Cockerham, Lytham St Anne's, Mellor; Oswaldtwistle, Preston Whalley **GM:** Ashton under Lyne, Bolton, Brooklands, Daisy Hill, Didsbury, Halebarns, Hyde, M/cc 2AGs + 2Libs, Marple, Rochdale, Swinton, Walmsley, Wigan, Worsley **MS:** Allerton, Bidston, Birkenhead(2), Edgehill, Frankby, Gateacre, Halewood, Knotty Ash, L'pool C WAG + Lib, Mossley Hill, New Ferry, Prescot, Sefton Park, Tue Brook, Wallasey, Whiston, Woolton **CH:** Alderley Edge, Aldford, Chelford, Chester (2), Crewe, Congleton, Eaton Hall, Knutsford, Macclesfield, Mottram St Andrew, Neston, Saighton, Sutton, Tabley, Wilmslow(2), Widnes **NS:** Berkhamstych, Brown Edge, Cheddleton, Chesterton, Endon, Leek(2), Madeley, Onecote

Ref: MacCarthy, F., *William Morris* 1994; Sewter, Charles, *The Stained-Glass Work of William Morris and his Circle*, 1975

Morris & Co. (1875–1947) see **Morris, William**

Morris, Marshall, Faulkner & Co. (1861–75) see **Morris, William**

Myres, Thomas Harrison (fl. 1859–1910)
Architect. He was articled to W. Poulson of Warrington 1859–64 and then spent two years with E. M. Barry, remaining as his assistant until 1867. He set up in his own practice in 1869. He appears to have spent five years in London 1879–84 but returned to Lancashire where he lived in Preston and Blackpool. He worked in partnership as Myres & Veevers and as Myres, Veevers and W. Myres. He became a FRIBA in 1889.

See: **LA:** Cuerdon.

Ref: *RIBA*, *Directory*, 2001.

Neatby, W. J. (1860–1910)
Architect and ceramics designer. He trained as an architect but then went to work at Burmantofts for the Leeds Fireclay Co. as a designer and painter of glazed architectural ceramic ware. In 1889 he joined Doulton of Lambeth and until 1900 was head of the architectural decoration department. The decoration of the Fish, Game and Poultry Department at Harrods, Knightsbridge is an example of his surviving work. In 1900 he set up his own practice with E. Hollyer Hayes at 15 Percy St, London W1 as designers and manufacturers of furniture, metalwork and stained glass. They were known as Neatby, Evans & Co.

See: **LA:** Blackpool **GM:** M/c MMU

Ref: Gray, A. S., *Edwardian Architecture*, 1985

Nesfield, Eden William (1833–88)
Architect. Born at Bath he was the son of W. A. Nesfield the landscape gardener. He was educated at Eton and 1851–53 became a pupil of William Burn and then, 1853–56, of his uncle, Anthony Salvin. He travelled on the continent for a year before setting up in practice on his own in 1860. From 1863 he shared offices in 30 Argyll St with his friend Richard Norman Shaw (qv) but both men ran independent practices. Between them they developed *The Old English* style of domestic architecture based on the vernacular of south west Surrey and north east Sussex. Nesfield worked on country houses and on smaller projects on country estates.

See: **MS:** West Derby Village (2) **CH:** Crewe Hall (2)

Ref: Girouard, M., *The Victorian Country House*, 1990; Obit. *RIBAJ*, 10 (1903) pp. 396–400; *Builder*, 54 (31.3.1888), pp. 225–29 & 54 (7, 14.4.1888), pp. 244, 269

Newton, Ernest (1856–1922)
Architect. Educated at Uppingham School, he was articled to Norman Shaw (qv) in 1873 and

acted as his assistant until 1879 when he set up his own practice at 14 Hart St WC1. He was a founder member of the AWG. He is best known for the design of smaller country houses in the South of England, including Buller's Wood, Chislehurst, Kent and Red Court, Haslemere 1894. His houses are characterised by white barge boards, white window frames and semi-circular domed porches. His interiors were often panelled and painted white with wide inglenooks. He wrote *A Book of Houses,* 1890 and *A Book of Country Houses,* 1903. He was President of the RIBA 1914–17.

See: **MS** Port Sunlight **CH:** Bollington, Prestbury

Ref: Newton, W. G., *The Work of Ernest Newton R.A.*, 1925; Obit. *RIBAJ*, 29 (1922), pp. 191, 212; *Builder*, 122 (3.2.1922), pp. 180–81

Nicholson, Archibald Keighley (1867–1937)
Stained-glass artist. He was brother to the architect Charles Nicholson (qv) and Sydney Nicholson founder of the Royal School of Church Music. He began training in architecture with Henry Wilson (qv) but late in the 1890s he took to stained glass, teaching himself both the art and the craft. He set up his own studio in Gower St, moving to Circus Rd and then founding the AKN Studio in St Johns Wood. His first work, made in 1899, can be seen at Wonersh Church, Surrey. Over the next forty years his work peppered the country from Jesmond to Southampton. He preferred simple colour schemes as the basis of his work using bright red, a full blue and pure yellow stain. He used a number of style devices including flying scrolls describing the scene, rainbows and rays. He also executed background landscapes in grisaille. He maintained complete control over all the work that left his studio.

See: **CU:** Armathwaite, Bowness, Carlisle Cath + (3), Eaglesfield, Greystoke, Heversham, Levens, Natland, Plumbland **LA:** Aughton, Fleetwood **GM:** Leigh, Marple, Middleton **CH:** Ashton Heyes, Chester Cath + (1), Frodsham, Malpas, Mobberley, Prestbury

Ref: Obit. *BSMGP Journal*, 7, no. 1 (1937)

Nicholson, Charles (1867–1949)
Architect. Brother to A. K. Nicholson (qv) and Sydney Nicholson who founded the Royal School of Church Music. He was educated at Rugby and New College Oxford before being articled to J. D. Sedding (qv). He carried on the practice with Henry Wilson (qv) after Sedding's death in 1891. He set up his own practice in 1893 and was in partnership 1895–1916 with H. C. Corlette and later with T. R. Rushton. He was a skilled draughtsman and water-colour artist. He was elected to the AWG in 1898. He was consulting architect to seven cathedrals.

See: **CU:** Carlisle Cath **CH:** Burton (2), Chester, Macclesfield

Ref: Gray, A. S., *Edwardian Architecture*, 1985; Obit. *Builder*, 176 (11.3.1949), p. 300; *The Times* (5.3.1949)

North, Herbert Luck (1871–1941)
Architect. Educated at Uppingham and Jesus College Cambridge, he was articled to Henry Wilson (qv) 1892–95 during which time he was involved in the restoration work at Tintagel. He attended classes at Tipton St and South Kensington Museum. He was assistant to Edwin Lutyens 1896–98 and to William Pite 1899. He set up in independent practice in London in 1900 and in Llanfairfechan in 1901. He wrote *Old Cottages in Snowdonia* 1924 and *Old Churches in Arllechwedd* 1906.

See: **CU:** Windermere

Ref: RIBA, *Directory of British Architects*, 2001; Drury, M., *Wandering Architects*, 2000; Obit. *Builder* (28.2.1941), p. 129; *RIBAJ* (May 1941), p. 124

Nuttgens, Joseph E. (1892–1982)
Stained-glass artist. Born at Aachen of a German father and an English mother. The family returned to England in 1894. Joseph attended a Catholic elementary school until the age of 14 and attended evening classes in art at Harrow. In 1908 he was recruited to draw cartoons by Arthur A. Orr and worked with him for eight years also attending the Central School of Arts and Crafts in London. There, he came under the influence of Christopher Whall. He took a studio at the Glass House in Lettice St where he became an assistant to Karl Parsons (qv) and later to Martin Travers (qv). At the outbreak of the Great War he was interned as a German in Scotland. In 1918, he was recruited by Anning Bell (qv) to run the stained-glass Department at the RCA but lost the job because of his German connections. He went to work in Chipping Campden with Paul Woodroffe (qv) after which he set up his own studio in Buckinghamshire, settling eventually at Piggotts Hill near Eric Gill's (qv) enclave. It is estimated that Nuttgens made over 300 windows on his own account and there is no formal reckoning of the number he executed for other designers. He was elected to the AWG in 1921 and was still working when he died at the age of 90. He was probably the last surviving student of Christopher Whall (qv).

See: **CU:** Ravenstonedale **LA:** Burnley, Chorley, Ormskirk **GM:** Swinton **MS:** Aigburth, St Helens **CH:** Bickley

Ref: Nuttgens, P., 70 Years Work, *JBSMGP*, 18, no. 1 (1983–1984)

Oakley, Frank Page (b. 1862)
Architect. Born in London, the son of a clergyman, he was educated in Brighton and at Malvern. He was articled to J. P. St Alban in London and attended the RA Schools in 1881. He also studied under James Brooks in London

and J. S. Crowther in Manchester. He set up on his own account, in Manchester in 1887.

See: **GM:** Littleborough **CH:** Bollington

Ref: Tracy and Pike, *Manchester and Salford at the Close of the C19* (nd) no. 2

Oddie, John William (1839–1923)
Amateur decorative artist. Oxford don. Founder of the Keswick Sketching Club, he was a member of the original committee drawn together by Mrs Rawnsley in establishing the Keswick School of Industrial Arts in 1884. Oddie allowed the school to use his designs for teaching and producing goods for sale, provided the designs were returned to him at the end of the session. His name disappears from the KSIA minute book after April 1885. In 1888, '89 and '90 he showed work at the Arts and Crafts Exhibition Society in London and in 1889 at the Exhibition of Decorative and Applied Art at the Walker Art Gallery, Liverpool, giving his address as 'Lyswick Hall School of Art, Keswick'.

See: **CU:** Hutton in the Forest.

Ref: PRO Carlisle, *KSIA archive*; Holland, J., 'Margaret Vane: A Chatelaine's Legacy', 1999; PRO Liverpool, WAG Exhibition catalogues

Oliver, George Dale (1851–1928)
Architect. George Dale Oliver was the son of a Newcastle architect. He was articled to G. E. Street (qv), then worked in Birkenhead before going to Carlisle as assistant and later a partner to Crosby Hetherington. He was responsible for many important buildings in Carlisle and was architect for locals schools, churches and chapels. He was appointed County Architect for Cumberland on the death of C. J. Ferguson in 1904. On Hetherington's death he was joined by Oliver Dodgshun, (1854–1927) whom he had first met in Street's office.

See: **CU:** Carlisle, Kirkbride

Ref: Obits: *RIBAJ* 35 (1928), p. 427; *Builder* 138 (11.5.28), p. 820

Ormerod & Pomeroy
Architects. John Ormerod was born in Bolton 1874 and attended Bolton High School and Whalley Royal Grammar School. He was articled 1891–95 to J. J. Bradshaw and J. Bradshaw-Gass and attended Manchester Technical School and Bolton School of Art. He qualified in 1897 and worked for a year in the Designs Branch of the War Office. He set up in independent practice in 1898 and lectured at Bolton Technical School. Ernest James Pomeroy was born in 1877 and articled 1894–97 to Llanfield C. Greenwood of Southampton, remaining there as his assistant until 1899. He became assistant to John Ormerod in 1899 and set up independent practice in 1902 but returned to take up a partnership with Ormerod in 1904. He died in 1950.

See: **MS:** Port Sunlight

Ref: RIBA, *Directory*, 2001

Owen, Segar (1874–1929) see **Owen, William** and **Segar**

Owen, William (1846–1910) and **Segar**
Architects. William Owen was articled to John Lowe of Manchester and was assistant to James Redford. He set up on his own in Warrington in 1869 where he established a large and successful general practice. After doing work at Lever Brothers' factory in Warrington he became a close friend of William Lever becoming a Director of the Company in 1897. He was the first architect to be employed at Port Sunlight. Segar Owen was articled to G. E. Street (qv) in London and trained at the RA Schools. He became his father's junior partner in 1898. The practice was pre-occupied with work at Port Sunlight for many years.

See: **MS:** Port Sunlight; Thornton Hough **CH:** Thelwall, Warrington

Ref: Gray, A. S., *Edwardian Architecture*, 1985; Hubbard & Shippobottom, *A Guide to Port Sunlight*, 1988

Pain & Blease
Architects. Coard Squarey Pain was born in Battersea 1851 and educated at Winchester. He was articled to Railence & Squarey of Salisbury. Much of his work was in the fields of surveying and engineering. He was a Fellow of the Surveyors Institute and president of Liverpool Engineering Society. He was the senior partner in the firm of Pain & Blease with offices at North John St, Liverpool. No information on Blease.

See: **MS:** Port Sunlight

Ref: *Gores Directory*, 1911

Paley & Austin (1868–1942)
Architects. Based in Lancaster, they became the premier church-building practice in the North West. The firm began in 1842 with Edmund Sharp, (qv) who took his nephew E. G. Paley into partnership in 1854. The firm did its best work after 1868 when Paley was joined by H. J. Austin. The quality of design and execution of the firm's work was sustained over a period of fifty years while the name changed to Paley and Austin, then to Paley, Austin and Paley; to Austin and Paley and in its years of decline, back to Paley and Austin. Like John Douglas (qv) who had been an assistant there, the firm's work was clearly influenced by Pugin and Ruskin. They used gothic forms and took great pains to place their buildings in their landscapes and to use local materials and craftsmen of very high quality. To this extent at

least, the firm exhibited Arts and Crafts credentials.

See: **CU:** Barbon (Paley) Barrow in Furness(3), Beetham, Brathay, Dalton in Furness, Finsthwaite, Flookburgh, Heversham, Keswick, Natland, Saint Bees, Walton, Windermere **LA:** Blackburn, Blackpool, Cockerham, Fleetwood, Leck, Lytham St Anne's **GM:** Altrincham, Atherton (2), Blackley, Bolton, Burnage, Daisy Hill, Ordsall, Stockport, Wigan **MS:** Kirkby, Mossley Hill (2), St Helens **CH:** Alderley Edge, Alsager, Knutsford, Widnes.

Ref: Price J., *Sharpe, Paley and Austin*, 1998

Parlby, George (1856–1944)
Stained-glass artist. He worked for Powell of Whitefriars and exhibited forty-four designs for stained glass at the RA 1906–44. He was elected to the AWG in 1899.

See: **GM:** Wigan

Ref: *Royal Academy Exhibitions 1905–1970*

Parsons, Karl (1884–1934)
Stained-glass artist. Born at Peckham and christened Charles Bergmann Parsons. He was educated at Haberdashers at New Cross in South London. In 1899, aged fifteen, he was apprenticed to Christopher Whall (qv) working in Hammersmith and at Lowndes and Drury, then in Chelsea. He attended Whall's classes at the London County Council Central School of Arts and Crafts and in 1900 became his assistant in the studio. By 1904 he was also assisting with teaching at the Central School becoming the principal teacher in stained glass 1906–29. He took over teaching duties from Whall at the RCA. He was a member of the Arts and Crafts Exhibition Society though not of the AWG. In 1908 he set up his own studio in the Glass House and collaborated there with Christopher Whall in completing the windows for Cape Town Cathedral. His own first commission was for St Alban's Hindhead. He worked for a short time with Louis Davis and in 1913 Joseph Nuttgens (qv) introduced him to Harry Clarke (qv) with whom he became firm friends. Parsons was conscripted into the army in 1916 and survived to return to the Glass House and teaching at the Central Schools in 1918. He employed assistants during the 1920s to help with his War Memorial work, including E. L. Armitage and Leonard Potter both of whom had been his pupils. In 1929 he resigned his teaching post and took his family to Shalbourne in Wiltshire where he set up his studio, but following a series of strokes he was forced to return to London where he died in 1934.

See: **CH:** Alsager.

Ref: William Morris Art Gallery, *Karl Parsons*, 1987

Payne, Edward Raymond (1906–91)
Stained-glass artist. Born in Birmingham, he was the son of Henry Payne the stained-glass artist and his artist wife, Edith Gere. The family moved to Amberley in Gloucestershire in 1909 and set up a studio to produce stained glass, frescoes, embroidery and mosaics. Edward was educated at Cheltenham College and at St George's Harpenden. In 1923 he attended the RCA in London. He worked in London until 1936 when his father became ill and he returned to Amberley to help complete outstanding commissions. He set up his own stained-glass studio at nearby Box Hill. Like his father, he worked with a well-thumbed copy of Christopher Whall's *Stained-Glass Work* in the studio.

See: **CU:** Arnside.

Ref: Moss, R., *Edward Payne*, 1995

Payne, Henry Albert (1868–1940)
Landscape and portrait painter, stained-glass artist and fresco painter. He was born at Kings Heath, Birmingham and studied art at Birmingham School of Art under Edward R. Taylor. He became a teacher of Art at the Municipal School of Art *c.* 1884. He exhibited at the Royal Birmingham School of Arts from 1898 and also at the RA and the Paris Salon. He was a member of the Birmingham Group which included art teachers Arthur and Georgina Gaskin, Sidney Meteyard, Charles Gere and Gere's two sisters, one of whom Edith, was a student at the college in the 1890s. She and Payne were married in 1901. In 1900 as the leading stained-glass artist at the School of Art he was sent to learn more about stained glass from Christopher Whall (qv) at the Lowndes and Drury Workshop in London. From *c.* 1900 Payne also accepted commissions from the Bromsgrove Guild (qv). With other members of the Birmingham Group he provided the painted décor for the Guild's highly acclaimed Art Nouveau bedroom in the Prince of Wales Pavilion at the 1901 Exposition Universelle in Paris. In 1902 the Group worked on the private chapel at Madresfield Court Nr Malvern, Worcester where some of the finest of the Bromsgrove Guild's work can be seen including murals and stained glass by Payne. He showed a cartoon for a stained-glass window, under the Guild's banner, at the Arts and Crafts Exhibition Society in 1903. In 1909, he moved to Amberley in Gloucester, where St Loe's House, the former school house, became not only his home but also a studio. In 1910 Payne was commissioned to do a mural in the House of Lords and *c.* 1912 the Loe's Guild was founded by Edith and Henry, modelled on Arts and Crafts principles, to undertake new work in frescoes, stained glass, embroidery and mosaics. In 1916, Henry Payne was one of the eight artists, who were asked to paint a mural

on one of the eight bays in the *Hall of Heroes* at the Burlington House Arts and Crafts Exhibition.

See: **CH:** Saighton Grange

Ref: Waters, *Dictionary of British Artists*, 1975; Moss, R., *Edward Payne*, 1995; Watt, *The Bromsgrove Guild*, 1999

Pearce, Walter John (1857–1942)
Stained-glass artist. Born in Brighton, he was moved to a children's home in London aged 10, after both his parents died. He was first apprenticed to a cabinet maker and then to a firm of painters and decorators in London. He moved to Manchester with his wife and children, and set up in business there in about 1890. By 1898 his firm appears in the Slater's' Directory of Manchester as 'Artists in Stained and Painted Glass' with an address at 12 & 14 Albert St. The workshop was moved to premises at 41 Gartside St, Manchester and then to Wilmslow in the early 1920s. Little is known of how the firm was organised or when it made the change from painting and decorating to stained glass. Nevertheless, it was clearly a flourishing enterprise and Pearce must have had considerable assistance in the workshop. An undated catalogue, still bearing the Gartside St address, claims that 'During the last few years work has been executed for 7,000 buildings.' Walter Pearce was a member of the Council of the Northern Art Workers' Guild at the time of the 1898 exhibition (when Gustave Hiller was Joint Hon. Sec.) and in 1903 he was Master of the Guild. In addition to writing the preface to the catalogue of the 1903 exhibition, he contributed an article entitled *Windows of Coloured Glass*. He taught painting and decorating at the Manchester School of Technology and wrote a standard text book *Painting and Decorating* in 1898 which ran into seven editions before being re-written in 1963. He also wrote occasionally for the *Journal of Decorative Art* and his work featured on occasions in *The Studio*.

See: **LA:** Blackpool(2), Oswaldtwistle **GM:** Ashton upon Mersey, Burnage, Bury, Chadderton, Clifton, Denshaw, Didsbury (2), Heaton Moor, Littleborough, M/cc, Patricroft, Rochdale, Rusholme, Victoria Park **CH:** Ashley, Bollington (2)

Ref: *Census 1901*; *Unpublished notes on WJ Pearce by David J Pearce*; M/c City Library, *Catalogues of the Exhibitions of the Northern Art Workers' Guild*, 1898 and 1903

Pearson, John Loughborough (1817–97)
Architect. Born in Durham, the son of a watercolour painter, Pearson was articled to Ignatius Bonomi, the County Surveyor of Durham. He remained there for ten years working on country houses and churches in both medieval and classical styles. In 1841 he went to London working first in the office of Anthony Salvin and then for Philip Hardwicke. He set up his own practice in 1844.

See: **MS:** Sefton Park, Thurstaston

Ref: Smart, G. M., 'J. L. Pearson' in *Muscular Churches*, pp. 112–41; Obit. *RIBAJ* (Nov.1947), p. 39

Pegram, Henry Alfred (1862–1937)
Sculptor. Born in London. He showed an early talent winning prizes in the National Art Competitions in 1881 and 1883 at the West End School of Art. In 1883, he entered the RA Schools, sponsored by Thomas Heatherly, Principal of Heatherly Academy, winning more prizes in 1882, 1884 and 1886. He worked as an assistant to Hamo Thorneycroft (qv) 1887–*c.* 1891. His bronze relief, Ignis Fatuus, which showed the influence of Alfred Gilbert (qv), exhibited in 1889 gained him recognition. His work became increasingly flamboyant as can be seen in the bronze candelabra in the nave of St Paul's Cathedral. His work includes the reliefs at the entrance to the Imperial Institute in South Kensington 1891–92, the frieze for the United University Club in Suffolk St for Reginald Blomfield (qv) *c.* 1906 and the monument to Edith Cavell in Norwich. He also had commissions from abroad. He was elected to the AWG in 1890, and became ARA in 1904 and RA in 1922.

See: **MS:** L'pool C, Mossley Hill AG

Ref: Beattie Susan, *The New Sculpture*, 1983; Gray, A. S., *Edwardian Architecture*, 1985

Pennington, Thomas Frederic (1853–1918)
Architect. Born in Kendal, he was articled in his home town to Stephen Shaw and stayed in his office after qualifying until he went as an assistant to Alfred Waterhouse (qv) in 1875.

See: **CU:** Kendal.

Ref: Obit. *RIBAJ*, 25 (1918), p. 121

Pepper, Elizabeth see **Langdale Linen**

Pilkington Tile Co. (1891–) and **Royal Lancastrian Pottery** (1903–38)
The firm was established at Clifton Junction, near Manchester by brothers Edward and Alfred Pilkington in 1891 to make tiles from the local clay found during coal mining operations. William Burton a chemist who had previously worked for Wedgwood was appointed manager and was ably assisted by his brother Joseph. As chemists both were interested in the development of glazes. Tile production was hugely successful. Lewis Day (qv) acted as an advisor and design consultant and contributed designs for tiles and later pottery, along with other well-known names including Walter Crane (qv), C. F. A. Voysey (qv), Frederic Shields (qv) and Alphonse Mucha. The firm also employed its own artists the first being John Chambers, their chief designer, and Joseph Kwiatowski. Lawrence Hall, William S. Mycock and T. F. Evans joined in the 1890s.

Albert Hall, Albert Barlow and Gladys M. Rodgers arrived in the 1900s and were followed by the tube-lining expert Edmund Kent in 1910. All these artists designed patterns for tiles which were carried out by a small army of painters. The Burton brothers' success in developing glazes led to the opening of the Lancastrian Pottery in 1903. The new art studio was headed by Gordon Forsyth (qv) who was appointed as chief artist to lead a team of both men and women including Richard Joyce, Charles Cundall, Gladys Rodgers, W. S. Mycock and Annie Burton in designing for these ground-breaking new lustre glazes. Crystalline, opalescent, transmutation and flambé glazes were followed by ever more successful developments and from 1905 the new pottery was exhibited at home and abroad. *Royal Lancastrian Ware* enjoyed a hey-day up until the First World War when artists, including Forsyth left for war service and demand for this luxury market fell. The firm recovered and was more successful than ever during the 1920s producing a different range of glazed ware until the recession of the 1930s. In 1937 the pottery department was closed down and in 1938 the firm became known as Pilkington Tiles Ltd.

See: **CU:** Eskdale Green **LA:** Burnley, Lancaster Uni, Padiham, Preston AG **GM:** Ashton under Lyne, Bramhall, BuryAG, M/c AG, Salford AG, Victoria Park **MS:** L'pool C WAG **CH:** Chester Mus, Willington **NS:** Hanley AG

Ref: Cross, A. J., *Pilkington's Royal Lancastrian Pottery and Tiles*, 1980

Pilkington, Margaret (1891–1974)
Born at Pendleton, Salford but moved with her family to Alderley Edge, Cheshire in 1906. She attended Manchester College of Art 1911–13 and then went to London, where she attended the Central School of Art part time, then full time at the Slade. While in London she met the Pissaro family, who ran the Eragny Press and spent some of her spare time assisting Lucien Eragny with the printing of the finely illustrated limited edition books that he published. She became interested in print making. The Great War put an end to her London studies and she returned to Cheshire to do her part for the war effort, doing social work in the deprived parts of Manchester and teaching Art to the Ancoats Girls Club – a task she continued to do well into the 1920s. In between times, she continued with her drawing and print making, buying her own printing press which was installed in the family home. She also designed some nursery tiles which were fired at the family works at Clifton. During the 1920s she exhibited with the new Society of Wood Engravers and in 1924 she became a full member and also its Honorary Secretary, a post she held for the next 30 years. In 1920 she founded the Red Rose Guild of Art workers arranging annual exhibitions of the work of original artists and craft workers mainly from the North West. After WW2 the Guild was one of the organisations which amalgamated to form the Crafts Council. Her other major contribution to Manchester was her tireless work with both the Manchester and Whitworth Art Galleries. She sat on both Art Gallery Committees and in 1936 became Honorary Director of the Whitworth. Over the years she acquired a personal collection of paintings and sculpture, including works by Henri Toulouse Lautrec, Ben Nicholson, Henry Moore and Barbara Hepworth with the idea of leaving it to the Whitworth. She continued to champion the crafts until her death in 1974.

See: **GM:** Horwich

Ref: Whitworth Art Gallery, *Margaret Pilkington*, Leaflet, Friends of Whitworth, 1999

Pite, Arthur Beresford (1861–1934)
Architect. He was educated at Kings College School and University College London. He entered the South Kensington School of Design in 1876 and was articled initially to Habershon and Fawkner. In 1880 he entered the office of John Belcher and stayed until 1897 when he set up on his own account. He was an innovative architect who enjoyed dabbling with different styles, He designed buildings, mainly churches, abroad as well as in southern England. He was elected to the AWG in 1884. He became a teacher and was Professor of Architecture at the RCA in South Kensington 1900–23.

See: **GM:** Cheadle Hulme **CH:** Burton

Ref: Gray, A. S., *Edwardian Architecture*, 1985; Obit. *RIBAJ* (8.12.1934), pp. 152, 212 & *RIBAJ* (22.12), p. 277; *Builder* (30.11.1934), p. 925 & *Builder* (7.12), p. 969

Platt, John Edgar (1886–1967)
Artist. Born in Leek, he was educated at Newcastle under Lyne High School and at the Nicholson Institute, Leek. He trained at the RCA 1905–08 and returned to Leek in 1910 to be the Head of the Art School where he remained until *c*. 1919. During this time he contributed much of the art work to his local church, All Saints', Leek. He was Head of Applied Art at Edinburgh College of Art 1921–23, Principal of Leicester School of Art 1923–29 and Principal of Blackheath School of Art in London from 1930–40. During the Second World War he was an official war artist to the Ministry of Transport and many of his wartime paintings are held in the Imperial War Museum. He exhibited regularly at the RA. His particular interest was in woodcuts and he was President of the Society of Gravure Printers in Colour from 1939–53. He published a handbook *Colour Woodcuts* in 1958. His paintings and prints can be seen at Manchester

Art Gallery, the Whitworth Art Gallery Manchester, Oldham Art Gallery and the Atkinson Gallery in Southport.

See: **NS:** Leek

Ref: Stafford PRO *Archives of All Saints, Leek*; Leek Library *Local newspaper cuttings*; Chapman, H., *Colour Wood Cuts of John Edgar Platt*, 1999

Pomeroy, Frederick William (1856–1924)
Sculptor. Born in London. During an apprenticeship with a firm of architectural carvers, he attended Lambeth School of Art and from 1880–5 he went to the RA Schools winning the gold medal and a Travelling Studentship. He also studied in Paris and Rome. He did the carving and statuary work on many public buildings often in collaboration with the architect E. W. Mountford. His statues of eminent people can be seen in city centres and parks all round the country. He exhibited regularly at the Arts and Crafts Exhibition Society and was a member of the AWG from 1887, becoming Master in 1907.

See: **CU:** Carlisle Cath **LA:** Lancaster TH **GM:** Oldham **MS:** L'pool C (3), Mossley Hill AG **CH:** Chester Cath + (1)

Ref Gray, *Edwardian Architecture*, 1985; Cavanagh, *Public Sculpture of Liverpool*, 1997

James Powell & Sons of Whitefriars (1834–)
In 1834, James Powell, a London wine merchant and entrepreneur bought the glass factory at Whitefriars and set about learning the art of glass making. Powell had the benefit of the research and experiments of Charles Winton, a lawyer with a particular interest in glass, which enabled the firm to make much better quality pot-metal glass. A large part of the firm's business was stained-glass windows. Edward Burne-Jones was first commissioned to design stained-glass windows for the firm in 1856. Powell supplied coloured flat glass to Morris, Marshall Faulkner and Co. when they set up their stained-glass business in 1861. Henry Holiday became Powell's chief designer when Burne-Jones left to work for Morris Marshall Faulkner & Co. in 1862.

James Powell also made table glass. While the firm originally produced the elaborate cut-glass so prized by Victorians and so reviled by Ruskin, they were at the fore-front of the production of light, simple, undecorated shapes, which reflected changes in taste in the 1870s. Many designs were by architects Philip Webb and Thomas G. Jackson. The firm had produced glasses specially for William Morris's home, the Red House to Webb's design *c.* 1860 and then made a range of glasses exclusively for Morris, Marshall, Faulkner & Co. When James Powell's grandson Harry, an Oxford graduate who had specialised in chemistry, joined the firm in 1871, table glass designs became increasingly innovative with the introduction of new techniques and new forms of glass and decoration including opalescent effects. Inspiration was frequently drawn from Roman, Medieval and Venetian glass. The firm's glassware was exhibited at all the major Arts and Crafts Exhibitions. James Powell was a member of the AWG from 1886 and Harry from 1890.

See: **CU:** Ambleside, Barbon, Bridekirk, Calder Bridge, Cotehill, Finsthwaite, Keswick, Mealsgate, Muncaster, Pennington, Ravenstonedale, Soulby, Temple Sowerby, Vale of Lune, Warwick on Eden, Watermillock **LA:** Blackburn, Church, Great Harwood, Leck, Lytham St Annes, Ormskirk, Upholland, Whittingham **GM:** Ashton upon Mersey, Bolton, M/cc. AG + MMULib, Monton, Prestwich, Rusholme, Wigan(2) **MS:** L'pool Cath + WAG , Sefton Village, St Helens, Thornton Hough, Wallasey, Woodchurch **CH:** Alsager, Chester Cath, Congleton, Macclesfield, Saughall, Styal **NS:** Caverswall

Ref: Rudoe & Coutts, 'The Table Glass Designs of Philip Webb and T. G. Jackson for James Powell & Sons, Whitefriars', *DASJ*, 16 (1992)

Preston Edward Carter (1885–1965)
Sculptor, painter. Born in Liverpool, he studied at the School of Architecture and Applied Art at Liverpool University but joined the Sandon Terrace Studios when the University School of Applied Art was amalgamated with the Liverpool School of Art in 1905. In his early years he was mainly a painter not taking up sculpture seriously until after WW1. His most prestigious work is in Liverpool's Anglican Cathedral.

See: **MS:** L'pool C + Cath + UniAG

Ref: Cavanagh, *Public Sculpture in Liverpool*, 1997; Compton, A., ed., *Edward Carter Preston*, 1999

Preston, Richard Bassnett (ob. 1934)
Architect. Born in Manchester and educated privately, he was articled to J. S. Crowther (1820–93) of Manchester becoming his managing assistant. In 1880 he set up on his own at the Diocesan Chambers Manchester, specialising in church architecture. He was an ARIBA and a member of the Manchester Society of Architects.

See: **LA:** Colne, Foulridge, Nelson **GM:** Blackrod, Leigh, Monton, Prestwich, Rochdale

Ref: *RIBA*, Directory, 2001; Pike, *Contemporary Biographies*

Prynne, George Halford Fellowes (1853–1927)
Architect. Son of a vicar, he attended Chard College Somerset and Haileybury. He emigrated to Canada in 1871 to take up farming but was attracted to architecture and trained in Toronto. On his return to England he worked for G. E. Street (qv) and entered the RA Schools in 1876. He finished St Peter's Plymouth

after Street's death in 1881. Much of his work involved additions and alterations to churches.

See: **CU:** Skirwith

Ref: Gray, *Edwardian Architecture*, 1985; Obit. *RIBAJ* (21.5.27), pp. 494–95: *Builder* (20.5.27), p. 802

Pugin, A. W. N. (1812–52)
Architect. Being the ultimate exponent of the Gothic style, Pugin's architectural philosophy was a major influence in the development of the Arts and Crafts Movement. He had an over-riding belief that all buildings should be based on the mediaeval and therefore be of Gothic design. He propounded three main principles: first, that function must determine form; that all features must be necessary for convenience, construction or propriety of the design; that all ornament should consist of enrichment of the essential construction of the building only. Whilst Arts and Crafts architects did not insist on pointed arches, they certainly adhered to these three principles. Pugin was a tireless worker with obsessive attention to detail, insisting on designing everything from the floor plan to the door knobs. His insistence on excellence in the craftsmanship applied to his designs led to a new awakening in craft training. Pugin did a huge amount of work for Sir Charles Barry in the planning and execution of the Houses of Parliament.

See: **CU:** Warwick Bridge **GM:** Bramhall, Hulme **CH:** Macclesfield

Ref: Architectural Association, *Great British Architects*, 1981; Atterbury & Wainwright, eds, *Pugin, a Gothic Passion*, 1994; Obit. *Builder*, 10 (25.9.1852), pp. 605–06

Ramsden, Omar (1873–1939)
Designer. Born in Sheffield. His father's firm produced silver-plated table cutlery so he was naturally apprenticed to a silversmith in 1887. After attending Sheffield School of Art from 1890 he moved to London in 1897 and entered into a partnership with his friend Alwyn C. E. Carr. The partnership lasted until about 1919. Ramsden is said to have been more of a designer and entrepreneur than a craftsman. Both Ramsden and Carr were elected to the AWG in 1904.

See: **GM:** Northenden.

Ref: Birmingham City Museum & Art Gallery, *Omar Ramsden*, 1973

Rathbone, Harold Steward (1858–1929)
Painter, designer and poet. He was a member of a wealthy Liverpool non-conformist family which had strong links with the art world. He studied at the Slade School of Art and in Paris and travelled in Europe. He had lessons from Ford Madox Brown (qv) during the period Brown was doing the Manchester Town Hall murals. A member of the Liverpool Academy, he exhibited there and in London and Paris. He collected paintings, pottery and manuscripts. He is credited with 'discovering' Frank Brangwyn when he was sketching in the V & A. In 1894 he co-founded the Della Robbia Pottery in Birkenhead with sculptor Conrad Dressler (qv).

See: **MS:** Birkenhead AGs + Lib, Wallasey **CH:** Sandiway

Ref: Williamson Art Gallery, *Della Robbia Pottery Birkenhead*, 1980

Rathbone, Richard Llewellyn Benson (1864–1939)
Designer and metalworker. Born at Menai Bridge, Anglesey, he belonged to an influential Liverpool family. He attended Cambridge University and trained in metalwork with W. A. S. Benson in London. He had a workshop in Liverpool *c.* 1890 and at his family home at Manadwyn, Menai Bridge *c.* 1895. He gave instruction in copper and brass work at evening classes at the Arts Sheds, Liverpool University from 1897–1902. In 1902, he moved to London to take charge of metalwork at the Sir John Cass Institute, becoming head of its Art School three years later. He also taught at the Central School of Arts and Crafts but maintained his workshops at Menai, Anglesey and in London. Much of his metalwork involved producing metal fittings and metal ware for other designers. Later in his career he developed unit metalwork particularly for jewellery which was marketed as Junit sets and he wrote several publications on it. He was a member of the AWG from 1892, being its Hon. Secretary 1909–13, and a member of the Arts and Crafts Exhibition Society.

See: **GM:** Prestwich **MS:** Aigburth, L'pool C TH +WAG, Sefton Park

Ref: Walker Art Gallery, *The Art Sheds 1894–1905*, 1981; WAG *archives on R. Ll. Rathbone;* Karlin, *Jewelry & Metalwork*, 1993; *The Studio*, 1 (1893) & 19 (1900)

Rawnsley, Edith (*c.* 1846–1916)
Born Edith Fletcher in Bolton-le-Moors, Lancashire, she lived for most of her early life in Ambleside. Her parents were admirers of John Ruskin's teaching and she grew up to share their views and to have a love of beauty in art, literature and music. She was a talented artist and a skilful craftswoman. In 1878 she married the Reverend Hardwicke Drummond Rawnsley who was vicar first at Wray and then in 1883 at Crosthwaite. The couple set up evening classes in Keswick in 1884 to help working men and boys to fill their leisure time during the long winter evenings. Eventually, the School also took girls and women. Edith Rawnsley managed the night school, superintended the metalwork classes and played a leading role in the development of the Keswick School of Industrial Arts (qv). She continued her conscientious management of the School as well as providing designs for metalwork and other new crafts taken on as the

School expanded. Though the KSIA appointed its first Director in 1890, Edith continued to be a controlling influence in the chair of the Management Committee. She died in December 1916.

See: **CU:** Barrow, Coniston Mus, Keswick Mus+(1)

Ref: PRO Carlisle *KSIA Archives*; Rawnsley, Eleanor, *Canon Rawnsley An Account of his Life*, 1923

Rea, Ada Hope Russell (b. 1861)
Writer and sculptor. Born in Liverpool. Her life is undocumented. She wrote *The Tuscan & Venetian Artists, their thought and work* which was published in 1898, followed in 1900 by *Donatello, il Maestro di chi sanno* and in 1905 *Peter Paul Rubens*. In 1904 she made the terracotta font at St Bega's at Eskdale Green. In August 1891 she signed the visitors' book at the Keswick School of Industrial Arts giving her address as 60 Belsize Park Gardens, London. By 1912 she was living in Letchworth Garden City. She was a theosophist and was involved in founding the Theosophical Education Trust.

See: **CU:** Eskdale Green

Ref: *Census 1901*; Carlisle PRO, *KSIA archives, Visitors' Book;* Whitehaven PRO, *Archive on Gatehouse, Eskdale Green*

Redfern, Harry (1861–1950)
Architect. Educated at Abingdon, Berkshire and articled to Henry Woodyer (1816–96). He became assistant to William Butterfield in 1877 and set up in practice with Glaswegian architect J. J. Stevenson 1896–1908. He designed new buildings for Christ's College and did other work at Magdalene College, Cambridge. At Oxford he designed the Science Laboratories and did work at Oriel and St John's Colleges. He continued the work originally initiated in 1891 by his partner designing interiors of Orient Liners. He was chief architect to the State controlled Liquor Licensing Board 1915–45. Much of this work was in Carlisle. He was elected to the AWG in 1902.

See: **CU:** Carlisle (4)

Ref: Gray, A. S., *Edwardian Architecture*, 1985; Obit. *RIBAJ* (April, 1950), p. 245; *Builder* (19.5.1950), p. 669

Rees, Thomas Taliesin (1865–1943)
Architect. He was apprenticed to Edmund Legge, Son & Co. (building contractors) in Birkenhead 1881–83 and articled to the Birkenhead architects Mills and Fletcher 1883–87 before attending University College, London. He travelled in France and Belgium after which he returned to Birkenhead where he set up his own practice in 1892. By 1918 he was in partnership with Richard Holt working in Liverpool where he exhibited occasionally at the WAG 1903–26.

See: **MS:** Port Sunlight (2)

Ref: RIBA, *Directory*, 2001; *Builder*, 165 (3.12, 1943), p. 458

Reid, James Eadie (b. 1859)
Artist. Born in Dundee and educated at Edinburgh University. He went to London where he became a pupil and assistant to Sir William Richmond during the installation of the mosaics in St Paul's Cathedral. From 1890 he became a member of Ashbee's Guild of Handicraft, decorating and painting Guild furniture and illustrating their pamphlets. He moved to the North East of England and became involved with the Gateshead Stained-Glass Company. He also worked with Gerald Horsley on a number of churches. By 1908 he had returned to London where he exhibited until 1917. After the Great War, he designed and executed many war memorials particularly in the West Country and in particular at Worcester Cathedral.

See: **MS:** Aigburth **NS:** Chesterton, Hanley, Ipstones

Ref: Hall, Marshall, *Artists of Northumbria*, 1982

Reilly, Charles Herbert (1874–1948)
Architect. Educated at Merchant Taylors' School, Great Crosby and Queen's College, Cambridge after which he spent two years in his father's office before becoming a pupil of John Belcher. He lectured at Kings College, London and in 1904 was appointed Professor of Architecture at Liverpool University. He had a special interest in town planning and is known for his 'Reilly Plan' for the City. He wrote for *Country Life* and for building and architectural magazines. He was knighted in 1944.

See:. **LA:** Accrington **MS:** Port Sunlight

Ref: Gray, A. S., *Edwardian Architecture*, 1985; Richmond, P., *Marketing Modernism – the architecture and influence of Charles Reilly*, 2001; Obit. *RIBAJ* (Feb. 1948), pp. 175, 212 & 228; *Builder* (6.2.48), p. 161

Reynolds, W. Bainbridge (1845–1935)
Trained as an architect with J. P. Seddon and spent some time in the office of G. E. Street (qv) before specialising in the design and manufacture of metalwork at his workshop in Clapham. His ecclesiastical work is to be found in Westminster Abbey and the cathedrals of York, Canterbury, Durham, Liverpool, Llandaff and Norwich. He also made fittings for C. F. A. Voysey (qv) and was elected to the AWG in 1888.

See: **CU:** Isel **LA:** Whalley **MS:** L'pool Cath

Ref: Gray, A. S., *Edwardian Architecture*, 1985, Obit. *RIBAJ* (11.5.1935), p. 789

Reynolds-Stephens, William Ernest (1862–1943)
Sculptor. Born of British parents in the USA but educated in England and Germany. He entered the RA schools in 1884 where he trained as a sculptor and became a member of the AWG in 1887. He was part of the New Sculpture movement and produced beautiful decorative work in the manner of Alfred

Gilbert (qv) and experimented with materials. His major work is the decoration of St Mary the Virgin at Great Warley in Essex 1901–05.

See: **LA:** Preston **MS:** L'pool C WAG, Port Sunlight AG **CH:** Warrington AG

Ref: Gray, A. S., *Edwardian Architecture*, 1985; *The Studio*, 51 (1911); Obit. *Builder* (5.3.1943), p. 225

Rhind, William Birnie (1855–1933)
Sculptor. Born in Edinburgh. He studied under his father the sculptor John Rhind. He attended the School of Design, Edinburgh and then the Life School of the Royal Scottish Academy. He executed architectural sculpture, public statues and memorials. He practised mainly in Edinburgh where he did sculpture for the central doorway over the Scottish Portrait Gallery and the groups 'Sculpture' and 'Religion' on the Glasgow Art Gallery. He exhibited at the RSA 1878–1929.

See: **LA:** St Annes **MS:** L'pool Uni, Wallasey

Ref: Cavanagh, *Public Sculpture in Liverpool*, 1997; Gray, A. S., *Edwardian Architecture*, 1985.

Rice, Bernard Charles (ob.1934)
Stained-glass artist. Born in Birmingham. He attended the Munich School of Art and then worked at a studio in Innsbruck. He returned to England in 1919 and worked for Williams and Gamon of Chester. Very little is known of his life and work.

See: **CH:** Neston

Ref: Information supplied by Deanne Mangold, Swansea Glass Studio

Robson, Philip Appleby (1871–1951)
Architect. Born in Liverpool but educated on the south coast at Lancing College. He was articled to J. L. Pearson in 1888 and attended Blackheath School of Art. He qualified in 1896 and practiced in Westminster and in Manchester 1919–22.

See: **MS:** Huyton

Ref: Obit. *RIBAJ* (April, 1952), p.230

Rope, Ellen Mary (1855–1934)
Sculptor and modeller. Born in 1855 in Bloxhall, Suffolk, she was from a family of prosperous farmers. In 1870 she attended Nottingham Place School, Marylebone, which was set up by Octavia Hill. She then attended Ipswich School of Art and in 1877 went to the Slade School of Art. She took a course in sculpture and modelling led by Alphonse Legros in 1880, which was to set her on the career for which she is best known. Her first job however was as an illustrator and painter but in 1884 after the acceptance of some of her low reliefs by the R.A. she decided to concentrate on sculpture. In 1886 she became a designer for the new Birkenhead-based Della Robbia pottery and from 1889 was a regular exhibitor at all the Arts and Crafts Exhibition Society's events. From 1890 she was never without commissions which came from many different sources. In 1893 she created four six-foot reliefs for the entrance of the Women's building at the Chicago World Columbian Exposition and the following year Octavia Hill asked her to do a series of bas reliefs for the Women's University Settlement in Southwark. Much of her work was for churches and she was a member of the Church Crafts League. From 1903 she shared a studio with her niece Dorothy Rope moving in 1913 to Fulham Road and later to Deodar Road, Putney. Memorials became a significant part of her work after the Great War.

See: **CU:** Brampton **MS:** Birkenhead, Knotty Ash, Liverpool

Ref. Exhibition catalogue. *Ellen Mary Rope, the Poet Sculptor*, 1997

Rope, Margaret Agnes (1882–1953)
Stained-glass artist. Born in Shrewsbury in 1882, she was brought up as a catholic. Educated at home and then from 1901 at the Municipal School of Art, Birmingham where she learnt enamelling from Sidney Meteyard and from 1901 she studied stained glass with Henry Payne. During her nine years at the School she won many scholarships and awards. From 1909 she worked from her home at The Priory in Shrewsbury, where she made the east window at Shrewsbury Roman Catholic Cathedral. From 1911 she worked in a rented studio at the Glass House in Fulham which she shared with her cousin Margaret Edith Aldrich Rope (qv). In September 1923 she became a Carmelite nun but continued to design and paint stained glass in a small studio set up in the convent at Woodbridge in Suffolk having the glass cut and fired at The Glass House. During her career she produced some sixty windows. They are notably strong in design with bright colours and with great attention to glass painting. Many of her windows portray English martyrs, the Annunciation and the lives of the Saints.

See: **GM:** Stockport **MS:** Hoylake, Oxton **CH:** Macclesfield, Warrington

Ref: William Morris Gallery, *Women Stained-Glass Artists of the Arts and Crafts Movement*, 1985

Rope, Margaret Edith Aldrich (1891–1988)
Stained-glass artist. Born in Leiston Suffolk, her family nickname was Tor. She was the younger cousin of Margaret Agnes Rope (qv) and niece of Ellen Mary Rope (qv). Her sister Dorothy was also a sculptor. She was educated first at home and then at Wimbledon High School, Chelsea School of Art and the LCC Central School of Arts. Here she specialised in stained glass under Karl Parsons (qv) and Alfred Drury. From 1911 she worked at the Glass House in Fulham with her cousin Margaret.

During WW1 she joined the Women's Land Army and returned to the Glass House afterwards where her first major commission was for St Chad's Headingley, Leeds *c.* 1923. In about 1926 she moved to 61 Deodar Road, Putney. During the Second World War she assisted Joan Howson (qv) at children's hospitals in North Wales. Post war she moved back to 89 Deodar Road, which she shared with her friend and pupil, Clare Dawson. Over fifty years she produced over 100 windows during which time her style developed, becoming simpler in later years. She used a tortoise as her logo.

See: **GM:** Ardwick

Ref: Rope, Arthur, Website: www.*arthur.rope.clara.net/torbio.htm*

Rosencrantz, Baron Arild (1870–1964)
Decorative and stained-glass artist, sculptor and illustrator. Born at Fredriksborg Castle in Denmark in April 1870, he was the son of a Danish diplomat who died before Arild was three years old. He spent much of his childhood travelling with his Scottish born mother Julia Louise Mackenzie. Aged 16 he went to Rome to study with fresco painter Professor Modesto Faustini followed by two years at L'Académie Julian in Paris. He exhibited at the exhibitions of the Rose and Croix Society of which he became a member. In 1894–95 he learnt the art of stained glass in the studio of John la Farge in New York where he made the five-light window in opalescent glass for Wickhambreaux church in Kent. In 1898 he settled in London where he soon established himself as a portrait painter and decorative artist. His decorative work included stained glass, book illustration, sculpture and murals. He decorated the dining hall of Claridge's Hotel in 1901. In 1912 he moved to Switzerland to assist Rudolf Steiner with a project in Dornach. He returned to England in 1925 where he taught, exhibited his work annually and designed stage sets and costumes for two theatres. He returned to Copenhagen in 1939 and remained there living on the family estate of Rosenholm. He continued to paint, lecture and exhibit for the next twenty years.

See: **LA:** Blackpool

Ref: Website www.arildrosencrantz.dk

Roslin, Louis Frederick (1878–1949)
Sculptor. Born in London. He studied at the City and Guilds College and at the Royal Academy Schools. He exhibited widely, sometimes under the name of L. Fritz Roselieb.

See: **LA:** Oswaldtwistle, Rawtenstall, Blackley

Ref: Johnson & Greutzner, *Dictionary of British Art*, 1999

Rossetti, Dante Gabriel (1828–82)
Painter and poet. Born in London the son of an Italian émigré who was a poet and scholar and Professor of Italian at Kings College, London. His mother was a private teacher. Rossetti attended Sass's Drawing Academy and entered the RA Schools in 1846. He briefly became a private pupil of Ford Madox Brown (qv). He was one of the original Pre-Raphaelite Brotherhood and in 1850 he published *The Germ*, the journal of the PRB. In 1854 he met Ruskin (qv) who became a friend and patron. He took William Morris (qv) and Edward Burne-Jones (qv) into his circle in the mid 1850s and they maintained a long, if sometimes strained, friendship. Rossetti was a member of the Morris, Marshall, Faulkner & Co. business, contributing painting on furniture and stained-glass cartoons. His paintings are best known for 'seductive yet aloof beauties, flame haired femmes fatales placed in dream-like settings laden with symbolism' (Treheurtz, see below)

See: **CU:** Carlisle **GM:** Oldham AG, M/ccAGs **MS:** L'pool C WAG, Mossley Hill AG, Port Sunlight AG

Ref: Treheurtz et al., *Dante Gabriel Rossetti*, 2003; Tickner, L., *Dante Gabriel Rossetti*, 2003

Ruskin, John (1819–1900)
Artist, writer and critic. Born in London, he was an only child, whose over-protective parents were ambitious for his future. He was taught at home where his talent for art and writing poetry showed themselves early. His parents took him on frequent visits to France and Italy. In 1837 he entered Christ Church, Oxford and completed his degree in 1842. In 1843 he published the first volume *of Modern Painters*, in which he urged artists to seek Truth in Nature, a view shared by the Pre-Raphaelite Brotherhood. *The Seven Lamps of Architecture* was published in 1849 and *the Stones of Venice* (1853), which includes a chapter on *The Nature of Gothic*. Ruskin looked back to medieval times when the medieval craftsman was valued for his craft and took pride in creating the finest of work. He compared this period with the ever-growing effects of industrialisation in which the machine controlled the individual and took away the skills of the craftsman and the joy and pride which came from hand work. He made a plea for a return to the skills of the artist and craftsman. As a practical demonstration of his beliefs he founded the Guild of St George in 1871 to support the establishment of small self-sufficient enterprises to preserve local crafts. Meanwhile in 1869 his literary and artistic talent was recognised when he was made Slade Professor of Art at Oxford but as well as his university work in 1870 he started writing *Fors Clavigera* a monthly letter on moral, social and economic issues to the 'Workmen and Labourers of Great Britain'. Ruskin's writings had a powerful effect on the architects, craftsmen and philanthropists of his

time, including William Morris (qv), A. H. Mackmurdo (qv) and Charles R. Ashbee (qv) who set up their great undertakings in response to his teachings.

See: **CU:** Ambleside AG, Coniston Mus +1, Keswick Mus **LA** : Lancaster Uni Lib **GM:** Oldham AG

Ref: Hilton T., *John Ruskin*, 2002

Ruskin Linen Industry (1889–*c.* 1914)
Established by Marian Twelves, a follower of Ruskin, who had managed the Langdale Linen Industry 1884–89. In 1889, she set up spinning, weaving and embroidery classes in a disused woollen mill, St Kentigern's, on Penrith Rd, Keswick. The classes ran in association with the Keswick School of Industrial Arts. The work produced was exhibited nationally and won many awards. The class was responsible for making the pall for Alfred Lord Tennyson's coffin. In 1892 Marian Twelves broke with the KSIA and set up her home and business in High Hill, Crosthwaite. The industry was run along the lines set up by Ruskin's Guild of St George to which it became affiliated in 1902. Marian Twelves retired in 1917 and the firm was continued by Ada Hooper who had been her co-partner in the business. After the Great War demand for hand-made work fell and the business gradually died out leaving just one or two spinners and weavers to carry on the work as a hobby.

See: **CU:** Ambleside AG, Coniston Mus +1

Ref: Ruskin Museum, *Archives*; Benjamin, F. A., *The Ruskin Linen Industry of Keswick*, 1974; Chapman, S. T., 'Arts, Crafts and Heritage in Victorian Lakeland' in *Armitt Library Journal*, I, 1998 pp. 38–63; Haslam, Sara E., *John Ruskin and the Lakeland Arts Revival*, 2004

Ruskin Pottery
Founded in 1898 by Edward Taylor (1838–1912), head of Birmingham School of Art 1878–*c.* 1898 and his son William Howson (1876–1935) in a former malt house in Smethwick. It was initially known as Birmingham Tile Pottery. Edward Taylor's interest in oriental ceramics and the glazes on Chinese porcelain, led him to experiment with glazes. He is said to have spent his savings of £15,000 on developing and perfecting the flambé and soufflé glazes which made his pottery unique. In 1902 the firm, upholding the Ruskin teaching of the superiority of hand-crafted artefacts, took on the name Ruskin Pottery. Howson Taylor destroyed all the recipes for his glazes shortly before he died in order to prevent them being copied.

See: **CU:** Coniston AG **MS:** Bramall Hall **NS:** Hanley AG

Ref: Rushton, J. H., *Ruskin Pottery*, 1975; Atterbury & Henson, *Ruskin Pottery*, 1993

Salisbury, Frank Owen (1874–1962)
Painter and stained-glass artist. He was educated at home in Harpenden, Hertfordshire where he was taught painting by his brother H. J. Salisbury. Later he attended Heatherley's School and the RA Schools, London in 1893. He exhibited at the RA and is best known for large historical paintings such as those in Liverpool Town Hall. He was elected to the AWG in 1914 and published his autobiography *Portrait and Pageant* in 1944.

See: **MS:** Bidston, L'pool TH **CH:** Tabley

Ref: Waters *Dictionary of British Arts*, 1975

Sanders, J. N. see **Barraclough & Sanders**

Schenck, Frederick E. E. (b. 1850)
Sculptor. Born in Scotland. He trained at Edinburgh and Hanley Schools of Art and taught at Hanley. In the 1880s he worked for several potteries and moved to London *c.* 1888. Schenck is best known for his relief sculptures on municipal buildings which included Bath Municipal Chambers, Stafford Council Hall and Oxford Town Hall. He exhibited at the RA 1886–1907.

See: **CH:** Crewe

Ref: Waters, *Dictionary of British Artists*, 1975; Gray, A. S., *Edwardian Architecture*, 1985

Schmaltz, Herbert Gustave (1856–1935)
Painter of genre, biblical, historical and flower subjects. Born at Ryton, County Durham where his father was German consul in Newcastle upon Tyne. He attended Newcastle School of Art and the South Kensington and RA Schools. He exhibited at the RA from 1879. Schmaltz visited the Holy Land in 1890 where he collected material for his biblical works. After WW1 he signed himself Herbert Carmichael, taking his mother's maiden name. His flower paintings are signed 'Angelico'. He was a member of the AWG from 1884.

See: **GM:** Bramhall

Ref: Waters, *Dictionary of British Artists*, 1975

Scott, Mackay Hugh Baillie (1865–1945)
Architect and designer. He was articled to Major Charles E. Davis the city Architect of Bath. He spent the first part of his career in the Isle of Man where after acting as assistant to surveyor Fred Sanderson, he established his own practice in 1892 at Red House which he built for himself. He built several notable houses on the island as well as receiving commissions in England and on the continent. In 1901 he moved to Bedford where he designed furniture made by John White at the Pyghtle Works, Bedford. Baillie Scott's design of the Manxman piano is iconic. He was a prolific writer, frequently published in *The Studio*. He was highly thought of and much written about on the continent where he did design work for

the Duke of Hesse and Princess Marie of Romania. He won the major prize in the *House of the Art Connoisseur* competition in Darmstadt. Later in his career he became involved in the Garden City movement, designing one of his most successful pieces of work, Waterlow Court for Hampstead Garden Suburb. His major pre-occupation was with the design of homes for ordinary people making best use of the space available to fit the needs of the family. In 1919 he took his former assistant A. E. Beresford as a partner in the firm which was highly successful in building many designer houses for the middle classes in pleasant suburban areas.

See: **CU:** Bowness **CH:** Knutsford

Ref: Haigh, D., *Baillie Scott, the Artistic House*, 1995; Kornwulf, J., *M. H. Baillie Scott and the Arts and Crafts Movement*, 1972

Seale
A family of sculptors. J. W. Seale was working from *c.* 1858 producing architectural sculpture in London. The work of G. W. Seale, probably his son, is found further a field although he was based in Brixton. He was responsible for decorative carving on St Michael's church Lyndhurst, Hampshire and St Clements Church Boscombe (1882–83). He was frequently commissioned by J. D. Sedding to do sculptural work in his churches, often in the execution of intricate marble or alabaster reredoses. Gilbert Seale fl. 1900 worked as a sculptor, modeller and plasterer. He worked with E. W. Mountford on Battersea Town Hall (1892–93) and at the Old Bailey (1900–07). His son Barney Seale was a portrait sculptor.

See: **LA:** Blackburn AG

Ref: Ward-Jackson, *Public Sculpture in the City of London*, 2003

Sedding, John Dando (1838–91)
Architect. From 1858 he spent five years in the office of G. E. Street (qv) in London before joining his brother Edmund in his Cornwall practice. After his brother's early death he moved to Bristol to set up his own practice in 1868 but returned to London in 1875. He was appointed Diocesan architect to Bath and Wells in 1880. Sedding was a founder member of the AWG and his office was the training ground for some notable Arts and Crafts architects and designers: Henry Wilson (qv), John Paul Cooper (qv), Arthur Grove, Ernest Gimson, S. Barnsley, A. H. Powell, Fellowes Prynne (qv) and Charles Nicholson(qv). His main work was church building and restoration. His most famous church is Holy Trinity, Sloane St one of the major examples of Arts and Crafts work. Unfortunately he died before the work was completed and it fell to his colleague Henry Wilson to finish the job. Sedding was a designer and practitioner in stone carving and metalwork. He was a passionate gardener and his book *Garden Craft Old and New* was published in 1891.

See: **GM:** M/cc AG, Marple **MS:** Mossley AG **NS:** Leek

Ref Wilson, H., *A Memorial of the late John Sedding*, London, 1892

Sellers, James Henry (1861–1954)
Educated at the elementary school in Oldham, Sellers started work for a local architect as an office boy. He went on to work in architects' offices in Liverpool, Birmingham, London and in York (for WG Penty). He became Assistant County Architect at Carlisle under George Dale Oliver (qv). In 1899 he set up his own practice in Oldham and then established an informal joint practice with Edgar Wood at 78 Cross St, Manchester. Both architects were interested in building with reinforced concrete and represented the cutting edge of northern architects in the first decade of the C20. Sellers, like Wood, was a talented furniture designer.

See: **CU:** Kirklinton **GM:** Fairfield, Heaton Moor, M/cc AGs +CLib+1, Middleton, Oldham, Swinton **CH:** Mere.

Ref: Gray, A. S., *Edwardian Architecture*, 1985; Archer, J., 'Edgar Wood and J Henry Sellers' in *Victorian Architecture*, Ed. Ferriday M., 1973; Treuhertz, J., *Partnership in Style, Edgar Wood and J. Henry Sellers*, 1975

Shakerley, Irene see **Dunlop, Irene**

Sharpe, J. (fl. 1912)
Sharpe was a wood carver believed to be from Hensingham near Whitehaven but local Trade Directories reveal nothing of him or his work place. If he was an amateur, he was exceptionally good.

See: **CU:** Seascale

Sharpe, Edmund (1809–77)
Architect. Edmund Sharpe established the practice in Lancaster that was to become Paley & Austin. He was an expert in the Gothic styles but is perhaps more readily remembered for his famous 'pot' churches, so called because of his use, at the request of the manufacturer, of terracotta building blocks and mouldings. The churches faced great criticism from the Ecclesiologists of the day but are still standing 150 years later albeit one is short of its tower.

See: **LA:** Bamber Bridge, Blackburn, Lancaster **GM:** Bolton, Rusholme, Walmsley, Wigan **MS:** St Helens **CH:** Davenham

Ref: Jolly, R., *Edmund Sharpe: a Lancaster Architect*, 1977; Obit. *Builder*, 35 (19 & 26.5.1877), pp. 491–93, p. 521; 35 (2.6.1877), pp. 550, 562

Shaw, Richard Norman (1831–1912)
Architect. Born and educated mainly in Edinburgh. The family moved to London in 1846 where he entered the London office of

William Burn and remained there for seven years. He attended the RA Schools from 1849 where he studied under Professor C. R. Cockerell. In Burn's office he met W. Eden Nesfield (qv) and together they used their leisure to visit and draw cathedrals in France and England. After three years in the office of Anthony Salvin, Nesfield's uncle, and four years as chief assistant to G. E. Street, Shaw and Nesfield set up their individual practices sharing rooms in Argyll St, London in 1863. Although they never worked together they developed the 'Old English' style based on the vernacular architecture of Kent, Sussex and Surrey. Shaw moved on from Old English and built up a large, successful and prestigious practice. His assistants of the 1870s (Ernest Newton (qv) 1873, E. S. Prior 1874, Mervyn Macartney (qv) 1877, William Lethaby (qv) 1879, Gerald Horsley (qv) 1879 were to become the collective founders of the AWG in 1884. Shaw is probably best known for his large country houses like Cragside, Northumberland (1870) and Merrist Wood in Surrey (1877) and for New Scotland Yard on Victoria Embankment (1888–90). He also built a small number of delightful Arts and Crafts churches.

See: **MS:** L'pool C (2), Sefton Park **CH:** Thurstaston (2) **NS:** Leek (4), Meerbrook

Ref: Saint, A., *Richard Norman Shaw*, 1976; Gray, A. S., *Edwardian Architecture*, 1985; Obit. *RIBAJ* (23.11.1912), pp. 55–56; *Builder* (22.11.1912), pp. 598–601; (29.11.1912), pp. 35–36, 643–44 ; (20.12.1912), p. 745

Shelmerdine, Thomas (1845–1921)
Architect and surveyor. Born in Broughton, near Manchester and educated at the Royal Institution, Liverpool. He was Liverpool Corporation's Surveyor and Architect for over forty years 1871–1914. As well as large public works such as St Johns Gardens (1904), the Hornby Library (1906), and the City Transport Offices (1905–07), Shelmerdine was also responsible for a number of small Carnegie Free Libraries built around the city in different styles. Shelmerdine's other recorded interest was golf being a life member of the West Lancashire Club.

See: **MS:** Garston, L'pool C (2), Sefton Park, Toxteth

Ref: PRO Liverpool, *Proceedings of Liverpool City Council: Tabulated Returns as to Salaries 1900–41*

Shields, Frederic James (1833–1911)
Painter, illustrator, stained-glass designer. Born in Hartlepool but moved to London with his family in 1836 where he attended Clement Danes Charity School. He followed his father to Manchester in 1847 where he was apprenticed to a lithographer and later worked for the printers Bradshaw & Blacklock. He became a close friend of Rossetti and Madox Brown and developed a reputation as a painter and illustrator. He was a deeply religious man and approached his ecclesiastical work with great reverence toiling over his stained glass and mosaic work. He spent the last years of his life painting the walls of the chapel in Bayswater Rd designed for Mrs Gurney by Herbert Horne. The chapel was totally destroyed in the Second World War.

See: **GM:** M/cc, Reddish **CH:** Chester, Eaton Hall, Parkgate

Ref: Mills, E., *The Life and Letters of Frederic J. Shields*, 1912.

Shrigley & Hunt (1874–1982)
Stained-glass window designers and manufacturers, ecclesiastical decorators. The stained-glass business was founded in 1874 by Arthur Hunt when he took over the church-decorating firm of Hudson and Shrigley based at Castle Hill, Lancaster. His firm aimed to supply lighter, more natural and intelligible interpretations of religious teaching in ecclesiastical stained-glass and to extend the business into the domestic market. His success owed much to the artists and designers he employed. Carl Almquist (qv), trained by Henry Holiday (qv), was appointed as chief designer in 1874 and Edward Holmes Jewitt (qv) arrived in 1877. These two men were responsible for most of the design work for more than 40 years, though Hunt employed other full time and freelance artists over the years. The firm was started at a time of change in the stained-glass industry and set off in the footsteps of the 1870s leaders of change such as Morris & Co. and Henry Holiday at Powell's. They followed, not in the sense of being stylistic copyists, but rather seeking to emulate the quality of their draughtsmanship and design. Whilst the firm tended to cling to the 'architectural frame' of plinths and crocketted pinnacles abjured by Morris and the later Arts and Crafters, Almquist and Jewitt were not to be faulted on the quality of their drawing and colour sense. Always commercially responsive to costs and their clients' ambitions, there are noticeable differences in the firm's windows as some clients chose expensive 'Antique' or 'Norman' glass and others took less expensive options. The firm had a successful working relationship with Lancaster-based church architects Paley & Austin. As well as continuing their church-decoration business Shrigley & Hunt also produced art tiles many of which bear similarities to designs by William De Morgan and Morris & Co. Hunt died in 1917. The firm continued for another 65 years for the last 32 of which the business was run by Joseph Fisher.

See: **CU:** Ambleside, Barbon, Bardsea, Broughton in Furness, Finsthwaite, Flookburgh, Kendal, Kirkby Lonsdale **LA:** Blackpool, Garstang, Lancaster (2), Oswaldtwistle, Over

Wyresdale **GM:** Burnage, Daisy Hill, Stockport **MS:** Eccleston, Great Crosby, Newton le Willows **CH:** Pulford, Thelwall, Warrington, Widnes, Wilmslow (2)

Ref: Walter, W., *Stained Glass from Shrigley and Hunt*, 2003

Siddall, Gertrude M. (b. 1877)
Artist. Information is scant. Gertrude was born in Chester to John and Elizabeth Siddall who ran two businesses, an opticians and an umbrella workshop in which three of their sons worked. Gertrude was an art student in 1901 and must have continued with her art for in 1910, she painted the beautiful organ screen to commemorate the life of Edward VII in Christ Church, Chester, where a member of her family was in the choir.

See: **CH:** Chester

Ref: *1901 Census*, Chester PRO, *Christ Church, Chester archives*

Simpson, Arthur W. (1857–1922)
Furniture maker and woodcarver. Born in Kendal, he was the son of a devout Quaker family and attended the Society of Friends schools in Leeds and Kendal. He was informally apprenticed to a cabinet maker at the age of 14 but left Kendal in 1875 to take up a new apprenticeship as a woodcarver at Gillows of Lancaster, attending Lancaster School of Art in the evenings. He worked briefly in Leicester as one of 30 carvers in a workshop, before returning to Kendal and setting up on his own, a venture which failed for lack of commissions. In 1882 he went to London and eventually found work in William Aumonier's (qv) wood-carving studio in Tottenham Court Road. At the end of that year he joined architect and designer G. Faulkner Armitage (qv) in Altrincham where he stayed for three years. In 1885 he returned to Kendal and set up in business. In addition to designing, making and carving furniture, Simpson spent much of his time teaching, mainly at evening classes in nearby villages like Burneside or Crook and also at the Keswick School of Industrial Art. He exhibited at the Arts and Crafts Exhibition Society in 1889 and was a committee man as well as an exhibitor at the Kendal Arts, Crafts and Loan Exhibition in 1891. He also contributed to the series of Summer Exhibitions at Coniston after 1906. In 1912 Simpson had a stand at the Ideal Homes Exhibition with Voysey (qv) on one side and George Walton on the other. In 1901 the firm opened a show room called *The Handicrafts* in Windermere which sold complete home furnishings. Arthur Simpson's talent was such that he was asked to design and make furniture or do wood-carving for many leading architects and designers of the day including C. F. A. Voysey, Dan Gibson (qv), M. H. Baillie Scott (qv), W. G .Collingwood (qv)and the Morton family. His work adorns many churches throughout the country. He was a friend of C. F. A. Voysey who designed his house, 'Littleholme', in 1910. He became a member of the AWG in 1913. Illness overtook him in 1920 and the firm continued through his son Hubert. Simpson's quirk was that he would not carve the human figure and most of the figure work associated with his work is said to have been carried out by William Aumonier Jr.

See: **CU:** Bowness (3), Burneside, Carlisle, Coniston Mus, Crosby-on-Eden, Kendal AG, Kirkby Stephen, Low Wray, Old Hutton, Rusland, Staveley **GM:** Darwen, Prestwich

Ref: Davidson, E., *The Simpsons of Kendal*, 1978

Simpson, Frederick Moore (1855–1928)
Architect. He was articled to G. F. Bodley (qv) and entered the RA Schools in 1880 and subsequently worked in the office of C. J. Ferguson (qv) in Carlisle. In 1894 he became Professor of Architecture at the University of Liverpool and at the University of London 1903–19. He is best known in Liverpool for his design of the statue of Queen Victoria in Derby Square with Willink and Thicknesse with whom he co-operated on a number of occasions. In London he designed buildings for University College including the department of Physiology. He wrote *A History of Architectural Development* in 1922.

See: **MS:** L'pool C (2)

Ref: Gray, A. S., *Edwardian Architecture*, 1985; Obit. *RIBAJ* (23.6.1928), p. 571; *Builder* (22.6.1928), p. 1062 and *Builder* (29.6.1928), p. 1102

Simpson, James Lomax (1882–1977)
Architect. Son of Jonathan Simpson (qv), he studied at Liverpool University and was articled to Grayson & Ould (qv). He set up on his own in Liverpool in 1905, occasionally helping out in his father's practice as well as being employed by Lever Brothers. In 1910 he was appointed Head of the Architecture Department at Lever Brothers and became a director of the firm in 1917. He was a talented and versatile architect and worked for the company overseas as well as at Port Sunlight.

See: **MS:** Port Sunlight (3), Thornton Hough (4)

Ref: Hubbard & Shippobottom, *Port Sunlight Village*

Simpson, Jonathan (1850–1937)
Architect. A native of Bolton, and a life long friend of William Hesketh Lever. He practised in Bolton doing largely domestic work, eclectic in style but with an Arts and Crafts influence. He later worked for London transport and the University of London.

See: **GM:** Bolton **MS:** Port Sunlight (3)

Ref: Hubbard & Shippobottom, *Port Sunlight*, 1988

Sleigh, Bernard (1872–1954)
Painter. He was born in Birmingham and studied at Birmingham School of Art. He was a

member of the Bromsgrove Guild. A painter in oils and water colour, he also did murals, wood engravings and designed stained glass and fabrics.

See: **MS:** Wallasey

Ref: Watts, *Bromsgrove Guild*, 1999; Cooper, R., 'Bernard Sleigh, Artist and Craftsman,' *DASJ*, 1997

Smith, Arthur Jackson (b. 1854)
Joiner, carpenter, woodcarver. Born in Flintham Notts he lived in Sale, where he is recorded as working in 1897 at Albion Grove as a joiner and in 1901 as a cabinet maker. From 1902–04 he may have worked away from the area as he is not recorded in the trade directories He had returned by 1905 when his business seems to have expanded as he had a work address in Wycliffe Place, Hope Rd and a home address in Eaton Rd. He remained in Sale until *c.* 1915. Perhaps this was when he retired to Coniston.

See: **CU:** Windermere

Smith, Gerald Edward Roberts (1883–1959)
Stained-glass artist. Born at Melbury, Dorset and educated at Sandbach School, Cheshire and at Chester Art School. He was apprenticed to Edward Frampton. In 1906 he joined A. K. Nicholson at his St Johns Wood Studios where he stayed and continued to run the studio after Nicholson's death. He was one of the first members of the British Society of Master Glass Painters and Chairman from 1958 until his death.

See: **CU:** Barrow, Carlisle (2), Natland, Windermere **GM:** Royton **CH:** Mobberley

Ref: Obit. *BSMGSJ*, 13, no. 1 (1959–60)

Smith, George Herbert Tyson (1883–1972)
Sculptor. Born in Liverpool and apprenticed to a letter cutter. He took evening classes in clay modelling, stone carving and plaster moulding at Liverpool College of Art. He also studied drawing under Augustus John in the Department of Architecture and Applied Art at Liverpool University. After WW1 he established a successful studio working mainly in Liverpool. In the 1920s he collaborated on a number of war memorials. He was also responsible for the busts of George V and Queen Mary on either side of the Liverpool entrance to the Mersey Tunnel. He was a member of the active and influential Sandon Studios Society and its President from 1956.

See: **LA:** Accrington, Fleetwood **MS:** Birkenhead, L'pool C, Mossley AG

Ref: Cavanagh, *Public Sculpture in Liverpool*, 1997

Smithies, James (1861–1941)
Metalworker. Born at Middleton, Lancs where he grew up as a contemporary of Edgar Wood. He trained as a blacksmith and by 1894 had set up his own workshop at Alden Bank, Water Lane, Wilmslow. He moved subsequently to Manchester Rd, Wilmslow and had a show room at 19, Bridge St, Manchester (1911). He had a small workforce, which produced beautiful repoussé work in brass and copper for domestic, commercial and ecclesiastical situations. He exhibited with the Northern Art Workers' Guild and more widely at Arts and Crafts Exhibitions, gaining a national reputation.

See: **CU:** Eskdale Green **GM:** Didsbury, Middleton **CH:** Alderley Edge (2), Chester Wilmslow

Ref: 'Experts in their field: James Smithies, Wilmslow', *Cheshire Life*, 1980; *The Studio*, 21 (1901), p. 257

Spence, Thomas Ralph (1848–1918)
Architect, painter, decorator, stained-glass designer and wood carver. Born at Gilling near Richmond in North Yorkshire. He was trained in architecture and by the 1870s was operating his own practice in Newcastle on Tyne. He devoted much of his time to painting and sent work to the RA in 1876 and 1878. In 1888 he designed and decorated the superb St George's church at Jesmond and in 1889 he exhibited church furniture at the Exhibition of Decorative and Applied Art at the WAG in Liverpool. He designed stained glass for the Gateshead Stained-Glass Company and continued to exhibit his paintings.

See: **GM:** Monton

Ref: Marshall Hall, *Artists of Northumbria*, 1982

Stabler, Harold (1872–1945)
Designer and metalworker. Born in Levens near Kendal where his father was a teacher at the Boys' School. Stabler was apprenticed *c.* 1886 to Arthur Simpson (qv) and attended Kendal School of Art where he gained his Teacher's Certificate. In 1898 he became the first full-time head teacher at the Keswick School of Industrial Arts bringing a new flair and style into the school's approach to design. In 1900 he moved to Liverpool to work with Richard Llewellyn Rathbone (qv) in his metalwork business. They shared accommodation at 37 Northumberland Terrace, until 1902 when Stabler followed Rathbone to London to teach at the Sir John Cass Technical Institute. He married Phoebe McLeish (qv), the sculptor and the couple worked together on producing cloisonné work, jewellery, ceramic figures and plaques. They were partners and designers in the firm of Carter, Stabler & Adams pottery, later to be marketed as Poole Pottery. Harold designed and executed his own silver work but also produced designs for Wakely and Wheeler, the Goldsmiths & Silversmiths Company, London and for Adie Brothers of Birmingham. He was a founder member of the Design and Industries Association in 1915.

See: **CU:** Coniston Mus, Hutton in the Forest, Keswick, Levens, Winster **MS:** Birkenhead **CH:** Alderley Edge

Ref: Karlin, *Jewelry and Metalwork*, 1993; Davidson, *The Simpsons of Kendal*, 1978; WAG, *The Art Sheds*, 1981; *Census 1901*

Stabler, Phoebe née McLeish (1879–1955)
Artist, sculptor, jeweller. Born Liverpool. She studied at Liverpool University School of Architecture and Applied Art under C. J. Allen (qv) and Augustus John. She was awarded a travelling scholarship but used the money instead to go to the RCA in London. She designed the cover of the University Guild Magazine *The Sphinx*, Nov 1903. After she married Harold Stabler (qv) in 1906, moved to London and exhibited under her married name. (See Harold Stabler)

See: **MS:** L'pool WAG, Mossley Hill AG

Ref: WAG, *The Art Sheds*, 1981; Aldham Resource Centre Archives, *Art Sheds Register 1901–4*

Stevenson, William Grant (1849–1919)
Sculptor. Born in Ratho, Mid Lothian and educated at the parish school and then Edinburgh College of Art. He attended the Royal Scottish Academy Life Class gaining one gold and two silver medals. With his older brother, David Watson Stevenson (1842–1904), he set up in business as D. W. and G. Stevenson in Edinburgh. His best known works include statues on the Scott Monument in Edinburgh, Robert Burns in Kilmarnock and William Wallace in Duthie Park, Aberdeen 1883.

See: **CU:** Eamont Bridge

Ref: Web site: *Gazetteer for Scotland*. Web site: *sites.scran.ac.uk/scottmon/peter_peebles.htm*

Stokes, Leonard Aloysius Scott (1858–1925)
Architect. Born at Southport, Lancs. The family moved to London where he was articled to S. J. Nicholl of Kentish Town 1871–74 and for a further six years he worked in a number of famous offices including G. E. Street (qv), T. E. Collcutt, and Bodley (qv) & Garner. He entered the RA Schools in 1878 and won the Pugin Prize 1880 with which he travelled to France and Germany. He set up in practice in 1882. He was a Catholic and designed many Catholic churches and school buildings together with many attractive private houses. He married Edith Gaine, the daughter of the General Manager of the National Telephone Company, and he designed about twenty telephone exchanges during the ten years before the telephone system was merged with The Post Office in 1911. Stokes's work shows some of the influences of his old masters, Bodley and Collcutt but also his own independent spirit. Some characteristic features of his buildings include horizontal stone and brick bands tying into window heads and sills, cleft parapets, small oeuil de boeuf openings, arches and splayed archivolts. His best known work is perhaps the convent at All Saints, London Colney (1899–1903). He was elected to the AWG in 1886.

See: **MS:** Sefton Park

Ref: Gray, A. S., *Edwardian Architecture*, 1985; Drysdale, George 'The Work of Leonard Stokes' in *RIBAJ* (8.1.1927); Obit. *RIBAJ* (9.1.1926), pp. 48–50, *Builder* (1.1.1926), p. 7

Street, George Edmund (1824–81)
Architect. Articled to Owen Browne Carter in Winchester 1841–44, he worked in the London office of G. G. Scott until 1849 when he set up his own practice. In 1850 he was appointed diocesan architect of Oxford and he moved his office there. His first assistants were Edmund Sedding and Philip Webb (qv) but Norman Shaw (qv), William Morris (qv), and John Sedding (qv) were all articled to him. Street's very influential practice may therefore be described as 'first generation Arts & Crafts'. Street was a hard and demanding worker. He was a skilled draughtsman and designed down to the last detail. He was a staunch Ecclesiologist and a supporter of the Pre-Raphaelite Brotherhood. He believed that his own architecture should be a continuation and development of Gothic architecture not a replication of earlier buildings and he used all Gothic precedent not just the widely preferred English Decorated. He built many remarkable churches in both town and country and felt the materials for these should be different for they should be seen in their local context. From 1868–81 much of his time was spent in the design and building of the Royal Courts of Justice in London.

See: **CU:** Carlisle **GM:** Swinton **MS:** Barnston, Caldy, Walton, Whiston **NS:** Denstone, Hollington, Leek

Ref: Smart Jnr, C. M., *Muscular Churches*, 1989

Sugden, William (1820–92) and **Sugden, William Larner** (1850–1901)
Architects. William Sugden senior was articled to a Mr Fruer of Framlingham, Suffolk and came to Leek to oversee the building of the stations on the Churnet Valley railway line. He set up practice as an architect in the town in about 1849. William Larner Sugden was educated at Leeds Grammar School and joined his father's practice in 1866. He was a Committee member of SPAB. The Sugdens have left a considerable heritage in the buildings they designed in Leek.

See: **NS:** Leek (6)

Ref: Lovenbury, G. A., *The Sugdens of Leek*, 1975; Leek Civic Society, *Sugden & Son Architects of Leek – a Town Trail.*

Sumner, George Heywood Maunoir (1848–1940)
Designer, painter and etcher. Born at Alresford, Hampshire his father was a Fellow and Tutor of Balliol College Oxford. He was educated at Eton and Christchurch Oxford. He exhibited at

the RA 1880–83. He was an associate of the Century Guild from 1884 and provided paintings for the Fitzroy Picture Society. He designed stained glass, textiles and wallpapers and Alexander Morton, Morris & Co. and Jeffrey & Co. made use of his designs. Morris and Co. made his pattern *The Chase* into a tapestry. He designed many exquisite church and domestic embroideries. Examples of these are to be found in the Victoria & Albert Museum. He was a specialist in the art of sgraffito, a form of applied decoration in which the outside layer of plaster or clay is scratched through to expose a different coloured under coat beneath. This form of wall decoration was associated in the second half of the C19 with a Neo-Renaissance style but Sumner adapted the process to a quite different style of work in which often quite realistic pictures played an important part. He wrote and illustrated books on archaeology. He was a member of the AWG and became Master in 1894. He was also a founder member of the Arts and Crafts Exhibition Society.

See: **CU:** Croglin

Ref: Gray, A. S., *Edwardian Architecture*, 1985; Coatts, M. & Lewis, E., eds, *Heywood Sumner, Artist and Archaeologist*, 1986; *The Studio*, 13 (1898)

Swindley, James (fl. 1885)
Ornamental metalworker. He was a cousin of John Douglas and had a workshop at Handbridge Chester. He executed many of Douglas's designs for metalwork in and around Chester including the gates at Belgrave Lodge, 1890–91 and the gates and railings at Eccelston Lodge 1893–94 Eaton Hall, the Diamond Jubiliee Clock, Eastgate Chester 1897 and the gates at Mostyn Hall Flintshire 1896.

See: **CH:** Chester + Cath, Eaton

Ref: Hubbard, E., *John Douglas*, 1991

Talbot, John Joseph (1871–1902)
Architect. Born in Bolton, the son of a school teacher. He designed many houses at Port Sunlight where he lived *c.* 1896–97. He also did work at Thornton Manor for William Lever. His work is marked by quality of materials and execution, stylishness of design, thoroughness of work and careful attention to detailing. He exhibited at the RA. From 1896 until his early death in 1902 he was in partnership with William Gilmour Wilson, practising in Liverpool and Bolton.

See: **MS:** Oxton, Port Sunlight (also as Talbot & Wilson), Prenton, Thornton Hough

Ref: Hubbard and Shippobottham, *Port Sunlight*, 1988

Taylor, Charles, Thomas (b. 1862)
Architect. Born in Oldham. Educated at the High School and at Owens College he was articled 1878–83 to Edward Potts in Oldham and remained with him, as an assistant, until he started his own practice in 1892. He was in partnership with Roberts and Bowman.

See: **GM:** Levenshulme

Ref: Pike, *Contemporary Biographies*, p. 222

Taylor, James Medland (1834–1909)
Architect. Born at Stanford Rivers, near Ongar in Essex, he was first a pupil of Joseph Payne in Leatherhead and then articled to his uncle, James Medland, the County Surveyor of Gloucestershire. He worked in Cardiff with H. J. Paull and in Hampstead with S. S. Teulon before going to Haley & Son in Manchester. He was twenty-six when he set up on his own at St Anne's Churchyard, Manchester in 1860. He worked in partnership with his younger brother, Henry Taylor. J. M. Taylor did not exhibit with the Northern Art Workers' Guild but many of his buildings are imbued with the spirit of the movement and he demonstrates a degree of quirkery that demands attention and makes his work very interesting.

See: **LA:** Burnley **GM:** Cheadle Hulme, Gatley, Haughton, Haughton Green, Hyde, Kearsley, Levenshulme, Rochdale **MS:** St Helens (2) **CH:** Saughall

Ref: Pike, *Contemporary Biographies* – Architects, p. 222; Obit. *Builder* (12.6.1909), pp. 710–11

Thompson, Charles Edward (b. 1869)
Art metalworker. He was born in Liverpool. At the time of the 1901 Census Charles Thompson was working as an architectural draughtsman and also on his own account as an art metalworker. According to reports of students' work in *The Studio* Thompson attended evening classes in metalwork *c.* 1898–1901 at Liverpool School of Architecture and Applied Art and in 1902 he attended two evening classes a week for enamelling. He later won commissions for plaques commemorating the opening of some of the Liverpool libraries in which his great talent for metalwork was admirably demonstrated.

See: **MS:** Aigburth, Garston, L'pool Central Lib, St Helens, Toxteth

Ref: *Census 1901*; Aldham Roberts Centre Archives, Art Sheds Attendance Registers 1901–05; *The Studio*, 17, 21, 29, 39

Thompson, Robert 'Mouseman' (1876–1955)
Woodworker and carver. Thompson was born in Kilburn in North Yorkshire the son of the village joiner, carpenter and wheelwright. He began his working life as an apprentice mechanical engineer with a firm in Cleckheaton but gave it up *c.* 1896, to return to his home village and work with his father. Robert took to carving oak and in 1919 undertook some work for the chapel at Ampleforth College. This work was the first on which he used his mouse trade mark and the commission was the beginning of a very successful, high quality

business which continues today. The carved mouse appears on every piece produced by the firm since 1919, but it is not always easily seen.

See: **LA:** Colne, Downham, Tarleton **GM:** Northenden, Oldham **MS:** Sefton Village, St Helens

Ref: Thompson, J., *The Mouseman of Kilburn*, 1988

Thorneycroft, William Hamo (1850–1925)
Sculptor. Educated at Macclesfield Grammar School and University College School London, he received training in sculpture in his father's studio where he assisted him in the sculpting of 'Commerce' for the Albert Memorial. He attended the RA Schools in 1869. His forte was architectural sculpture exemplified in the celebrated Institute of Chartered Accountants' building. He received commissions for many public monuments and memorials but was equally at home modelling small-scale, New Sculpture statuettes. He was a member of the AWG 1884–1901 and was knighted in 1917.

See: **CU:** Carlisle Cath **LA:** Preston Mus **GM:** M/cc, Shaw **CH:** Knutsford

Ref: Gray, A. S., *Edwardian Architecture*, 1985; Beattie, S., *New Sculpture*, 1983; Manning, E., *Marble and Bronze*, 1882

Tiffany Glass
Louis Comfort Tiffany (1843–1933) was the son of the New York jeweller and store owner. In 1876 he went to Paris to study painting and became interested in the art of stained glass. On his return home in 1879 he founded an interior design company and in 1885 established the Tiffany Glass Co. He experimented with creating iridescent effects in blown glass and in 1894 he patented the 'favrile' glass for which his name is so famous. The firm produced other types of decorative glass and also metalwork including candlesticks, lamps and vases in bronze and copper. The firm went bankrupt in 1932 after he had retired.

See: **LA**: Accrington **GM:** MMULib

Ref: Paul, T., *The Art of Louis Comfort Tiffany*, 1987; Arwas, V., *Tiffany*, 1979

Tinworth, George (1844–1913)
Ceramicist. Born in Walworth, London, he had little formal schooling and worked from the age of fourteen in his father's small wheelwright shop. In his spare time he would whittle and carve figures in wood and stone and though untaught he developed a considerable skill. In 1861 he went to Lambeth School of Art and then to the RA Schools where in 1867 he won a Silver Medal for a Study from Life. He first exhibited at the RA in 1866, the year in which he joined Doulton (qv) as a pottery modeller. At Doulton he designed and made the decorated stoneware pottery which became known as 'Doulton Ware'. From 1874 Tinworth made terracotta panels with biblical themes and gained many commissions including a reredos for York Minster. For light relief he also designed comical groups of animals in human situations. He was described as the man who made the name of Doulton world famous from the 1870s.

See: **CH:** Capesthorne

Ref: Eyles & Irvine, *Doulton Lambeth Wares*, 2002

Todd, Arthur (fl. 1908–35)
Stained-glass artist. He exhibited eight times at the Walker Art Gallery, Liverpool between 1908 and 1919 with addresses in Heywood and Lytham St Anne's. He was working in Heywood, Lancs *c.* 1935.

See: **LA:** Blackpool

Ref: Johnson and Greutzner, *Dictionary of British Art*, 5, 1999.

Toft, Albert (1869–1949)
Sculptor. Born in Birmingham, he was educated at Stoke on Trent. He was first apprenticed as a modeller at Elkington & Co. the Birmingham metalwork firm and then to Wedgwood's Pottery. He attended Hanley and Newcastle under Lyme Schools of Art 1881–83 and studied at the South Kensington Schools under Lanteri. His early work was as a portraitist in terracotta but in the 1890s he became a member of the New Sculpture Movement. At the turn of the century he took up public sculpture doing figures of Queen Victoria and many war memorials, including the figures representing the armed services at Birmingham's Hall of Memory 1923–24. Toft was a member of the AWG 1891–1920. He wrote *Modelling and Sculpture*, a sculptor's manual in 1924.

See: **LA:** Preston AG **GM:** Chadderton, Rochdale AG **MS:** L'pool WAG

Ref: Ward-Jackson, *Public Sculpture in the City of London*, 2003; *The Studio*, 66 (1916)

Toogood, Rev J. H. (fl. 1907–46)
Wood carver. Vicar of Plemstall in Cheshire from 1907 to 1946.

See: **CH:** Plemstall

Townsend, C. Harrison (1851–1928)
Architect. Born at Birkenhead, where he attended the local school and was subsequently articled to the architect Walter Scott in Liverpool. In 1880 he joined T. L. Banks who had an office in Whitehaven. He was a partner in the firm from 1884 until he left to set up on his own in London in 1888. He was a leading light in the Arts and Crafts Movement becoming a member of the AWG 1888 and its Master in 1903.

See: **CU:** Kirkland

Ref: Gray, A. S., *Edwardian Architecture*, 1985; Obit. *RIBAJ* (12.1.1929), p. 211 and *Builder* (4.1.1929), p. 30

Townshend, Caroline Charlotte (1878–1944)
Stained-glass artist. Born in London the daughter of an architect who trained under G. E. Street and was a friend of J. D. Sedding. She spent five years studying at St Andrews in Scotland and a further two years at the Slade in London. She decided to take up stained-glass work *c.* 1900 and became an assistant and pupil of Christopher Whall. She attended his classes until 1903 when she set up on her own in collaboration with Lowndes and Drury. In 1906 she took a studio in the newly opened Glass House in Fulham. In 1912 she met Joan Howson who became her trainee. After a period of war work Townshend and Howson entered upon a lifelong partnership working first in the Glass House and from the mid 1920s from a studio in Deodar Rd, Putney. During World War Two Townshend opened evacuee centres in North Wales assisted by Joan Howson and other stained-glass artists.

See: **CU:** Burneside, Eskdale Green, Seascale **MS:** Fazakerley, Gateacre **CH:** Widnes

Ref: William Morris Gallery, '*Women Stained-Glass Artists*, 1985

Travers, Howard Martin Otto (1886–1948)
Stained-glass artist and illustrator. Born in Godmanchester he was educated at Tonbridge School in Kent. He was articled to Ninian Comper and attended the Royal College of Art 1904–08 taking his Diploma in Architecture in 1908. He won the award of the Grand Prix de Paris for Stained Glass in 1925. He taught at the RCA from 1925–48.

See: **MS:** Runcorn

Ref: Blagden-Gamlen, P. E., *Martin Travers 1886–1948 A hand list of his Work*, 1977

Truefitt, George (1824–1902)
Architect. He had a large practice in Manchester designing houses, churches and banks. His work shows the influence of his travels as a young man through France and Germany. A major commission was the work he did for Sir W. Cunliff Brooks in Aberdeenshire.

See: **GM:** Ashton upon Mersey, Partington

Ref: Obit. *RIBAJ*, 9 (1902), p. 461 and *Builder* 83 (16.8.1902), p. 153

Twelves, Marian see **Langdale Linen** and **Ruskin Linen Industry**

Vale Press (1894–1904)
Established in 1894 at Warwick St, off Regent St, London by Charles Ricketts, an engraver, in partnership with Llewelyn Hacon, a wealthy lawyer interested in the arts. It moved to 17 Craven St the Strand in 1899. Ricketts and his lifelong friend Charles Haslewood Shannon, an artist and engraver collaborated on many of the illustrations. Each book was designed throughout by Ricketts: the watermark, typeface, wood engravings, bindings etc. Forty-six titles were produced including a thirty-nine volume Shakespeare.

See: **Cu:** Carlisle AG **GM:** M/cc Libs, MMUlib **MS:** L'pool C Lib, Uni Lib

Ref: Cave, R., *The Private Presses*, 1983

Voysey, Charles Francis Annesley (1857–1941)
Architect and designer. He was educated at home by his clergyman father with a brief period at Dulwich School. In 1874 he was articled to J. P. Seddon and spent a year as his assistant. After a short time with Saxon Snell, he worked in George Devey's (qv) office in 1880. He set up on own in 1882. He was an independent thinker and an idealist, who went back to first principles in realising his designs. His watch word was 'fitness for purpose'. He built many small country houses and holiday homes and developed his easily recognisable style. He also designed wallpapers, fabrics, carpets, furniture and metal ware. He worked for a time for the Liquor Control Board which was based in Carlisle. He was a member of the AWG and it's Master in 1924.

See: **CU:** Kendal, Bowness (3) **GM:** M/cc Whitworth AG **MS:** L'pool WAG, Mossley AG **CH:** Alderley Edge

Ref: Hitchmough, W., *C F A Voysey*, 1995

Walker, Leonard (1877–1965)
Stained-glass artist. Born in Ealing he studied at St John's Wood Art School where he later became a teacher and Principal. Stylistically, he kept painting to a minimum and allowed the qualities of the glass and the lead lines to define his subjects. He became a member of the AWG in 1914.

See: **CU:** Gt Asby **NS:** Hartshill

Ref: *Ely Museum* notes on exhibits; Obit. *BSMGP*, 14, no. 2, 1965

Walmsley, Bernard Deane (1893–1985)
Stained-glass artist. Born at Blackburn, the son of Luke S. Walmsley, who was a fine-art dealer, carver and gilder. His mother Harriet née Kenyon was born at Lytham, Lancashire and the family moved there, from Blackburn, in the early 1900s. Bernard was educated at the Lytham Grammar School and then attended the Municipal School of Art in Liverpool. He returned to Lytham St Anne's and with his father, opened a stained-glass studio in the town. In 1922 he married Beatrice Partington who was the daughter of a painter and an accomplished artist. While Beatrice joined the firm as a book-keeper she is said to have been responsible for much design work. In 1929 the Walmsleys closed the studio at St Anne's and moved their operation to an idyllic setting at Chapel Stile in Langdale where they set up a new studio under the old name 'St Anne's Studio'. Here they continued to produce

beautiful windows while aiming at self-sufficiency in their three-acre garden and supplementing their income by selling art work to the summer tourists. In addition to windows the Walmsleys designed glass vases and plaques blown by Hartley Wood & Co. in Sunderland.

See: **CU:** Ambleside, Chapel Stile
LA: Blackburn, Church, Rochdale

Ref: Mr and Mrs D. Furness, *Walmsley family archives*

Ward, William Henry (1865–1924)
Architect. Born at Iver in Buckinghamshire the son of a vicar, he was educated at Repton and Clare College, Cambridge. He was articled to Sir Arthur Blomfield 1890–92 and went into the office of George & Peto 1892–93. He worked briefly with Dan Gibson in Windermere before becoming assistant to Edwin Lutyens 1894–98. He set up his own practice in Charlotte St, London and did a range of different building-work including a group of houses in Hampstead Garden Suburb. He also designed furniture for the Church Craft League and was elected to the AWG in 1910. He wrote *Sixteenth Century French Chateaux and Gardens* (1909) and *The Architecture of the Renaissance in France* (1911).

See: **CU:** Bassenthwaite **MS:** Fazakerley

Ref: Gray, *Edwardian Architecture*, 1985; Obit. *Builder* (14.3.1924), pp. 407, 414 and *Builder* (28.3.1924), p. 488

Wardle, Elizabeth see **Leek Embroidery Society**

Ware and Rathbone (1890–1900)
The partnership was established at the end of 1890 with an office at 6 The Temple, Dale St, Liverpool. Edmund Ware (1852–1934) had spent thirteen years as assistant to Edmund Kirby and Edmund Rathbone (1863–1924), a member of the wealthy and influential Liverpool Rathbone family, had just terminated his partnership with Mackmurdo (qv) and Horne. The work done by the Ware-Rathbone partnership has yet to be researched but it is known they designed the Baptist Church School in Serpentine Road, Wallasey in 1896 (now demolished) and in the following year went on to do the acclaimed Manor Road Unitarian Church also in Wallasey. Both partners were involved with Della Robbia Pottery, the enterprise of Edmund's brother Harold Rathbone (qv). Ware was a member of its prestigious Controlling Board along with Holman Hunt, G. F. Watts and others while Edmund designed occasional pieces of pottery and promoted its use for architectural decoration. When the partnership was dissolved, Ware set up on his own at Exchange St Liverpool, which was his office for the next thirty years. Rathbone went into a brief partnership with R. T. Beckett, a nephew of John Douglas (qv). Much of his time however was involved with the art world. He organised exhibitions at the Walker Art Gallery and other venues and also exhibited at them. In *c.* 1905 he established the City Beautiful Wayside Café at 15 Harrington St, a place where artist, writers and thinkers could meet.

See: **MS:** Wallasey

Ref: L'pool PRO *Kirby archives, WAG exhibition catalogues & Gore's Directories;* L'pool Uni. Lib. *Rathbone Archives*; Private archives of the Rathbone family; Liverpool PRO; Bisson, R. B., *The Sandon Studio Society and the Arts*, 1965

Warham Guild
Ecclesiastical decorative artists. The Guild was founded in 1912 and made church ornaments and vestments to very high standards. It was supported by an Advisory Committee headed by Percy Dearmer until 1936. As well as providing vestments, altar cloths, wood and metalwork it had a wider remit. It offered advice and help, both architectural and ecclesiological, on any queries regarding the fabric of a church. Its headquarters were in Margaret St, London, in a building owned by Mowbrays. When this firm merged with Wippells and relocated to Exeter in 1969 the Guild was also transferred and virtually disappeared.

See: **CH:** Chester

Ref: Website: www///.anglicansonline.org/special/warham *A Brief History of the Warham Guild*

Waterhouse, Alfred (1830–1940)
Architect. Born at Aigburth, Liverpool, he was educated at Friends School Tottenham and articled 1848–53 to Richard Lane, Manchester. He commenced practice in Manchester in 1853 and moved to London 1865. His son Paul joined him in the practice in 1891. Although he is particularly associated with the Gothic Revival in his earlier work, which included the Manchester Asssize Courts 1859 (now demolished) and Manchester Town Hall 1868–77, he worked in a variety of styles often using polychromy and terracotta. He was a prolific architect best known for his public buildings all over the country including work at Oxford and Cambridge colleges, the Natural History Museum, South Kensington, the Royal Institute of Chartered Surveyors in Parliament Square and many banks and insurance company buildings. Other notable buildings include the Metropole Hotel Brighton and Eaton Hall (now demolished) near Chester for the Duke of Westminster. He became a FRIBA in 1861 and was its President 1888–91. He gained many awards, was an associate member of the RA and a member of many Academies in Europe. He was a frequent assessor of architectural competitions. Although he was not a member of the AWG, he frequently used artists and craftsmen who were members, in the decoration of his buildings.

See: **GM:** Brooklands, M/cc (2), Reddish, Rochdale **MS:** L'pool uni **CH:** Eaton Hall

Ref: Cunningham & Waterhouse, *Alfred Waterhouse: Biography of a Practice*, 1992; Fawcett, J., ed., *Seven Victorian Architects 1976*; Obit. *RIBAJ*, 12, (30.9.1905) pp. 605, 609–18 & 13 (11.11.1905), p. 11–12; *Builder*, 89 (26.8. 1905), pp. 231, 237–38 & 89 (2.9.1905), p. 253–54

Watkins E. Stanley (fl. 1909)
Decorative artist. Described in the *Studio Yearbook* for 1909 as a designer of ecclesiastical decoration, including stained-glass windows, painted panels for reredoses and triptychs, marble and Venetian mosaics and memorial brasses. He lived in Ealing, London.

See: **GM:** Oldham

Ref: *Studio Year Book*, 1909, p. 79

Watts, George Frederick (1812–1904)
Painter and sculptor. Born in London, he was the son of a piano maker and tuner. He attended the RA schools 1835 having previously spent time in the studio of sculptor William Behnes. The first painting which brought him notice was 'Caractacus' which won him £300 in 1842. He spent some time in Italy and returned to England in 1847. He became an eminent portrait painter but preferred large allegorical subjects at which he excelled. He was also a sculptor being one of those painters who, like Leighton, made plaster models to help in the composition of his paintings. He worked on the grand scale in his statue of Hugh Lupus now at Eaton Hall. He was 'the most revered figure in British art after 1880'. (Oxford Dictionary of Art. OUP 1988.)

See: **LA:** Preston AG **GM:** Bury AG **MS:** L'pool WAG **CH:** Eaton Hall

Ref: Wilton, A. and Upstone, R., ed., *The Age of Rossetti, Burne-Jones and Watts*, 1997; Gould, V., *G. F. Watts, the Last Great Victorian*, 2004; Fine Art Society *British Sculpture 1850–1910*, 1968

Watt, Richard Harding (1842–1913)
Merchant and amateur architect. Watts was a qualified teacher of drawing but made his living as a glove merchant. He travelled widely, spending his time sketching buildings. His particular interest was in Italian and Islamic architecture. He lived in Knutsford and designed buildings for the town which he felt would enhance it. Most of his developments were around Drury Lane and Legh Road but the Kings Coffee House now the Belle Epoque restaurant was in the centre of the town. He paid architects to carry out his ideas using clay models instead of drawings to explain his ideas.

See: **CH:** Knutsford

Ref: Gray, *Edwardian Architecture*, 1985

Webb, Harry (fl 1920)
Metalworker with a workshop on Carrington Road, Ashton upon Mersey. He made memorial plaques for the local churches.

See: **GM:** Ashton upon Mersey (2)

Ref: Trade Directories, Sale Library

Webb, Phillip Speakman (1831–1915)
Architect. One of the great influences on the Arts and Crafts movement. Son of an Oxford doctor he was educated at Ayno Foundation Grammar School in Northamptonshire. He was articled to John Billing of Reading in 1848 and then worked briefly for Bidlake & Lovatt in Wolverhampton. He returned to Oxford in 1854 and joined the office of G. E. Street (qv). There he met William Morris (qv) and became part of his circle of friends. He set up his own practice in 1858 and after designing 'The Red House' at Bexley Heath for Morris in 1859, he helped establish the firm of Morris, Marshall, Faulkner & Co. in 1861. In 'The Firm', Webb was responsible for the overall design of the stained-glass work, he designed quarries and was very good at animals! He also designed furniture, wallpaper, metal ware, glass ware and embroidery. Along with Charles Faulkner and Morris he founded the Society for the Protection of Ancient Buildings (SPAB) in 1877. He designed country houses only for clients who would appreciate his craft and allow him a free hand. He built for George Howard, later Earl of Carlisle, both in London and at Brampton near Carlisle. 'Standen' the house he built near East Grinstead in 1892 is now owned by the National Trust. He designed from first principles believing that an architect must have knowledge of the craft of building and must appreciate local traditions and materials.

See: **CU:** Brampton (3), Troutbeck **GM:** Wigan **MS:** L'pool WAG. **NS:** Cheddleton

Ref: Lethaby, W. R., *Philip Webb and his Work*, 1935, OUP; Jack, George, 'An appreciation of Philip Webb' *A. R.* 1915. Kirk, S., *Philip Webb*, 2005

Weingartner, Louis (*c.* 1864–*c.* 1936)
Sculptor. Born in Lucerne, Switzerland, he trained and worked in Florence in the jewellery trade for some twenty years before moving to England. By 1902 he was working in London with Joseph Hodel (qv) as an art metalworker. In 1904 he became the chief designer of sculpture and metalwork at the Bromsgrove Guild (qv) where he stayed until 1921 when he left the Guild to join Walter Gilbert (qv) at H. H. Martyn (qv) in Cheltenham. He retired to Switzerland in c. 1933 and died there after falling under a tram at the age of 72.

See: **MS:** L'pool Cath, Prescot **CH:** Crewe

Ref: Watt, The *Bromsgrove Guild*, 1999

Whall, Christopher (1849–1924)
Painter and stained-glass artist. The inspiration of the Arts and Crafts stained-glass school at the turn of the century. He was educated at Rossall School, Lancashire and entered the RA Schools in 1867 with a view to becoming a

painter. After completing his training he found work assisting other artists in their studios and exhibited some work himself. From 1876 he travelled in Europe for 4 years. On his return to England he worked as a freelance designer for large stained-glass firms including John Hardman & Co. and James Powell & Sons. This experience with commercialism led him to see the importance of being able to carry out the whole process, from design to finish, himself. He married Florence Chapman in 1884 and set up his own studio workshop in a converted cow shed next to his cottage at Stonebridge near Dorking. He taught himself all the techniques of the craft. As an early member of the AWG, which he joined in 1889, he had many contacts with architects and designers and became the trail-blazer for the art of stained glass, working closely with John Sedding (qv), Henry Wilson (qv), William Lethaby (qv) etc. From 1898 he taught at the Central School of Arts and Crafts and later at the RCA. Many subsequently famous artists were trained by him and have the stamp of the Christopher Whall School including Karl Parsons (qv), Edward Woore (qv), and Paul Woodroffe (qv). In 1898 he started on his major commission – some 150 lights in the Lady Chapel of Gloucester Cathedral. From 1899 he moved to 19 Shaftesbury Rd, Ravenscourt Park in West London where he set up a new studio but continued to use Lowndes and Drury for processes other than designing and cartooning. He shared his knowledge of the art through his book *Stained Glass Work* published in 1904 and he promoted his art through his active involvement in the Arts and Crafts Exhibition Society and by showing at major exhibitions. He was Master of the AWG in 1912. Illness caused his retirement from the business in 1922.

See: **CU:** Carlisle Cath, Killington
LA: Fleetwood, Swinton, Whalley
GM: Cheadle, Marple, Middleton
CH: Macclesfield, Tabley, Thelwall
NS: Denstone

Ref: Cormack, P., *Christopher Whall*, 1999

Whall and Whall see **Whall, Veronica**

Whall, Veronica (1887–1967)
Stained-glass artist. Born at Stonebridge near Dorking in Surrey, she was one of the five children of the leading stained-glass artist, Christopher Whall (qv). Veronica learned the art and craft of stained glass at her father's knee, in the studio and by attending his classes at the Central School of Arts and Crafts. By the age of thirteen she had designed the figure of St Catherine in the Lady Chapel at Gloucester Cathedral. She sat as a figure model for her father from time to time as well as doing work in the studio. The firm of Whall and Whall Ltd was created in 1922, with Veronica and her father as the sole directors, when he became ill. She carried on the management and work of the studio when her father died in 1924 making her last window in about 1953 before she retired to Huntingdon to rear goats.

See: **CU:** Aldingham, Keswick **LA:** Blackburn, Whalley **GM:** Cheadle, Middleton, Swinton

Ref: Cormack, P., *Women Stained-Glass Artists*, 1985

Whistler, Beatrice (1857–96)
Decorative artist. Born Beatrice Phillip, she was the daughter of a sculptor and presumably received her art education at home. At the age of eighteen in 1876 she married E. W. Godwin but continued to work as an artist. She assisted in the business by designing architectural terracotta, tiles, and wallpapers and by painting panels fitted in Godwin's furniture. From 1881 she began exhibiting at St Stephens Art Club under the name of Rix Birnie. When Godwin died in 1888 Beatrice married James McNeil Whistler.

See: **CU:** Great Orton

Ref: MacDonald, M. F., *Beatrice Whistler: Artist and Designer*, 1976

Willford, Thomas (1898–1963)
Stained-glass artist. Apprenticed to W. J. Pearce (qv) for whom he worked before setting up as Attwell and Willford in Grosvenor St, Manchester in the 1920s. The partnership was dissolved in the 1930s. Willford worked with Pointer until the end of WW2. He then set up his own workshop with his daughter at the Brabyns Studio in Marple. His work is not catalogued.

See: GM: Burnage, Levenshulme
MS: Bebington

Ref: Wilford family archive; *Cheshire Life*, Sept 1954, p. 37

Williams, Maurice Meredith (b. 1881)
Williams, Gertrude Alice (ob. 1934)
Born at Cowbridge in Glamorgan, Maurice Meredith Williams was a painter, designer and stained-glass artist. He studied at the Slade in London and in Paris and Italy. He married Gertrude Alice Williams who was a sculptor, decorative painter and a stained-glass artist. She was born in Liverpool and studied at the School of Architecture and Applied Art before spending time studying in Paris. The couple lived in Scotland from about 1905, and often worked in collaboration with Robert Lorimer (qv). They both exhibited at the RSA and the RA

See: **LA:** Fleetwood

Ref: Johnson and Greutzner, *Dictionary of British Artists 5*, 1999

Willink and Thicknesse
Architectural practice in Liverpool. William Edward Willink, son of a Liverpool vicar was educated at Liverpool College and King's

College Cambridge. He was articled to Alfred Waterhouse, set up practice in Liverpool in 1882 and was joined in 1884 by P. C. Thicknesse. Philip Coldwell Thicknesse was the son of the Bishop of Peterborough. He was educated at Marlborough and articled to Norman Shaw (qv) entering the RA Schools in 1880. In addition to their architectural work they designed the interiors of Booth Line and Cunard liners.

See: **MS:** L'pool C (3), Toxteth

Ref: Gray, A. S., *Edwardian Architecture*, 1985; Obit. Willink: *Builder* (28.3.1924), p. 503. Thicknesse: *RIBAJ* (6.3.1920), p. 211, *Builder* (5.3.1920), p. 283

Wilson, Henry (1864–1934)
Architect, designer, jeweller, decorator. Born in Liverpool, he later went to Kidderminster Art School and was articled to a Mr Squirhill in Maidenhead. He worked in the offices of J. Oldrid Scott, John Belcher and J. Beresford Pite before arriving in John Sedding's Office (qv) in 1888. This was an inspirational office charged with the enthusiasm of the change engendered by the Arts and Crafts Movement. With Sedding's untimely death in 1891, Wilson took over the office finishing off some of Sedding's most illustrious work including Holy Trinity, Sloane Square, London. Wilson went on to concentrate on church decoration and other decorative arts. He was one of the most gifted designers of his time in the field of metalwork, sculpture, stained glass and jewellery. Perhaps his best and most dramatic church work can be seen in St Bartholomew's in Brighton. From 1901 he taught metalwork at the RCA and at the Central School of Arts and Crafts. He also designed wallpaper for Jeffrey & Co. and fireplaces for Longden & Co. He was a member of the AWG and became its Master in 1917. He was an honorary member of the Northern Art Workers' Guild and President of the Arts and Crafts Exhibition Society 1915–22. He was the first editor of the Architectural Review.

See: **CU:** Barbon **LA:** Rawtenstall
GM: Brooklands, Marple, Swinton

Ref: Gray, A. S., *Edwardian Architecture*, 1985

Wilson, William Gilmour (*c.* 1856–1943)
Architect. Born in Rothesay, Strathclyde, he was a pupil of Robert Baldie of Glasgow for four years. He was an assistant first to Alexander Adamson and then to John Honeyman in Glasgow and William Owen (qv) in Warrington. He set up independent practice in 1880 and worked in Liverpool in 1894 and London in 1899. He was a partner of J. J. Talbot (qv) 1896–1902.

See: **MS:** Port Sunlight

Ref: RIBA, *Directory*, 2001

Wilson, H. Warren
Thought to be a pupil of Anning Bell *c.* 1920. He had his glass made up at Lowndes and Drury.

See: **CU:** Colton

Winstanley, Charles (fl. 1880)
Metalworker. Information is scant. Winstanley worked for the Century Guild *c.* 1882–90, during which time his address was The Forge, Bushill Park, Enfield. A. H. Mackmurdo described him in his autobiographical notes as 'one of the finest craftsmen in all manner of ironwork that England has ever had'. His name does not appear in the 1901 census.

See: **CH:** Wilmslow

Ref: *A. H. Mackmurdo archive* at William Morris Gallery, Walthamstow

Wood, Francis Derwent (1871–1926)
Born at Keswick, Cumberland, he studied at the Karlsruhe School of Art, Lausanne. He returned to England in 1889 and worked in London as a modeller for Maw and Co. and Coalbrookdale Iron Co. while attending the National Art Training School in South Kensington. He studied under Lanteri and won a National Scholarship. He then trained at the Slade School under Alphonse Legros and became his assistant and also assistant to Thomas Brock. He entered the RA Schools in 1894 aged twenty-three and won the Gold Medal and Travelling Studentship, which enabled him to go to Paris. He taught modelling at the Glasgow School of Art 1897–1901 and executed many pieces of architectural sculpture in the city, including the Mercantile Chambers in Bothwell St and Caledonian Chambers in Union St. He settled in London in 1901 and became a member of the AWG in the same year. He produced a wide range of work including many portrait busts, statues, memorials and architectural sculpture. In 1898 he assisted Thomas Brock with the Victoria Memorial in the Mall doing the emblems of Australia, the kangaroo and the ram. His best known work is the Machine-Gun memorial at Hyde Park Corner. He was Professor of Sculpture at the RCA 1918–23.

See: **MS:** L'pool C, Port Sunlight AG

Ref: Gray, A. S., *Edwardian Architecture*, 1985; Beattie, *The New Sculpture*, 1983

Wood, Edgar (1860–1935)
Architect, artist and furniture designer. Born in Middleton near Manchester the son of a cotton mill owner, he attended Queen Elizabeth's Grammar School, Middleton. He was articled to Mills & Murgatroyd in Manchester and set up his own practice in a disused cotton mill, owned by his father, in Suffield St, Middleton. His first work was in Middleton where he did Temple St Baptist Church. He moved his office

to Cross St, Manchester and entered into an informal partnership with J. Henry Sellers. Wood was an active founding member of the Northern Art Workers' Guild and was its Master in 1896. He was the leading Arts and Crafts architect in the North West designing schools, chapels and houses in a simple and individual style. Some of his work anticipates Art Deco. He was also a designer of furniture and jewellery. He retired from practice in 1922 and went to live in Italy.

See: **GM:** Bramhall, Chadderton, Fairfield, Hale, Heywood, M/cc Whitworth AG, Middleton (15), Oldham, Rochdale (4) +AG, Timperley, Victoria Park

Ref: Gray, A. S., *Edwardian Architecture*, 1985; Archer, J. H. G., *Edgar Wood, a Manchester 'Art Nouveau' Architect*, 1966; Archer, J. H. G., 'Edgar Wood and J Henry Sellers, A Decade of Partnership and Experiment', 1973

Woodroffe, Paul Vincent (1875–1954)
Stained-glass artist. Born at Madras in India he was educated in Lancashire at Stonyhurst College and at the Slade School of Art. He began his career as an illustrator and book designer.

He studied stained-glass work under Christopher Whall, working with him in his studio. In 1904 Woodroffe left London for Chipping Campden in the Cotswolds where he set up his studio and workshop producing stained glass for many churches in the UK and abroad. By 1938 he was living at Jayne's Court in the village of Bisley in Gloucestershire.

See: **CU:** Urswick **LA:** Stoneyhurst, Turton **GM:** M/cc **MS:** Aigburth, L'pool C, Formby, Prescot **CH:** Macclesfield

Ref: Waters, *Dictionary of British Artists*, 1975; Cormack, P., 'Paul Woodroffe' in *Originality and Design*, 2003

Woodhouse and Willoughby
Architects. John Henry Woodhouse (1847–1929) was born in Manchester and studied at the Manchester School of Art. He was articled to Philip Nunn in Manchester 1865 but transferred to Royle and Bennett. He remained there as assistant until he set up independent practice in 1872. George Harry Willoughby (b. 1859) was born in Stockport. He was articled to John Pierpont of Warrington 1875–79 and became an assistant to Royle and Bennett for two years. He set up in independent practice in 1883. The partnership Woodhouse and Willoughby was established in 1886.

See: **GM:** Bury AG, M/cc

Ref: Gray, A. S., *Edwardian Architecture*, 1985; RIBA, *Directory*, 2001

Woolfall & Eccles (1890–1919)
Architects practicing in Liverpool. John Woolfall (1838–1919) was born at Huyton and articled to E. Davis of Liverpool. He later became assistant to G. E. Grayson (qv) and in 1890 he set up in partnership with Eccles in Bank Buildings, 65 Castle St, Liverpool. Thomas Edgar Eccles (1865–1946) was educated at Uppingham School and articled to Grayson & Ould (qv) 1884–89. He was brother-in-law to Guy Dawber. The partnership designed schools, banks, churches and country houses mainly in the north and west of England.

See:. **MS:** Bidston, Hoylake

Ref: *Pike* 1911; RIBA, *Directory*, 2001; Woolfall Obit. *RIBAJ*, 26 (Mar. 1919), p. 118; Eccles Obit. *Builder*, 171 (26.7.1946), p. 98

Wooliscroft Pottery (fl 1850–1999)
Potters. The Wooliscroft Pottery was established in Stoke around 1850 making tiles. Its products extended over the years with three factories making a huge range of ceramic and brick floor and wall coverings. The business was taken over by Pilkington and production moved to Dorset. The factory closed around 1999.

See: **NS:** Leek

Ref: Godden, G., *British Pottery and Porcelain*, 1964

Woolner, Thomas (1825–92)
Sculptor and founder member of the Pre-Raphaelite Brotherhood. Born in Hadleigh Suffolk and educated locally and then in London where his family moved. His talent for art was such that aged 13 he went to study with Charles (a painter) and William Behnes (a sculptor), where he stayed for six years. In 1842 he entered the RA Schools and first exhibited at the RA in 1843. In his early years he was an exponent of 'Ideal' works – works based on history, mythology, poetry etc. He shared a studio in Stanhope St with Bernhard Smith and next door to John Hancock. In 1847 he met Rossetti (qv), Hunt and F. G. Stephens by which time he had come to share their belief in the need to turn to Nature to 'purify art'. He became the only sculptor member of the Pre-Raphaelite Brotherhood in 1848. Much of his work at this time was portrait medallions and he produced a series depicting contemporary poets. He also wrote poetry and published a volume of poems in 1863. In an attempt to raise funds he had a short but unsuccessful excursion to the gold fields of Southern Australia 1852–54. On his return his career as a portrait and monumental sculptor took off when in the mid 1850s he gained some influential patrons and some prestigious commissions such as the figures on the Oxford Museum, 1857 and Llandaff Cathedral, 1858. He was elected an ARA in 1871 and was Professor of Art at the RA 1877–79.

See: **GM:** M/cc **MS:** Walton

Ref: Read & Barnes, Pre-*Raphaelite Sculpture*, 1991

Woore, Edward (1880–1960)
Stained-glass artist. Born in Derby. He won a scholarship to the Central School of Arts and Crafts where he studied stained glass under Christopher Whall. Subsequently Whall offered him a position in his workshop where he later became manager. He served in the 1914–18 war during which he lost the sight in one eye. After the war he set up his own studio and workshop first in Peter's Square, Hammersmith and then in Deodar Rd, Putney. His early work is in the Christopher Whall style but has its own very recognisable character. He received commissions from all over the country and from New Zealand and South Africa. He was also a skilful painter in tempera and watercolour. During WW2 he moved to Bristol to work with his friend Arnold Robinson who made stained-glass windows as Joseph Bell & Son. He returned to work in his own studio in Putney in 1945 until he retired from active work in 1958 and moved to Wales where he died on 24 June 1960.

See: **LA:** Great Mitton, Whalley **GM:** Atherton (2) **MS:** Prescot, Wallasey

Ref: Obit. *JBSMGP*, 13, no. 2 (1960–61)

Worthington, Sir Percy Scott (1864–1939)
Architect. Educated at Clifton College and Corpus Christi College, Oxford and articled to his father Thomas Worthington. He studied at Manchester School of Art and University College, London. He was assistant to J. MacVicar Anderson in London before joining his father's practice as a partner in 1891. As well as having a large domestic practice the firm specialised in hospitals and also built churches and some buildings at Manchester University.

See: **CU:** Ambleside, Oxenholme
GM: Littleborough **MS:** Sefton Park
CH: Alderley Edge (4), Chelford, Cranage, Knutsford (2) **NS:** Leek

Ref: Gray, A. S., *Edwardian Architecture*, 1985; Obit. *RIBAJ* (14.8.1939), pp. 950–52, 983; *Builder*, (21.3.1939), p. 100

Wragge, George (b. 1863)
Metalworker, stained-glass window maker. Born in Bramshall near Uttoxeter in Staffordshire. In the 1890s he established a metalworking firm at the Wardry Works, Chapel St in Salford making iron gates and casement windows. The business expanded to include stained glass, leaded lights, mosaic and gesso work, furniture, electrical fittings, door furniture and metal plaques. He opened a second workshop in Chapel St called 'The Crafts' and had offices in London and Glasgow as well as agencies abroad. The firm's bread and butter work was metal casement windows and door furniture but it was also noted for its production of designer Arts and Crafts fittings. Much of his success was due to the talented artists he commissioned to do his design work. These included J. E. C. Carr (qv) from 1898, E. A. Taylor 1906–10 and Harry Fenton (qv) whose dates are not known. Wragge was a friend of the architect Edgar Wood (qv) who illustrated his catalogue. Wragge, in turn, made some of Wood's stained-glass windows and much of his furniture. The work the firm produced was regularly illustrated in *The Studio*. The firm continued well into the C20 though Wragge, who had been a founder member of the Northern AWG, retired from the business in *c.* 1908.

See: **LA:** Blackpool, Padiham, Worsthorne
GM: Ashton under Lyne, Clifton, Didsbury, M/cc (3), Timperley, Victoria Park (2)
MS: Bebington, L'pool C + TH **CH:** Knutsford, Runcorn

Ref: *1901 Census*; *The Studio*, 14 (1898); White, C., *The Enchanted World of Jessie King*, 1989

BIBLIOGRAPHY

UNPUBLISHED SOURCES

Evans, Stuart, 'Arthur Heygate Mackmurdo and the Century Guild', PhD dissertation, Manchester University (1976)

Hadley, Joan, 'Henry Holiday: Windows and Reredoses made by James Powell & Sons 1863–1914, National Art Library (Great Britain) Archive of Art and Design (2001)

——, 'Henry Holiday: Windows, Wall Paintings, Reredoses and Panels Made by Holiday's Workshop 1888–1905 and Lowndes & Drury at the Glasshouse 1906–1935', National Art Library, Archive of Art and Design (2001)

Holland, Jocelyne, 'Margaret Vane: A Chatelaine's Legacy', Dissertation, Leeds University, (1999)

Jezzard, Andrew, 'The Sculpture of George Frampton', Thesis, University of Leeds, Fine Art Dept (Leeds, 1999)

Liverpool University Department of Architecture and Applied Art (Art Sheds) Registers 1901–04 and the City School of Art Admission Registers 1905 in the Aldham Robarts Resource Centre archive, John Moore's University, Liverpool

Manchester Municipal School of Art Calendars and Minutes 1894–1930 in the Sir Kenneth Green Library archives, Manchester Metropolitan University

Martyn, H. H. archive at Gloucester Museum

Morris, Colin, 'History of Liverpool Regional College of Art 1825–1970', MPhil, Liverpool Polytechnic (1985)

Public Monuments and Sculpture Association, National Record Project Database (web site: PMSA.courtald.ac.uk)

Smith, Leslie, 'Charles J. Ferguson: a North Country Ecclesiastical Architect', PRO Kendal, ref. WDX1041

Woodroffe, Paul, archive at Cheltenham Museum

BOOKS

(* indicates those books which the authors recommend as providing a grounding in the Arts and Crafts Movement)

Adams, Maurice (ed.), *Modern Cottage Architecture* (London, Batsford, 1904)

Addleshaw, George, Dean of Chester, *Chester Cathedral: The Stained Glass, Mosaics, Monuments and Some of its Other Treasures*, 2nd edn (Gloucester, British Publishing Co., 1967)

Anscombe, Isabelle, *Arts and Crafts Style* (London, Phaidon, 1991)

Archer, John H. G., 'Edgar Wood and J. Henry Sellers: A Decade of Partnership and Experiment' in *Victorian Architecture*, ed by P. Ferriday (London, Jonathan Cape, 1973)

Architectural Association, *Great British Architects* (London, Architectural Association, 1981). Includes A. W. N. Pugin and C. F. A. Voysey

Armitage, E. Liddall, *Stained Glass: History, Technology and Practice* (London, L. Hill, 1960)

Arthur, Elizabeth, 'Ann Macbeth 1875–1948' in *Glasgow Girls: Women in Art and Design 1880–1920*, ed by J. Burkhauser (Edinburgh, Canongate, 1990)

Art Workers Guild, *Hugh Arnold: An Account of the Special Meeting Held March 31 1916* (London, Art Workers' Guild, 1916)

Arvas, Victor, *Tiffany* (London, London Academy, 1979)

Aslet, Clive, *The Last Country Houses* (New Haven and London, Yale U. P., 1982)

Atterbury, Paul, *Moorcroft: A Guide to Moorcroft Pottery, 1897–1990* (Shepton Beauchamp, Dennis & Edwards, 1990)

—— and Maureen Batkin, *The Dictionary of Minton* (Woodbridge, Antique Collectors' Club, 1990)

—— and Paul Henson, *Ruskin Pottery: The Pottery of Edward Richard Taylor and William Howson Taylor 1898–1933* (Baxendale Press, 1993)

—— and Clive Wainwright (eds), *Pugin: A Gothic Passion* (New Haven and London, Yale U. P. in association with the V&A, 1994)

Barnes, Joanna et al., *Ellen Mary Rope: The Poet Sculptor* (London, Joanne Barnes Fine Arts and H. Blairman & Sons, 1997)

Batchelor, John, *No Wealth but Life* (London, Pimlico, 2001)

Bayne, Simone, *Heaton, Butler & Bayne: A Hundred Years of Stained Glass* (Montreux, S. B. N. Bayne, 1986)

Beattie, Susan, *The New Sculpture* (New Haven and London, Yale U. P., 1983)

Benjamin, Frederick A., *The Ruskin Linen Industry of Keswick* (Beckermet, Michael Moon, 1974)

Bennett, Mary, *Artists of the Pre-Raphaelite Circle: The First Generation*, the works of the Galleries on Merseyside (London, Lund Humphries for National Museums and Galleries on Merseyside, 1988)

Birmingham City Museum and Art Gallery, *Omar Ramsden* (Birmingham, Kings Norton Press, 1973)

Bisson, R. F., *The Sandon Studios Society and the Arts* (Liverpool, Parry Books for the Sandon Studios Society, 1965)

Blagden-Gamlen, Peter E., *Martin Travers, 1886–1948: A Handlist of his Work* (London, The Ecclesiological Society, 1977)

Bowe, Nicola Gordon, *The Life and Work of Harry Clarke* (Dublin, Irish Academic Press, 1989)

——, David Caron and Michael Wynne, *Gazetteer of Irish Stained Glass* (Dublin, Irish Academic Press, 1988)

Bradford Art Galleries and Museums, *Burmantofts Pottery* (Bradford, Bradford Museums and Art Gallery, 1983)

Brandwood, Geoffrey, *Temple Moore: An Architect of the Late Gothic Revival* (Stamford, Paul Watkins, 1997)

Brown, Jane, *Gardens of a Golden Afternoon – The Story of a Partnership: Edwin Lutyens and Gertrude Jekyll* (Harmondsworth, Penguin, 1982)

——, *Lutyens and the Edwardians: An English Architect and his Clients* (London, Viking, 1996)

Bruce, Ian, *The Loving Eye and Skilful Hand* (Carlisle, Bookcase, 2001)

Brunton, Jennie, *The Arts and Crafts Movement in the Lake District* (Lancaster, Centre for North West Regional Studies, University of Lancaster, 2001)

Campbell, Kenneth, *Campbell, Smith & Company: The History of the Company and an Introduction to their Work* (London, Campbell, Smith & Co. Ltd, 1989)

*Carruthers, Annette, and Mary Greensted (eds), *Good Citizen's Furniture* (London, Lund Humphries with Cheltenham Art Gallery and Museums, 1994)

*——, —— (eds), *Simplicity or Splendour* (London, Lund Humphries with Cheltenham Art Gallery and Museums, 1999)

Cavanagh, Terry, *Public Sculpture of Liverpool* (Liverpool, Liverpool U. P., 1997)

Cave, Roderick, *The Private Presses* (New York and London, R. R. Bowker Co., 1983)

Chapman, Hilary, *The Colour Woodcuts of John Edgar Platt* (London, 20th Century Gallery, 1999)

Clay, Andrew et al., *British Sculpture in the Lady Lever Art Gallery* (National Museums and Galleries of Merseyside, 1999)

Clough, Matthew (ed.), *C. J. Allen, 1862–1956: Sculptor and Teacher* (Liverpool, University of Liverpool Art Collection, 2003)

Coatts, Margot and Elizabeth Lewis (eds), *Heywood Sumner: Artist and Archaeologist 1853–1940* (Winchester, Winchester City Museum, 1986)

Collins, Judith, *Eric Gill: The Sculpture, A Catalogue Raisonné* (London, Herbert Press, 1998)

Compton, Ann, *The Sculpture of Charles Sargeant Jagger* (Much Hadham, Henry Moore Foundation with Lund Humphries, 2004)

—— (ed.), *Edward Carter Preston 1885–1965: Sculptor, Painter, Medallist* (Liverpool, University of Liverpool Art Collections, 1999)

Cormack, Peter, 'Paul Woodroffe stained glass artist' in *Originality and Initiative: The Arts and Crafts Archives at Cheltenham*, ed by Mary Greenstead and Sophia Wilson (Cheltenham and Aldershot, Cheltenham Art Gallery and Museum in association with Lund Humphries, 2003)

——, *The Stained Glass Work of Christopher Whall 1849–1924* (Boston, Trustees of the Public Library of the City of Boston, 1999)

Cottle, Simon, *Sowerby Gateshead Glass* (Tyne and Wear Museums Service, 1986)

Crane, Walter, *An Artist's Reminiscences*, 2nd edn (London, Methuen, 1907)

Crawford, Alan, *C. R. Ashbee: Architect, Designer and Romantic Socialist* (Newhaven and London, Yale U. P., 1985)

*—— (ed.), *By Hammer and Hand: The Arts and Crafts Movement in Birmingham* (Birmingham, Birmingham Museums and Art Gallery, 1984)

Cross, A. J., *Pilkington's Royal Lancastrian Pottery and Tiles* (London, Richard Dennis, 1980)

Culme, John, *Directory of Gold and Silversmiths, Jewellers and Allied Trades 1838–1914 from London Assay Office Registers* (Antique Collectors Club, 1987)

*Cumming, Elizabeth, and Wendy Kaplan, *The Arts and Crafts Movement* (London, Thames and Hudson, 1991)

Cunningham, Colin, and Prudence Waterhouse, *Alfred Waterhouse 1830–1905: Biography of a Practice* (Oxford, Clarendon Press, 1992)

*Davey, Peter, *Arts and Crafts Architecture* (London, Phaidon, 1995)

Davidson, Eleanor, *The Simpsons of Kendal: Craftsmen in Wood 1885–1952* (Lancaster, University of Lancaster Visual Arts Centre, 1978)

Dictionary of National Biography (Oxford, OUP, 1993)

Dixon, R., and S. Muthesius, *Victorian Architecture* (London, Thames & Hudson, 1995)

Dolman, Bernard (ed.), *A Dictionary of Contemporary Artists, 1929* (Woodbridge Antique Collectors Club, 1981)

Donnelly, Michael, *Glasgow Stained Glass: A Preliminary Study* (Glasgow, Glasgow Museums and Art Galleries, 1981)

Dorment, Richard, *Alfred Gilbert: Sculptor and Goldsmith* (London, Royal Academy of Arts with Weidenfeld & Nicholson, 1986)

Drury, Michael, *Wandering Architects: In Pursuit of the Arts and Crafts Ideal* (Stamford, Shaun Tyas, 2000)

Edwards, Margaret, *The Studios of Lancaster's Artists in Stained Glass* (Lancaster, Lancaster City Museums, 1974)

Eyles, Desmond, and Louis Irvine, *The Doulton Lambeth Wares* (Shepton Beauchamp, Richard Dennis, 2002)

Fawcett, Jane (ed.), *Seven Victorian Architects* (London, Thames & Hudson, 1976)

Ferriday, Peter (ed.), *Victorian Architecture* (London, Jonathan Cape, 1963)

Fine Art Society, *Peter Pan and Eros, Sir George Frampton & Sir Alfred Gilbert: Public and Private Sculpture in Britain, 1880–1940* (London, Fine Arts Society, 2002)

——, *British Sculpture 1850–1914* (London, Fine Arts Society, 1968)

Fisher, A., *The Art of Enamelling upon Metal* (London, The Studio, 1906)

Fitzgerald, Penelope, *Edward Burne Jones* (Stroud, Sutton, 2003)

Fletcher, Ian, *Rediscovering Herbert Horne* (Greensboro, N. Carolina, ELT Press, 1990)

Ford, Ford Madox, *Ford Madox Brown: A Record of his Life and Work* (New York, AMS Press, 1972)

Freeman, Jennifer M., *W. D. Caröe: His Architectural Achievement* (Manchester, Manchester U. P., 1990)

Gallery Lingard, *Horatio Walter Lonsdale, 1844–1919: Architectural Artist* (London, Gallery Lingard, 1984)

Garlick, A., *Burmantofts Pottery*, illustrated by T. Raffles Davison (Leeds, Museum of Leeds, 1991)

Gaze, Delia (ed.), *Concise Dictionary of Women Artists* (London, Fitzroy Dearborn, 2001)

Girouard, Mark, *The Victorian Country House*, 4th edn (New Haven and London, Yale U. P., 1990)

Gould, Veronica Franklin, *G. F. Watts: The Last Great Victorian* (New Haven and London, Yale U. P., 2004)

Graves, Arthur A., *Royal Academy of Arts: A Complete Dictionary of Contributors and their Work from its Foundation in 1769 to 1904*, 8 vols (London, Henry Grave & Co., 1905–06)

Gray, A. Stuart, *Edwardian Architecture: a Biographical Dictionary* (Ware, Wordsworth Editions, 1985)

Greenwood, Martin, *The Designs of William De Morgan* (Shepton Beauchamp, Dennis & Wiltshire, 1989)

Haigh, Diane, *Baillie Scott: the Artistic House* (London, Academy Editions, 1995)

Halen, Widar, *Christopher Dresser: A Pioneer of Modern Design* (London, Phaidon, 1990)

Hall, Marshall, *Artists of Northumbria*, Artists of the Region Series, 2nd edn (Newcastle, Marshall Hall Associates, 1982)

Harrison, Martin, *Victorian Stained Glass* (London, Barrie and Jenkins, 1980)

Hartwell, Clare, *Pevsner Architectural Guides: Manchester* (London, Penguin, 2001)

Haslam, Malcolm, *The Martin Brothers: Potters* (London, Richard Dennis, 1978)

——, *English Art Pottery 1865–1915* (Woodbridge, Antique Collectors Club, 1975)

Haslam, Sara E., *John Ruskin and the Lakelands Arts Revival, 1880–1920* (Whitchurch, Merton, 2004)

Hilton, Tim, *John Ruskin* (New Haven and London, Yale U. P., 2002)

Hitchmough, Wendy, *C. F. A. Voysey* (London, Phaidon Press, 1995)

Holiday, Henry, *Reminiscences of my Life* (London, Heinemann, 1914)

Hubbard, E., *The Work of John Douglas* (London, The Victorian Society, 1991)

——, and M. Shippobottom, *A Guide to Port Sunlight Village* (Liverpool, Liverpool U. P., 1988)

Hussey, Christopher, *The Life of Sir Edwin Lutyens* (Woodbridge, Antique Collectors Club, 1984)

Irvine, Louise, and Paul Atterbury, *Gilbert Bayes Sculptor 1872–1953* (Shepton Beauchamp, Richard Dennis, 1998)

Jack, George, 'An Appreciation of Philip Webb' in *Edwardian Architecture and its Origins*, ed by Alistair Service (London, Architectural Press, 1975)

Jacques, Anne G., *Leek Embroidery* (Staffordshire Libraries and Archives, 1990)

——, *The Wardle Story: A Victorian Enterprise* (Leek, Churnet Valley Books, 1996)

Johnson and Greutzner, *Dictionary of British Art*, Vol. 5, *British Artists 1880–1940* (Woodbridge, Antique Collectors Club, 1999)

Jolley, Robert, *Edmund Sharpe 1809–1877: A Lancaster Architect* (Lancaster, Visual Arts Centre, University of Lancaster, 1977)

Jones, Joan, *Minton: The First 200 Years of Design and Production* (Shrewsbury, Swan Hill Press, 1993)

Karlin, E. Z., *Jewelry and Metalwork in the Arts and Crafts Tradition* (USA, Schiffer, 1993)

Keyte, Owen, *The Annals of a Century: Bridgeman's of Lichfield, 1878–1998* (S.I.1993)

Kidson, J. Herbert, *Records of St Margaret's Church, Prestwich* (1927)

Kirk, Sheila, *Philip Webb: Pioneer of Arts and Crafts Architecture* (Chichester, Wiley-Academy, 2005)

Kornwulf, James D., *M. H. Baillie Scott and the Arts and Crafts Movement: Pioneers of Modern Design* (Baltimore and London, John Hopkin's Press, 1972)

Kuzmanovic, Natasha N., *John Paul Cooper: Designer and Craftsman of the Arts and Crafts Movement* (Stroud, Sutton, 1999)

Lambourne, Lionel, *The Aesthetic Movement* (London, Phaidon Press, 1996)

Lethaby, W. R., *Philip Webb and his Work* (Oxford, OUP, 1935)

Lomax, Abraham, *Royal Lancastrian Pottery* (Bolton, Lomax, 1957)

Lovenbury, G. A., *The Sugdens of Leek: A Brief History of a Family Business* (Leek, Leek Post and Times, Newspaper House, 1975)

*MacCarthy, Fiona, *William Morris, A Life for Our Time* (London, Faber & Faber, 1994)

MacDonald, Margaret F., *Beatrice Whistler: Artist and Designer* (Glasgow, Hunterian Art Gallery, 1997)

Manning, Elfrida, *Marble and Bronze: The Art and Life of Hamo Thorneycroft* (London, Trefoil, 1982)

Marsh, Jan, *Pre-Raphaelite Women* (London, Phoenix, 1998)

Mawson, Thomas Hayton, *The Life and Work of an English Landscape Architect: An Autobiography* (London, Batsford, 1927)

——, *The Art and Craft of Garden-Making*, 5th edn (London, Batsford, 1926)

Mills, Ernestine (ed.), *The Life and Letters of Frederic J. Shields* (London, Longmans, Green & Co., 1912)

Moore, Jerrold Northrop, *F. L. Griggs, 1876–1938: the Architecture of Dreams* (Oxford, Clarendon Press, 1999)

Moriarty, Catherine, *The Sculpture of Gilbert Ledward 1888–1960* (Much Hadham, Henry Moore Foundation with Lund Humphries, 2003)

Moss, Rachel, *Edward Payne 1906–1991* (London, Moss & Glass, 1995)

National Association of Decorative and Fine Arts Societies, *Church Records* (London, NADFAS , 1973–)

*Naylor, Gillian, *The Arts and Crafts Movement* (London, Studio Vista, 1971)

Newman, Teresa, *Ford Madox Brown and the Pre-Raphaelite Circle* (London, Chatto & Windus, 1991)

Newton, W. G., *The Work of Ernest Newton R. A.* (London, Architectural Press, 1925)

*Parry, Linda, *Textiles of the Arts and Crafts Movement* (London, Thames & Hudson, 1988)

——, *William Morris Textiles* (New Jersey, Crescent Books, 1994)

Paul, Tessa, *The Art of Louis Comfort Tiffany* (Baldock, Herts, The Apple Press, 1987)

Pearson, Fiona, *Goscombe John at the National Museum of Wales* (Cardiff, National Museum of Wales, 1979)

Pevsner, Nikolaus, *Buildings of England and Wales* (London, Penguin): *Cheshire* (1971), *Cumberland and Westmorland* (1967), *North Lancashire* (1969), *South Lancashire* (1969), *Staffordshire* (1974)

Powers, Alan, *Oliver Hill: Architect and Lover of Life 1887–1968* (London, Methuen, 1989)

Price, James, *Sharpe, Paley and Austin: A Lancaster Architectural Practice, 1836–1942* (Lancaster, Centre for North West Regional Studies, University of Lancaster, 1998)

Proctor, Helen, *The Holy Grail Tapestries Designed by Edward Burne-Jones, William Morris and J. H. Dearle for Morris & Co.* (Birmingham, Birmingham Museum and Art Gallery, 1997)

Ransom, Will, *Private Presses and Their Books* (NewYork and London, R. R. Bowker Co., 1929)

Rawnsley, Eleanor, *Canon Rawnsley, An Account of his Life* (Glasgow, Maclehose, Jackson & Co., 1923)

Read, Benedict and Joanna Barnes (eds), *Pre-Raphaelite Sculpture: Nature and Imagination in Sculpture 1848–1914* (London, Henry Moore Foundation in association with Lund Humphries, 1991)

RIBA, *Directory of British Architects 1824–1914* (London and New York, Continuum, 2001)

Richards, J. M. (ed.), *Who's Who in Architecture 1400 to the Present Day* (London, Weidenfeld & Nicholson, 1977)

*Richardson, Margaret, *Architects of the Arts and Crafts Movement* (London, Trefoil, 1983)

Richmond, Peter, *Marketing Modernisms: The Architecture and Influence of Charles Reilly* (Liverpool, Liverpool U. P., 2001)

Ridley, Jane, *Edwin Lutyens: His Life, his Wife, his Work* (London, Pimlico, 2003)

Robinson, Joy, *Relatively Rathbone* (Richmond, Trotman, 1992)

Royal Academy of Arts, *Pre-Raphaelite and Other Masters: The Andrew Lloyd Webber Collection* (London, Royal Academy of Arts, 2004)

——, *Royal Academy Exhibitions 1905–70*, 6 vols (Wakefield, E. P. Publishing, 1973–83)

Ruston, James H., *Ruskin Pottery* (West Bromwich, Metropolitan Borough of Sandwell, 1975)

Saint, Andrew, *Richard Norman Shaw* (London and New Haven, Yale U. P., 1976)

Savage, Peter, *Lorimer and the Edinburgh Craft Designers* (Edinburgh, Paul Harris Publishing, 1980)

Schoeser, Mary, *The Watts Book of Embroidery: English Church Embroidery 1833–1953* (London, Watts & Co. Ltd, 1998)

Sellars, Jane, *Women's Works* (Liverpool, National Museums and Galleries of Merseyside, 1988)

Service, Alastair, *Edwardian Architecture* (London, Thames & Hudson, 1977)

Sewter, A. C., *The Stained Glass of William Morris and his Circle* (Newhaven and London, Yale U. P., 1975)

Sharples, Joseph, *Pevsner Architectural Guides: Liverpool* (Newhaven and London, Yale U. P., 2004)

Shrigley, Ruth (ed.), *Inspired by Design: The Arts and Crafts Collection of the Manchester Metropolitan University*, introductory essay by John Davies (Manchester, Manchester City Art Galleries, 1994)

Smart Jnr, C. M., *Muscular Churches: Ecclesiastical Architecture of the High Victorian Period* (Fayetteville and London, Arkansas U. P., 1989)

Smith, Greg and Sarah Hyde (eds), *Walter Crane 1845–1915: Artist, Designer and Socialist* (London, Lund Humphries in association with Whitworth Art Gallery, Manchester University, 1989)

Smith, Leslie, *The Stained Glass in the Churches of the Anglican Diocese of Carlisle* (Kendal, Cumberland and Westmorland Antiquarian and Archaeological Society, 1994)

Soros, Susan Weber (ed.), *E. W. Godwin: Aesthetic Movement Architect and Designer* (New Haven and London, Yale U. P., 1999)

Spalding, Frances, *Dictionary of British Art*, Vol. 6, *20th Century Painters and Sculptors* (Woodbridge, Antique Collectors Club, 1990)

Speel, Erika, *Dictionary of Enamelling* (Aldershot, Ashgate Publishing, 1998)

Spencer, Christopher and Geoffrey Wilson, *Elbow Room: The Story of John Sydney Brocklesby, Arts and Crafts Architect* (Redhill, Ainsworth & Nelson, 1984)

Stansky, Peter, *Redesigning the World: William Morris, the 1880s and the Arts and Crafts* (Palo Alto California, Society for the Promotion of Science and Scholarship, 1996)

Stuart, Dennis, *Dear Duchess* (London, Victor Gollanz Ltd, 1982)

Surtees, Virginia, *The Artist and the Autocrat: George and Rosalind Howard, Earl and Countess of Carlisle* (Salisbury, Michael Russell, 1988)

Thompson, James, The Mouseman of Kilburn: The Story of Robert Thompson and the Church Mouse (Clapham, Lancaster, Dalesman, 1988)

—— (ed.), *The Diary of Ford Madox Brown* (Newhaven and London, Yale U. P., 1981)

Tickner, Lisa, *Dante Gabriel Rossetti*, British Artist Series (London, Tate Publishing, 2003)

Tilbrook, Adrian (ed.), *Truth, Beauty and Design: Victorian, Edwardian and Later Decorative Art* (London, Tilbrook and Fischer Fine Art Ltd, 1986)

Tracy and Pike, *Manchester and Salford at the Close of the 19th Century*, no. 2

Trade Directories: Bulmer's, Kelly's, Gore's, Slater's

Treheurtz, Julian, *Partnership in Style: Edgar Wood and J. Henry Sellers* (Manchester, Manchester City Art Gallery, 1975)

——, Elizabeth Prettejohn and Edwin Becker, *Dante Gabriel Rossetti* (Zwolle, Waanders for Van Gogh Museum Amsterdam and The Walker, Liverpool, 2003)

Victoria & Albert Museum, *Victorian Church Art* (London, HMSO, 1971)

Walker Art Gallery, *The Art Sheds, 1894–1905* (Liverpool, Merseyside County Council, 1981)

Walters, William, *The Stained Glass from Shrigley & Hunt of Lancaster and London* (Lancaster, Centre for North West Regional Studies, University of Lancaster, 2003)

Ward-Jackson, Philip, *Public Sculpture of the City of London* (Liverpool, Liverpool U. P., 2003)

Waters, Grant, *Dictionary of British Artists Working 1900–1950* (Eastbourne, Fine Art Trade Press, 1975)

Watkin, D., *The Architecture of Basil Champneys* (Cambridge, Newnham College, 1989)

Watt, Quintin (ed.), *The Bromsgrove Guild: An Illustrated History* (Bromsgrove, Bromsgrove Society, 1999)

Whall and Whall Ltd, *List of Windows*, (London, 1929)

White, Colin, *The Enchanted World of Jessie M. King* (Edinburgh, Canongate, 1989)

Whitworth Art Gallery, *Margaret Pilkington*, Leaflet (Friends of Whitworth, 1999)

Wildman, Stephen and John Christian, *Edward Burne-Jones: Victorian Art-Dreamer* (New York, Metropolitan Museum of Art, 1998)

Wilgress, Jane, *Alec Miller: Guildsman and Sculptor in Chipping Campden* (Chipping Campden, Campden and District Archaeological and Historical Society, 1987)

William Morris Gallery, *Henry Holiday 1839–1927* (London, Borough of Waltham Forest, 1989)

——, *Karl Parsons 1884–1934* (London, Borough of Waltham Forest, 1987)

——, *Women Stained Glass Artists of the Arts and Crafts Movement* (London, Borough of Waltham Forest, 1985)

Williams, Canon G. A., *Rachel Kay-Shuttleworth 1886–1967* (Kendal, Wilson, 1968)

Williamson Art Gallery and Museum, *Della Robbia Pottery 1891–1906* (Birkenhead, Metropolitan Borough of Wirral, 1980)

Wilson, Henry, et al., *A Memorial of the Late John Sedding* (London, B. T. Batsford, 1892)

Wilton, Andrew and Robert Upstone (eds), *The Age of Rossetti, Burne-Jones and Watts: Symbolism in Britain, 1860–1910* (London, Tate Gallery Publishing, 1997)

Wyke, Terry with Harry Cocks, *Public Sculpture of Greater Manchester* (Liverpool, Liverpool U. P., 2004)

Wynne, Michael, *Irish Stained Glass* (Dublin, Eason, 1977)

Yorke, Malcolm, *Eric Gill: Man of Flesh and Spirit* (London, Constable, 1981)

PERIODICALS

Allwood, Rosamond,'George Faulkner Armitage', *Furniture History*, 23 (1987)

Archer, John H. G., *Edgar Wood (1860–1938): A Manchester 'Art Nouveau' Architect* (Transactions of the Lancashire and Cheshire Antiquarian Society, 1963–64), pp. 153–87

Baldry A. L., 'Henry Holiday', *Walker's Quarterly*, 31–32 (1930)

Burman, Peter, 'A Stern Thinker and Most Able Constructor: Philip Webb', *Architectural History*, 42 (1999), pp. 1–23

Chapman S. T., 'Arts, Crafts and Heritage in Victorian Lakeland', *Armitt Library Journal*, 1 (1998), pp. 38–63

Collingwood, Gillian, 'George Faulkner Armitage – Cumbrian Connections,' *Quarto Magazine* (Kendal, Abbot Hall, April 1996)

Drysdale, George, 'The Work of Leonard Stokes', *RIBAJ* (8.1.1927)

Hardy, Emma, 'Farmer and Brindley', *Victorian Society Annual* (1993), pp. 4–17

Ellison, Norman F., Obit. 'Gustave Hiller', *North Western Naturalist*, 21 (Sept–Dec 1946), pp. 258–60

Hughes, Quentin, 'Before the Bauhaus. The Liverpool Experiment at the Liverpool School of Architecture and Applied Arts', *Architectural History*, 25 (1982), pp. 102–13

Jones, S., 'Champneys, an Under-rated Victorian' *Victorian*, 12 (Mar 2003), pp. 12–15

Slowe, Vicki, 'Alice Mary Gordon', *Quarto Magazine* (Kendal, Abbot Hall, Jan 1970)

Country Life

Garland, Madge, 'Fair Face in Many Guises: The Mosaic Hall at Peacock House, Holland Park' (29.3.1984), p. 830

'The Lesser Country Houses of To-day: Birket Houses, Winster, Lancashire, Designed by the Late Dan Gibson', Supplement (13.4.12), pp. 7–8,11

Newman, Carol, 'Gardens for Cocktail Time' (14.11.1996), pp. 50–53

Cheshire Life

Ellington, Robert, 'Restoration Piece', includes Sam Frodsham, 40, No. 5 (1974), p. 74

'Experts in their Field: James Smithies, Wilmslow' (June 1980), p. 70

'Thomas Wilford' (Sept 1954), p. 37

Journal of the British Society of Master Glass Painters (listed by artist)

Aikman,W., *Obit*, 13, no. 1 (1959–60), p. 364–65

Almquist, Carl, 'Carl Almquist His Life and Work' by B. R. Lövgren, 21, no. 10 (1997), pp. 11–40.

Bell, Robert Anning, *Obit*, 5, no. 33 (1934), p. 153

Camm, Florence, *Obit*, 13, no. 2 (1960–61), p. 445

Davies, A. J., *Obit*, 11, no. 3 (1953–54), p. 180

Day, Lewis, 'Lewis Foreman Day, Designer and Writer on Stained Glass, by D. M. Ross, 3, no. 1 (1929–30), p. 5 *et seq*.

Eden, F. C., 'Frederick Charles Eden' by W. I. Croome, 13, no. 4 (1962–63), pp. 554–57

Frampton, Edward, 'Edward Frampton, Master Glass Painter 1850–1929' by Alfred L. Wilkinson, 11, no. 2 (1952–53), p. 70

Geddes, Wilhelmina, 1887–1955, Her Life and Work, a Reappraisal by Nicola Gordon Bowe, 18, no. 3 (1988), pp. 275–96

Geddes, Wilhelmina, Obit.,12, no. 1 (1955–56), p. 69

Holiday, Henry, Obit., 2, no. 2 (1927), p. 105

Holiday, Henry, 'Henry Holiday 1839–1927' by Dennis and Joan Hadley, 29, no. 1 (1989–90), p. 48 *et seq*.

Howson, Joan, Obit., 14, no. 2 (1965), p. 111

Image, Selwyn, Obit., 3, no. 4 (1930), p. 204

Lowndes, Mary, 'Mary Lowndes: A Brief Overview of her Life and Work' by Ann O'Donoghue, 24, (2001), p. 38

Nicholson, Archibald, Obit., 7, no. 1 (1937), p. 52

Nuttgens, J. E., 'Seventy Years' Work: The Stained Glass of Joseph Edward Nuttgens 1892–1982' by Professor Patrick Nuttgens, 18, no. 1 (1983–84), p. 58 *et seq*.

Smith, G. E. R., Obit., 13, no. 1 (1959–60), pp. 367–68

Walker, Leonard, Obit., 14, no. 2 (1965), p. 112

Woore, Edward, Obit., 13, no. 2 (1960–61), p. 444

Journal of the Decorative Arts Society

Ceresole, Anne, 'The Work in Cloisonné of Clement Heaton', 20 (1996), pp. 34–42

Cooper, Roger, 'Bernard Sleigh: Artist and Craftsman, 1872–1954', 21 (1997), pp. 88–102

Davis, John, '"A most important and necessary thing": an Arts and Crafts Collection in Manchester', 18 (1994), pp. 15–24.

Eatwell, Ann, 'Gordon Mitchell Forsyth (1879–1952): Artist, Designer and Father of Art Education in the Potteries', 13 (1989), pp. 27–32

Evans, Stuart, 'The Century Guild of Artists at the International Inventions Exhibition, London, 1885', 21 (1997), pp. 46–53

Muter, Grant, 'Leon Solon and John Wadsworth: Joint Designers of Minton's Secessionist Ware', 9 (1985), pp. 41–49

Rose, Peter, 'William Arthur Smith Benson: A Pioneer Designer of Light Fittings', 9 (1985), pp. 50–57

——, 'The Coloured Relief Decoration of Robert Anning Bell', 14 (1990), pp. 16–23

Rudoe, Judy and Howard Coutts, 'The Table Glass Designs of Philip Webb and T. G. Jackson for James Powell & Sons, Whitefriars', 16 (1992), pp. 24–41

Rycroft, Elizabeth, 'Lewis Foreman Day, 1845–1910', 13 (1989), pp. 19–26

Walker, Robert Prescott, 'Conrad Dressler and the Medenham Pottery', 18 (1994), pp. 50–60

Werner, Alex, 'John Charles Lewis Sparkes, 1833–1907', 13 (1989), pp. 9–18

Studio Magazines and Year Books (listed by artist)

Bankart, G., 38 (1906), pp. 194–98; 39 (1907), pp. 147–50

Bell, R. Anning, 49 (1910), pp. 254–62, T. M. Wood, 'Mr Robert Anning Bell's Work as a Painter'

Bonnor, J. H., 79 (1920), pp. 12–20, A. Romney Green, 'John Houghton Bonnor: An Appreciation'

Carr, J. E. C., 14 (1898), pp. 124–25; 30 (1904), pp. 218–25, G. Ll. Morris, 'The Metalwork of John Carr',

Clark, James, 14 (1898), pp. 153–60, A. L. Baldry, 'The Work of James Clarke'

Cooksey, May, 19 (1900), pp. 131, 134; 45 (1909), pp. 144–46

Fenton, Harry, *Studio Year Book of Decorative Art* (1909), pp. 48–49

Fitzroy Picture Society, 1 (1893), pp. 28–29

Frampton, George, 54 (1912), pp. 35–43

Hilton, Agnes, 25 (1902), p. 56; 30 (1904), p. 164

Hilton, Robert, 14 (1898), p. 283; 25 (1902), p. 55; 27 (1903), p. 213; 30 (1904), pp. 162–64; 36 (1906), p. 264; *Studio Year Book of Decorative Art* (1907 and 1910)

Hodel, Joseph, 37 (1906), pp. 135, 137; *Studio Year Book of Decorative Art* (1909), p. 140

Kay, Ida Lillian, 25 (1902), p. 203

Lee, Thomas Stirling, *Obit*, 68 (1916), pp. 175–77

Mackmurdo, A. H., 16 (1899), pp. 183–92

MacNair, Herbert and Frances Macdonald, 26 (1902), pp. 97–101, 103

Mallows, C. E., 44 (1908), pp. 181–88; 45 (1909), pp. 31–42, 180–88; 46 (1909), pp. 120–28

Martin, Alfred, 36 (1906), pp. 80–81

Martin, William Alison, 30 (1904), p. 67

Moira, Gerald, 20 (1900), pp. 148–56; A. L. Baldry, 'Prof Moira's Recent Mural Decoration', 40 (1907), pp. 24–34

Rathbone, R. Ll., 1 (1893), pp. 240–41; 19 (1900), pp. 272–73

Reynolds Stephens, W. E., 51 (1911), pp. 260–74, A. L. Baldry, 'Recent Decorative Work and Sculpture by Mr Reynolds Stephens'

Smithies, James, 21 (1901), pp. 257–58

Sumner, Heywood, 13 (1898), pp. 152–63, Gleeson White 'The Work of Heywood Sumner'

Thompson, C. E., 17 (1899), pp. 189–90; 21 (1901), pp. 133, 136; 29 (1903), p. 294; 39 (1907), p. 68

Toft, Albert, 66 (1916), pp. 18–28

Watkins, Stanley, *Studio Year Book of Decorative Art* (1909) p. 79

Wragge, George, 14 (1898), pp. 128–29

ACKNOWLEDGEMENTS

ACROSS THE NORTH WEST of England there are many hundreds of people who helped us, often unknowingly, with this book and we would like to thank them all. Among them are:

The very many clergymen of all denominations and their wives, church wardens and volunteers who made our visits to churches possible, often providing valuable information and frequently waiting patiently while we had a last look or took a last photograph.

The staff in the local studies, archive and private collection sections of public and university libraries: the Armitt at Ambleside, the Public Libraries at Ambleside, Bolton, Carlisle, Dublin Central, Horwich, Keswick, Lancaster Central, Leek, Lichfield, Liverpool Central, Macclesfield, Manchester Central, Nelson, Padiham, Preston, Salford and Windermere. Staff at the John Rylands Library Manchester University, Sir Kenneth Green Library Manchester Metropolitan University, Sidney Jones Library Liverpool University, the Birmingham Municipal School of Art archives at the University of Central England, William Salt Library Stafford, Also to staff at the RIBA library and the National Art Library at the V&A and to Ron Travis manager of Liverpool Community libraries.

The staff at Public Record Offices at Carlisle, Barrow, Chester, Kendal, Lancaster, Liverpool, Manchester, Preston, Stafford and Whitehaven and The Diocesan Registrars and staff in the registries of Carlisle, Blackburn, Lichfield, Liverpool, and Manchester.

The curators and assistants of Museums, Art Galleries and country houses: Abbot Hall, Blackwell, Blackburn Museum, Brantwood, Bury Museum and Art Gallery, Chester Museum, Ruskin Museum, Coniston, Gawthorpe Hall, Harris Museum and Art Gallery, Haworth Art Gallery, Hutton in the Forest, Keswick Museum, Lancaster Museum, Liverpool Museum, Gallery Oldham, Penrith Museum, Rochdale Museum and Art Gallery, Salford Museum, Peter Scott Gallery Lancaster University, Towneley Hall, Tullie House, Turton Tower, the National Museums, Liverpool, the Wirral Museums, Liverpool University Art Gallery, Manchester Art Gallery, M/c School of Art Collection at Manchester Metropolitan University and the Whitworth Gallery.

To other organisations who have made information available to us: The Art Workers Guild, The Society of Antiquaries, the Archive of Art and Design, London and the National Inventory of War Memorials at the Imperial War Museum.

Thanks also to the owners of: 'Broadleys', the Windermere Motor Boat Racing Club; Capesthorne Hall Mr and Mrs Bromley Davenport; Eaton Hall, His Grace the Duke of Westminster; Hutton in the Forest, Lord and Lady Inglewood; 'Gate house', the Outward Bound Trust and to the previous owners of 'Tirley Garth', Moral Re-Armament, all of whom kindly allowed us to visit and photograph their houses, gardens or chapels.

Thank you for making us welcome to the heads of Abbeygate College Saighton, Denstone College Denstone, Pownall Hall School Wilmslow, Queen Elizabeth Grammar School Blackburn, Rossall School Fleetwood, Stonyhurst College Lancashire and St Bees School St Bees Head Cumbria.

We have consulted many individuals, some of whom had special knowledge in their field and were kind enough to share it. Thank you Chris Blanchett Tile historian, Peter Cormack at Walthamstow Museum, John Davis at Manchester Metropolitan University, Stuart Evans at University of Arts London, Alan Rhodes of Rhodes and Day architects Windermere, Joseph Sharples of the History Dept at Liverpool University, and Vicki Slowe at the Coniston Museum — and others whose special knowledge about particular people or buildings has been invaluable: Dean and Doreen Furness of Chapel Stile, John Garbett of Allithwaite, Mrs Bridget Gledhill of Menai, Brian Hobson of Alderley Edge, Deanne Mangold of Swansea Glass Studio, David Pearce of Worsley, Mr and Mrs J. Rathbone of Formby, Jessica Scott of Siddington, Cheshire and Len Smith and George Harrison previously connected with Salford Unitarian church.

To Jean Turnbull of the Centre for North West Regional Studies and author Jennie Brunton who unknowingly gave us the encouragement in the early days to keep going, to John Archer, Ronald Brunskill, and Andor Gomme for their wisdom, advice and support and especially to Alan Crawford for his encouragement, for reading our script and for making invaluable suggestions from which we learned a great deal.

To the Mark Fitch Fund whose generous grant helped to make publication a reality.

To Derek Brown and Jackie Maidment, the talented producers of our book, who shared our enthusiasm for it and with great equanimity and skill, saw it though to publication.

To good friend June Plymen who corrected our script, to friends who gave us moral support and finally to our family whose interest over the years and whose involvement in numerous ways with our book has meant so much to us. This book is dedicated to them.

Barrie and Wendy Armstrong

NOTES

THE AUTHORS would like to hear of any examples of the work of the Arts and Crafts Movement in the North West which did not come to light during their research for this book. If you would like to contribute information of this kind to their ongoing database, please e-mail a description, together with location and access details to **AandChandbook@aol.com**.

The following pages may be used for noting down any such discoveries.

NOTES

NOTES

NOTES